JEREMY
SORESE

CURVEBALL

NOBROW
LONDON-
NEW YORK

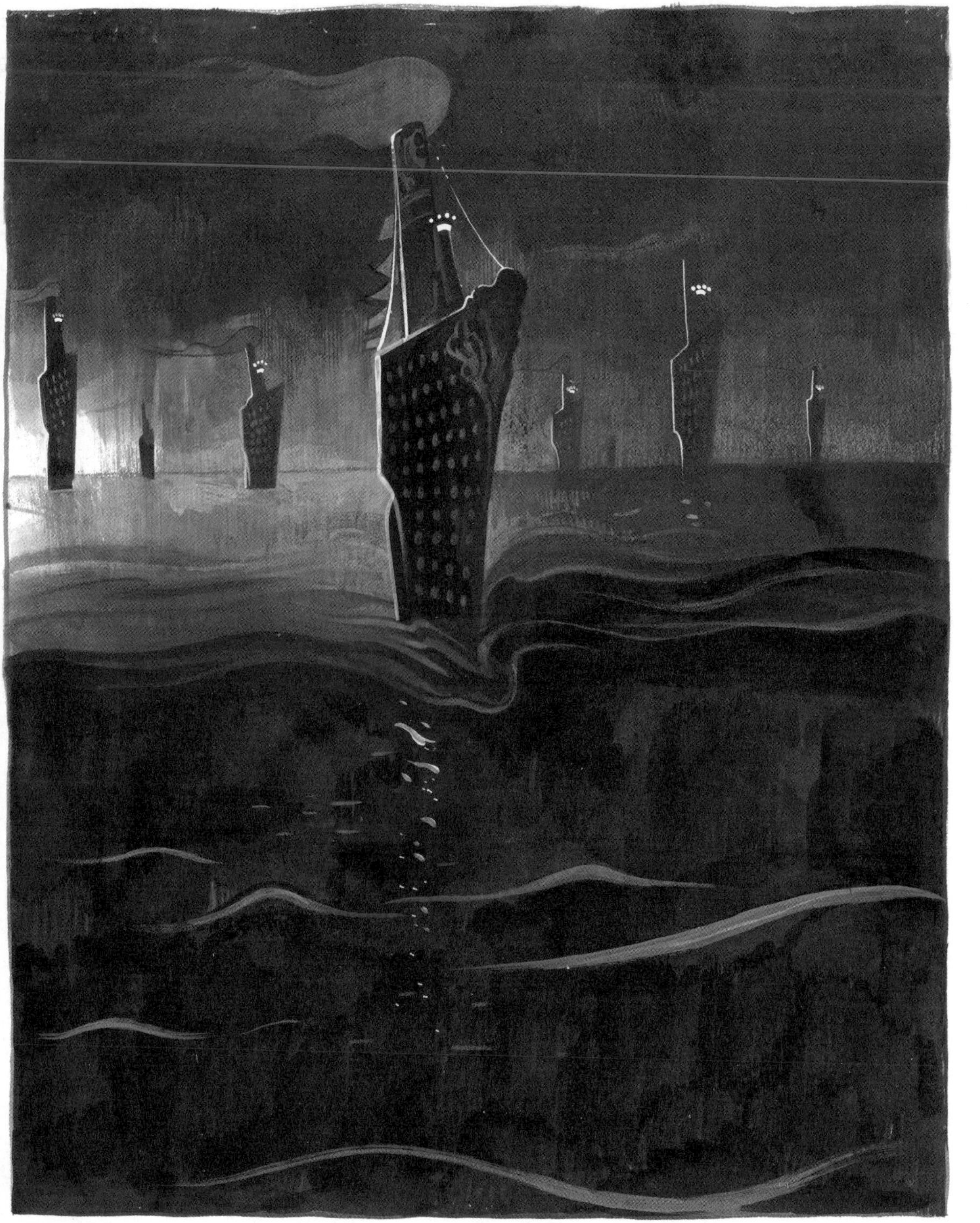

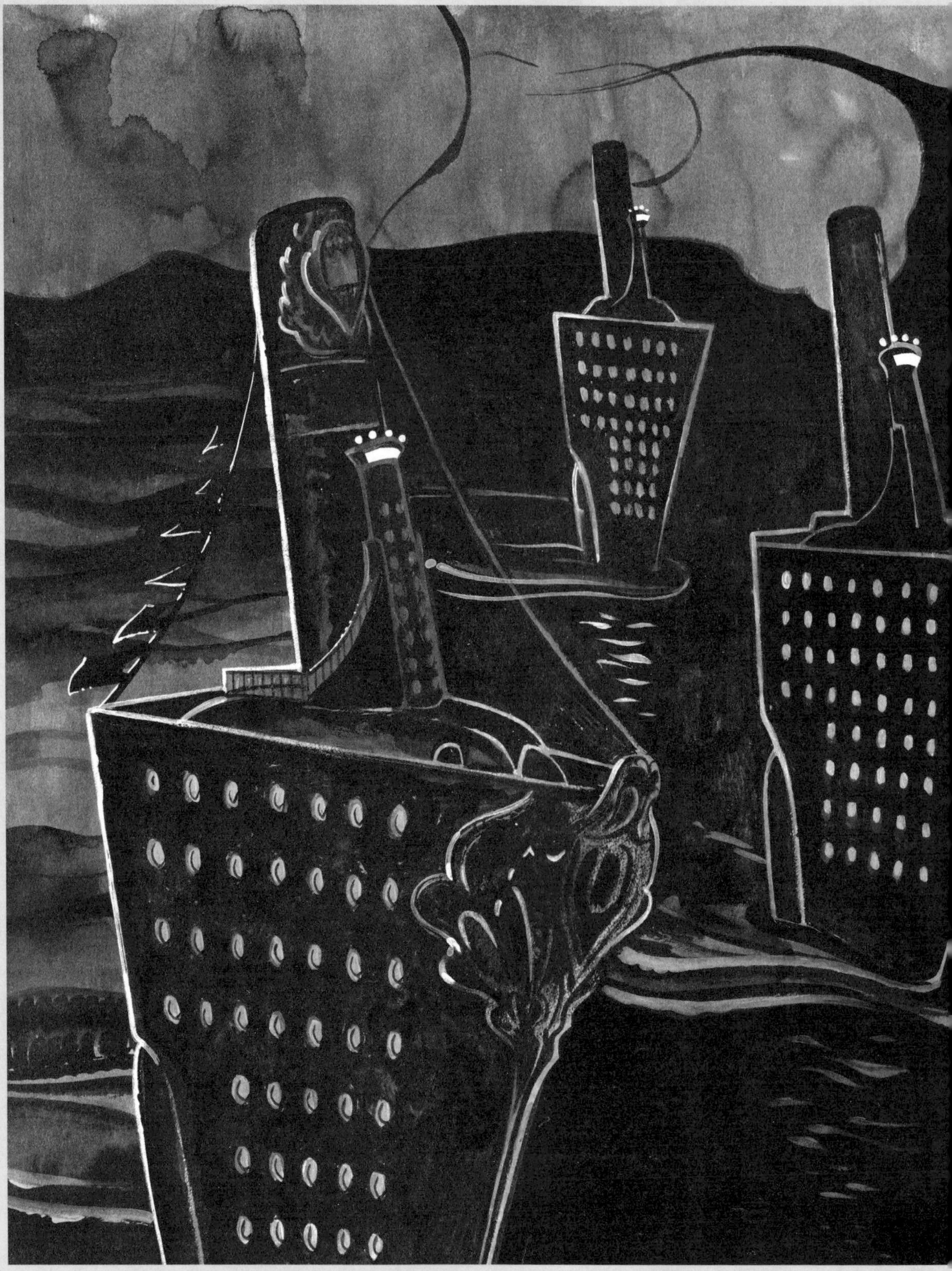

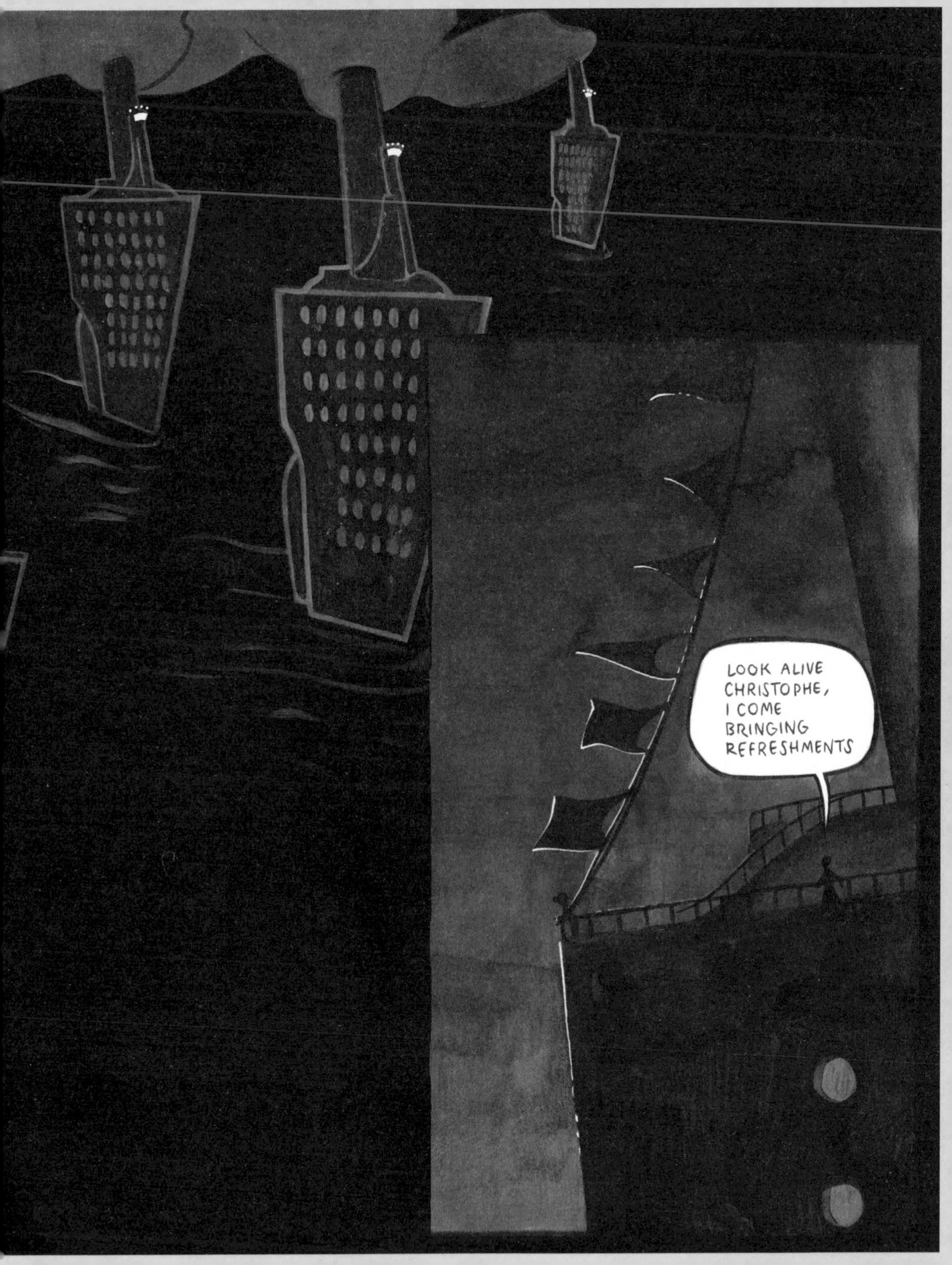
LOOK ALIVE CHRISTOPHE, I COME BRINGING REFRESHMENTS

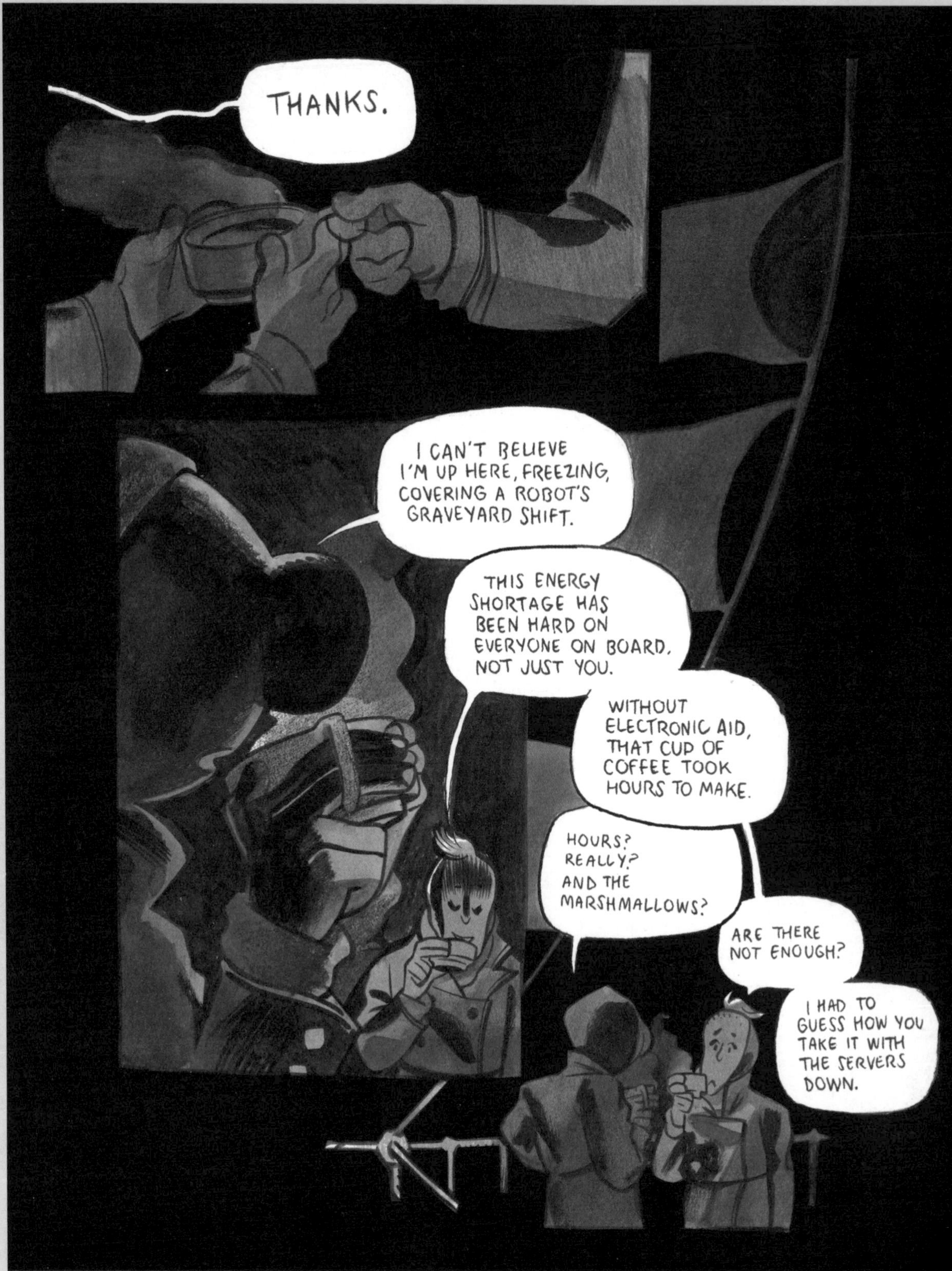
THANKS.
I CAN'T BELIEVE I'M UP HERE, FREEZING, COVERING A ROBOT'S GRAVEYARD SHIFT.
THIS ENERGY SHORTAGE HAS BEEN HARD ON EVERYONE ON BOARD, NOT JUST YOU.
WITHOUT ELECTRONIC AID, THAT CUP OF COFFEE TOOK HOURS TO MAKE.
HOURS? REALLY? AND THE MARSHMALLOWS?
ARE THERE NOT ENOUGH?
I HAD TO GUESS HOW YOU TAKE IT WITH THE SERVERS DOWN.

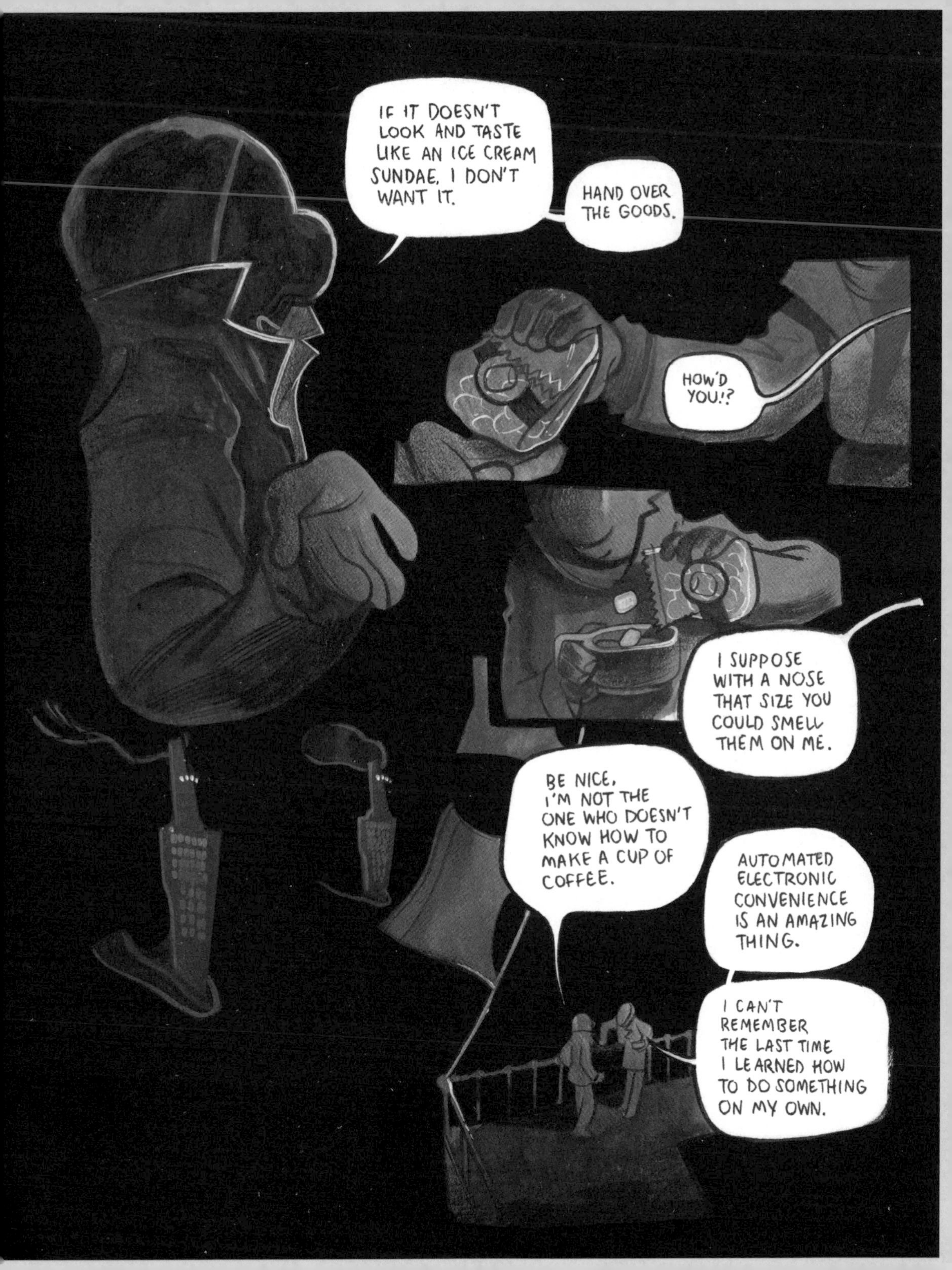
IF IT DOESN'T LOOK AND TASTE LIKE AN ICE CREAM SUNDAE, I DON'T WANT IT.
HAND OVER THE GOODS.
HOW'D YOU!?
I SUPPOSE WITH A NOSE THAT SIZE YOU COULD SMELL THEM ON ME.
BE NICE, I'M NOT THE ONE WHO DOESN'T KNOW HOW TO MAKE A CUP OF COFFEE.
AUTOMATED ELECTRONIC CONVENIENCE IS AN AMAZING THING.
I CAN'T REMEMBER THE LAST TIME I LEARNED HOW TO DO SOMETHING ON MY OWN.

I JUST DON'T SEE THE POINT.
?
DID YOU SEE THAT?
IT WAS PROBABLY JUST GARBAGE.

TAKE THIS. I NEED TO REPORT THAT, WHATEVER IT WAS.
YOU'RE WASTING YOUR TIME, THE CAPTAIN GETS BORED EASILY...
...ESPECIALLY WITH VAGUE HUNCHES ABOUT THE UNNKNOWN
CREAK

PERMISSION TO SPEAK FREELY, SIR?
PERMISSION GRANTED. WHAT'S ON YOUR MIND SAILOR?
I BELIEVE I SAW AN UNIDENTIFIED OBJECT OFF OF STARBOARD.
AWWW, DID IT SPOOK YOU? NEXT TIME I'LL REMEMBER TO KEEP THE NIGHTLIGHT ON.

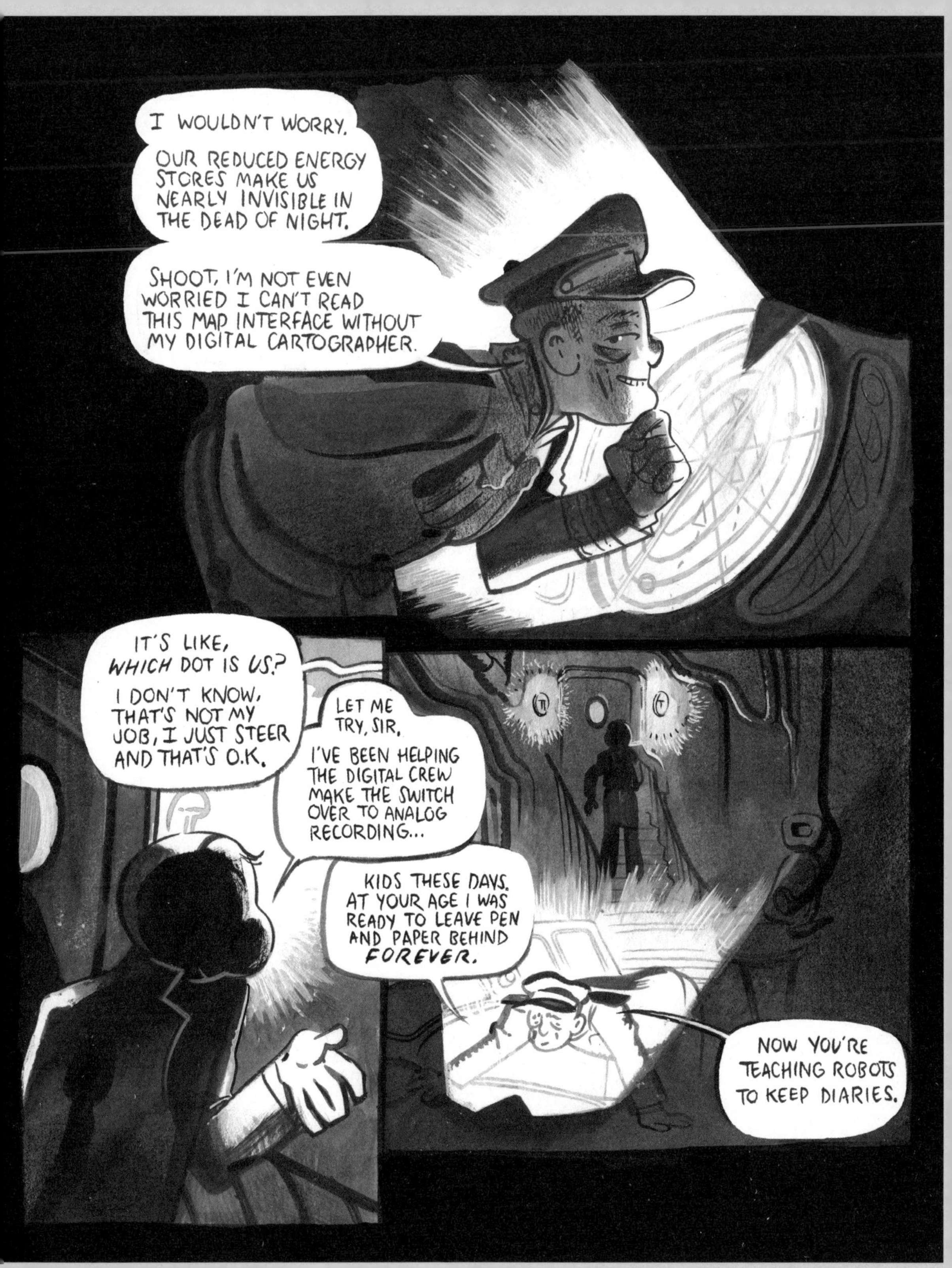
I WOULDN'T WORRY.
OUR REDUCED ENERGY STORES MAKE US NEARLY INVISIBLE IN THE DEAD OF NIGHT.
SHOOT, I'M NOT EVEN WORRIED I CAN'T READ THIS MAP INTERFACE WITHOUT MY DIGITAL CARTOGRAPHER.
IT'S LIKE, *WHICH* DOT IS *US*?
I DON'T KNOW, THAT'S NOT MY JOB, I JUST STEER AND THAT'S O.K.
LET ME TRY, SIR.
I'VE BEEN HELPING THE DIGITAL CREW MAKE THE SWITCH OVER TO ANALOG RECORDING...
KIDS THESE DAYS. AT YOUR AGE I WAS READY TO LEAVE PEN AND PAPER BEHIND *FOREVER*.
NOW YOU'RE TEACHING ROBOTS TO KEEP DIARIES.

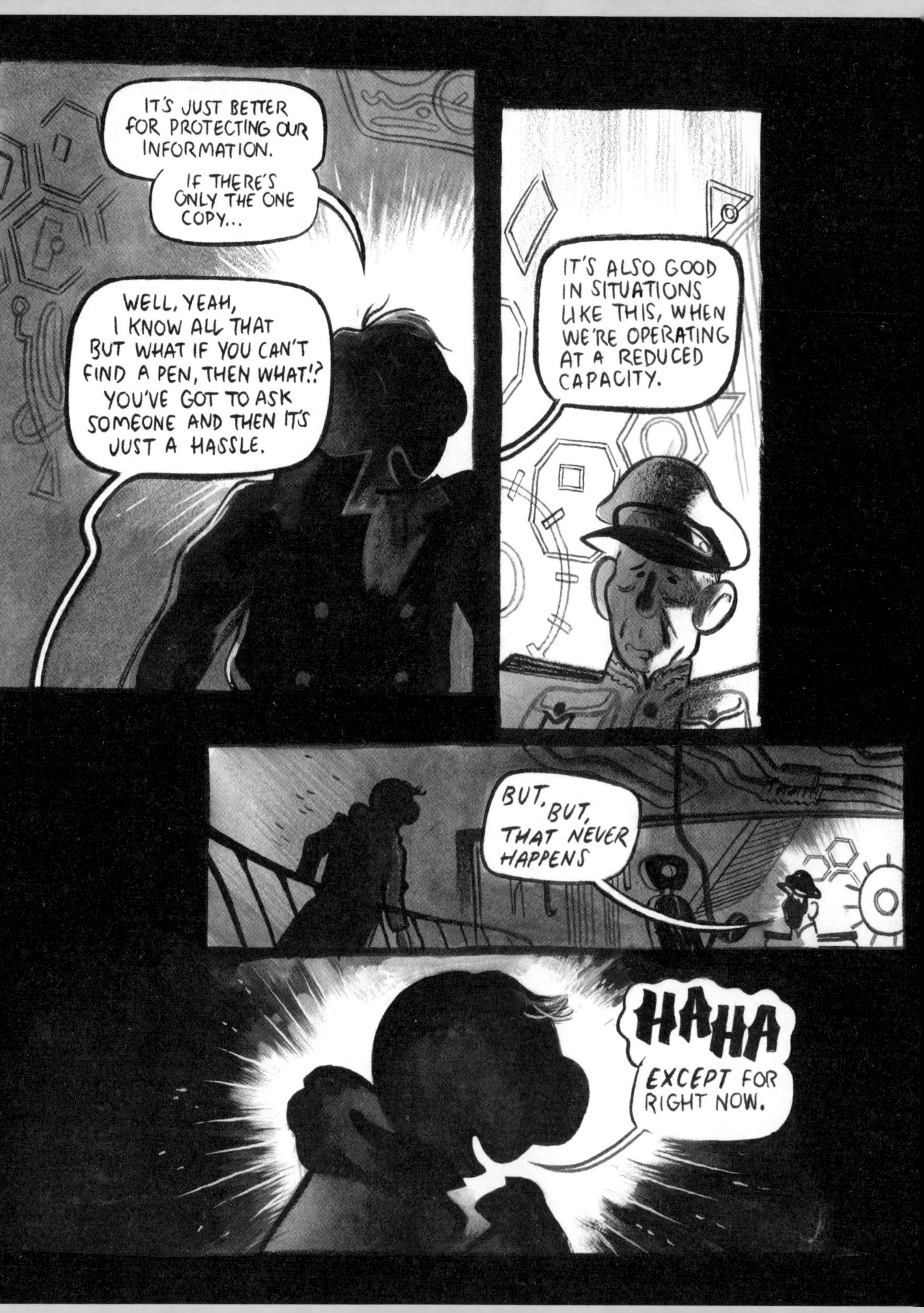
IT'S JUST BETTER FOR PROTECTING OUR INFORMATION.
IF THERE'S ONLY THE ONE COPY...
WELL, YEAH, I KNOW ALL THAT BUT WHAT IF YOU CAN'T FIND A PEN, THEN WHAT!? YOU'VE GOT TO ASK SOMEONE AND THEN IT'S JUST A HASSLE.
IT'S ALSO GOOD IN SITUATIONS LIKE THIS, WHEN WE'RE OPERATING AT A REDUCED CAPACITY.
BUT, BUT, THAT NEVER HAPPENS
HAHA
EXCEPT FOR RIGHT NOW.

LIFE IS TOO SHORT TO LIVE IN FEAR! QUIT WORRYING, WHY ADD THE STRESS?
BUMP
oof
WHOA

SIR, I THINK THE ENEMY IS PLANNING AN ATTACK FROM BELOW!
WHAT MAKES YOU THINK THAT, SAILOR?
WE MAY HAVE JUST HIT A BUMP IN THE ... OCEAN.
SIR, WE SHOULD PREPARE FOR AN ATTACK!
YOU COULD BE WRONG. THESE THINGS CAN BE HARD TO PREDICT. LET'S JUST WAIT AND SEE...

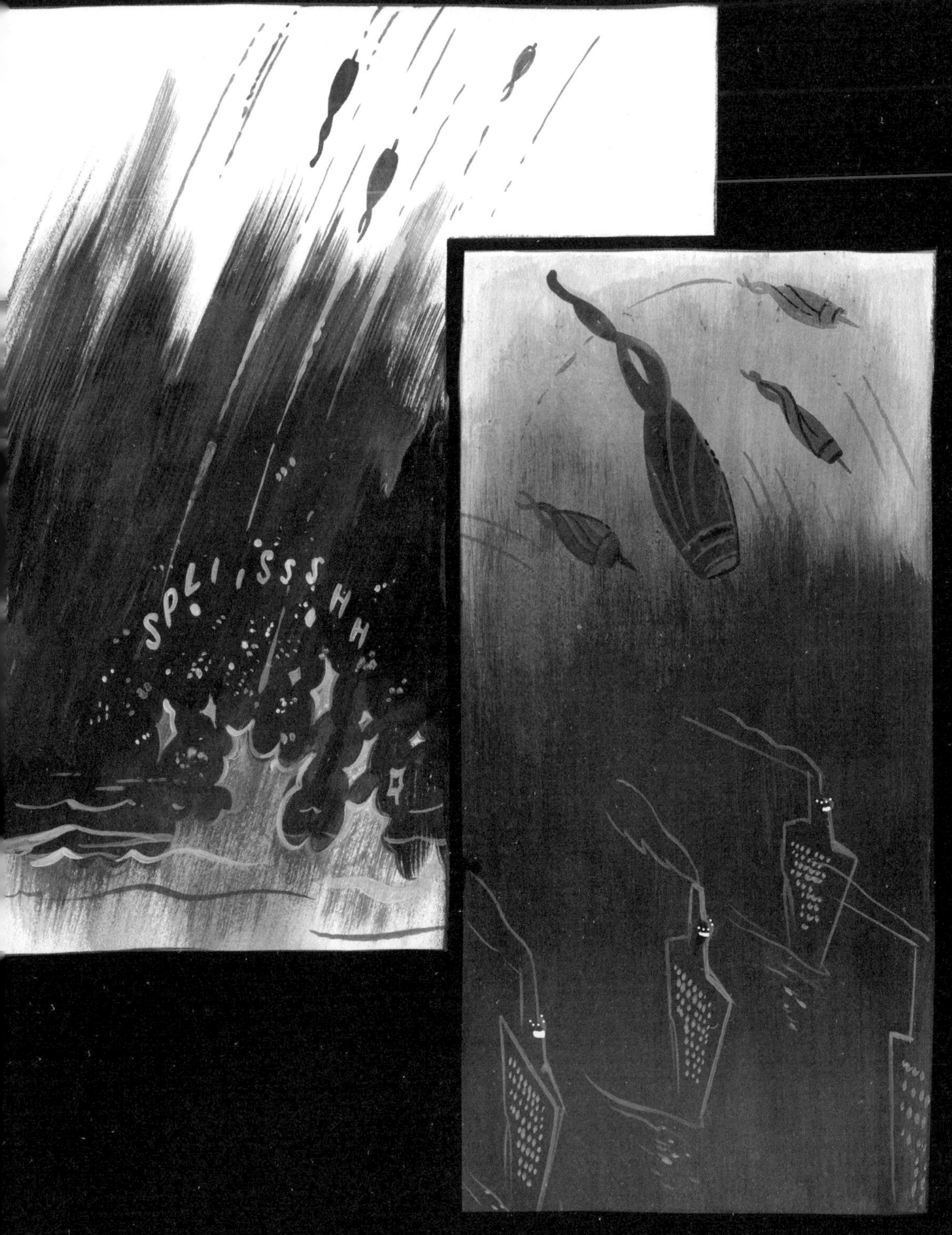
SPLIISSSHH

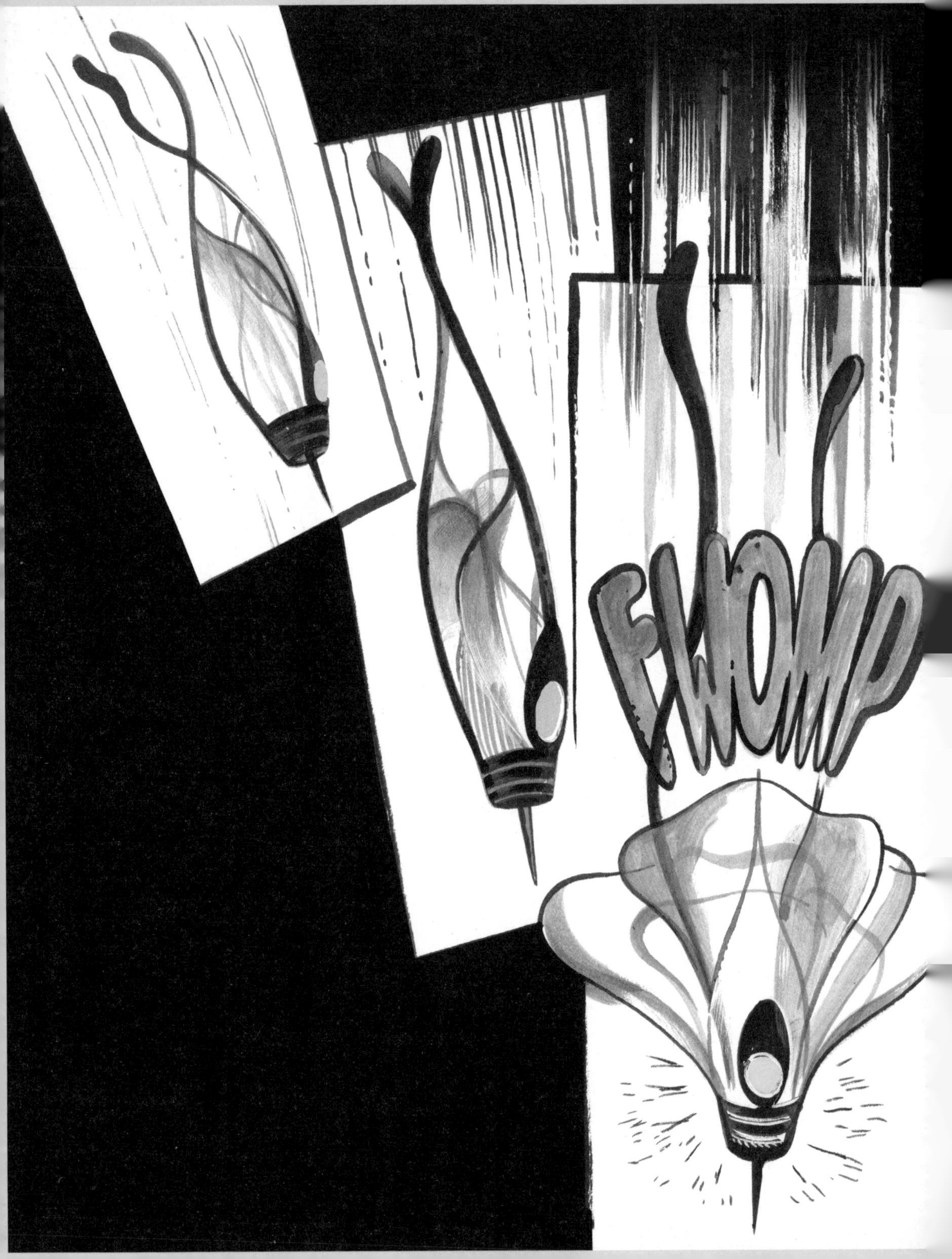
FWOMP

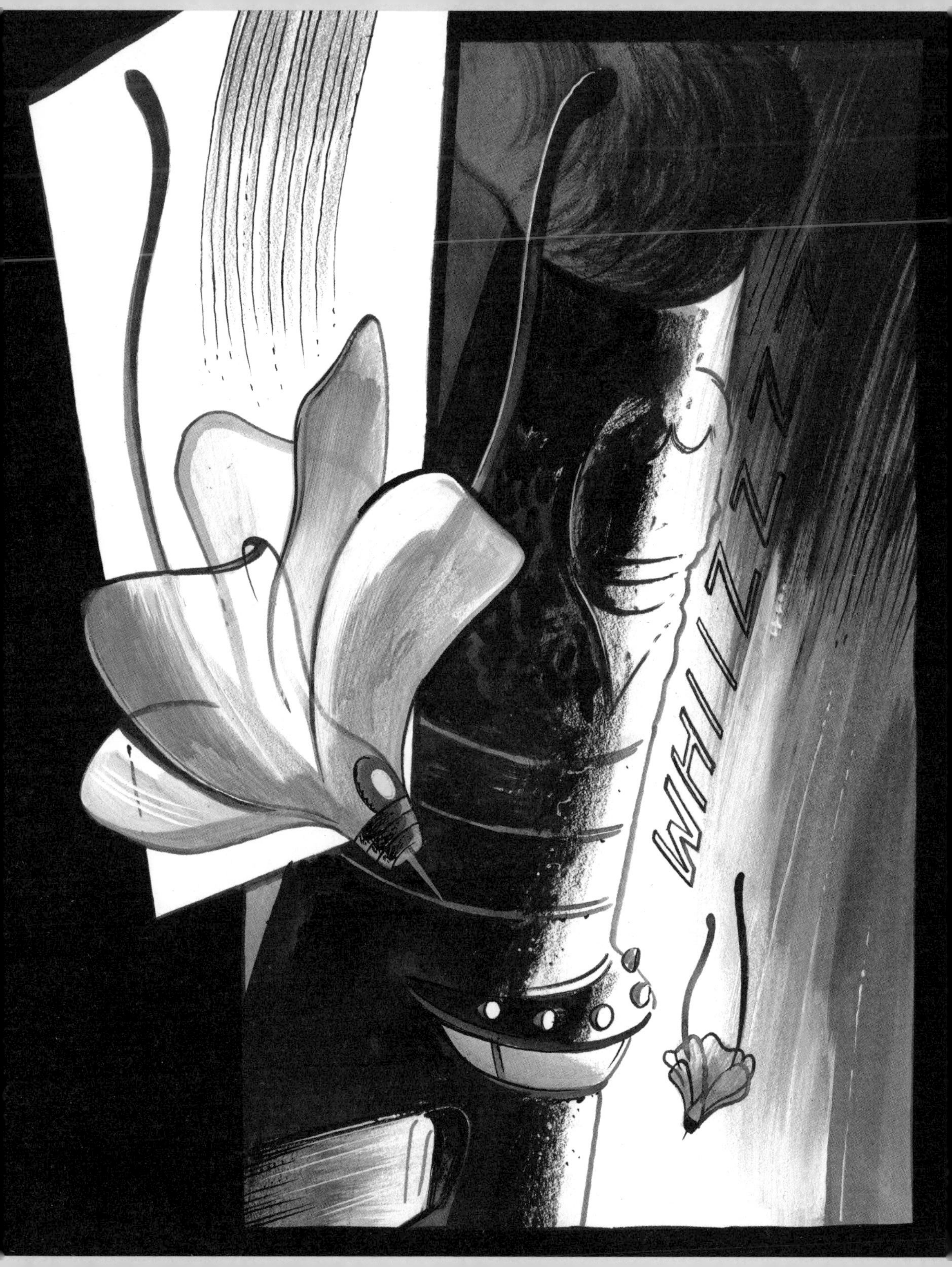
WHIIZZZZ

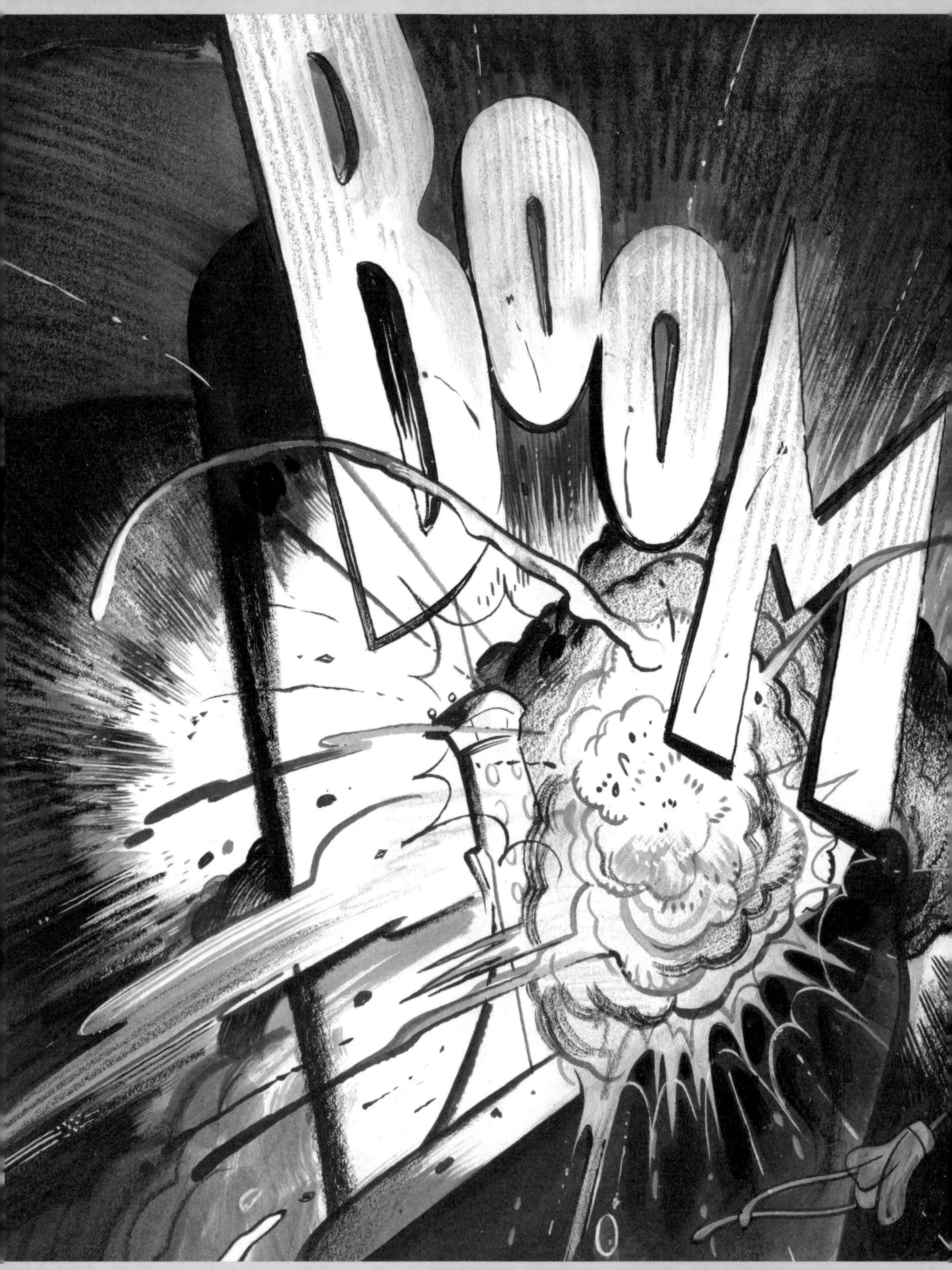
BOOM

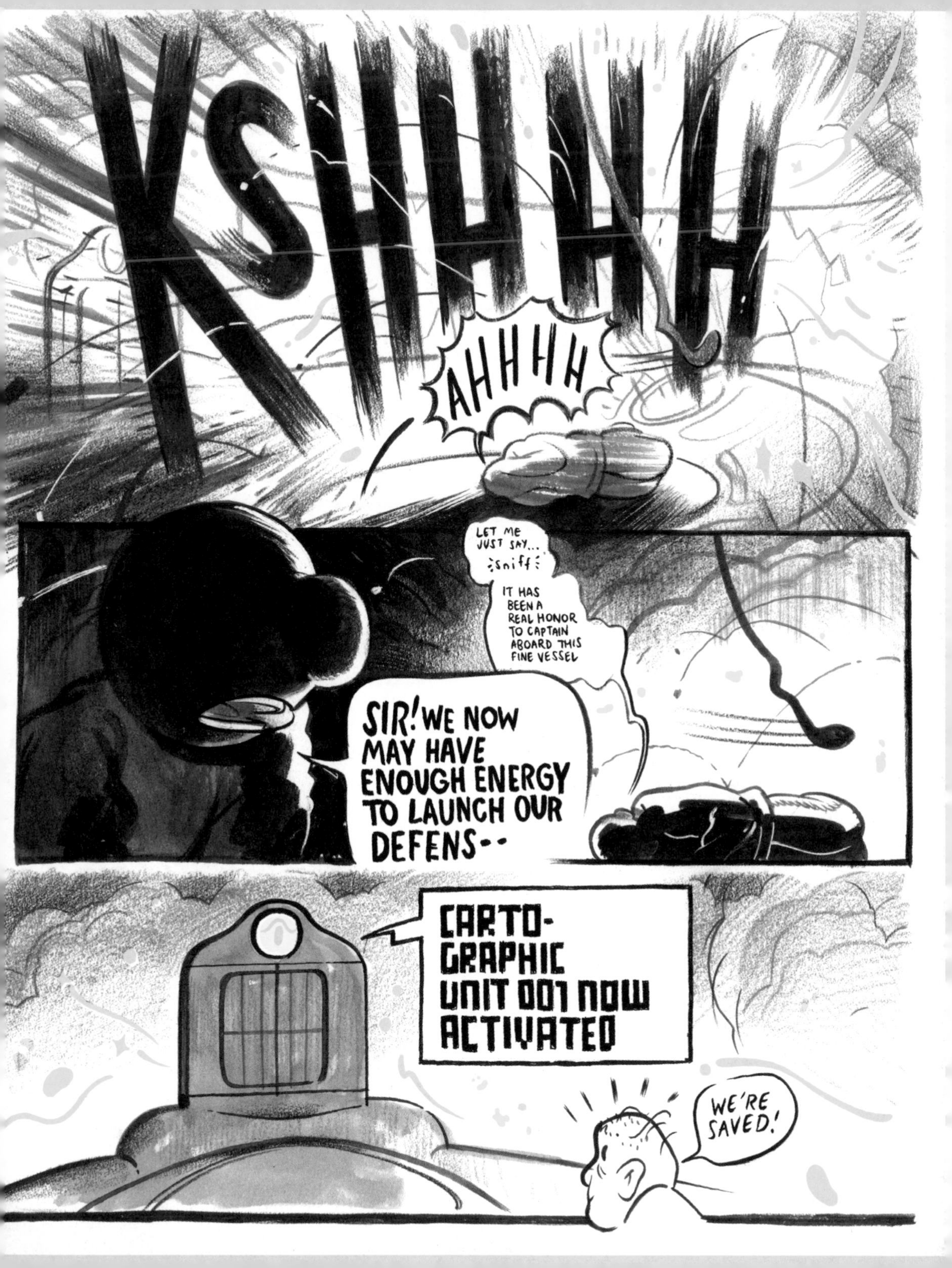
KSHHHHH
AHHHHH
LET ME JUST SAY... sniff
IT HAS BEEN A REAL HONOR TO CAPTAIN ABOARD THIS FINE VESSEL
SIR! WE NOW MAY HAVE ENOUGH ENERGY TO LAUNCH OUR DEFENS--
CARTO-GRAPHIC UNIT 001 NOW ACTIVATED
WE'RE SAVED!

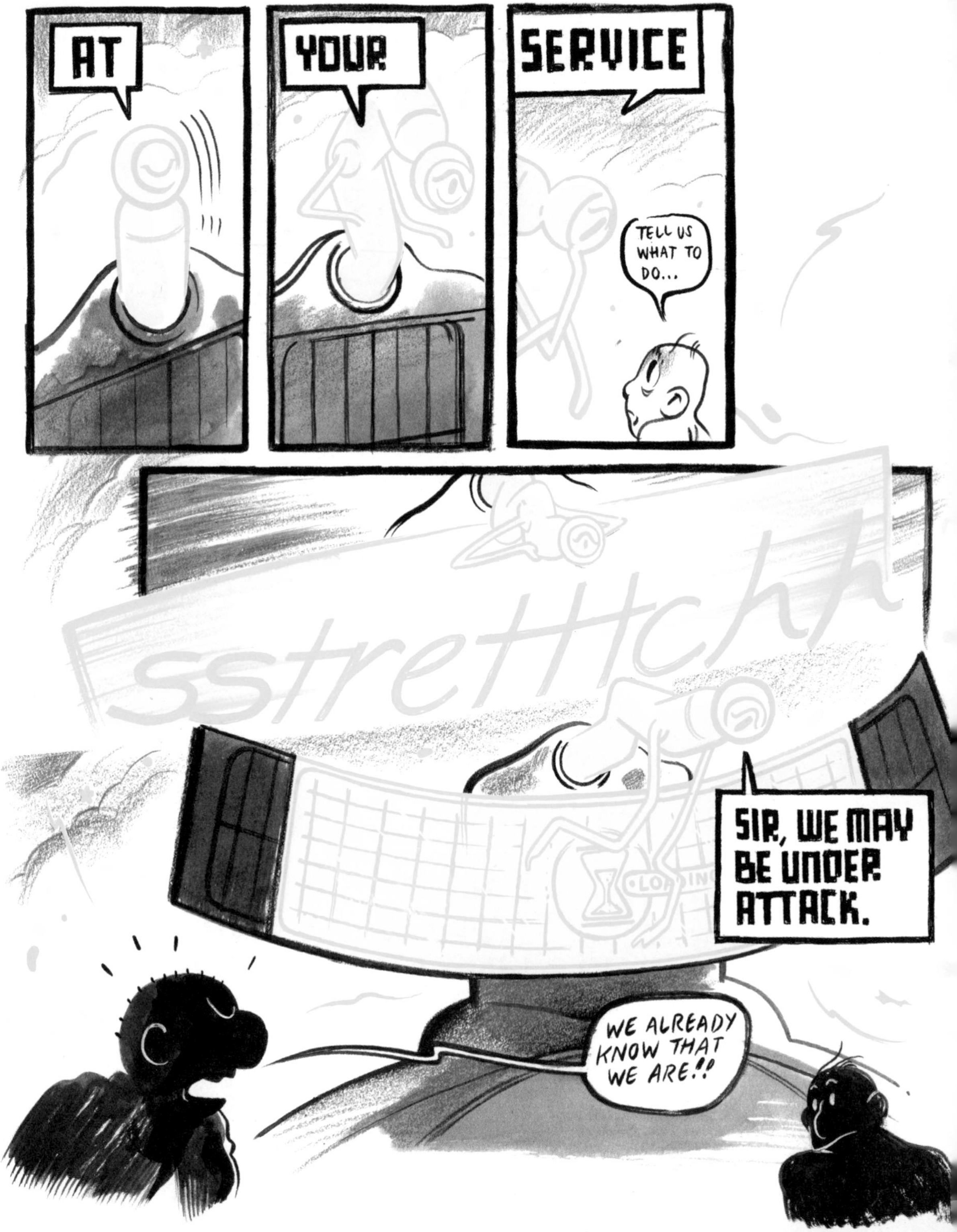
AT
YOUR
SERVICE
TELL US WHAT TO DO...
sstretTchh
SIR, WE MAY BE UNDER ATTACK.
WE ALREADY KNOW THAT WE ARE!!

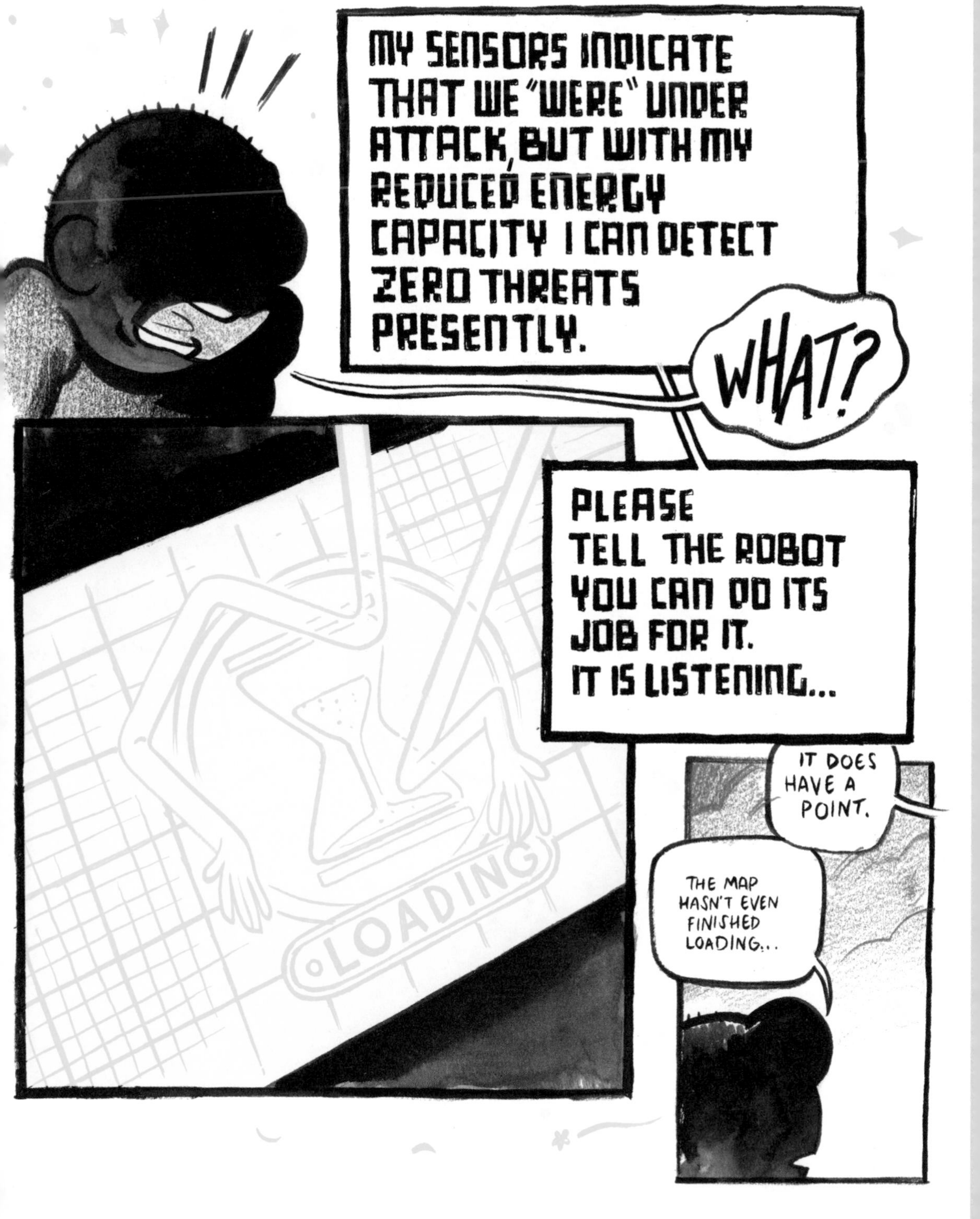
MY SENSORS INDICATE THAT WE "WERE" UNDER ATTACK, BUT WITH MY REDUCED ENERGY CAPACITY I CAN DETECT ZERO THREATS PRESENTLY.
WHAT?
PLEASE TELL THE ROBOT YOU CAN DO ITS JOB FOR IT. IT IS LISTENING...
LOADING
IT DOES HAVE A POINT.
THE MAP HASN'T EVEN FINISHED LOADING...

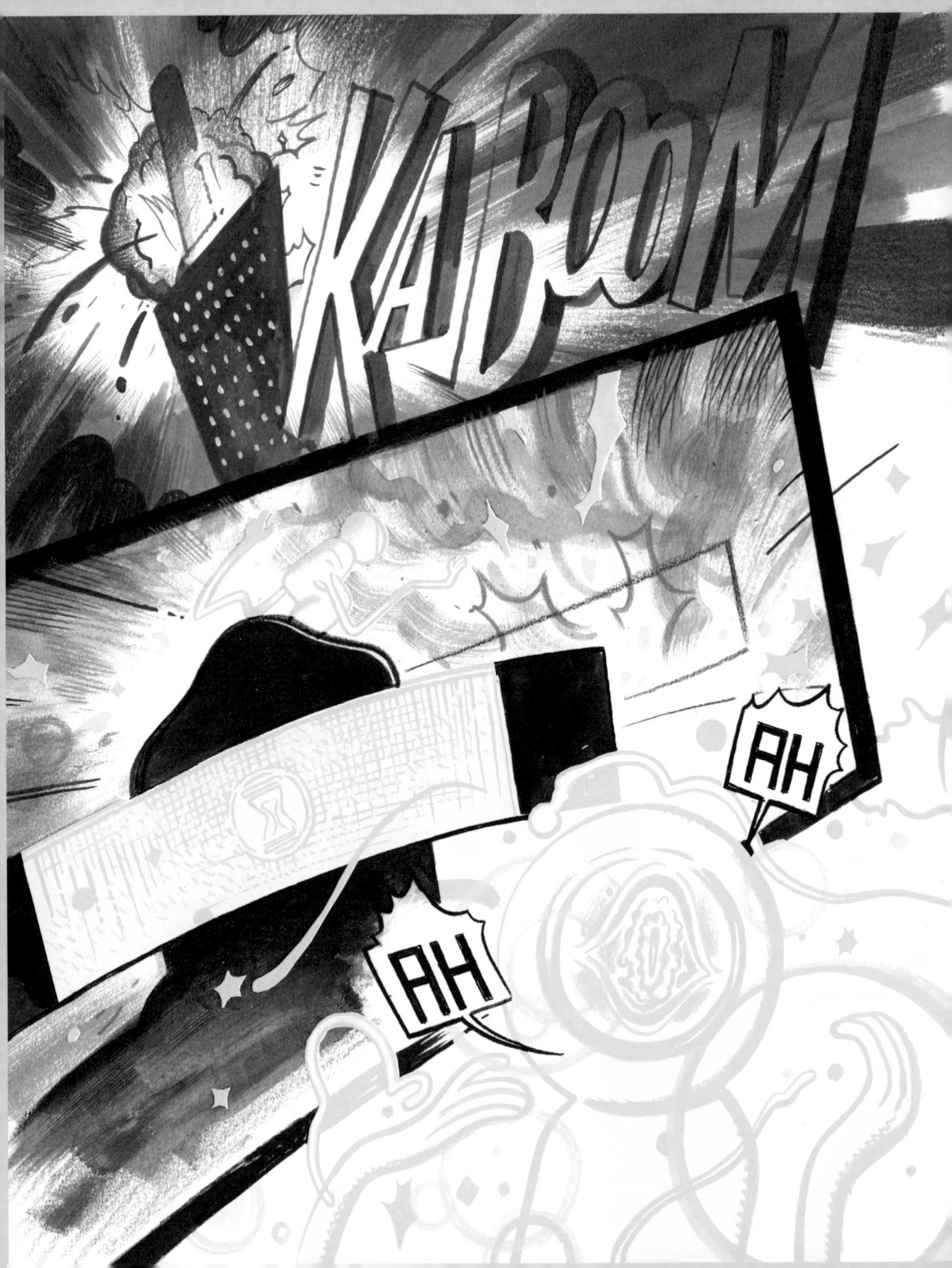
KABOOM
AH
AH

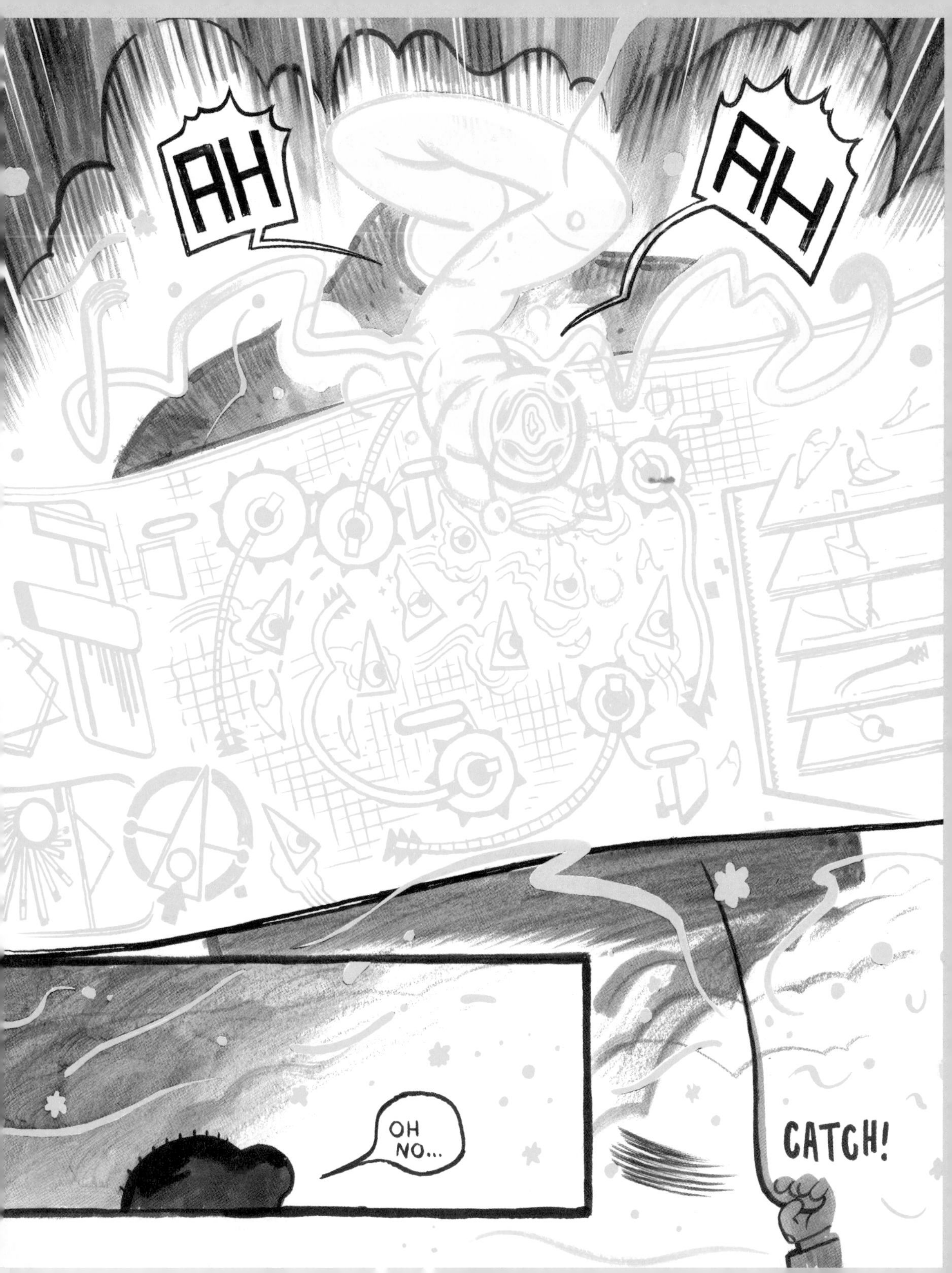
AH
AH
OH NO...
CATCH!

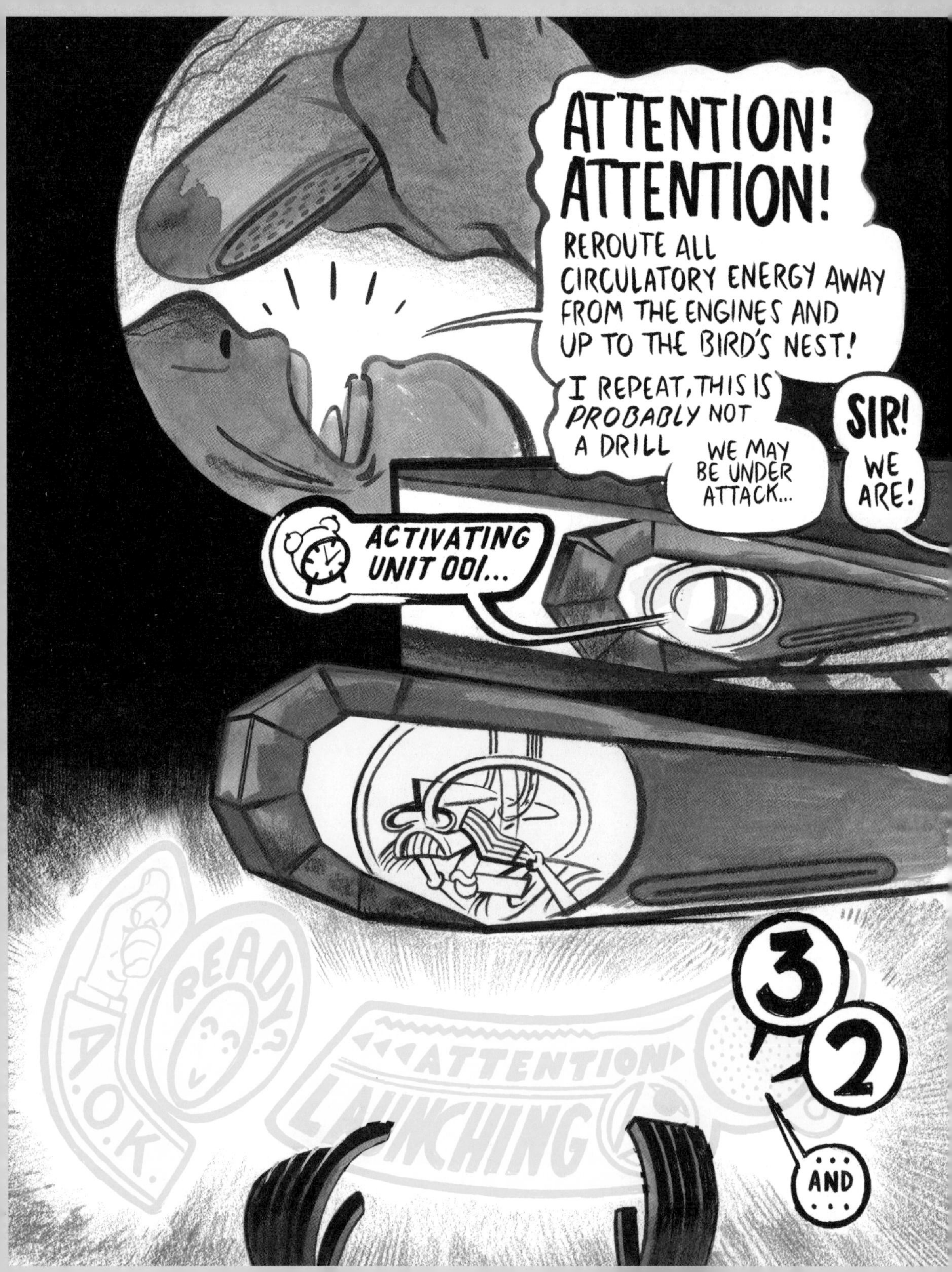
ATTENTION! ATTENTION!
REROUTE ALL CIRCULATORY ENERGY AWAY FROM THE ENGINES AND UP TO THE BIRD'S NEST!
I REPEAT, THIS IS *PROBABLY* NOT A DRILL
WE MAY BE UNDER ATTACK...
SIR!
WE ARE!
ACTIVATING UNIT 001...
A.O.K.
READY?
ATTENTION
LAUNCHING
3
2
...AND...

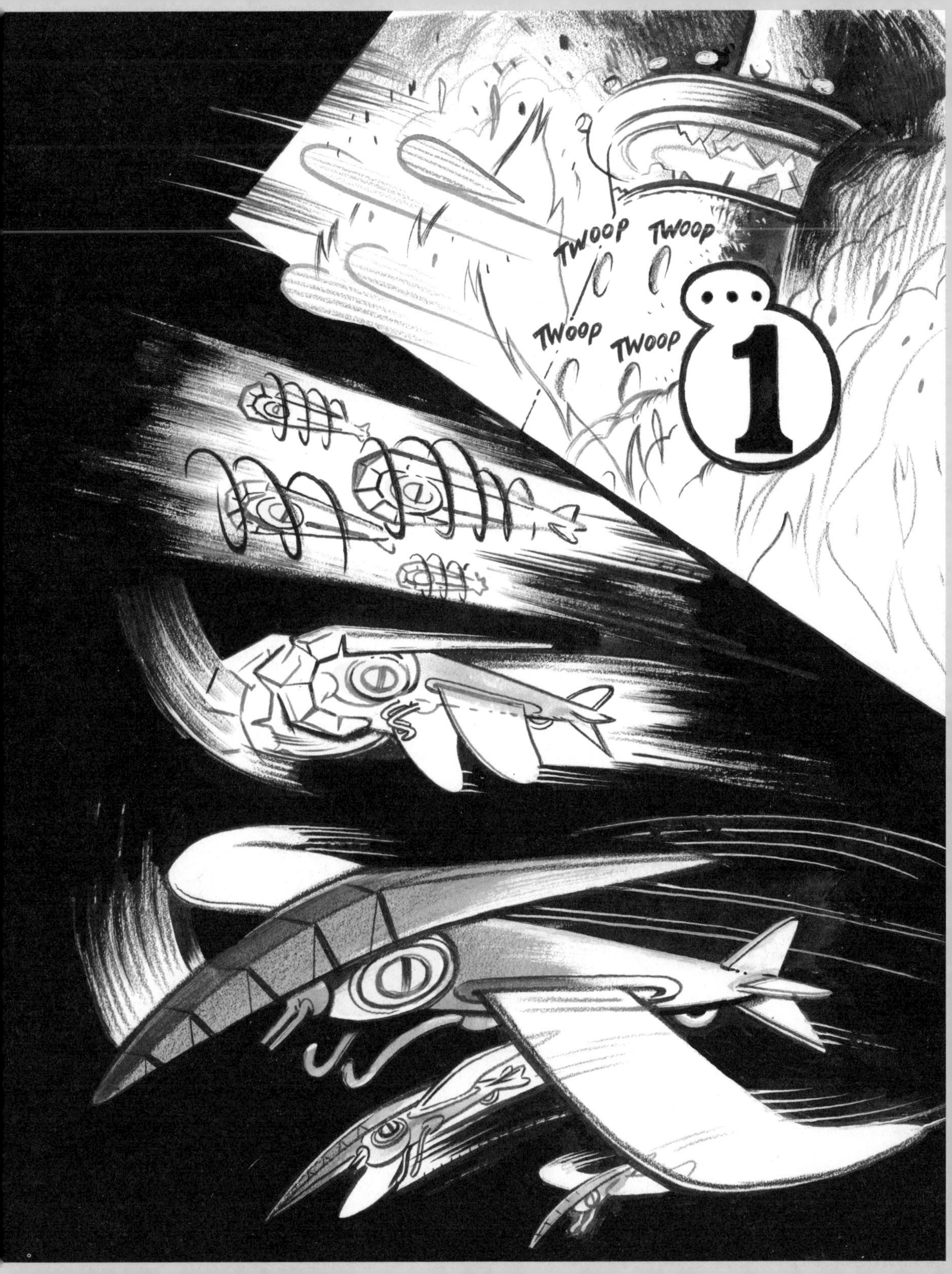
TWOOP TWOOP
TWOOP TWOOP
1

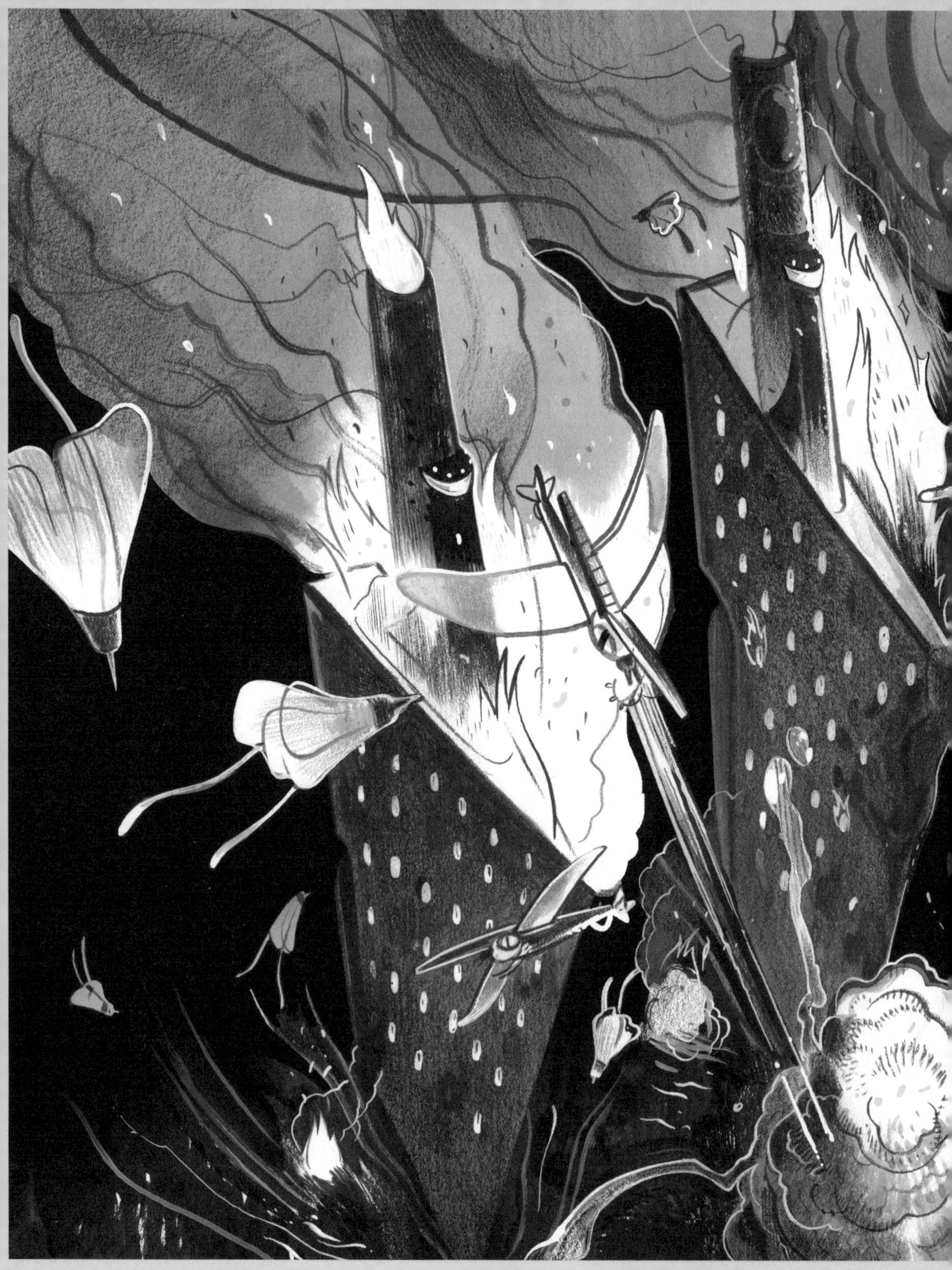

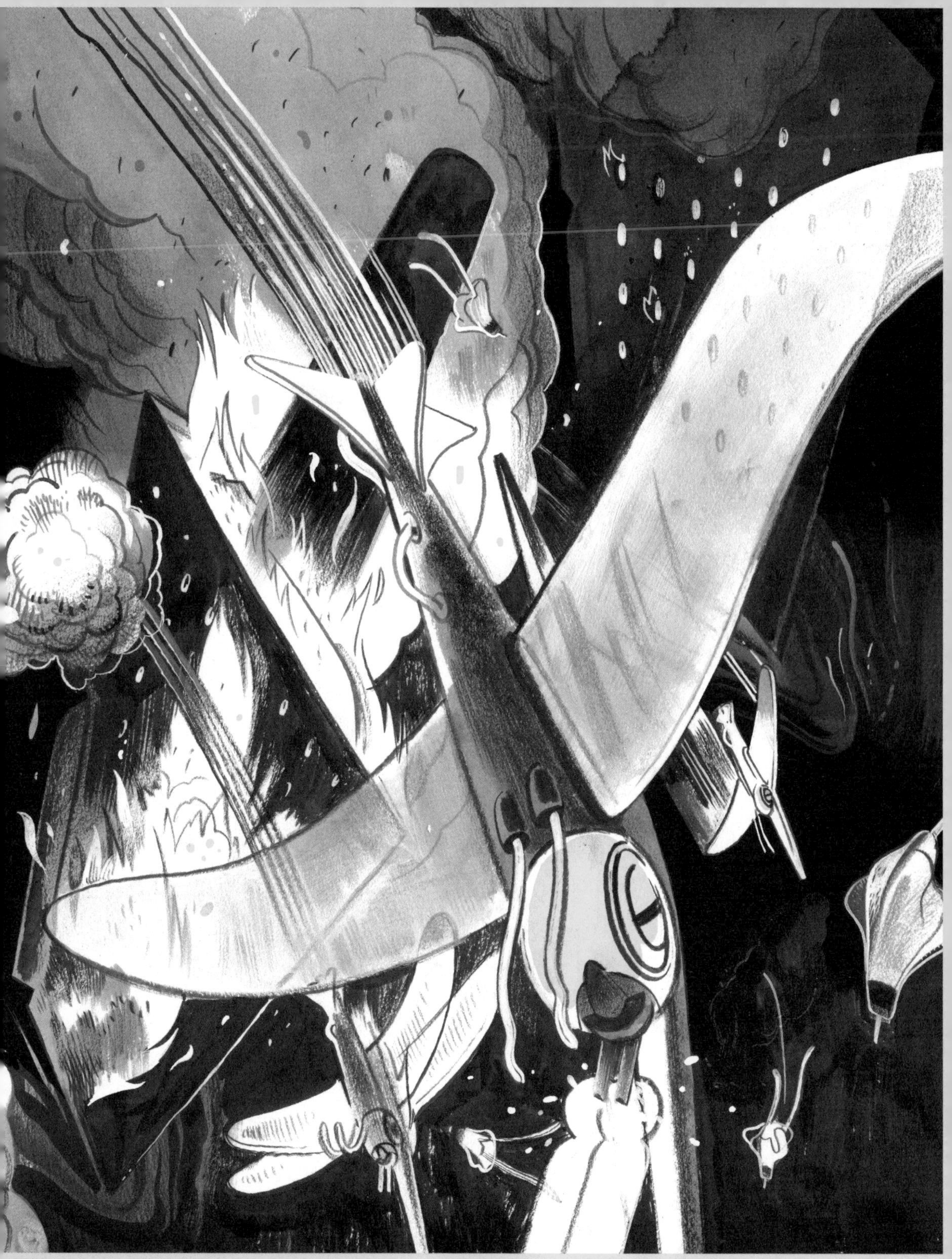

I GUESS THE TRICK NOW IS TO SURVIVE LONG ENOUGH FOR OUR ENERGY STORES TO REPLENISH.

FINGERS CROSSED.

RIGHT, SAILOR?

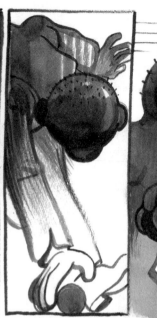

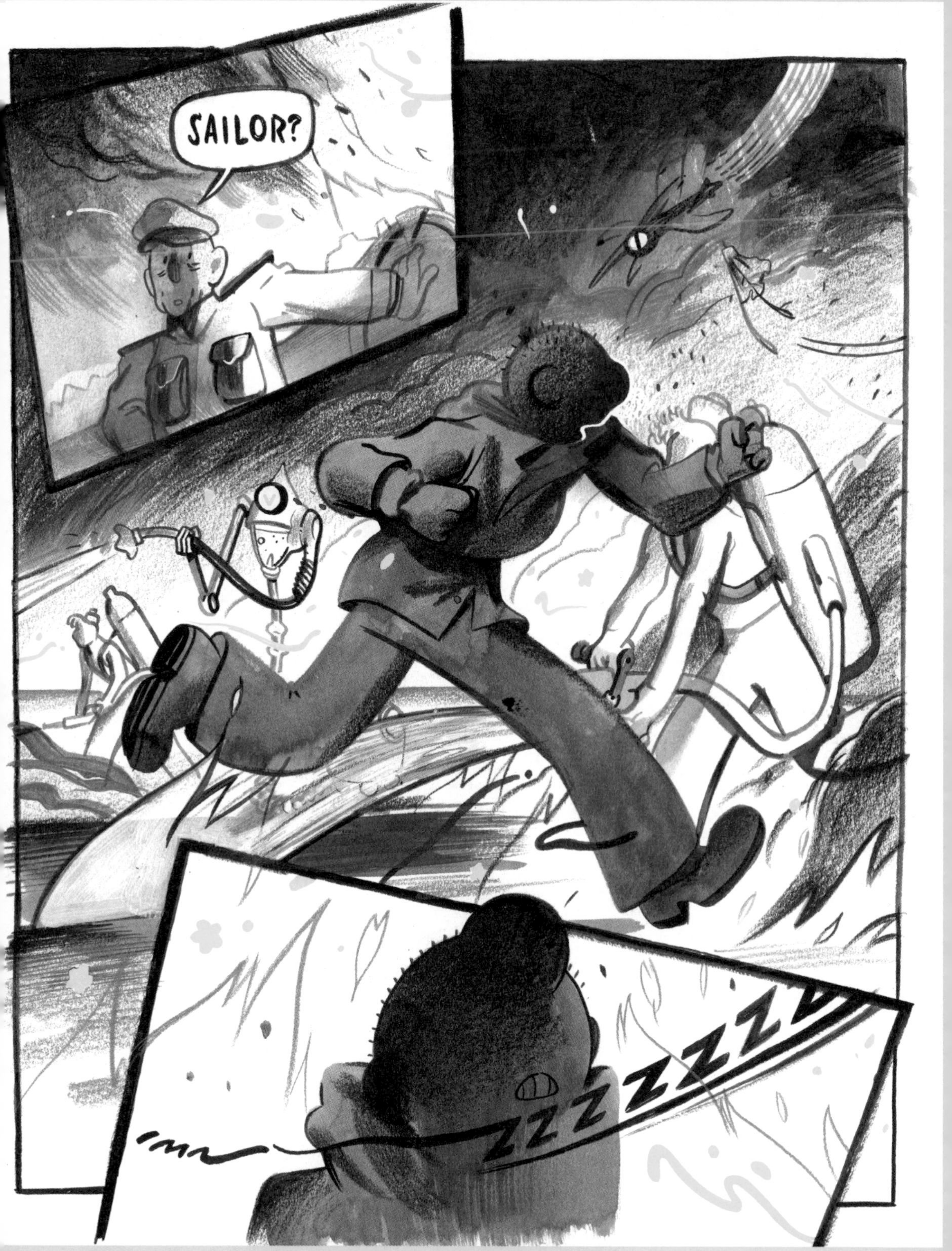
SAILOR?
ZZZZZZZZ

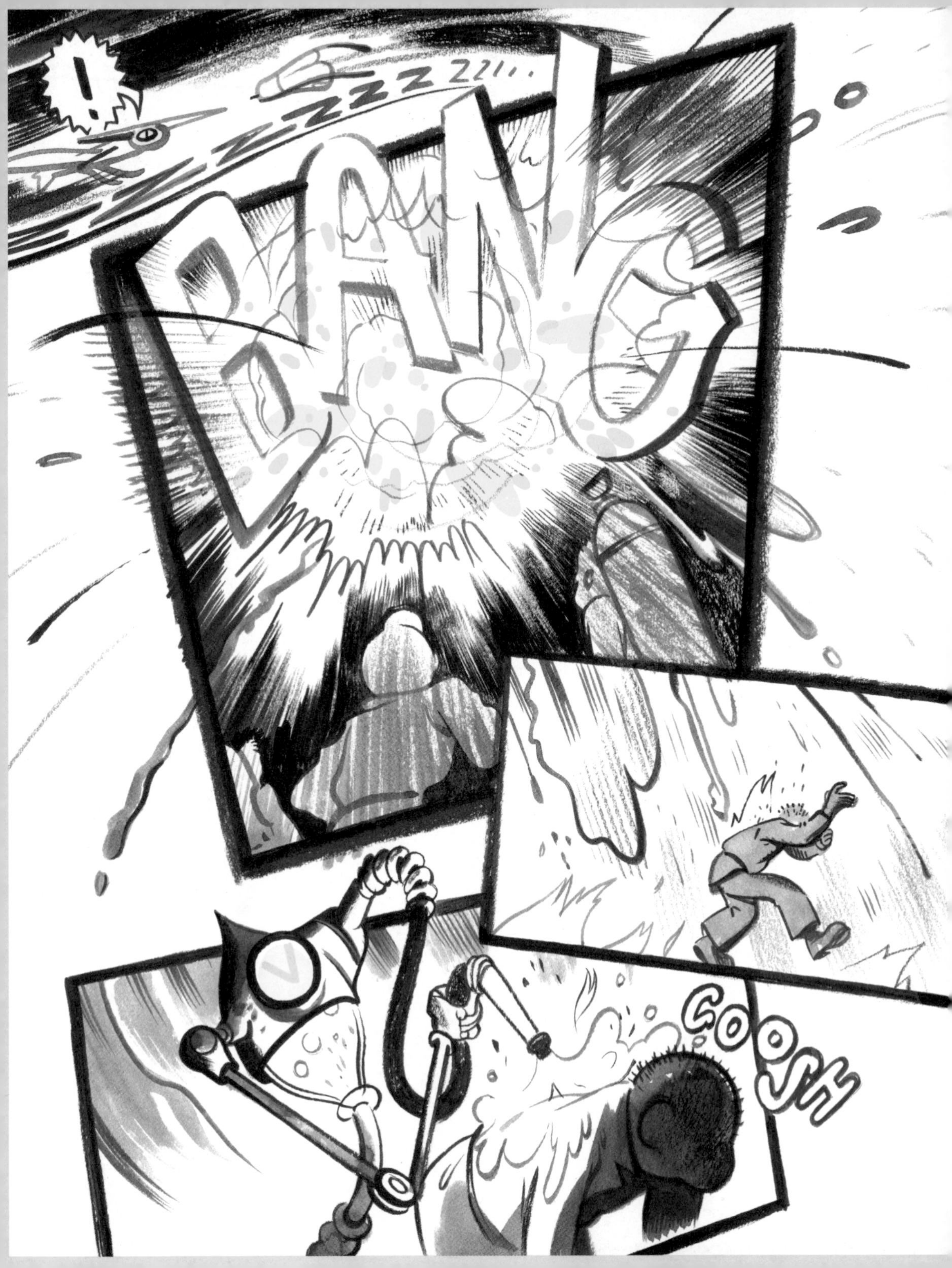
!
ZZZZZZZZZZZ...
BANG
GOOSH

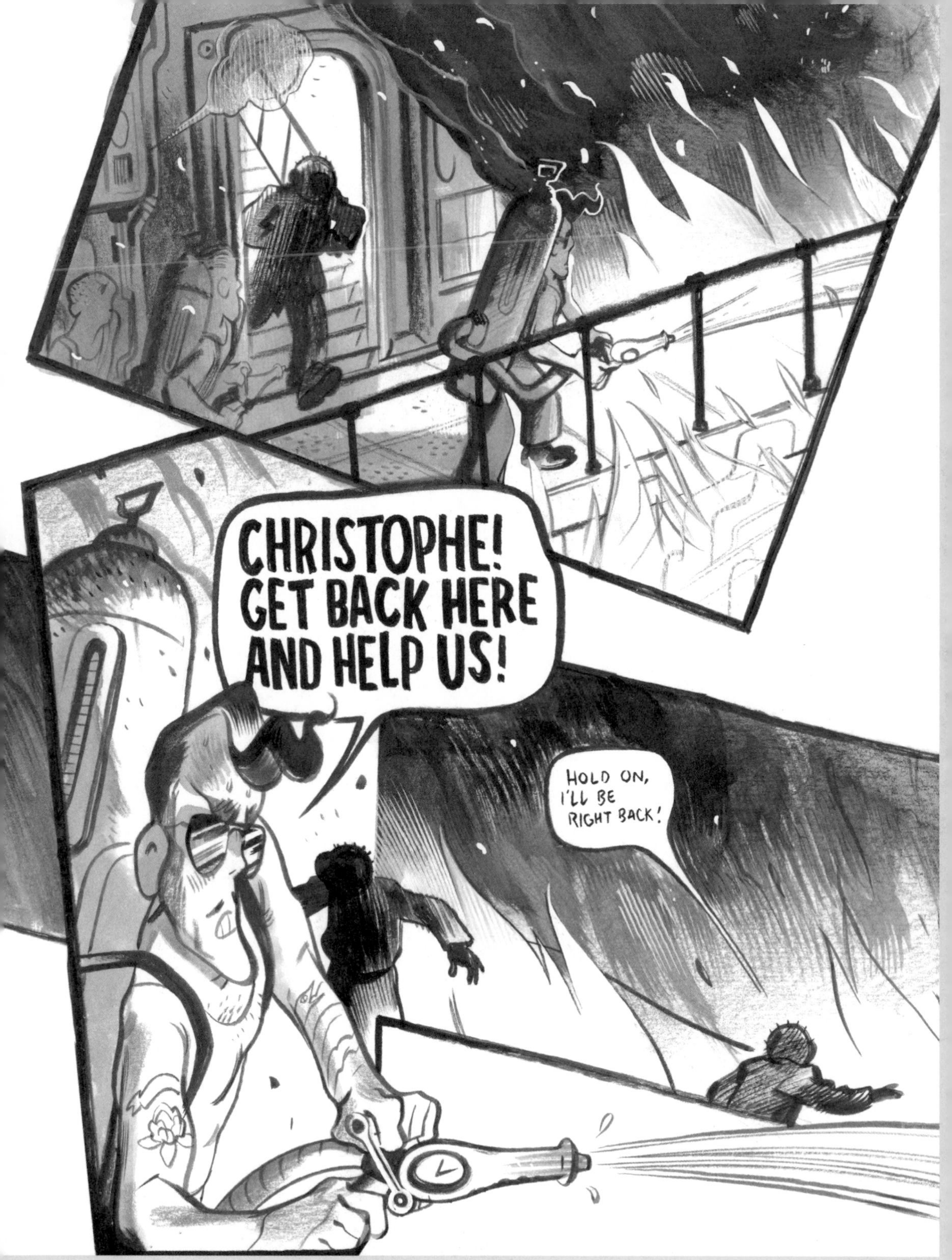
CHRISTOPHE! GET BACK HERE AND HELP US!
HOLD ON, I'LL BE RIGHT BACK!

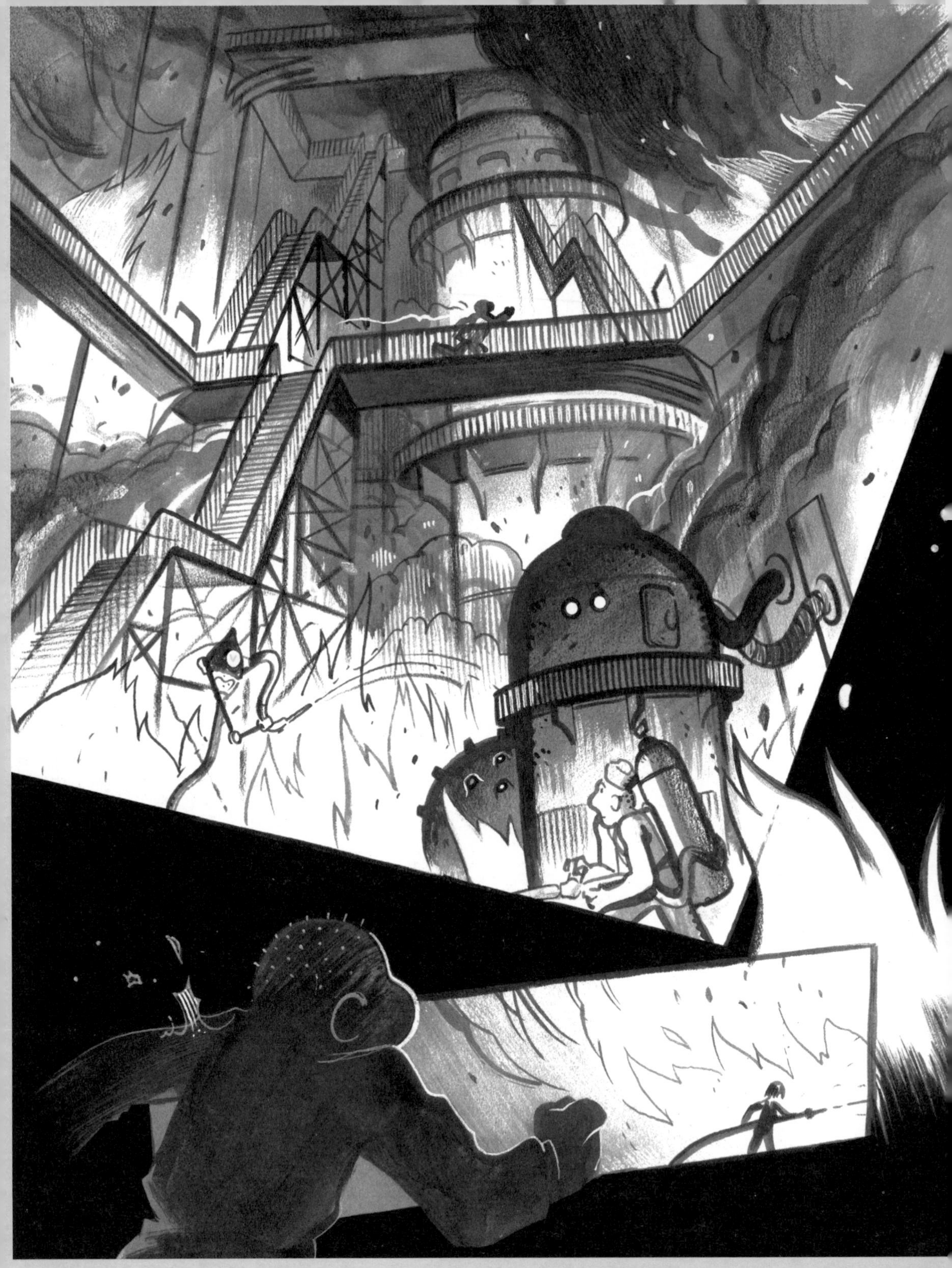

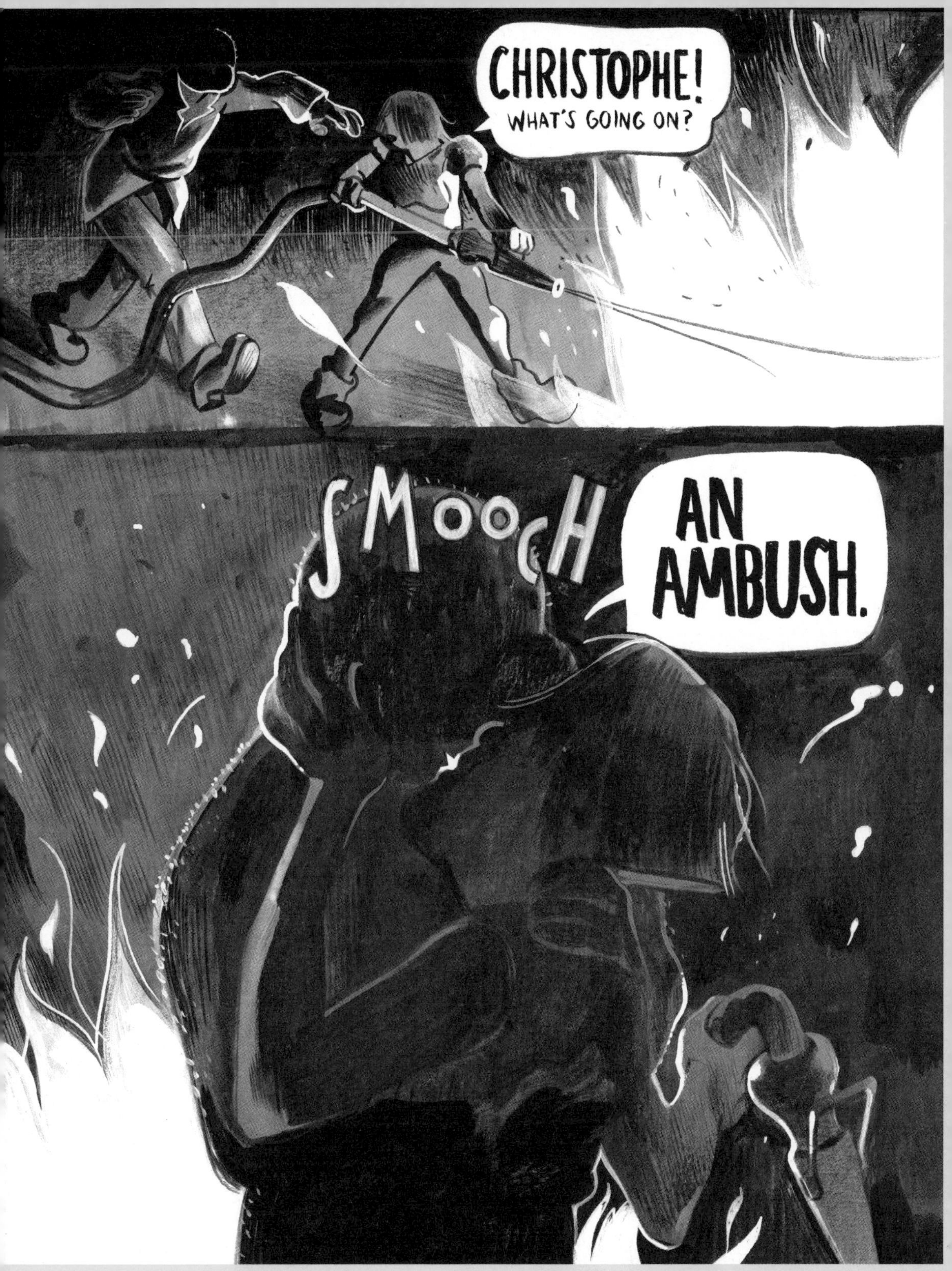
CHRISTOPHE! WHAT'S GOING ON?
SMOOCH
AN AMBUSH.

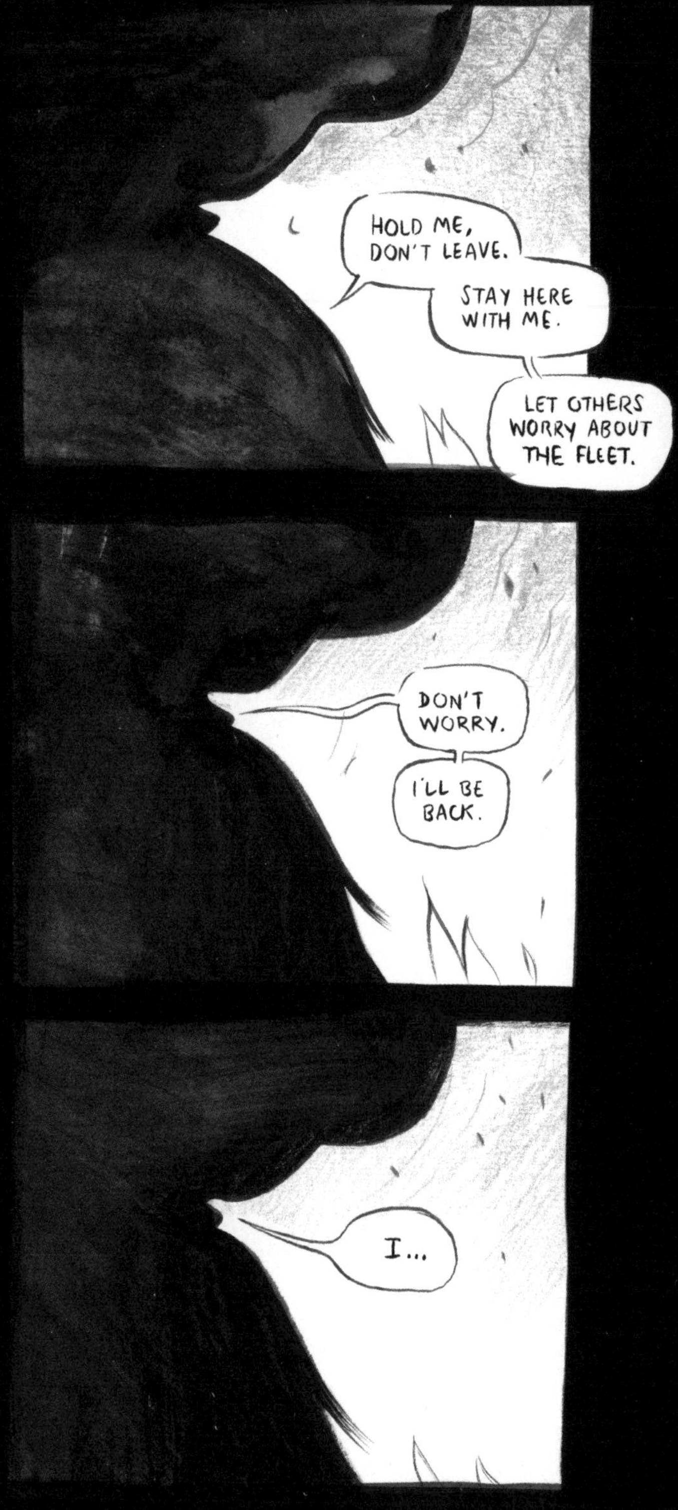
HOLD ME, DON'T LEAVE.
STAY HERE WITH ME.
LET OTHERS WORRY ABOUT THE FLEET.
DON'T WORRY.
I'LL BE BACK.
I...

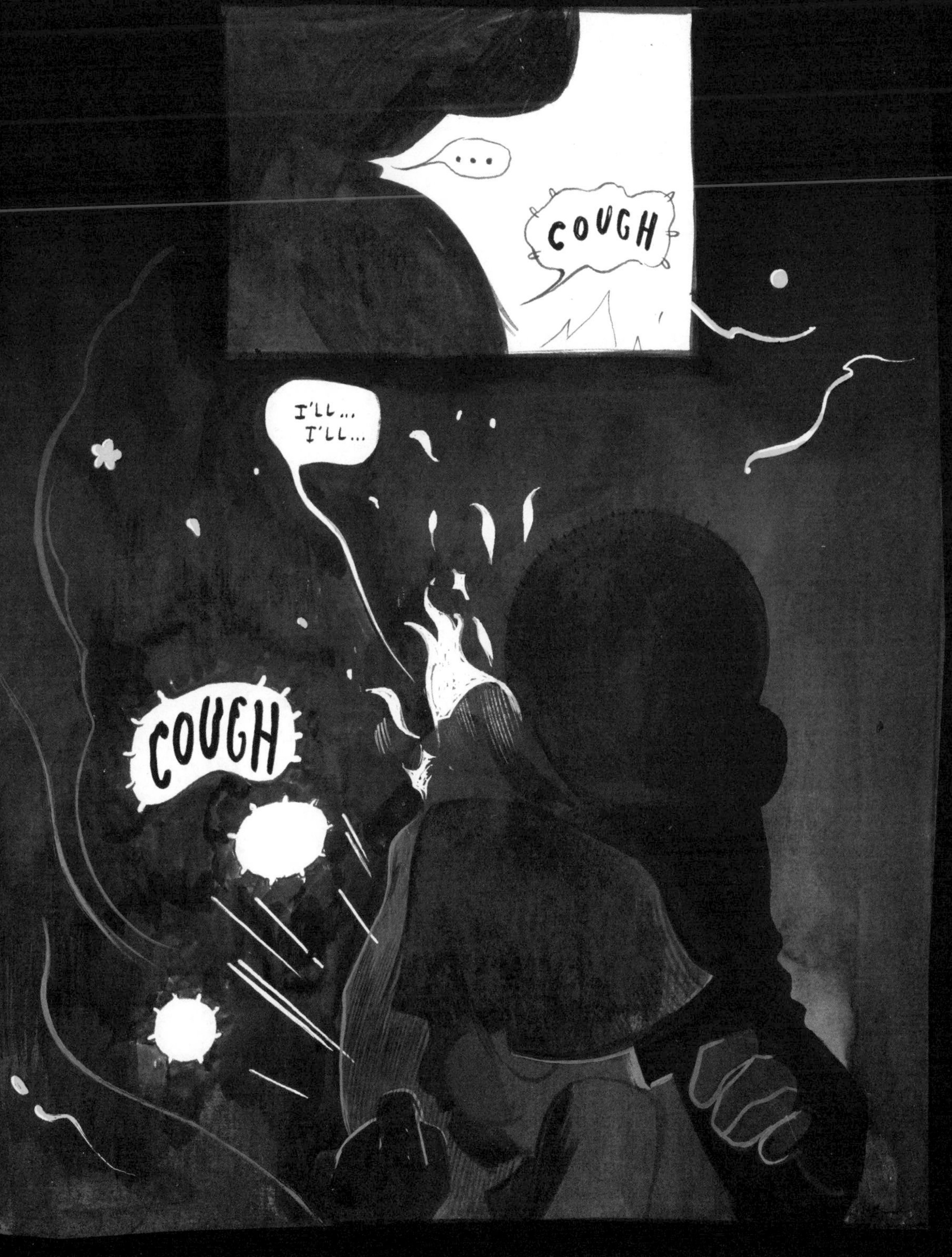
...
COUGH
I'LL... I'LL...
COUGH

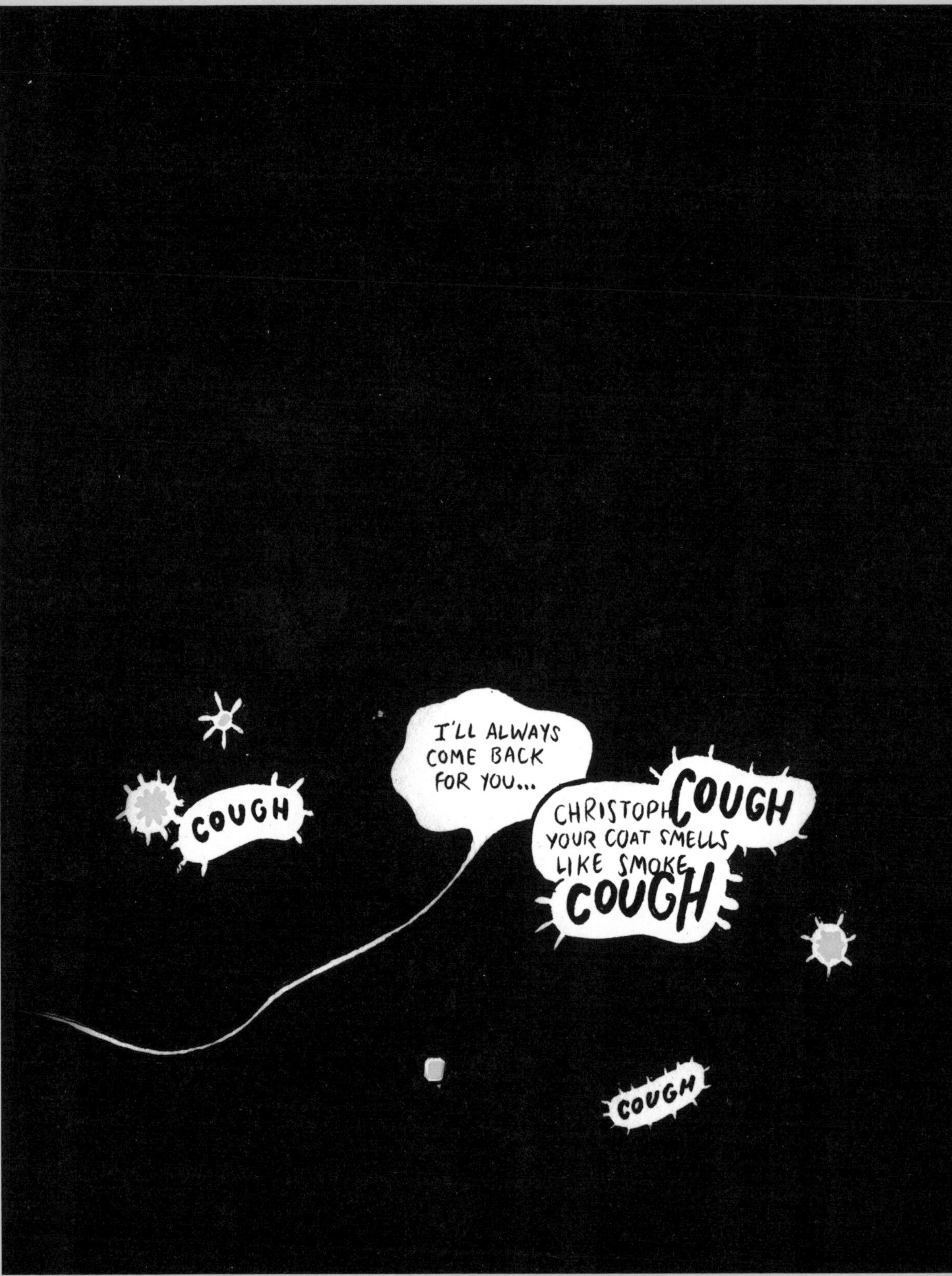
COUGH
I'LL ALWAYS COME BACK FOR YOU...
CHRISTOPH COUGH
YOUR COAT SMELLS LIKE SMOKE
COUGH
COUGH

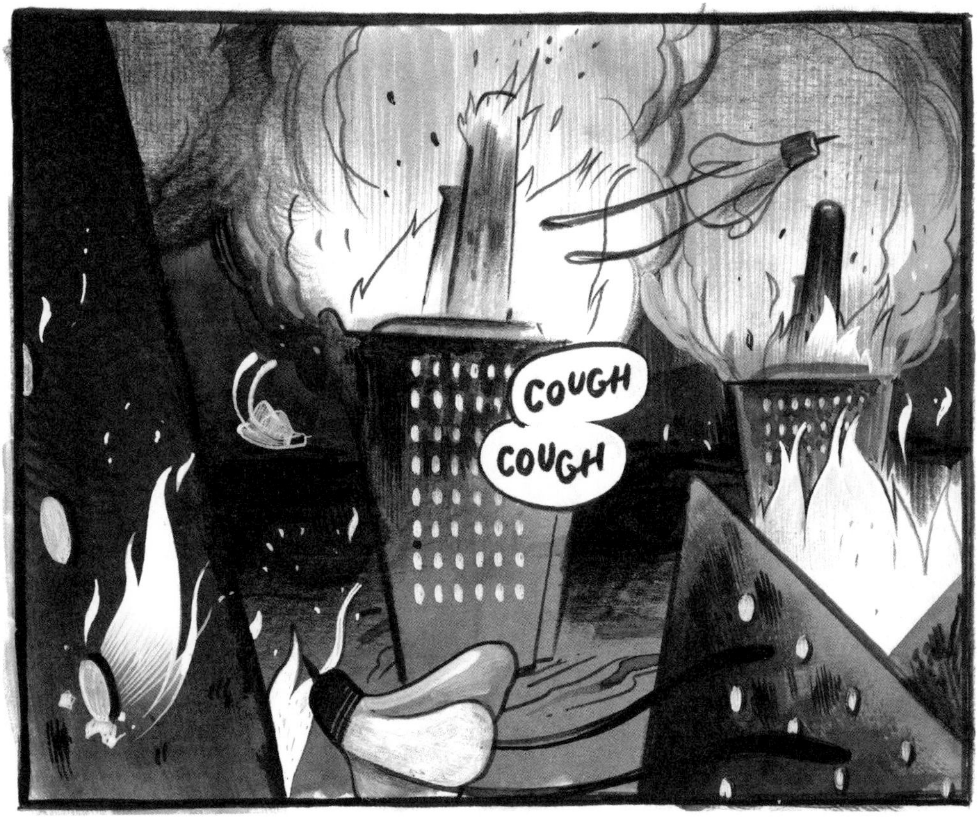
COUGH
COUGH

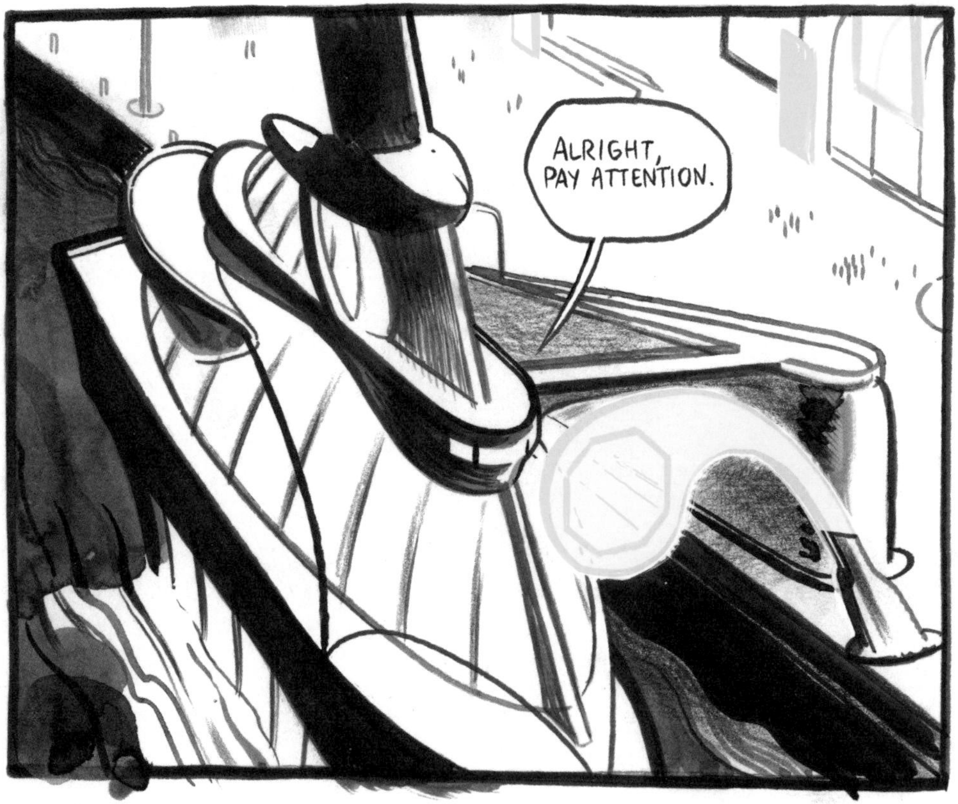
ALRIGHT, PAY ATTENTION.

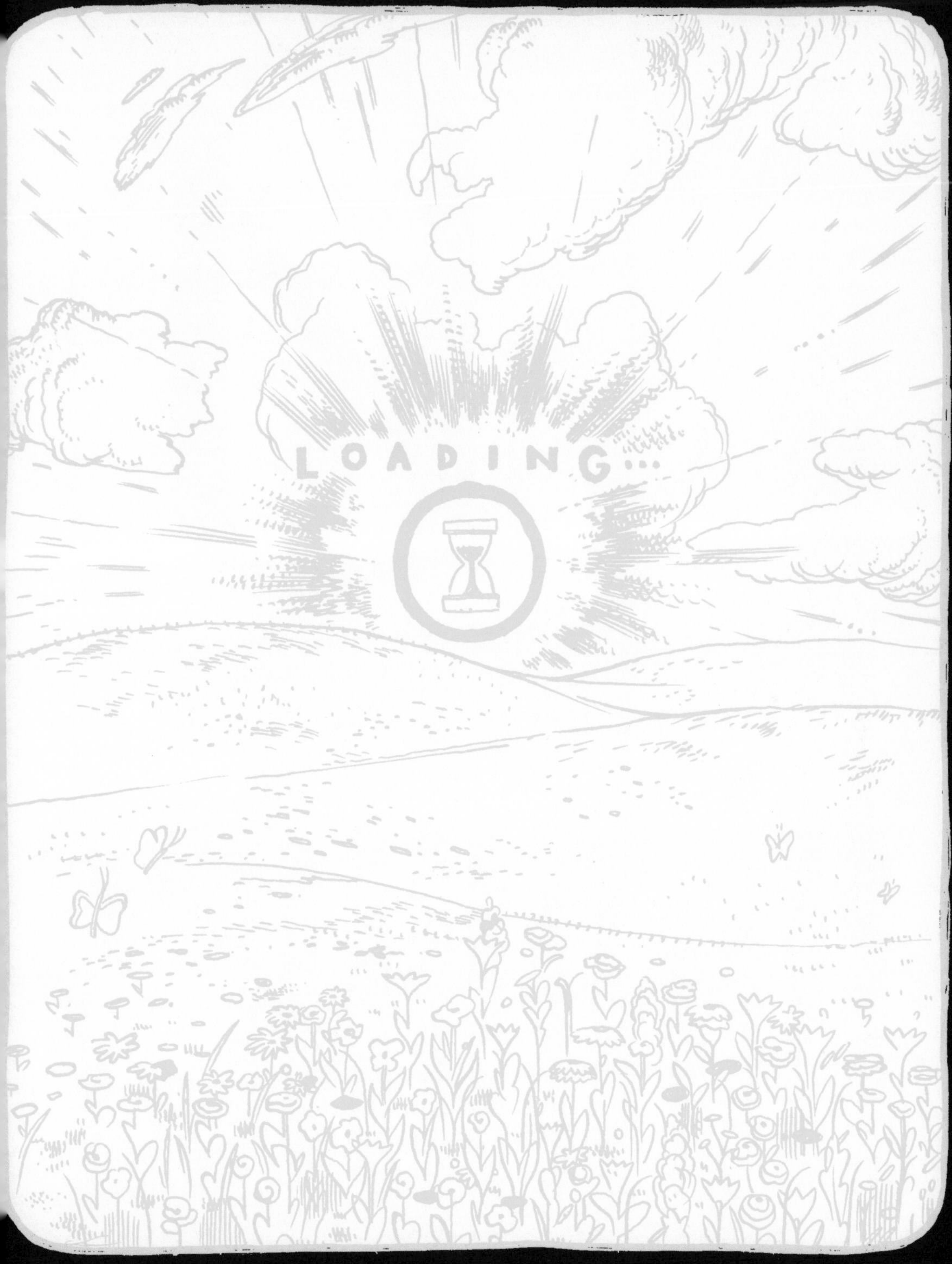
LOADING...

WHAT
EXACTLY,
IS ZERO?

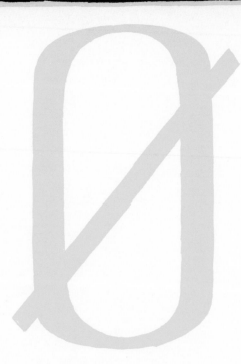

IN TODAY'S CULTURAL CLIMATE,
WHERE SPACE IS TIGHT,
AND OUR SCHEDULES EVEN
TIGHTER, WHAT IS...

NOTHING?

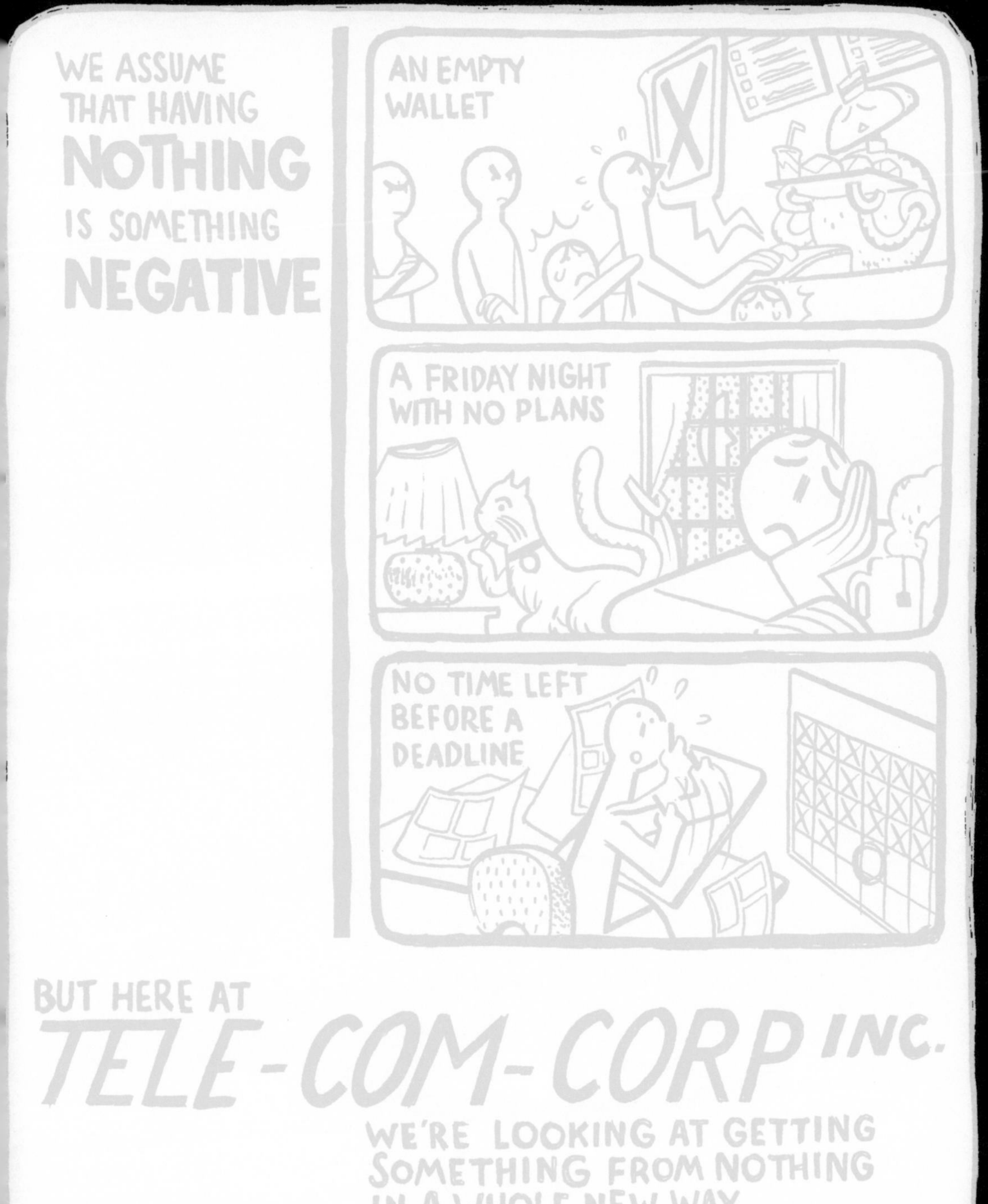
WE ASSUME THAT HAVING NOTHING IS SOMETHING NEGATIVE
AN EMPTY WALLET
A FRIDAY NIGHT WITH NO PLANS
NO TIME LEFT BEFORE A DEADLINE
BUT HERE AT TELE-COM-CORP INC.
WE'RE LOOKING AT GETTING SOMETHING FROM NOTHING IN A WHOLE NEW WAY.

BECAUSE EVERYTHING,
        INCLUDING OUR NATURAL RESOURCES,
            DEPENDS ON HOW YOU LOOK AT IT.

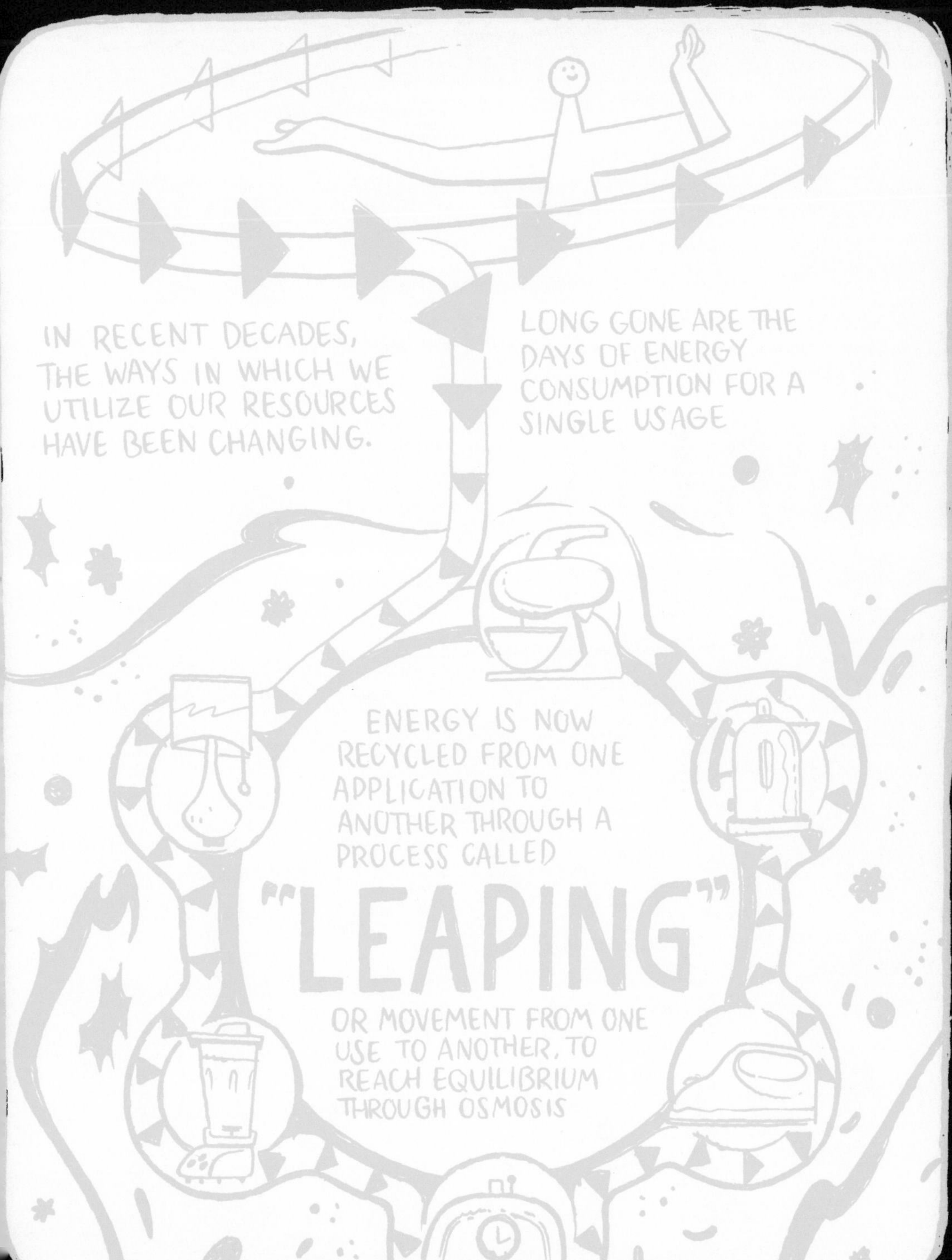
IN RECENT DECADES, THE WAYS IN WHICH WE UTILIZE OUR RESOURCES HAVE BEEN CHANGING.
LONG GONE ARE THE DAYS OF ENERGY CONSUMPTION FOR A SINGLE USAGE
ENERGY IS NOW RECYCLED FROM ONE APPLICATION TO ANOTHER THROUGH A PROCESS CALLED
"LEAPING"
OR MOVEMENT FROM ONE USE TO ANOTHER, TO REACH EQUILIBRIUM THROUGH OSMOSIS

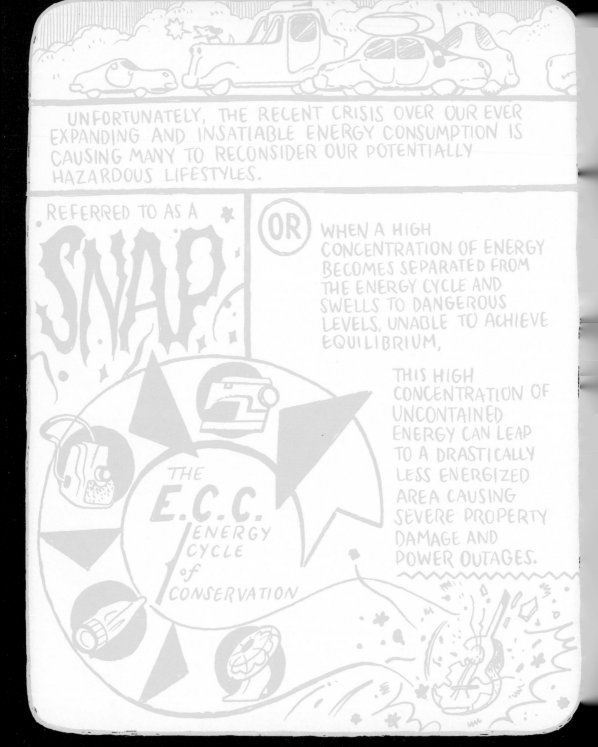

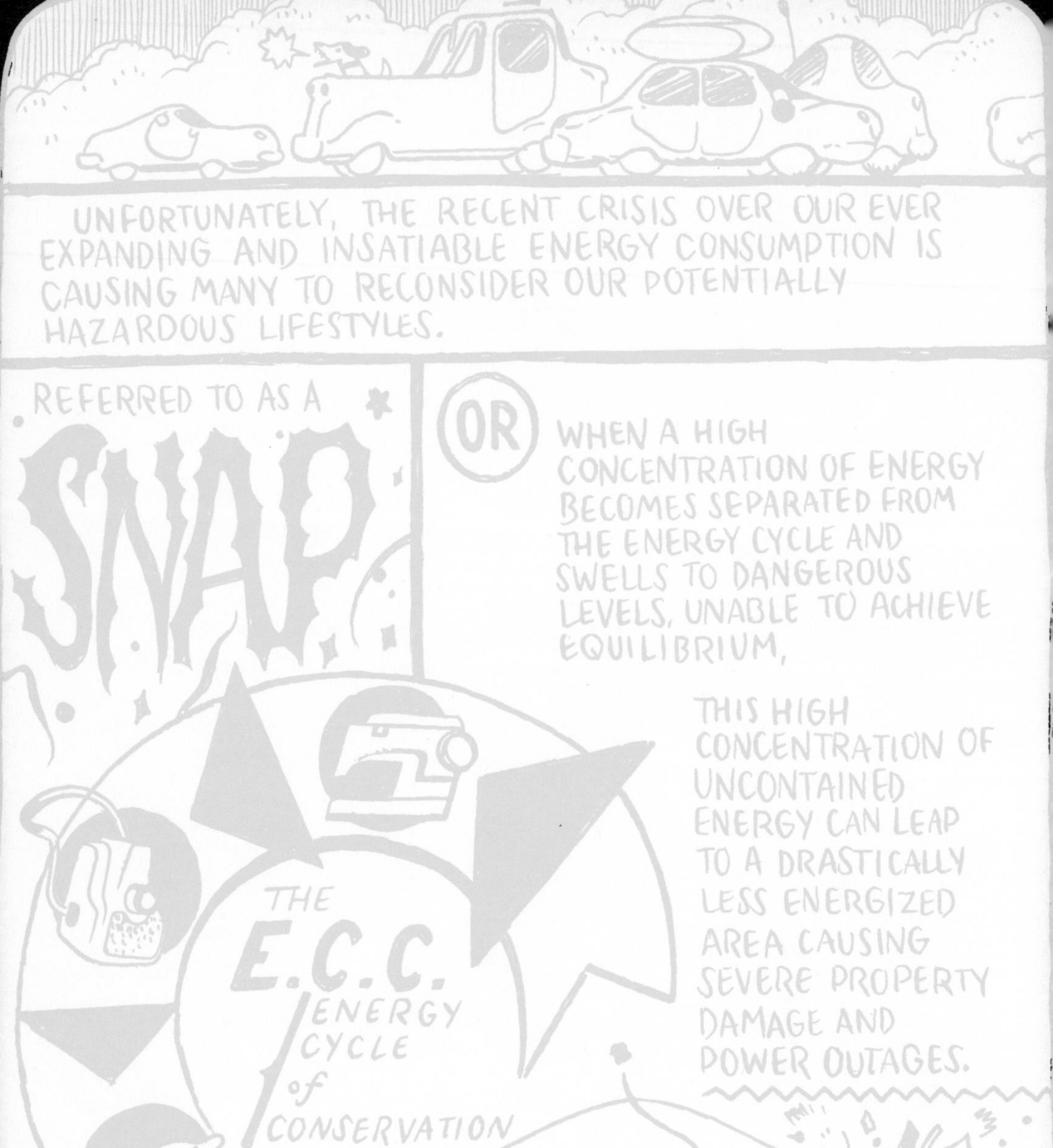
UNFORTUNATELY, THE RECENT CRISIS OVER OUR EVER EXPANDING AND INSATIABLE ENERGY CONSUMPTION IS CAUSING MANY TO RECONSIDER OUR POTENTIALLY HAZARDOUS LIFESTYLES.
REFERRED TO AS A
SNAP
OR
WHEN A HIGH CONCENTRATION OF ENERGY BECOMES SEPARATED FROM THE ENERGY CYCLE AND SWELLS TO DANGEROUS LEVELS, UNABLE TO ACHIEVE EQUILIBRIUM,
THIS HIGH CONCENTRATION OF UNCONTAINED ENERGY CAN LEAP TO A DRASTICALLY LESS ENERGIZED AREA CAUSING SEVERE PROPERTY DAMAGE AND POWER OUTAGES.
THE
E.C.C.
ENERGY
CYCLE
of
CONSERVATION

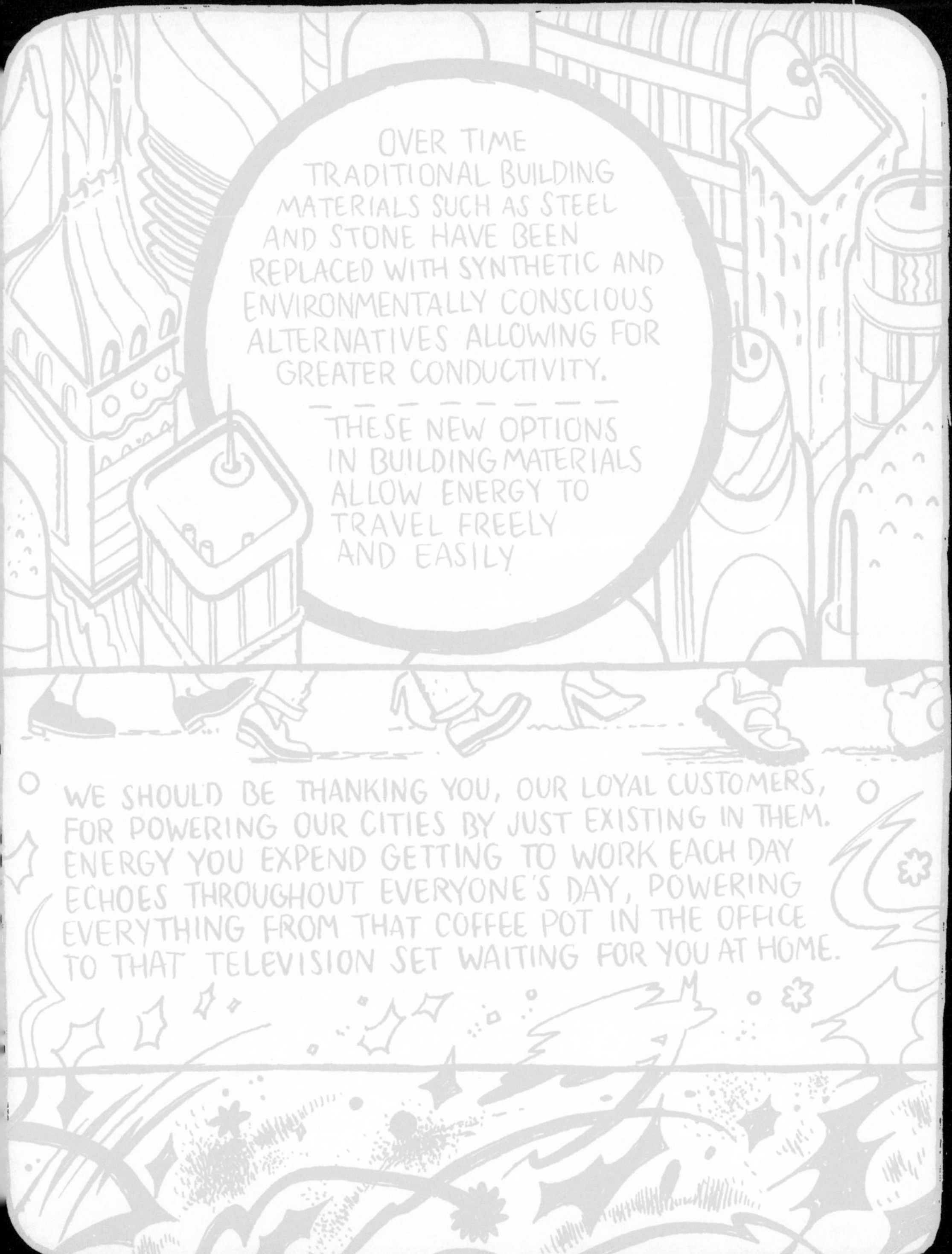
OVER TIME TRADITIONAL BUILDING MATERIALS SUCH AS STEEL AND STONE HAVE BEEN REPLACED WITH SYNTHETIC AND ENVIRONMENTALLY CONSCIOUS ALTERNATIVES ALLOWING FOR GREATER CONDUCTIVITY.
THESE NEW OPTIONS IN BUILDING MATERIALS ALLOW ENERGY TO TRAVEL FREELY AND EASILY
WE SHOULD BE THANKING YOU, OUR LOYAL CUSTOMERS, FOR POWERING OUR CITIES BY JUST EXISTING IN THEM. ENERGY YOU EXPEND GETTING TO WORK EACH DAY ECHOES THROUGHOUT EVERYONE'S DAY, POWERING EVERYTHING FROM THAT COFFEE POT IN THE OFFICE TO THAT TELEVISION SET WAITING FOR YOU AT HOME.

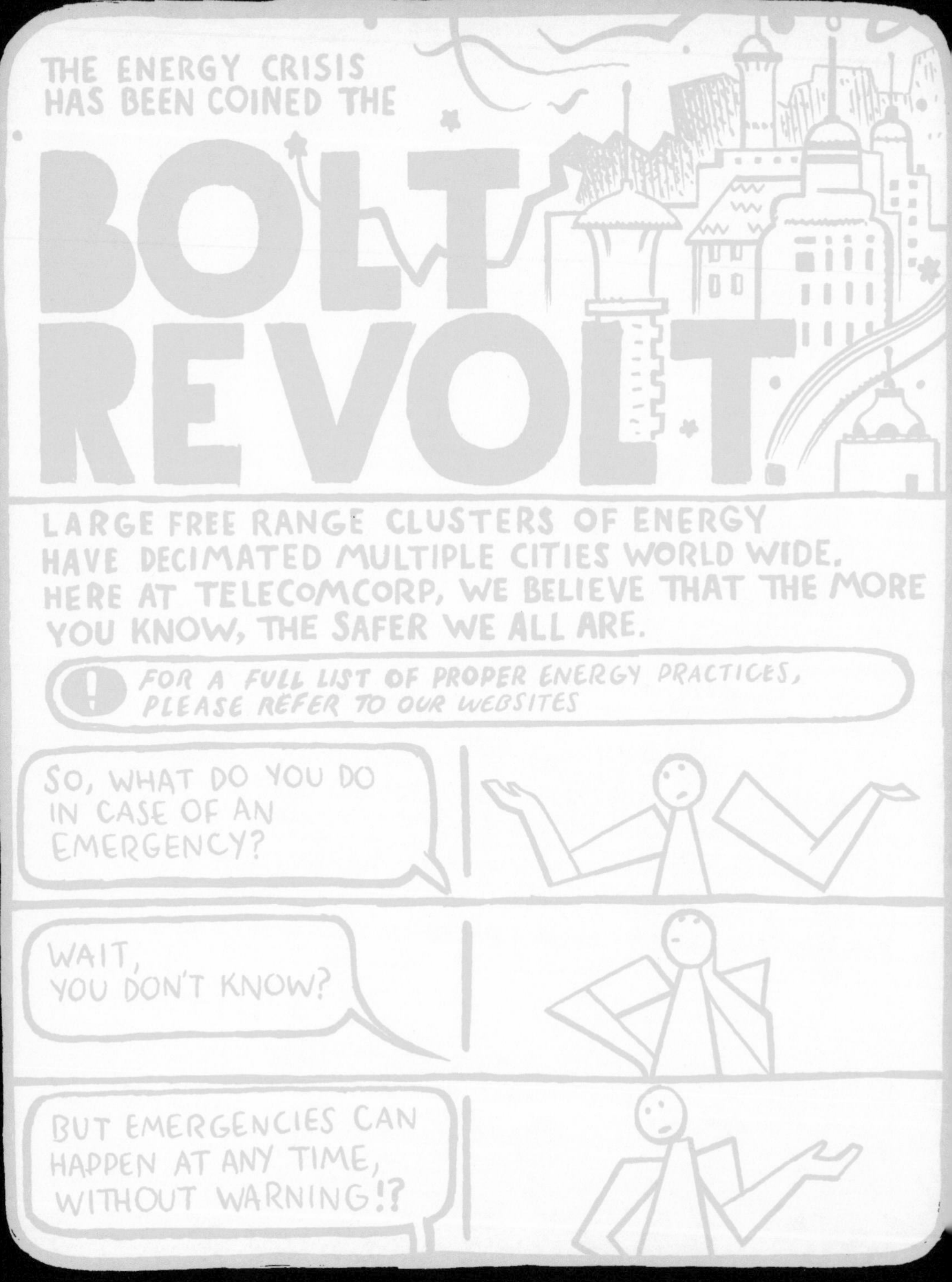
THE ENERGY CRISIS HAS BEEN COINED THE
BOLT REVOLT
LARGE FREE RANGE CLUSTERS OF ENERGY HAVE DECIMATED MULTIPLE CITIES WORLD WIDE. HERE AT TELECOMCORP, WE BELIEVE THAT THE MORE YOU KNOW, THE SAFER WE ALL ARE.
FOR A FULL LIST OF PROPER ENERGY PRACTICES, PLEASE REFER TO OUR WEBSITES
SO, WHAT DO YOU DO IN CASE OF AN EMERGENCY?
WAIT, YOU DON'T KNOW?
BUT EMERGENCIES CAN HAPPEN AT ANY TIME, WITHOUT WARNING!?

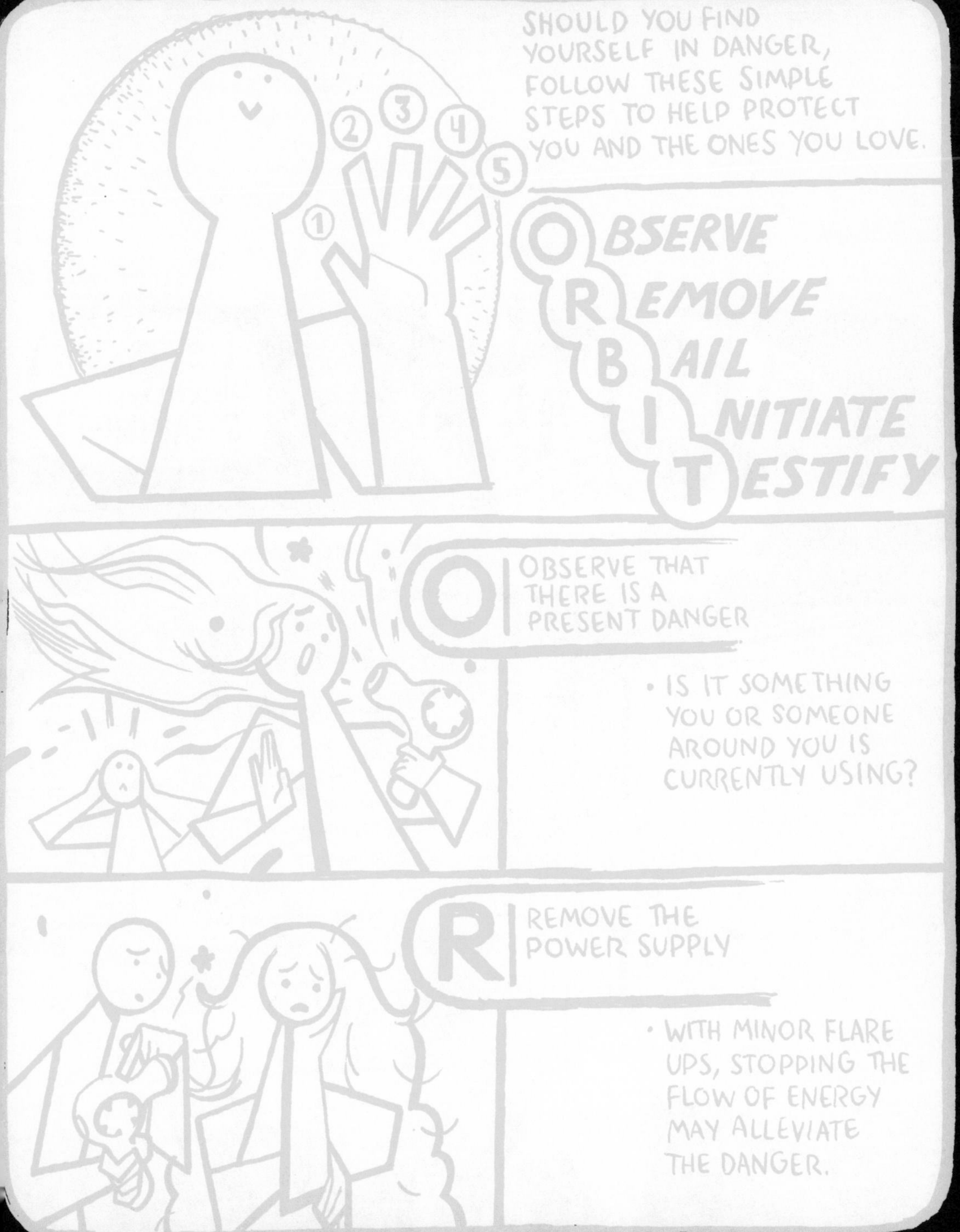
SHOULD YOU FIND YOURSELF IN DANGER, FOLLOW THESE SIMPLE STEPS TO HELP PROTECT YOU AND THE ONES YOU LOVE.
1
2
3
4
5
OBSERVE
REMOVE
BAIL
INITIATE
TESTIFY
O
OBSERVE THAT THERE IS A PRESENT DANGER
• IS IT SOMETHING YOU OR SOMEONE AROUND YOU IS CURRENTLY USING?
R
REMOVE THE POWER SUPPLY
• WITH MINOR FLARE UPS, STOPPING THE FLOW OF ENERGY MAY ALLEVIATE THE DANGER.

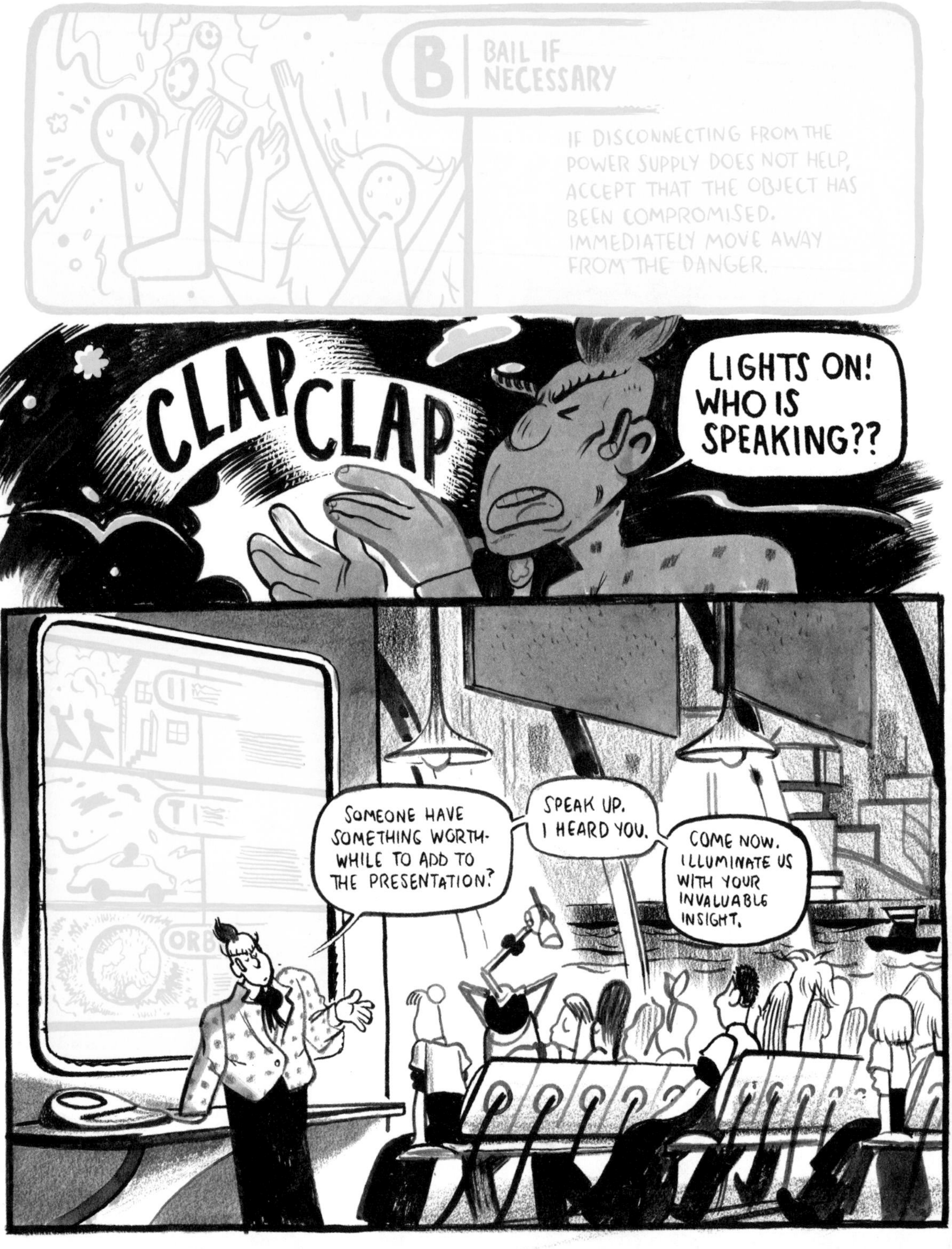
B
BAIL IF NECESSARY
IF DISCONNECTING FROM THE POWER SUPPLY DOES NOT HELP, ACCEPT THAT THE OBJECT HAS BEEN COMPROMISED. IMMEDIATELY MOVE AWAY FROM THE DANGER.
CLAP CLAP
LIGHTS ON! WHO IS SPEAKING??
SOMEONE HAVE SOMETHING WORTHWHILE TO ADD TO THE PRESENTATION?
SPEAK UP. I HEARD YOU.
COME NOW. ILLUMINATE US WITH YOUR INVALUABLE INSIGHT.
ORB

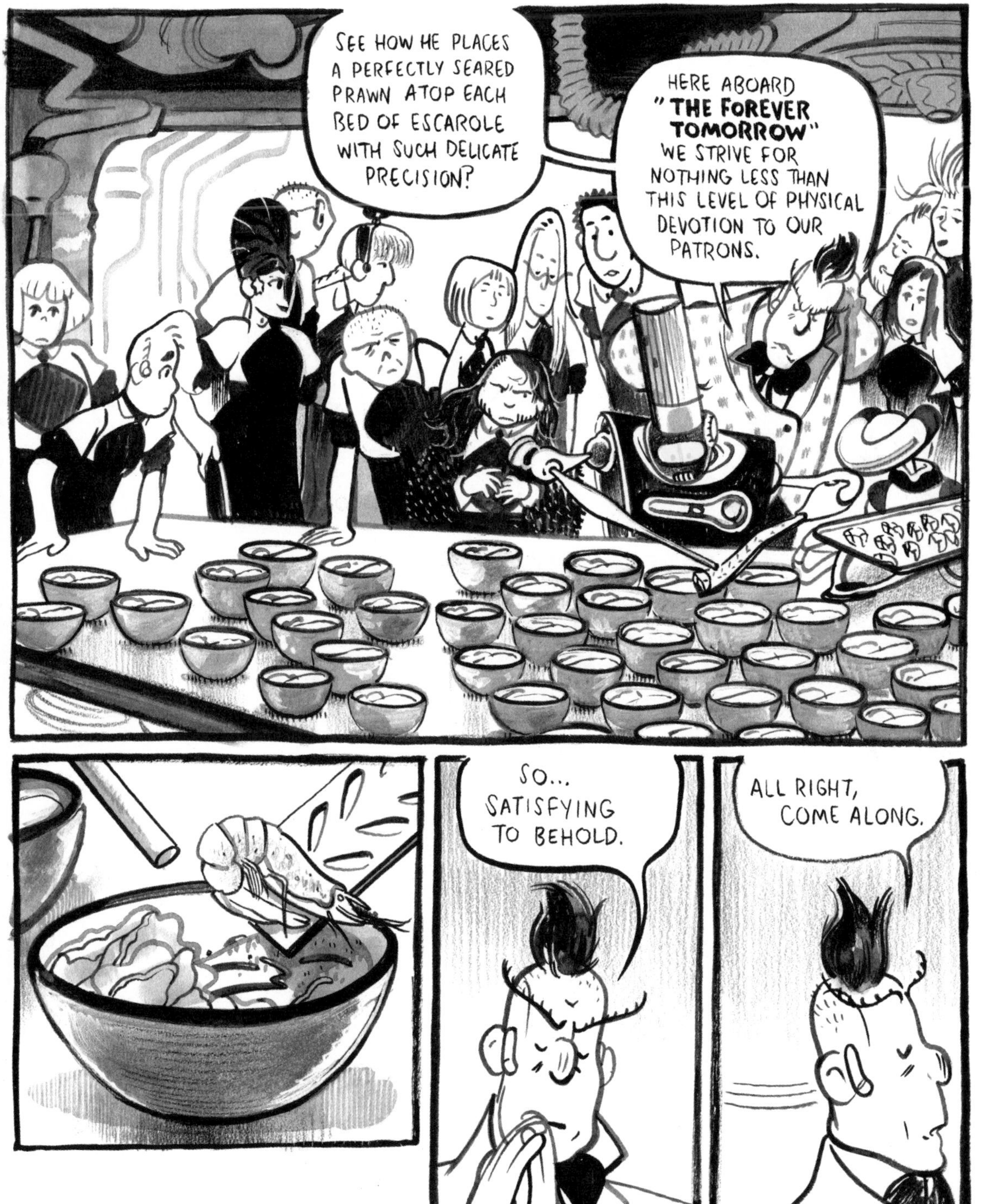
SEE HOW HE PLACES A PERFECTLY SEARED PRAWN ATOP EACH BED OF ESCAROLE WITH SUCH DELICATE PRECISION?
HERE ABOARD "THE FOREVER TOMORROW" WE STRIVE FOR NOTHING LESS THAN THIS LEVEL OF PHYSICAL DEVOTION TO OUR PATRONS.
SO... SATISFYING TO BEHOLD.
ALL RIGHT, COME ALONG.

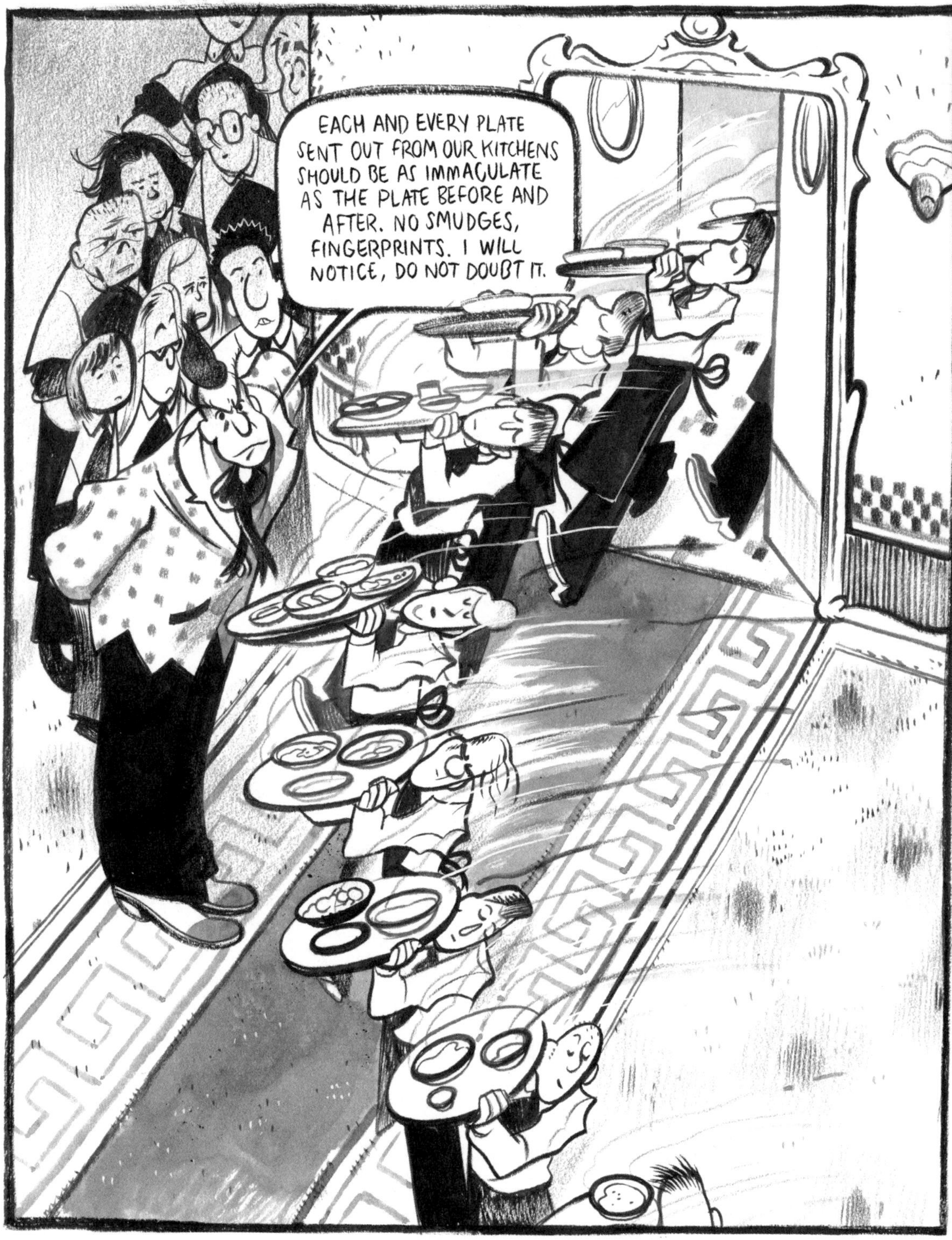
EACH AND EVERY PLATE SENT OUT FROM OUR KITCHENS SHOULD BE AS IMMACULATE AS THE PLATE BEFORE AND AFTER. NO SMUDGES, FINGERPRINTS. I WILL NOTICE, DO NOT DOUBT IT.

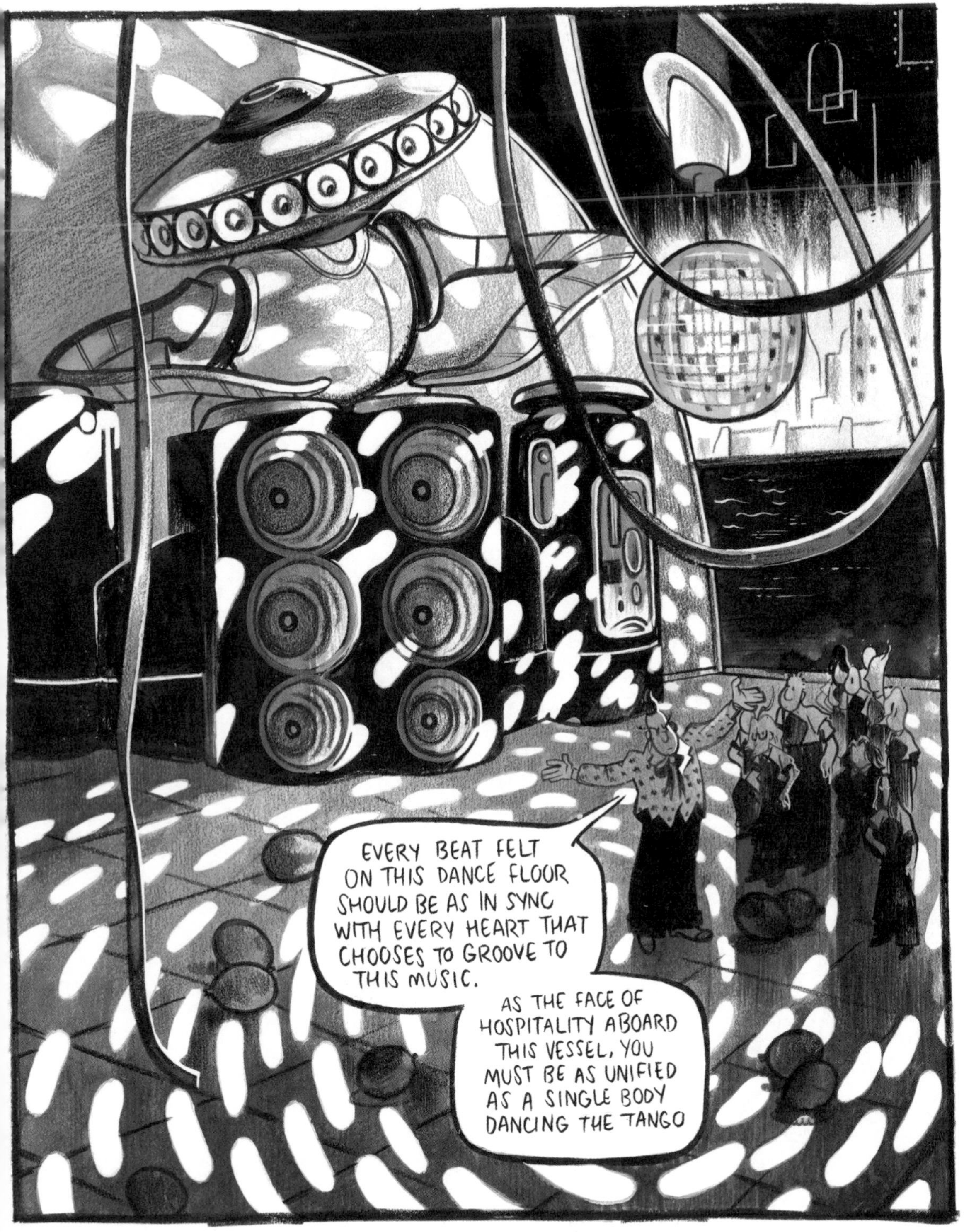
EVERY BEAT FELT ON THIS DANCE FLOOR SHOULD BE AS IN SYNC WITH EVERY HEART THAT CHOOSES TO GROOVE TO THIS MUSIC.
AS THE FACE OF HOSPITALITY ABOARD THIS VESSEL, YOU MUST BE AS UNIFIED AS A SINGLE BODY DANCING THE TANGO

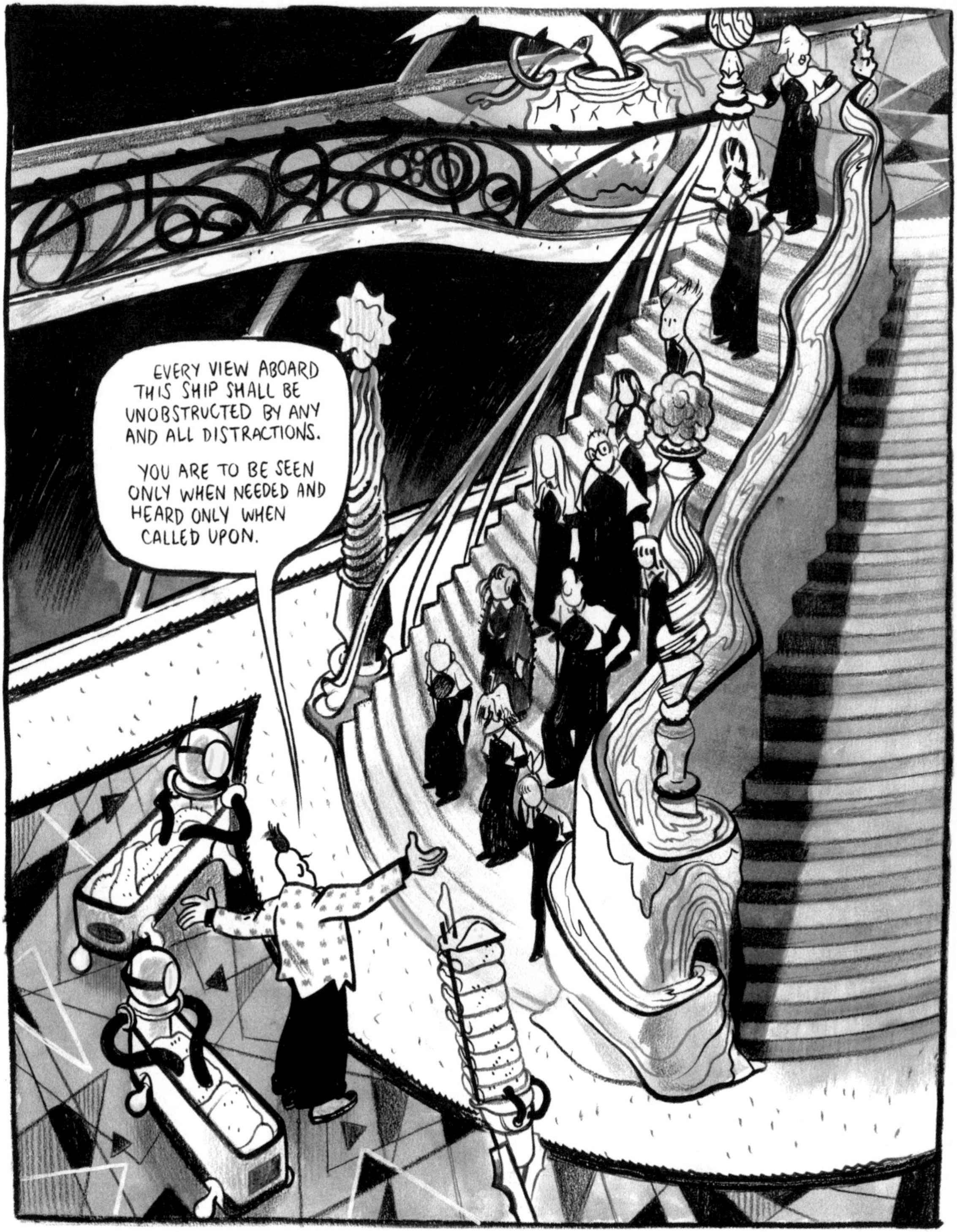
EVERY VIEW ABOARD THIS SHIP SHALL BE UNOBSTRUCTED BY ANY AND ALL DISTRACTIONS.
YOU ARE TO BE SEEN ONLY WHEN NEEDED AND HEARD ONLY WHEN CALLED UPON.

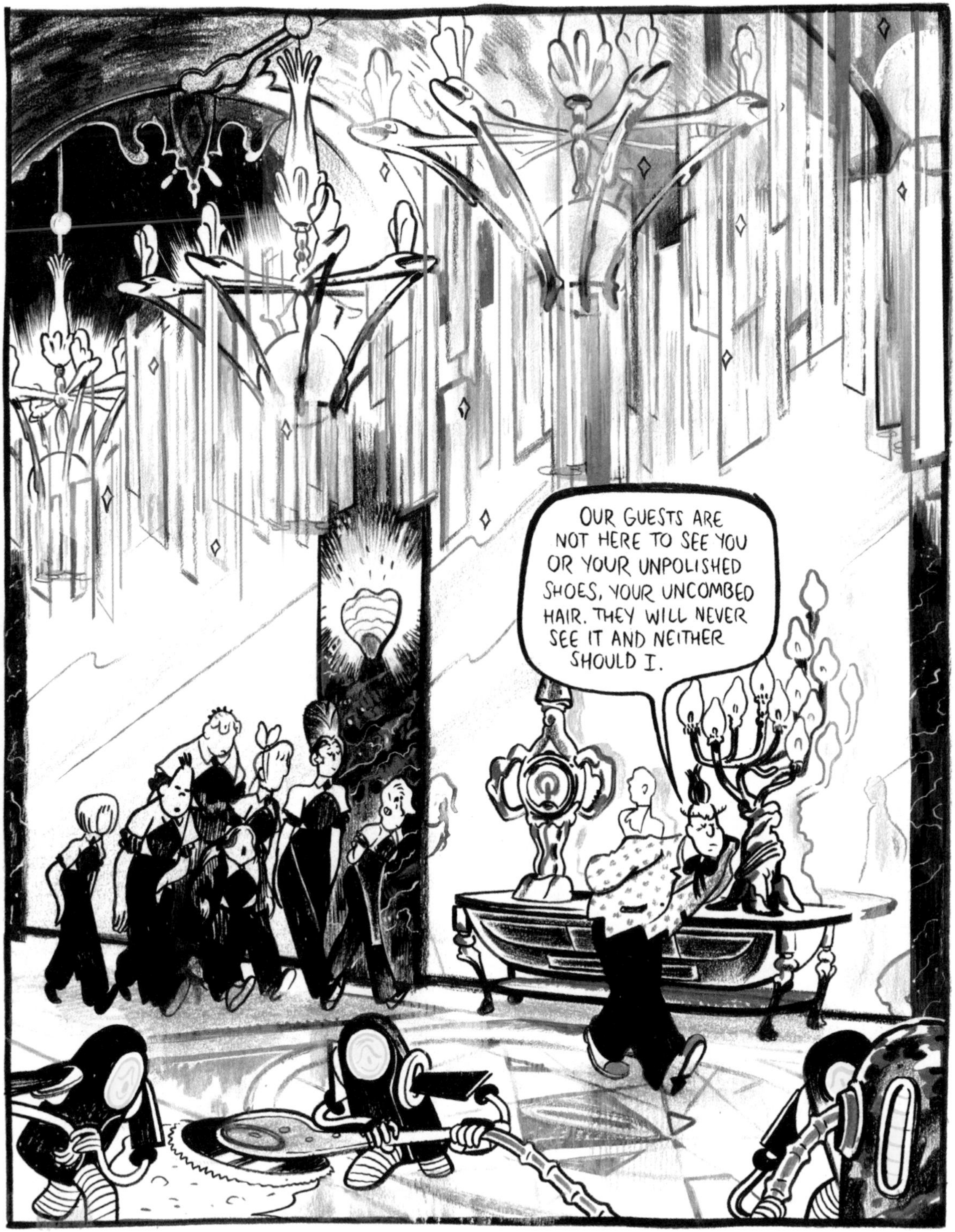
OUR GUESTS ARE NOT HERE TO SEE YOU OR YOUR UNPOLISHED SHOES, YOUR UNCOMBED HAIR. THEY WILL NEVER SEE IT AND NEITHER SHOULD I.

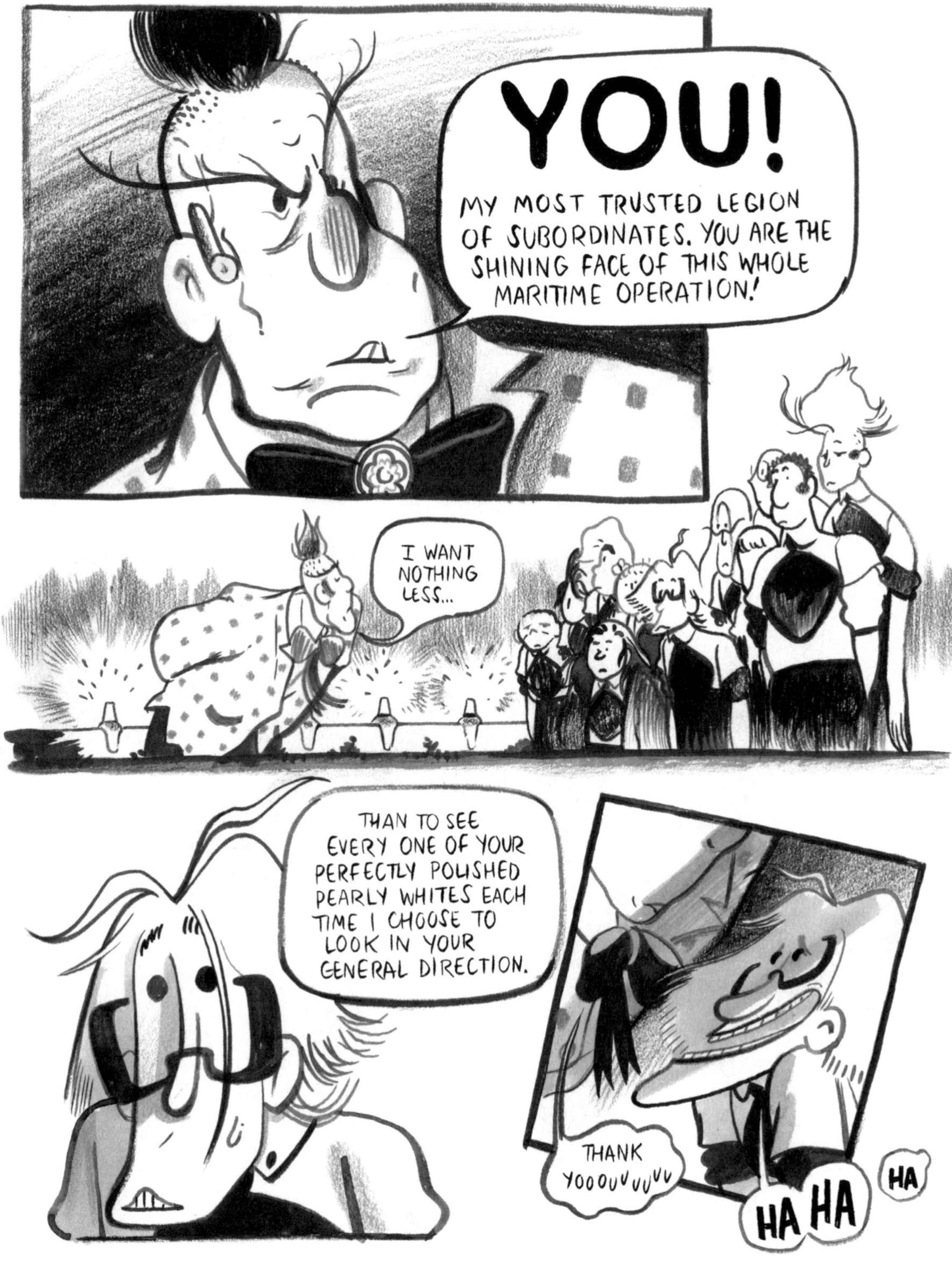
YOU!
MY MOST TRUSTED LEGION OF SUBORDINATES. YOU ARE THE SHINING FACE OF THIS WHOLE MARITIME OPERATION!
I WANT NOTHING LESS...
THAN TO SEE EVERY ONE OF YOUR PERFECTLY POLISHED PEARLY WHITES EACH TIME I CHOOSE TO LOOK IN YOUR GENERAL DIRECTION.
THANK YOOOUVVUVVV
HA HA
HA

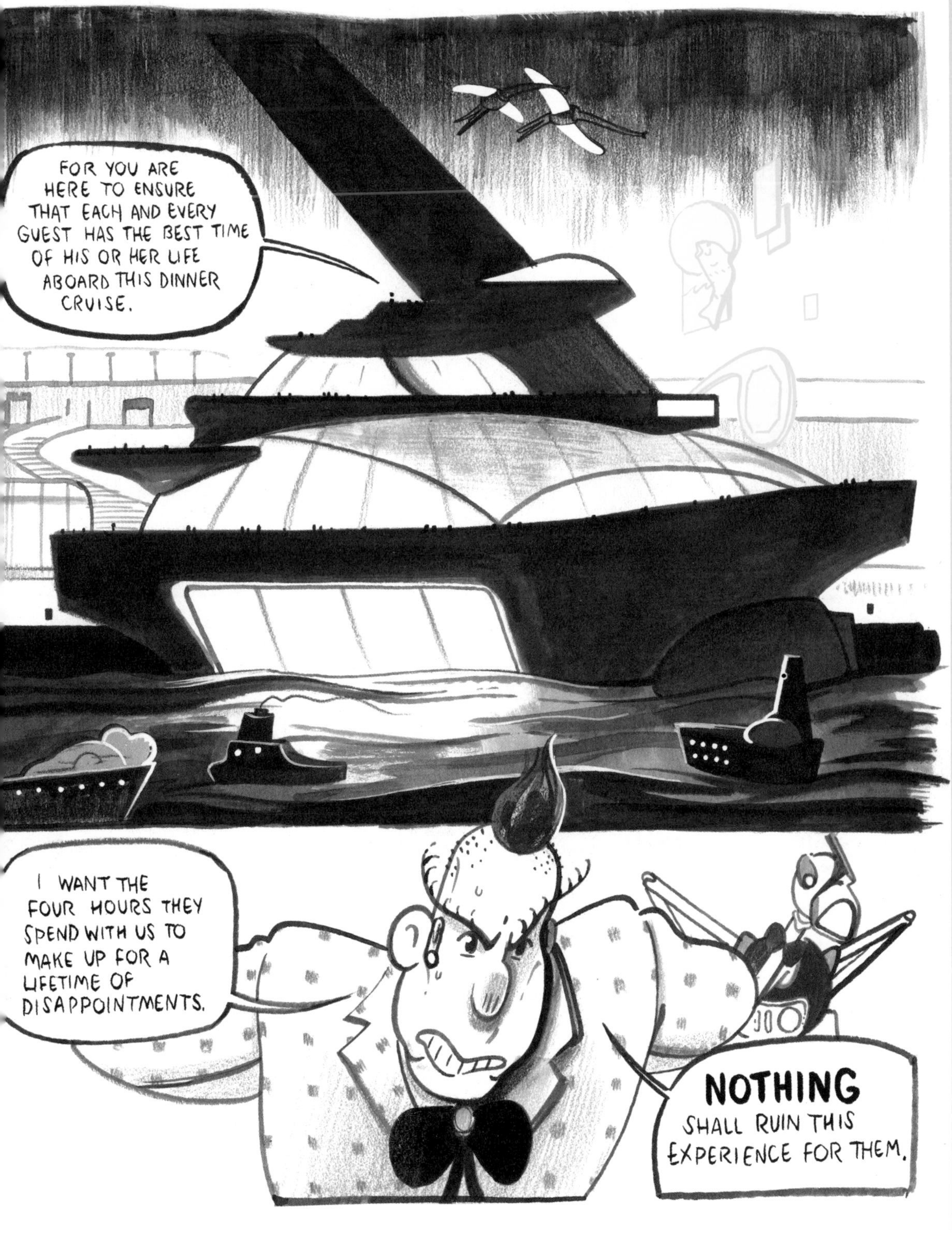
FOR YOU ARE HERE TO ENSURE THAT EACH AND EVERY GUEST HAS THE BEST TIME OF HIS OR HER LIFE ABOARD THIS DINNER CRUISE.
I WANT THE FOUR HOURS THEY SPEND WITH US TO MAKE UP FOR A LIFETIME OF DISAPPOINTMENTS.
NOTHING SHALL RUIN THIS EXPERIENCE FOR THEM.

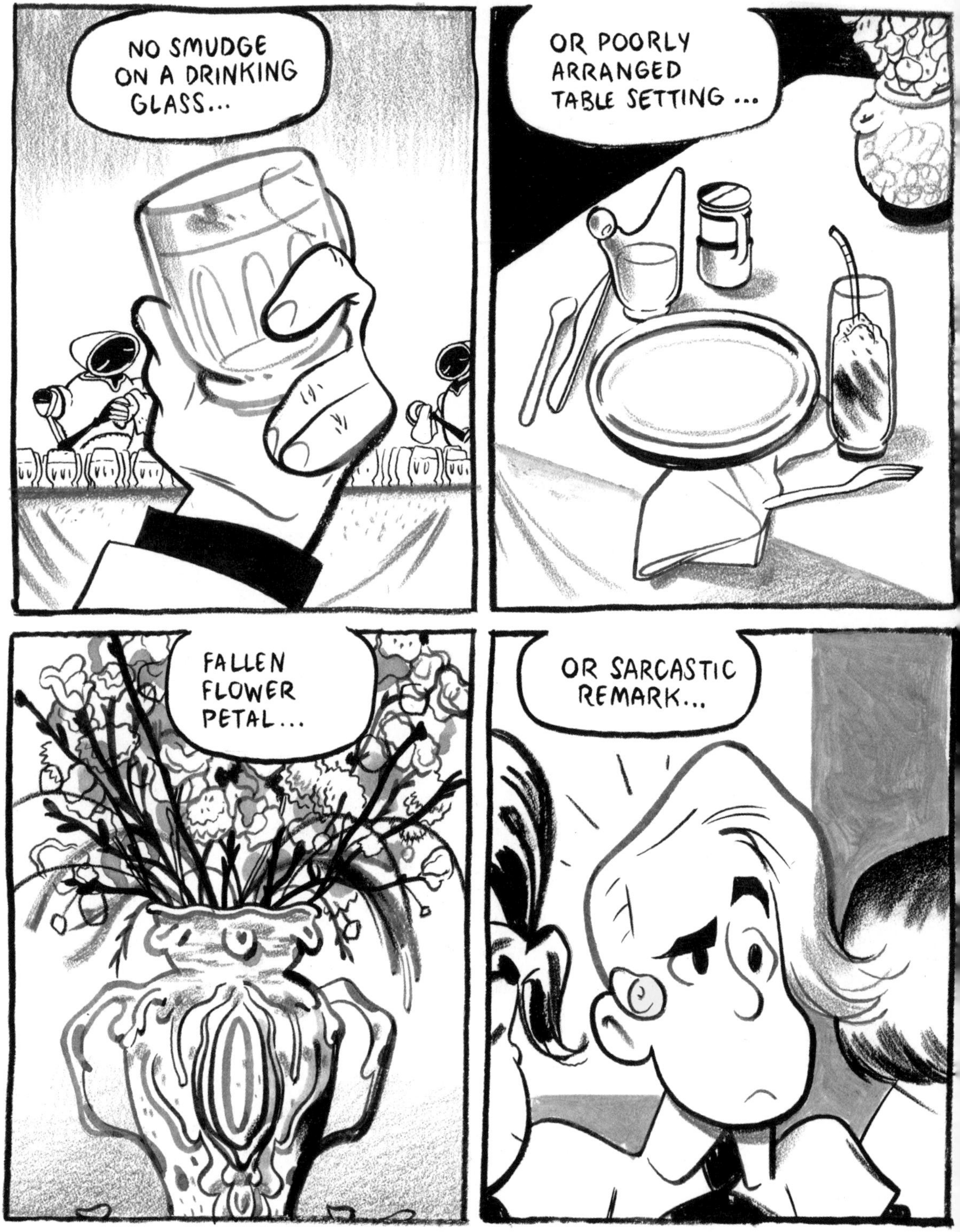
NO SMUDGE ON A DRINKING GLASS...
OR POORLY ARRANGED TABLE SETTING ...
FALLEN FLOWER PETAL...
OR SARCASTIC REMARK...

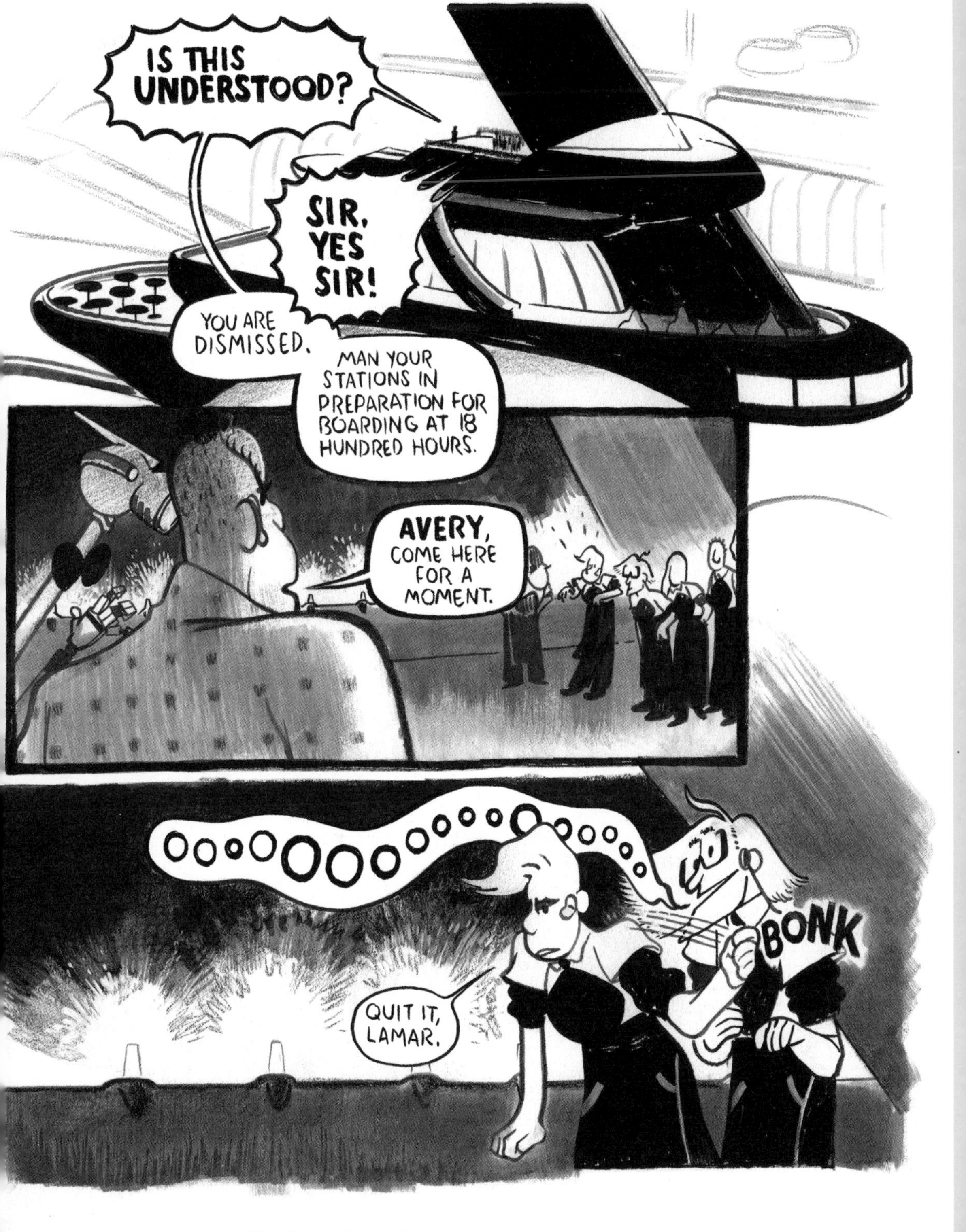
IS THIS UNDERSTOOD?
SIR, YES SIR!
YOU ARE DISMISSED.
MAN YOUR STATIONS IN PREPARATION FOR BOARDING AT 18 HUNDRED HOURS.
AVERY, COME HERE FOR A MOMENT.
BONK
QUIT IT, LAMAR.

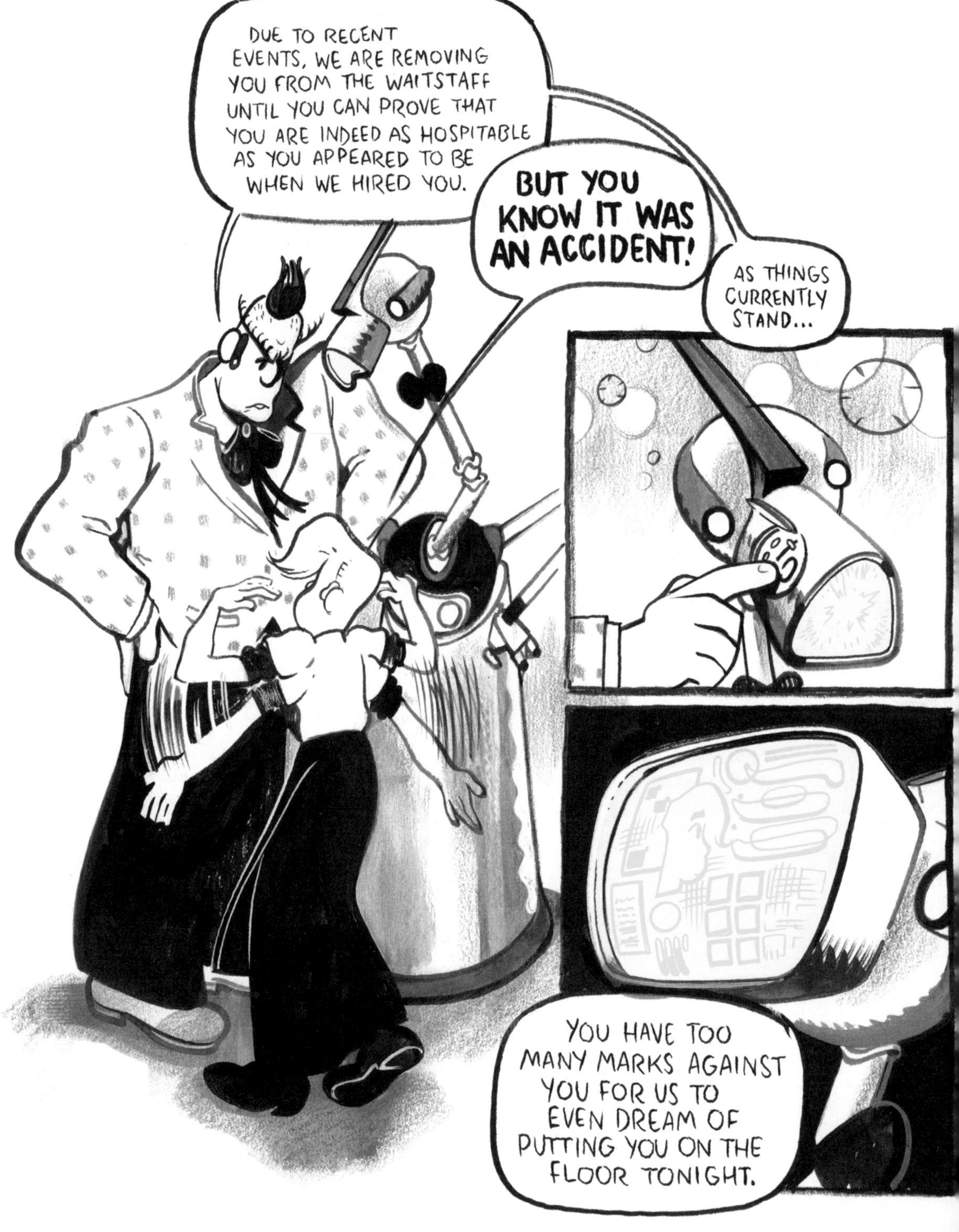
DUE TO RECENT EVENTS, WE ARE REMOVING YOU FROM THE WAITSTAFF UNTIL YOU CAN PROVE THAT YOU ARE INDEED AS HOSPITABLE AS YOU APPEARED TO BE WHEN WE HIRED YOU.
BUT YOU KNOW IT WAS AN ACCIDENT!
AS THINGS CURRENTLY STAND...
YOU HAVE TOO MANY MARKS AGAINST YOU FOR US TO EVEN DREAM OF PUTTING YOU ON THE FLOOR TONIGHT.

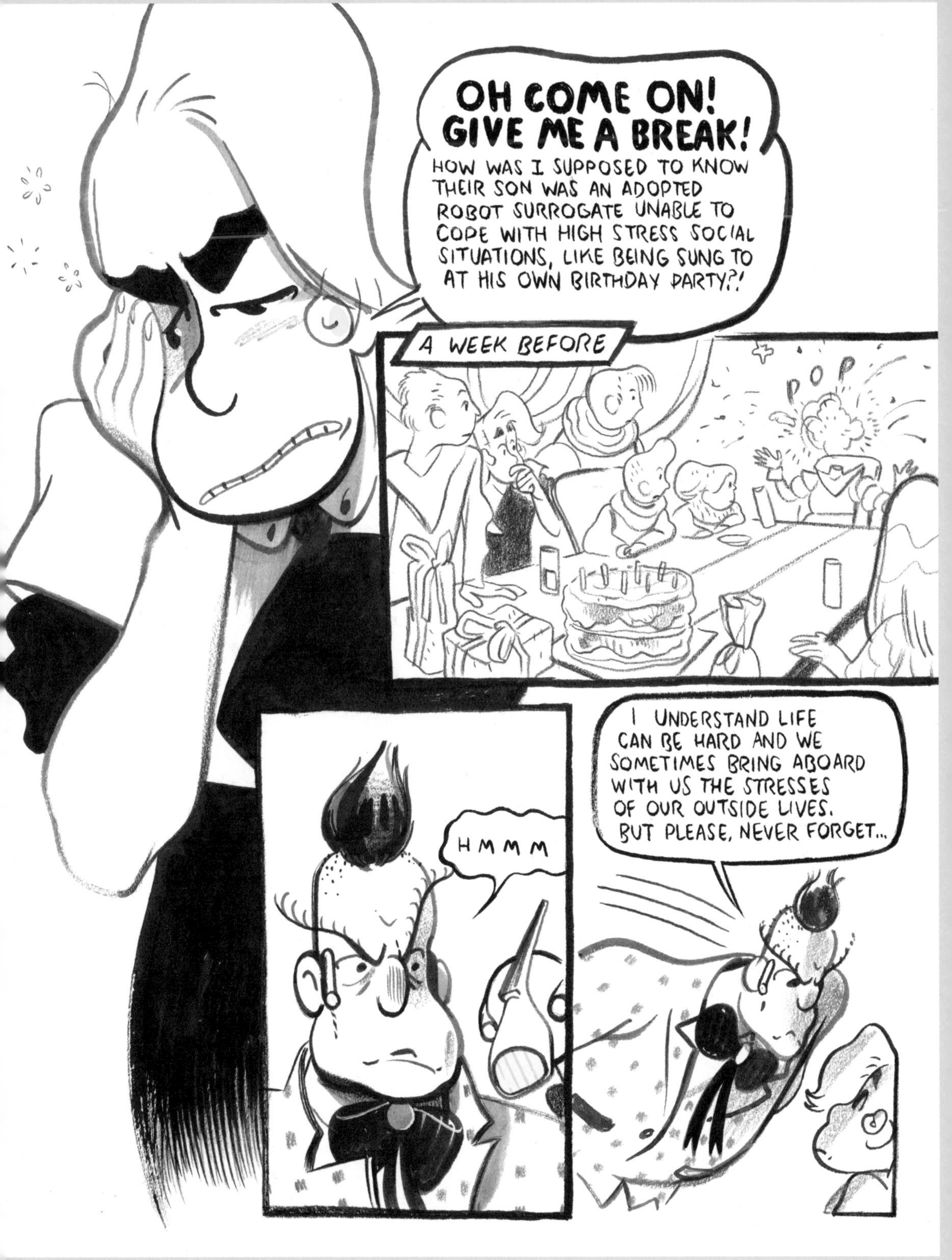
OH COME ON! GIVE ME A BREAK!
HOW WAS I SUPPOSED TO KNOW THEIR SON WAS AN ADOPTED ROBOT SURROGATE UNABLE TO COPE WITH HIGH STRESS SOCIAL SITUATIONS, LIKE BEING SUNG TO AT HIS OWN BIRTHDAY PARTY?!
A WEEK BEFORE
POP
HMMM
I UNDERSTAND LIFE CAN BE HARD AND WE SOMETIMES BRING ABOARD WITH US THE STRESSES OF OUR OUTSIDE LIVES. BUT PLEASE, NEVER FORGET...

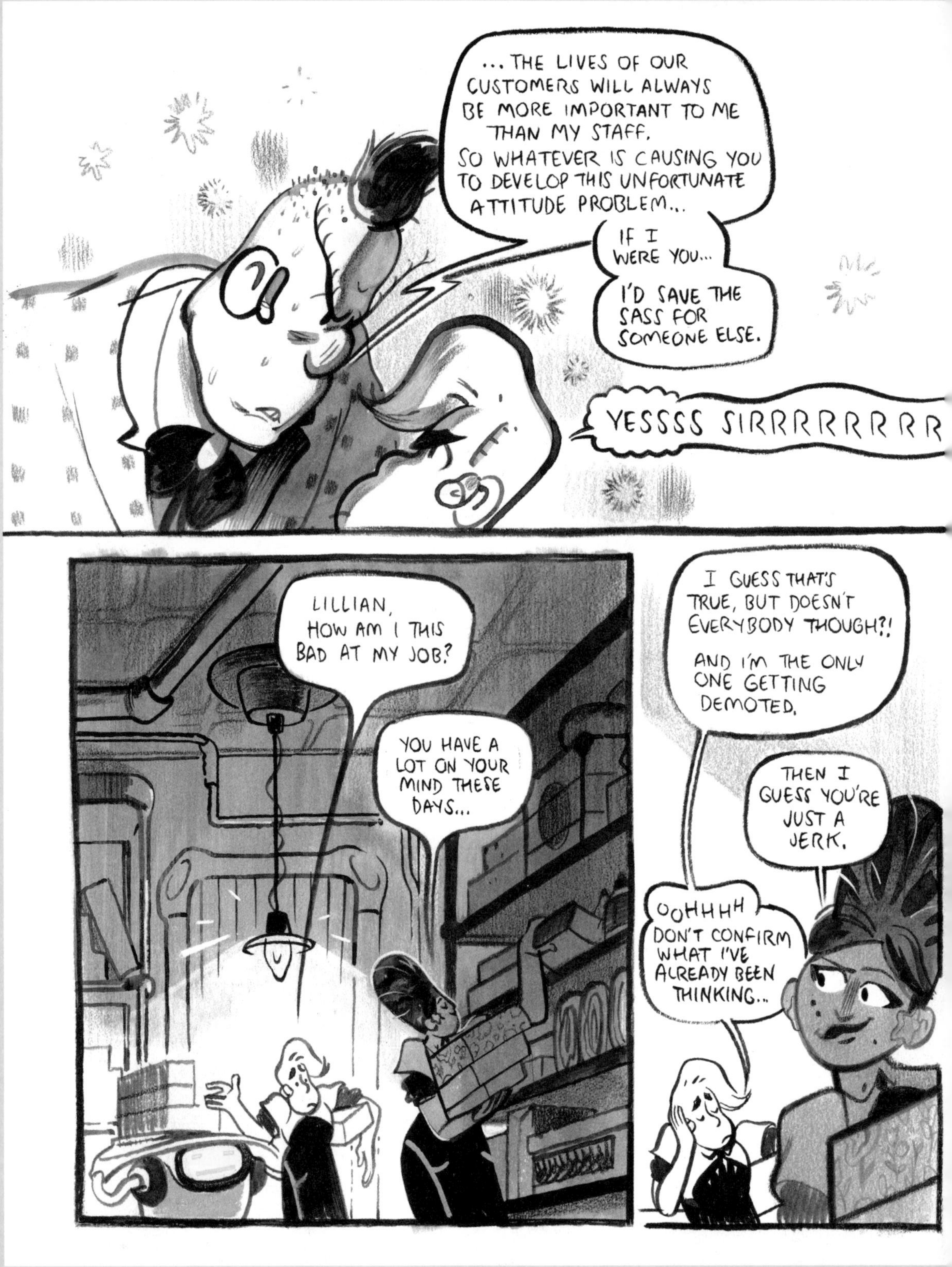
...THE LIVES OF OUR CUSTOMERS WILL ALWAYS BE MORE IMPORTANT TO ME THAN MY STAFF. SO WHATEVER IS CAUSING YOU TO DEVELOP THIS UNFORTUNATE ATTITUDE PROBLEM...
IF I WERE YOU...
I'D SAVE THE SASS FOR SOMEONE ELSE.
YESSSS SIRRRRRRRR
LILLIAN, HOW AM I THIS BAD AT MY JOB?
YOU HAVE A LOT ON YOUR MIND THESE DAYS...
I GUESS THAT'S TRUE, BUT DOESN'T EVERYBODY THOUGH?!
AND I'M THE ONLY ONE GETTING DEMOTED.
THEN I GUESS YOU'RE JUST A JERK.
OOHHHH DON'T CONFIRM WHAT I'VE ALREADY BEEN THINKING...

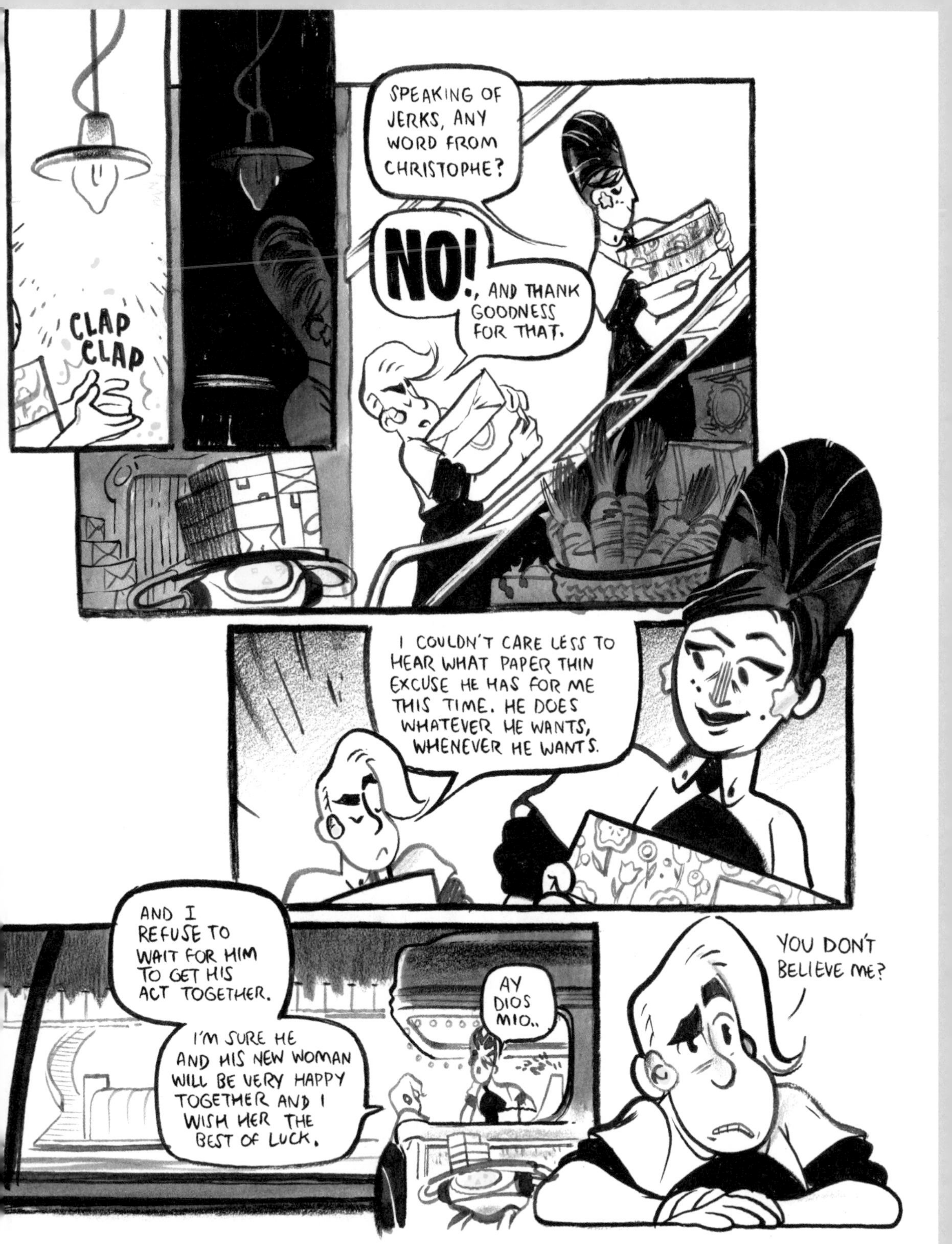
CLAP CLAP
SPEAKING OF JERKS, ANY WORD FROM CHRISTOPHE?
NO!, AND THANK GOODNESS FOR THAT.
I COULDN'T CARE LESS TO HEAR WHAT PAPER THIN EXCUSE HE HAS FOR ME THIS TIME. HE DOES WHATEVER HE WANTS, WHENEVER HE WANTS.
AND I REFUSE TO WAIT FOR HIM TO GET HIS ACT TOGETHER.
I'M SURE HE AND HIS NEW WOMAN WILL BE VERY HAPPY TOGETHER AND I WISH HER THE BEST OF LUCK.
AY DIOS MIO..
YOU DON'T BELIEVE ME?

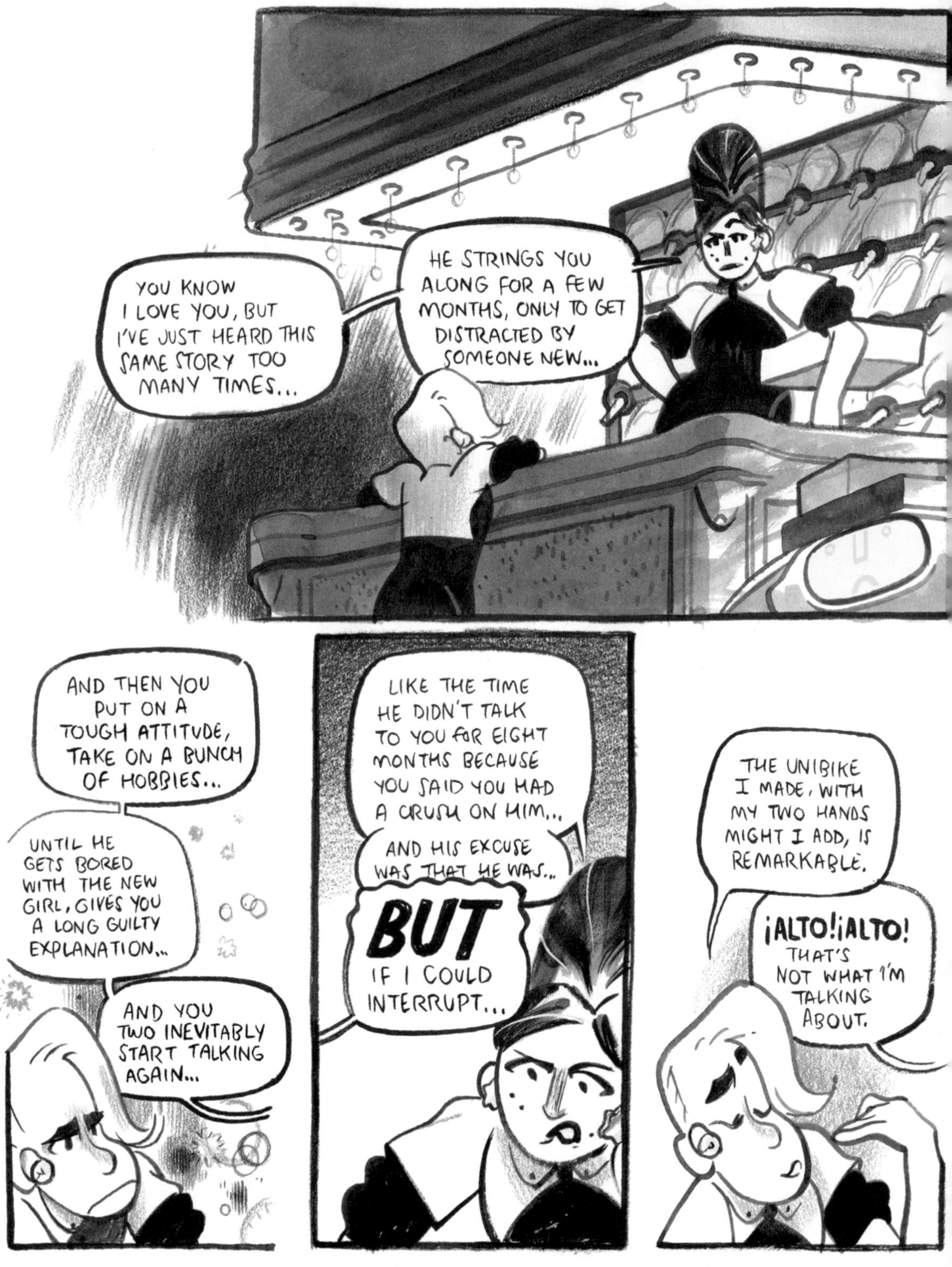
YOU KNOW I LOVE YOU, BUT I'VE JUST HEARD THIS SAME STORY TOO MANY TIMES...
HE STRINGS YOU ALONG FOR A FEW MONTHS, ONLY TO GET DISTRACTED BY SOMEONE NEW...
AND THEN YOU PUT ON A TOUGH ATTITUDE, TAKE ON A BUNCH OF HOBBIES...
UNTIL HE GETS BORED WITH THE NEW GIRL, GIVES YOU A LONG GUILTY EXPLANATION...
AND YOU TWO INEVITABLY START TALKING AGAIN...
LIKE THE TIME HE DIDN'T TALK TO YOU FOR EIGHT MONTHS BECAUSE YOU SAID YOU HAD A CRUSH ON HIM...
AND HIS EXCUSE WAS THAT HE WAS...
BUT IF I COULD INTERRUPT...
THE UNIBIKE I MADE, WITH MY TWO HANDS MIGHT I ADD, IS REMARKABLE.
¡ALTO! ¡ALTO! THAT'S NOT WHAT I'M TALKING ABOUT.

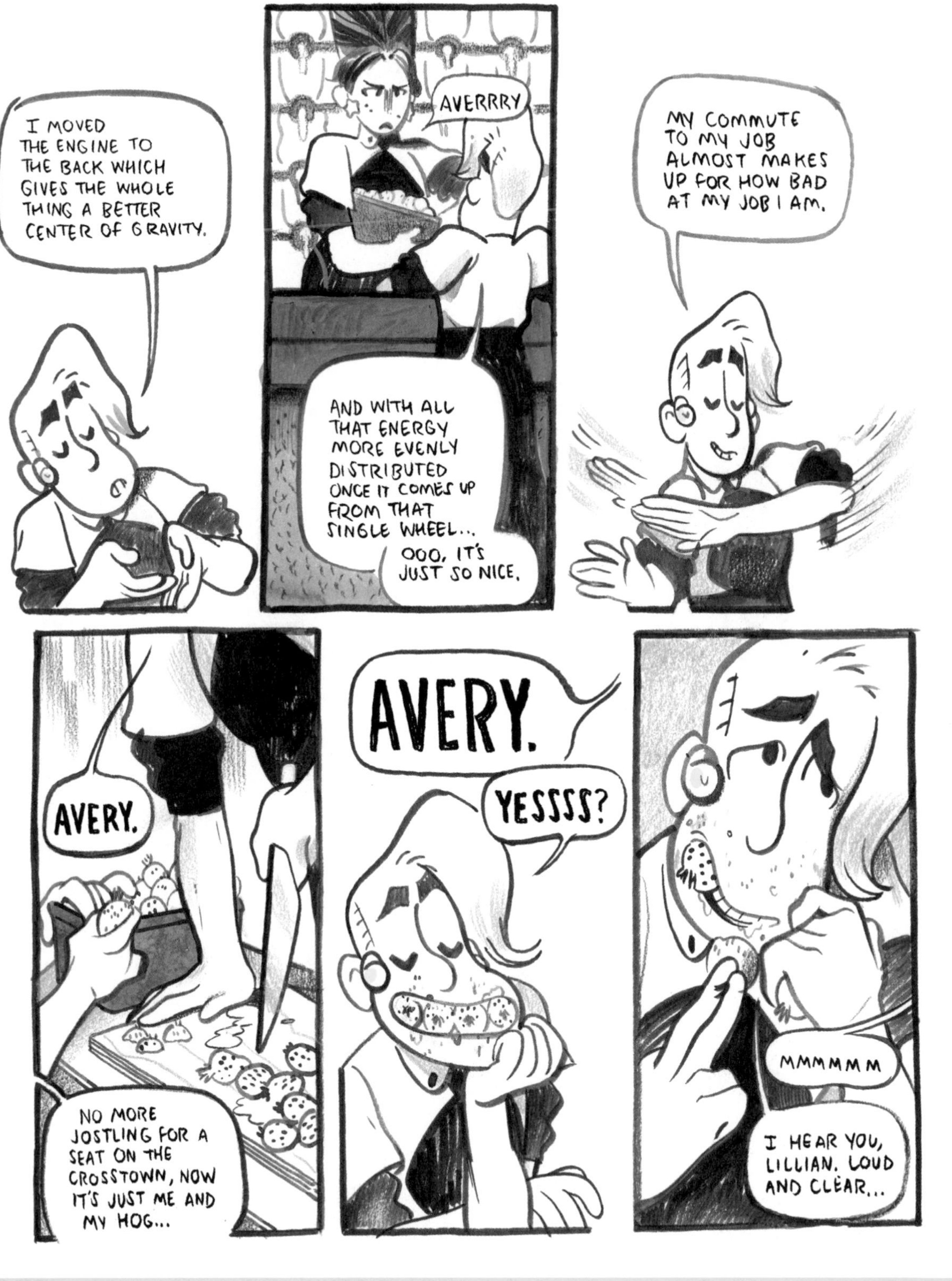
I MOVED THE ENGINE TO THE BACK WHICH GIVES THE WHOLE THING A BETTER CENTER OF GRAVITY.
AVERRRY
AND WITH ALL THAT ENERGY MORE EVENLY DISTRIBUTED ONCE IT COMES UP FROM THAT SINGLE WHEEL...
OOO, IT'S JUST SO NICE.
MY COMMUTE TO MY JOB ALMOST MAKES UP FOR HOW BAD AT MY JOB I AM.
AVERY.
NO MORE JOSTLING FOR A SEAT ON THE CROSSTOWN, NOW IT'S JUST ME AND MY HOG...
AVERY.
YESSSS?
MMMMMM
I HEAR YOU, LILLIAN. LOUD AND CLEAR...

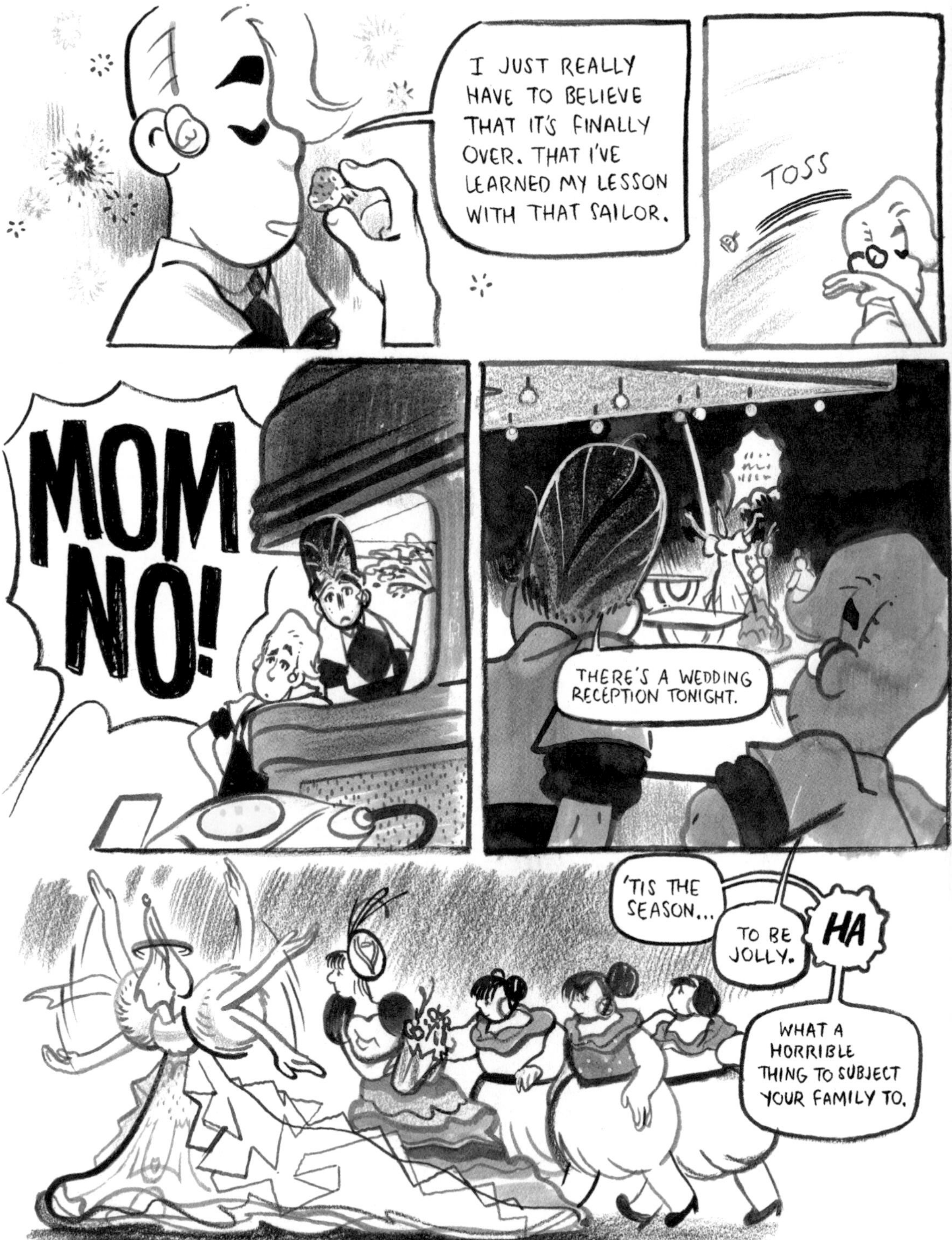
I JUST REALLY HAVE TO BELIEVE THAT IT'S FINALLY OVER. THAT I'VE LEARNED MY LESSON WITH THAT SAILOR.
TOSS
MOM NO!
THERE'S A WEDDING RECEPTION TONIGHT.
'TIS THE SEASON...
TO BE JOLLY.
HA
WHAT A HORRIBLE THING TO SUBJECT YOUR FAMILY TO.

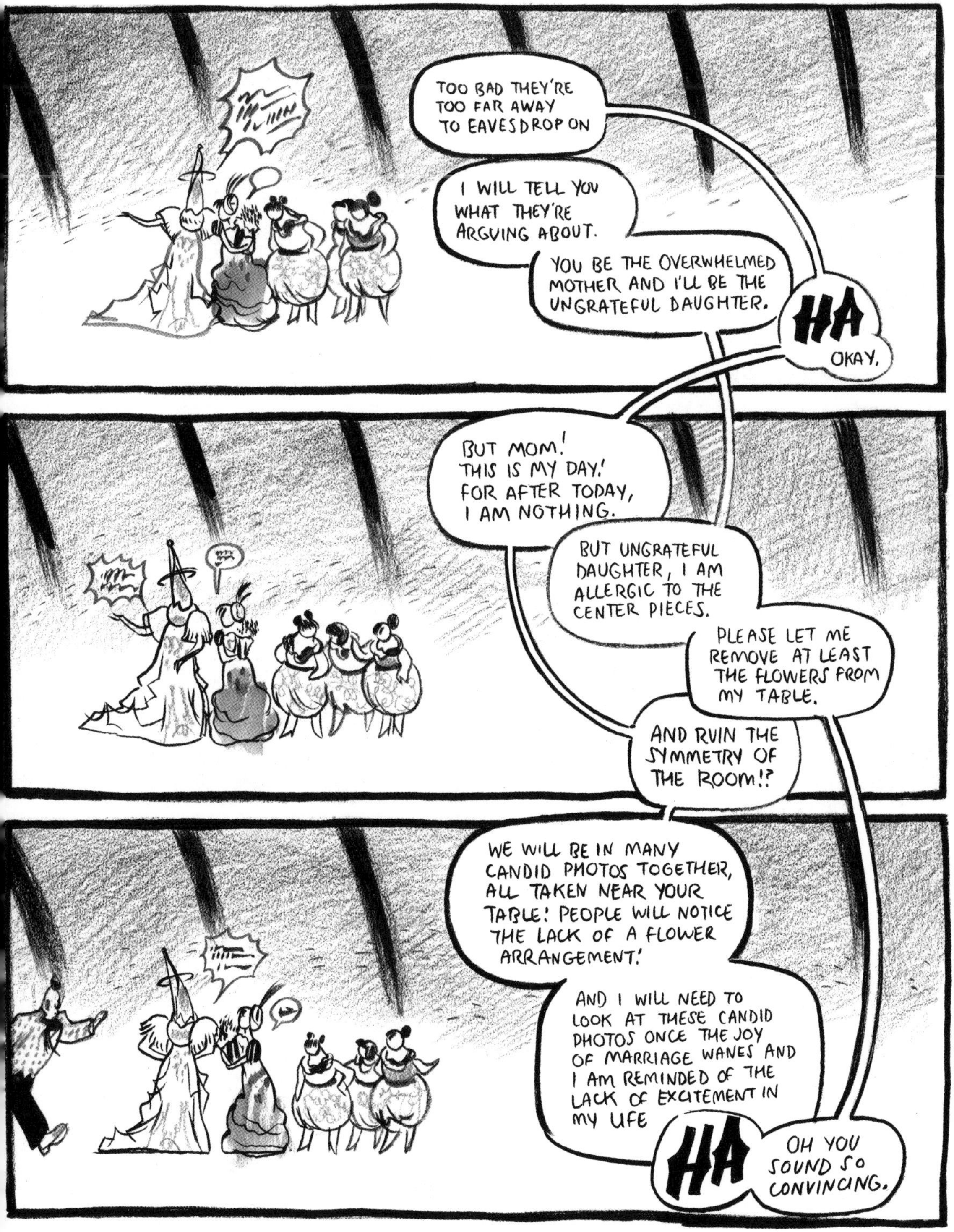
TOO BAD THEY'RE TOO FAR AWAY TO EAVESDROP ON
I WILL TELL YOU WHAT THEY'RE ARGUING ABOUT.
YOU BE THE OVERWHELMED MOTHER AND I'LL BE THE UNGRATEFUL DAUGHTER.
HA
OKAY.
BUT MOM! THIS IS MY DAY! FOR AFTER TODAY, I AM NOTHING.
BUT UNGRATEFUL DAUGHTER, I AM ALLERGIC TO THE CENTER PIECES.
PLEASE LET ME REMOVE AT LEAST THE FLOWERS FROM MY TABLE.
AND RUIN THE SYMMETRY OF THE ROOM!?
WE WILL BE IN MANY CANDID PHOTOS TOGETHER, ALL TAKEN NEAR YOUR TABLE! PEOPLE WILL NOTICE THE LACK OF A FLOWER ARRANGEMENT!
AND I WILL NEED TO LOOK AT THESE CANDID PHOTOS ONCE THE JOY OF MARRIAGE WANES AND I AM REMINDED OF THE LACK OF EXCITEMENT IN MY LIFE
HA
OH YOU SOUND SO CONVINCING.

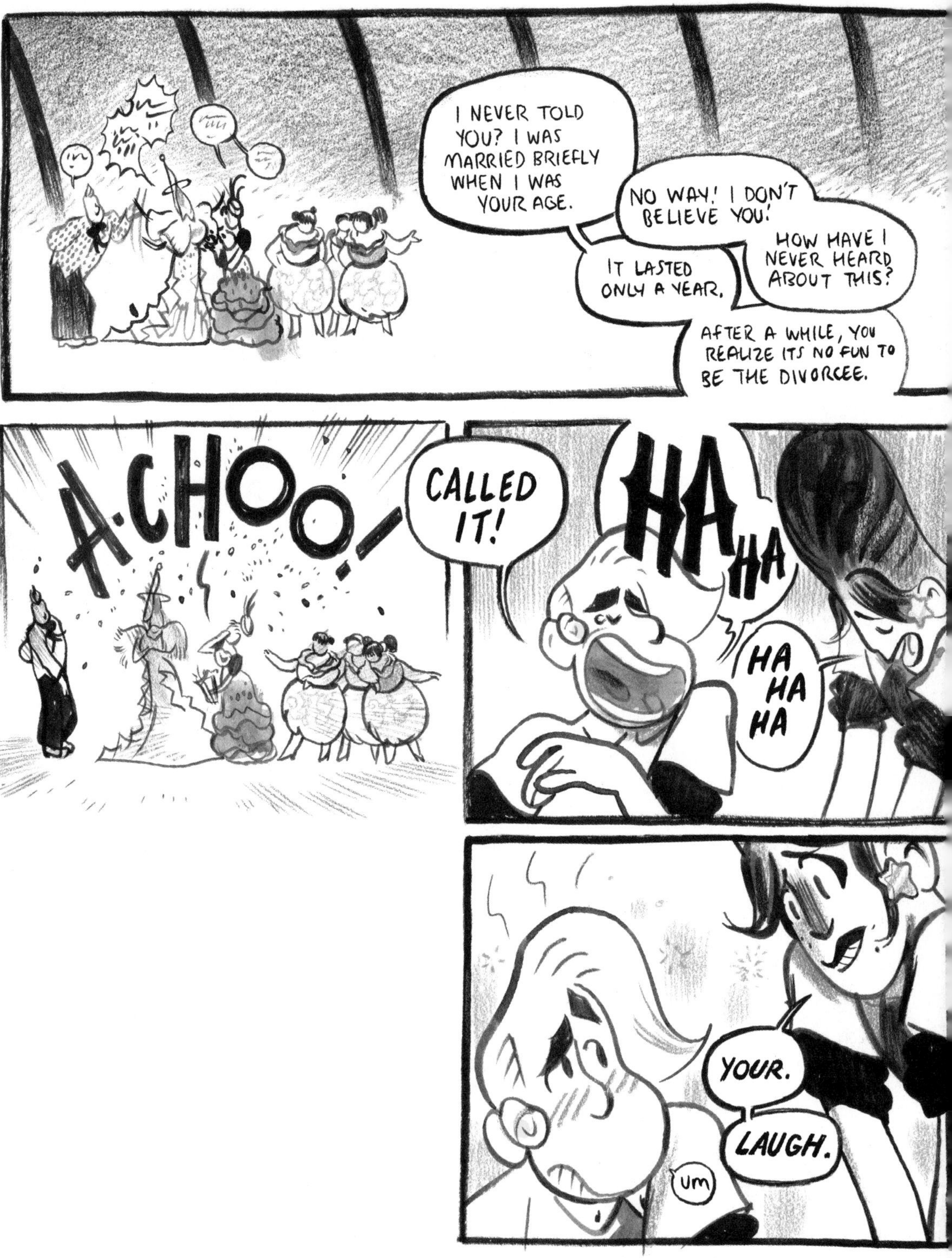
I NEVER TOLD YOU? I WAS MARRIED BRIEFLY WHEN I WAS YOUR AGE.
NO WAY! I DON'T BELIEVE YOU!
IT LASTED ONLY A YEAR.
HOW HAVE I NEVER HEARD ABOUT THIS?
AFTER A WHILE, YOU REALIZE ITS NO FUN TO BE THE DIVORCEE.
A-CHOO!
CALLED IT!
HA HA HA
HA HA HA
YOUR.
LAUGH.
um

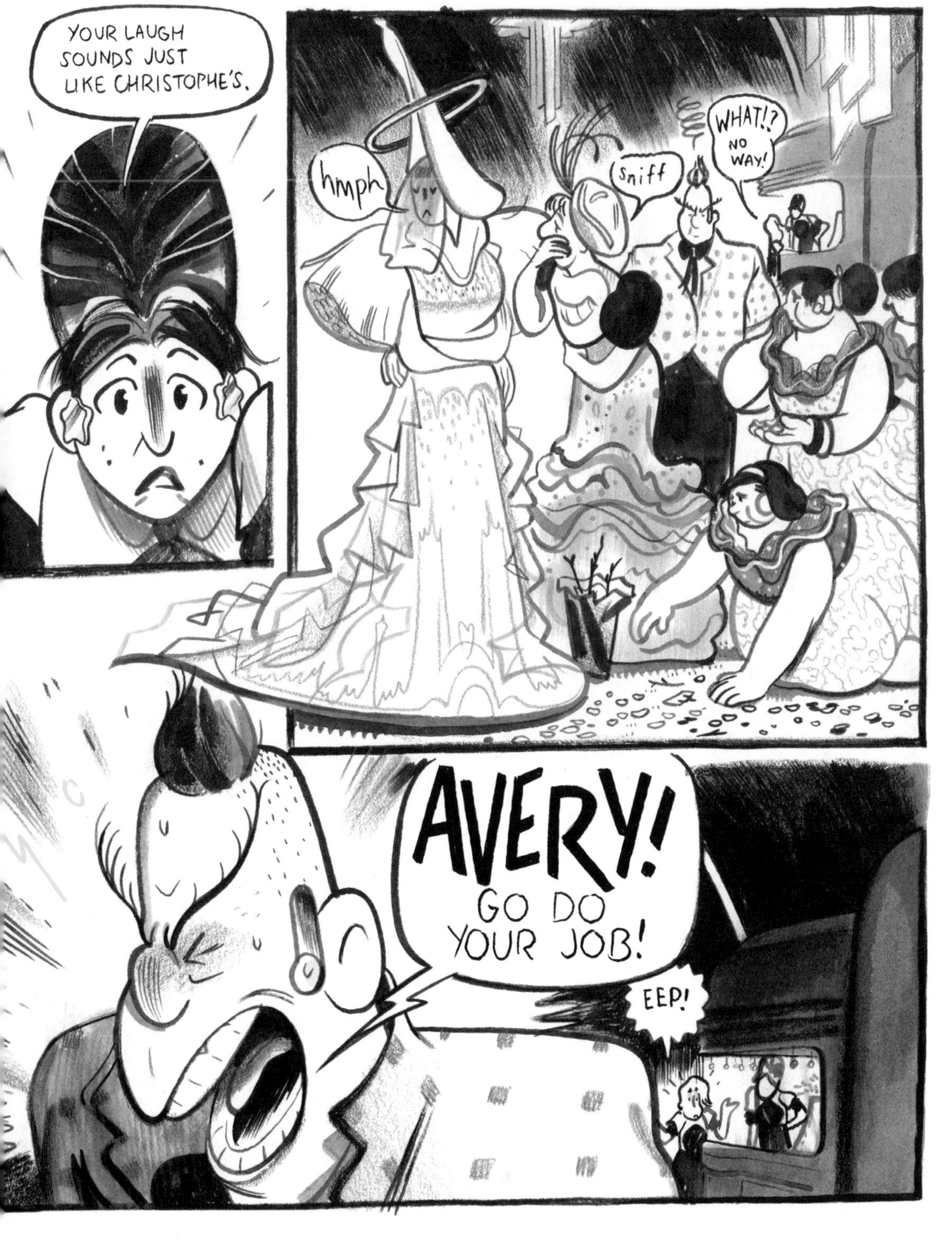
YOUR LAUGH SOUNDS JUST LIKE CHRISTOPHE'S.
hmph
sniff
WHAT!? NO WAY!
AVERY! GO DO YOUR JOB!
EEP!

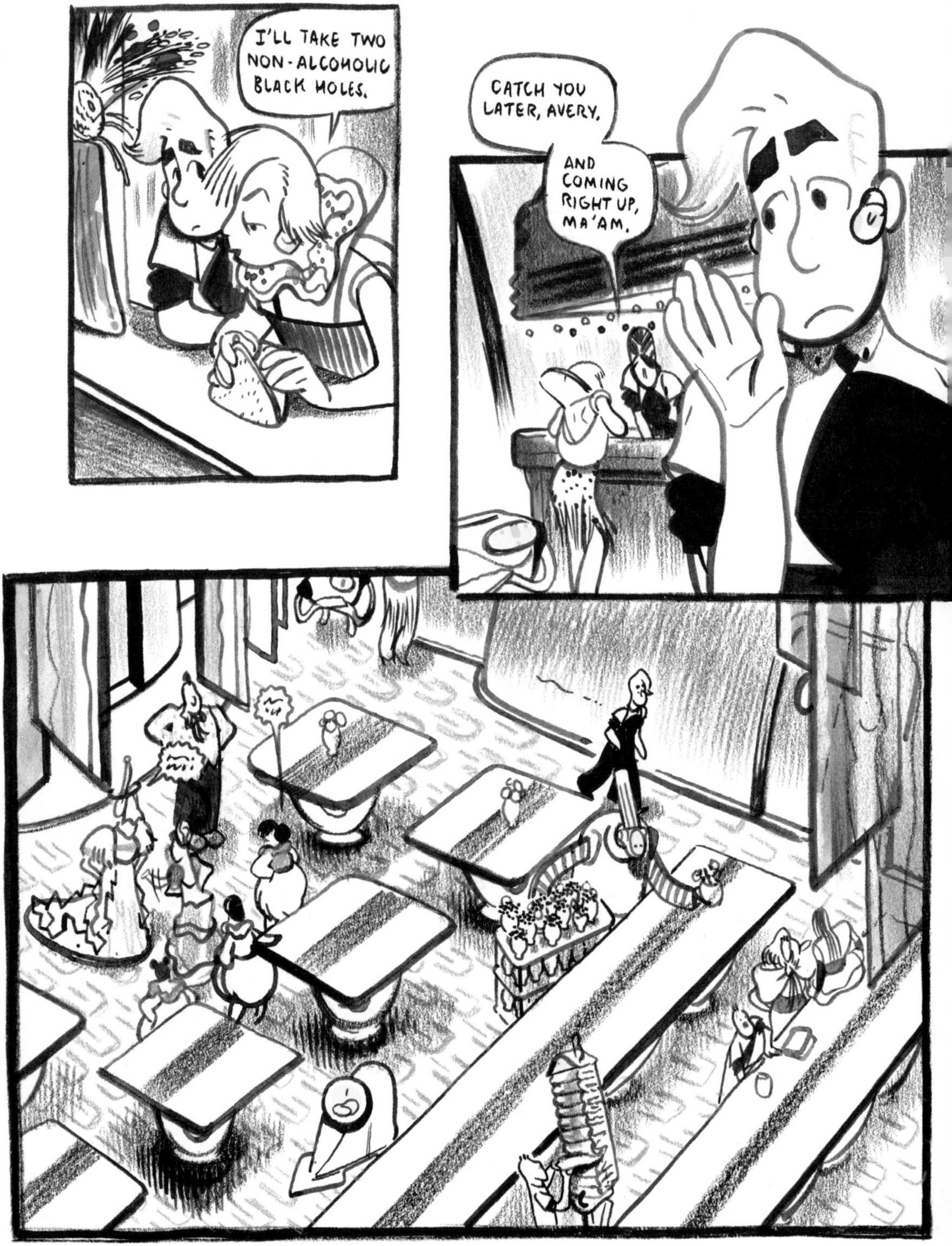
I'LL TAKE TWO NON-ALCOHOLIC BLACK HOLES.
CATCH YOU LATER, AVERY.
AND COMING RIGHT UP, MA'AM.

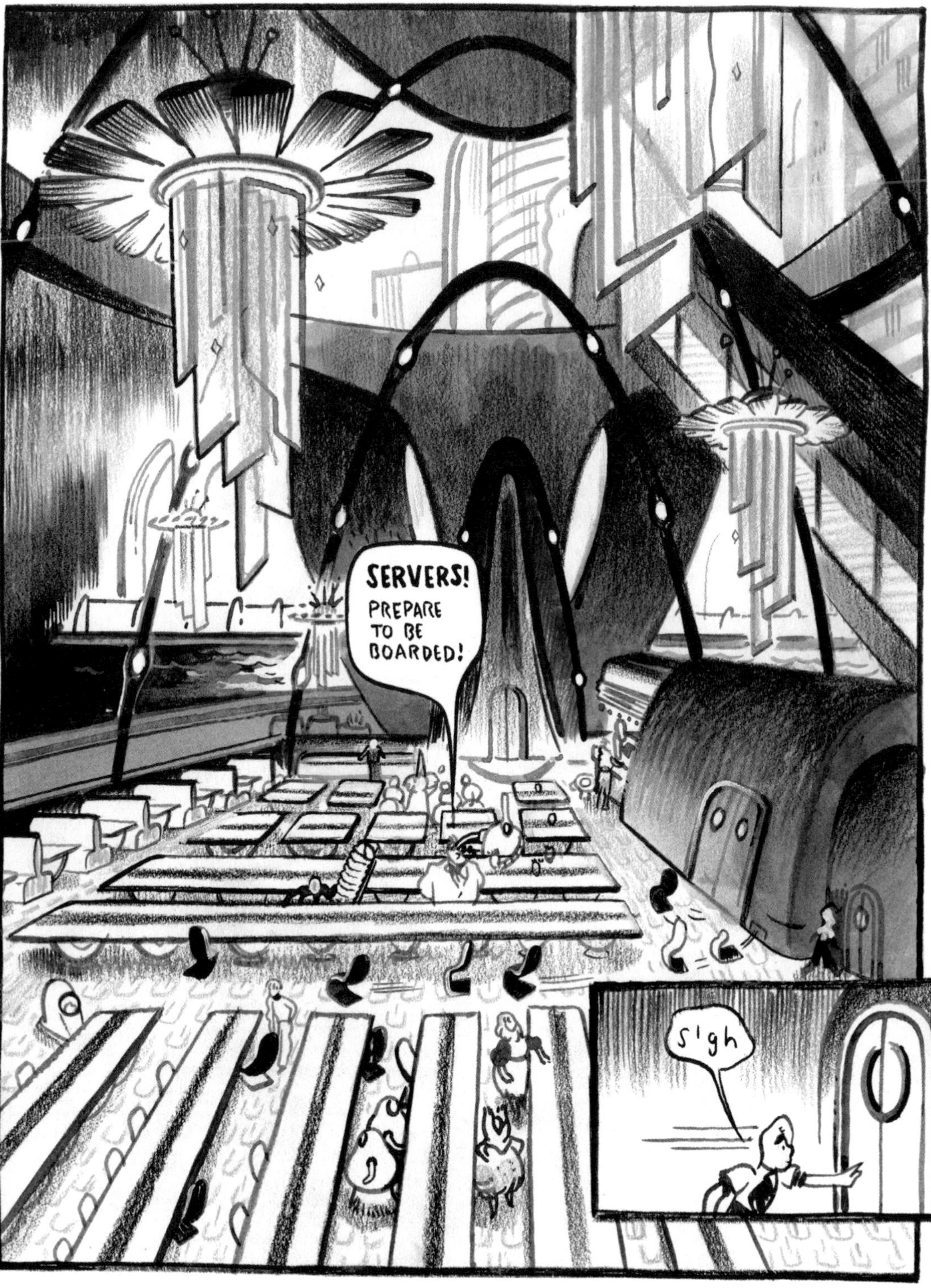
SERVERS! PREPARE TO BE BOARDED!
sigh

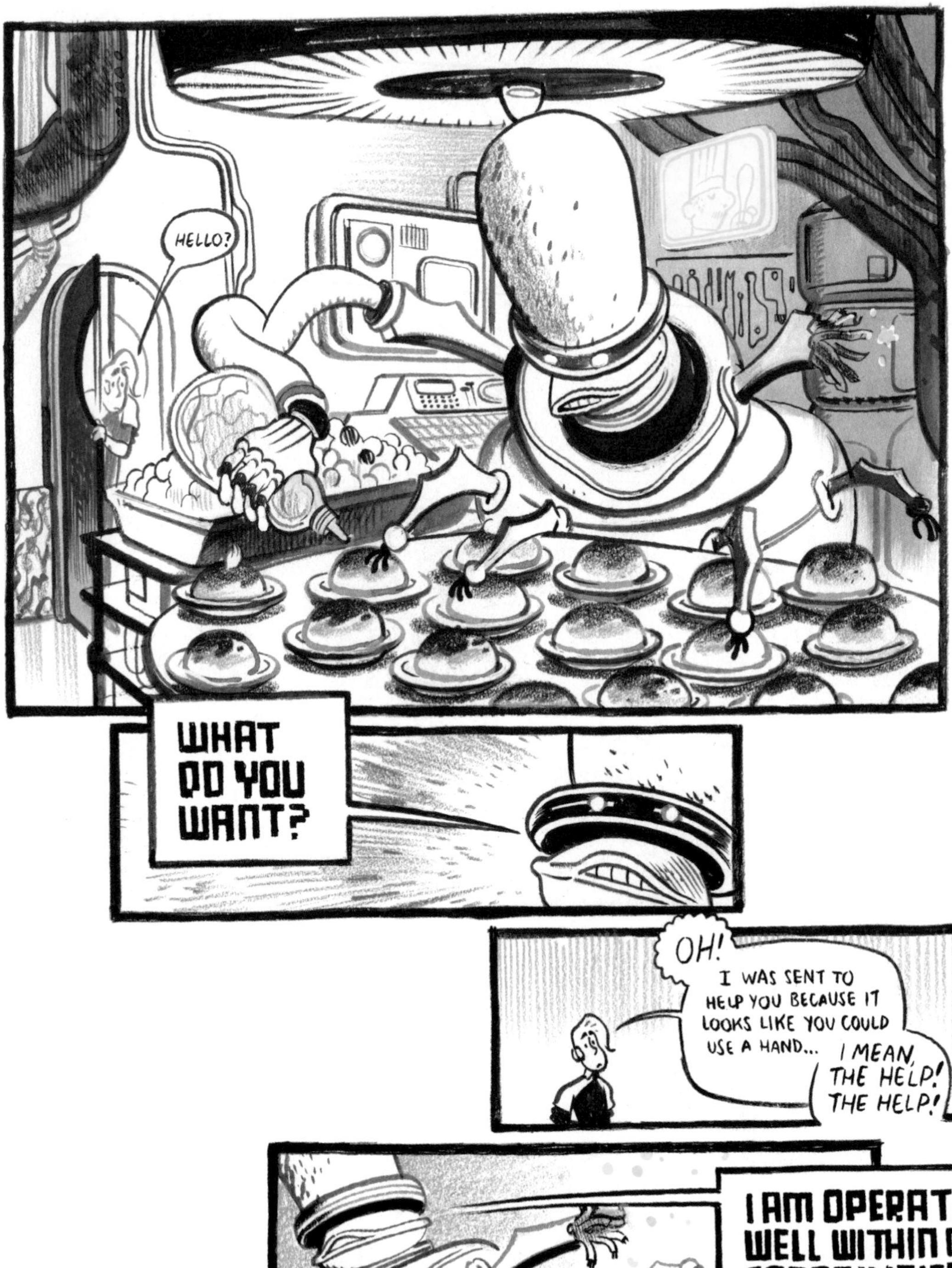
HELLO?
WHAT DO YOU WANT?
OH!
I WAS SENT TO HELP YOU BECAUSE IT LOOKS LIKE YOU COULD USE A HAND...
I MEAN, THE HELP! THE HELP!
I AM OPERATING WELL WITHIN MY CAPABILITIES.

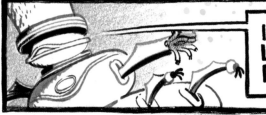

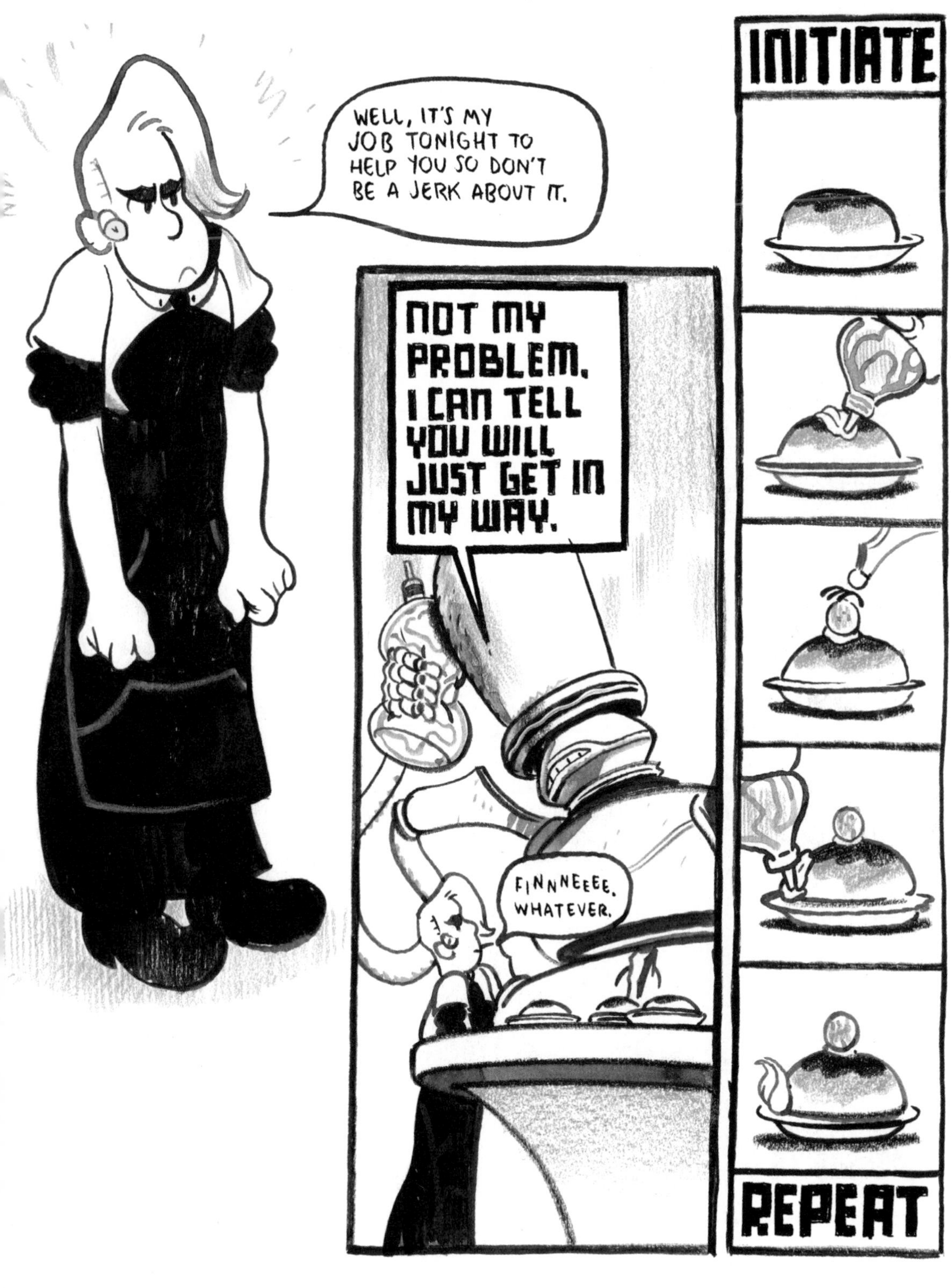
WELL, IT'S MY JOB TONIGHT TO HELP YOU SO DON'T BE A JERK ABOUT IT.
NOT MY PROBLEM. I CAN TELL YOU WILL JUST GET IN MY WAY.
FINNNEEEE. WHATEVER.
INITIATE
REPEAT

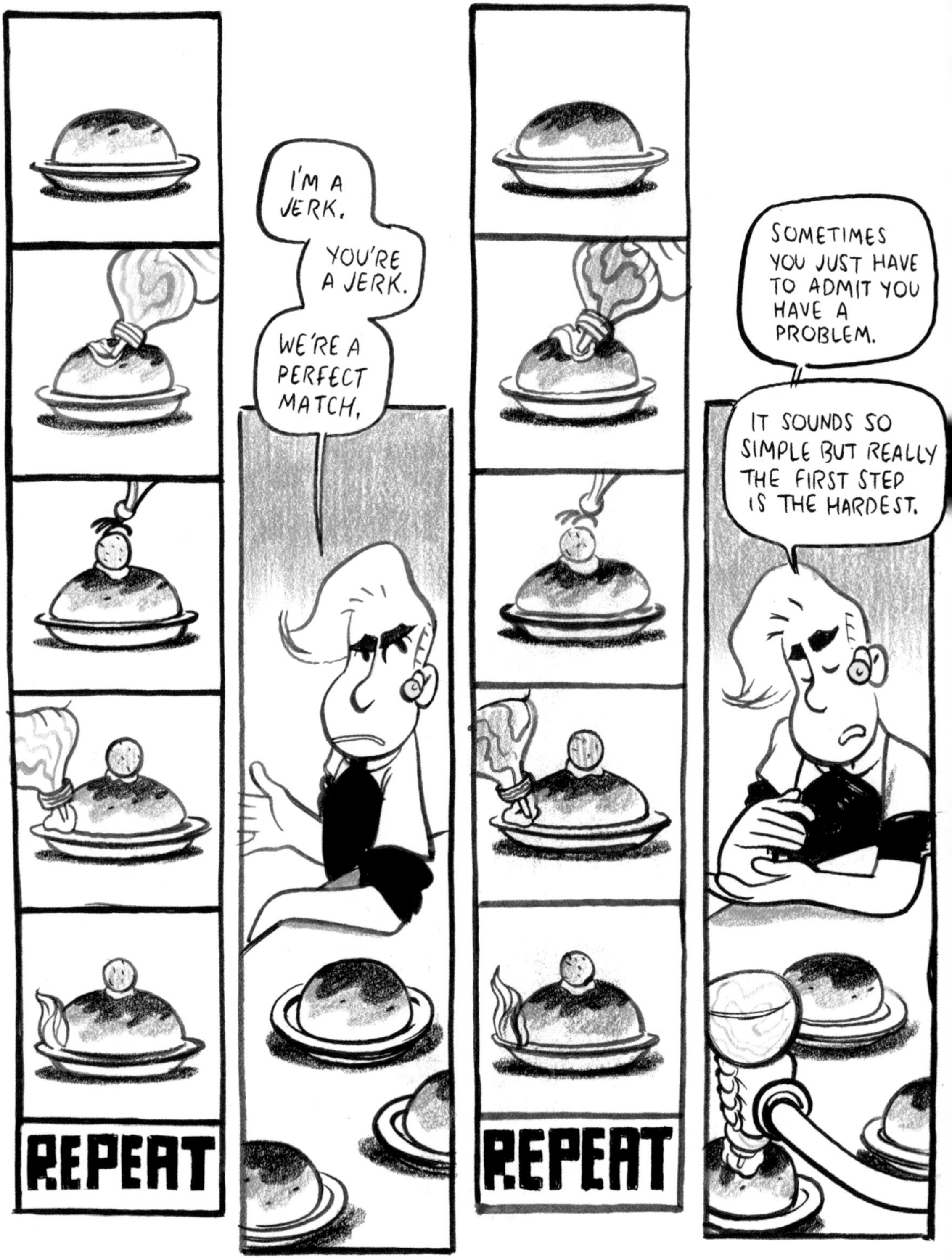

REPEAT
I'M A JERK.
YOU'RE A JERK.
WE'RE A PERFECT MATCH.
REPEAT
SOMETIMES YOU JUST HAVE TO ADMIT YOU HAVE A PROBLEM.
IT SOUNDS SO SIMPLE BUT REALLY THE FIRST STEP IS THE HARDEST.

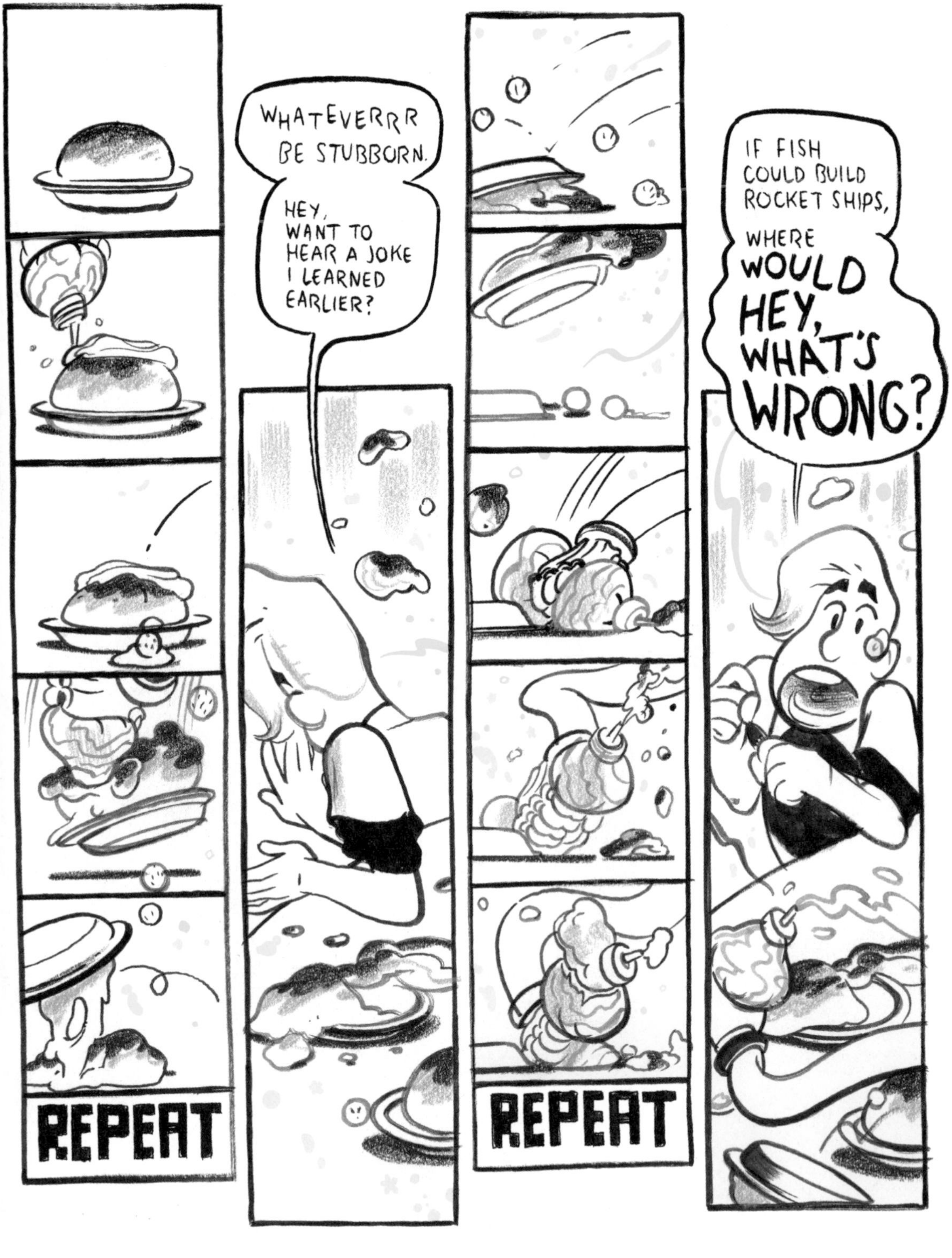
REPEAT
WHATEVERRR BE STUBBORN.
HEY, WANT TO HEAR A JOKE I LEARNED EARLIER?
REPEAT
IF FISH COULD BUILD ROCKET SHIPS,
WHERE WOULD
HEY, WHAT'S WRONG?

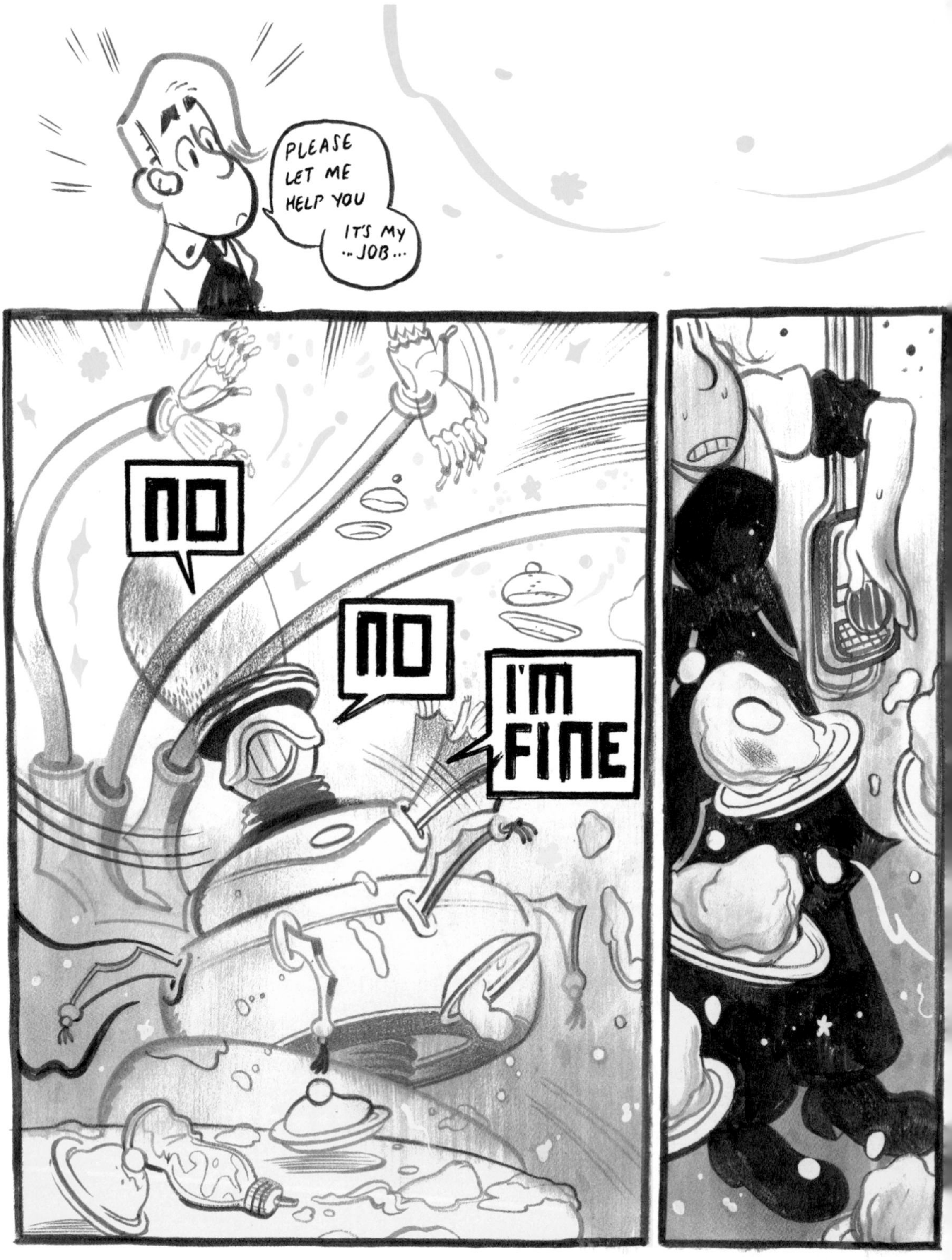
PLEASE LET ME HELP YOU
IT'S MY ..JOB...
NO
NO
I'M FINE

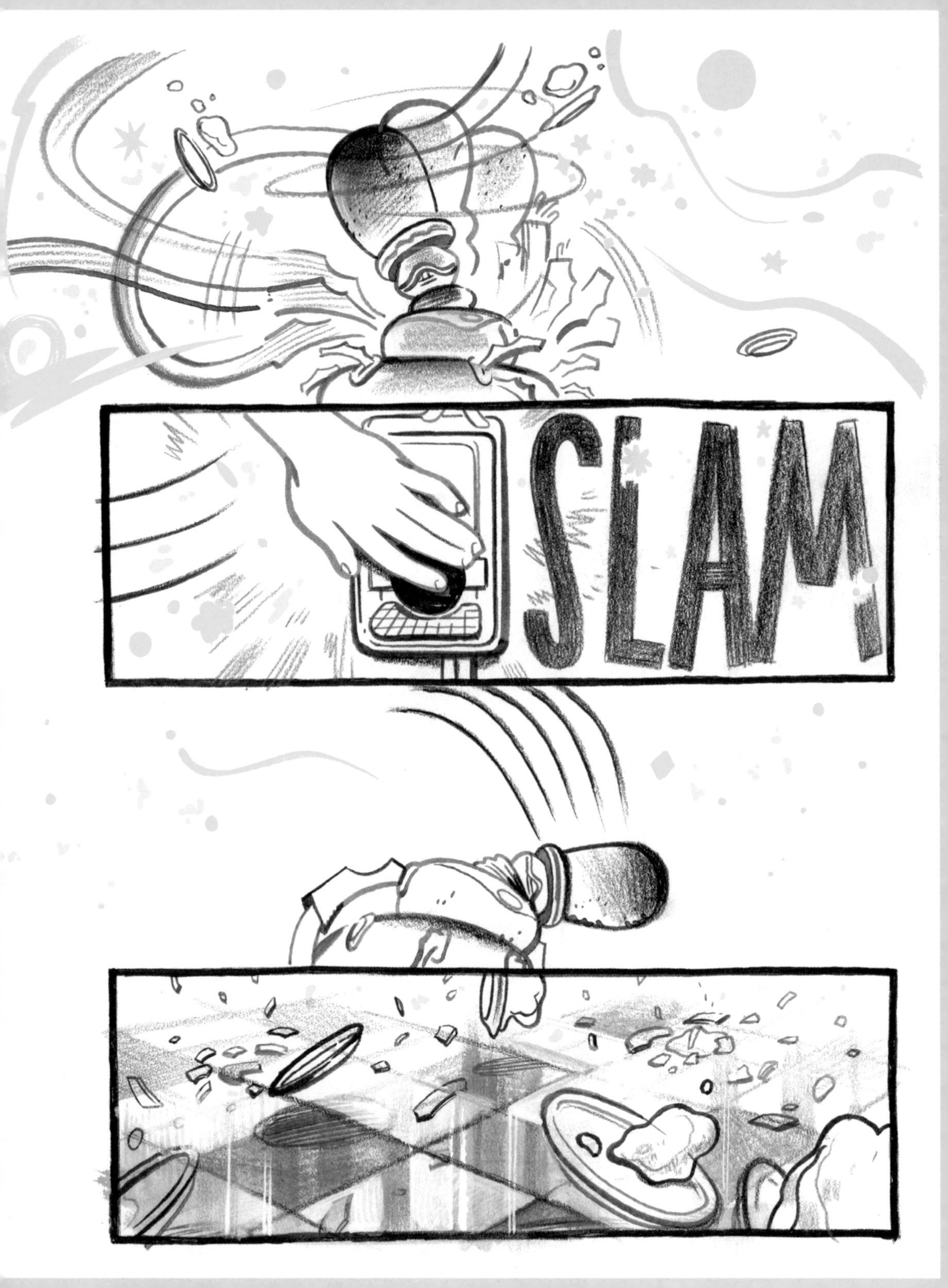
SLAM

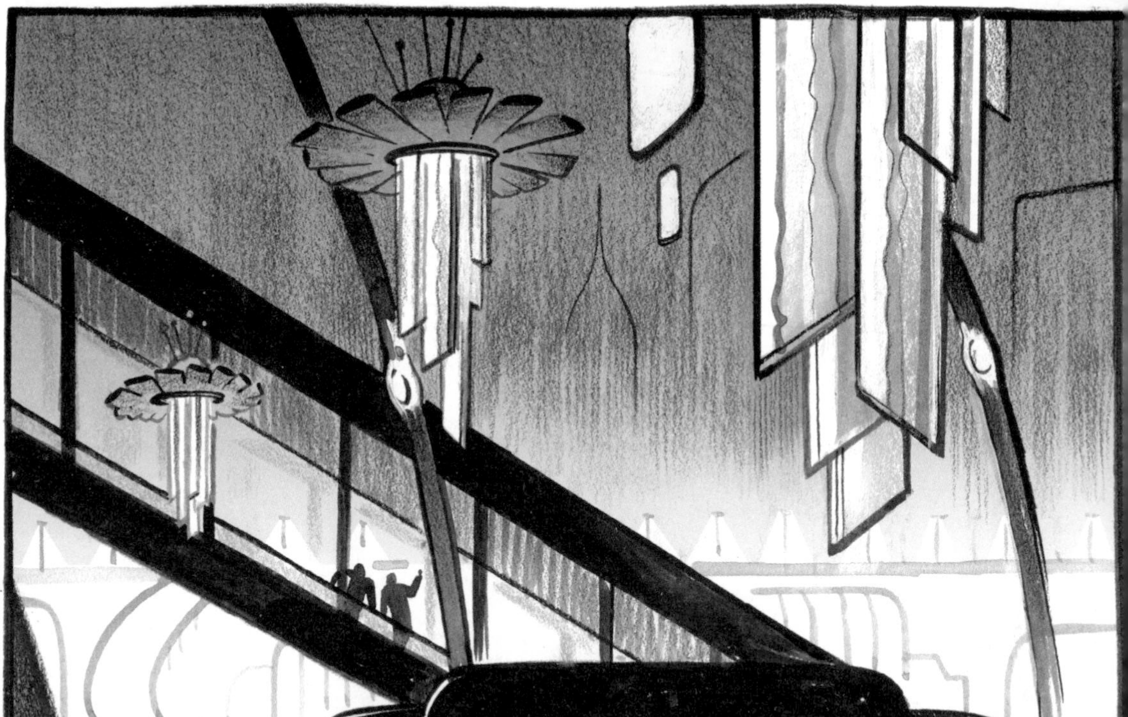

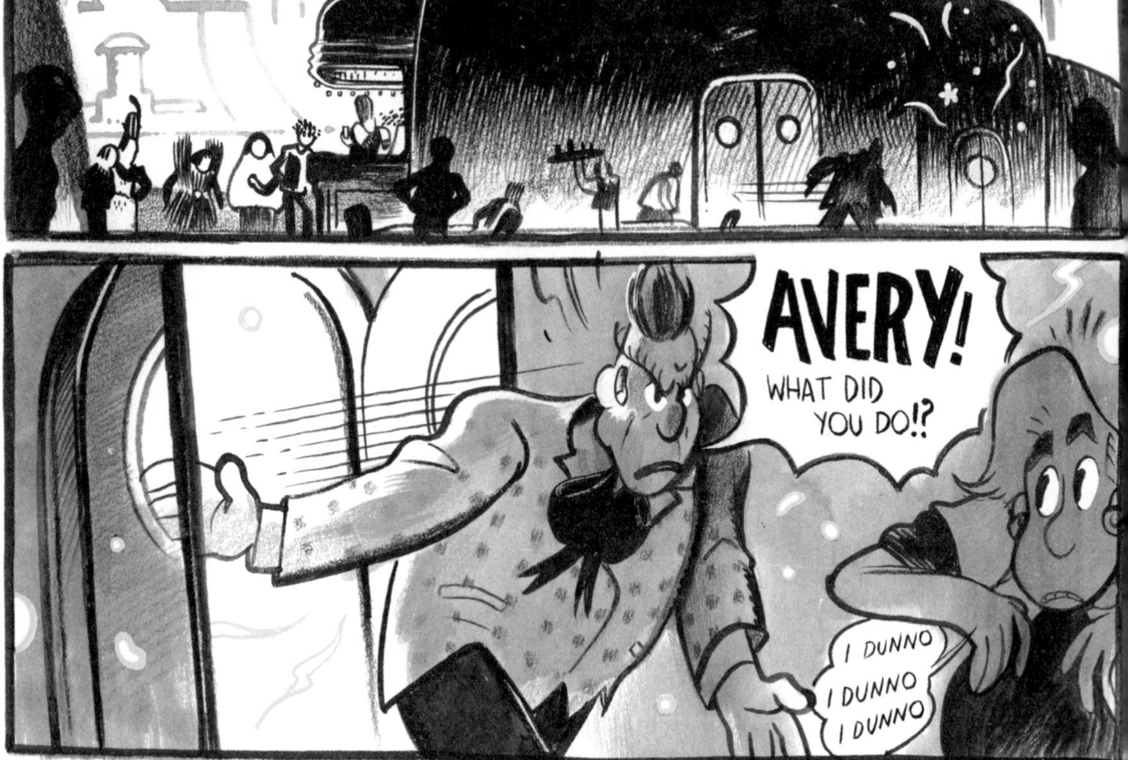
AVERY! WHAT DID YOU DO!?
I DUNNO I DUNNO I DUNNO

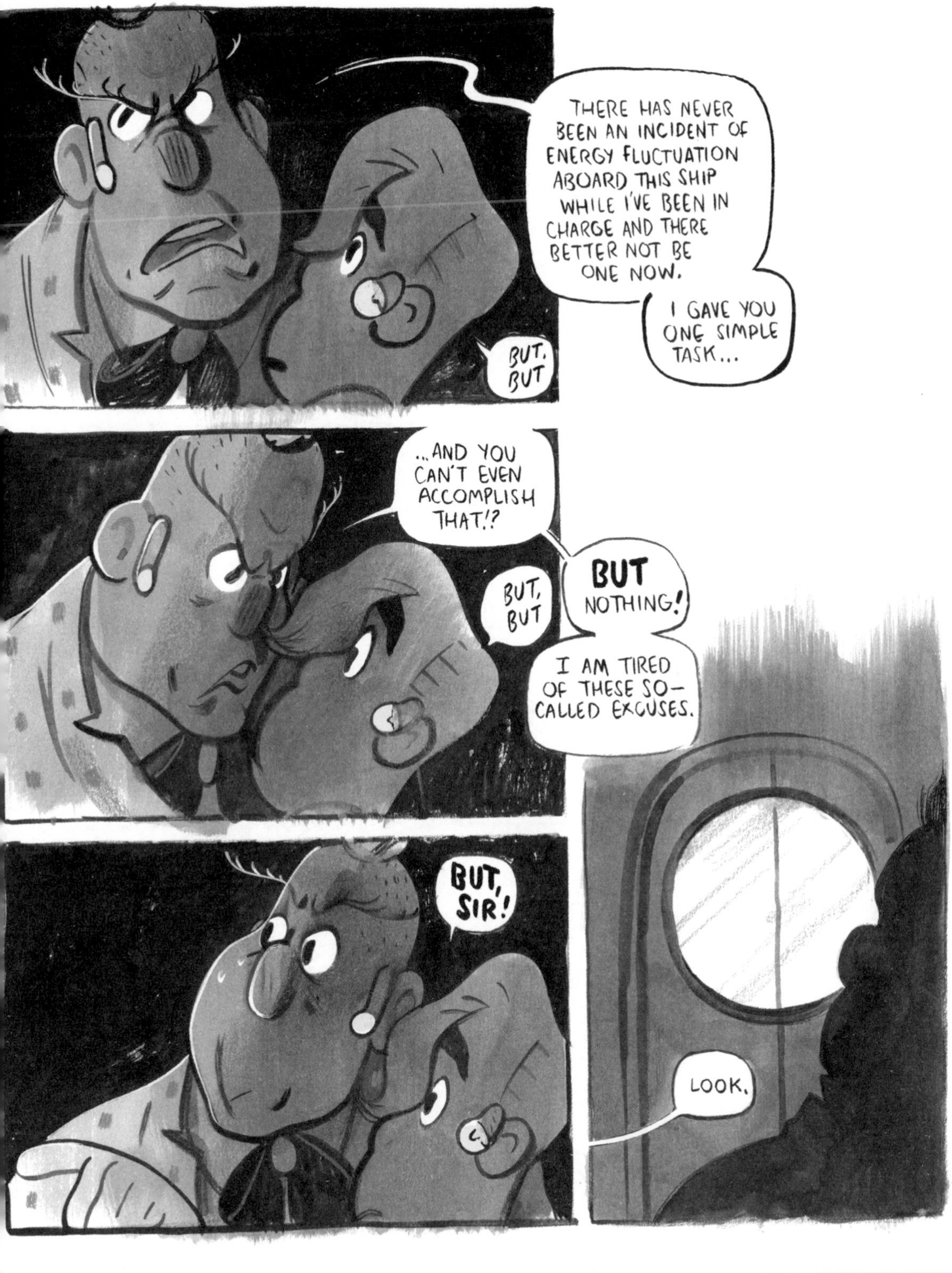
THERE HAS NEVER BEEN AN INCIDENT OF ENERGY FLUCTUATION ABOARD THIS SHIP WHILE I'VE BEEN IN CHARGE AND THERE BETTER NOT BE ONE NOW.
I GAVE YOU ONE SIMPLE TASK...
BUT, BUT
...AND YOU CAN'T EVEN ACCOMPLISH THAT!?
BUT, BUT
BUT NOTHING!
I AM TIRED OF THESE SO-CALLED EXCUSES.
BUT, SIR!
LOOK.

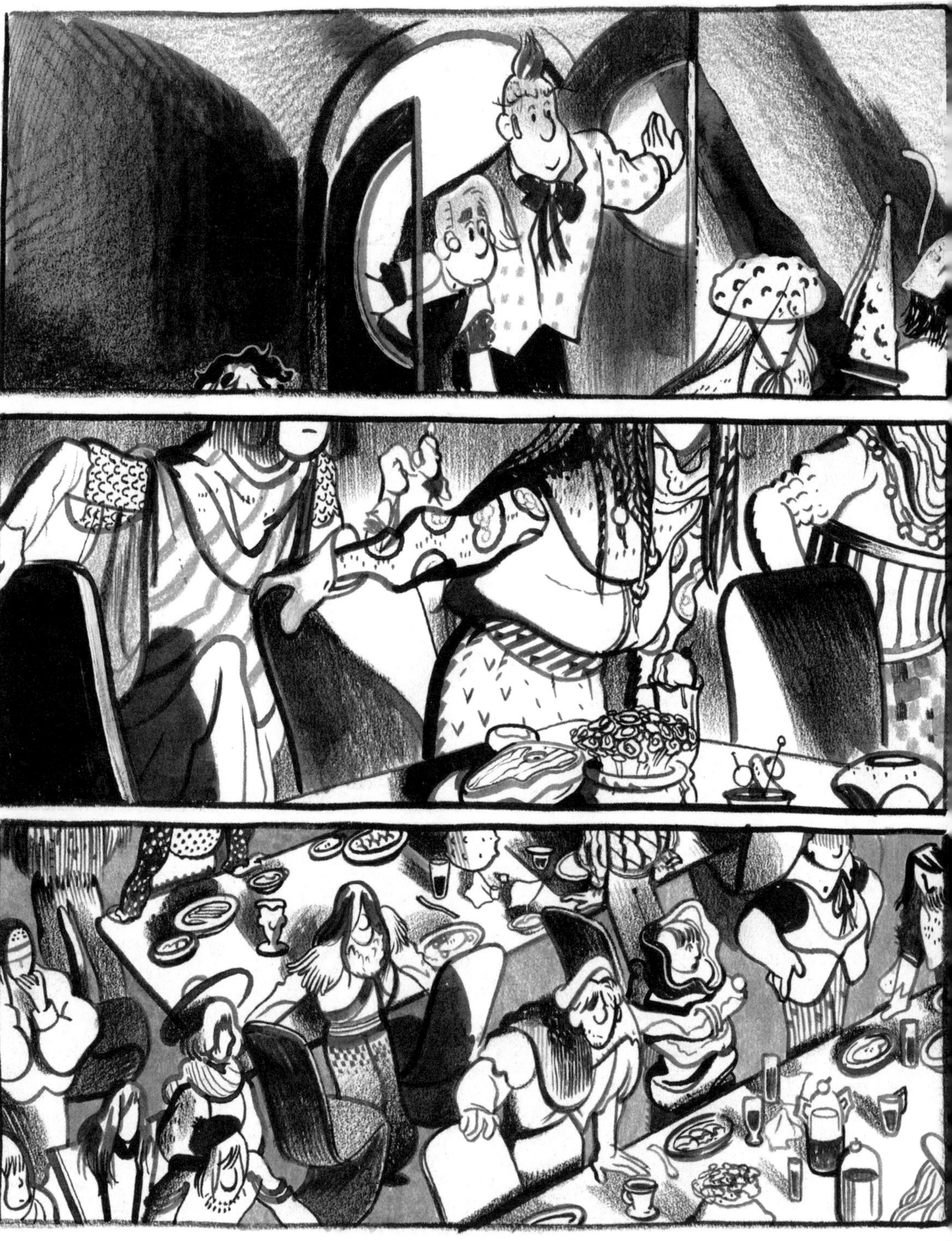

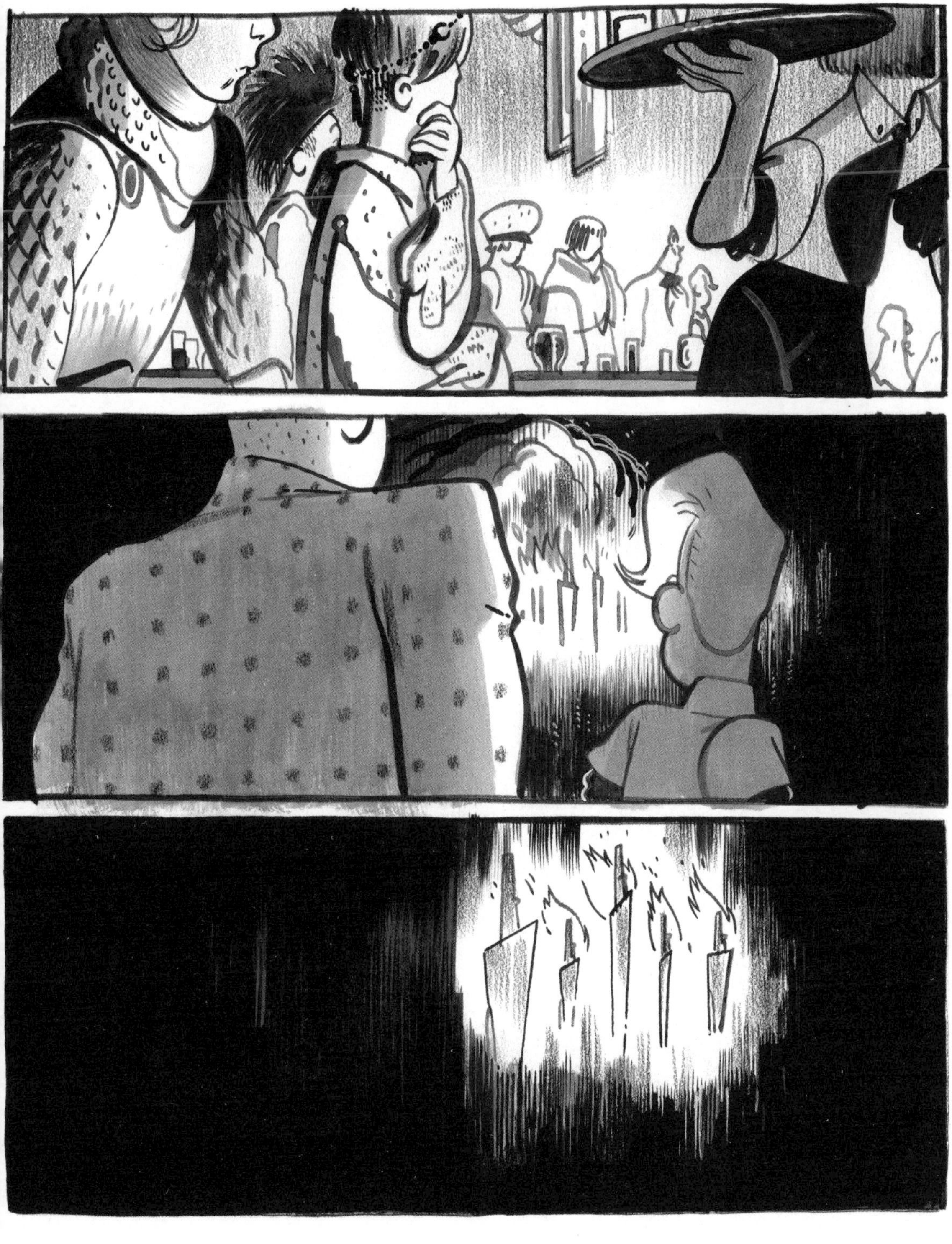

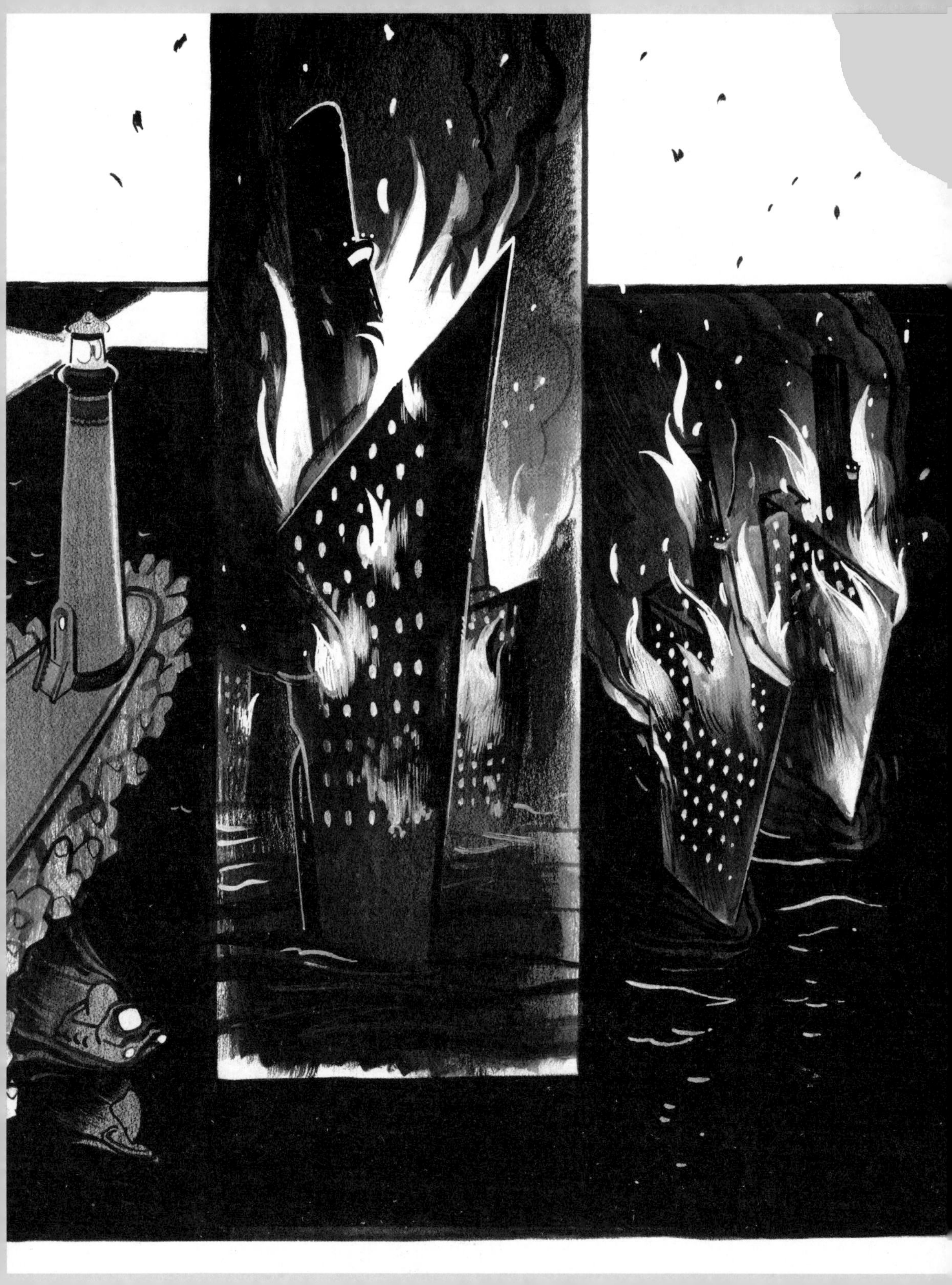

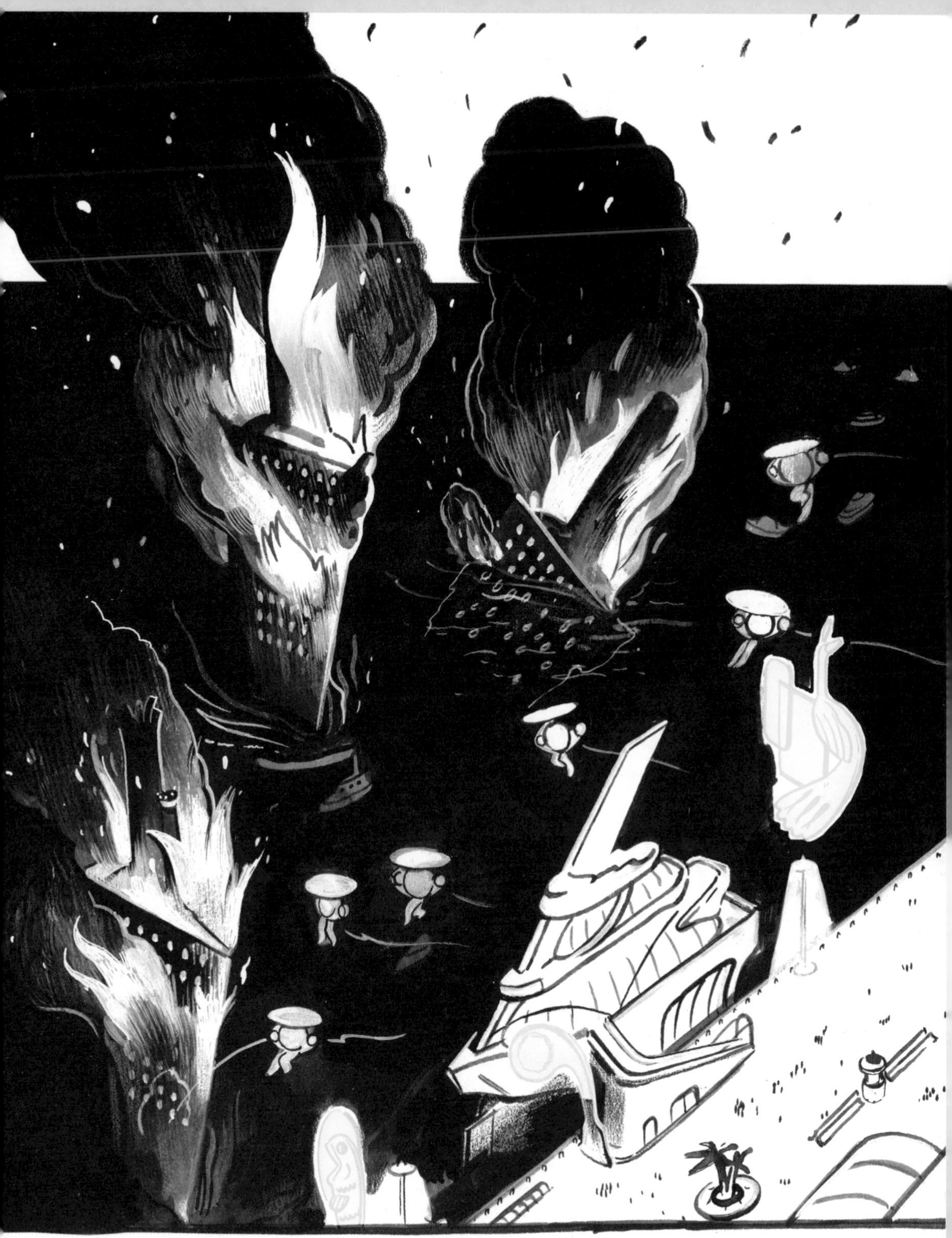

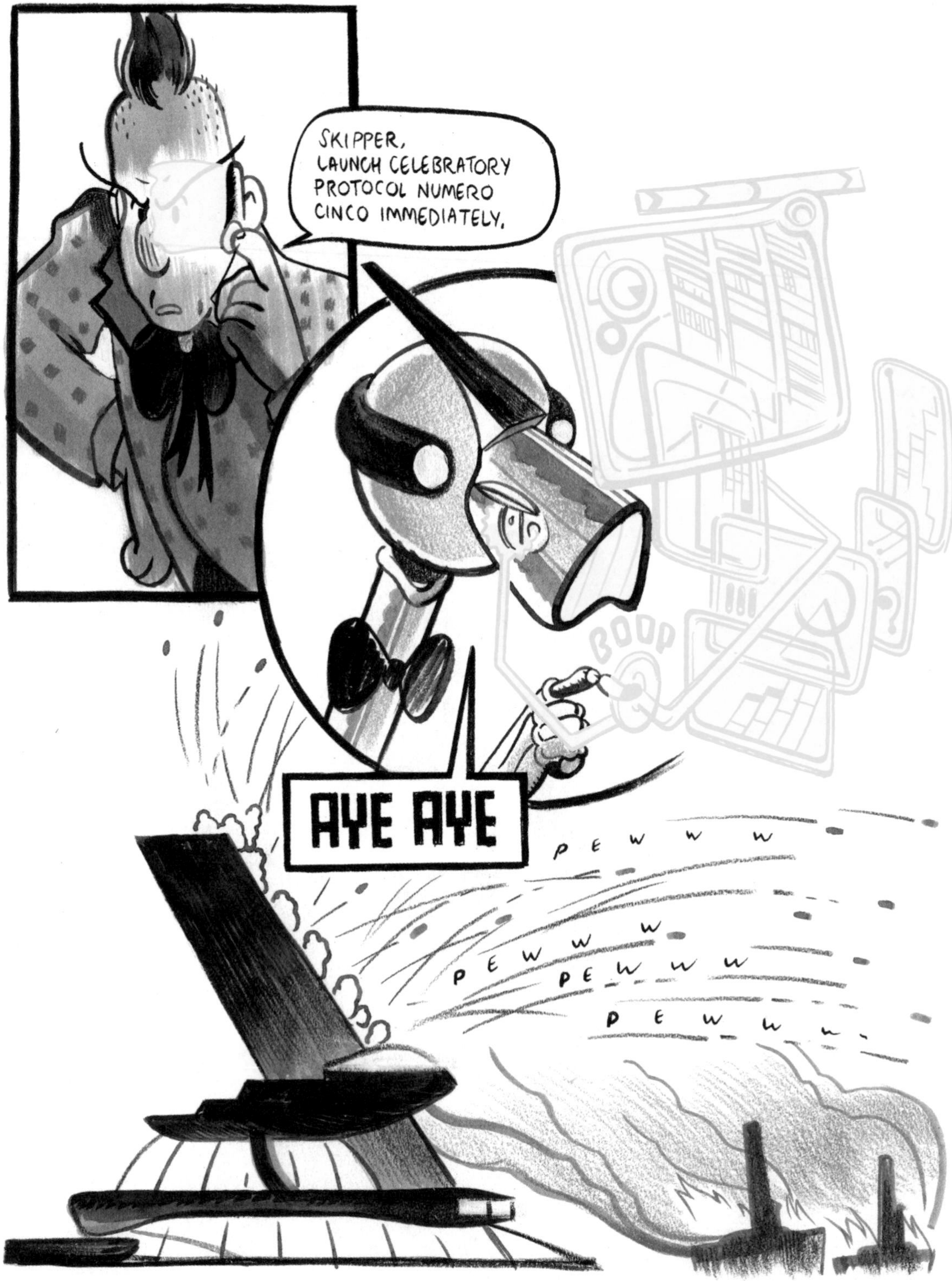
SKIPPER, LAUNCH CELEBRATORY PROTOCOL NUMERO CINCO IMMEDIATELY.
BOOP
AYE AYE
PEWWW
PEWWW
PEWWW
PEWWW

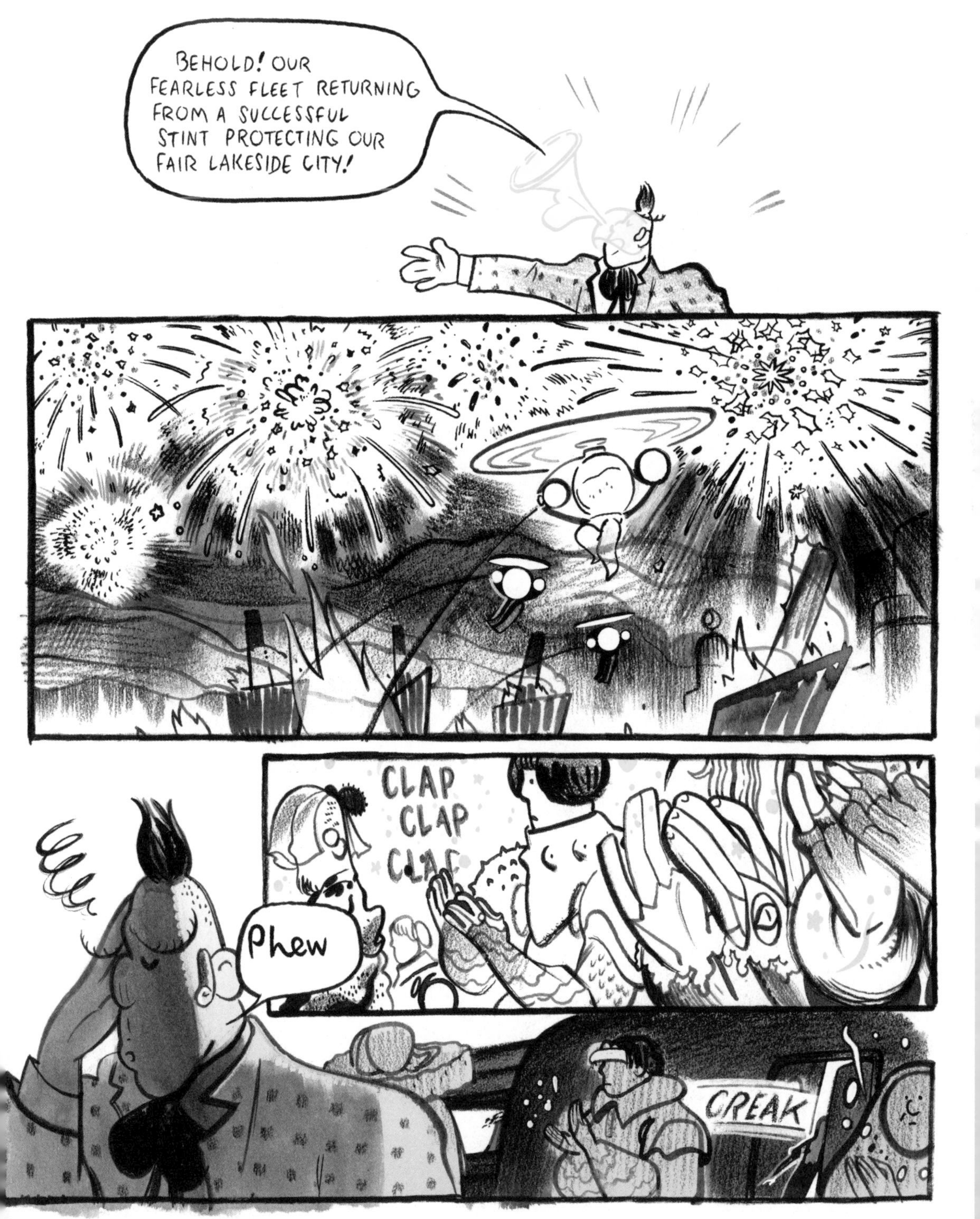
BEHOLD! OUR FEARLESS FLEET RETURNING FROM A SUCCESSFUL STINT PROTECTING OUR FAIR LAKESIDE CITY!
CLAP
CLAP
CLAP
Phew
CREAK

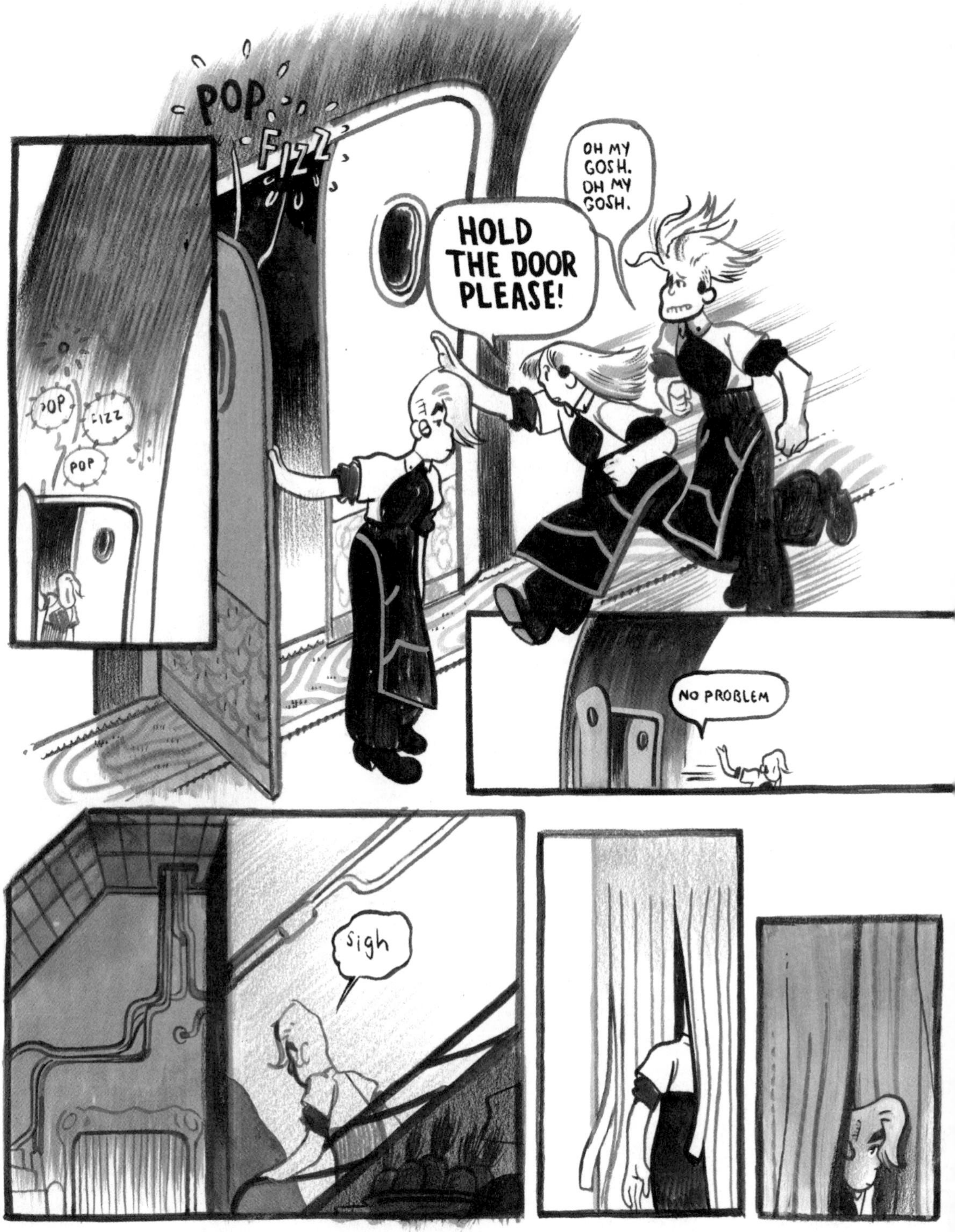
POP
FIZZ
POP
FIZZ
POP
OH MY GOSH. OH MY GOSH.
HOLD THE DOOR PLEASE!
NO PROBLEM
sigh

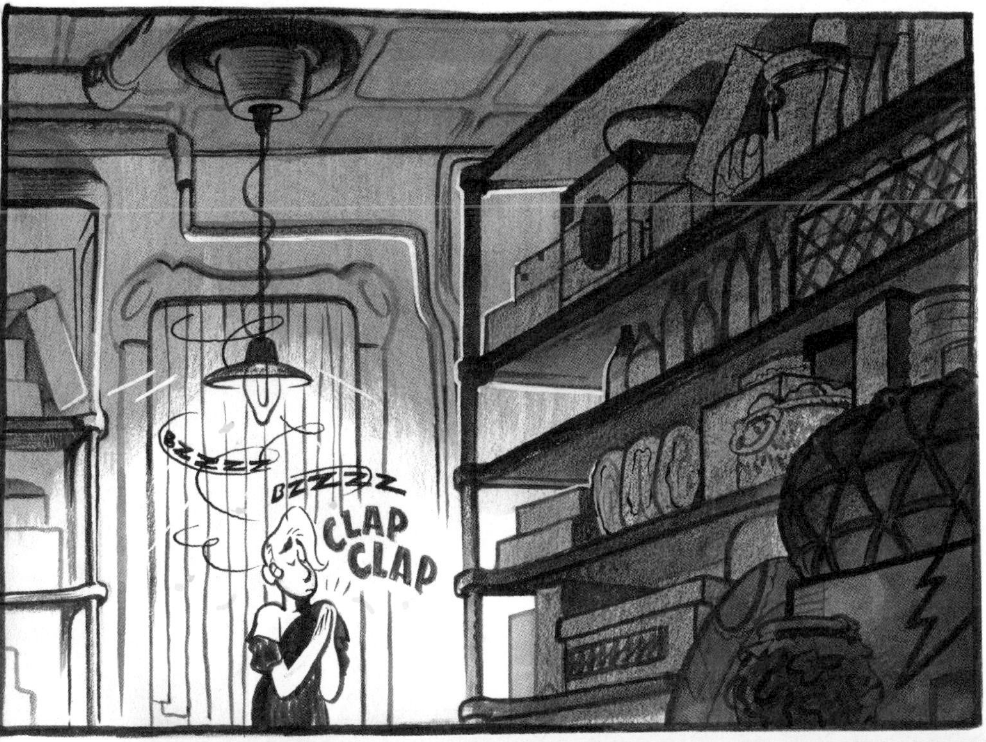
BZZZZZ
BZZZZ
CLAP CLAP

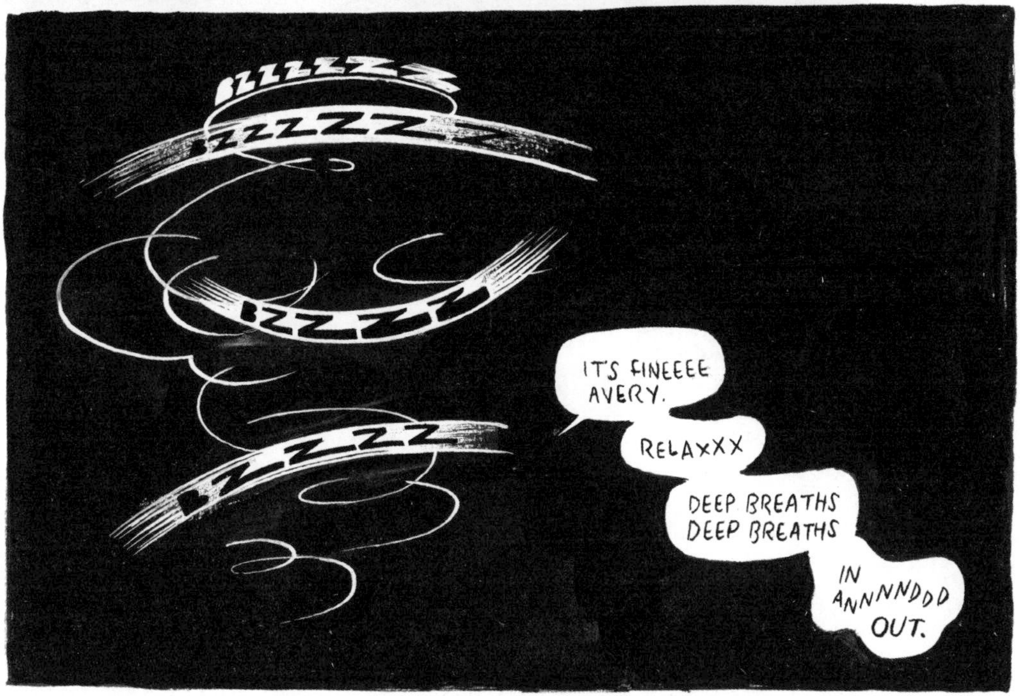
BZZZZZZ
BZZZZZZ
BZZZZZ
BZZZZZ
IT'S FINEEEE AVERY.
RELAXXX
DEEP BREATHS
DEEP BREATHS
IN ANNNNDDD OUT.

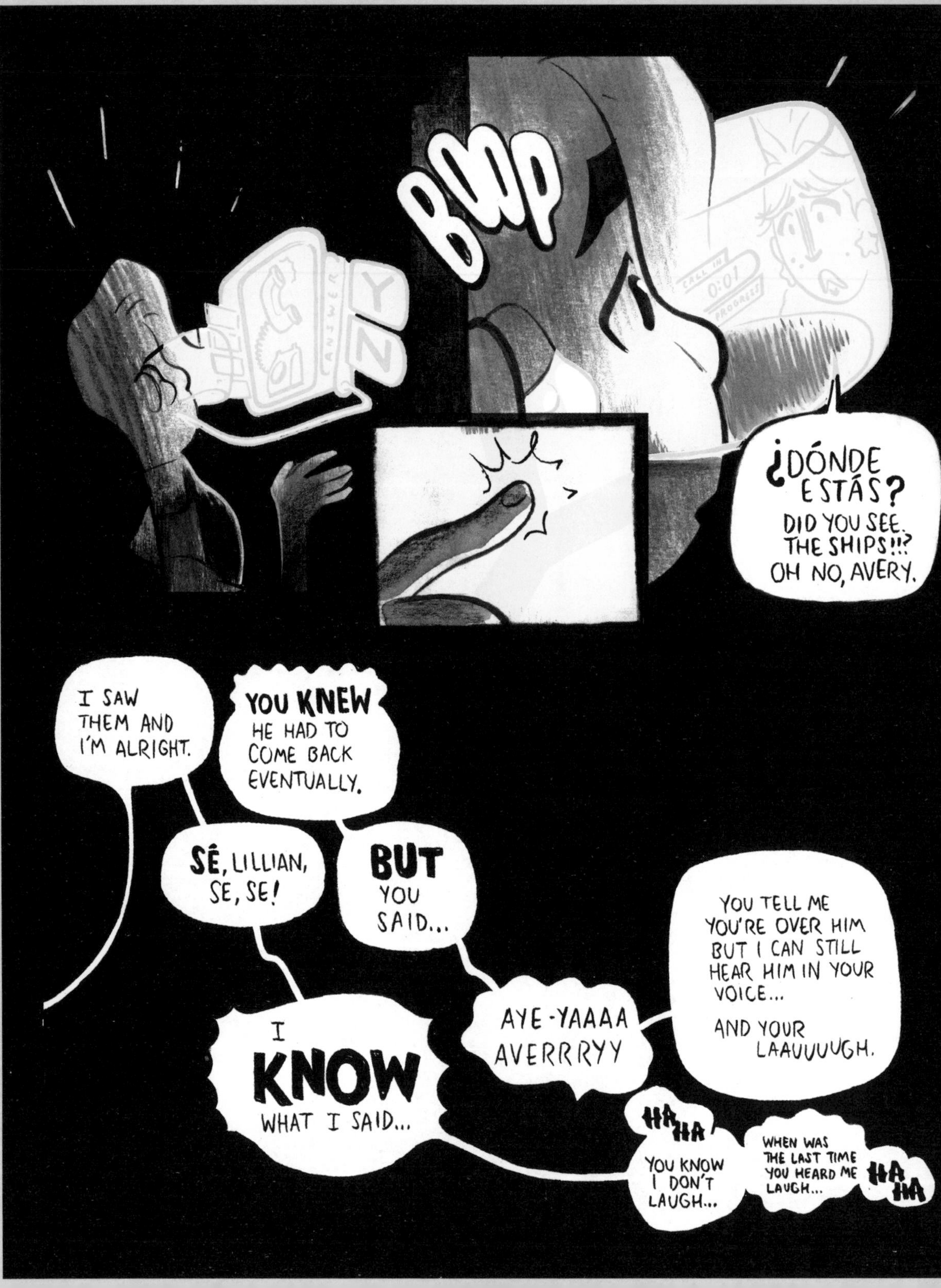
BOOP
CALL IN 0:01 PROGRESS
¿DÓNDE ESTÁS? DID YOU SEE THE SHIPS!!? OH NO, AVERY.
I SAW THEM AND I'M ALRIGHT.
YOU KNEW HE HAD TO COME BACK EVENTUALLY.
SÉ, LILLIAN, SE, SE!
BUT YOU SAID...
I KNOW WHAT I SAID...
AYE-YAAAA AVERRRYY
YOU TELL ME YOU'RE OVER HIM BUT I CAN STILL HEAR HIM IN YOUR VOICE...
AND YOUR LAAUUUUGH.
HA HA
YOU KNOW I DON'T LAUGH...
WHEN WAS THE LAST TIME YOU HEARD ME LAUGH...
HA HA

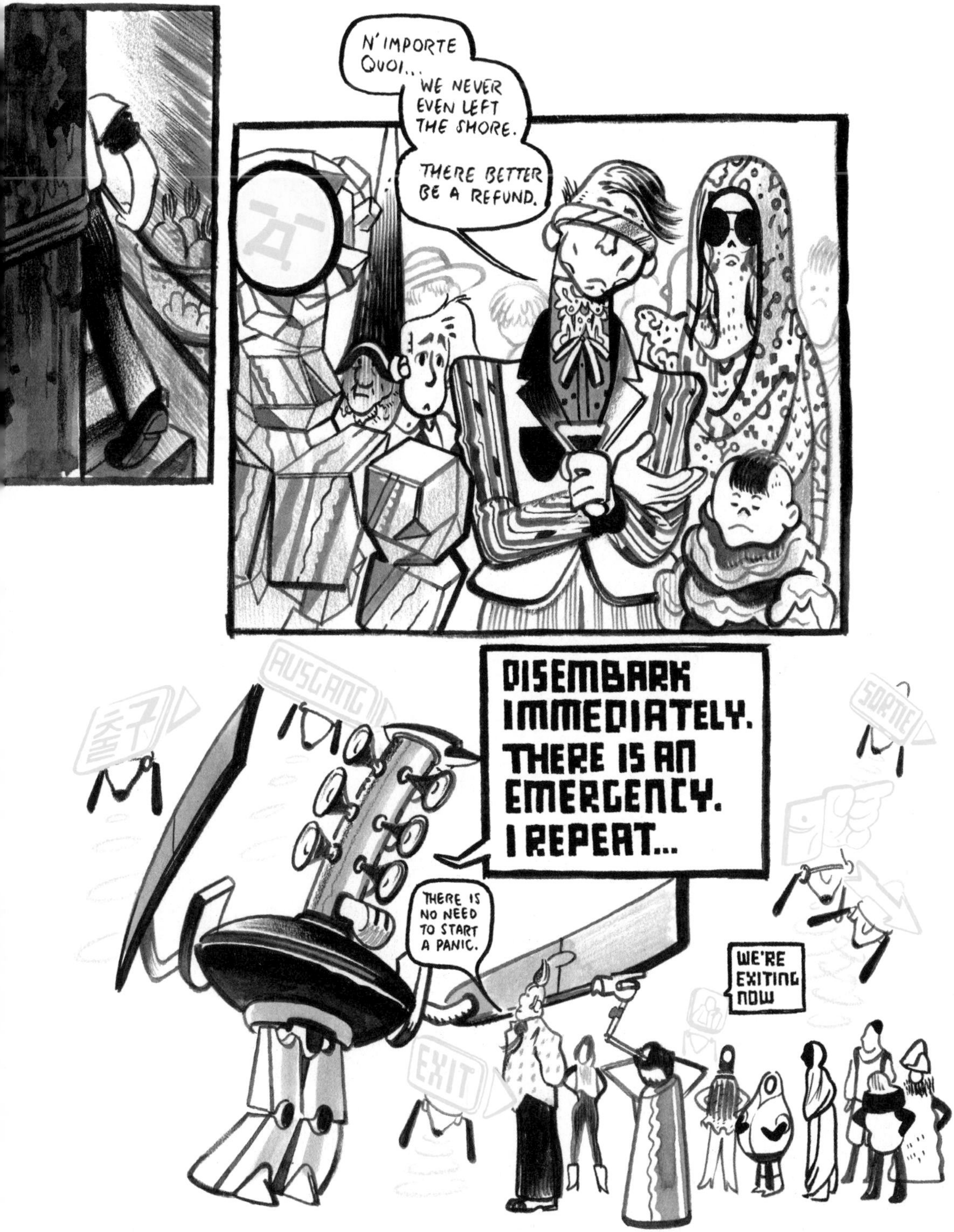
N'IMPORTE QUOI...
WE NEVER EVEN LEFT THE SHORE.
THERE BETTER BE A REFUND.
AUSGANG
SORTIE
DISEMBARK IMMEDIATELY. THERE IS AN EMERGENCY. I REPEAT...
THERE IS NO NEED TO START A PANIC.
WE'RE EXITING NOW
EXIT

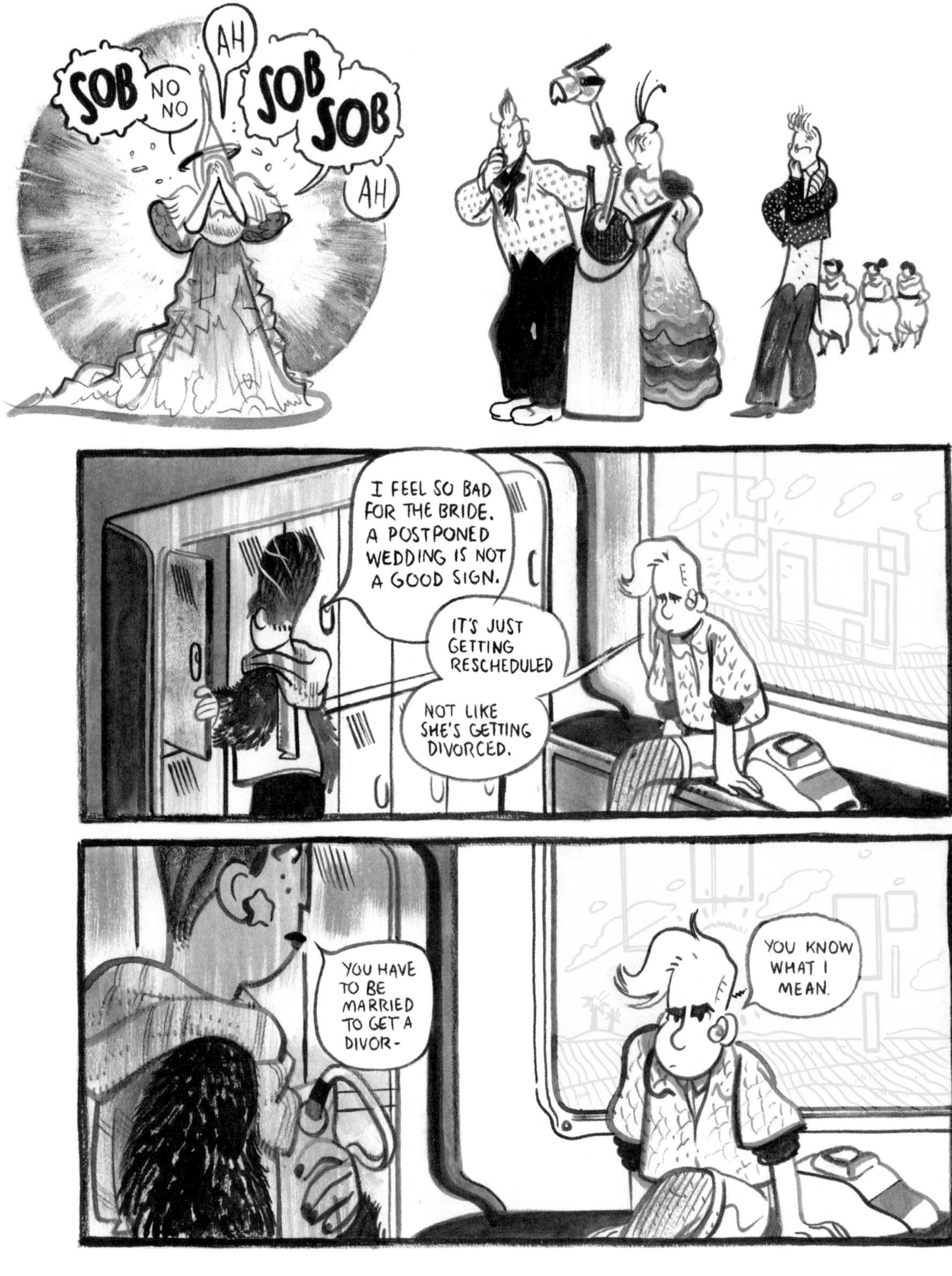
SOB
NO NO
AH
SOB SOB
AH
I FEEL SO BAD FOR THE BRIDE. A POSTPONED WEDDING IS NOT A GOOD SIGN.
IT'S JUST GETTING RESCHEDULED
NOT LIKE SHE'S GETTING DIVORCED.
YOU HAVE TO BE MARRIED TO GET A DIVOR-
YOU KNOW WHAT I MEAN.

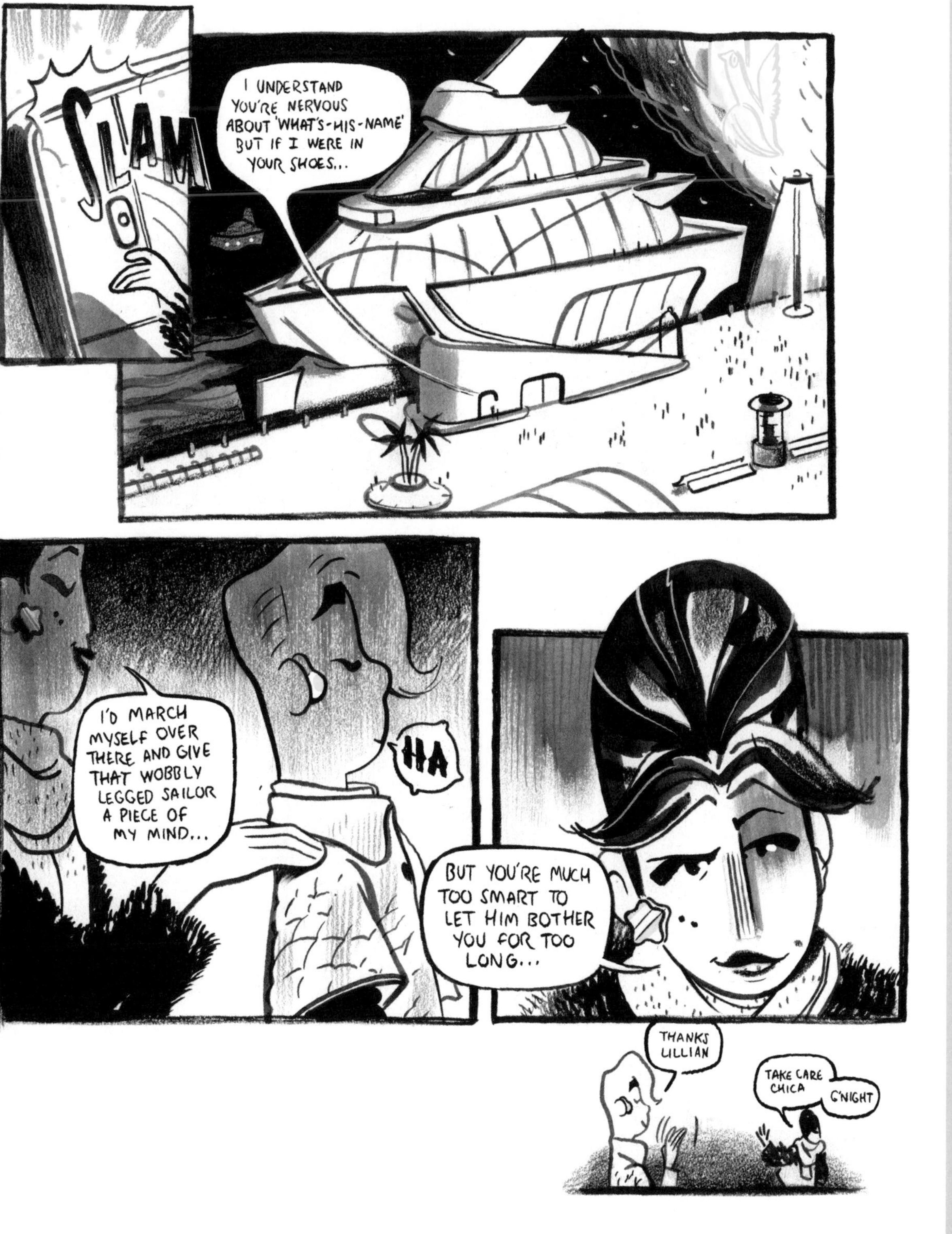
SLAM
I UNDERSTAND YOU'RE NERVOUS ABOUT 'WHAT'S-HIS-NAME' BUT IF I WERE IN YOUR SHOES...
I'D MARCH MYSELF OVER THERE AND GIVE THAT WOBBLY LEGGED SAILOR A PIECE OF MY MIND...
HA
BUT YOU'RE MUCH TOO SMART TO LET HIM BOTHER YOU FOR TOO LONG...
THANKS LILLIAN
TAKE CARE CHICA
G'NIGHT

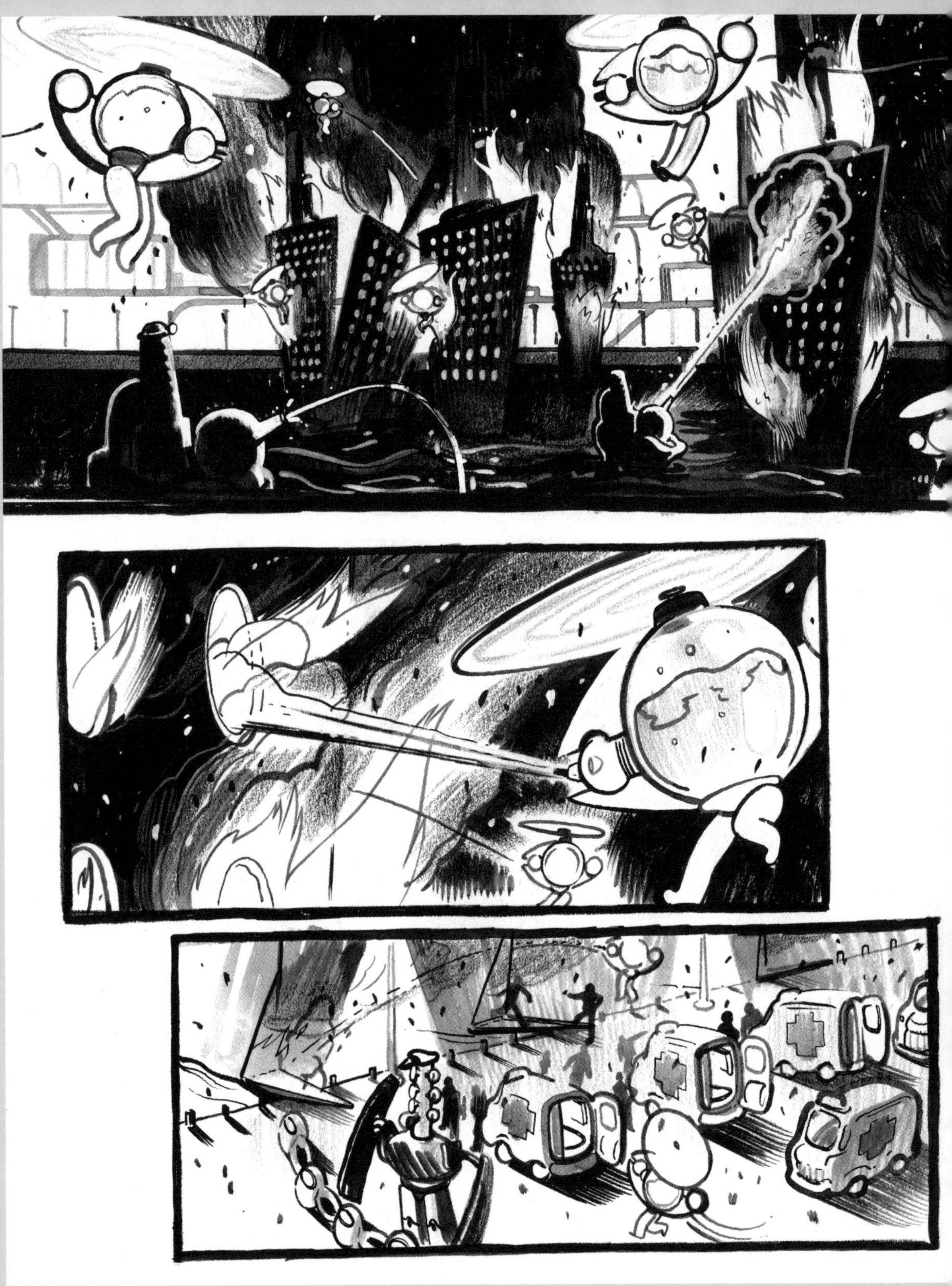

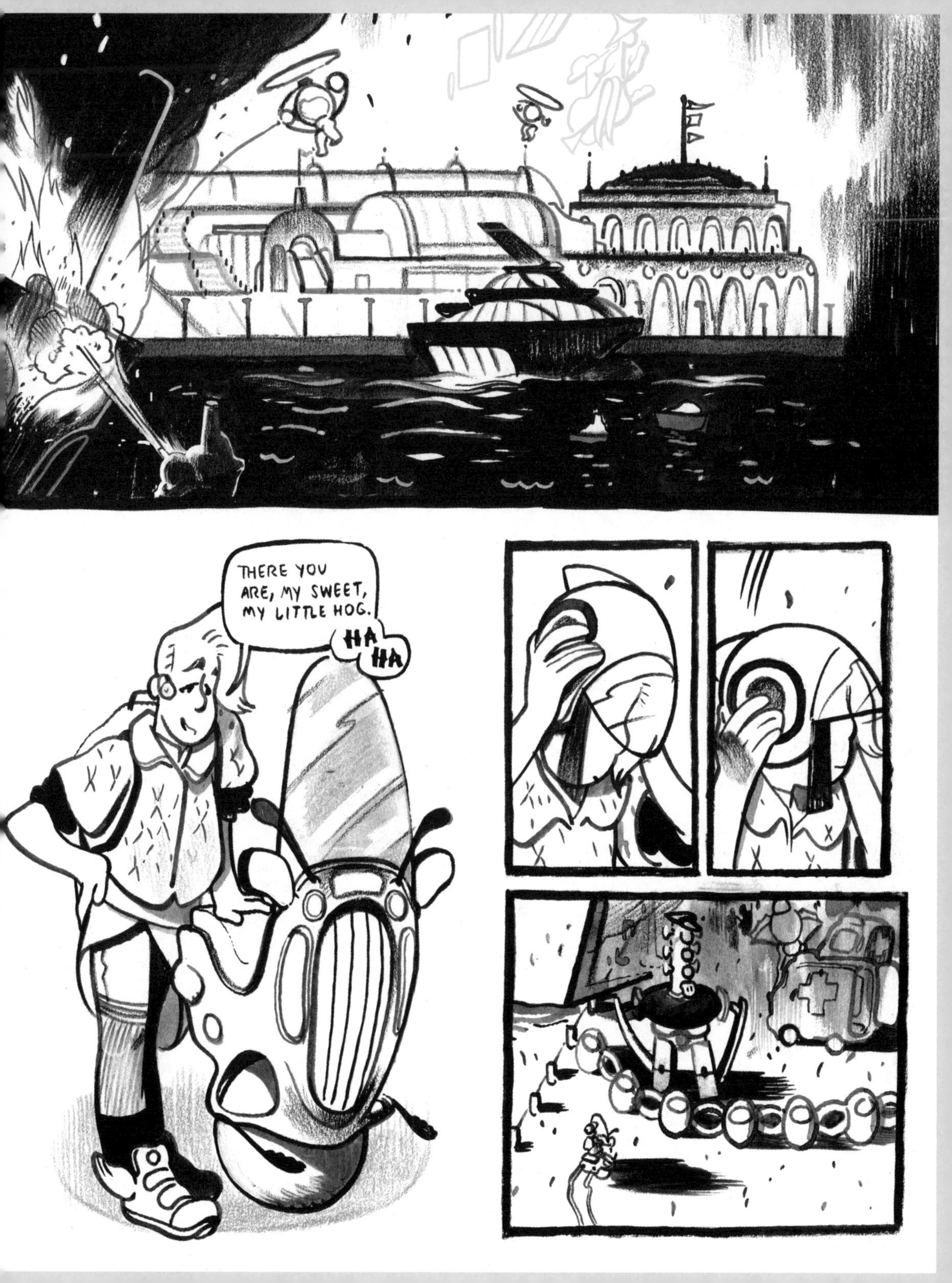
THERE YOU ARE, MY SWEET, MY LITTLE HOG.
HA HA

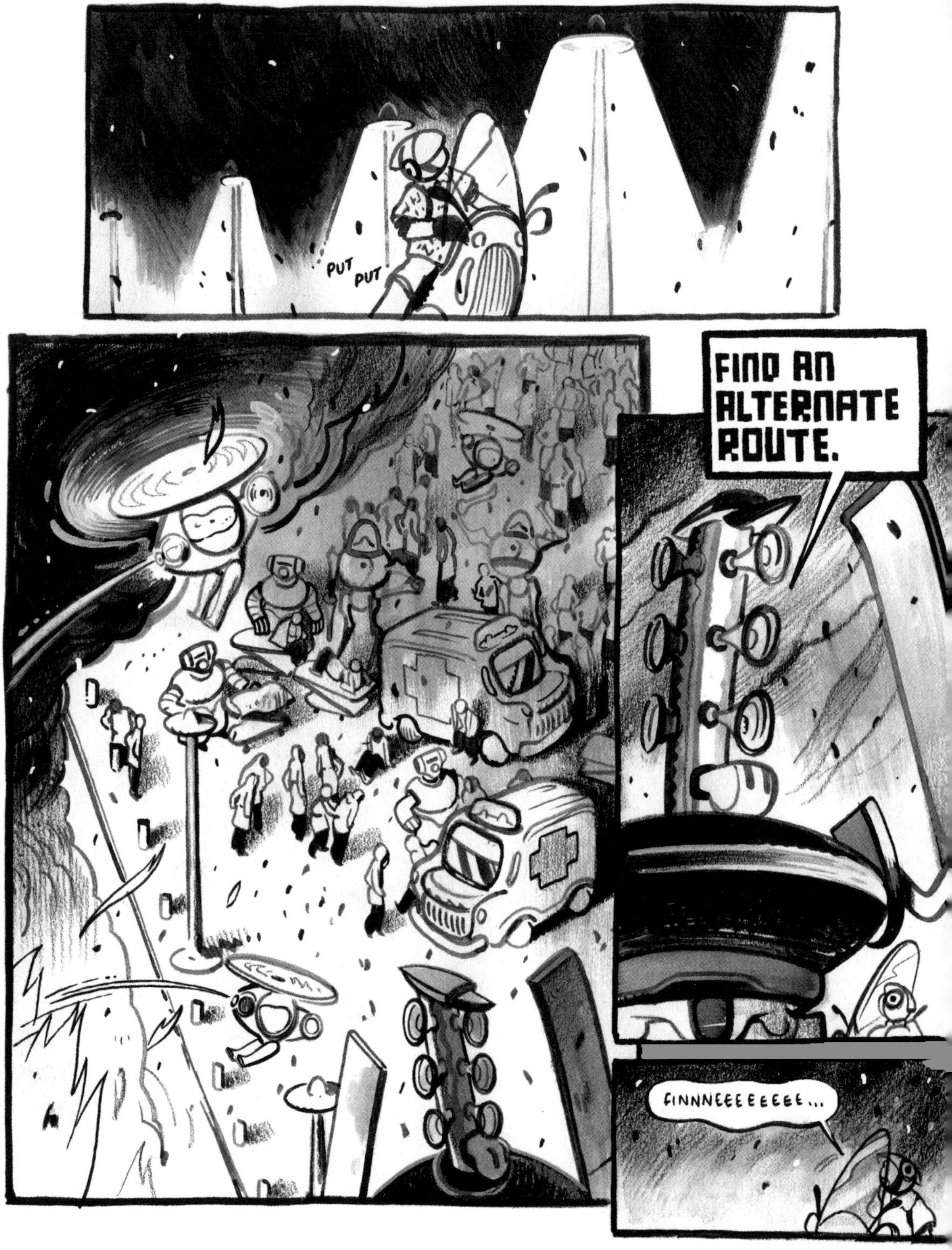
PUT
PUT
FIND AN ALTERNATE ROUTE.
FINNNEEEEEEEE...

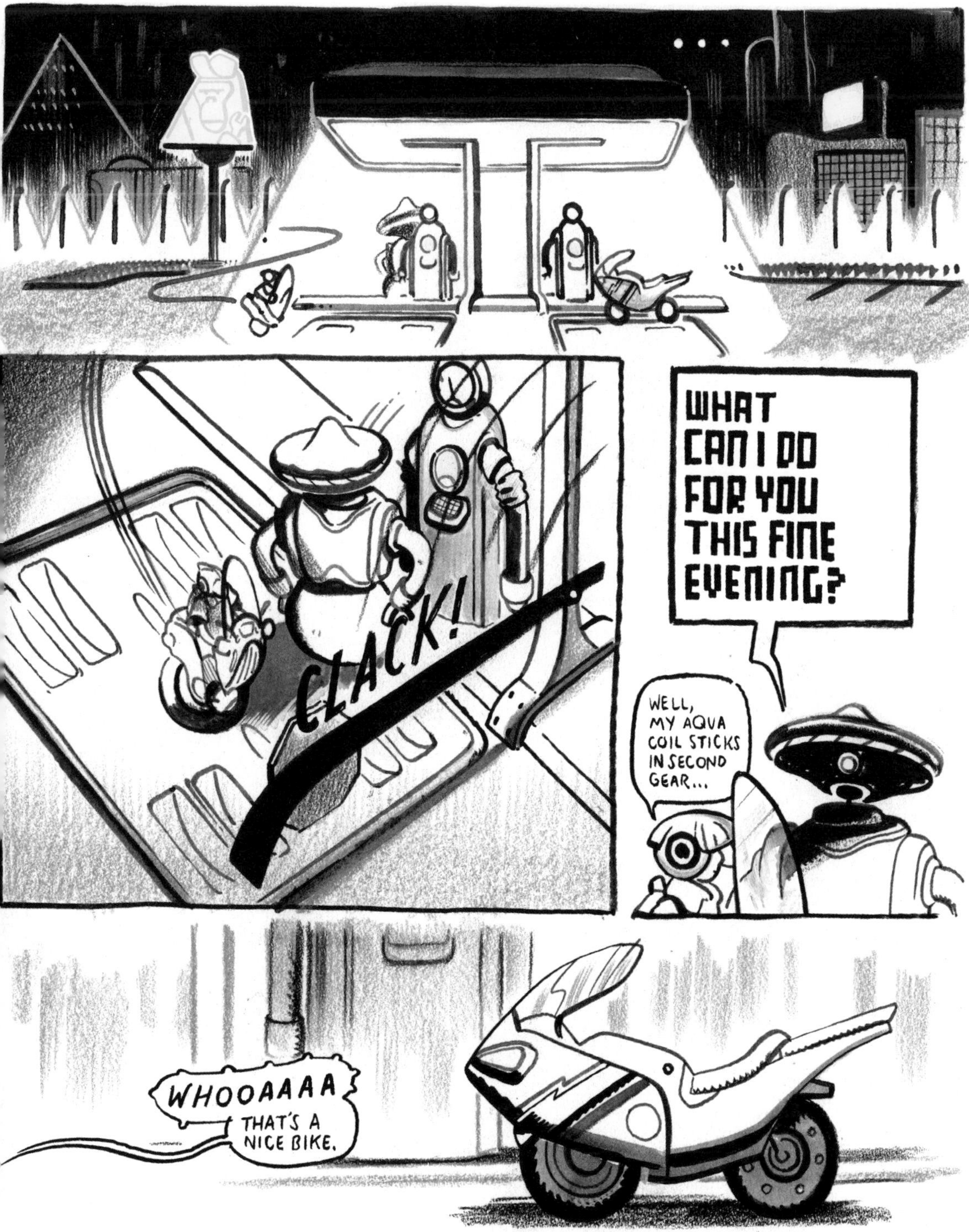
CLACK!
WHAT CAN I DO FOR YOU THIS FINE EVENING?
WELL, MY AQUA COIL STICKS IN SECOND GEAR...
WHOOAAAA
THAT'S A NICE BIKE.

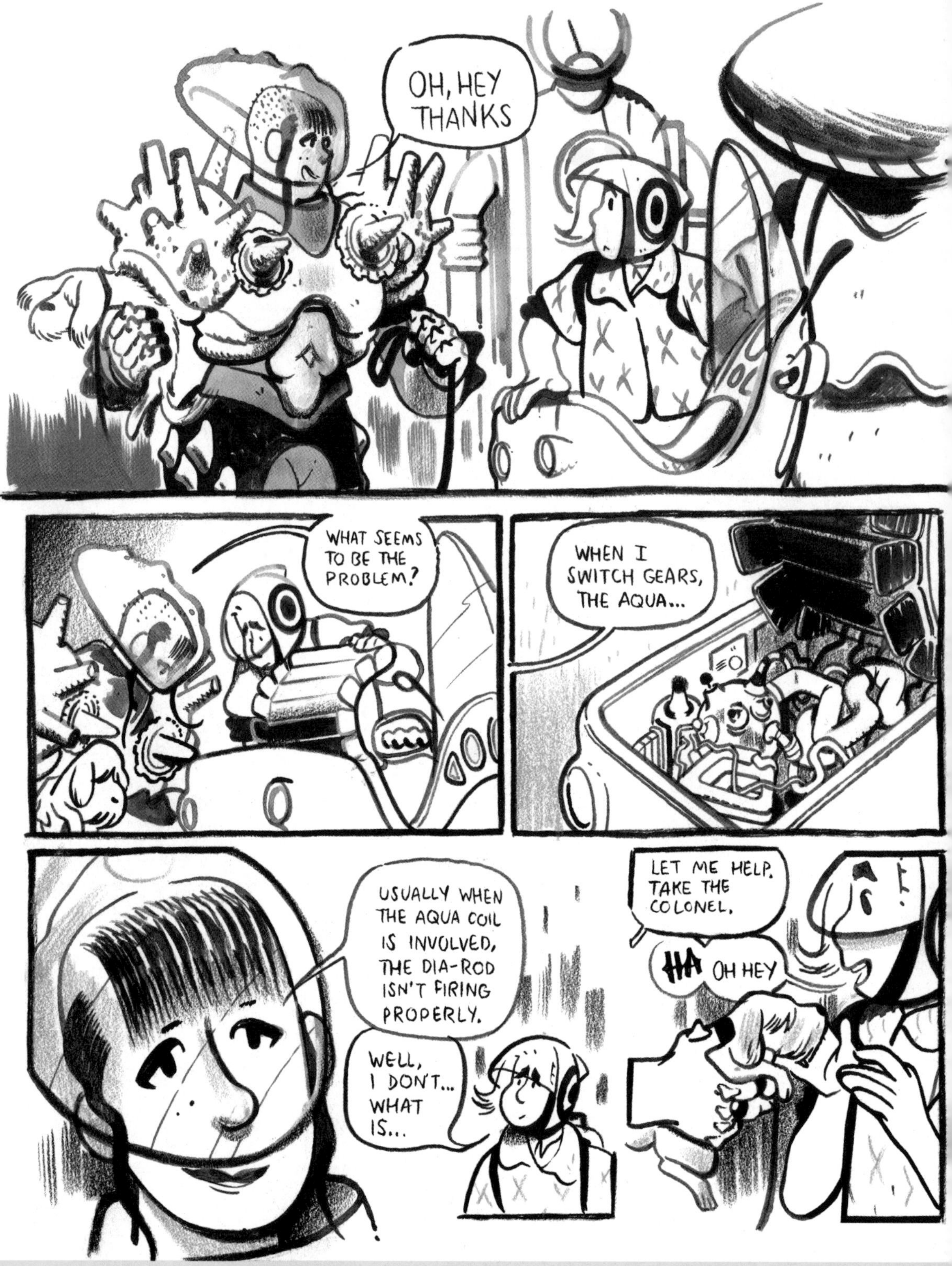
OH, HEY THANKS
WHAT SEEMS TO BE THE PROBLEM?
WHEN I SWITCH GEARS, THE AQUA...
USUALLY WHEN THE AQUA COIL IS INVOLVED, THE DIA-ROD ISN'T FIRING PROPERLY.
WELL, I DON'T... WHAT IS...
LET ME HELP. TAKE THE COLONEL.
HA OH HEY

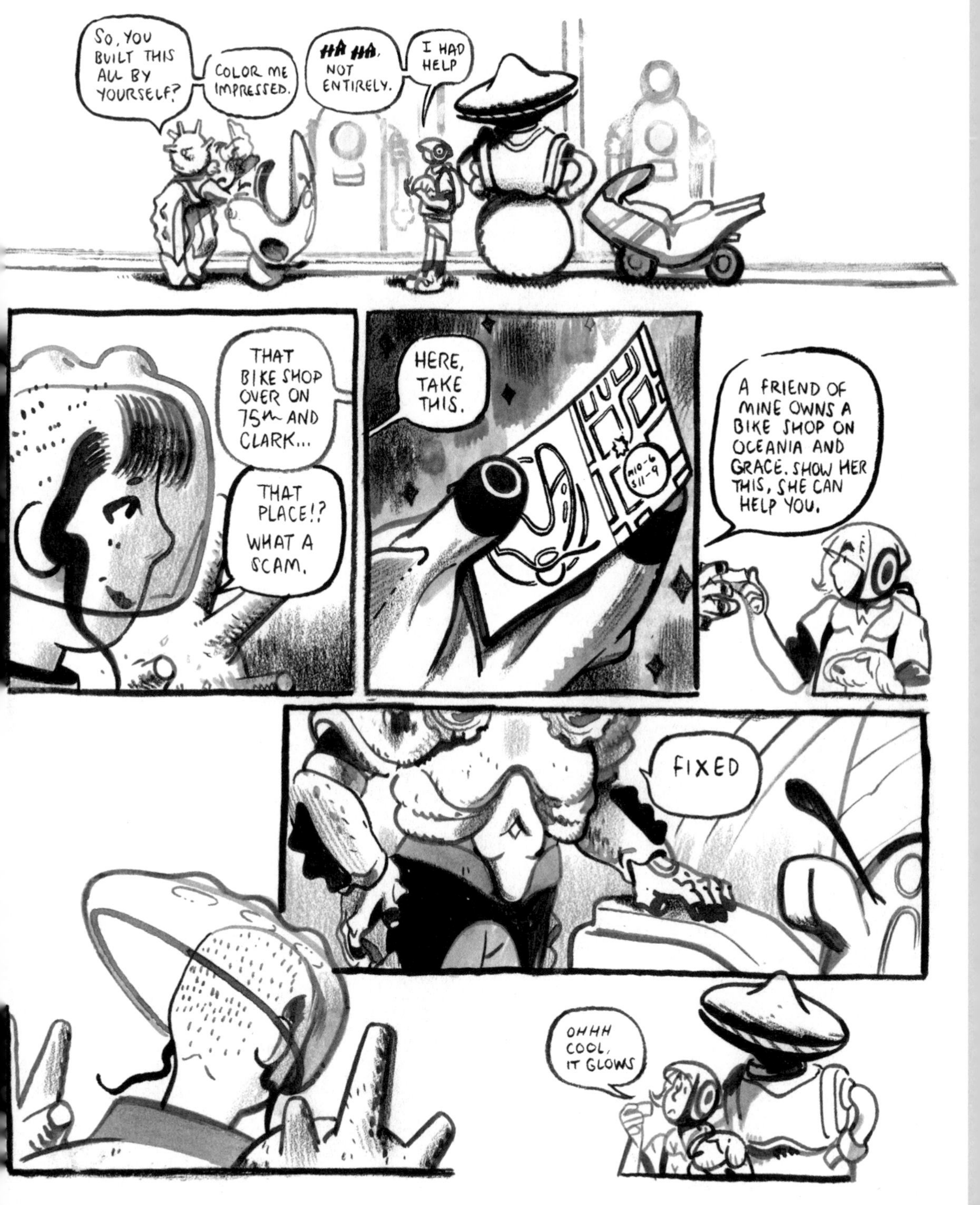

SO, YOU BUILT THIS ALL BY YOURSELF?
COLOR ME IMPRESSED.
HA HA, NOT ENTIRELY.
I HAD HELP
THAT BIKE SHOP OVER ON 75th AND CLARK...
THAT PLACE!? WHAT A SCAM.
HERE, TAKE THIS.
M10-6 S11-9
A FRIEND OF MINE OWNS A BIKE SHOP ON OCEANIA AND GRACE. SHOW HER THIS, SHE CAN HELP YOU.
FIXED
OHHH COOL, IT GLOWS

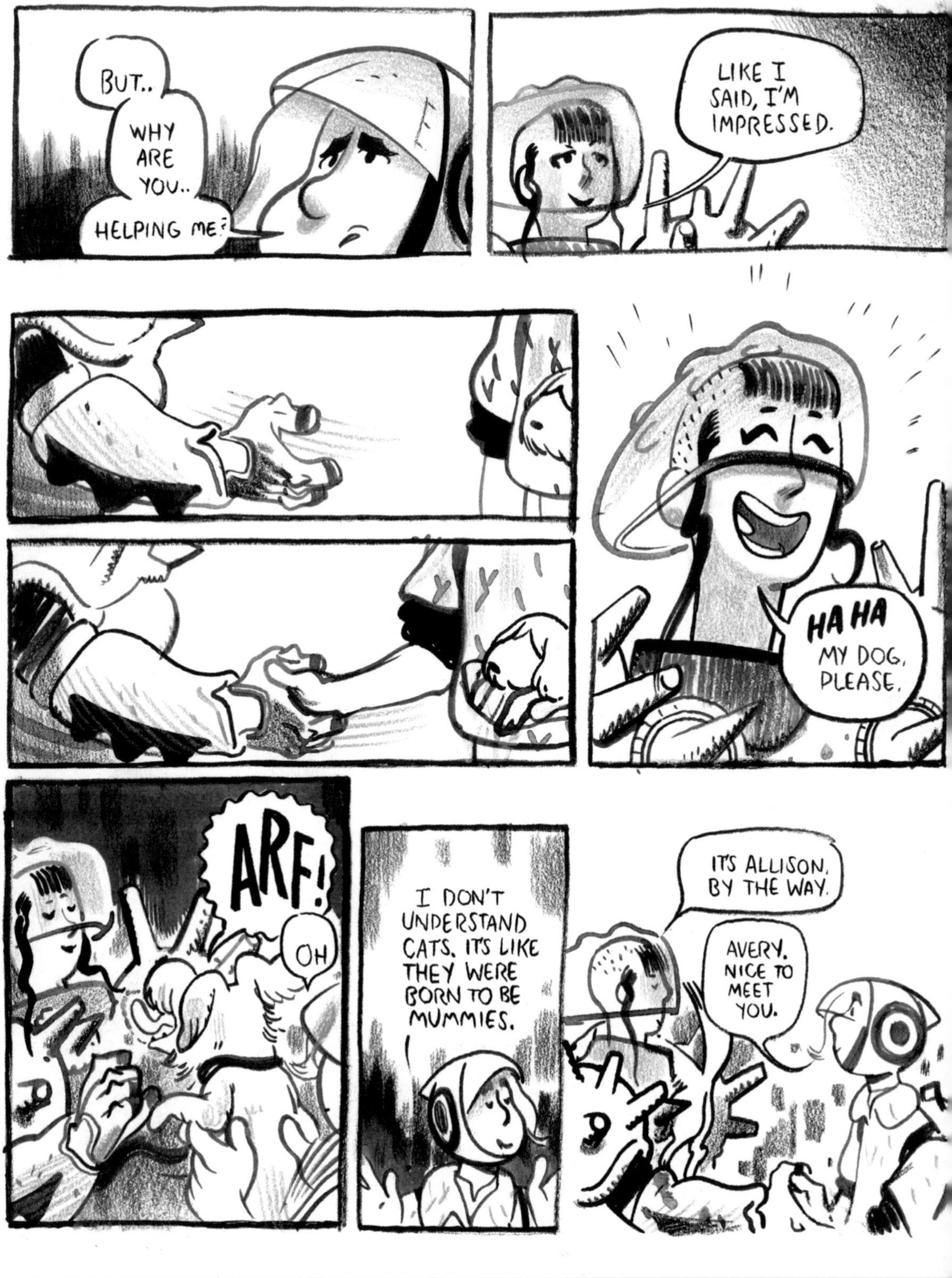
BUT..
WHY ARE YOU..
HELPING ME?
LIKE I SAID, I'M IMPRESSED.
HA HA
MY DOG, PLEASE.
ARF!
OH
I DON'T UNDERSTAND CATS. IT'S LIKE THEY WERE BORN TO BE MUMMIES.
IT'S ALLISON, BY THE WAY.
AVERY. NICE TO MEET YOU.

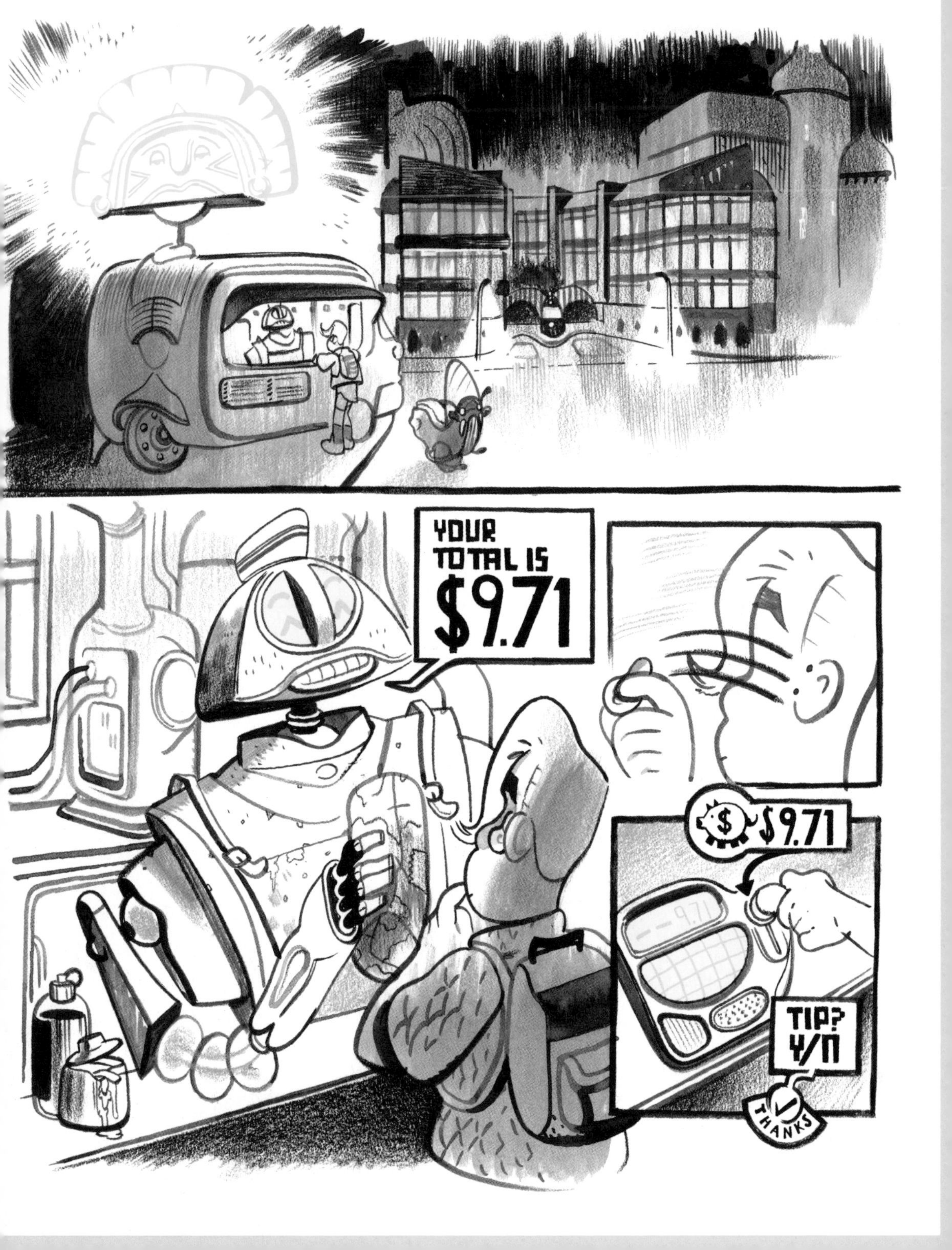
YOUR TOTAL IS $9.71
$9.71
TIP? Y/N
THANKS

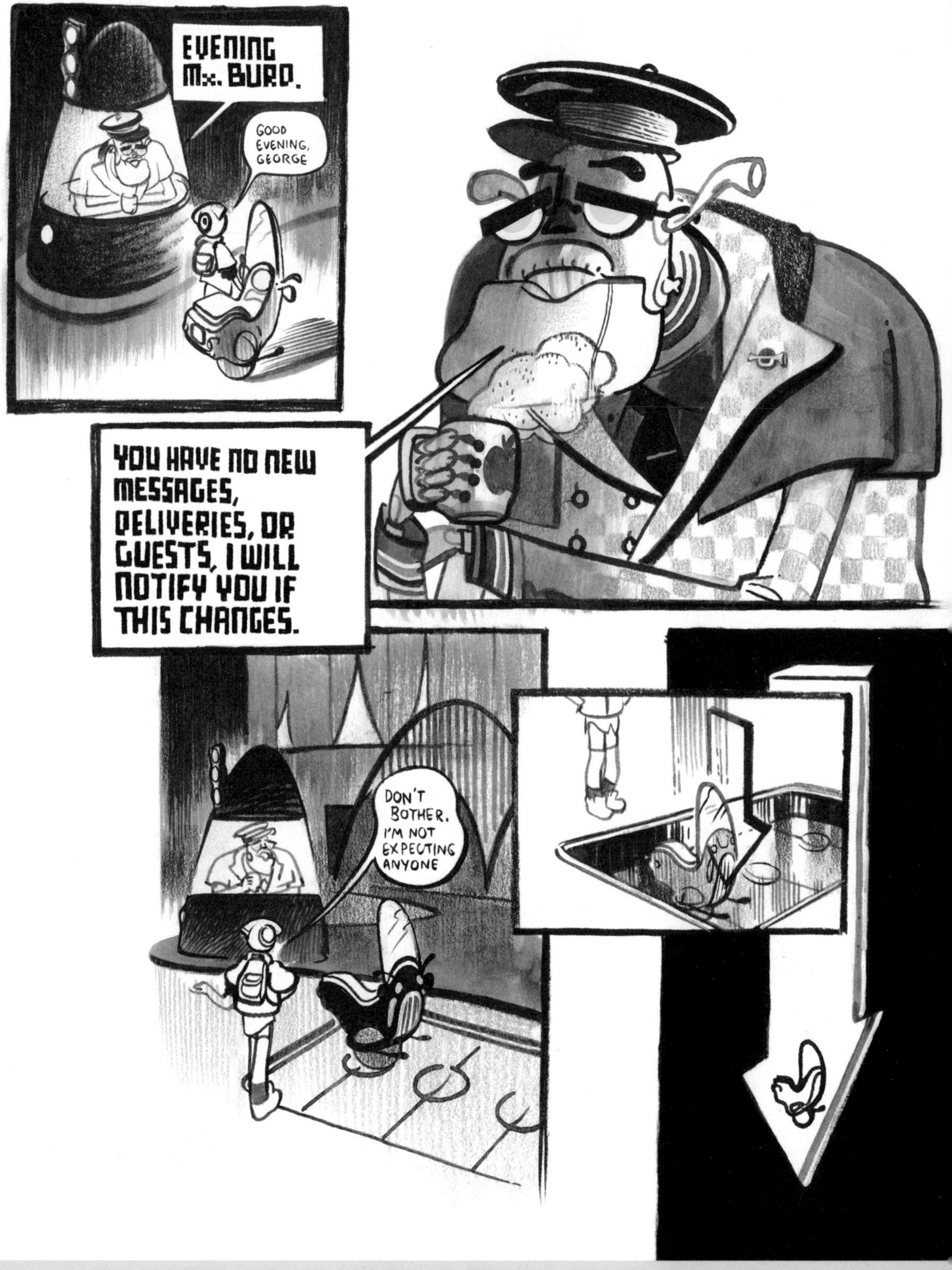
EVENING Mx. BURD.
GOOD EVENING, GEORGE
YOU HAVE NO NEW MESSAGES, DELIVERIES, OR GUESTS, I WILL NOTIFY YOU IF THIS CHANGES.
DON'T BOTHER. I'M NOT EXPECTING ANYONE

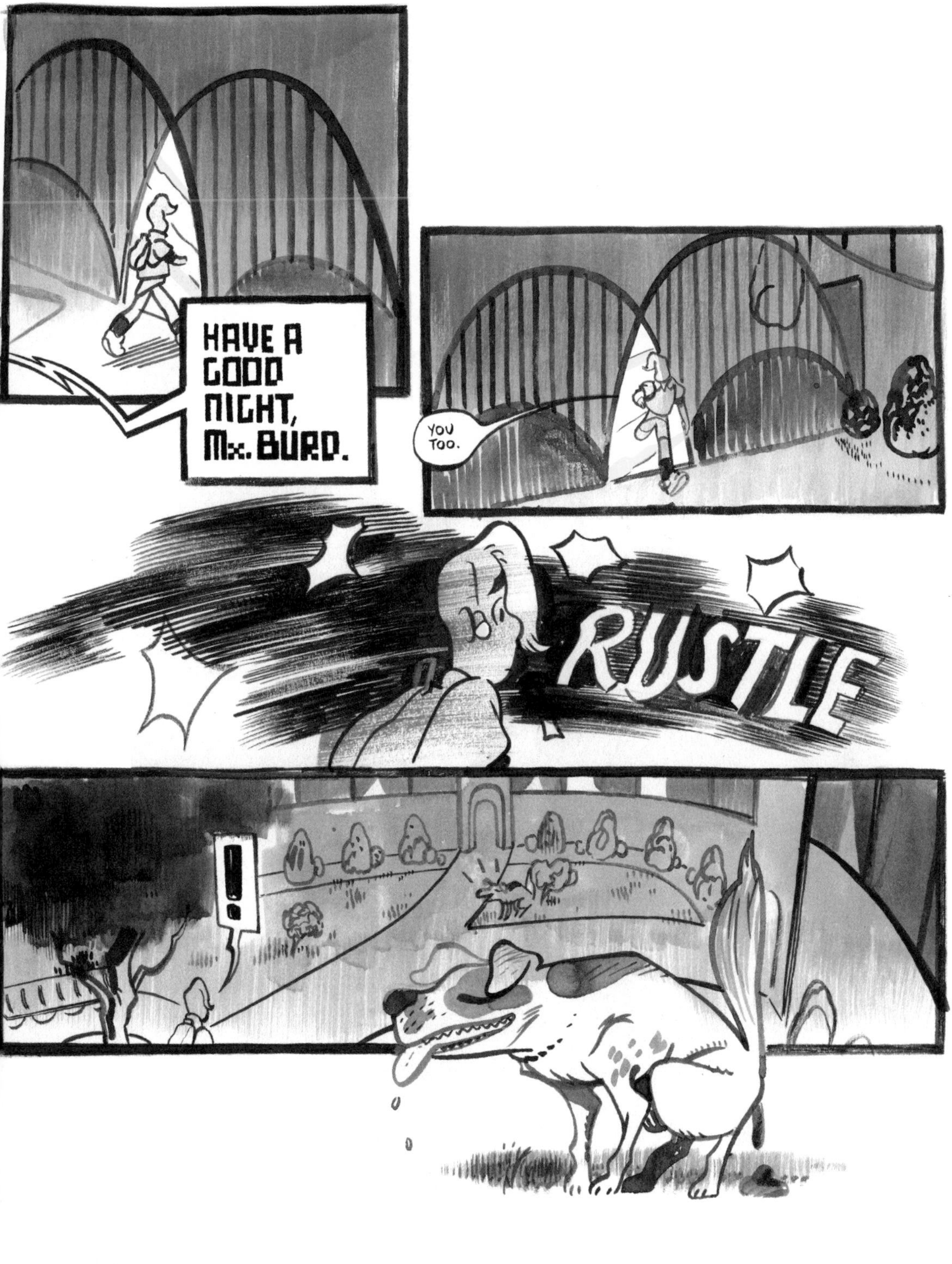
HAVE A GOOD NIGHT, Mx. BURD.
YOU TOO.
RUSTLE
!

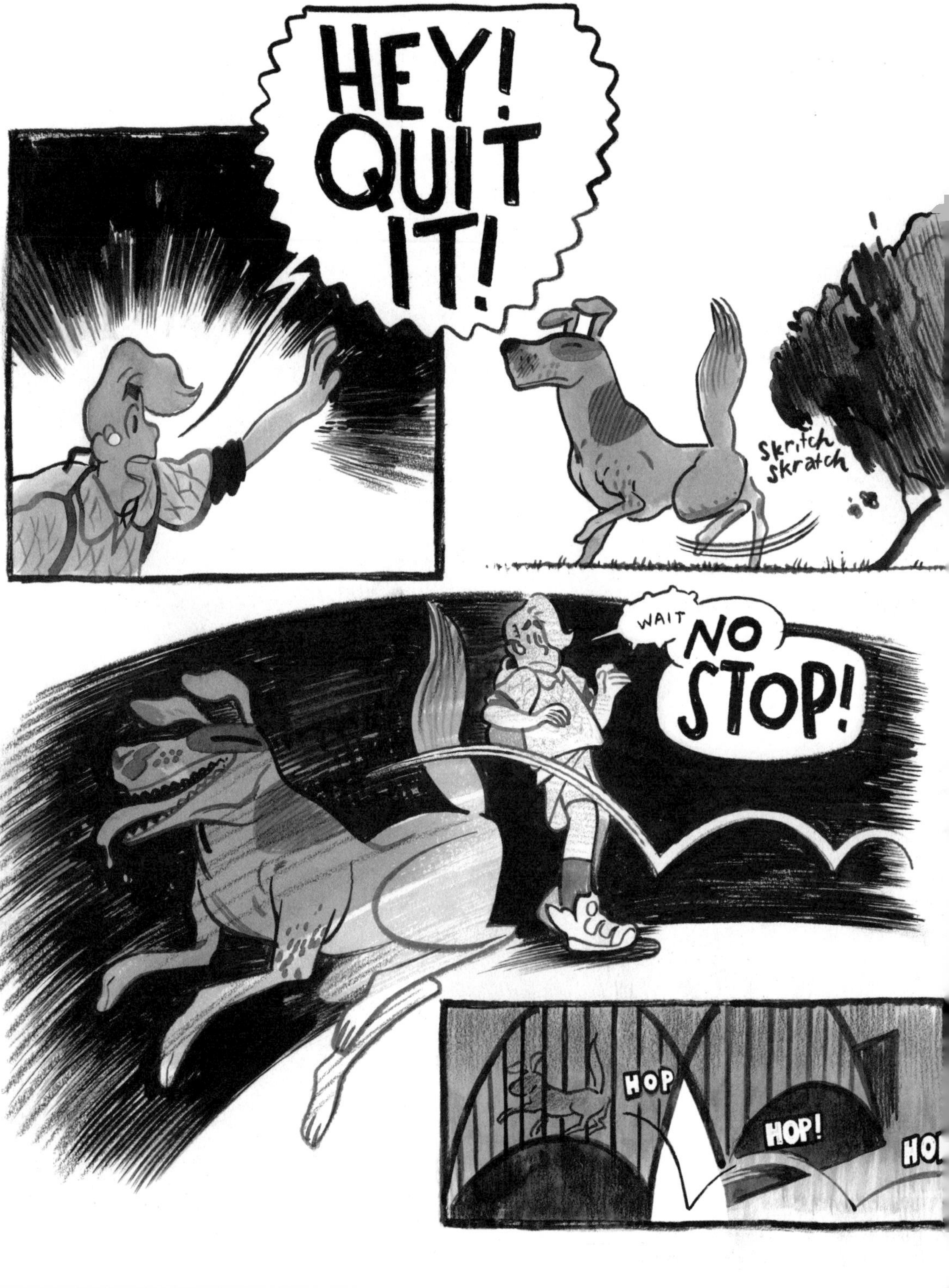
HEY! QUIT IT!
Skritch skratch
WAIT NO STOP!
HOP
HOP!

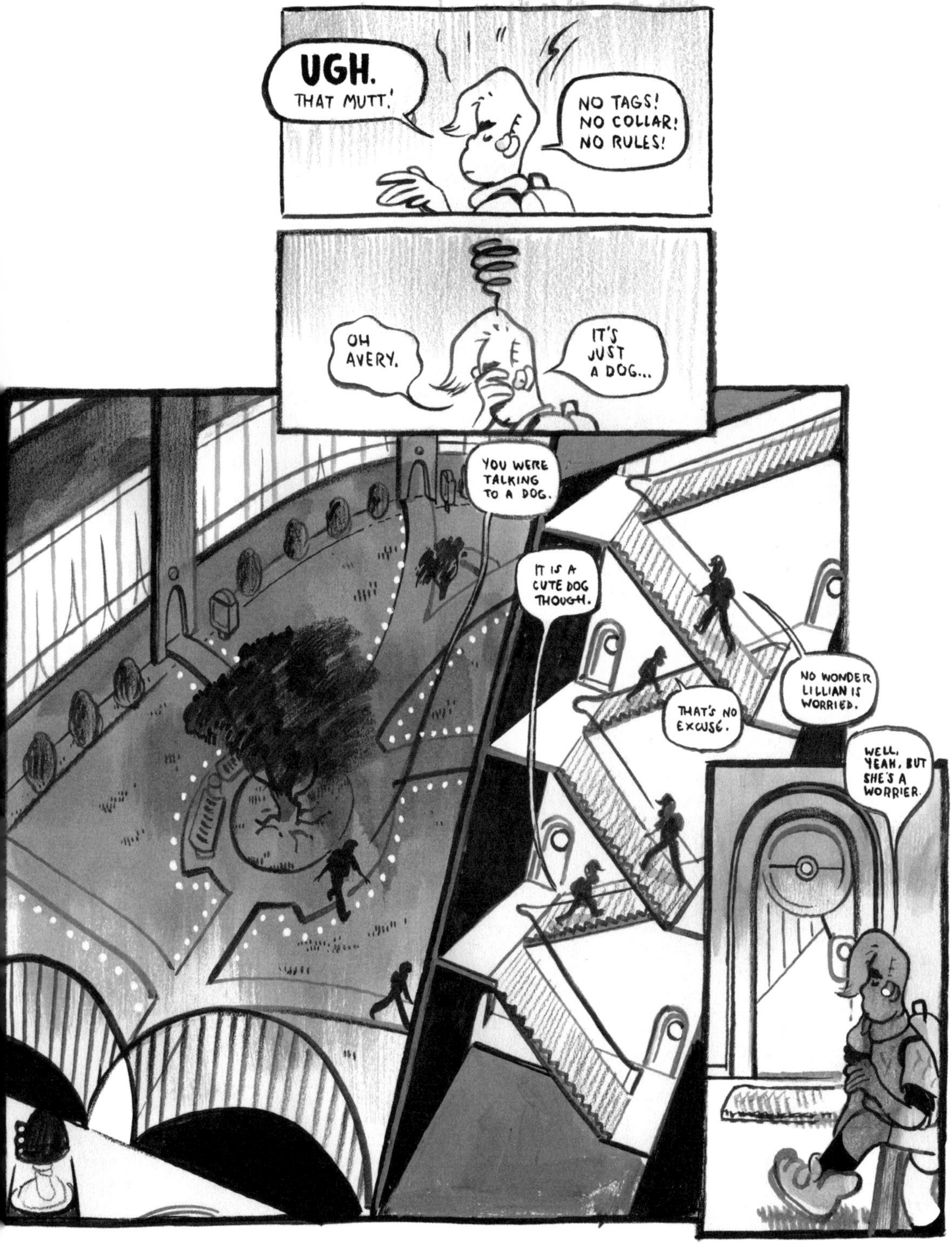
UGH. THAT MUTT!
NO TAGS! NO COLLAR! NO RULES!
OH AVERY.
IT'S JUST A DOG...
YOU WERE TALKING TO A DOG.
IT IS A CUTE DOG THOUGH.
THAT'S NO EXCUSE.
NO WONDER LILLIAN IS WORRIED.
WELL, YEAH, BUT SHE'S A WORRIER.

WELCOME HOME, AVERY.

WELCOME HOME, AVERY.

WHIRRRR

CLICK

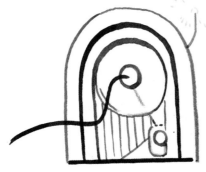

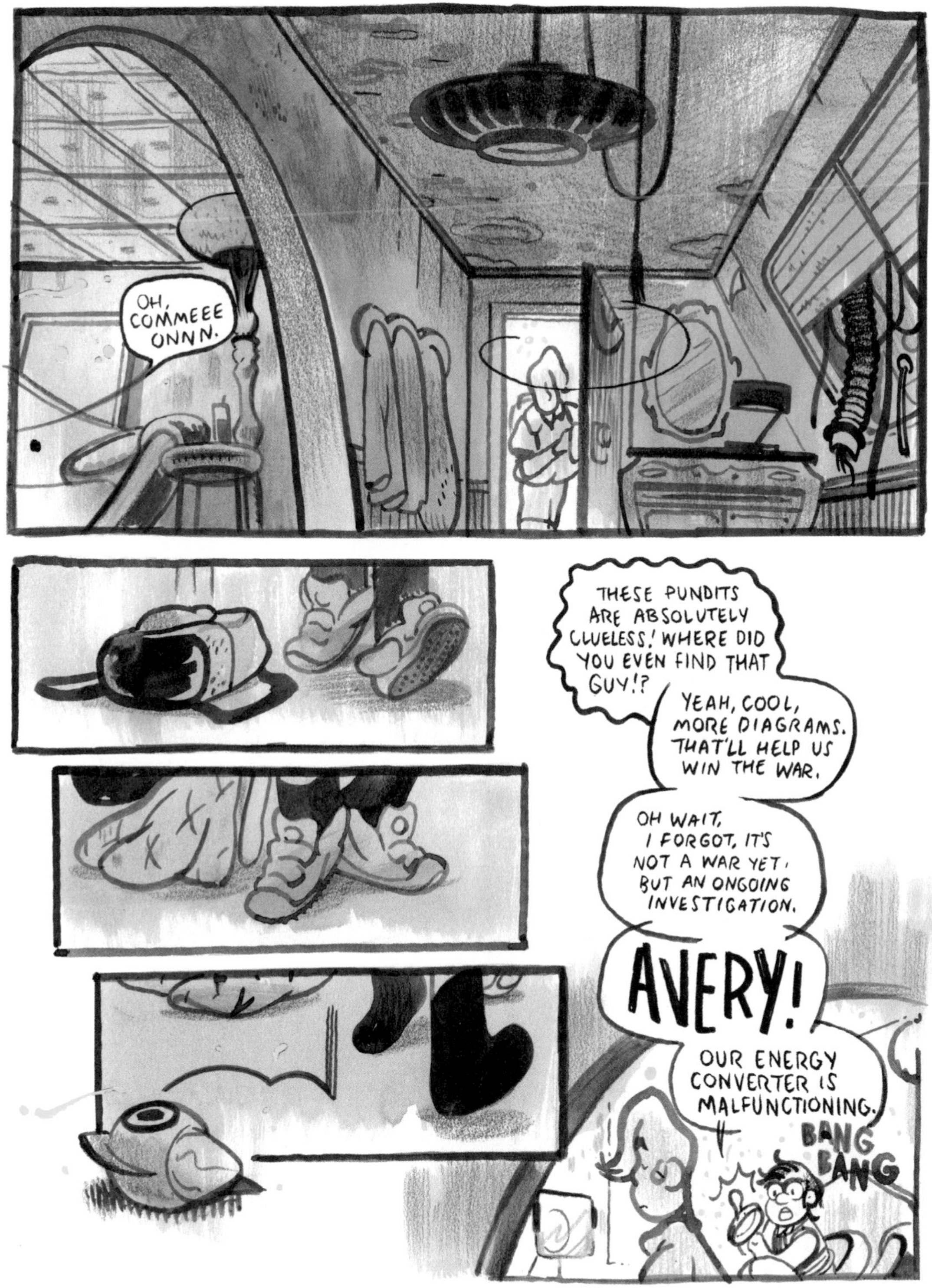
OH, COMMEEE ONNN.
THESE PUNDITS ARE ABSOLUTELY CLUELESS! WHERE DID YOU EVEN FIND THAT GUY!?
YEAH, COOL, MORE DIAGRAMS. THAT'LL HELP US WIN THE WAR.
OH WAIT, I FORGOT, IT'S NOT A WAR YET, BUT AN ONGOING INVESTIGATION.
AVERY!
OUR ENERGY CONVERTER IS MALFUNCTIONING.
BANG BANG

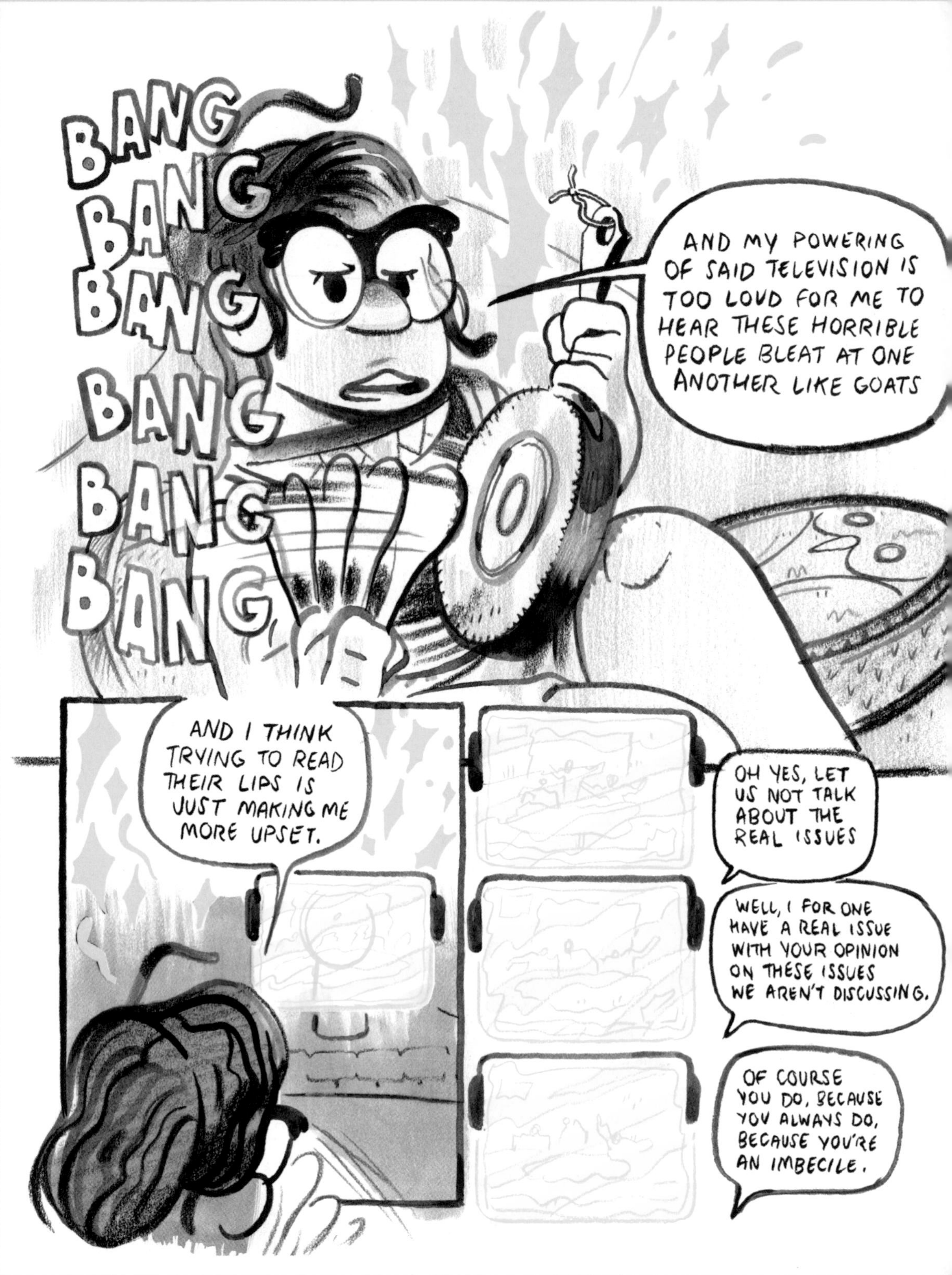
BANG BANG BANG BANG BANG BANG
AND MY POWERING OF SAID TELEVISION IS TOO LOUD FOR ME TO HEAR THESE HORRIBLE PEOPLE BLEAT AT ONE ANOTHER LIKE GOATS
AND I THINK TRYING TO READ THEIR LIPS IS JUST MAKING ME MORE UPSET.
OH YES, LET US NOT TALK ABOUT THE REAL ISSUES
WELL, I FOR ONE HAVE A REAL ISSUE WITH YOUR OPINION ON THESE ISSUES WE AREN'T DISCUSSING.
OF COURSE YOU DO, BECAUSE YOU ALWAYS DO, BECAUSE YOU'RE AN IMBECILE.

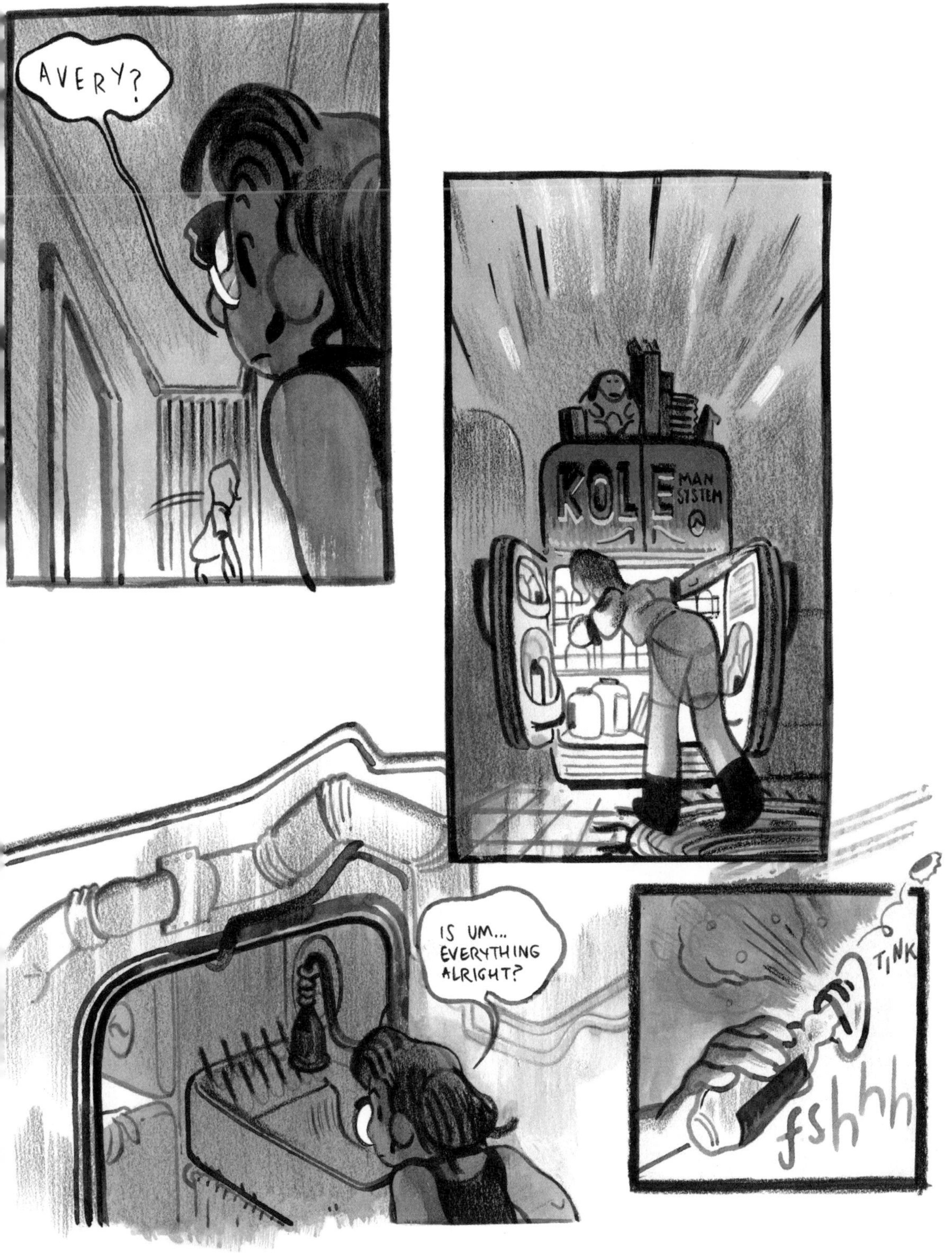
AVERY?
KOLE MAN SYSTEM
IS UM... EVERYTHING ALRIGHT?
TINK
fshhhh

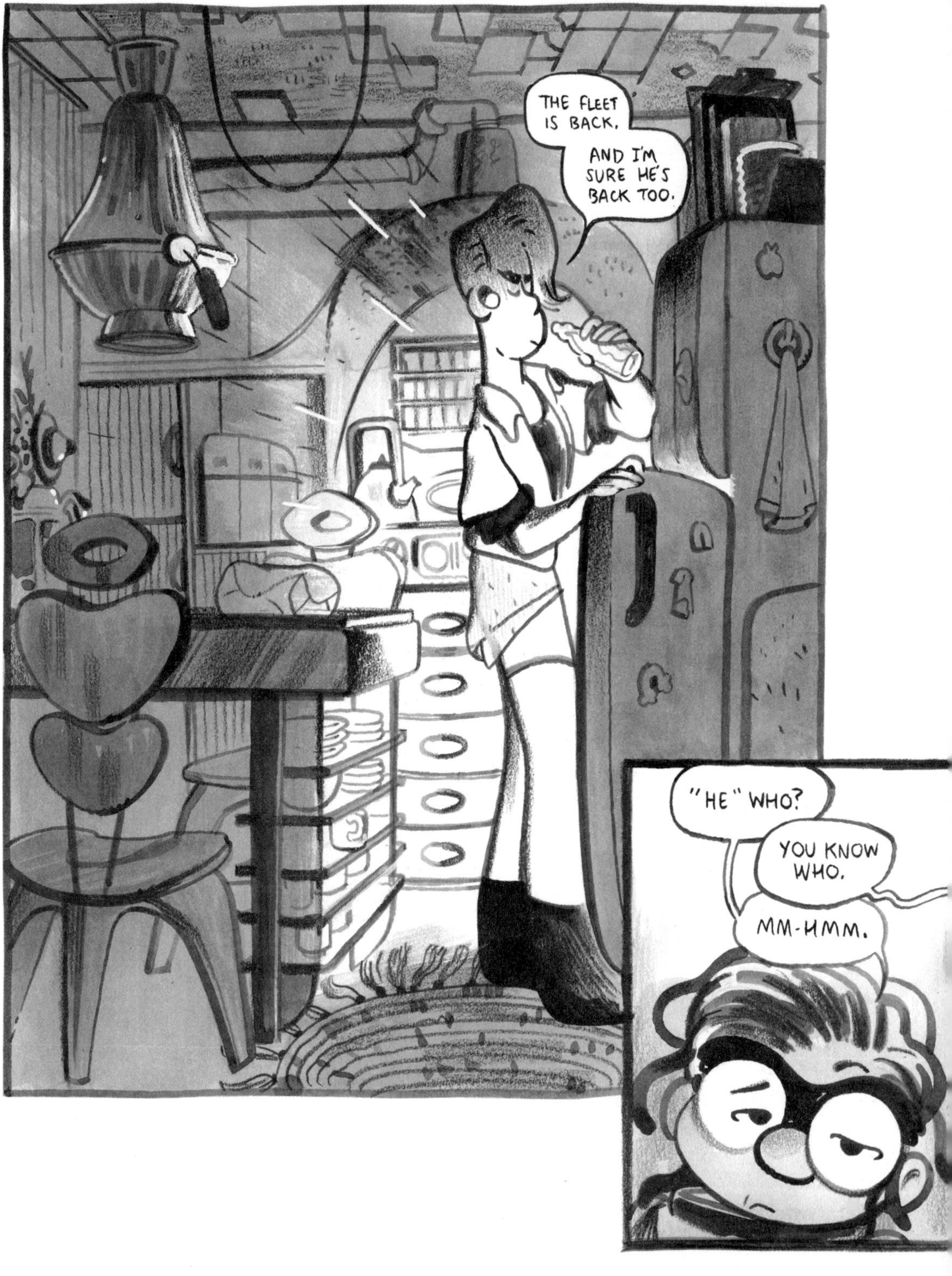
THE FLEET IS BACK.
AND I'M SURE HE'S BACK TOO.
"HE" WHO?
YOU KNOW WHO.
MM-HMM.

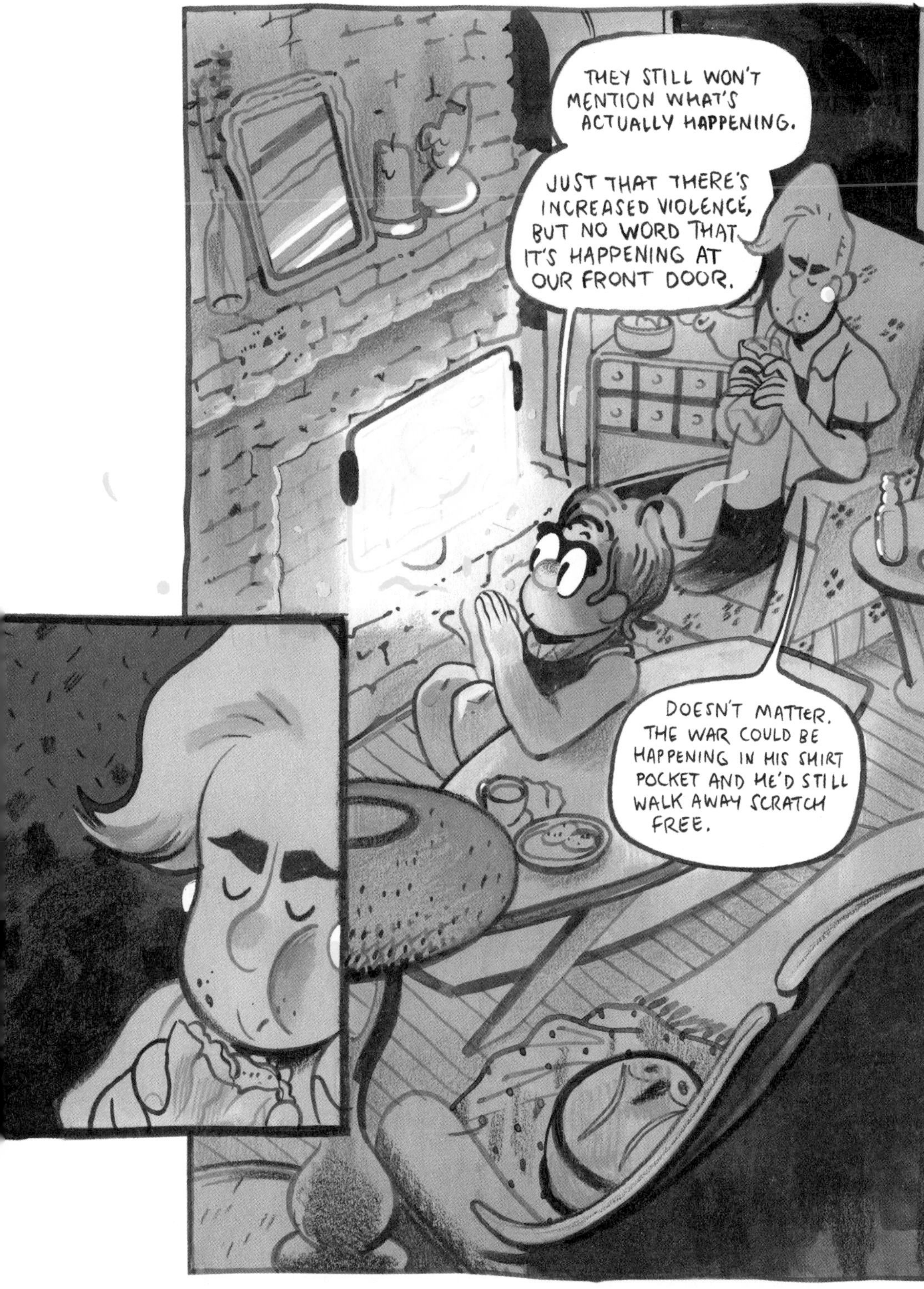
THEY STILL WON'T MENTION WHAT'S ACTUALLY HAPPENING.
JUST THAT THERE'S INCREASED VIOLENCE, BUT NO WORD THAT IT'S HAPPENING AT OUR FRONT DOOR.
DOESN'T MATTER. THE WAR COULD BE HAPPENING IN HIS SHIRT POCKET AND HE'D STILL WALK AWAY SCRATCH FREE.

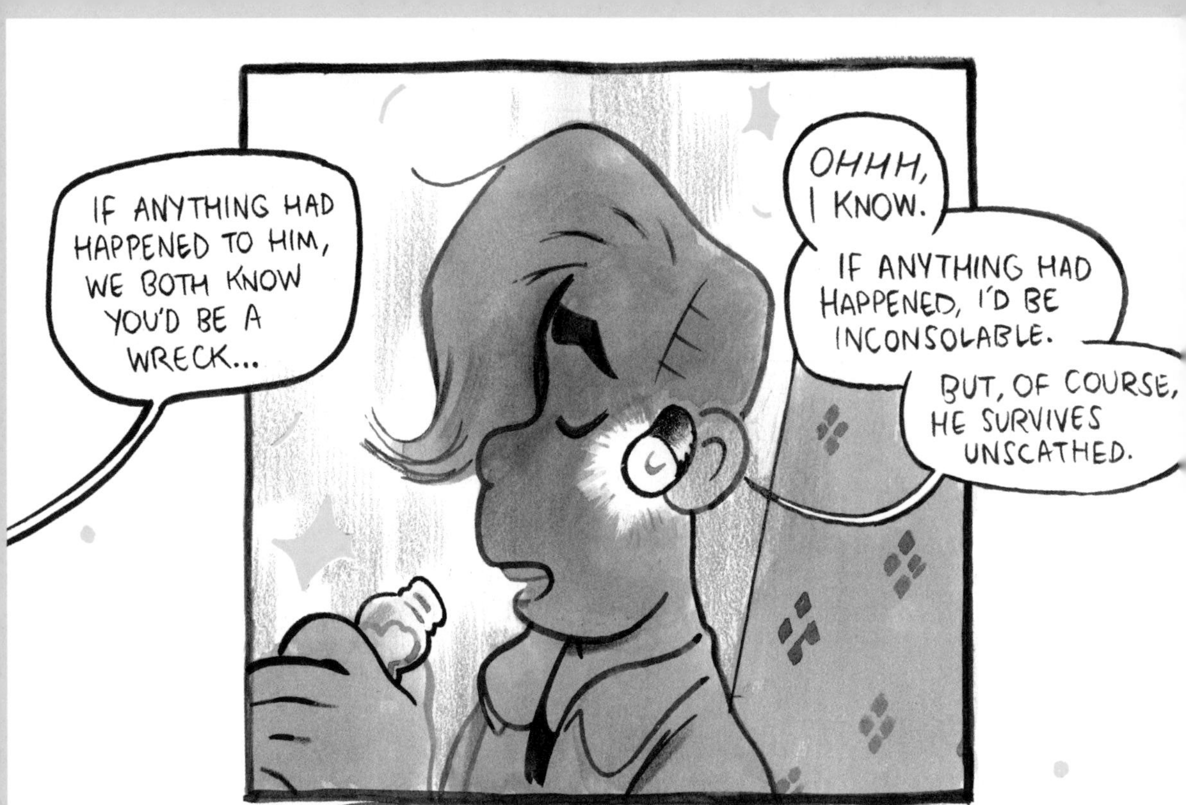
IF ANYTHING HAD HAPPENED TO HIM, WE BOTH KNOW YOU'D BE A WRECK...
OHHH, I KNOW.
IF ANYTHING HAD HAPPENED, I'D BE INCONSOLABLE.
BUT, OF COURSE, HE SURVIVES UNSCATHED.

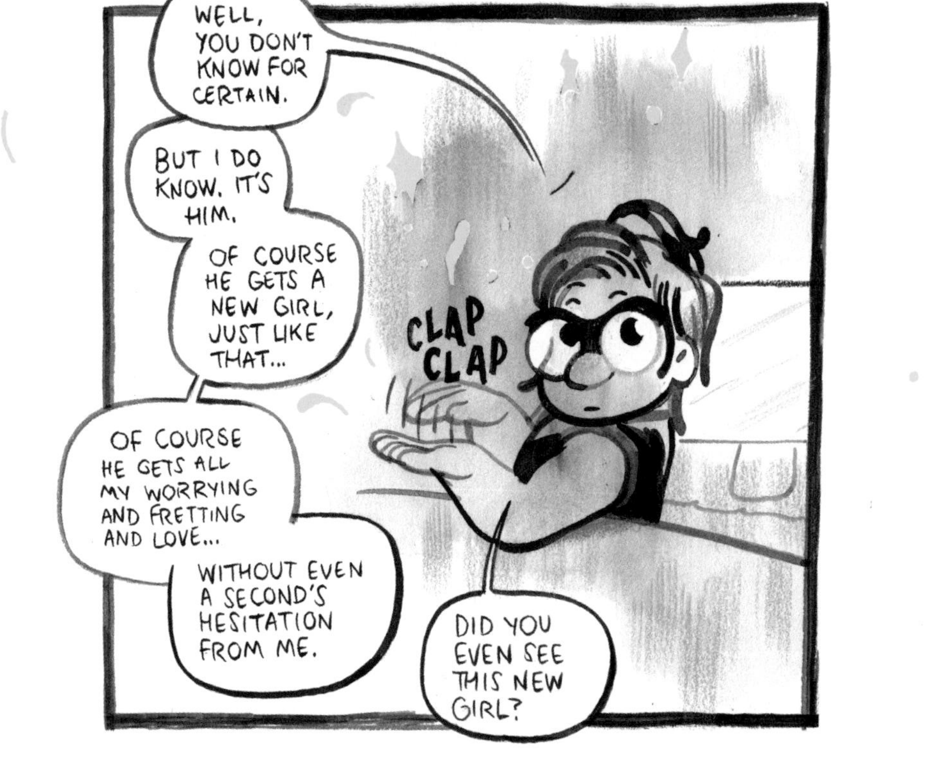
WELL, YOU DON'T KNOW FOR CERTAIN.
BUT I DO KNOW. IT'S HIM.
OF COURSE HE GETS A NEW GIRL, JUST LIKE THAT...
CLAP CLAP
OF COURSE HE GETS ALL MY WORRYING AND FRETTING AND LOVE...
WITHOUT EVEN A SECOND'S HESITATION FROM ME.
DID YOU EVEN SEE THIS NEW GIRL?

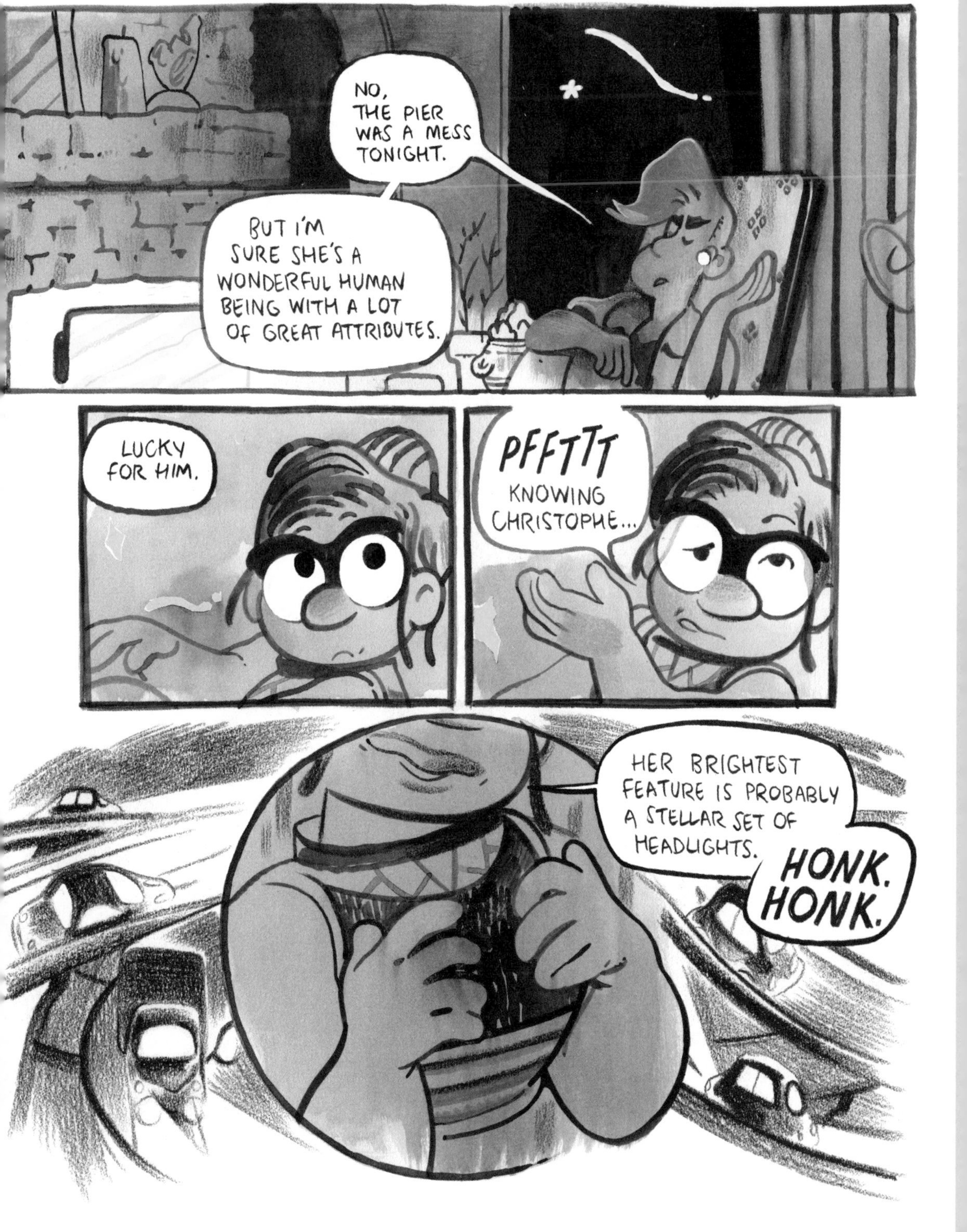
NO, THE PIER WAS A MESS TONIGHT.
BUT I'M SURE SHE'S A WONDERFUL HUMAN BEING WITH A LOT OF GREAT ATTRIBUTES.
LUCKY FOR HIM.
PFFTTT
KNOWING CHRISTOPHE...
HER BRIGHTEST FEATURE IS PROBABLY A STELLAR SET OF HEADLIGHTS.
HONK. HONK.

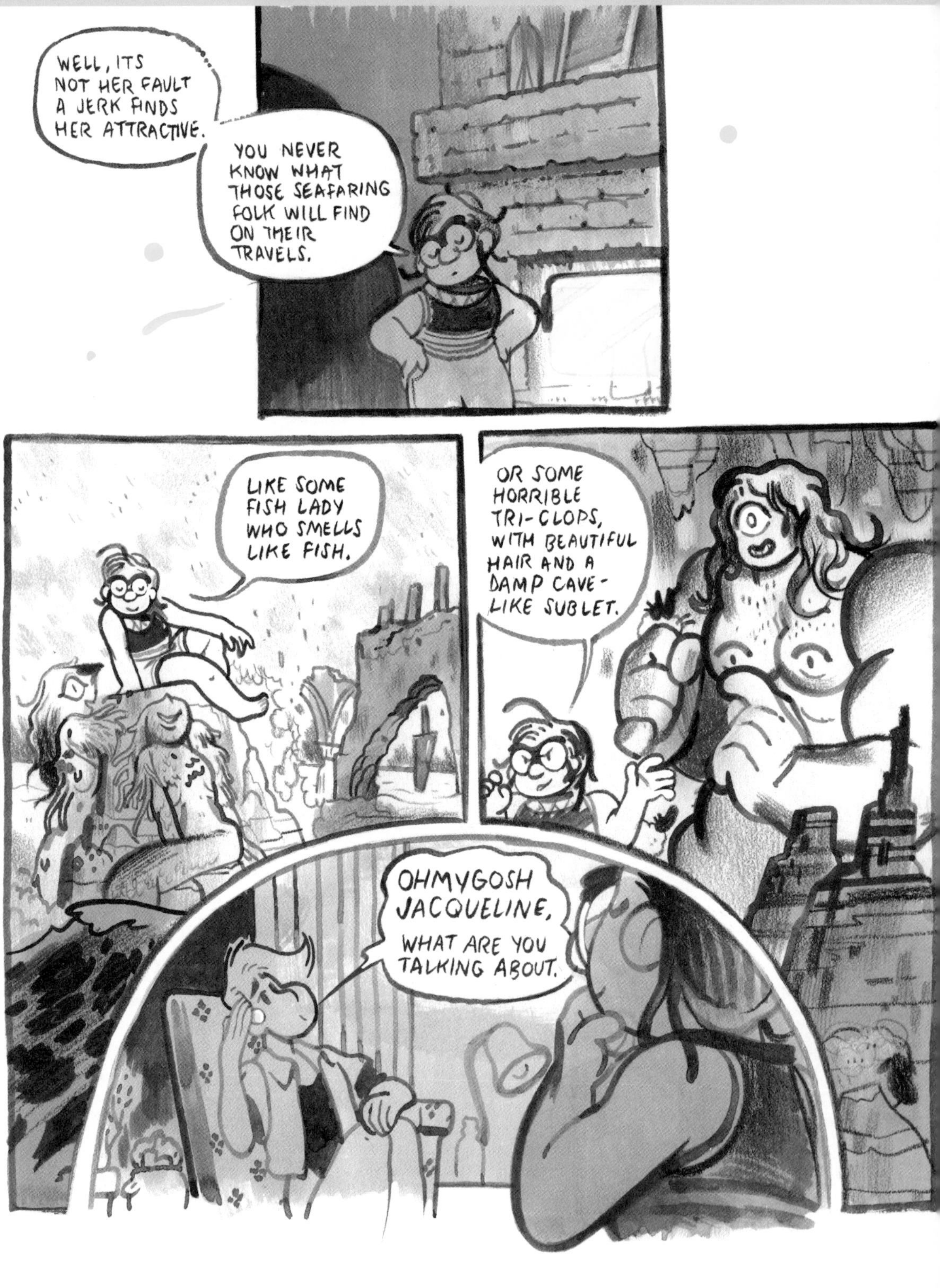
WELL, ITS NOT HER FAULT A JERK FINDS HER ATTRACTIVE.
YOU NEVER KNOW WHAT THOSE SEAFARING FOLK WILL FIND ON THEIR TRAVELS.
LIKE SOME FISH LADY WHO SMELLS LIKE FISH.
OR SOME HORRIBLE TRI-CLOPS, WITH BEAUTIFUL HAIR AND A DAMP CAVE-LIKE SUBLET.
OHMYGOSH JACQUELINE,
WHAT ARE YOU TALKING ABOUT.

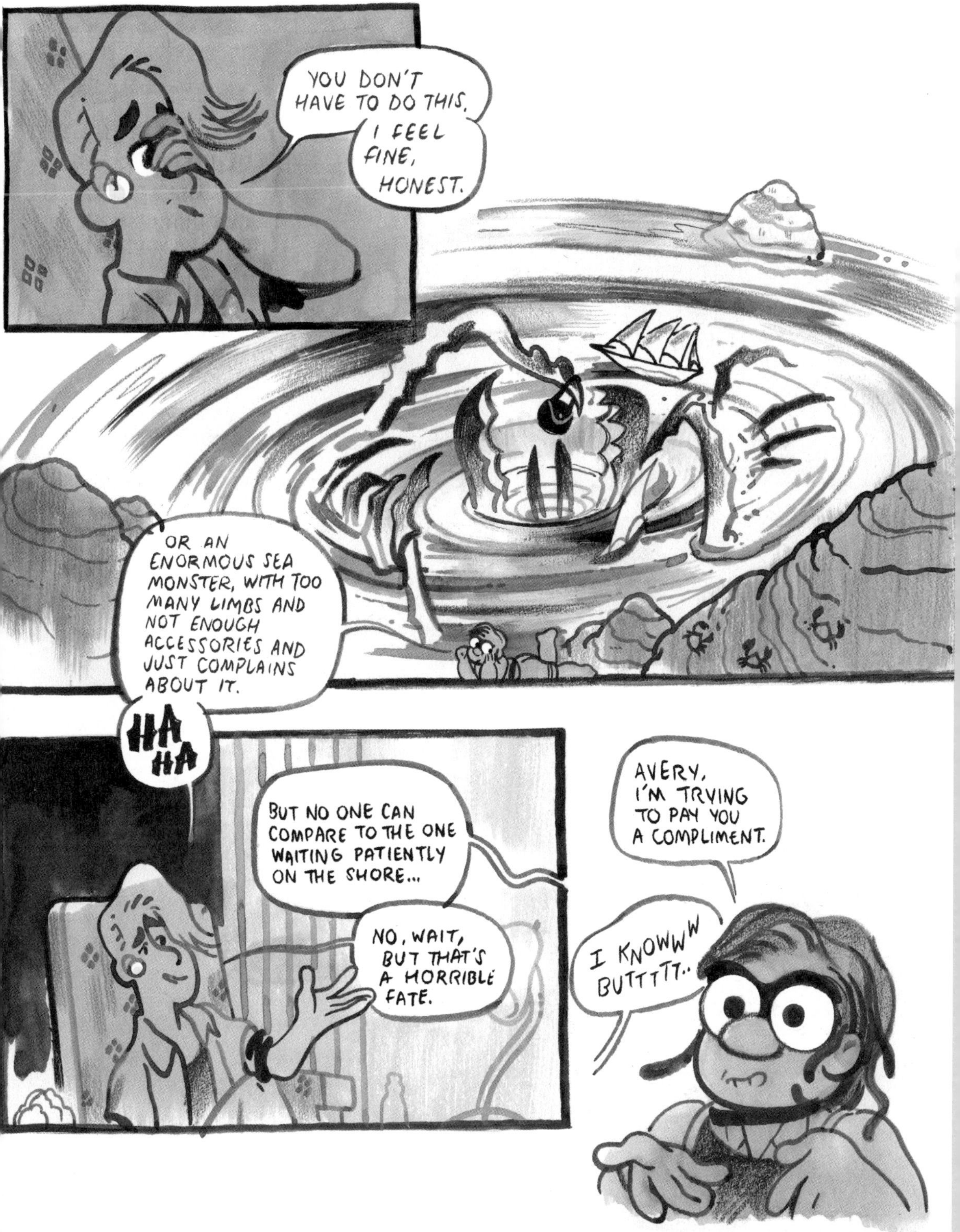
YOU DON'T HAVE TO DO THIS.
I FEEL FINE, HONEST.
OR AN ENORMOUS SEA MONSTER, WITH TOO MANY LIMBS AND NOT ENOUGH ACCESSORIES AND JUST COMPLAINS ABOUT IT.
HA HA
BUT NO ONE CAN COMPARE TO THE ONE WAITING PATIENTLY ON THE SHORE...
NO, WAIT, BUT THAT'S A HORRIBLE FATE.
AVERY, I'M TRYING TO PAY YOU A COMPLIMENT.
I KNOWWW BUTTTTT..

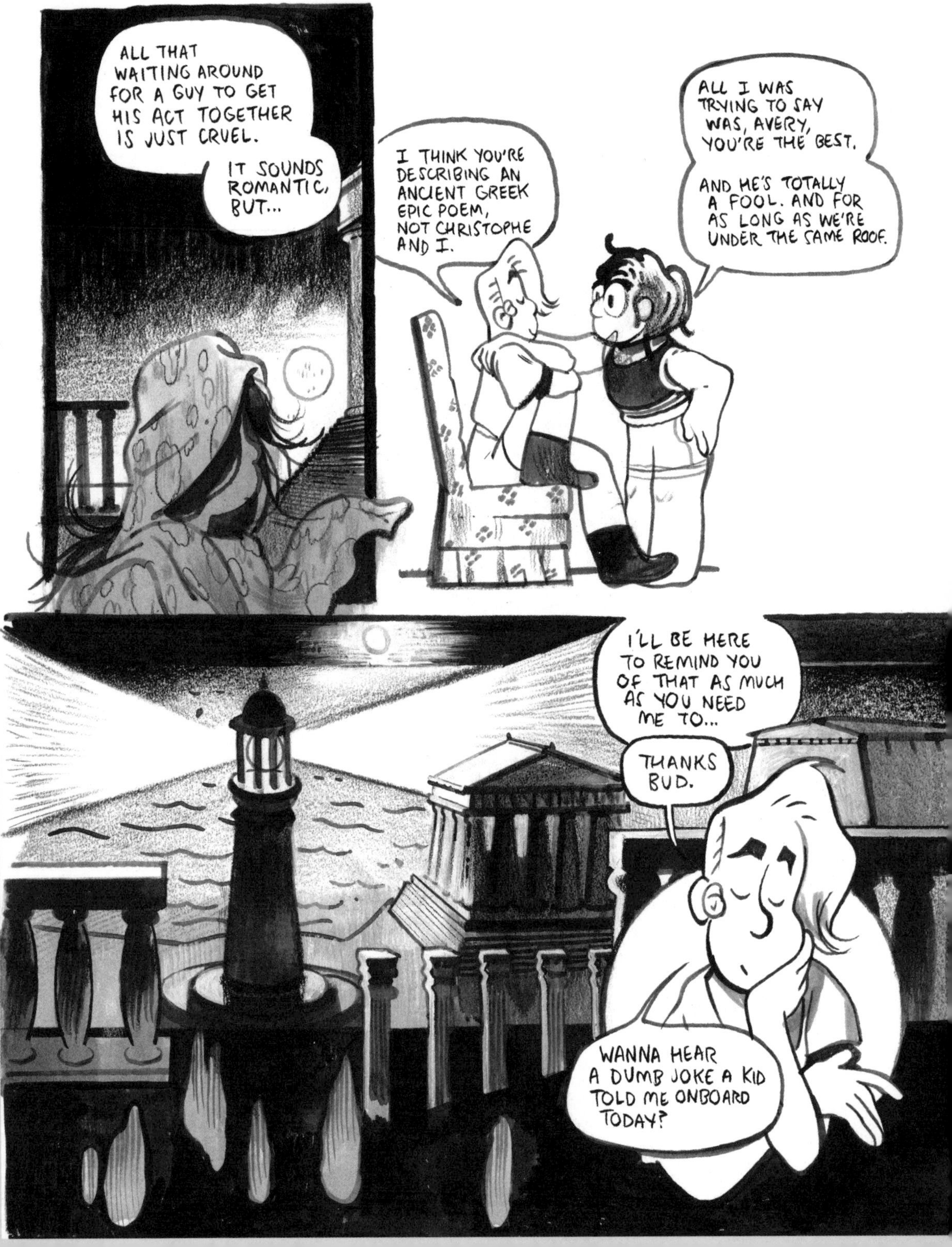
ALL THAT WAITING AROUND FOR A GUY TO GET HIS ACT TOGETHER IS JUST CRUEL.
IT SOUNDS ROMANTIC, BUT...
I THINK YOU'RE DESCRIBING AN ANCIENT GREEK EPIC POEM, NOT CHRISTOPHE AND I.
ALL I WAS TRYING TO SAY WAS, AVERY, YOU'RE THE BEST.
AND HE'S TOTALLY A FOOL. AND FOR AS LONG AS WE'RE UNDER THE SAME ROOF.
I'LL BE HERE TO REMIND YOU OF THAT AS MUCH AS YOU NEED ME TO...
THANKS BUD.
WANNA HEAR A DUMB JOKE A KID TOLD ME ONBOARD TODAY?

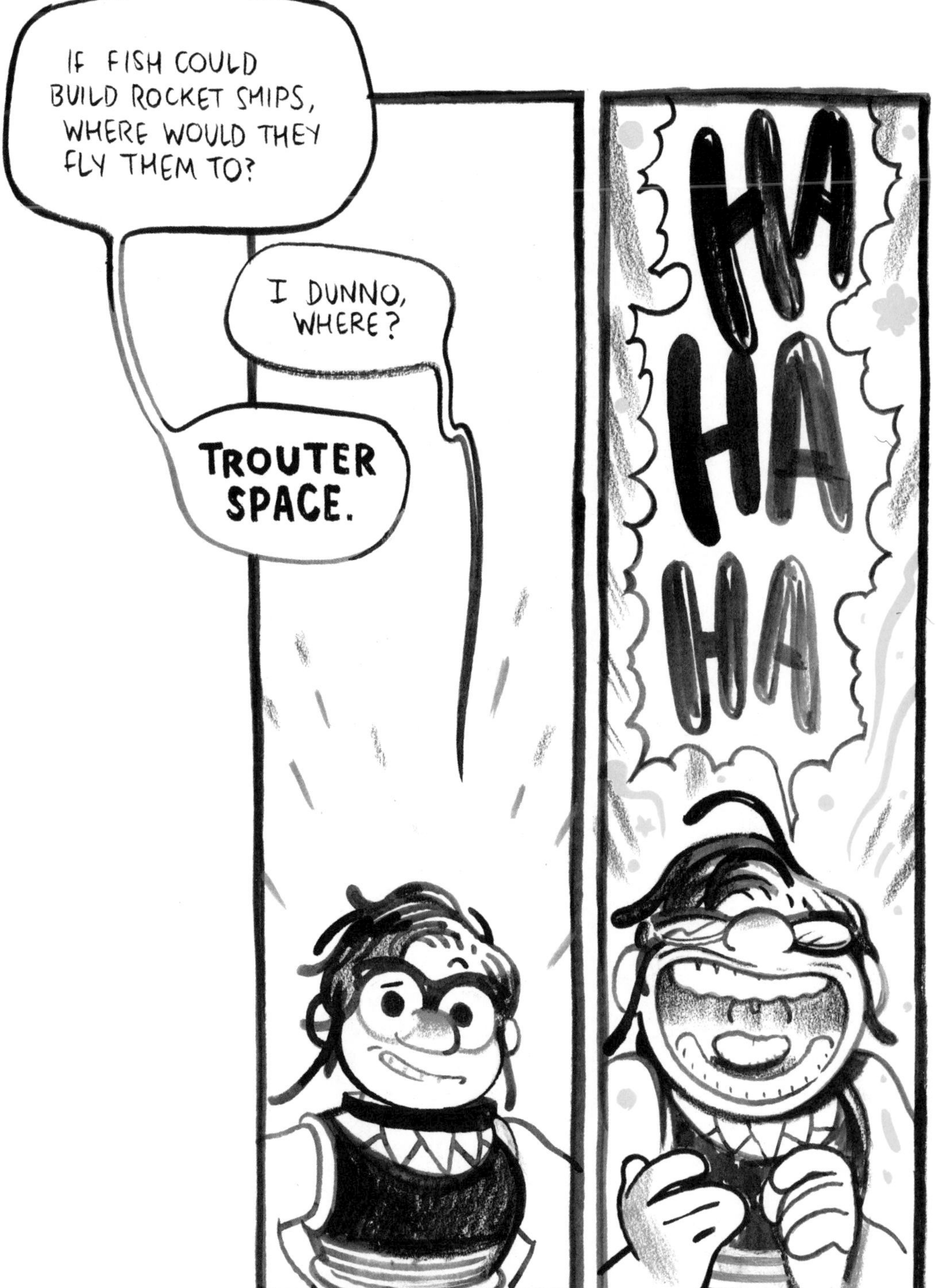
IF FISH COULD BUILD ROCKET SHIPS, WHERE WOULD THEY FLY THEM TO?
I DUNNO, WHERE?
TROUTER SPACE.
HA HA HA

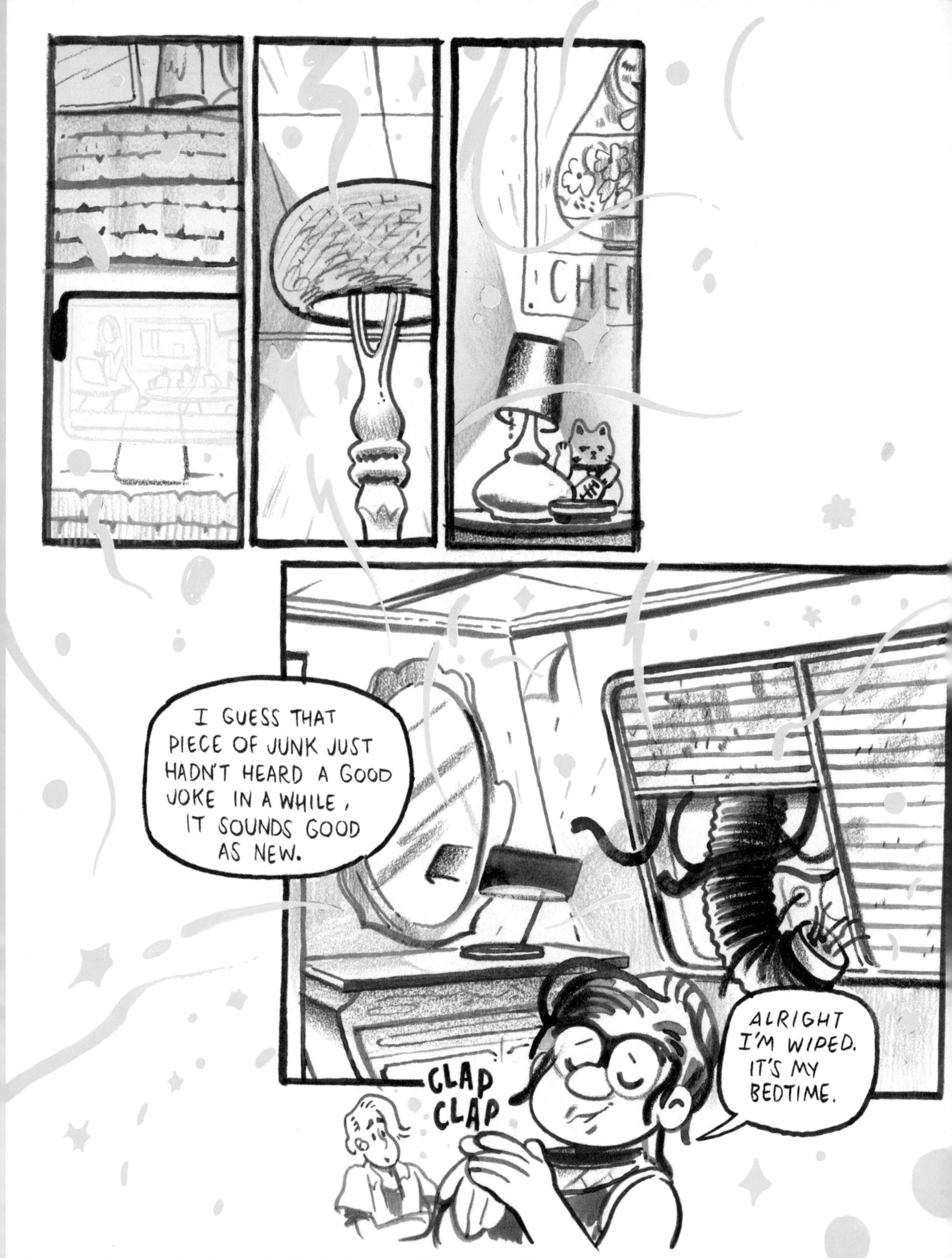
CHE
I GUESS THAT PIECE OF JUNK JUST HADN'T HEARD A GOOD JOKE IN A WHILE, IT SOUNDS GOOD AS NEW.
CLAP CLAP
ALRIGHT I'M WIPED. IT'S MY BEDTIME.

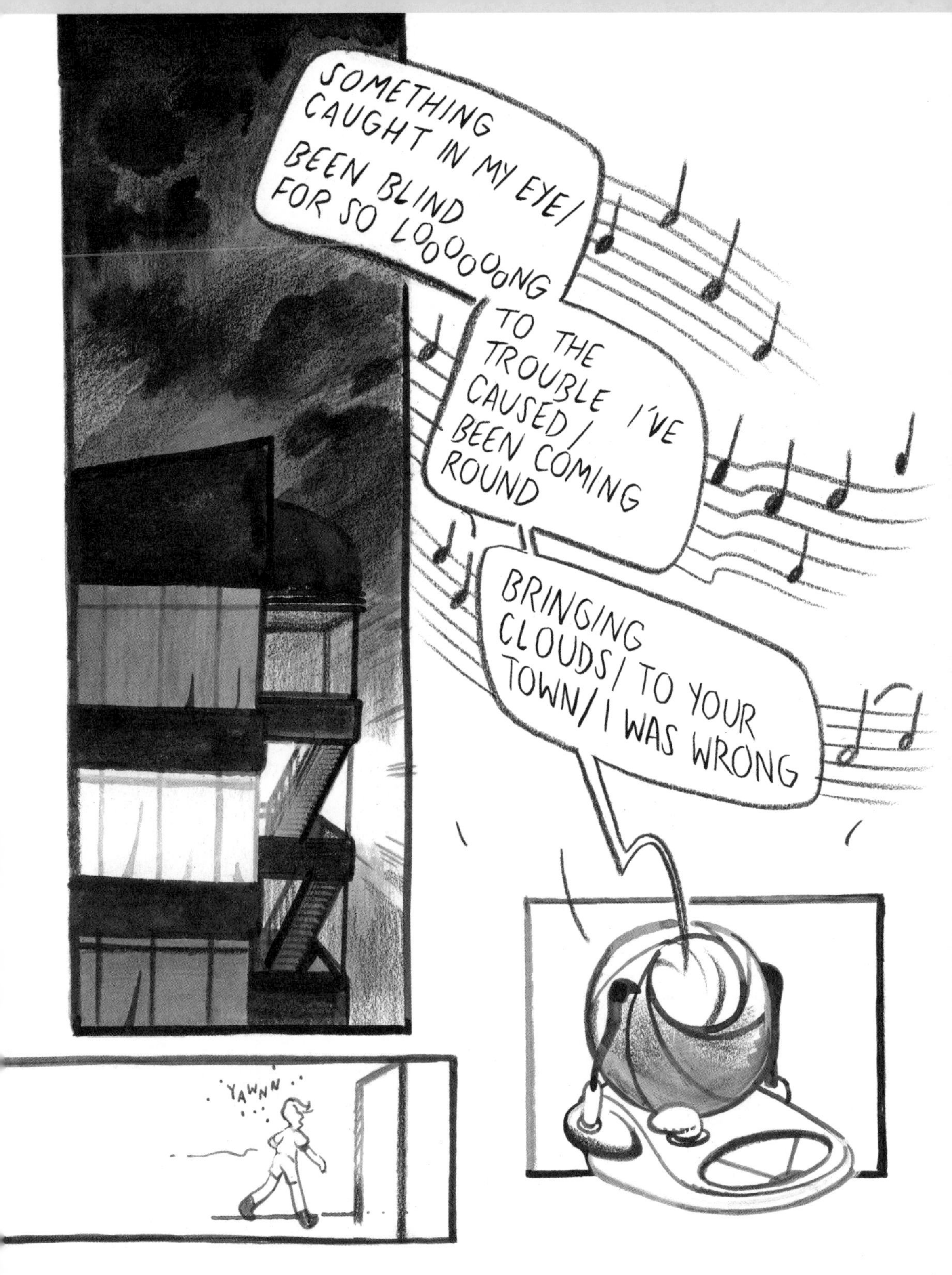
SOMETHING CAUGHT IN MY EYE/ BEEN BLIND FOR SO LOOOOOOONG
TO THE TROUBLE I'VE CAUSED/ BEEN COMING ROUND
BRINGING CLOUDS/ TO YOUR TOWN/ I WAS WRONG
YAWNN

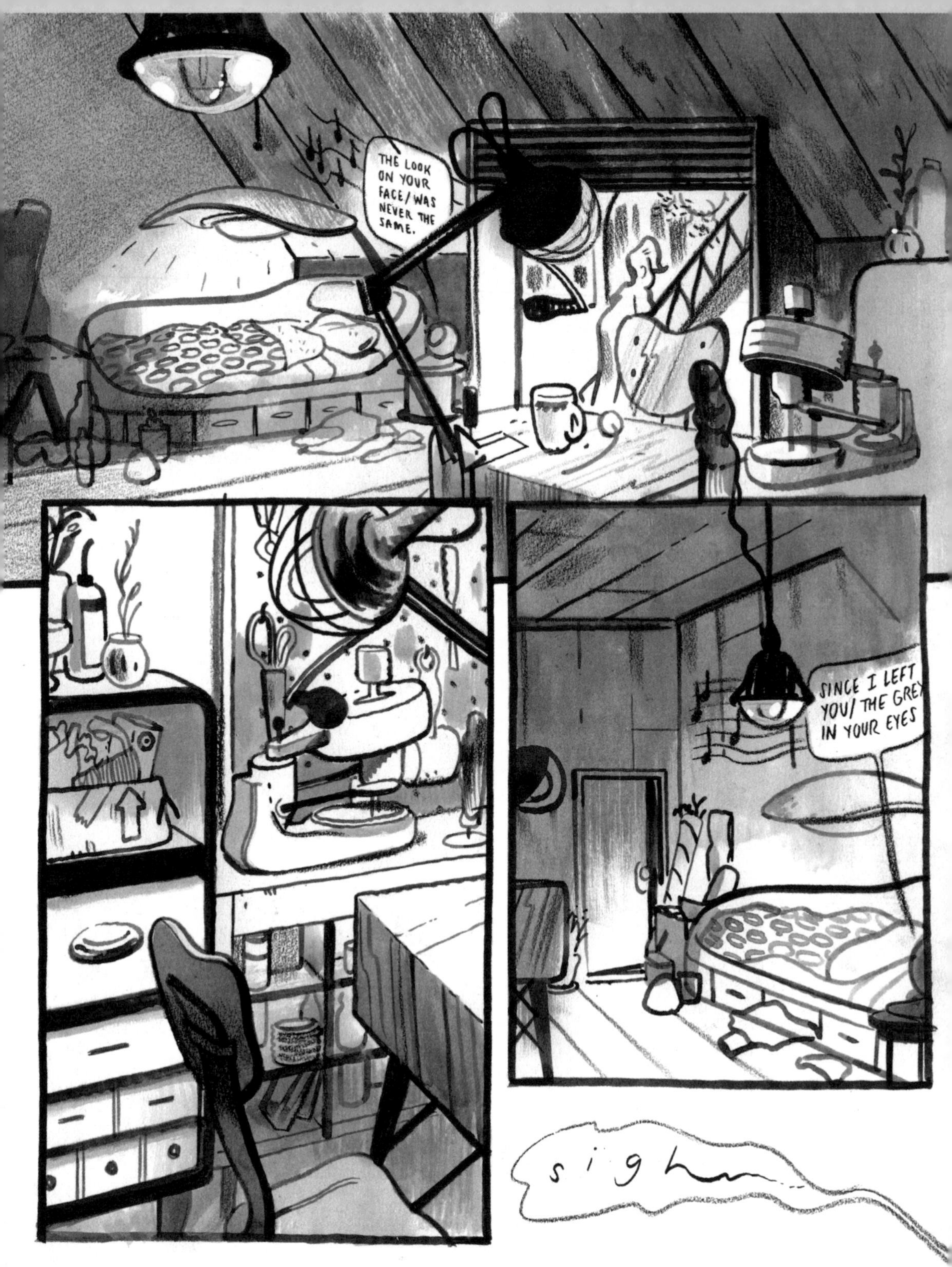
THE LOOK ON YOUR FACE/ WAS NEVER THE SAME.
SINCE I LEFT YOU/ THE GREY IN YOUR EYES
sigh...

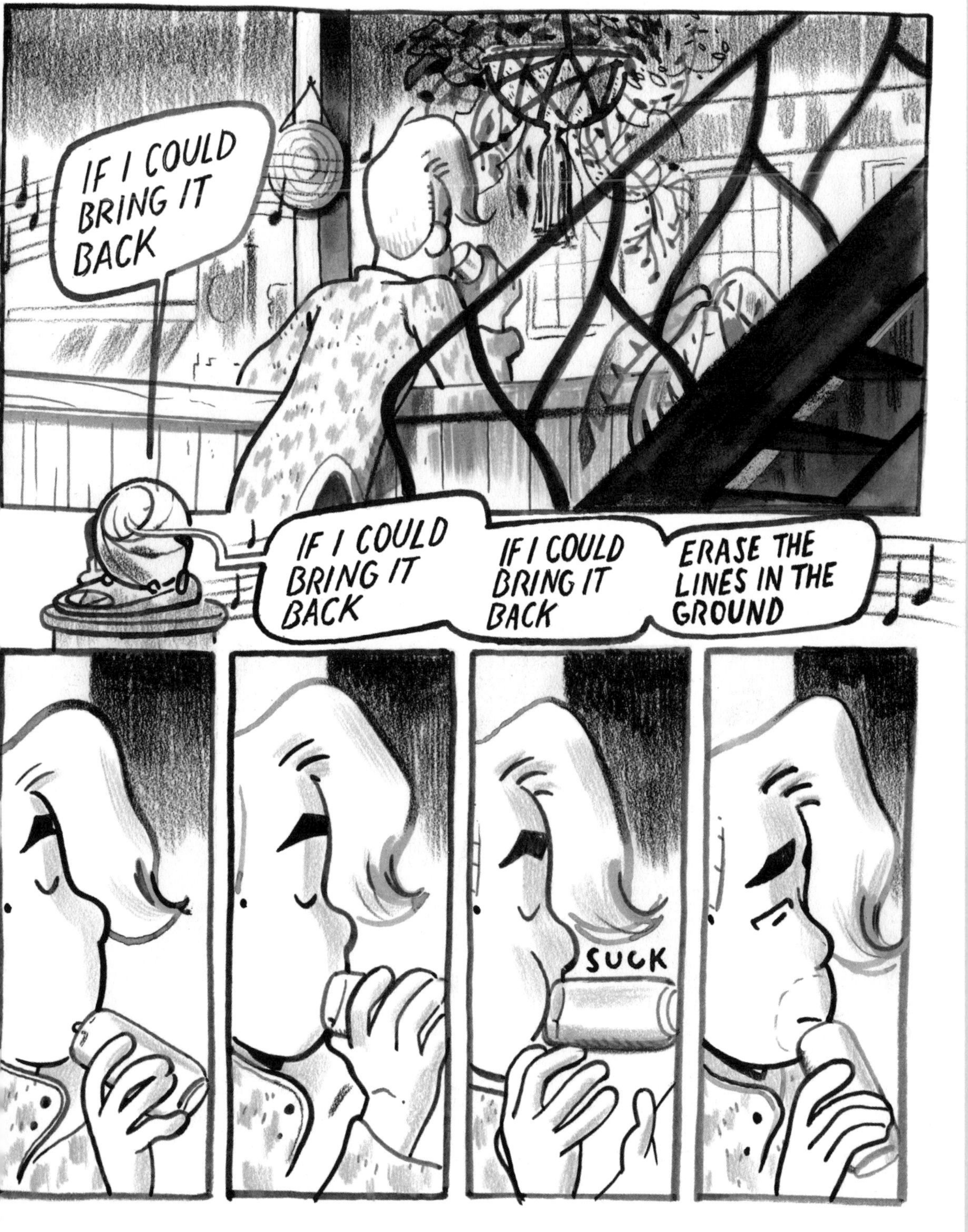
IF I COULD BRING IT BACK
IF I COULD BRING IT BACK
IF I COULD BRING IT BACK
ERASE THE LINES IN THE GROUND
SUCK

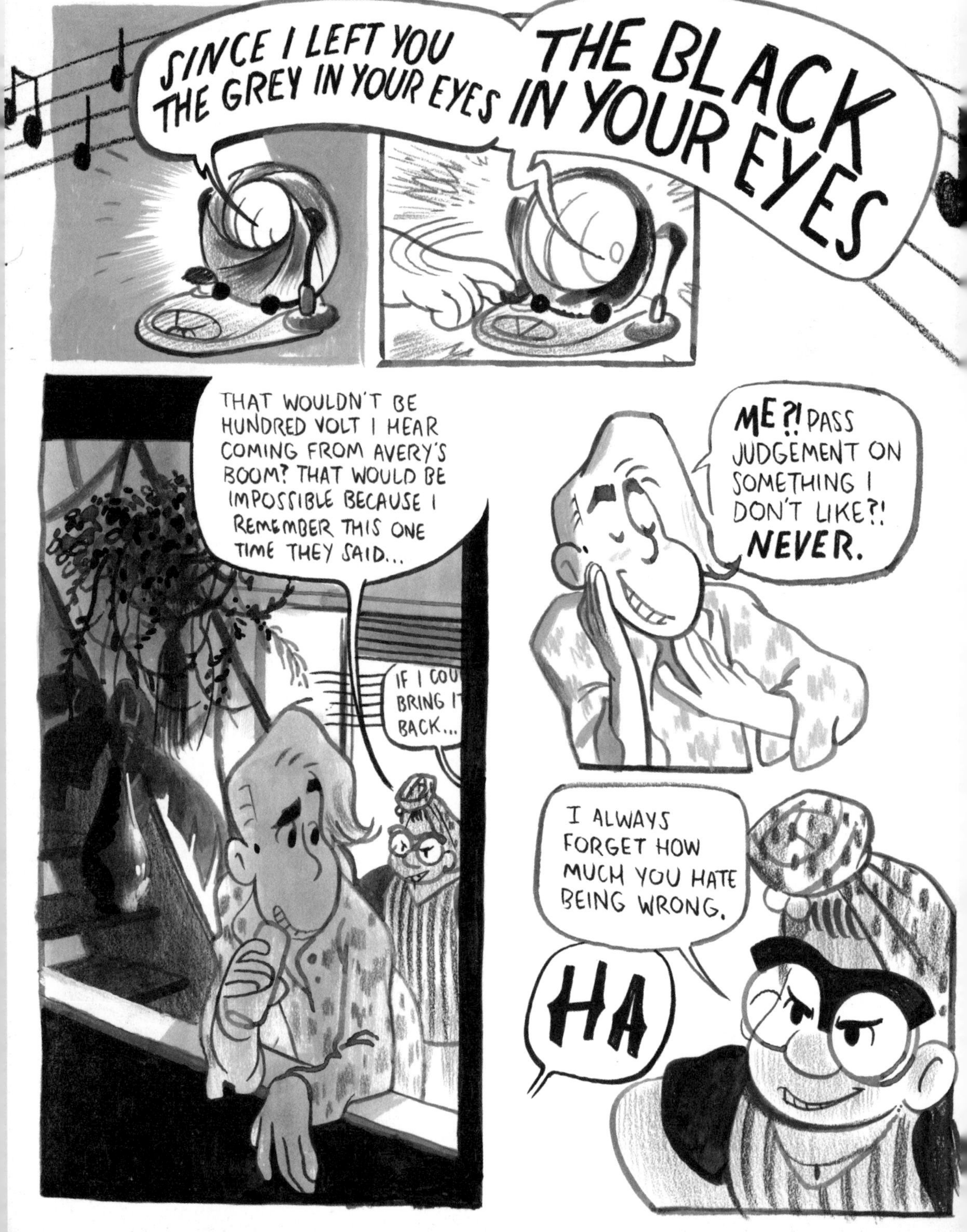
SINCE I LEFT YOU THE GREY IN YOUR EYES
THE BLACK IN YOUR EYES
THAT WOULDN'T BE HUNDRED VOLT I HEAR COMING FROM AVERY'S BOOM? THAT WOULD BE IMPOSSIBLE BECAUSE I REMEMBER THIS ONE TIME THEY SAID...
IF I COU BRING IT BACK...
ME?! PASS JUDGEMENT ON SOMETHING I DON'T LIKE?! NEVER.
I ALWAYS FORGET HOW MUCH YOU HATE BEING WRONG.
HA

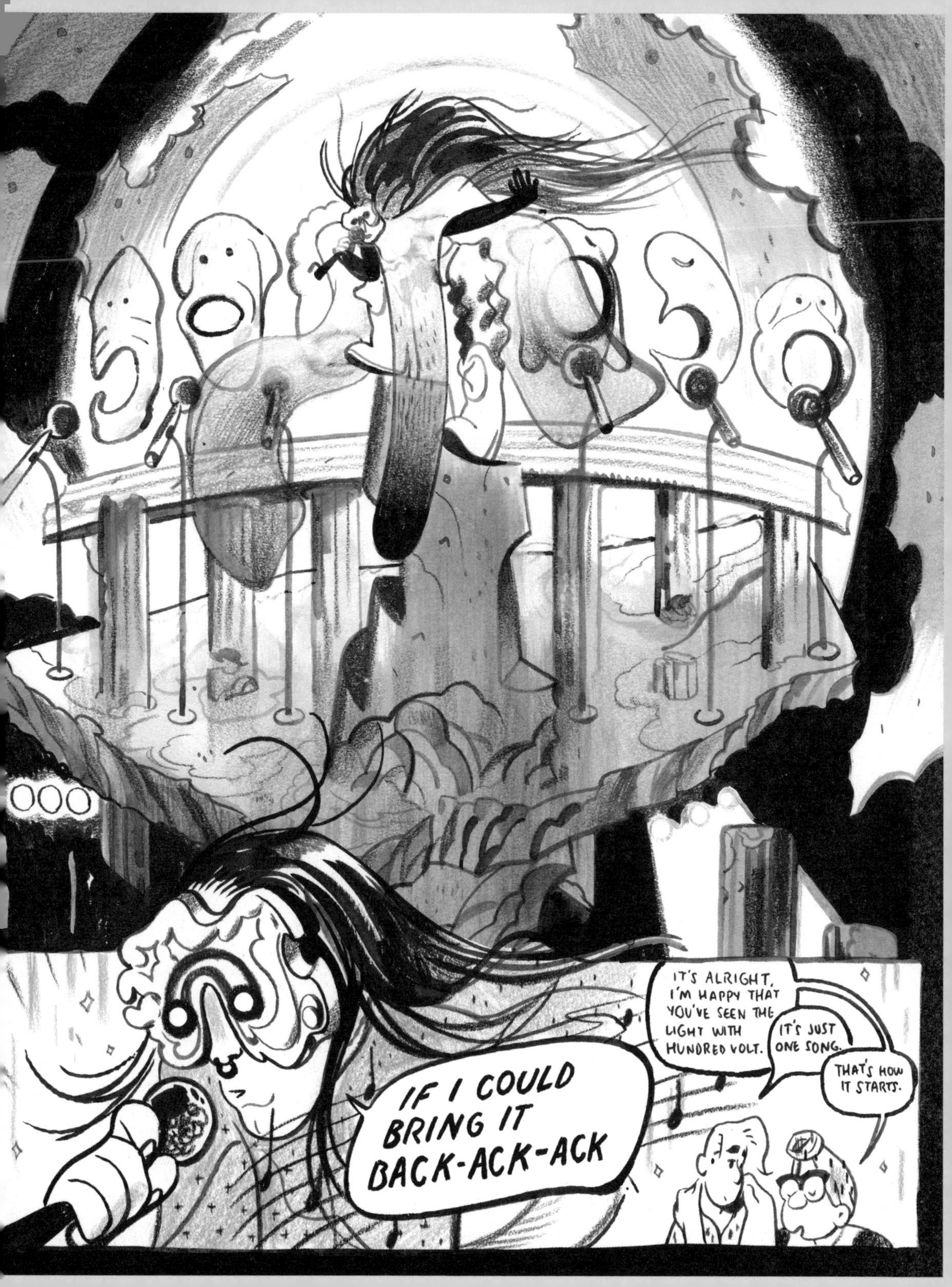
IF I COULD BRING IT BACK-ACK-ACK
IT'S ALRIGHT. I'M HAPPY THAT YOU'VE SEEN THE LIGHT WITH HUNDRED VOLT.
IT'S JUST ONE SONG.
THAT'S HOW IT STARTS.

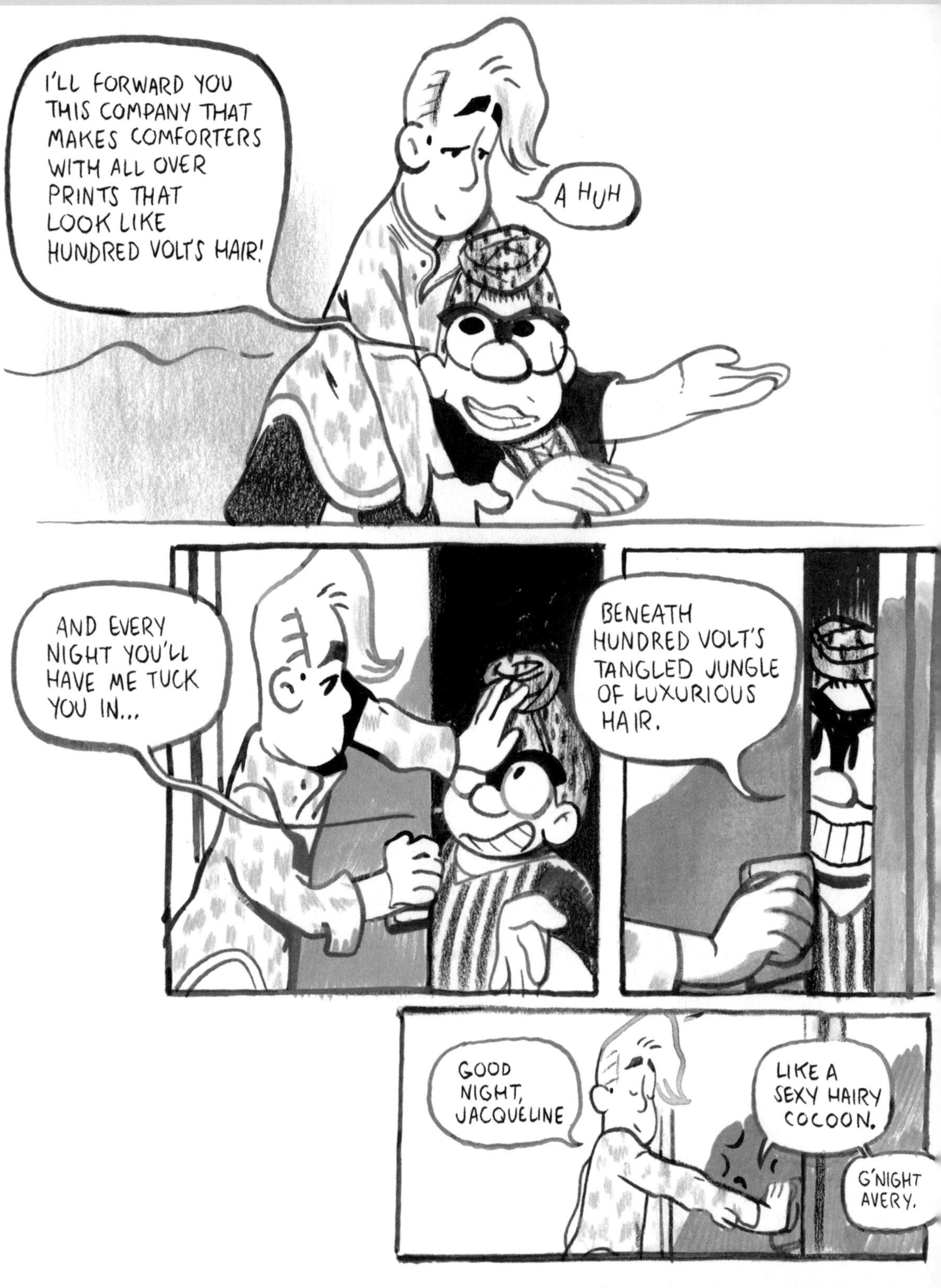
I'LL FORWARD YOU THIS COMPANY THAT MAKES COMFORTERS WITH ALL OVER PRINTS THAT LOOK LIKE HUNDRED VOLT'S HAIR!
A HUH
AND EVERY NIGHT YOU'LL HAVE ME TUCK YOU IN...
BENEATH HUNDRED VOLT'S TANGLED JUNGLE OF LUXURIOUS HAIR.
GOOD NIGHT, JACQUELINE
LIKE A SEXY HAIRY COCOON.
G'NIGHT AVERY.

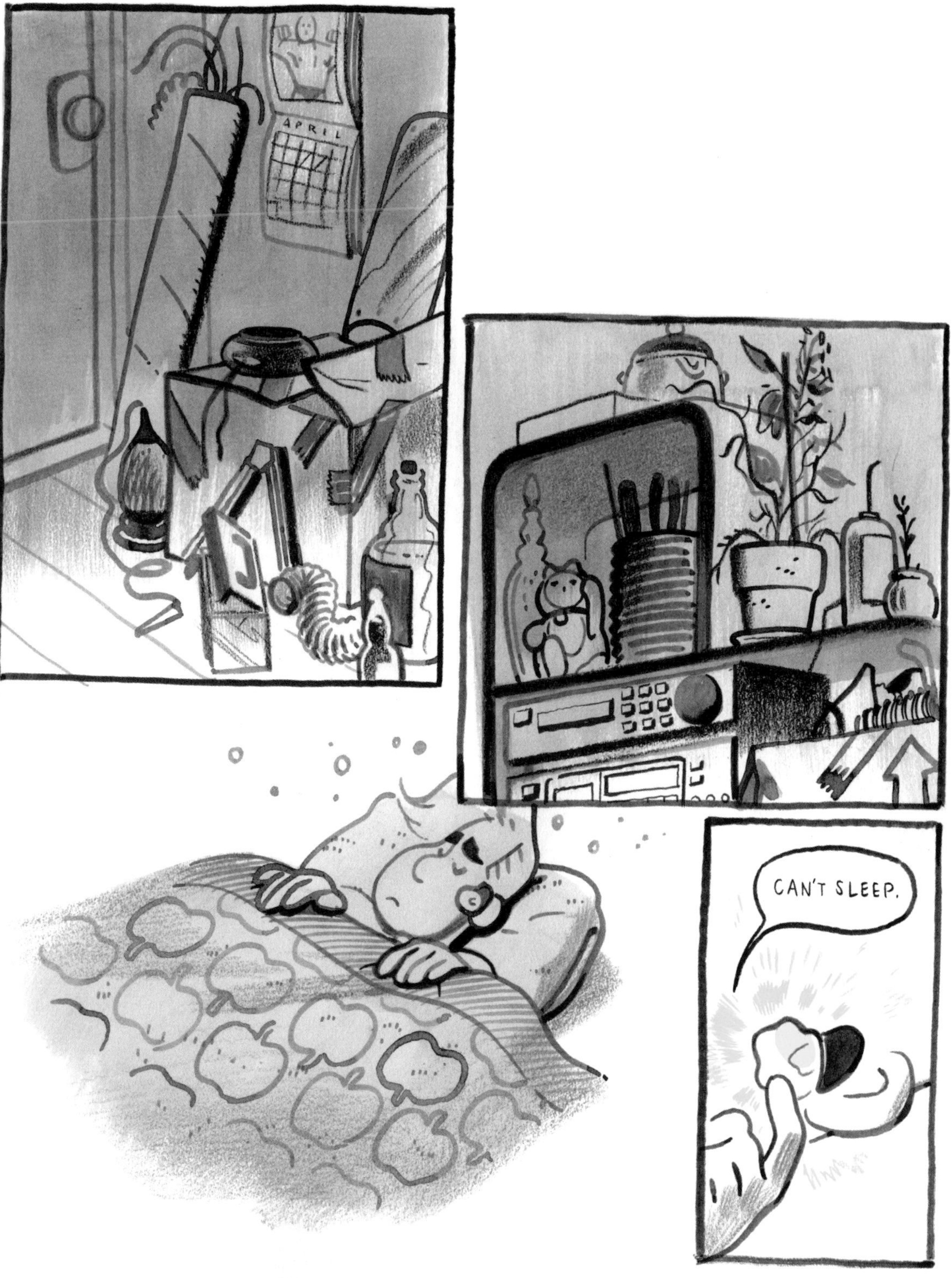
APRIL
CAN'T SLEEP.

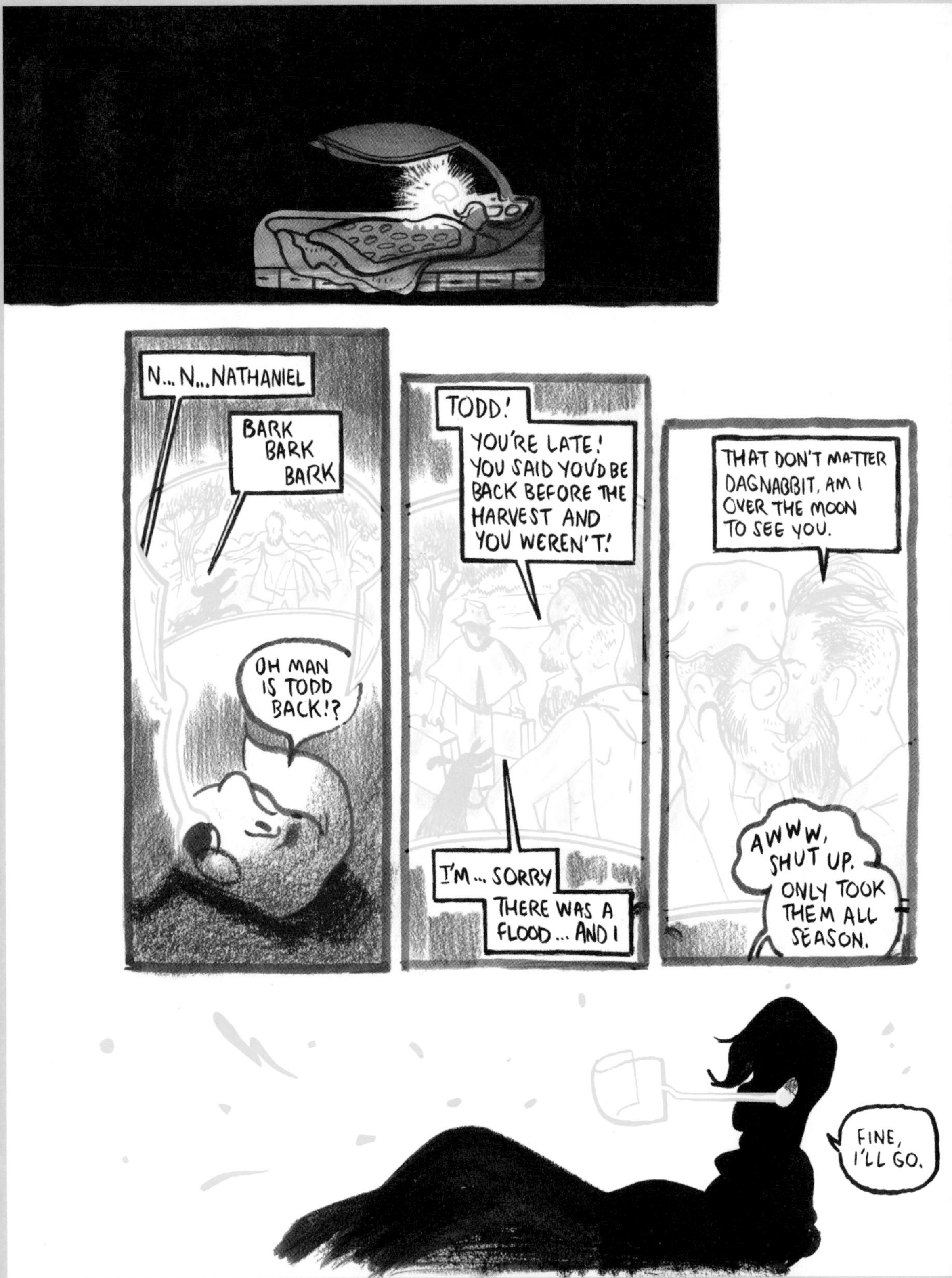
N... N... NATHANIEL
BARK BARK BARK
OH MAN IS TODD BACK!?
TODD!
YOU'RE LATE! YOU SAID YOU'D BE BACK BEFORE THE HARVEST AND YOU WEREN'T!
I'M... SORRY
THERE WAS A FLOOD... AND I
THAT DON'T MATTER DAGNABBIT, AM I OVER THE MOON TO SEE YOU.
AWWW, SHUT UP.
ONLY TOOK THEM ALL SEASON.
FINE, I'LL GO.

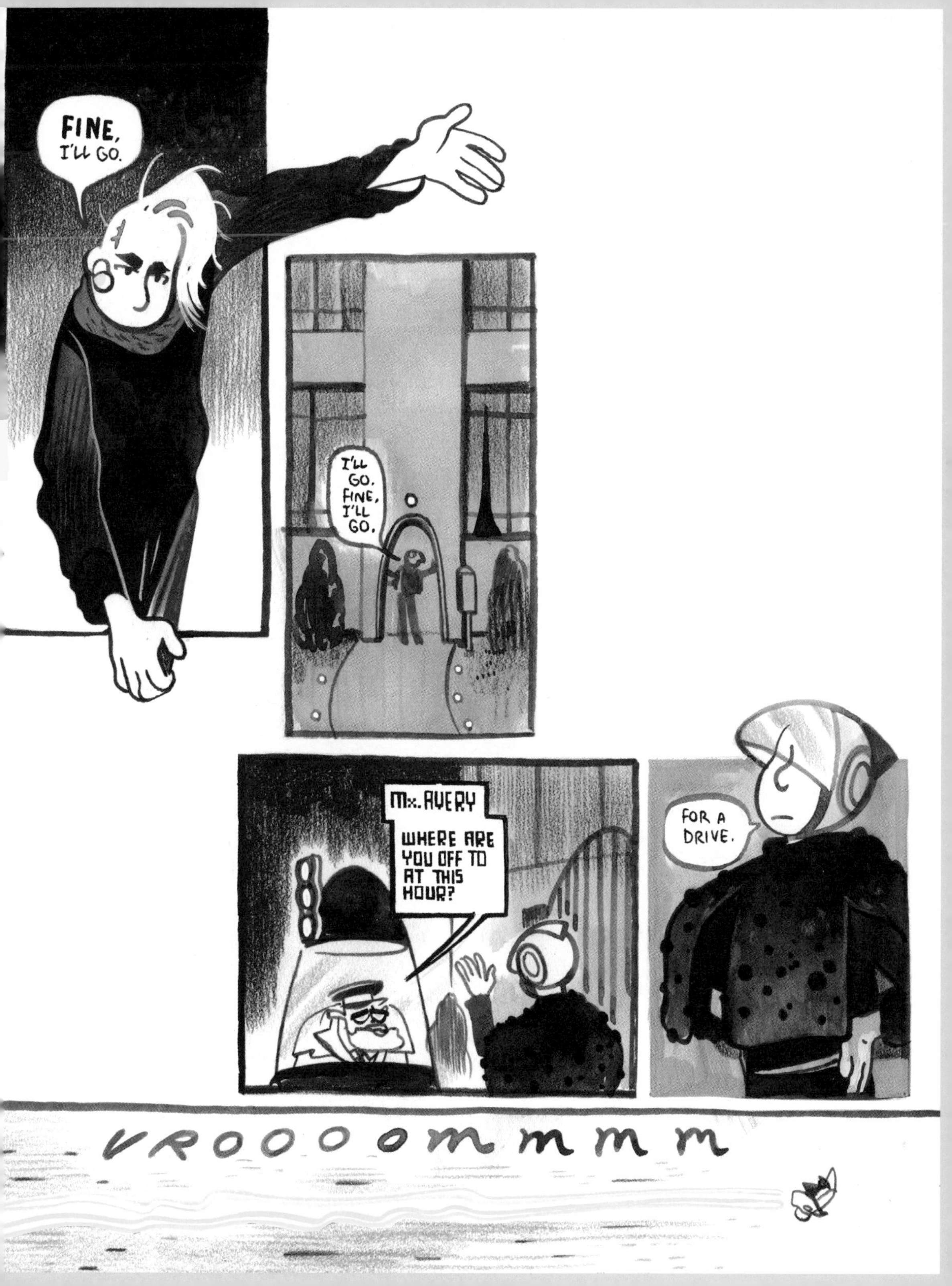
FINE, I'LL GO.
I'LL GO. FINE, I'LL GO.
Mx. AVERY
WHERE ARE YOU OFF TO AT THIS HOUR?
FOR A DRIVE.
VROOOOOMMMMM

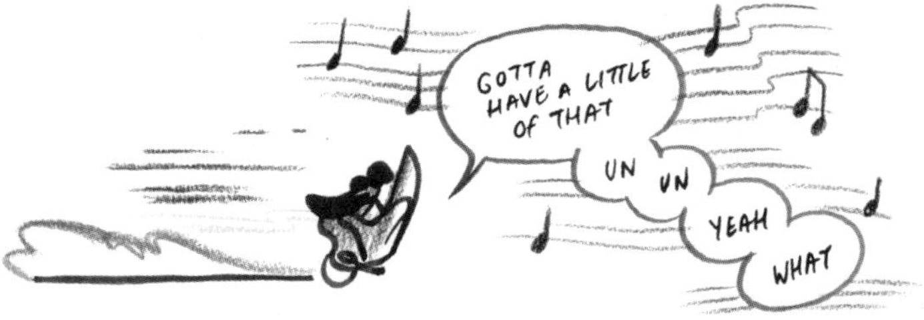
GOTTA HAVE A LITTLE OF THAT
UN
UN
YEAH
WHAT

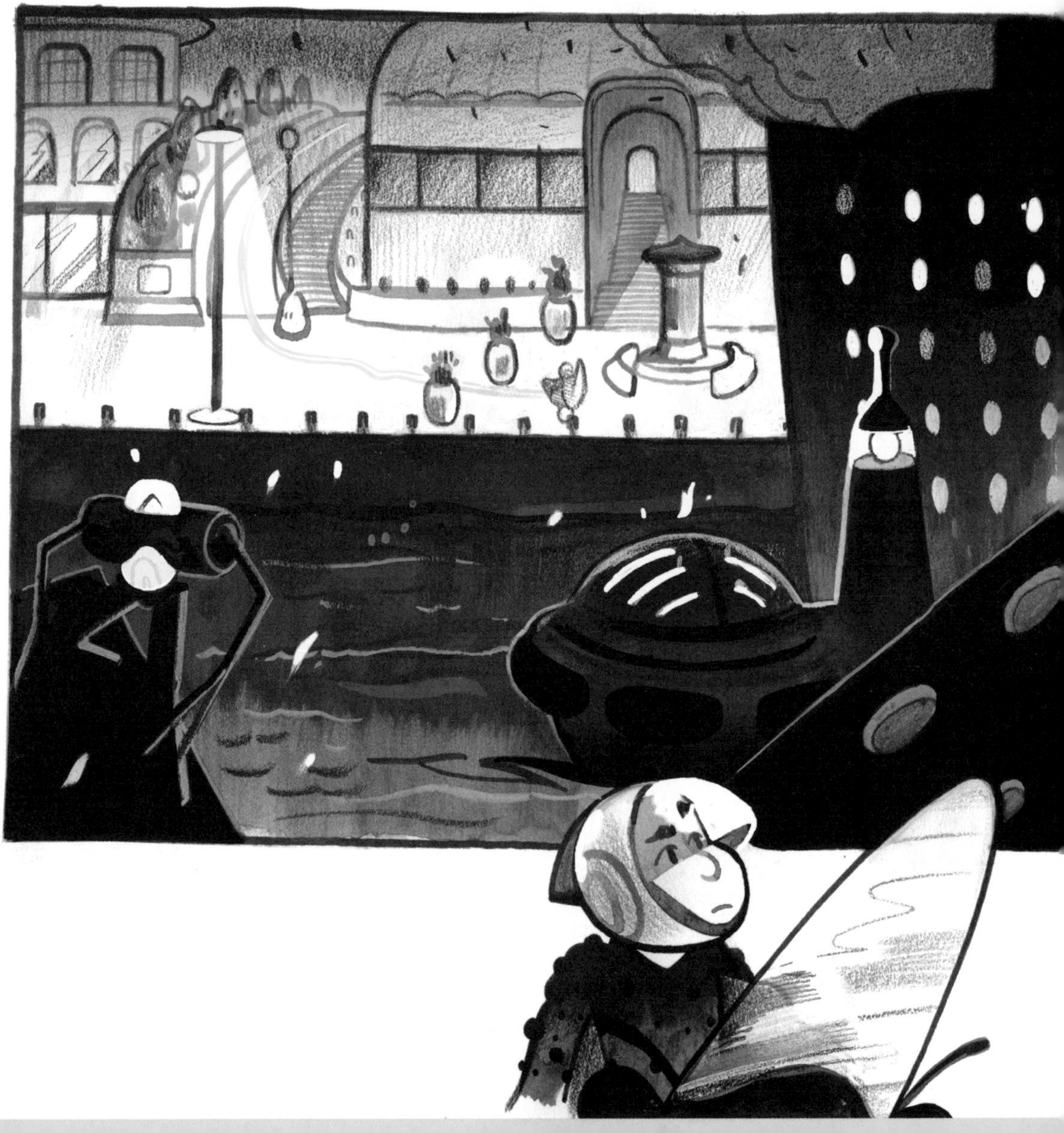

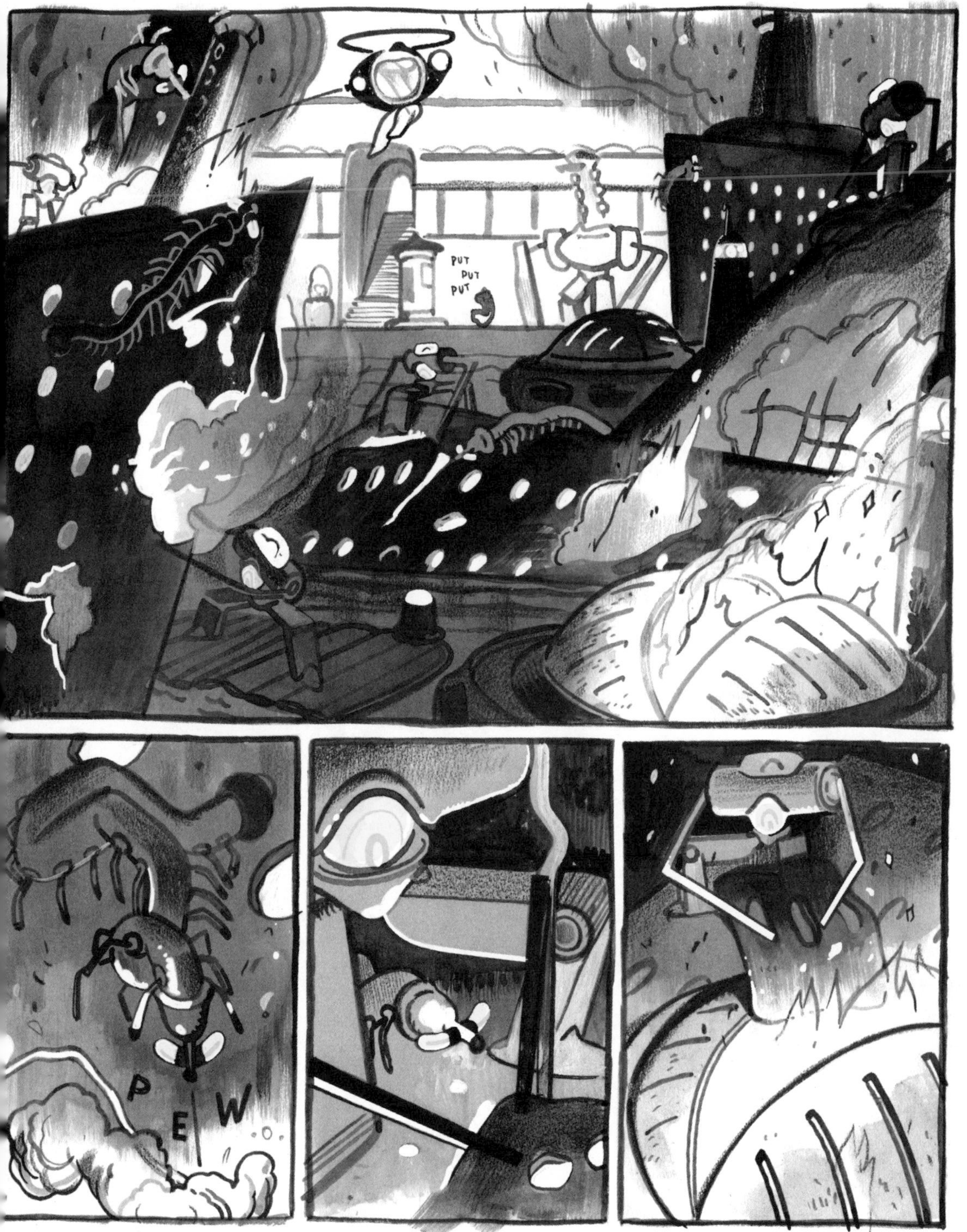
PUT PUT PUT
PEW

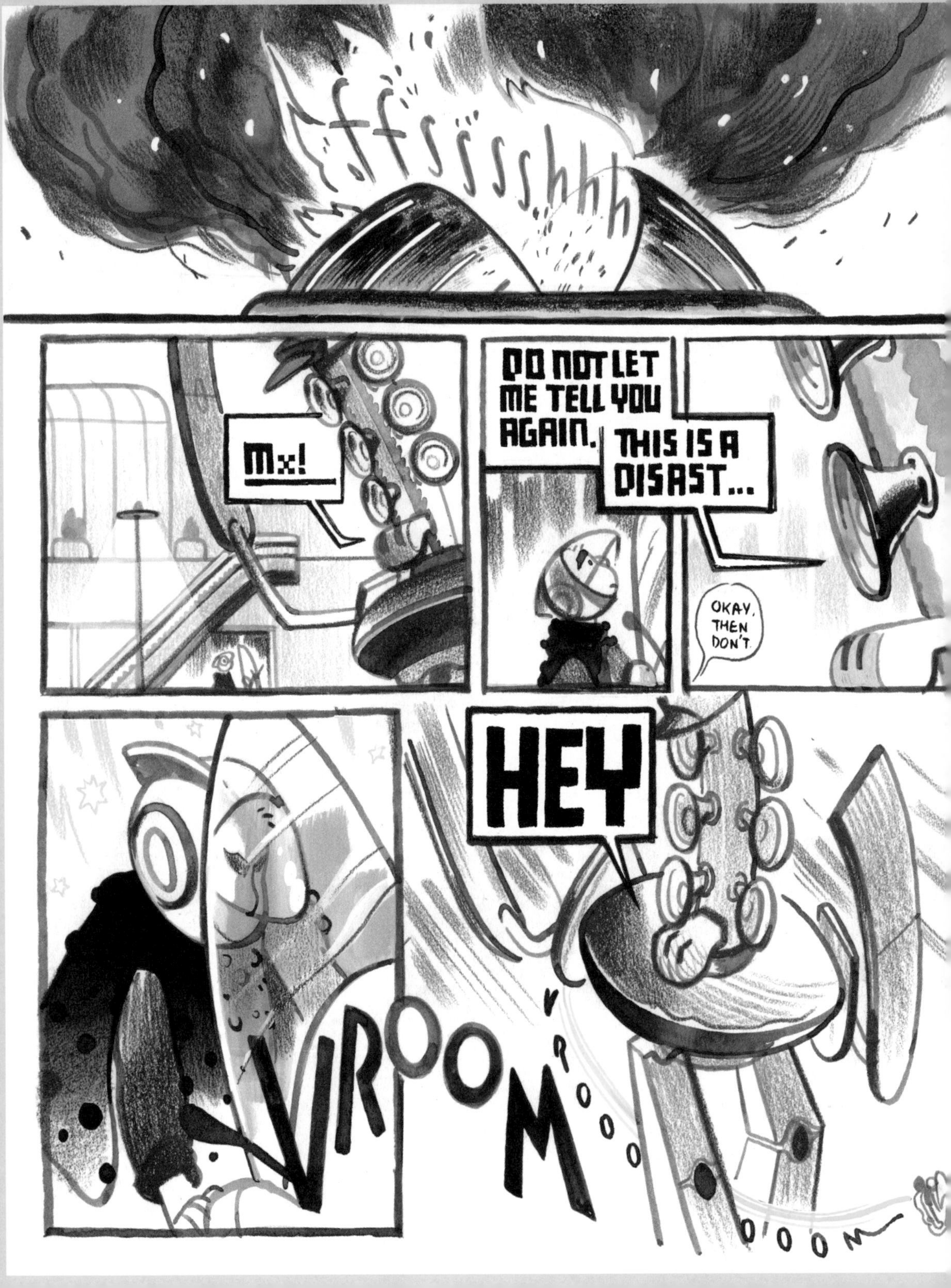
ffsssshhh
Mx!
DO NOT LET ME TELL YOU AGAIN.
THIS IS A DISAST...
OKAY, THEN DON'T.
HEY
VROOM
VROOOOOOOM

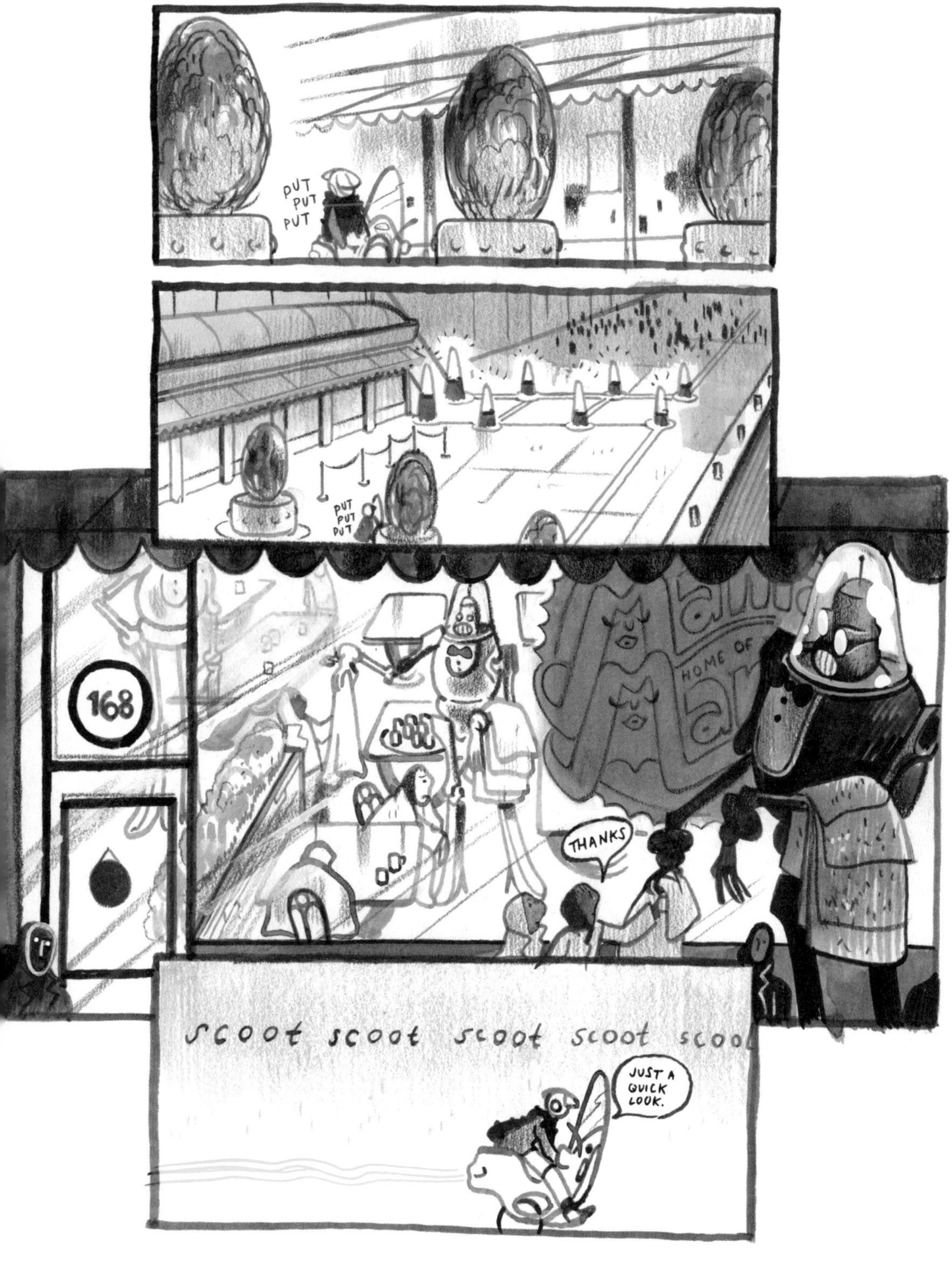
PUT
PUT
PUT
PUT
PUT
PUT
168
HOME OF
THANKS
scoot scoot scoot scoot scoo
JUST A QUICK LOOK.

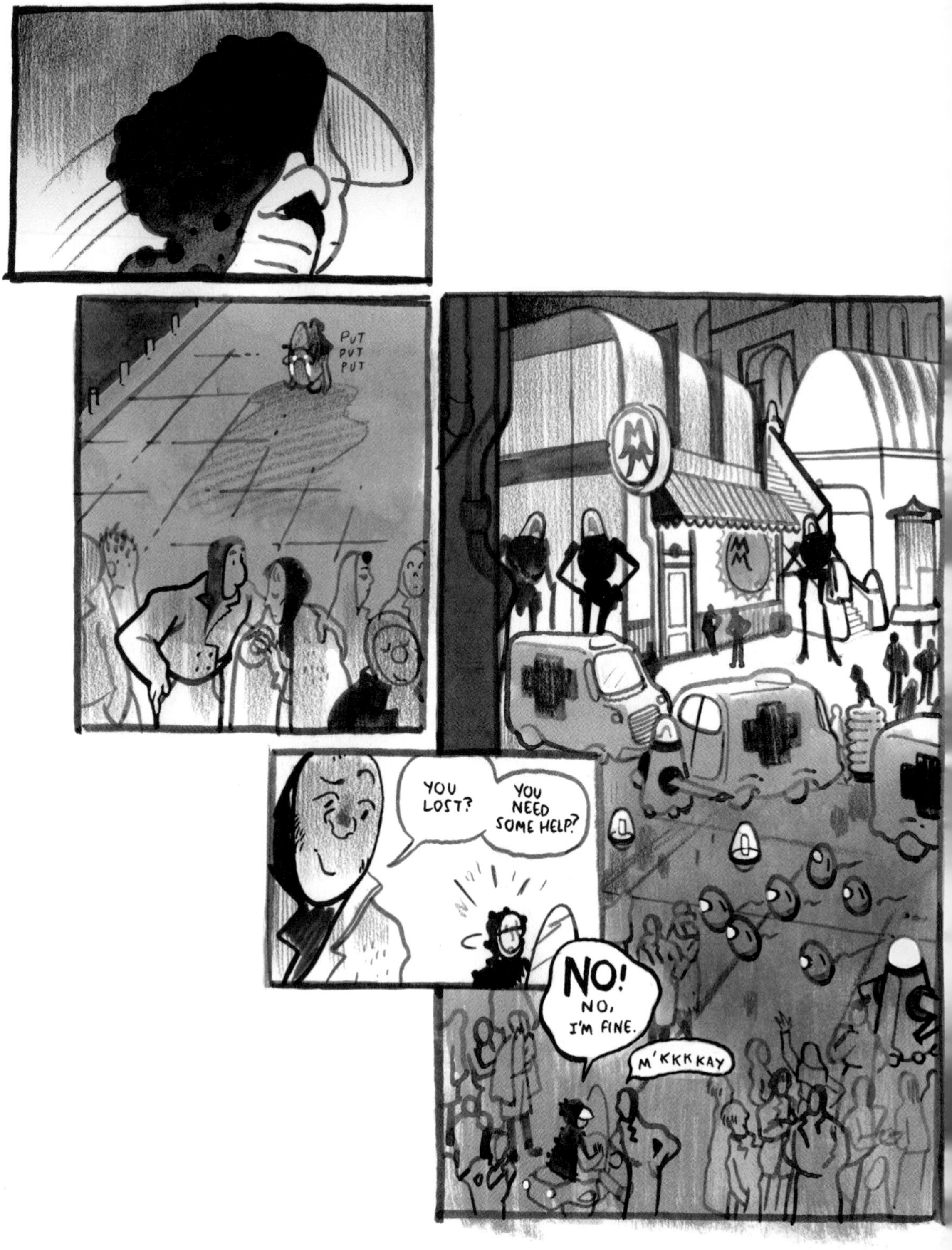
PUT PUT PUT
YOU LOST?
YOU NEED SOME HELP?
NO! NO, I'M FINE.
M'KKKKAY

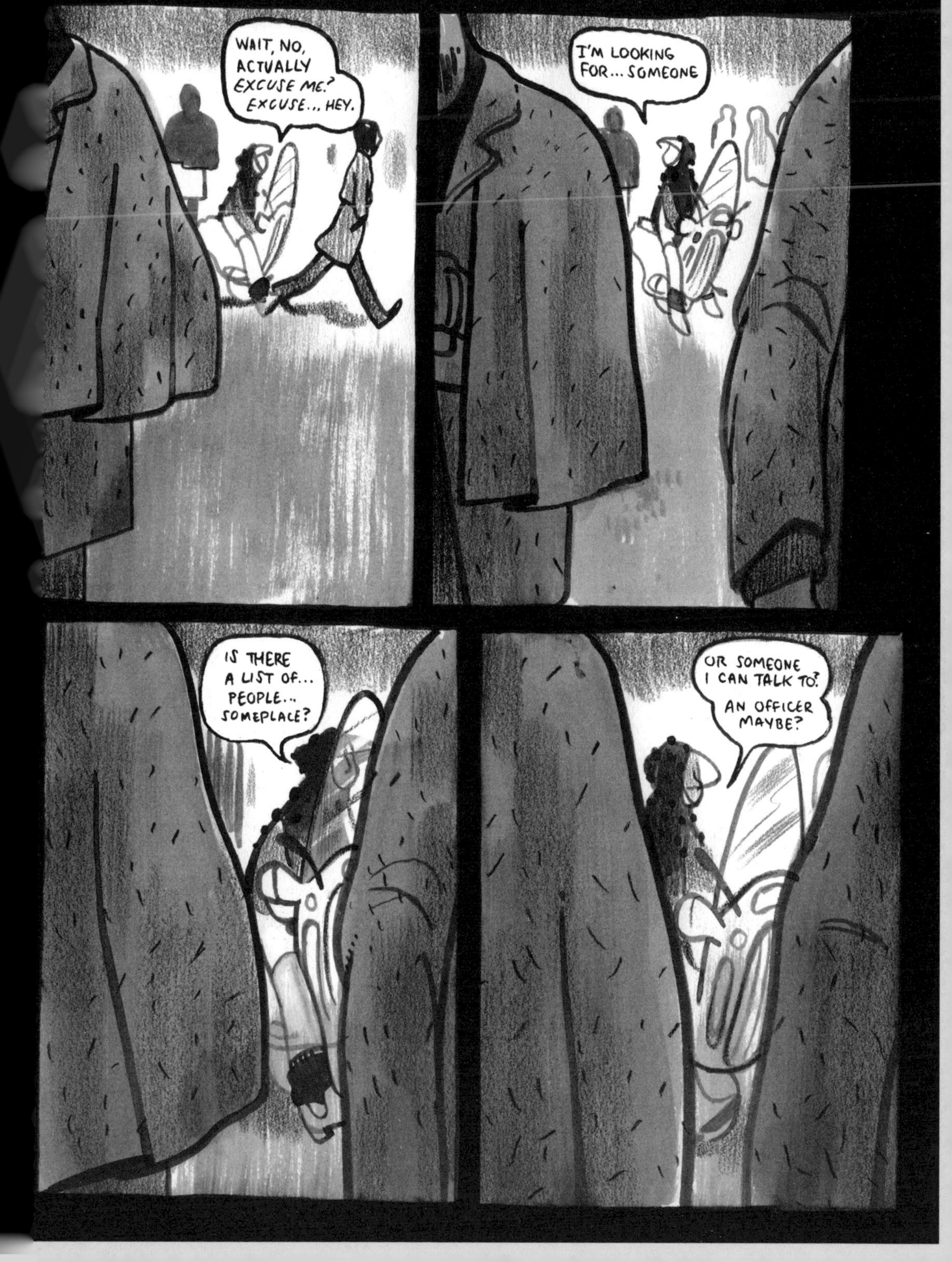
WAIT, NO, ACTUALLY EXCUSE ME? EXCUSE... HEY.
I'M LOOKING FOR... SOMEONE
IS THERE A LIST OF... PEOPLE... SOMEPLACE?
OR SOMEONE I CAN TALK TO?
AN OFFICER MAYBE?

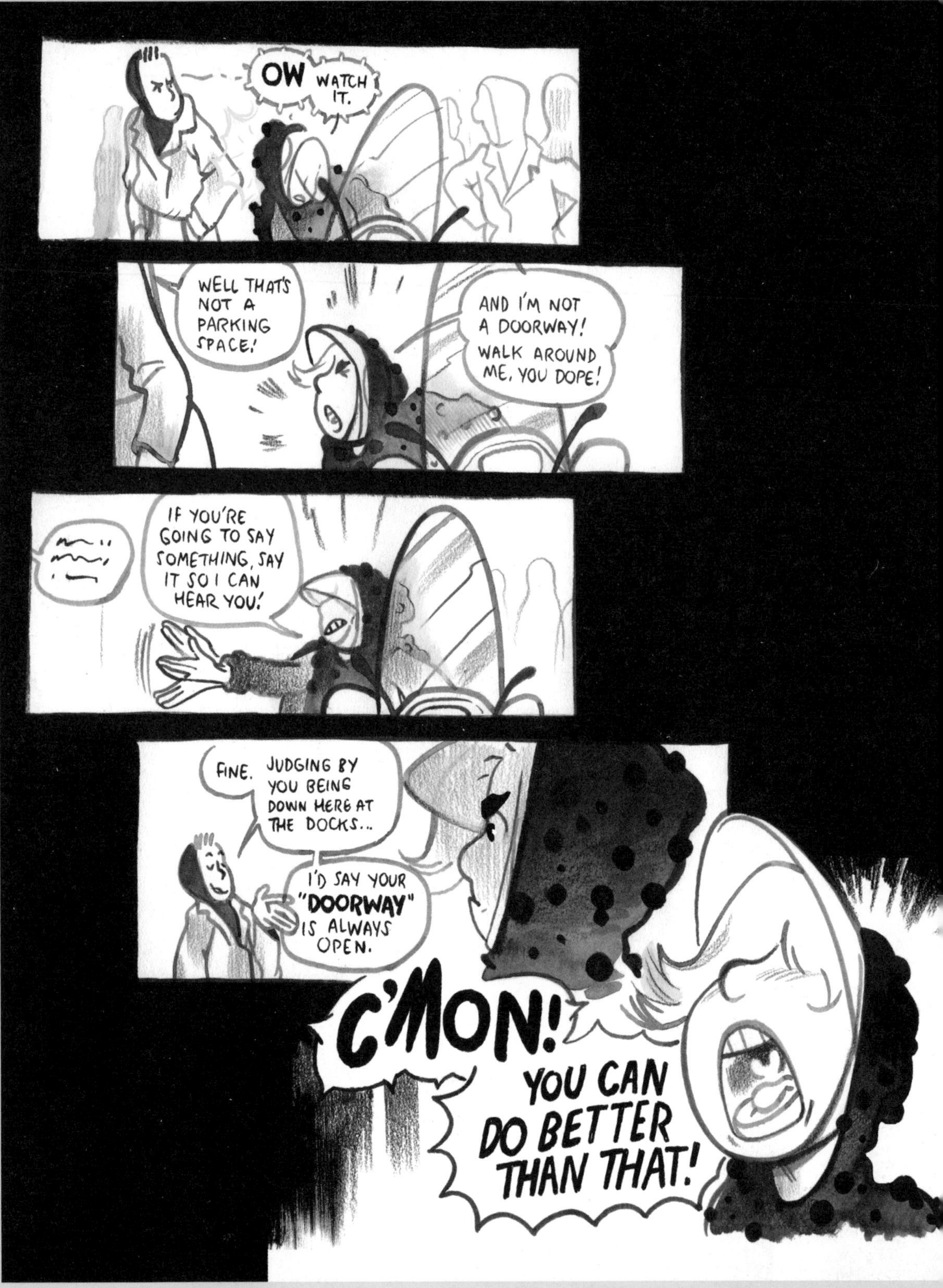
OW
WATCH IT.
WELL THAT'S NOT A PARKING SPACE!
AND I'M NOT A DOORWAY! WALK AROUND ME, YOU DOPE!
IF YOU'RE GOING TO SAY SOMETHING, SAY IT SO I CAN HEAR YOU!
FINE.
JUDGING BY YOU BEING DOWN HERE AT THE DOCKS...
I'D SAY YOUR "DOORWAY" IS ALWAYS OPEN.
C'MON!
YOU CAN DO BETTER THAN THAT!

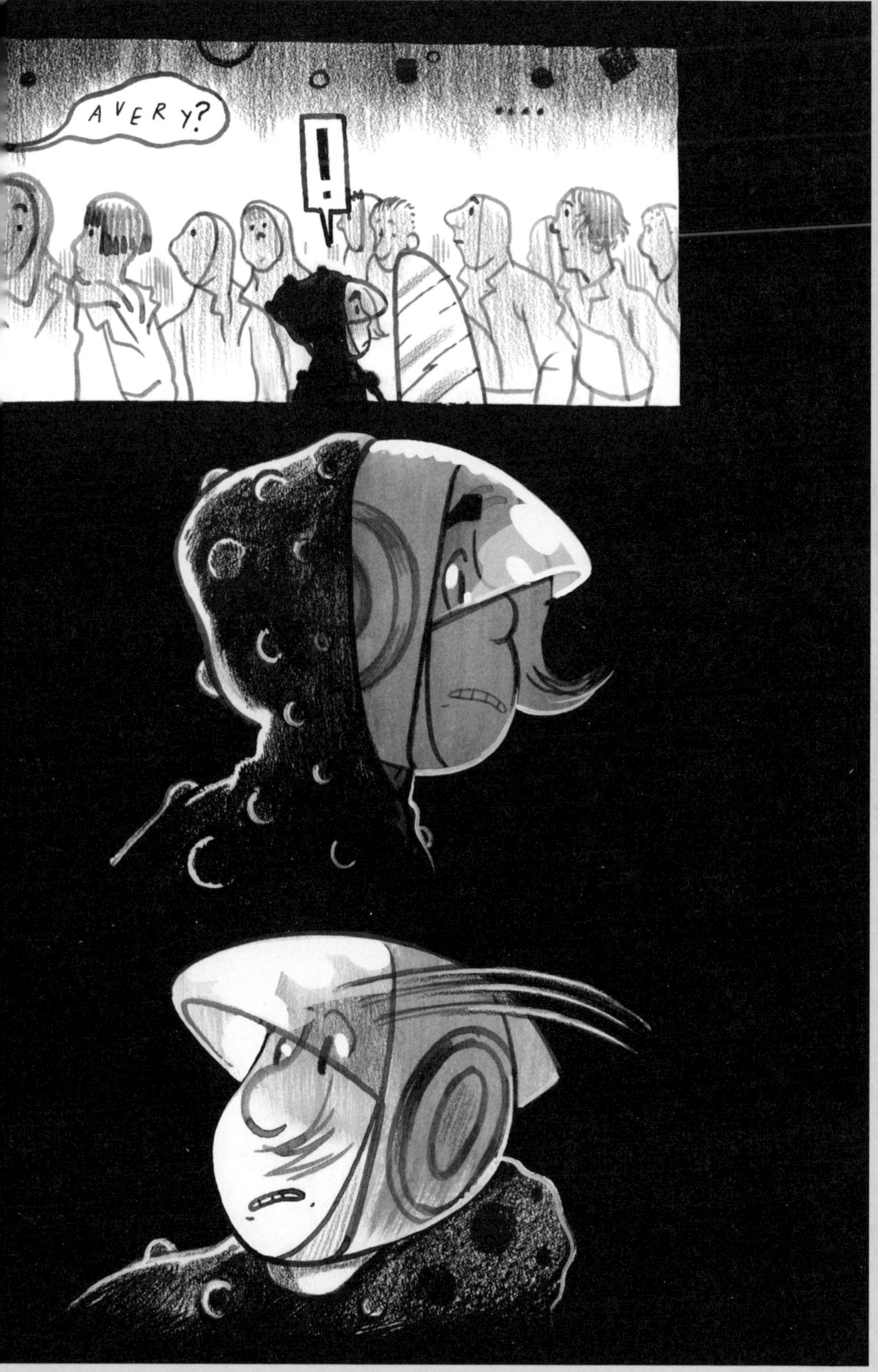
AVERY?
!

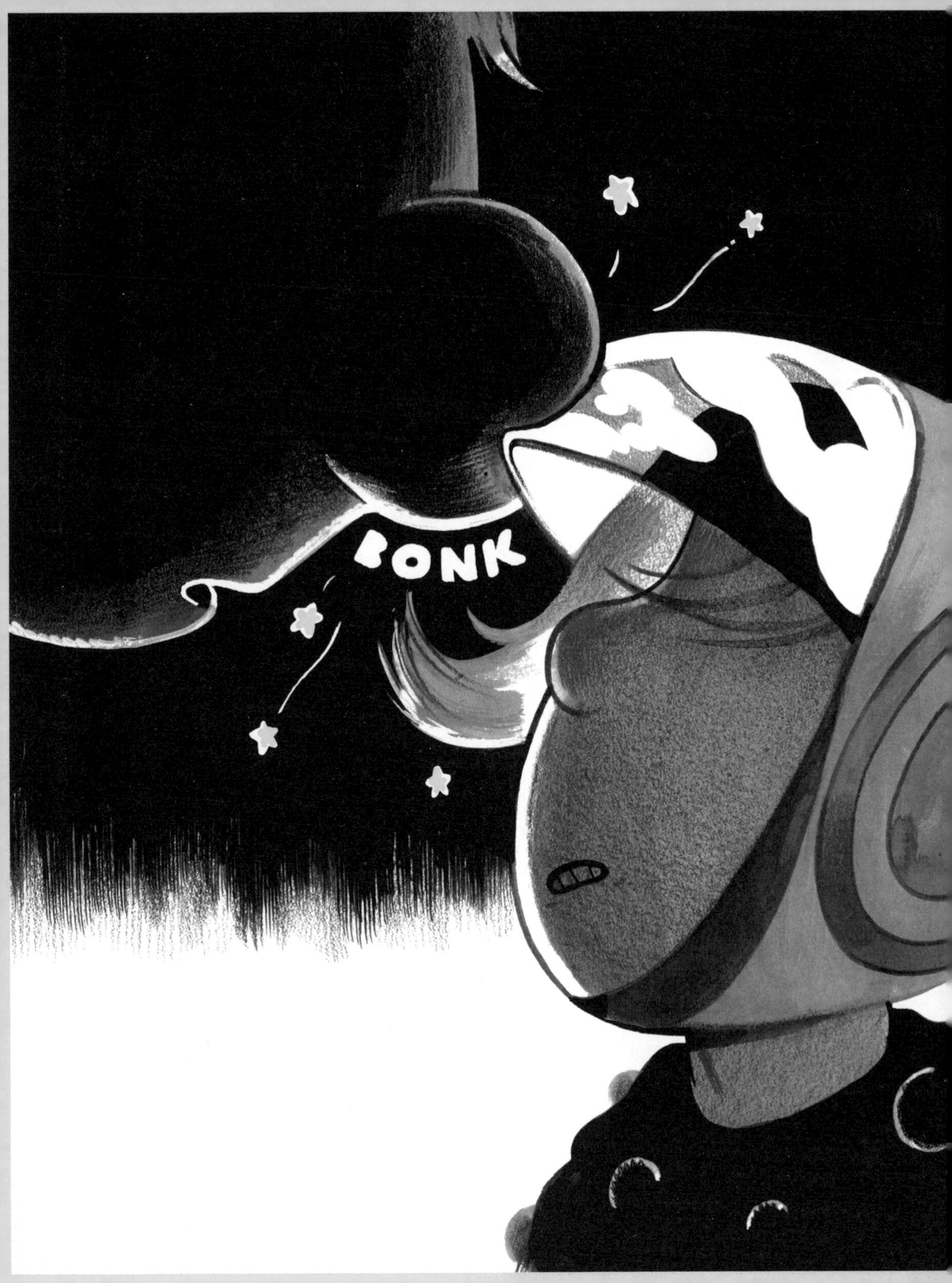
BONK

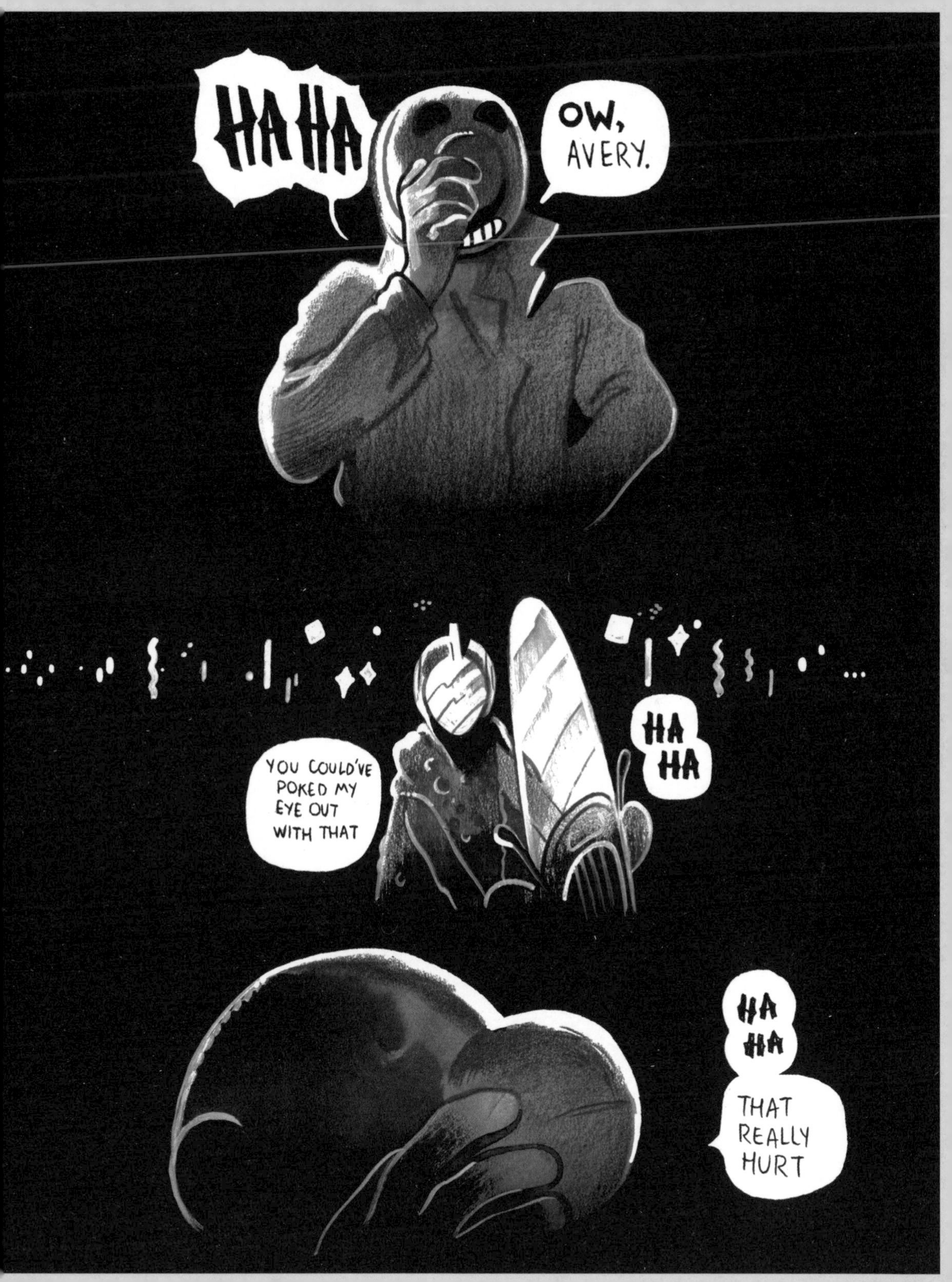
HAHA
OW, AVERY.
YOU COULD'VE POKED MY EYE OUT WITH THAT
HA HA
HA HA
THAT REALLY HURT

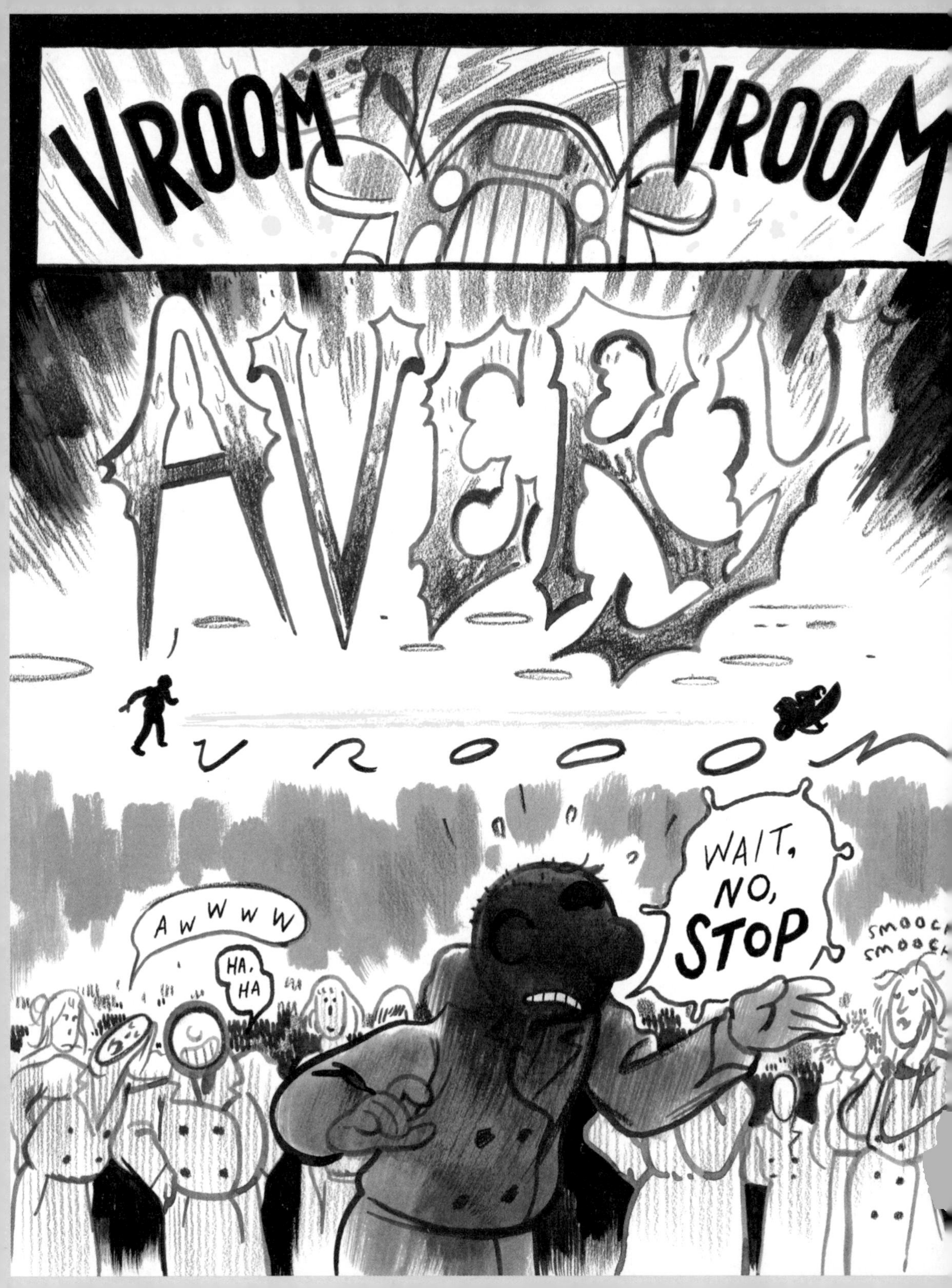
VROOM
VROOM
AVERY
VROOOOM
AWWWW
HA, HA
WAIT, NO, STOP

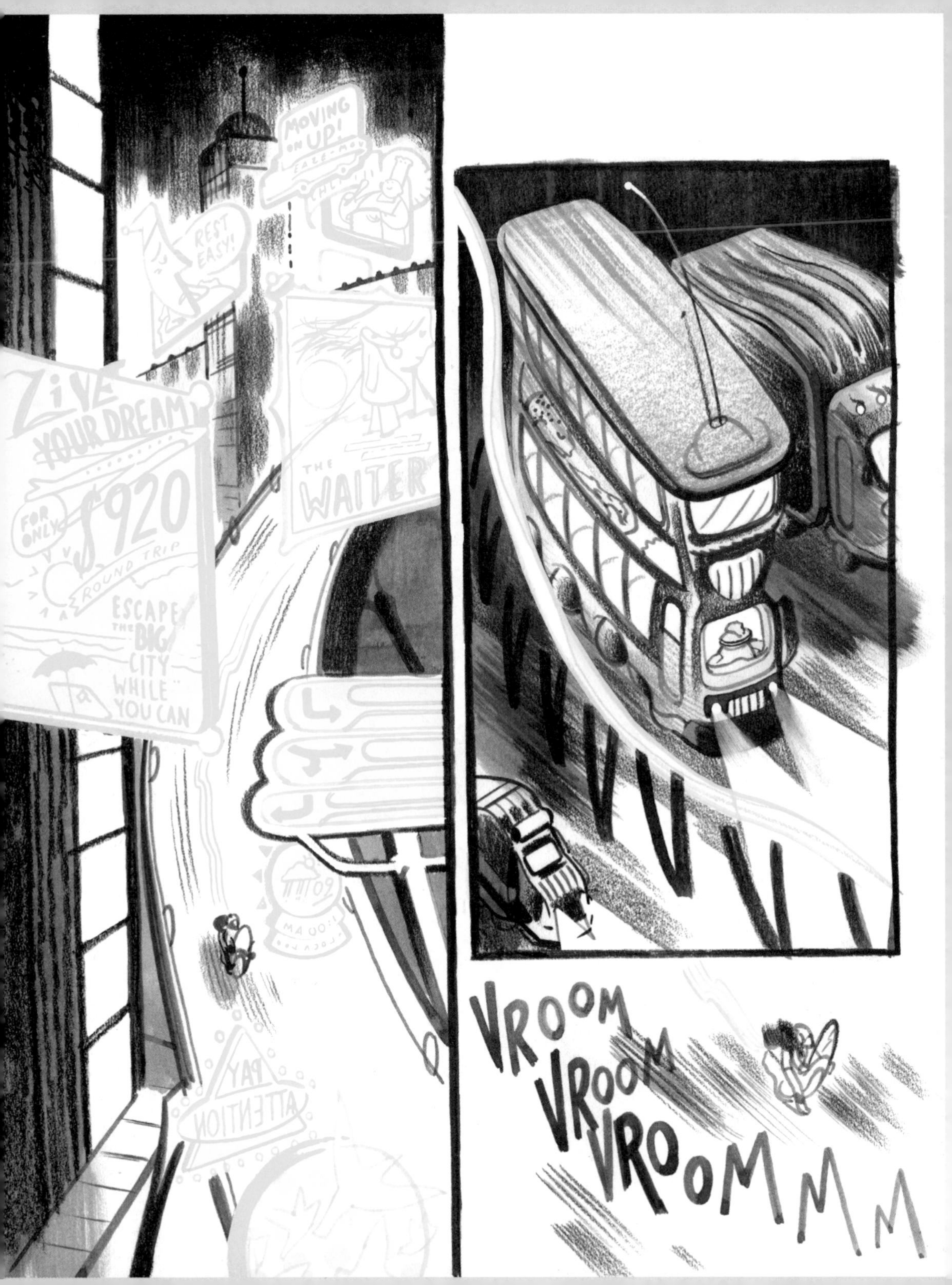
MOVING ON UP!
REST EASY!
LIVE YOUR DREAM
FOR ONLY $920 ROUND TRIP
ESCAPE THE BIG CITY WHILE YOU CAN
THE WAITER
PAY ATTENTION
VROOM
VROOM
VROOMMMM

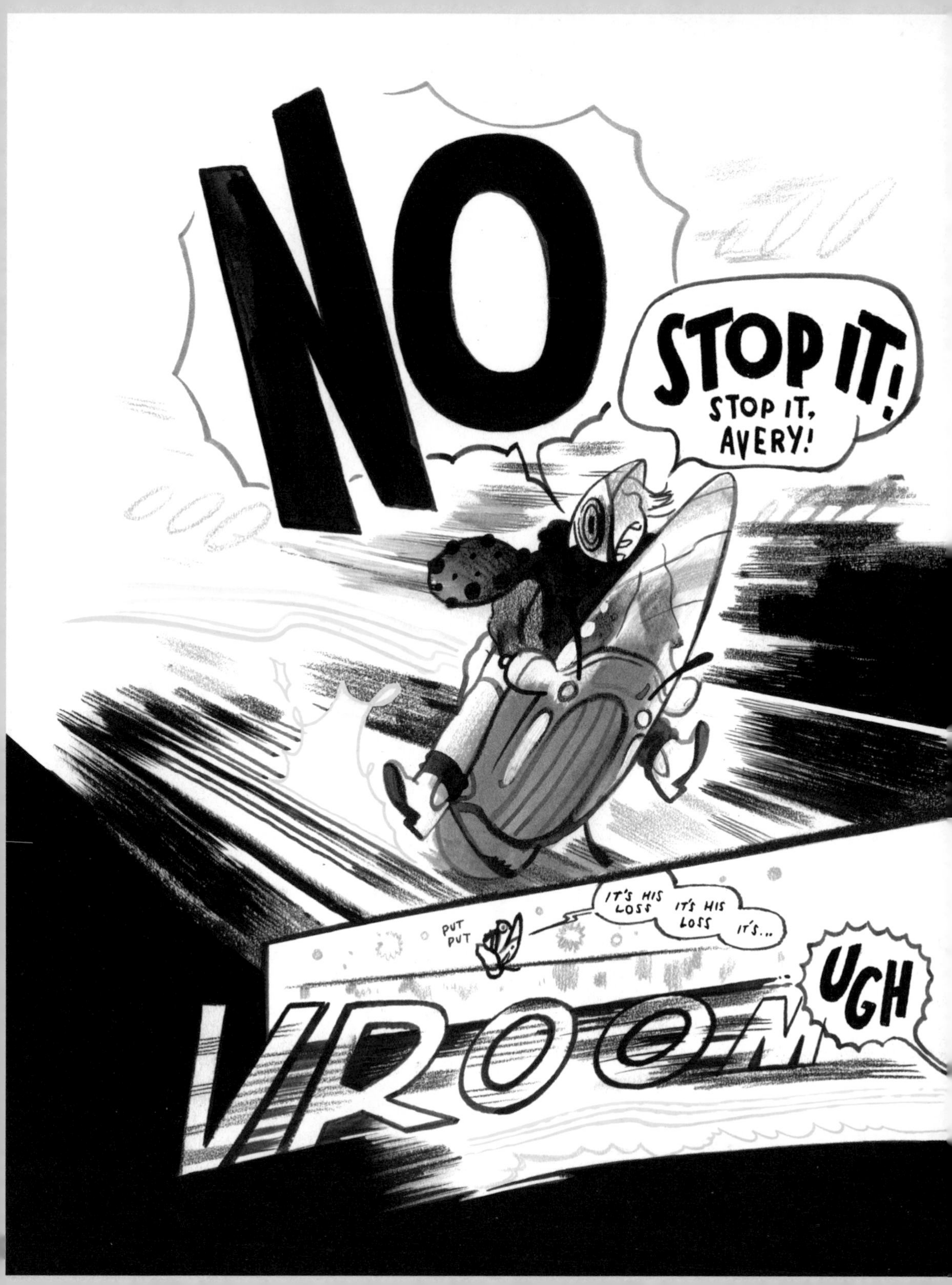
NO
STOP IT!
STOP IT, AVERY!
PUT PUT
IT'S HIS LOSS
IT'S HIS LOSS
IT'S...
VROOM
UGH

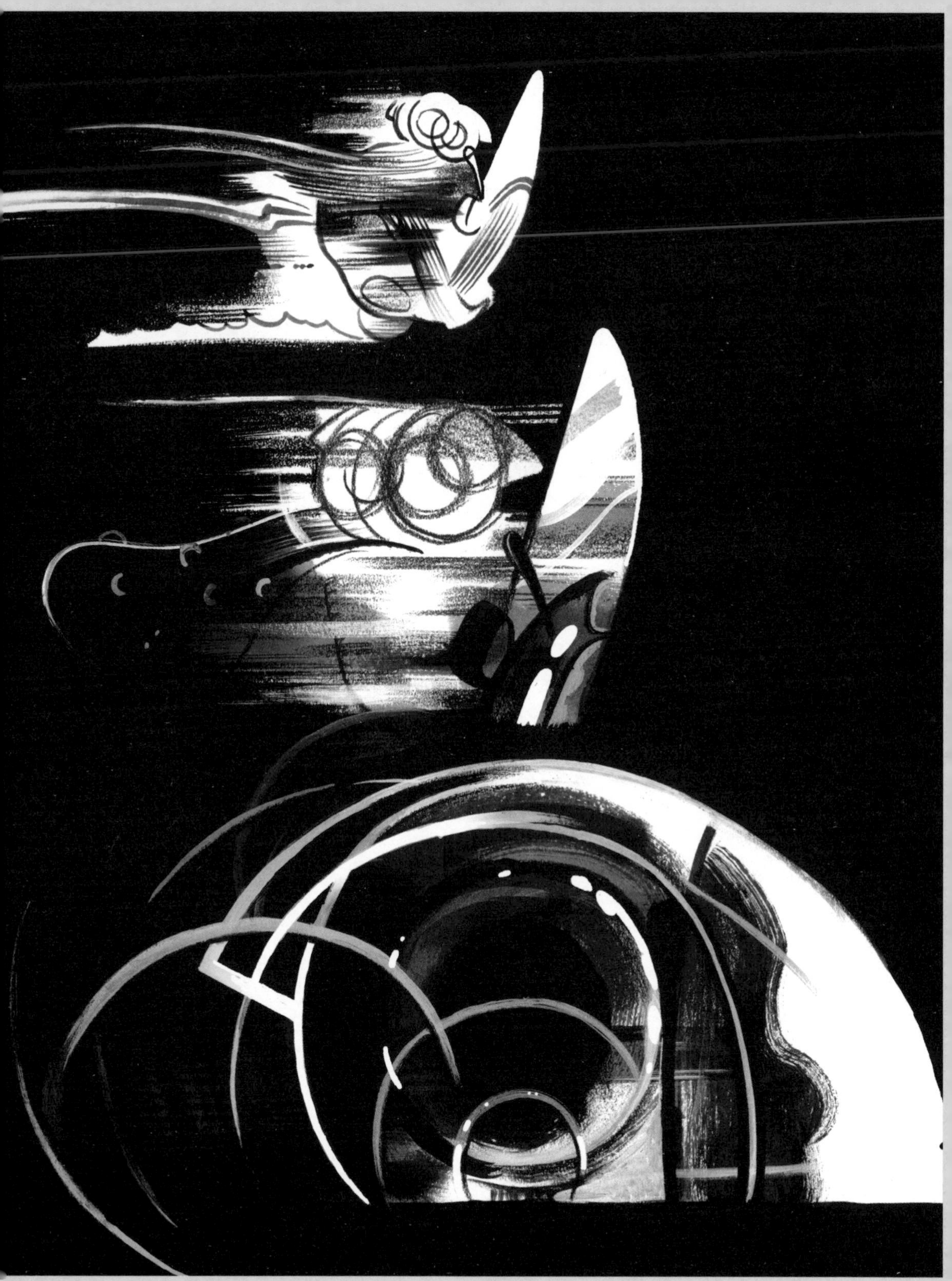

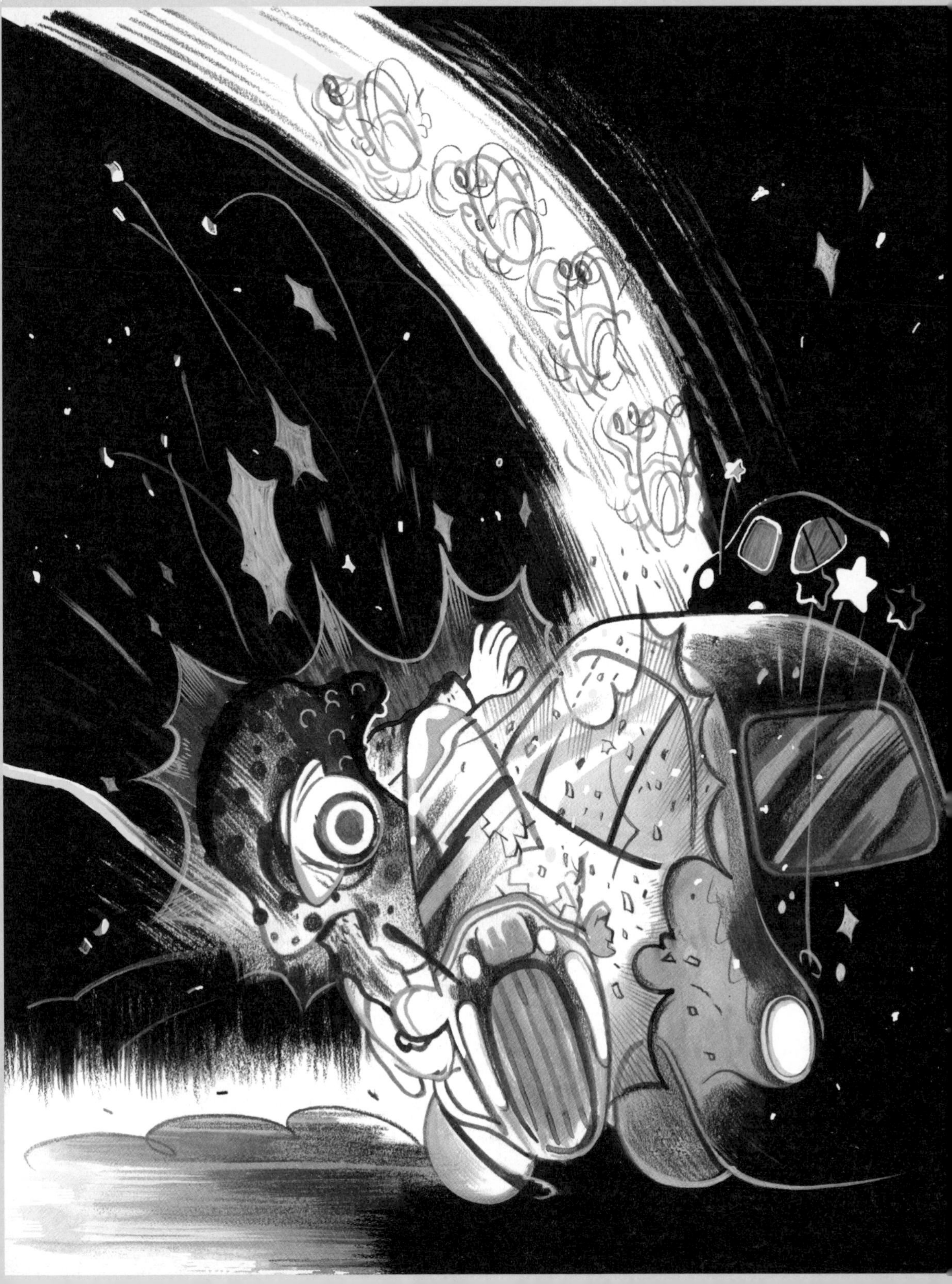

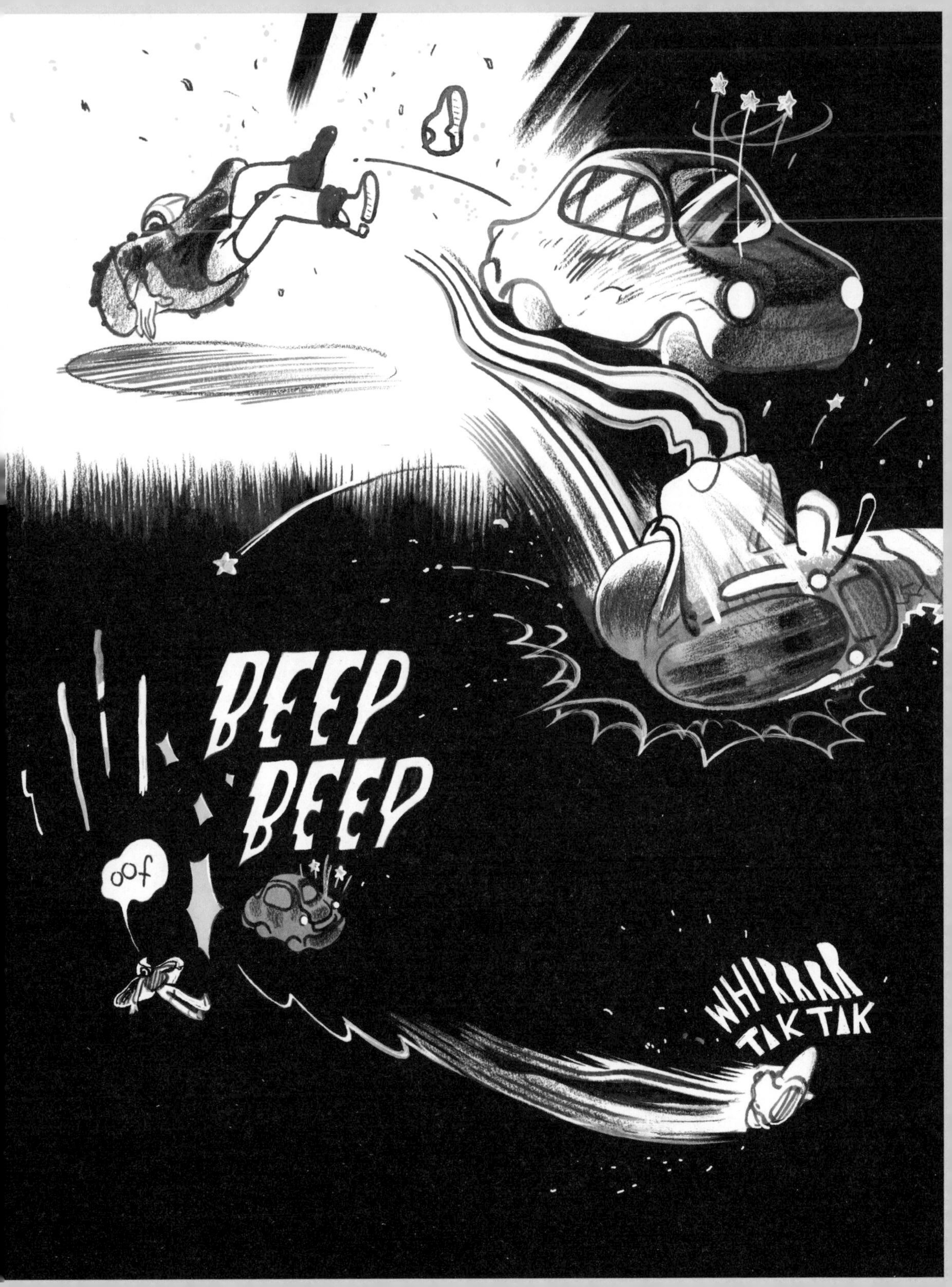
BEEP
BEEP
oof
WHIRRRR
TAK TAK

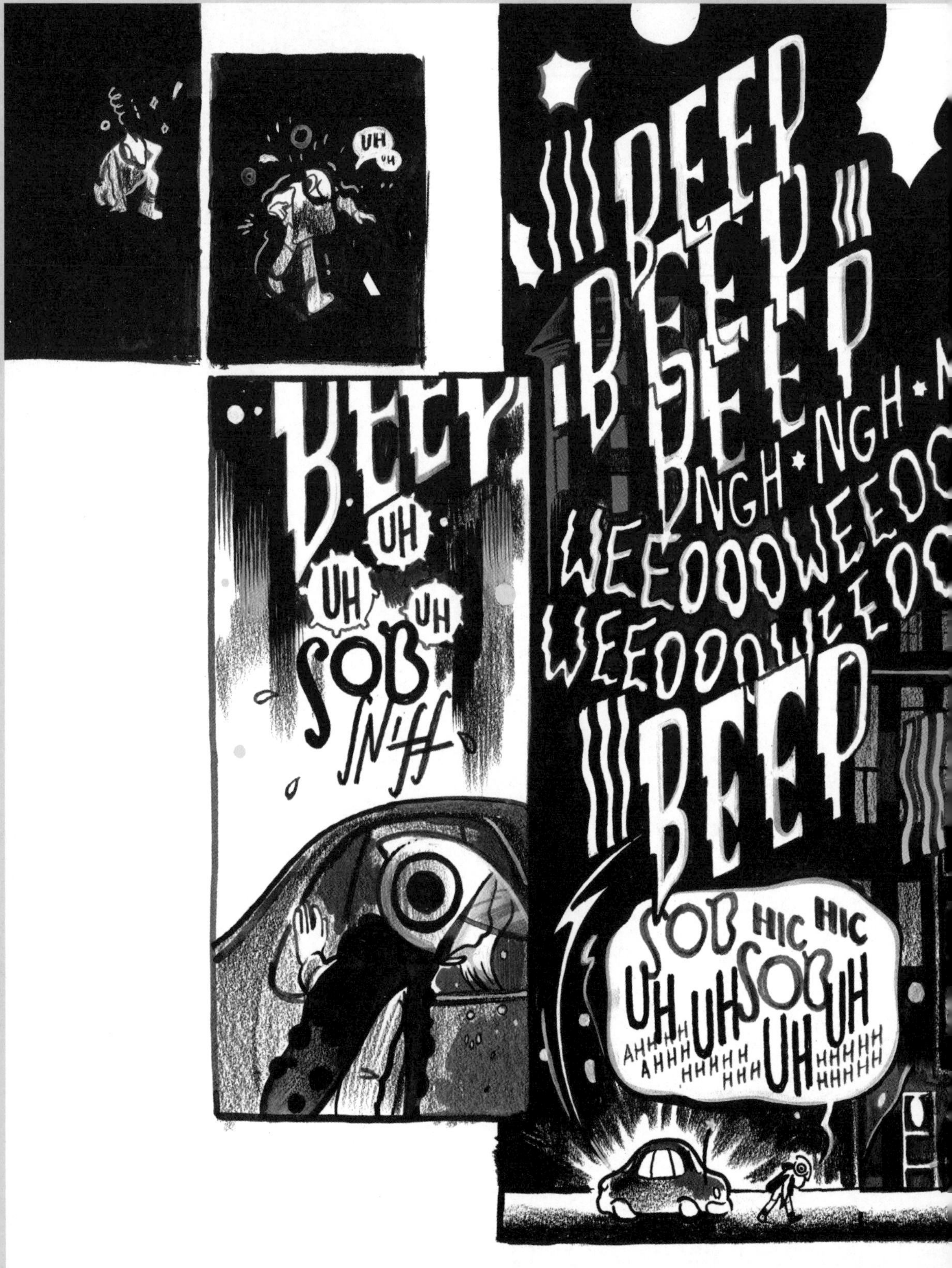

UH uh
BEEP
UH
UH
UH
SOB
SNIFF
BEEP
BEEP
BEEP
BEEP
NGH NGH NGH
WEEOOOWEEOO
WEEOOOWEEOO
BEEP
SOB HIC HIC
UH UH SOB UH
UH UH
AHHHH AHHHH HHHHH HHH HHHHH HHHHH

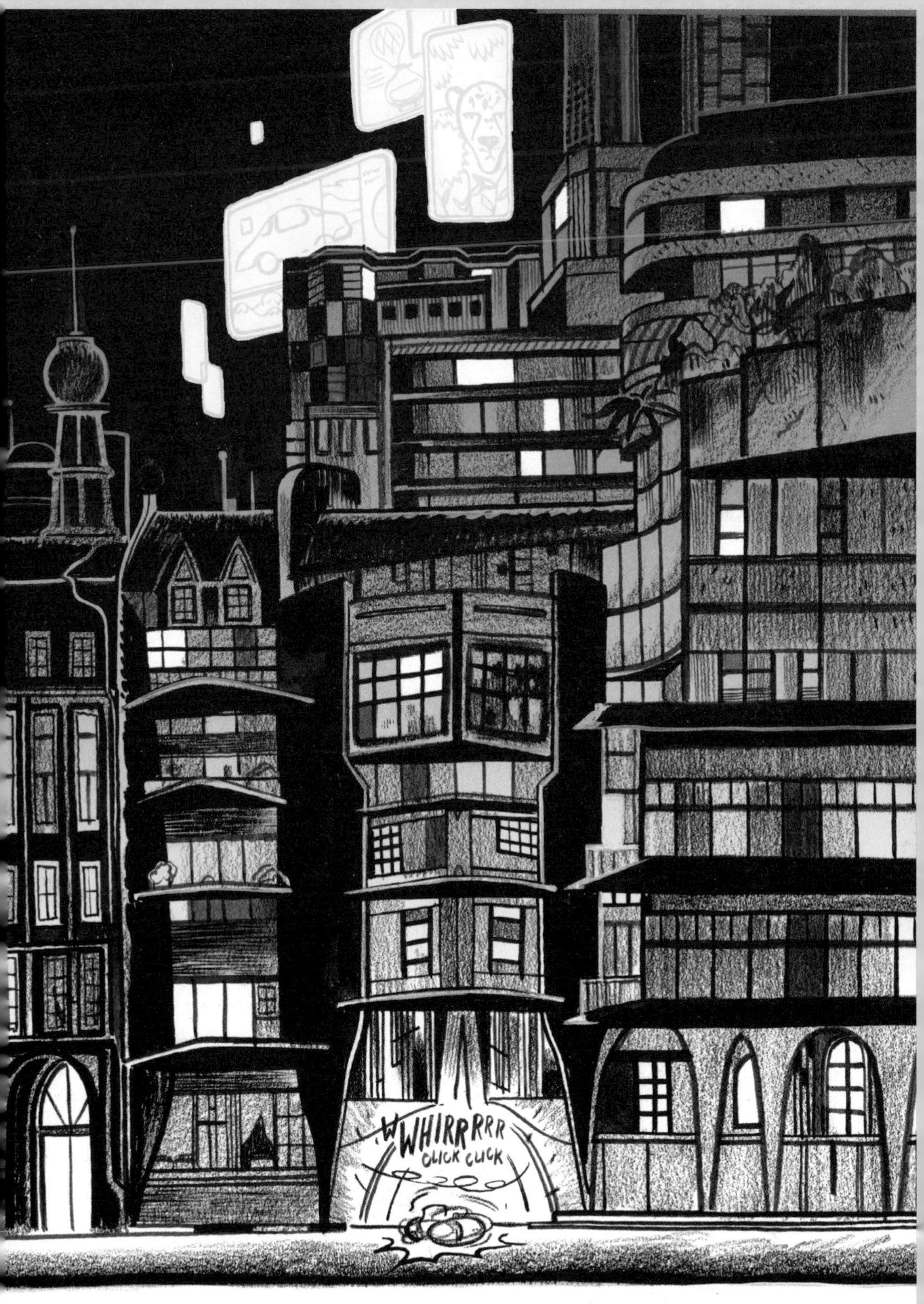
WWHIRRRRR
CLICK CLICK

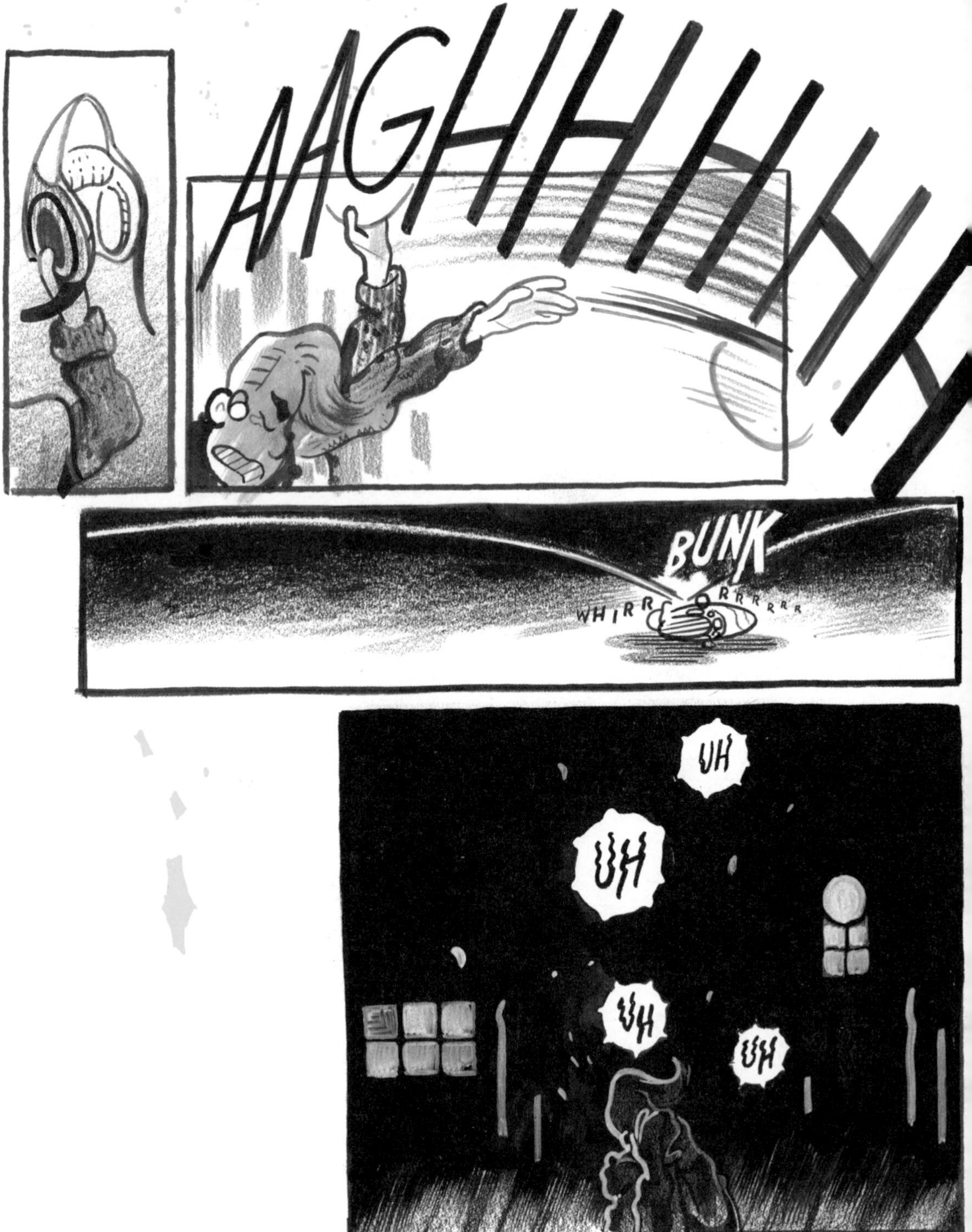
AAGHHHHHHHH
BUNK
WHIRRRRRRRRR
UH
UH
UH
UH

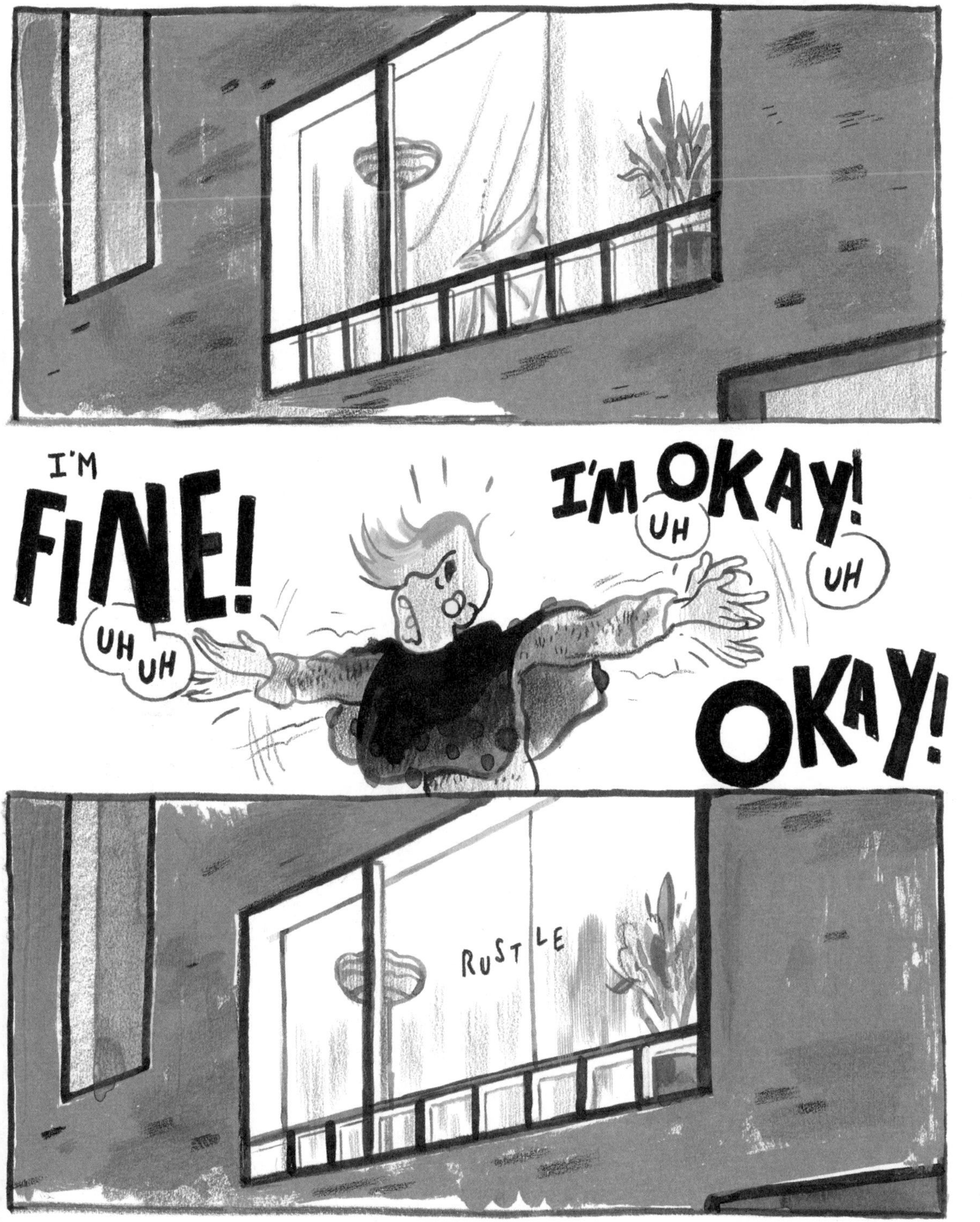
I'M FINE!
UH UH
I'M OKAY!
UH
UH
OKAY!
RUSTLE

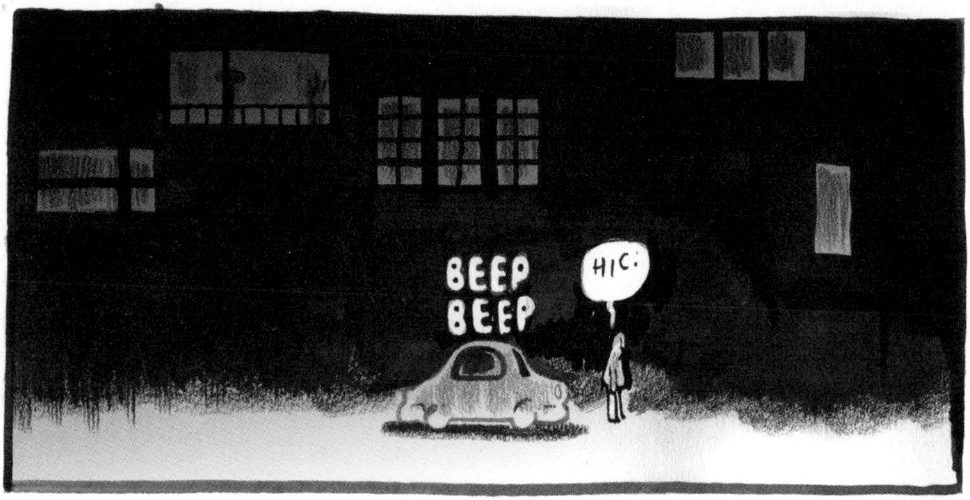
BEEP
BEEP
HIC:

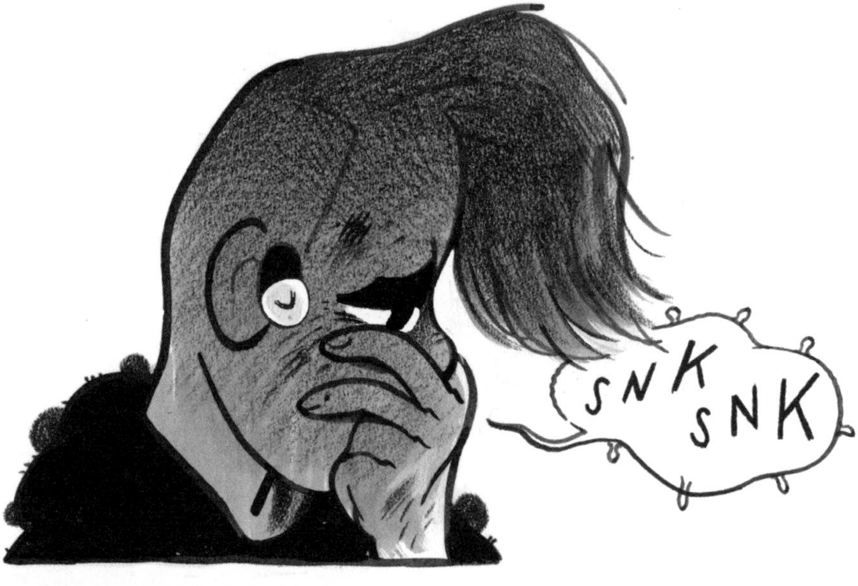
SNK
SNK

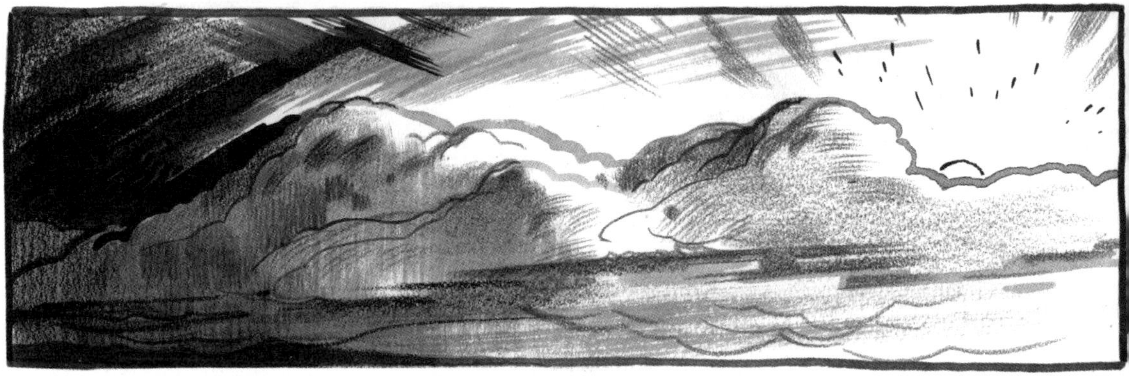

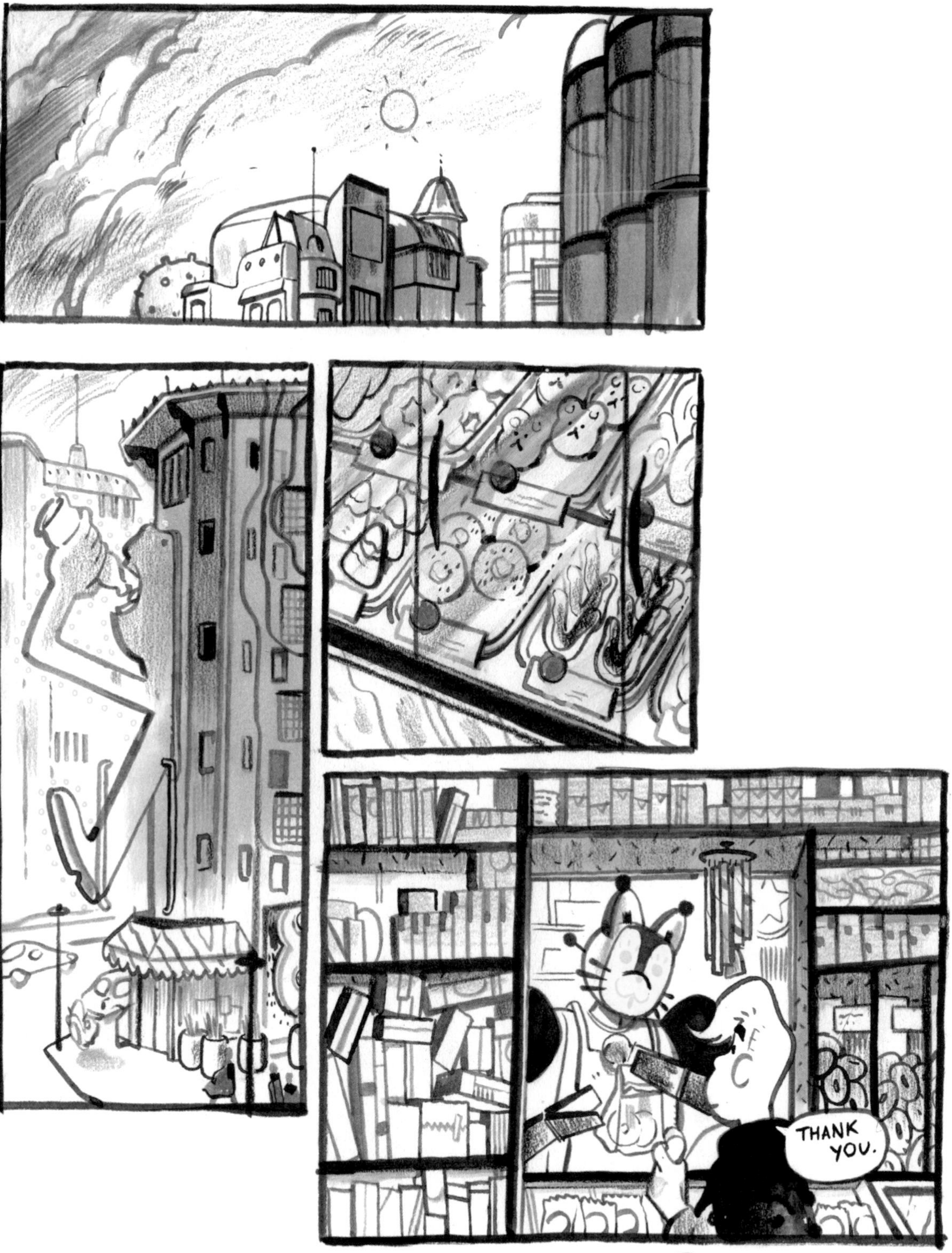
THANK YOU.

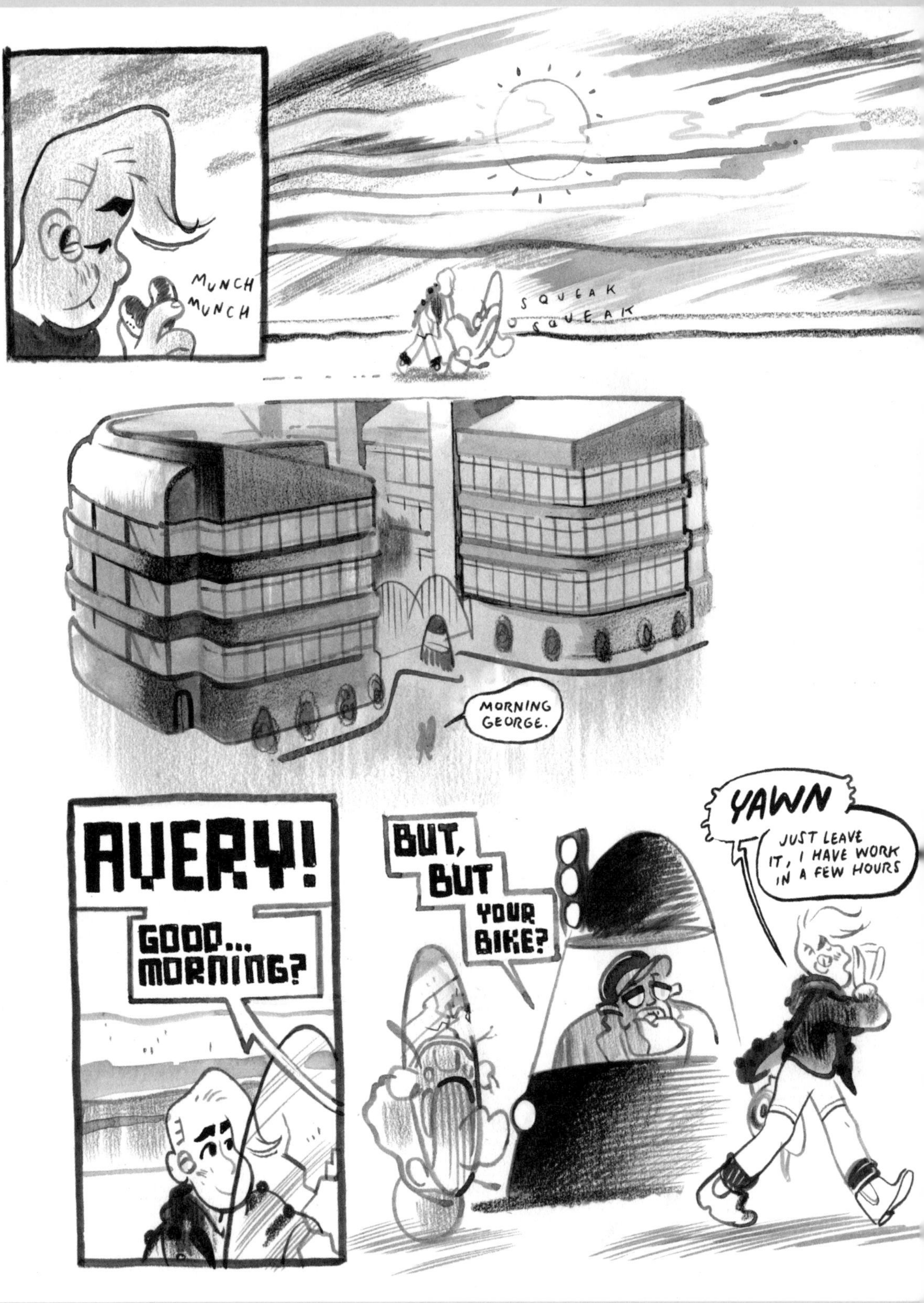
MUNCH
MUNCH
SQUEAK
SQUEAK
MORNING GEORGE.
AVERY!
GOOD... MORNING?
BUT, BUT
YOUR BIKE?
YAWN
JUST LEAVE IT, I HAVE WORK IN A FEW HOURS

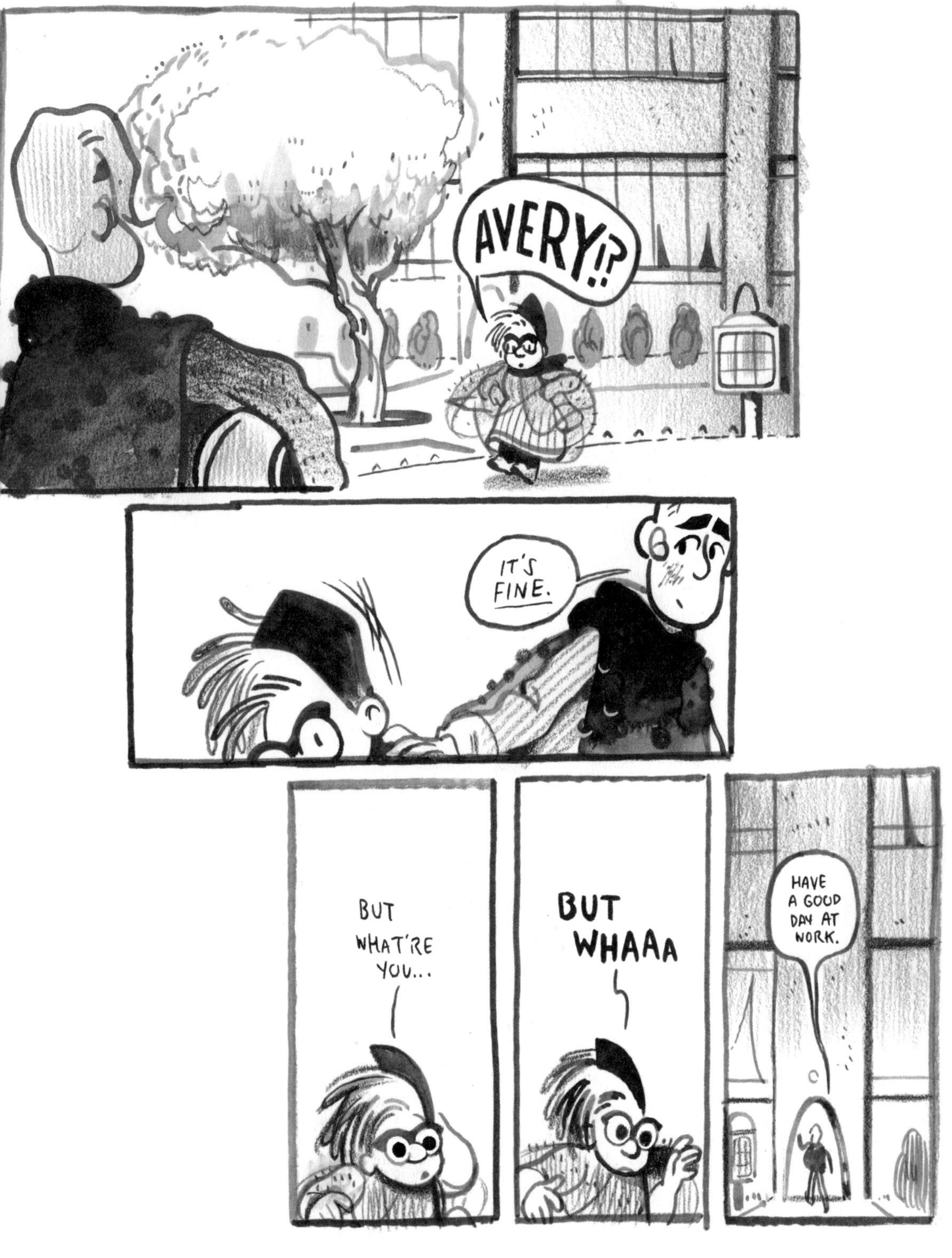
AVERY!?
IT'S FINE.
BUT WHAT'RE YOU...
BUT WHAAA
HAVE A GOOD DAY AT WORK.

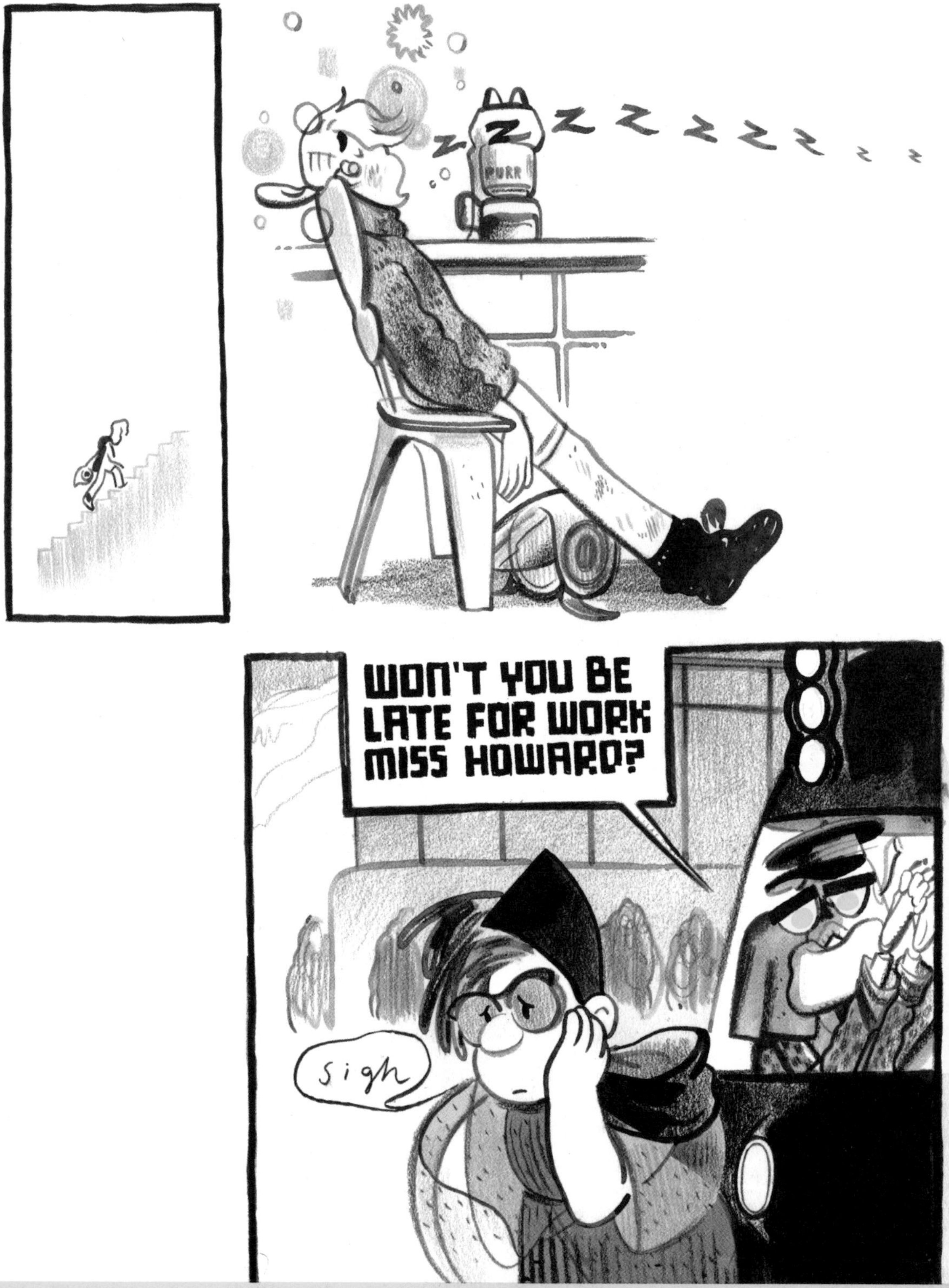
PURR
WON'T YOU BE LATE FOR WORK MISS HOWARD?
sigh

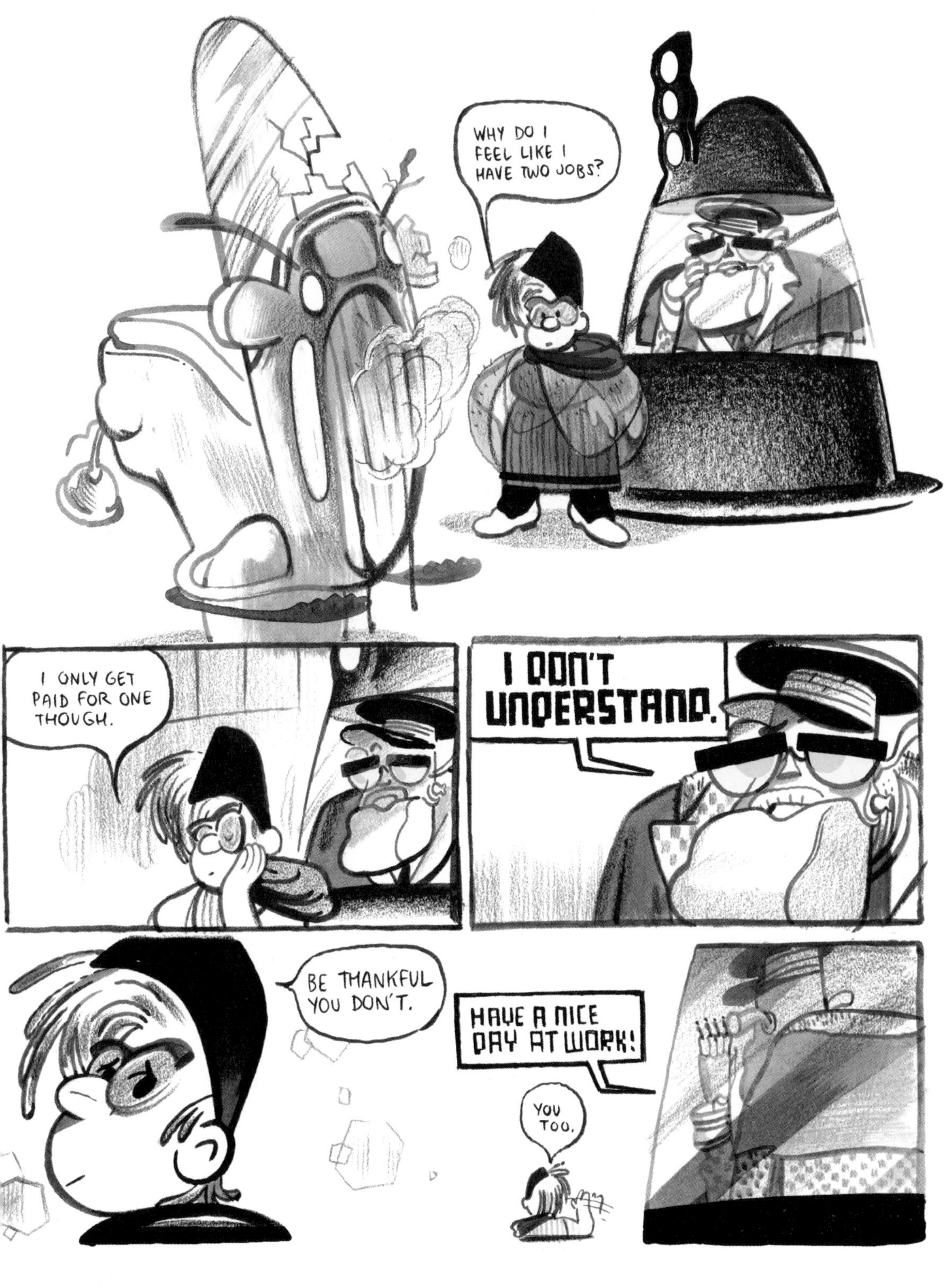
WHY DO I FEEL LIKE I HAVE TWO JOBS?
I ONLY GET PAID FOR ONE THOUGH.
I DON'T UNDERSTAND.
BE THANKFUL YOU DON'T.
HAVE A NICE DAY AT WORK!
YOU TOO.

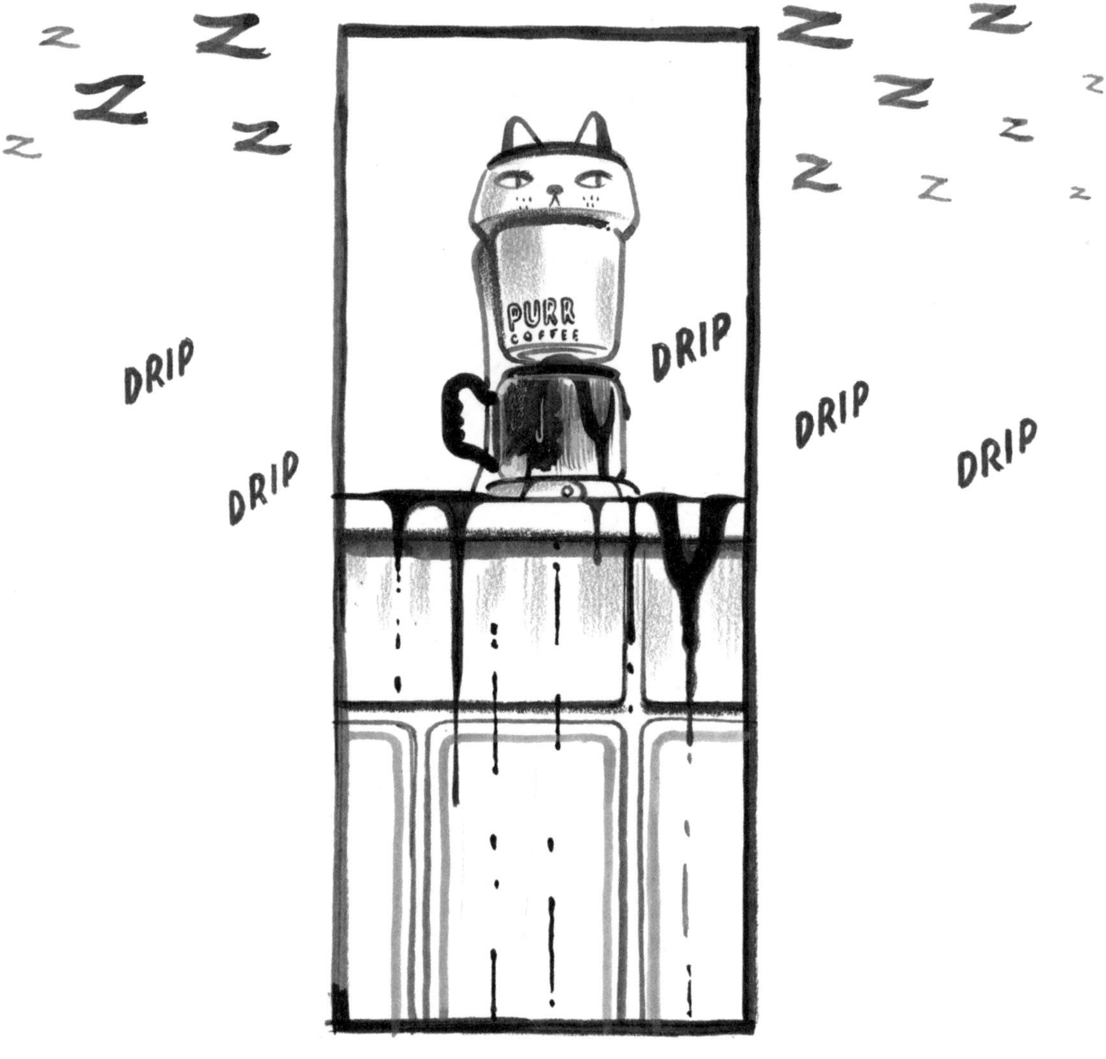
PURR
COFFEE
DRIP
DRIP
DRIP
DRIP
DRIP

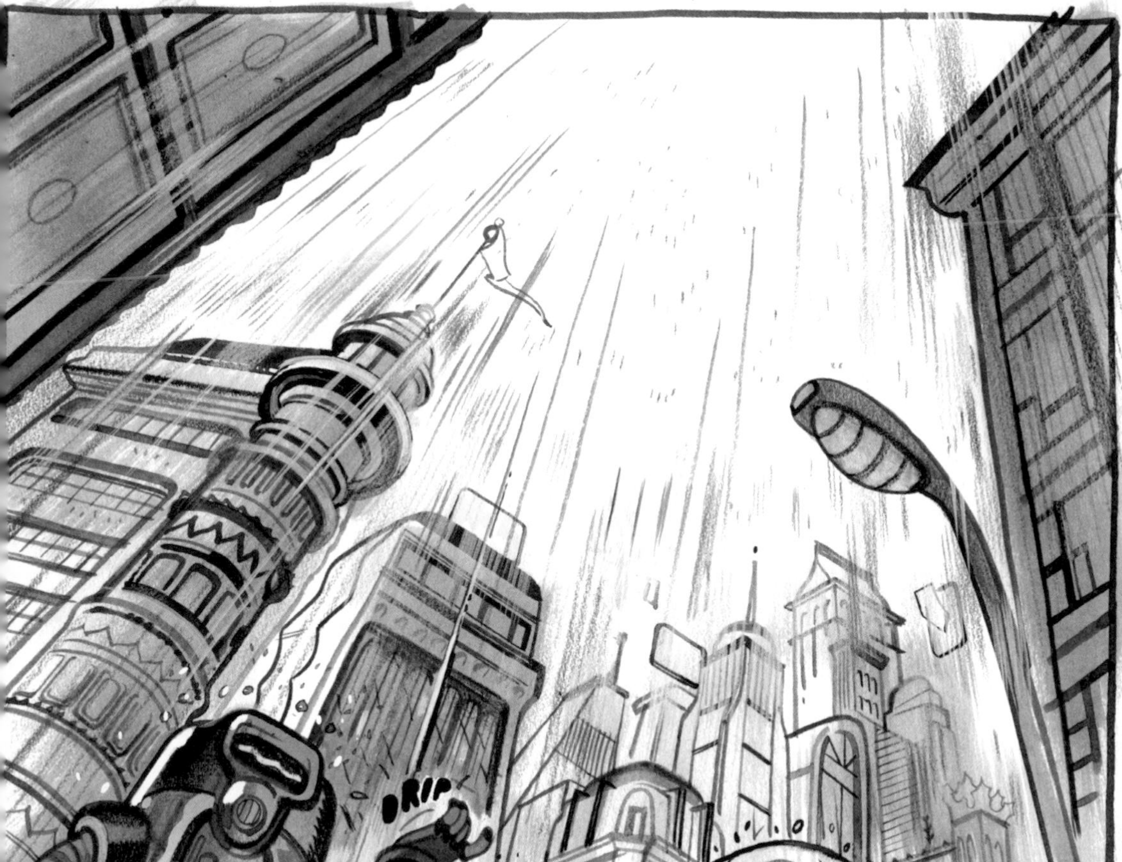
DRIP

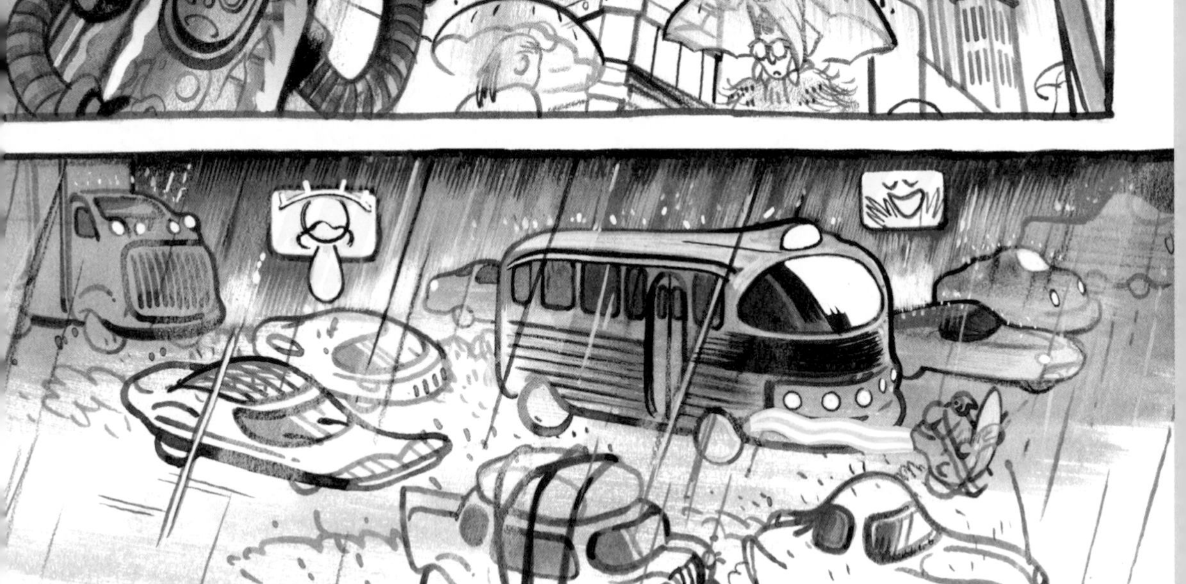

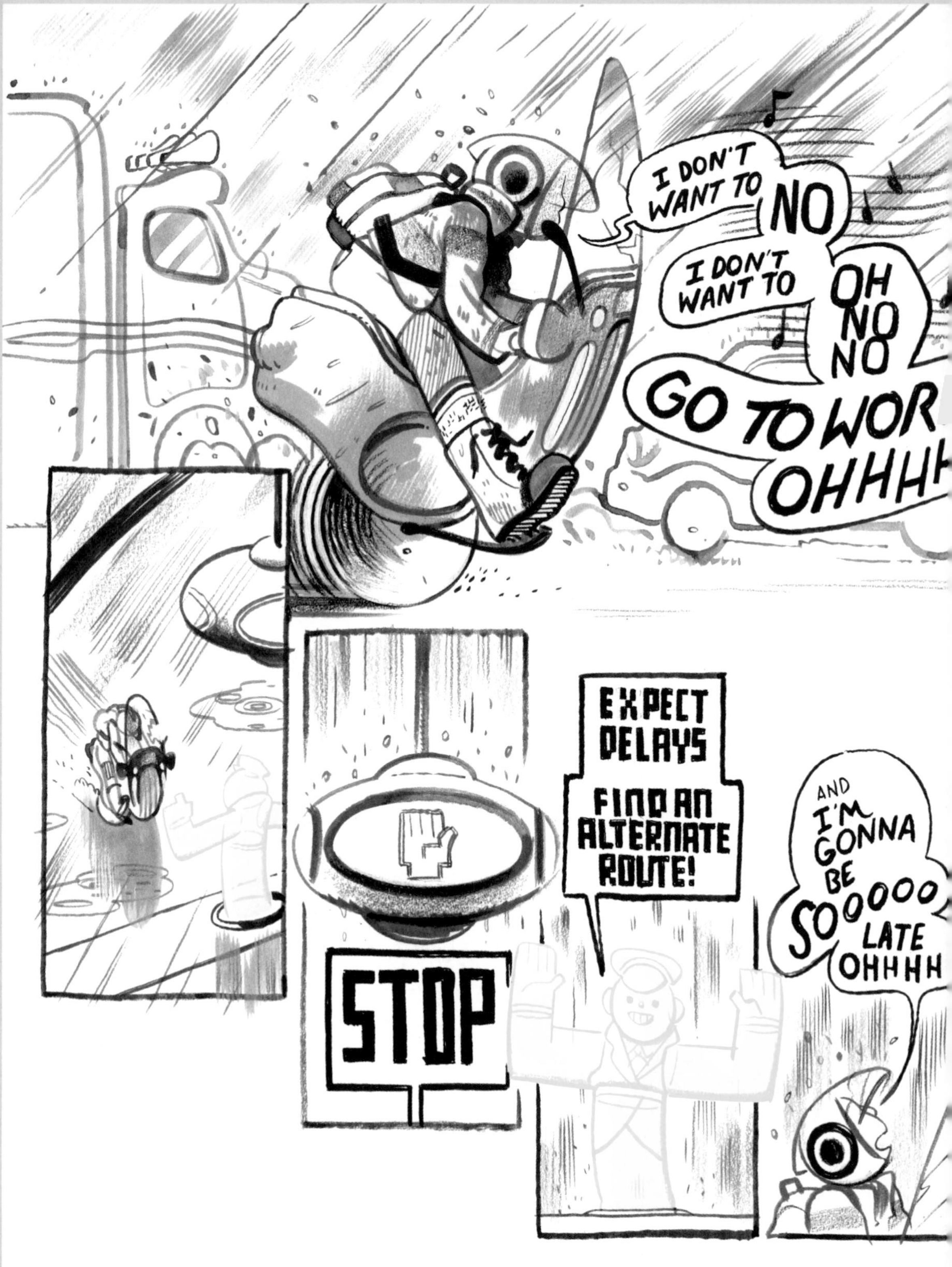

I DON'T WANT TO NO
I DON'T WANT TO OH NO NO NO
GO TO WOR
OHHH
EXPECT DELAYS
FIND AN ALTERNATE ROUTE!
STOP
AND I'M GONNA BE SOOOOO LATE OHHHH

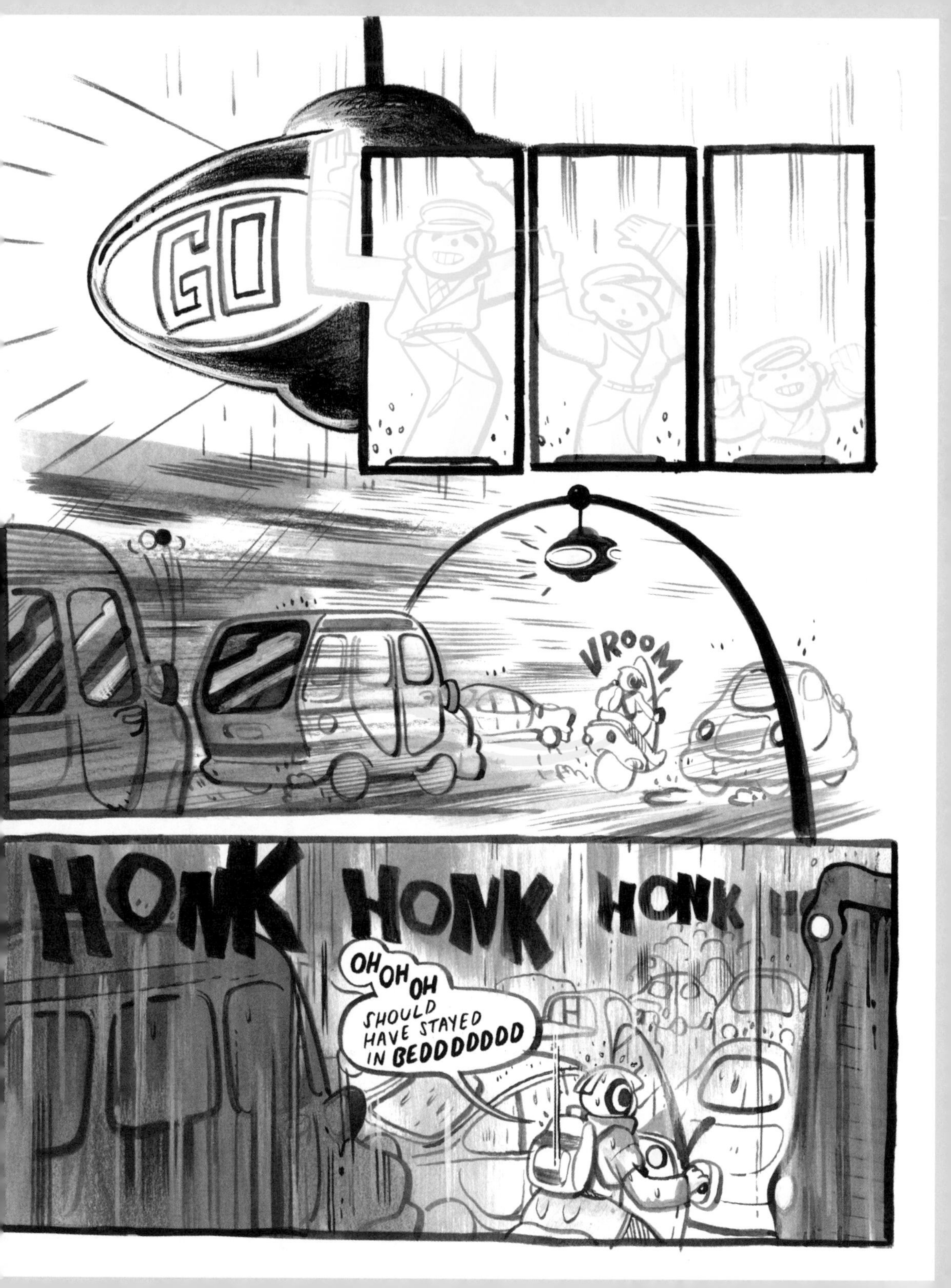
GO
VROOM
HONK HONK HONK
OH OH OH SHOULD HAVE STAYED IN BEDDDDDDD

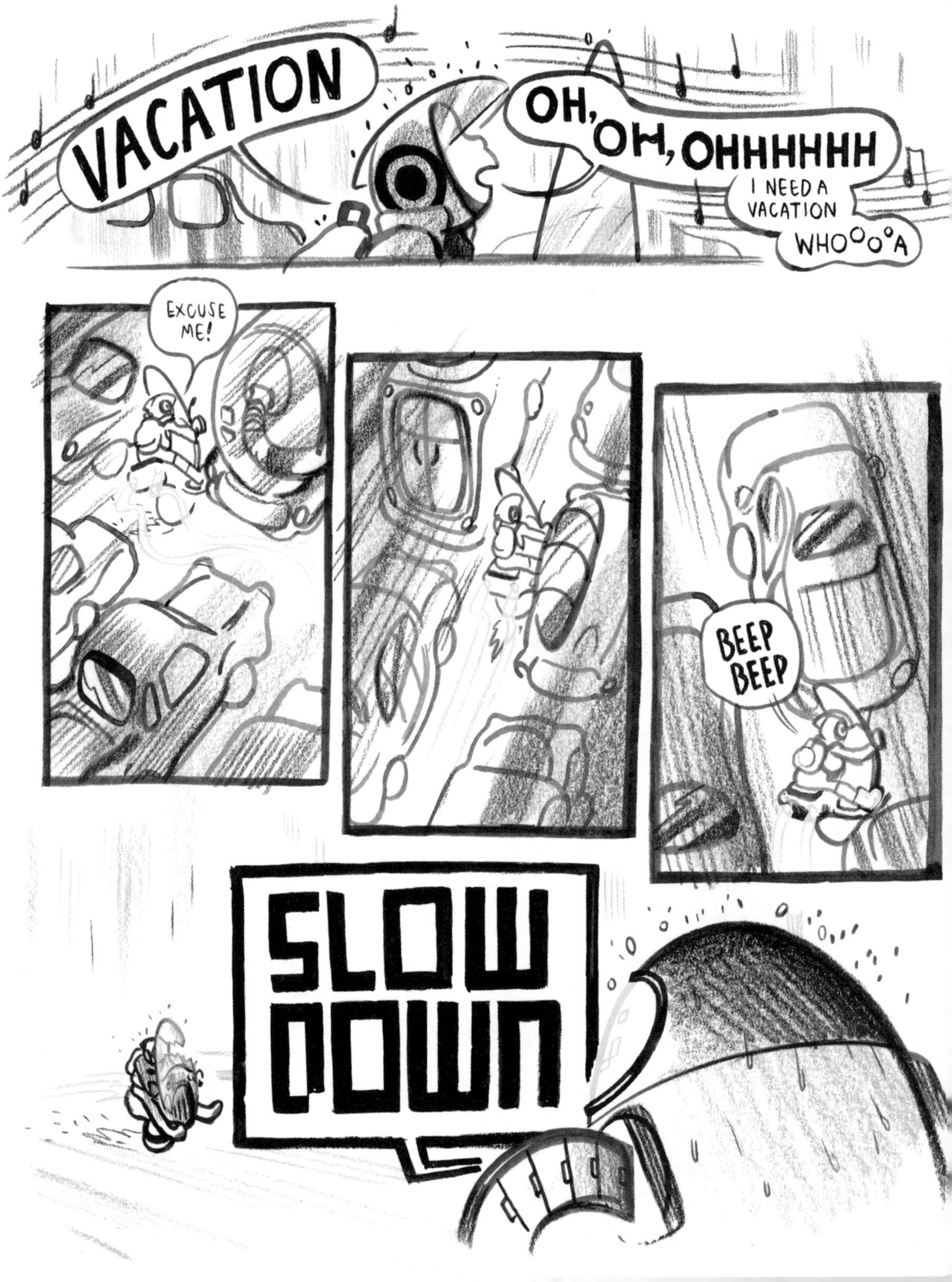
VACATION
OH, OH, OHHHHHH
I NEED A VACATION WHOOOOA
EXCUSE ME!
BEEP BEEP
SLOW DOWN

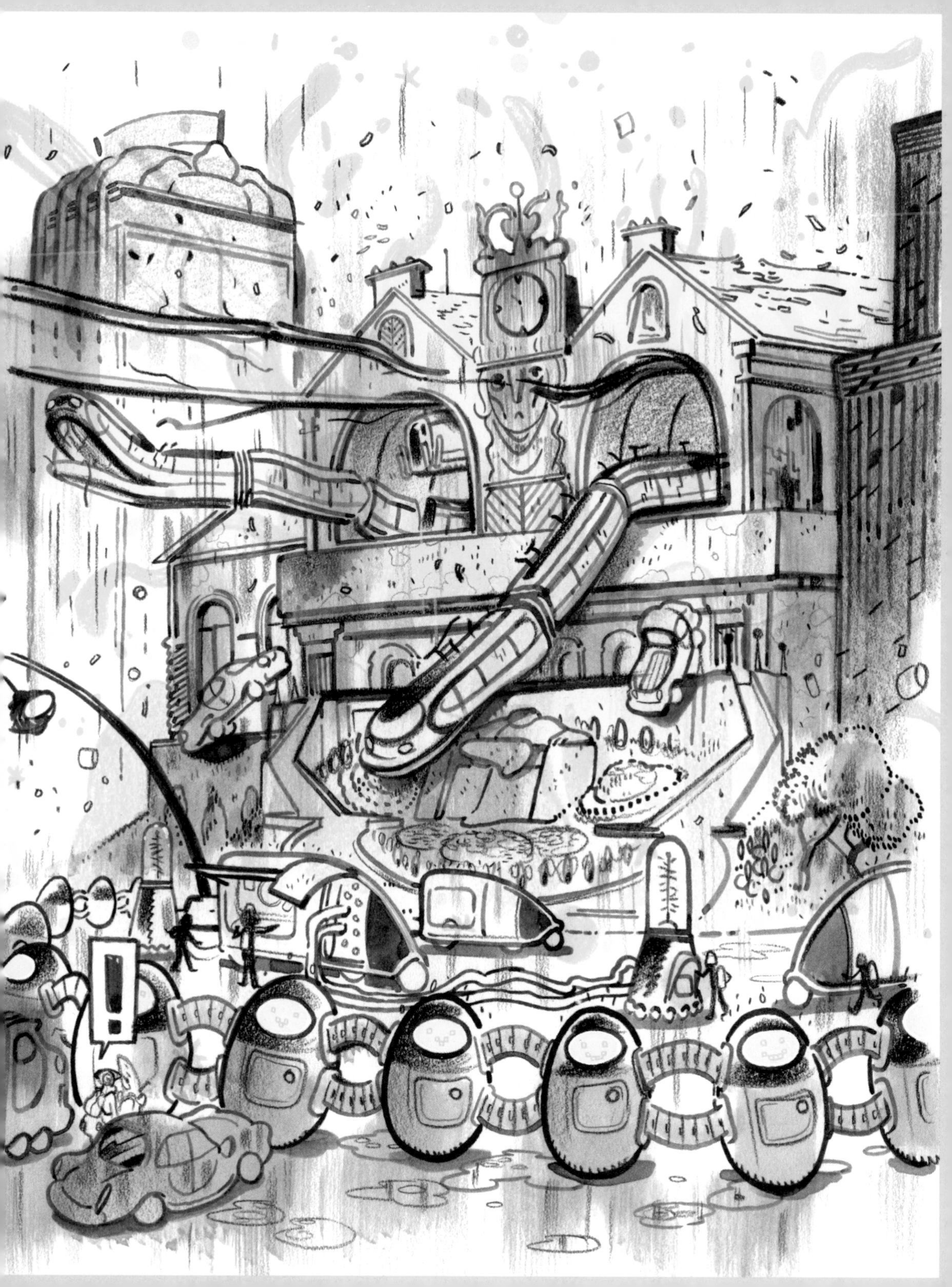
!

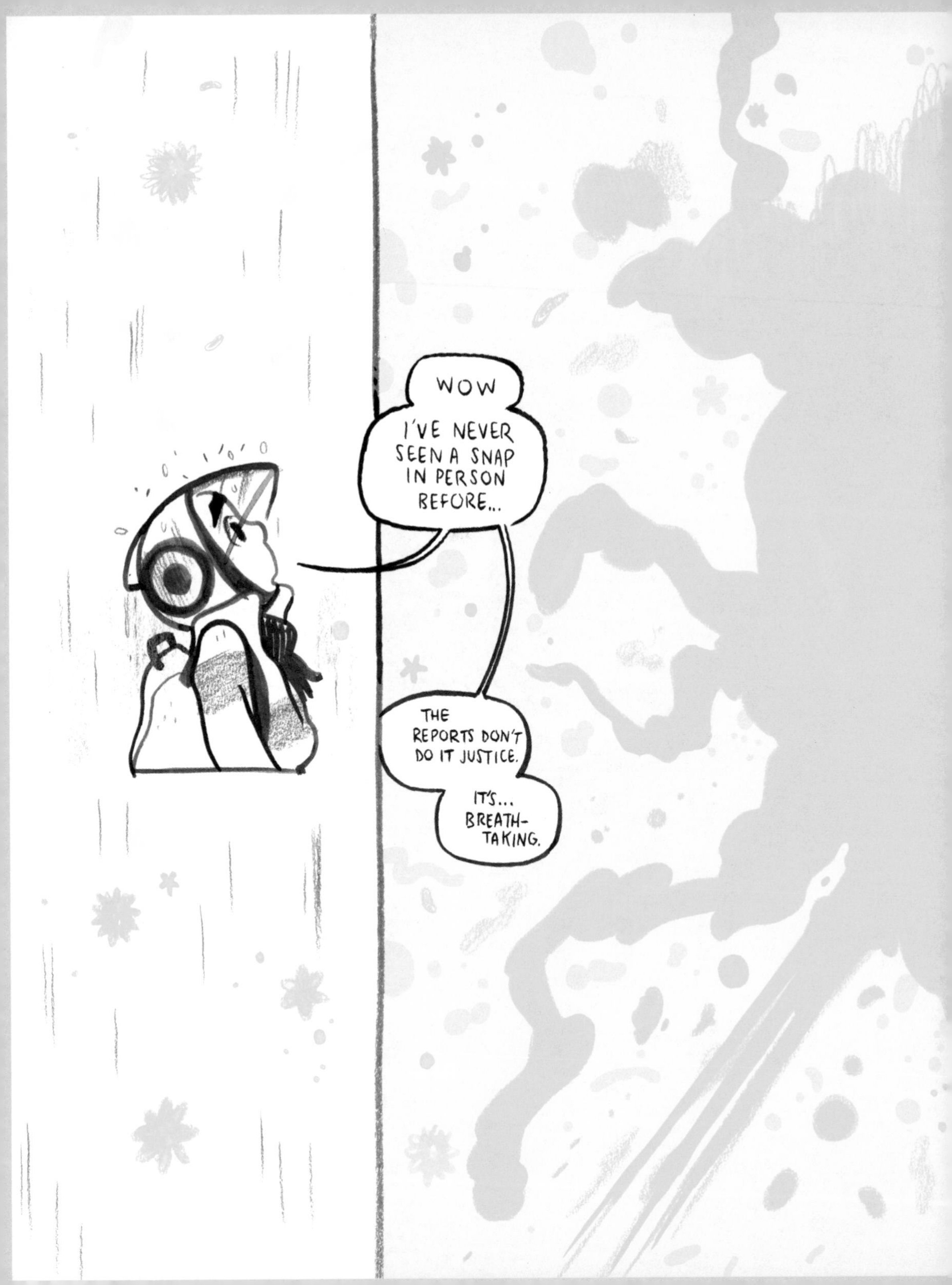
WOW
I'VE NEVER SEEN A SNAP IN PERSON BEFORE...
THE REPORTS DON'T DO IT JUSTICE.
IT'S... BREATH-TAKING.

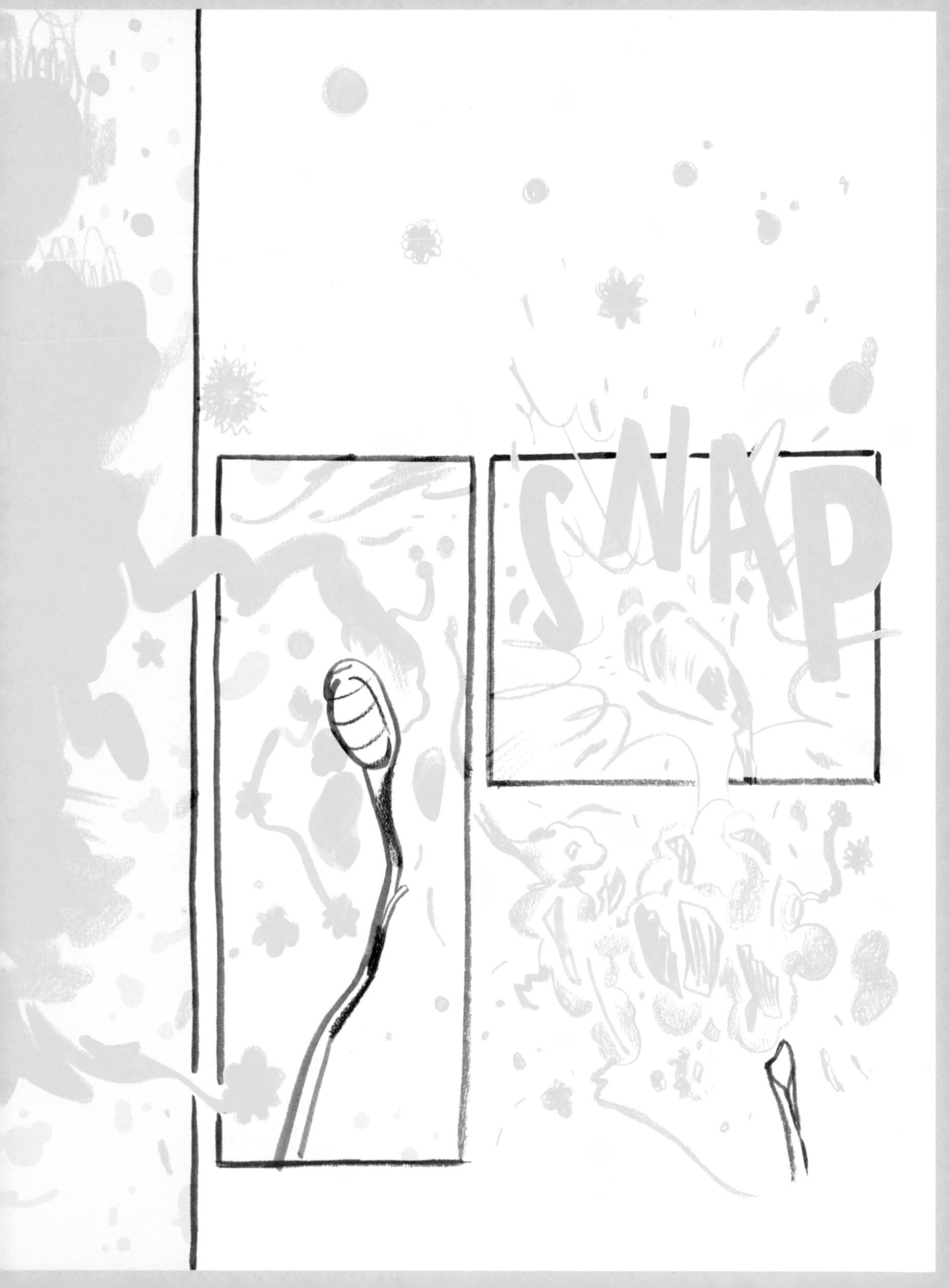
SNAP

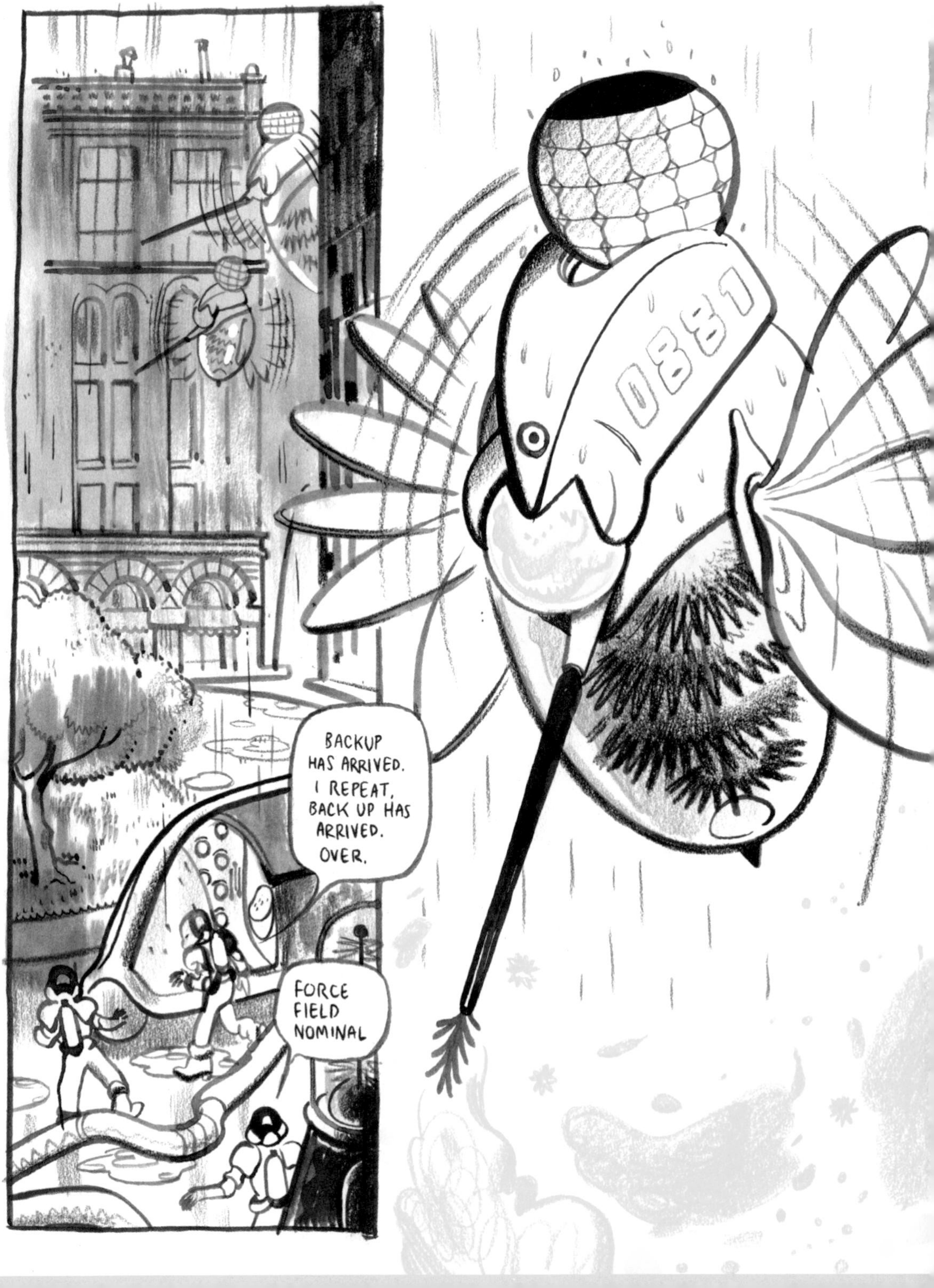
BACKUP HAS ARRIVED. I REPEAT, BACK UP HAS ARRIVED. OVER.
FORCE FIELD NOMINAL
0881

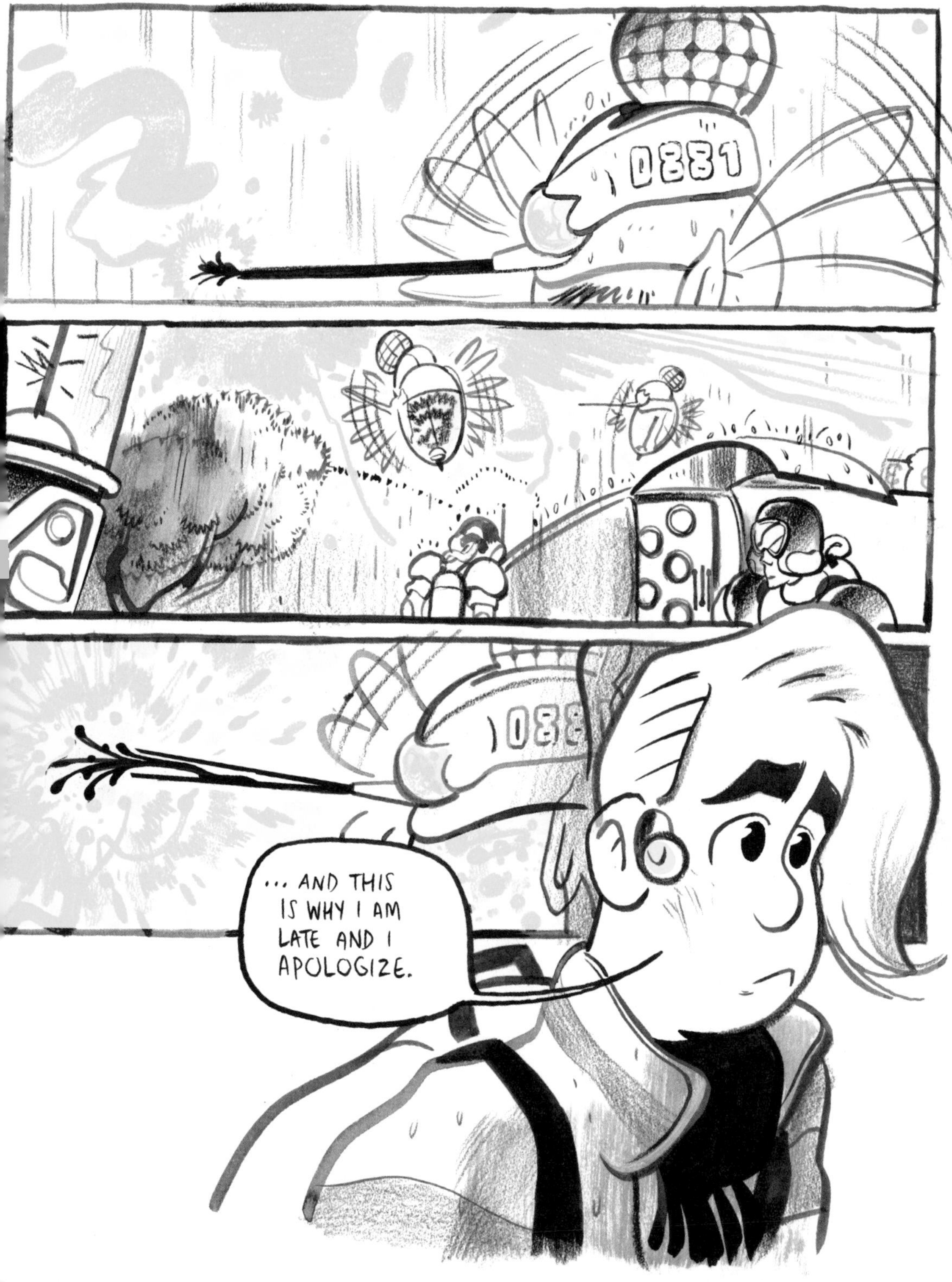
0881
0880
... AND THIS IS WHY I AM LATE AND I APOLOGIZE.

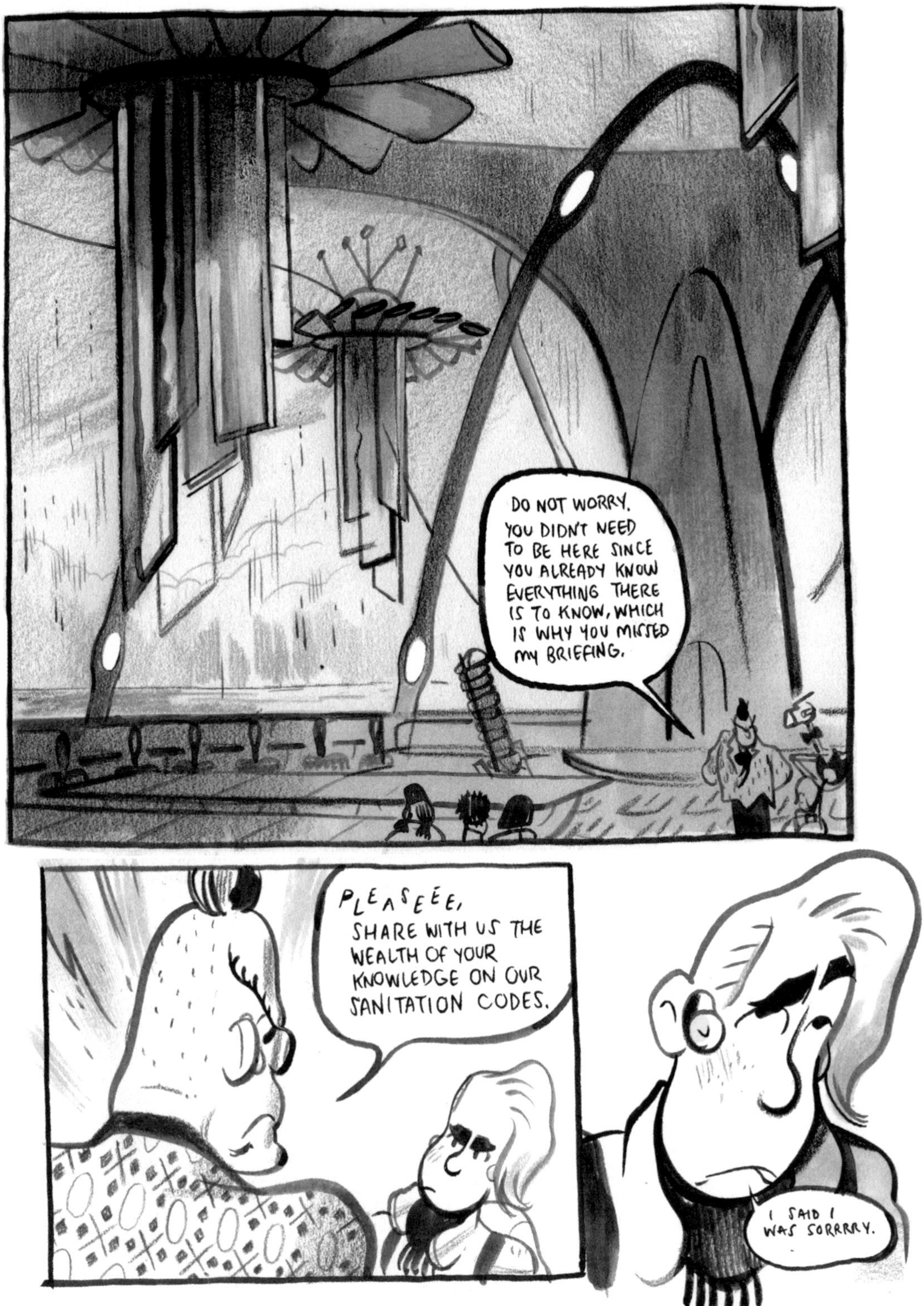
DO NOT WORRY. YOU DIDN'T NEED TO BE HERE SINCE YOU ALREADY KNOW EVERYTHING THERE IS TO KNOW, WHICH IS WHY YOU MISSED MY BRIEFING.
PLEASEEE, SHARE WITH US THE WEALTH OF YOUR KNOWLEDGE ON OUR SANITATION CODES.
I SAID I WAS SORRRRY.

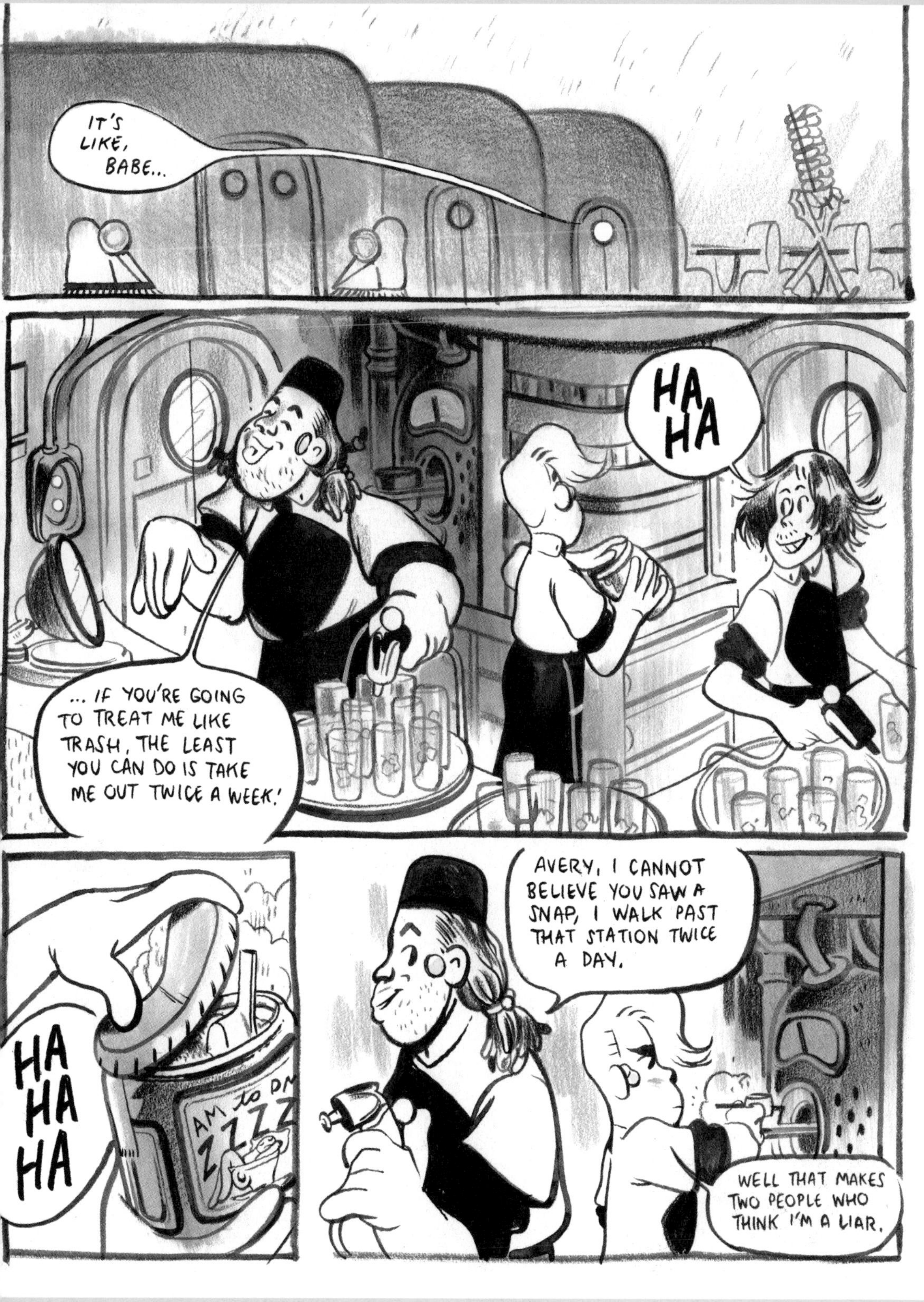
IT'S LIKE, BABE...
HA HA
... IF YOU'RE GOING TO TREAT ME LIKE TRASH, THE LEAST YOU CAN DO IS TAKE ME OUT TWICE A WEEK!
HA HA HA
AM to DM
ZZZZ
AVERY, I CANNOT BELIEVE YOU SAW A SNAP, I WALK PAST THAT STATION TWICE A DAY.
WELL THAT MAKES TWO PEOPLE WHO THINK I'M A LIAR.

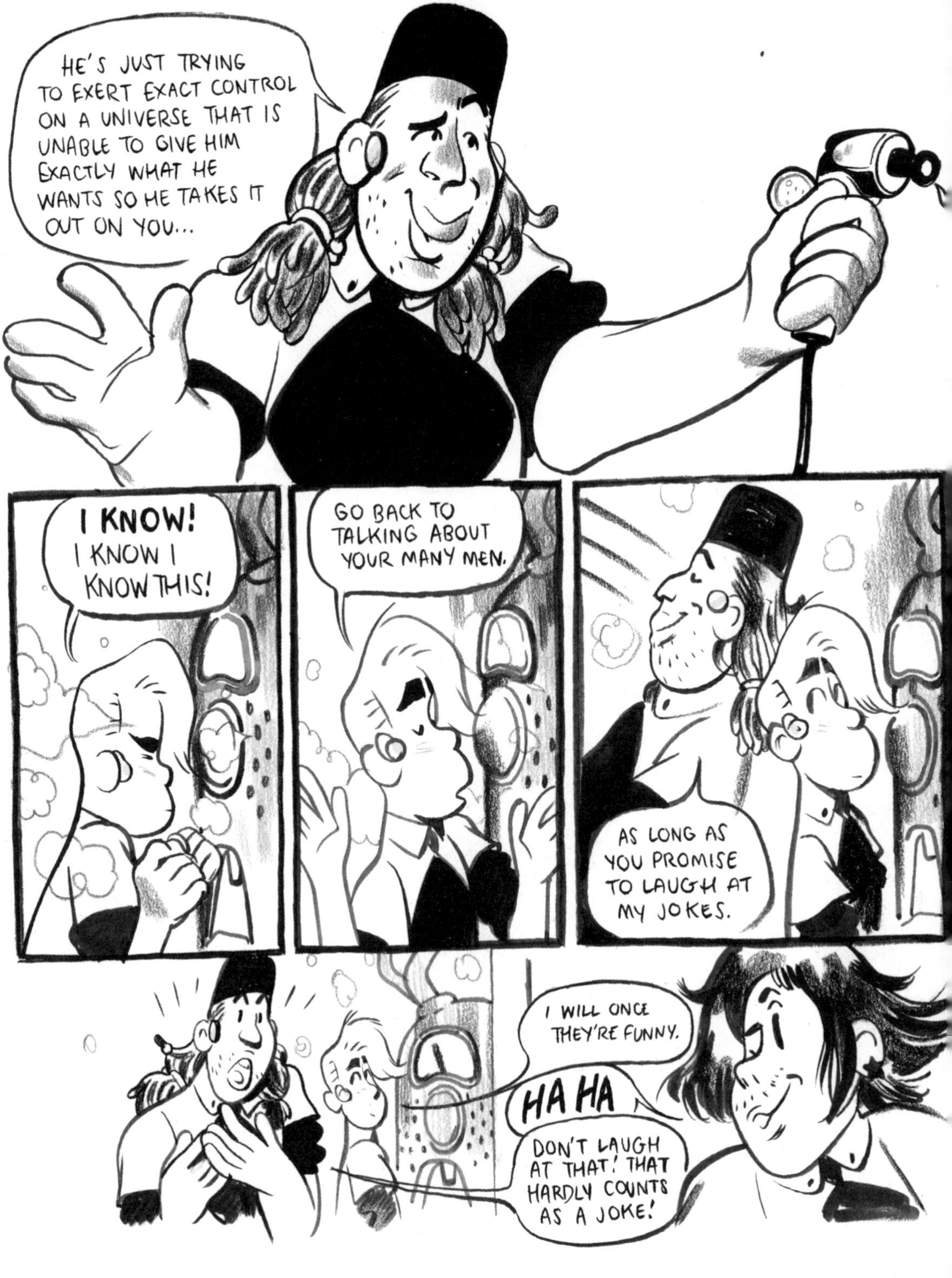
HE'S JUST TRYING TO EXERT EXACT CONTROL ON A UNIVERSE THAT IS UNABLE TO GIVE HIM EXACTLY WHAT HE WANTS SO HE TAKES IT OUT ON YOU...
I KNOW! I KNOW I KNOW THIS!
GO BACK TO TALKING ABOUT YOUR MANY MEN.
AS LONG AS YOU PROMISE TO LAUGH AT MY JOKES.
I WILL ONCE THEY'RE FUNNY.
HA HA
DON'T LAUGH AT THAT! THAT HARDLY COUNTS AS A JOKE!

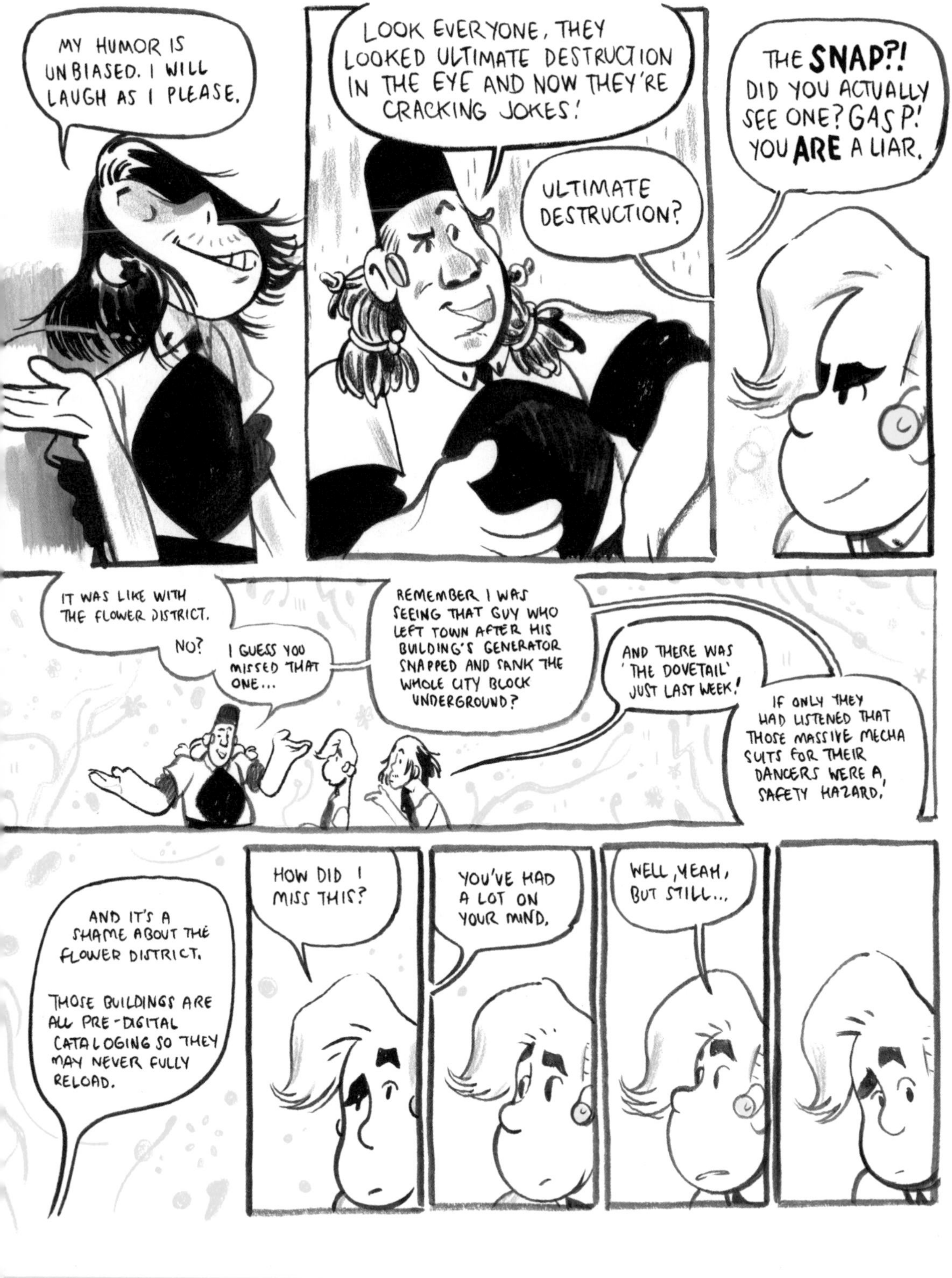
MY HUMOR IS UNBIASED. I WILL LAUGH AS I PLEASE.
LOOK EVERYONE, THEY LOOKED ULTIMATE DESTRUCTION IN THE EYE AND NOW THEY'RE CRACKING JOKES!
ULTIMATE DESTRUCTION?
THE SNAP?! DID YOU ACTUALLY SEE ONE? GASP! YOU ARE A LIAR.
IT WAS LIKE WITH THE FLOWER DISTRICT.
NO?
I GUESS YOU MISSED THAT ONE...
REMEMBER I WAS SEEING THAT GUY WHO LEFT TOWN AFTER HIS BUILDING'S GENERATOR SNAPPED AND SANK THE WHOLE CITY BLOCK UNDERGROUND?
AND THERE WAS 'THE DOVETAIL' JUST LAST WEEK!
IF ONLY THEY HAD LISTENED THAT THOSE MASSIVE MECHA SUITS FOR THEIR DANCERS WERE A SAFETY HAZARD!
AND IT'S A SHAME ABOUT THE FLOWER DISTRICT.
THOSE BUILDINGS ARE ALL PRE-DIGITAL CATALOGING SO THEY MAY NEVER FULLY RELOAD.
HOW DID I MISS THIS?
YOU'VE HAD A LOT ON YOUR MIND.
WELL, YEAH, BUT STILL...

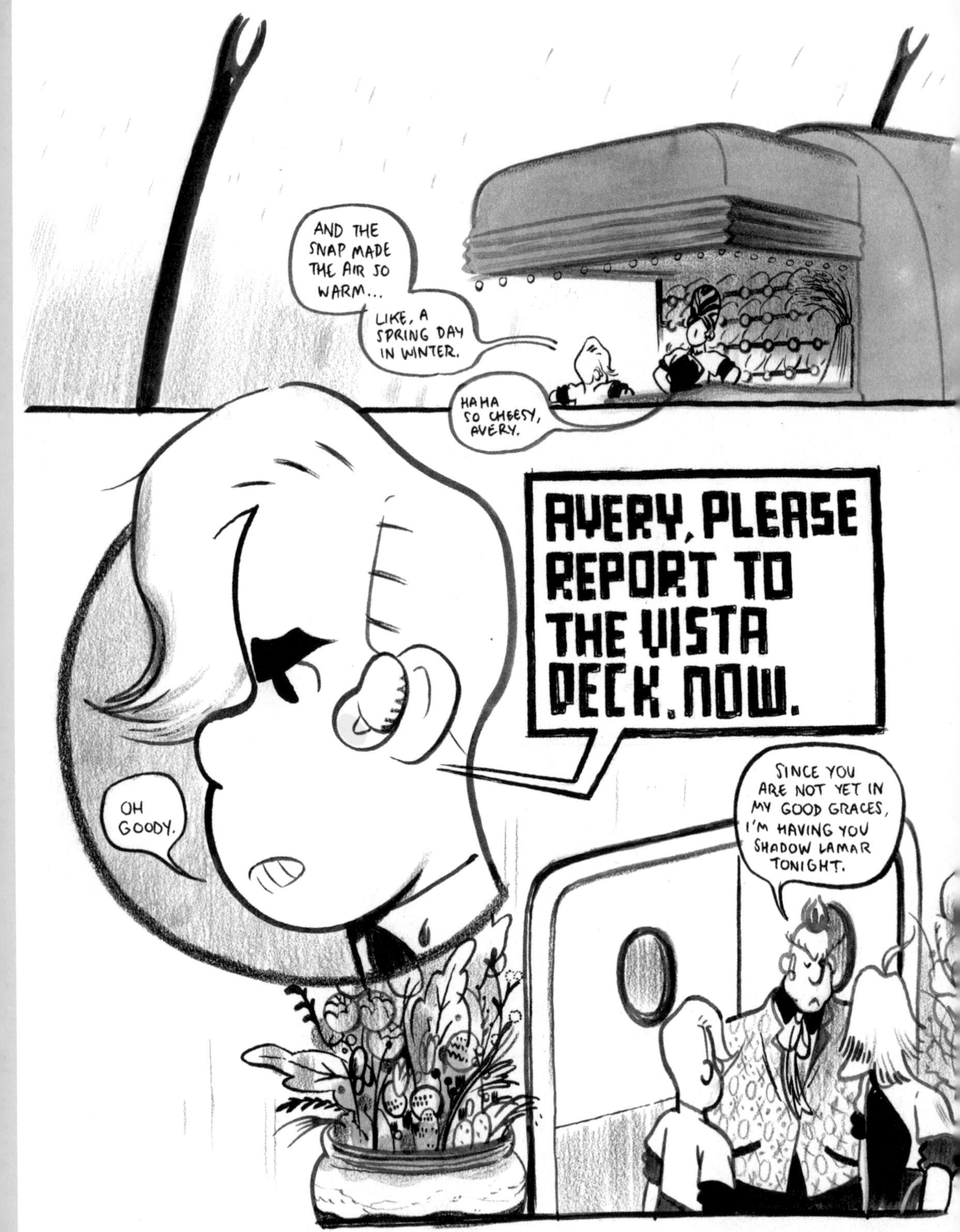

AND THE SNAP MADE THE AIR SO WARM...
LIKE, A SPRING DAY IN WINTER.
HAHA SO CHEESY, AVERY.
AVERY, PLEASE REPORT TO THE VISTA DECK. NOW.
OH GOODY.
SINCE YOU ARE NOT YET IN MY GOOD GRACES, I'M HAVING YOU SHADOW LAMAR TONIGHT.

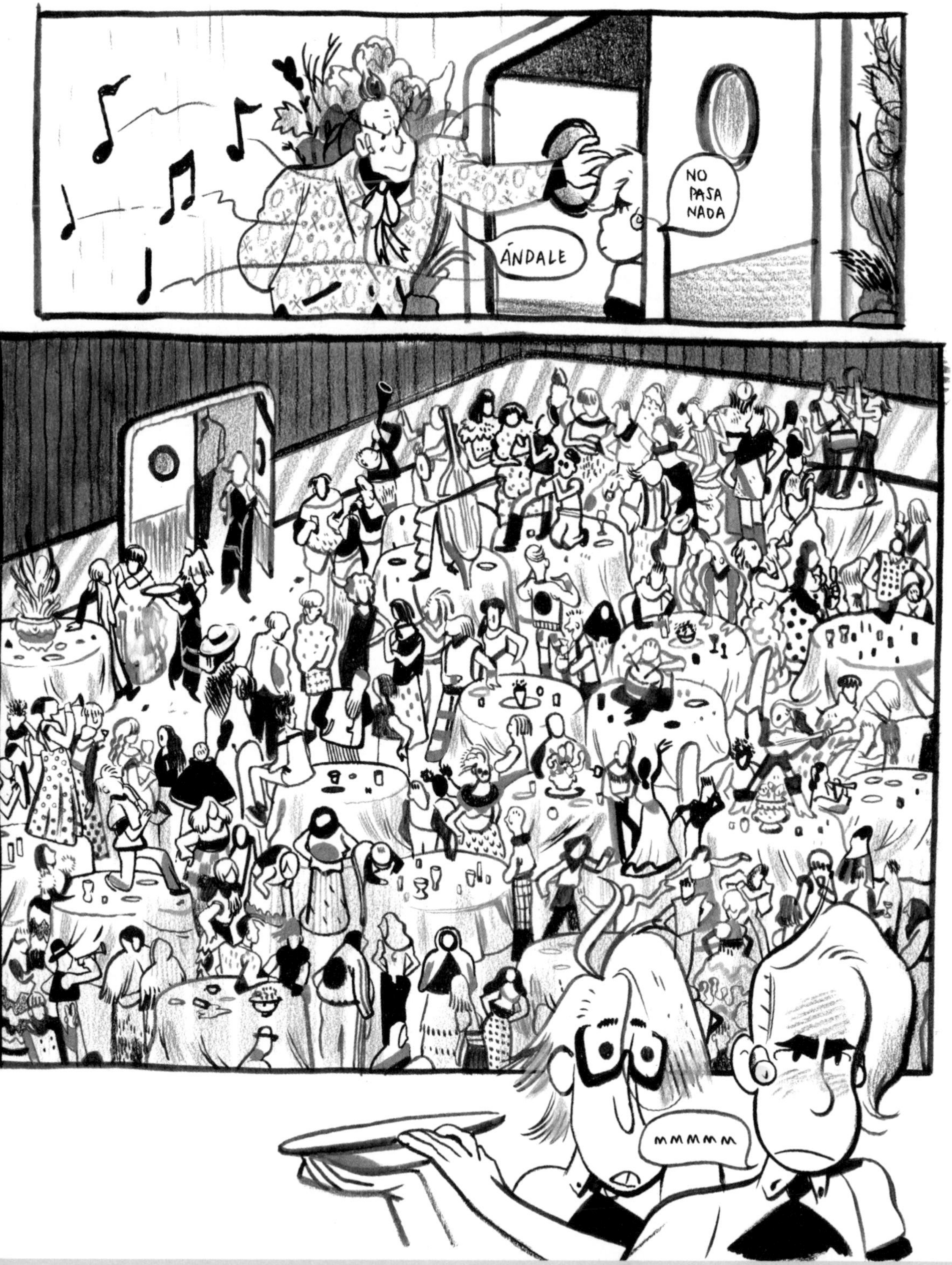
ÁNDALE
NO PASA NADA
MMMMM

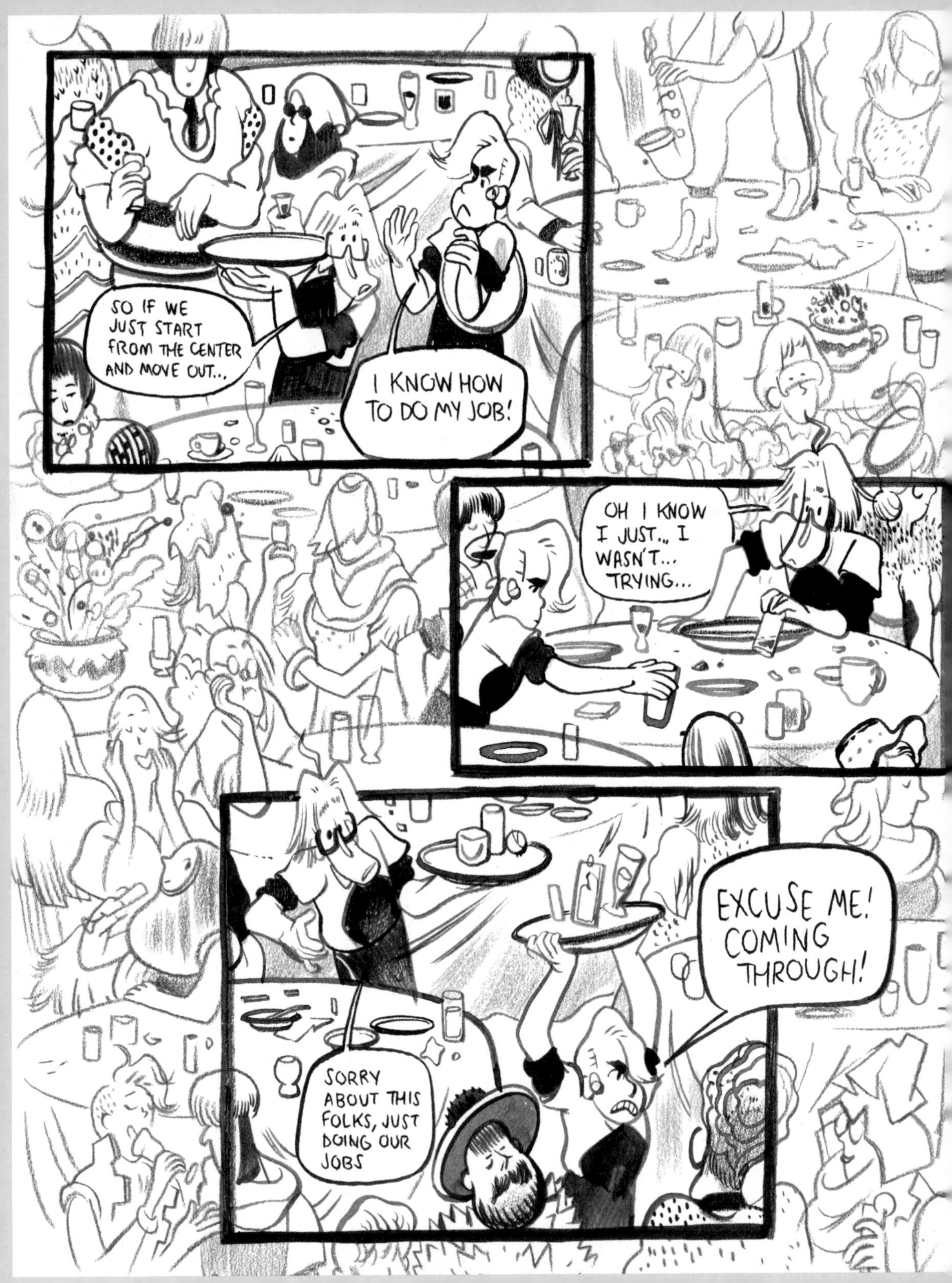
SO IF WE JUST START FROM THE CENTER AND MOVE OUT...
I KNOW HOW TO DO MY JOB!
OH I KNOW I JUST... I WASN'T... TRYING...
EXCUSE ME! COMING THROUGH!
SORRY ABOUT THIS FOLKS, JUST DOING OUR JOBS

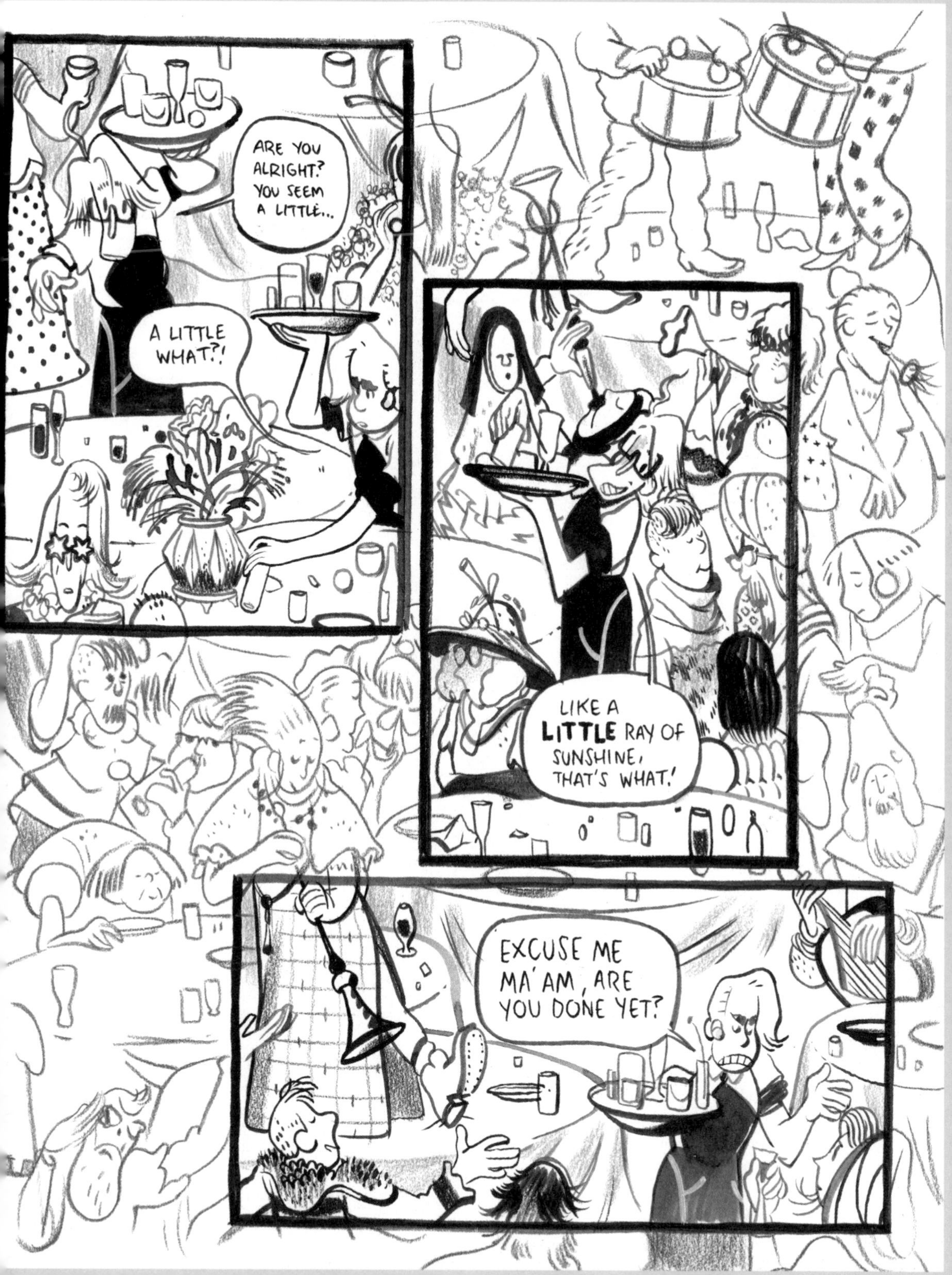
ARE YOU ALRIGHT? YOU SEEM A LITTLE...
A LITTLE WHAT?!
LIKE A LITTLE RAY OF SUNSHINE, THAT'S WHAT!
EXCUSE ME MA'AM, ARE YOU DONE YET?

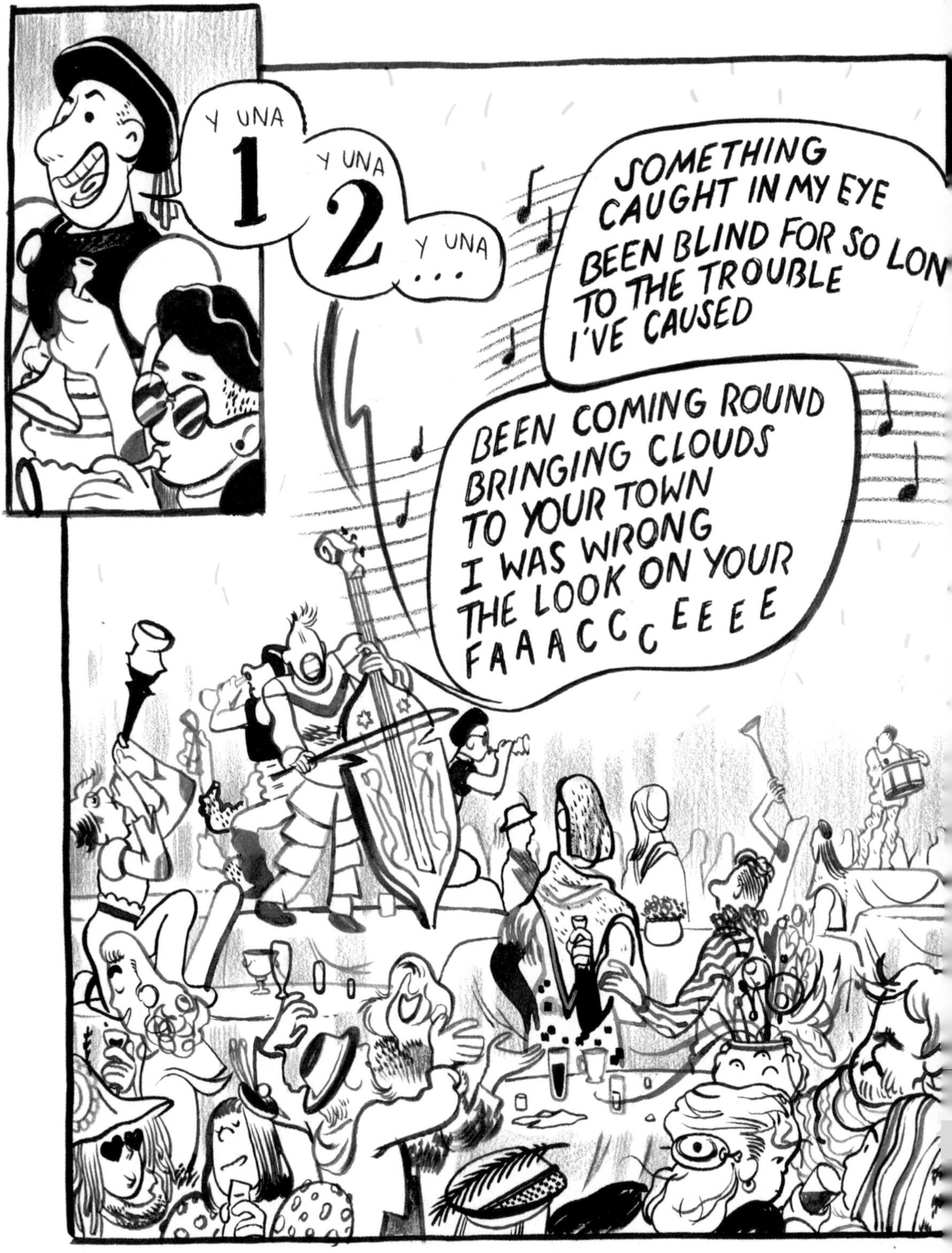
Y UNA 1
Y UNA 2
Y UNA . . .
SOMETHING CAUGHT IN MY EYE BEEN BLIND FOR SO LON TO THE TROUBLE I'VE CAUSED
BEEN COMING ROUND BRINGING CLOUDS TO YOUR TOWN I WAS WRONG THE LOOK ON YOUR FAAACCCEEEE

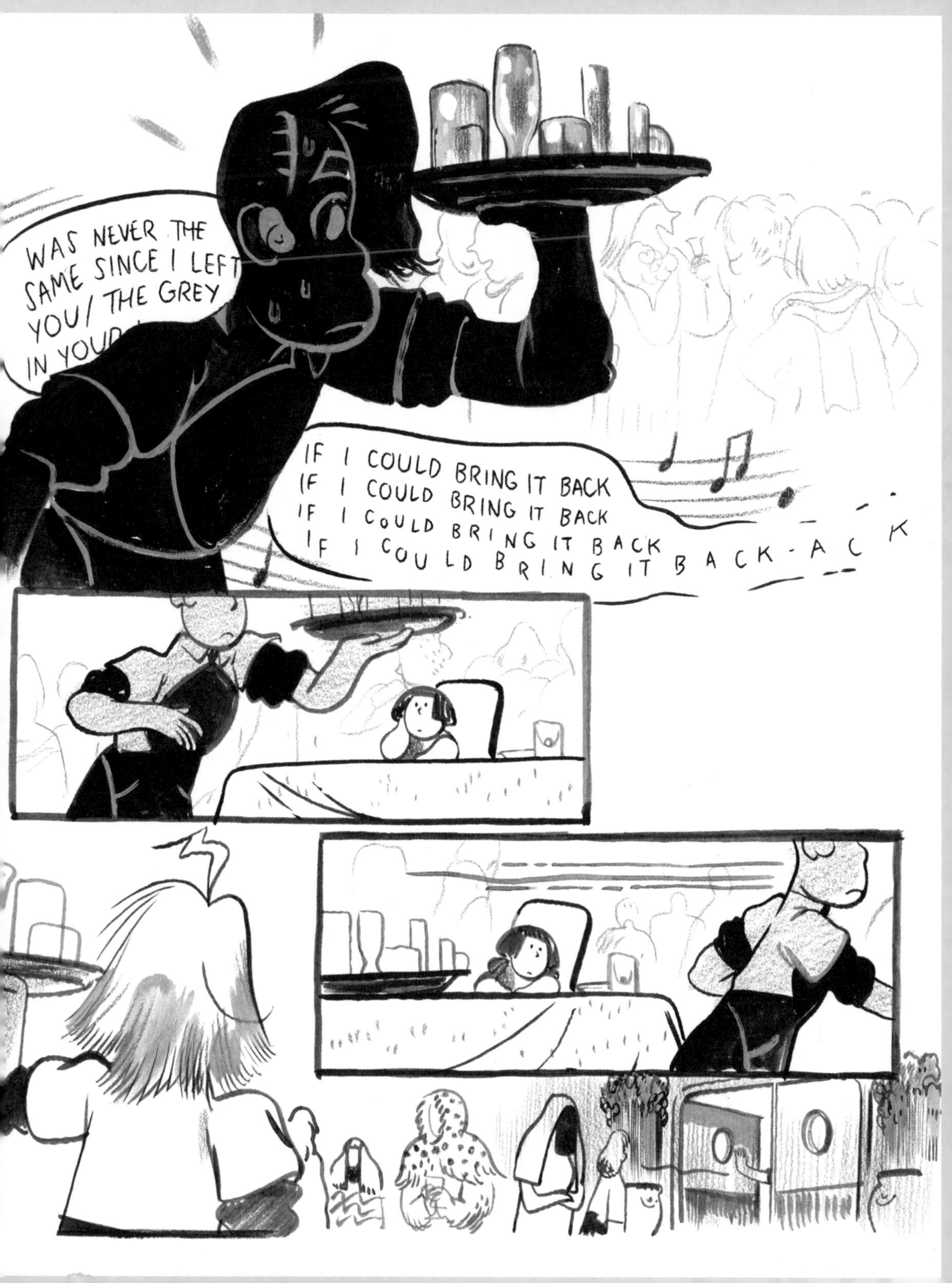

WAS NEVER THE SAME SINCE I LEFT YOU/ THE GREY IN YOUR
IF I COULD BRING IT BACK
IF I COULD BRING IT BACK
IF I COULD BRING IT BACK
IF I COULD BRING IT BACK
IF I COULD BRING IT BACK-ACK

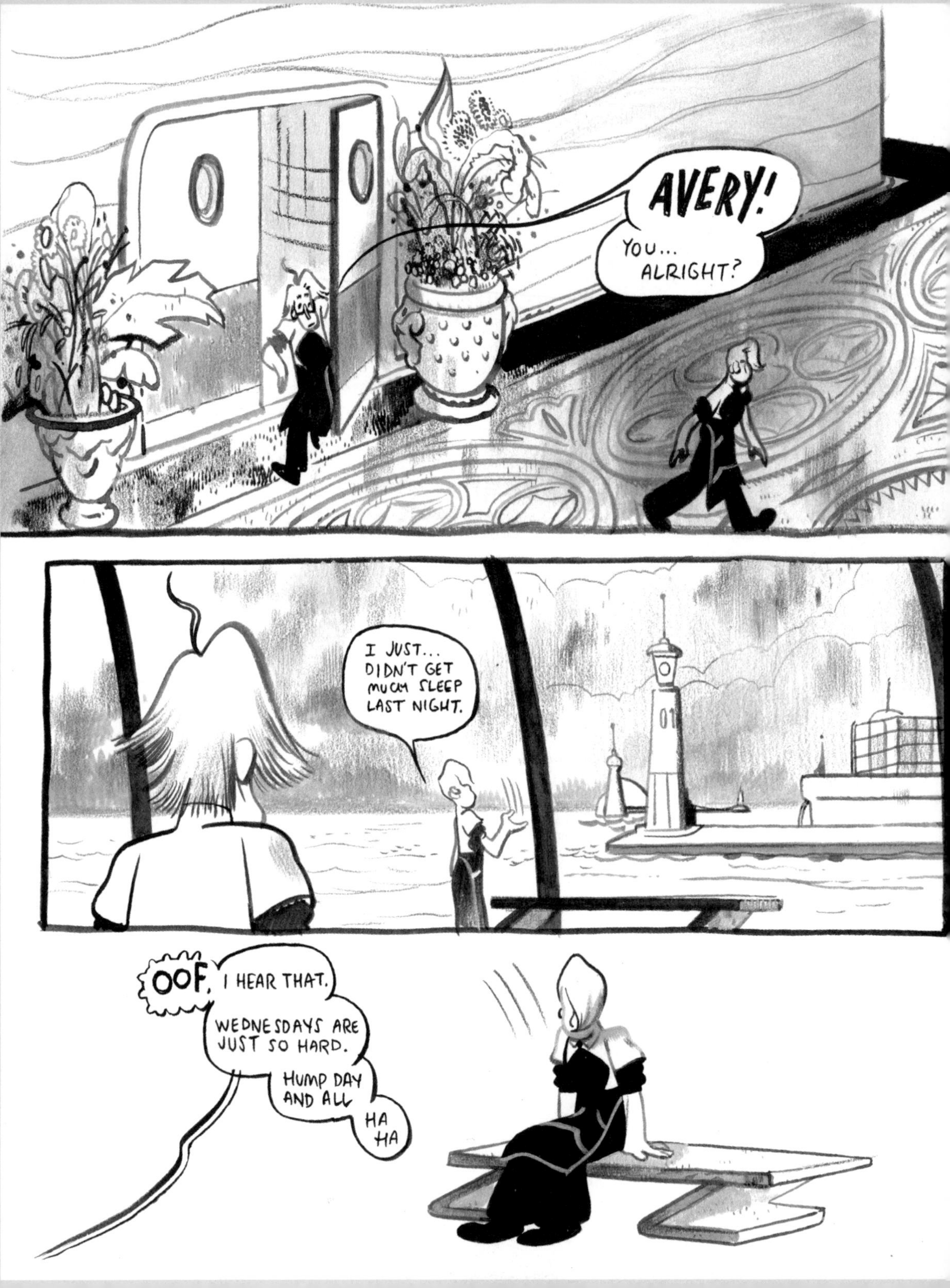
AVERY!
YOU... ALRIGHT?
I JUST... DIDN'T GET MUCH SLEEP LAST NIGHT.
OOF.
I HEAR THAT.
WEDNESDAYS ARE JUST SO HARD.
HUMP DAY AND ALL
HA HA

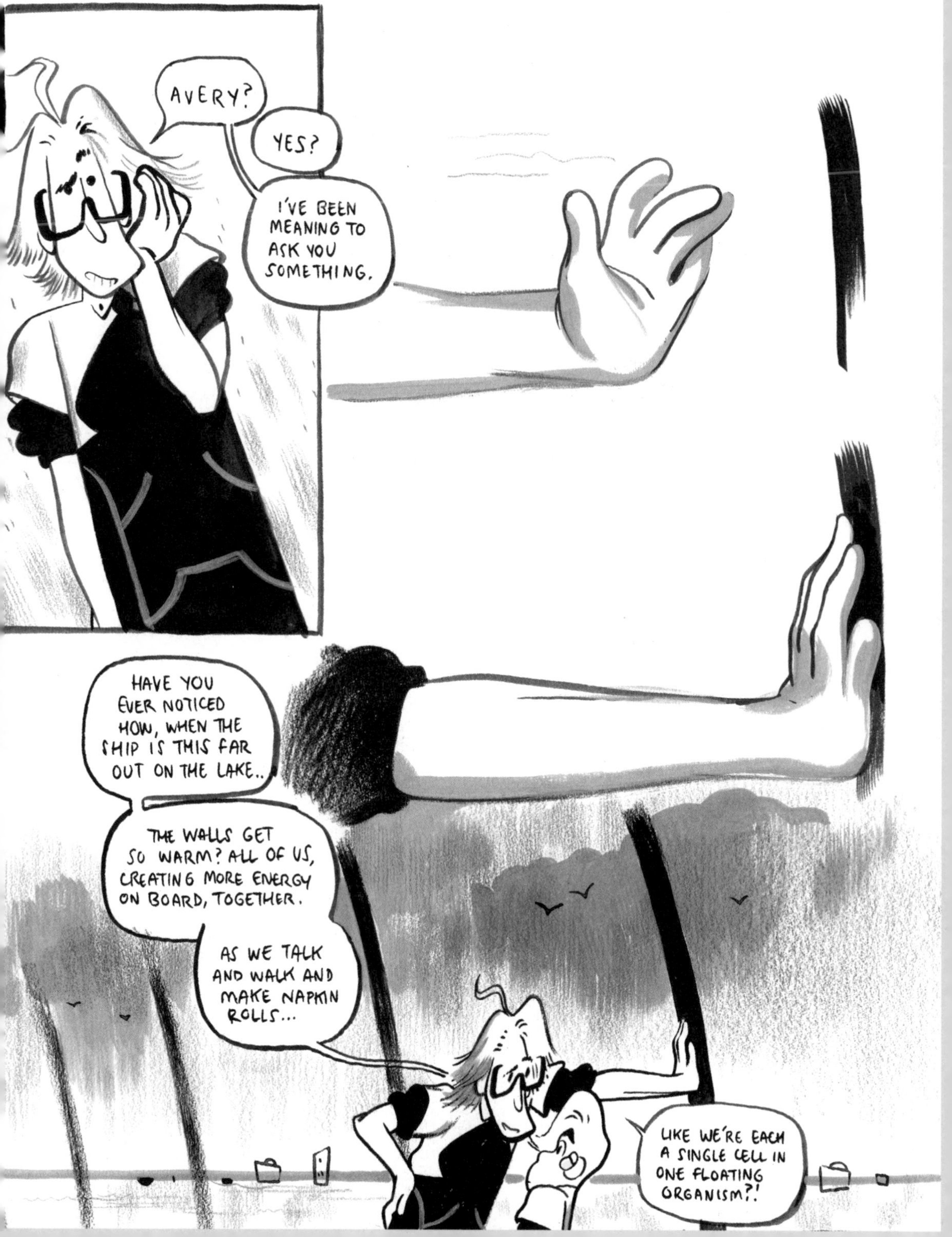
AVERY?
YES?
I'VE BEEN MEANING TO ASK YOU SOMETHING.
HAVE YOU EVER NOTICED HOW, WHEN THE SHIP IS THIS FAR OUT ON THE LAKE..
THE WALLS GET SO WARM? ALL OF US, CREATING MORE ENERGY ON BOARD, TOGETHER.
AS WE TALK AND WALK AND MAKE NAPKIN ROLLS...
LIKE WE'RE EACH A SINGLE CELL IN ONE FLOATING ORGANISM?!

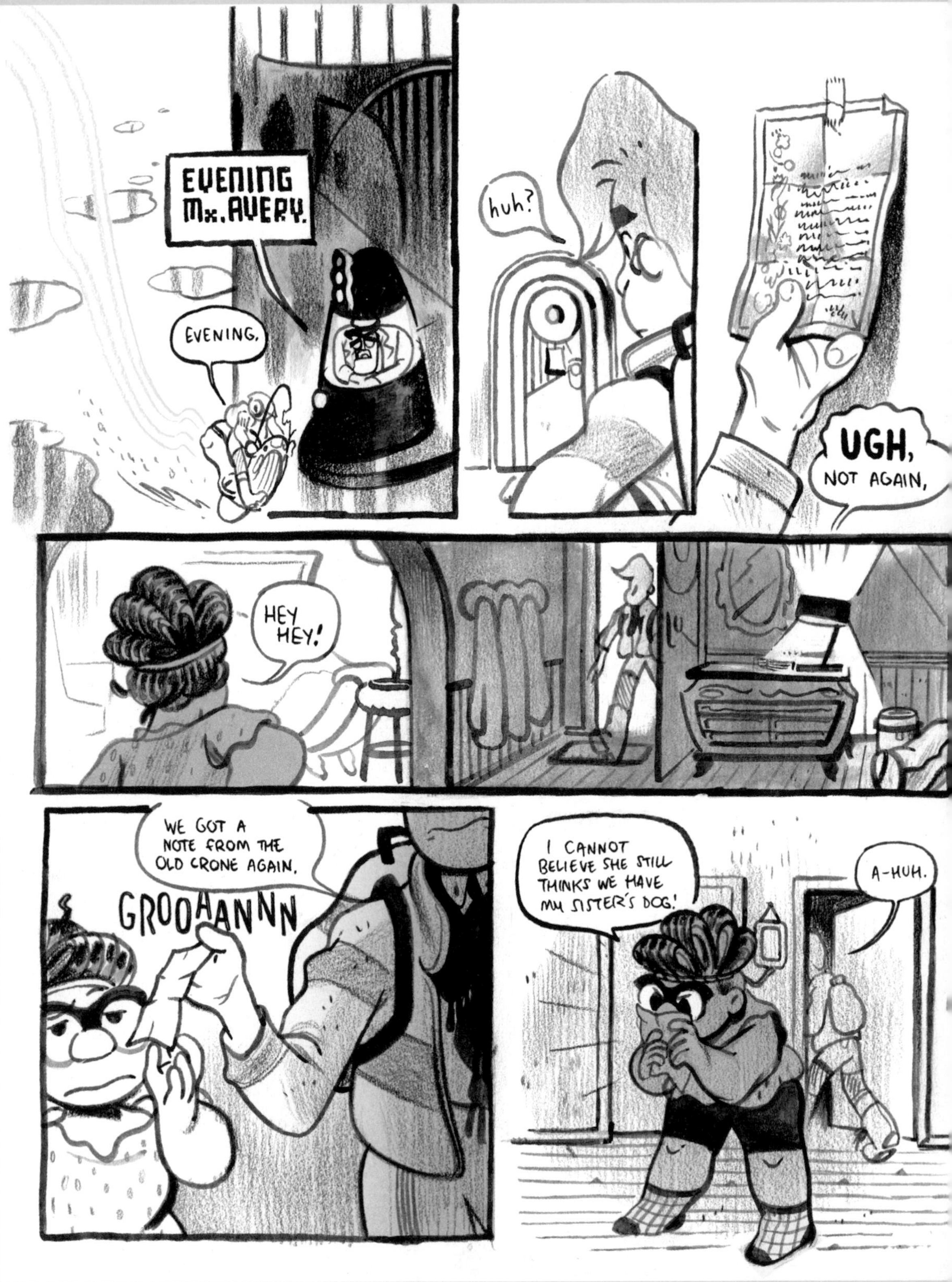
EVENING Mx. AVERY.
EVENING.
huh?
UGH, NOT AGAIN,
HEY HEY!
WE GOT A NOTE FROM THE OLD CRONE AGAIN.
GROOAANNN
I CANNOT BELIEVE SHE STILL THINKS WE HAVE MY SISTER'S DOG!
A-HUH.

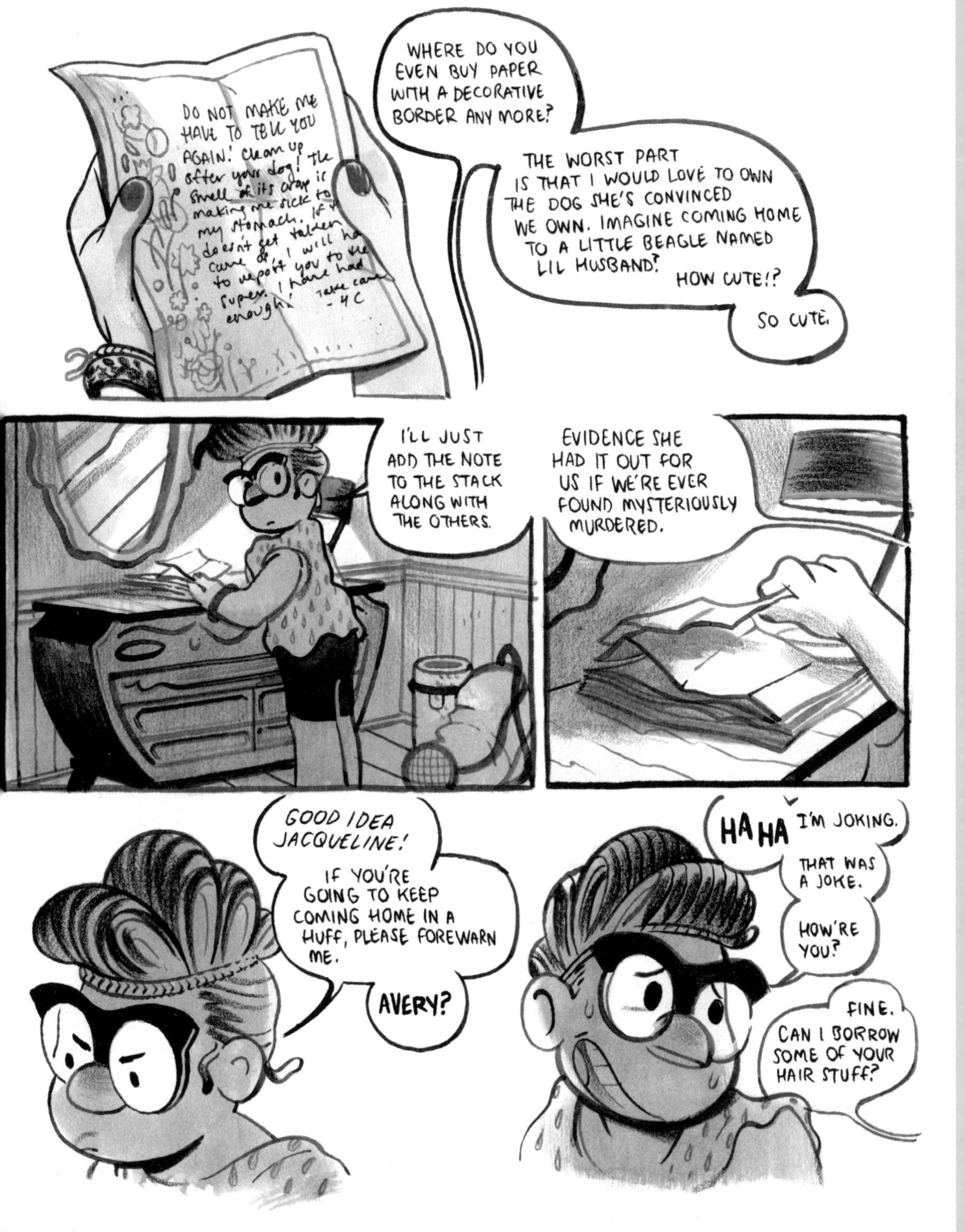

DO NOT MAKE ME HAVE TO TELL YOU AGAIN! Clean up after your dog! The smell of its crap is making me sick to my stomach. If it doesn't get taken care of, I will have to report you to the super. I have had enough! Take care -4C
WHERE DO YOU EVEN BUY PAPER WITH A DECORATIVE BORDER ANY MORE?
THE WORST PART IS THAT I WOULD LOVE TO OWN THE DOG SHE'S CONVINCED WE OWN. IMAGINE COMING HOME TO A LITTLE BEAGLE NAMED LIL HUSBAND?
HOW CUTE!?
SO CUTE.
I'LL JUST ADD THE NOTE TO THE STACK ALONG WITH THE OTHERS.
EVIDENCE SHE HAD IT OUT FOR US IF WE'RE EVER FOUND MYSTERIOUSLY MURDERED.
GOOD IDEA JACQUELINE!
IF YOU'RE GOING TO KEEP COMING HOME IN A HUFF, PLEASE FOREWARN ME.
AVERY?
HAHA I'M JOKING.
THAT WAS A JOKE.
HOW'RE YOU?
FINE. CAN I BORROW SOME OF YOUR HAIR STUFF?

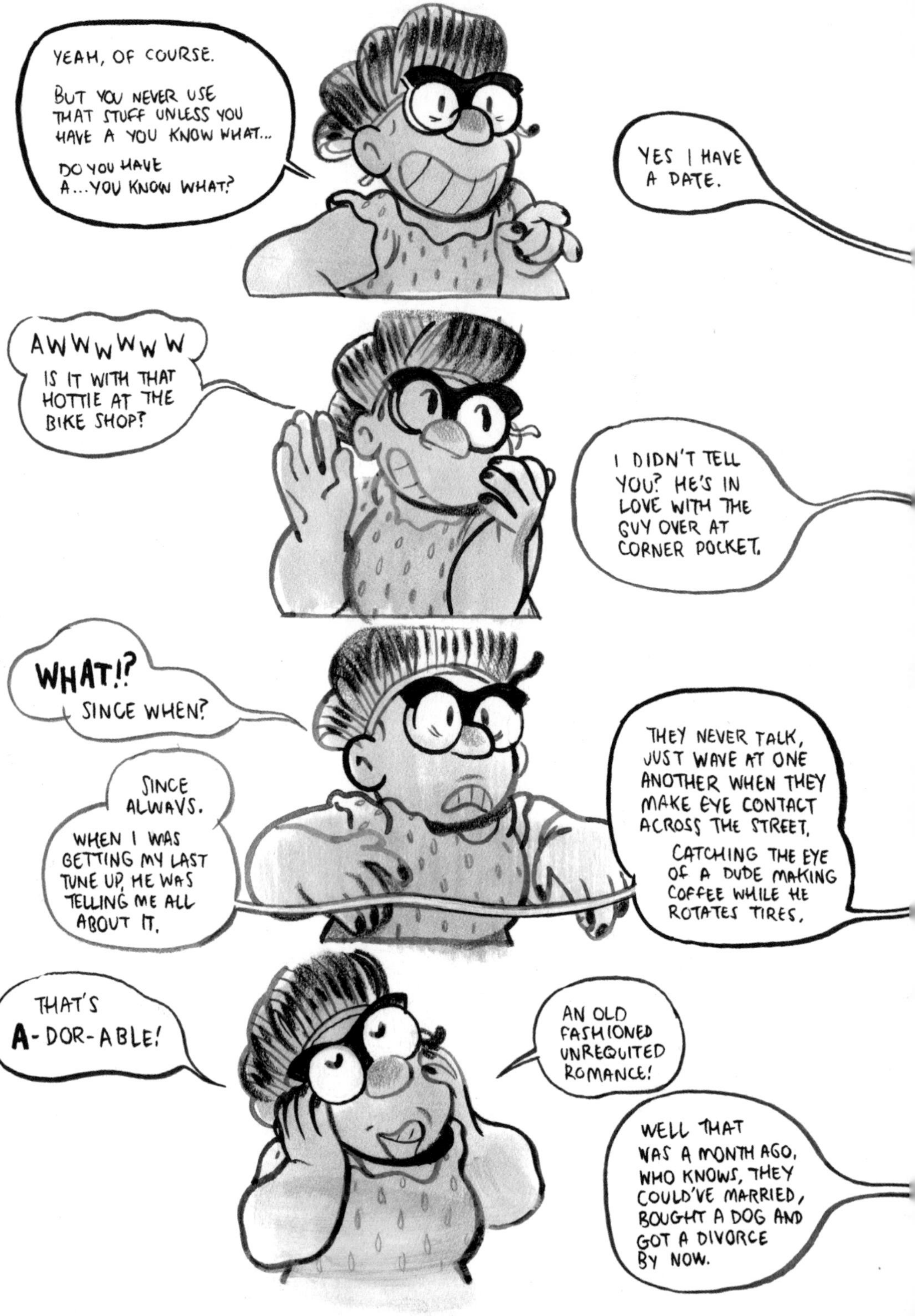
YEAH, OF COURSE.
BUT YOU NEVER USE THAT STUFF UNLESS YOU HAVE A YOU KNOW WHAT...
DO YOU HAVE A...YOU KNOW WHAT?
YES I HAVE A DATE.
AWWWWWWW
IS IT WITH THAT HOTTIE AT THE BIKE SHOP?
I DIDN'T TELL YOU? HE'S IN LOVE WITH THE GUY OVER AT CORNER POCKET.
WHAT!?
SINCE WHEN?
SINCE ALWAYS.
WHEN I WAS GETTING MY LAST TUNE UP, HE WAS TELLING ME ALL ABOUT IT.
THEY NEVER TALK, JUST WAVE AT ONE ANOTHER WHEN THEY MAKE EYE CONTACT ACROSS THE STREET.
CATCHING THE EYE OF A DUDE MAKING COFFEE WHILE HE ROTATES TIRES.
THAT'S A-DOR-ABLE!
AN OLD FASHIONED UNREQUITED ROMANCE!
WELL THAT WAS A MONTH AGO, WHO KNOWS, THEY COULD'VE MARRIED, BOUGHT A DOG AND GOT A DIVORCE BY NOW.

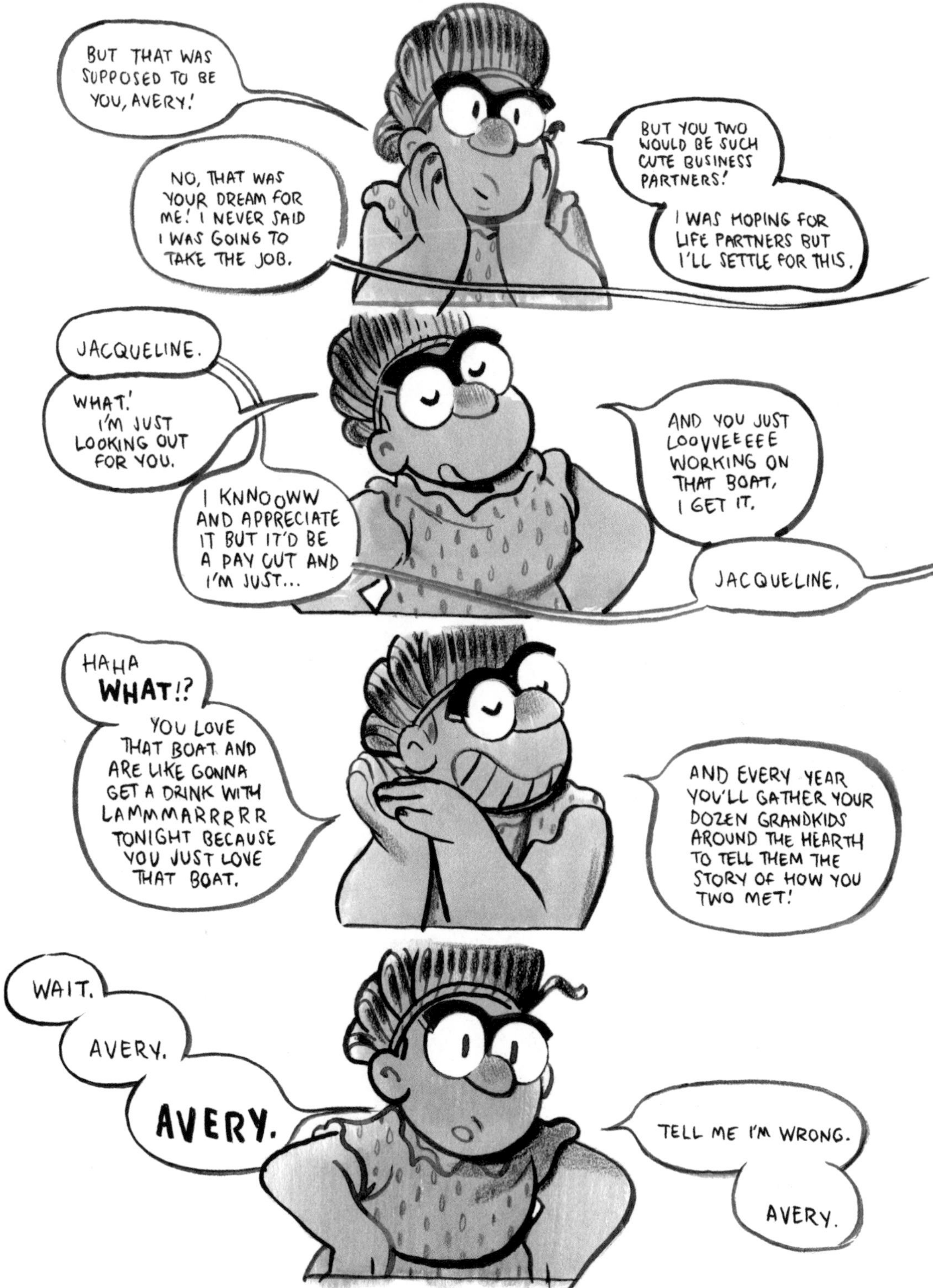
BUT THAT WAS SUPPOSED TO BE YOU, AVERY!
NO, THAT WAS YOUR DREAM FOR ME! I NEVER SAID I WAS GOING TO TAKE THE JOB.
BUT YOU TWO WOULD BE SUCH CUTE BUSINESS PARTNERS!
I WAS HOPING FOR LIFE PARTNERS BUT I'LL SETTLE FOR THIS.
JACQUELINE.
WHAT! I'M JUST LOOKING OUT FOR YOU.
I KNNOOWW AND APPRECIATE IT BUT IT'D BE A PAY CUT AND I'M JUST...
AND YOU JUST LOOVVEEEEE WORKING ON THAT BOAT, I GET IT.
JACQUELINE.
HAHA WHAT!?
YOU LOVE THAT BOAT AND ARE LIKE GONNA GET A DRINK WITH LAMMMARRRRR TONIGHT BECAUSE YOU JUST LOVE THAT BOAT.
AND EVERY YEAR YOU'LL GATHER YOUR DOZEN GRANDKIDS AROUND THE HEARTH TO TELL THEM THE STORY OF HOW YOU TWO MET!
WAIT.
AVERY.
AVERY.
TELL ME I'M WRONG.
AVERY.

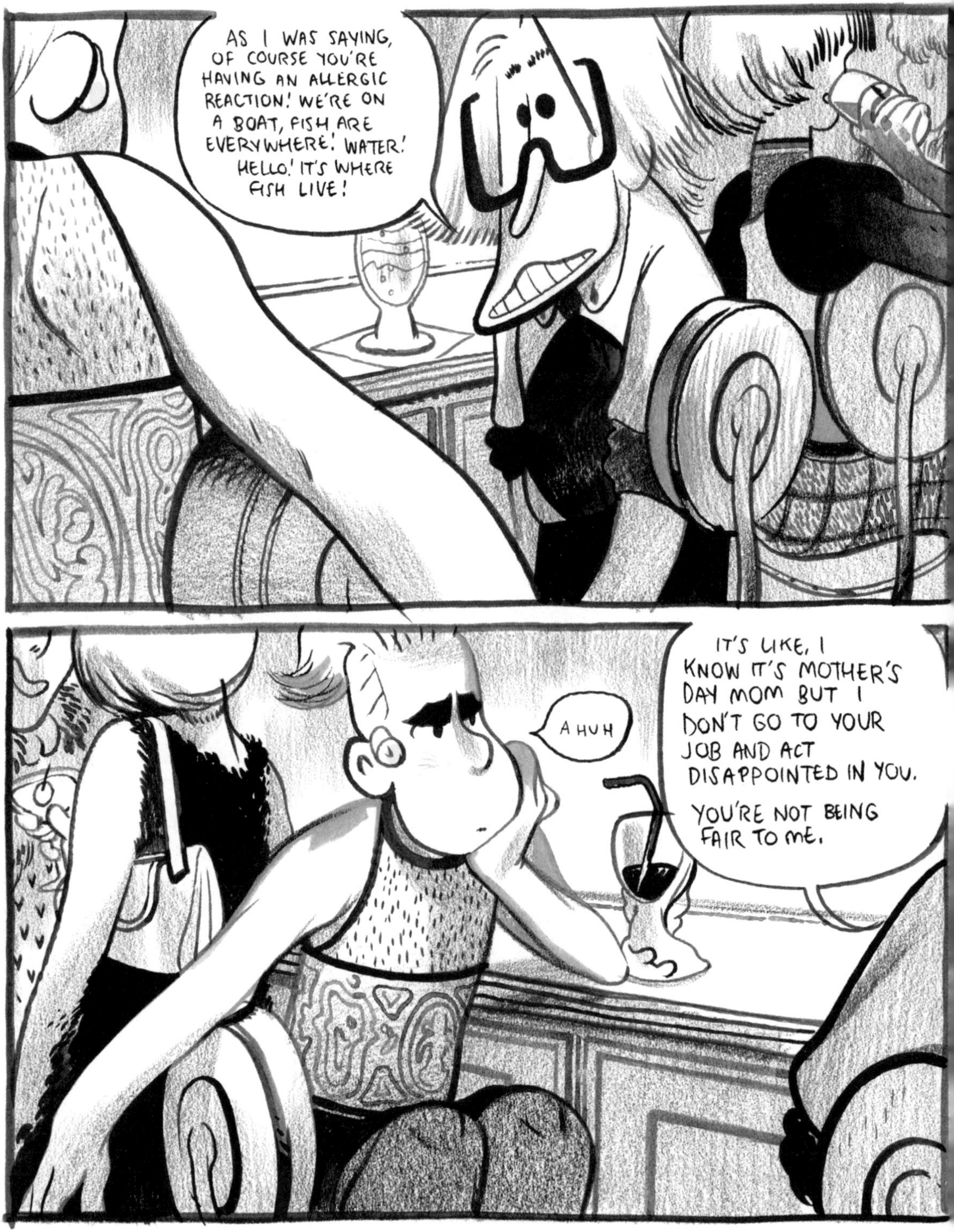
AS I WAS SAYING, OF COURSE YOU'RE HAVING AN ALLERGIC REACTION! WE'RE ON A BOAT, FISH ARE EVERYWHERE! WATER! HELLO! IT'S WHERE FISH LIVE!
AHUH
IT'S LIKE, I KNOW IT'S MOTHER'S DAY MOM BUT I DON'T GO TO YOUR JOB AND ACT DISAPPOINTED IN YOU.
YOU'RE NOT BEING FAIR TO ME.

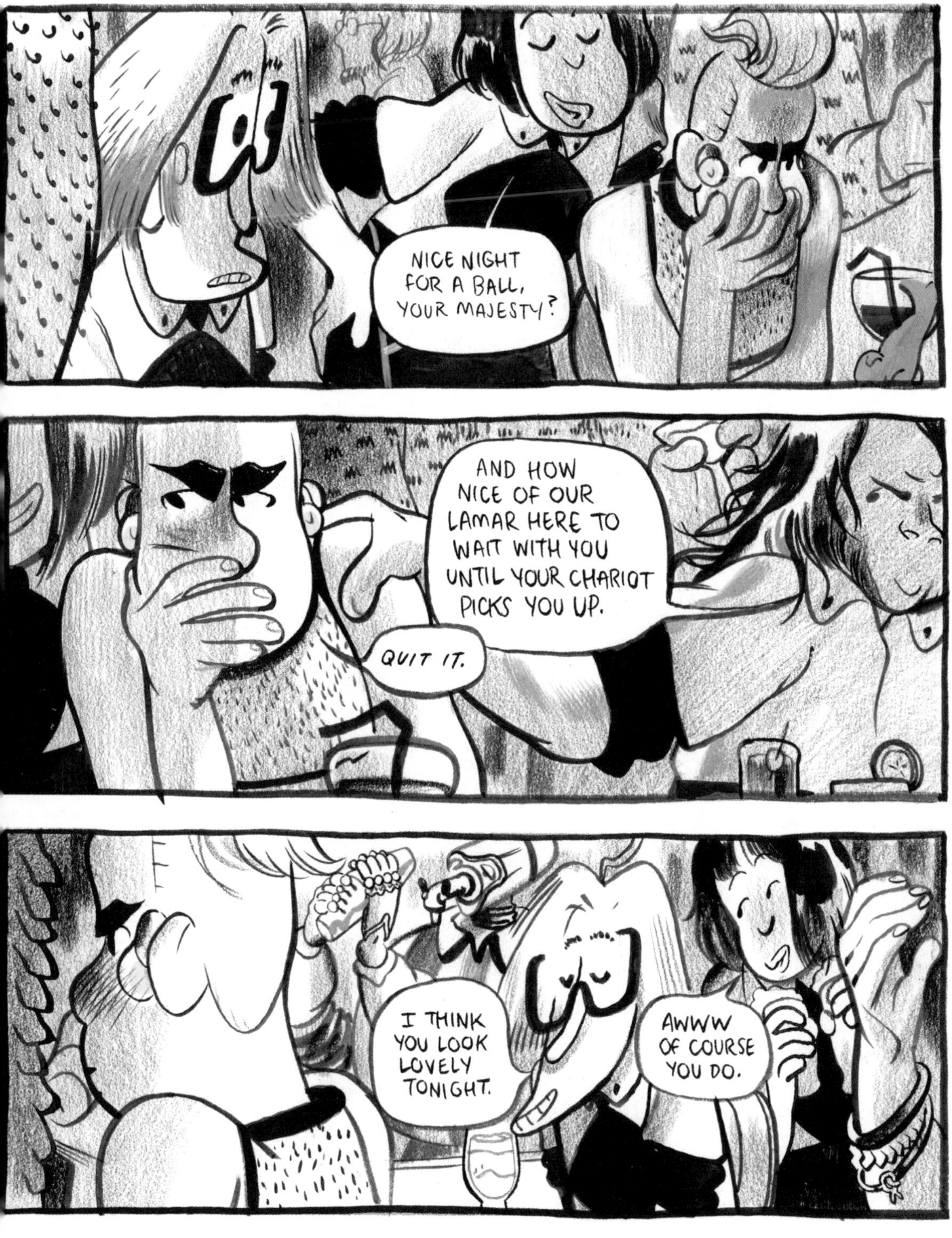
NICE NIGHT FOR A BALL, YOUR MAJESTY?
AND HOW NICE OF OUR LAMAR HERE TO WAIT WITH YOU UNTIL YOUR CHARIOT PICKS YOU UP.
QUIT IT.
I THINK YOU LOOK LOVELY TONIGHT.
AWWW OF COURSE YOU DO.

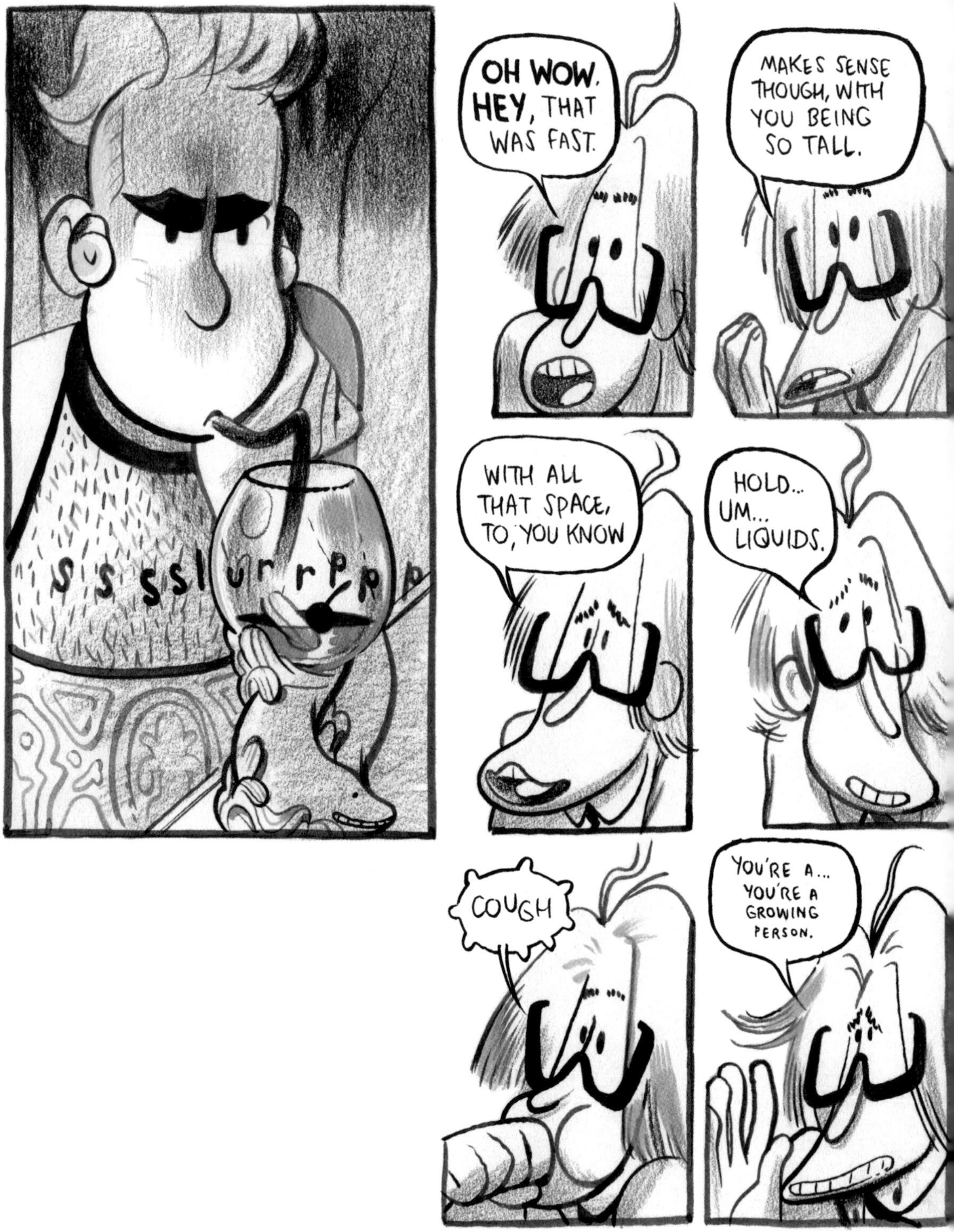
SSSSlurrppp
OH WOW. HEY, THAT WAS FAST.
MAKES SENSE THOUGH, WITH YOU BEING SO TALL.
WITH ALL THAT SPACE, TO, YOU KNOW
HOLD... UM... LIQUIDS.
COUGH
YOU'RE A... YOU'RE A GROWING PERSON.

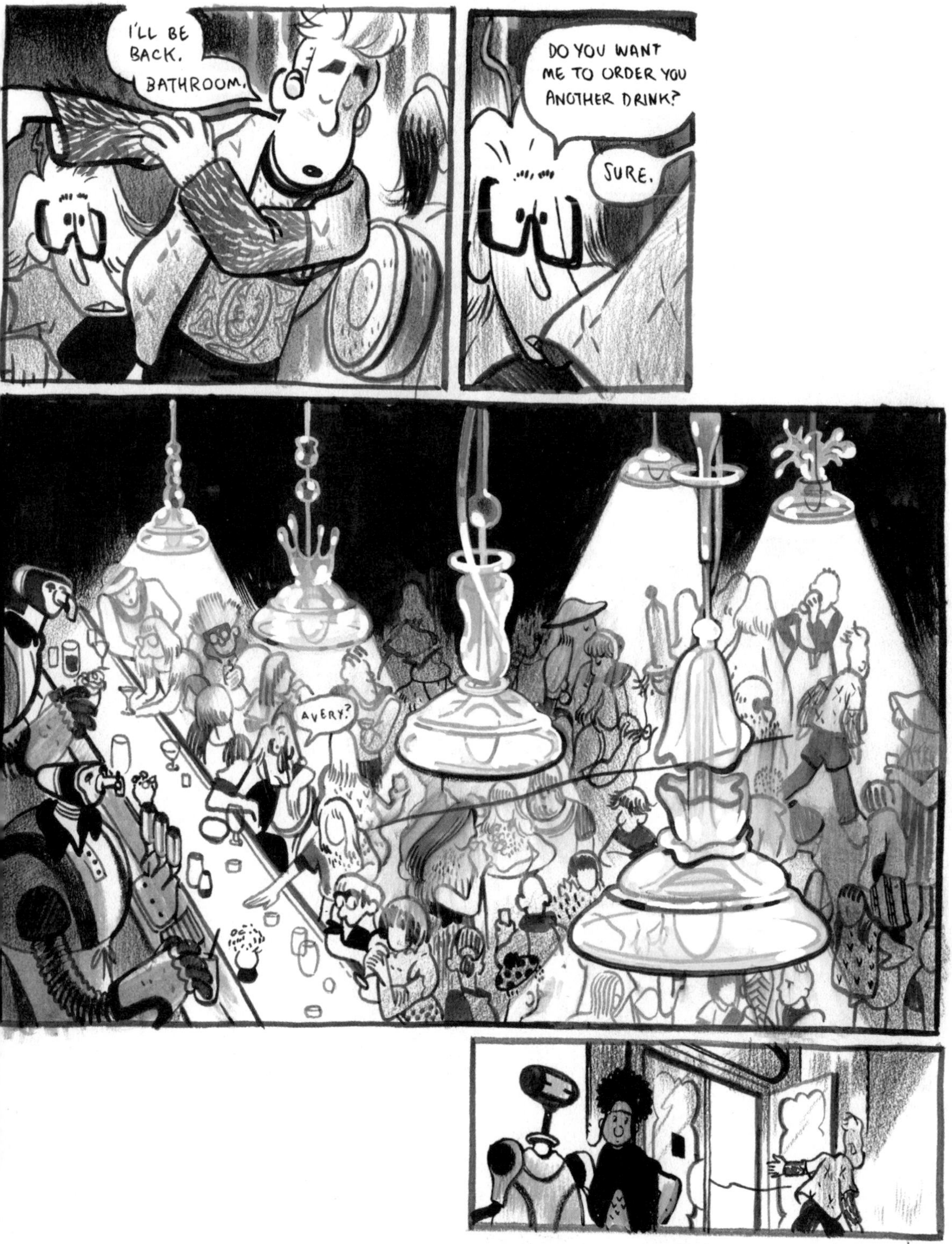

I'LL BE BACK.
BATHROOM.
DO YOU WANT ME TO ORDER YOU ANOTHER DRINK?
SURE.
AVERY?

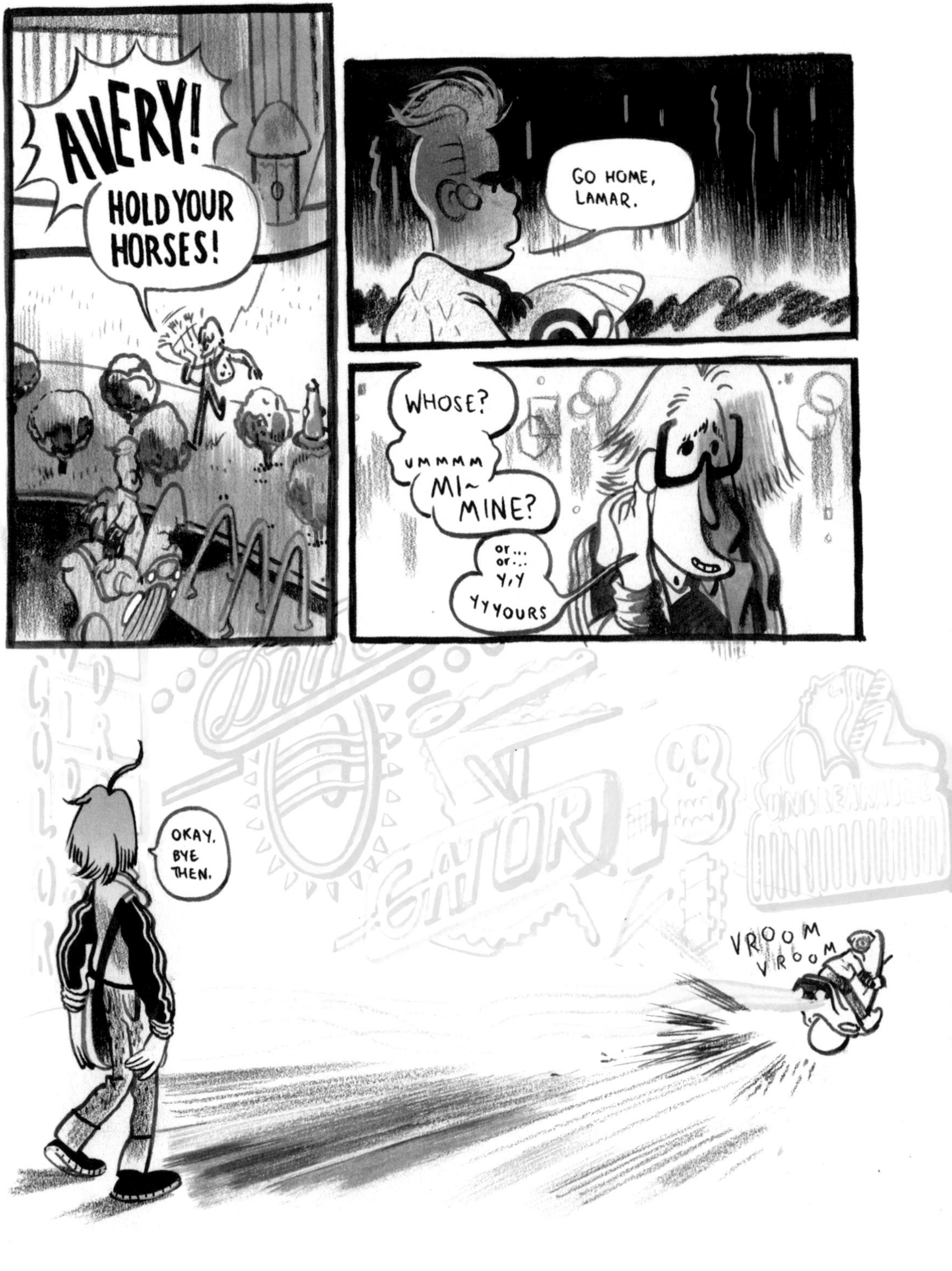

AVERY!
HOLD YOUR HORSES!
GO HOME, LAMAR.
WHOSE?
UMMMM
MI~ MINE?
or... or... Y, Y YYYOURS
OKAY. BYE THEN.
GATOR
VROOM VROOM

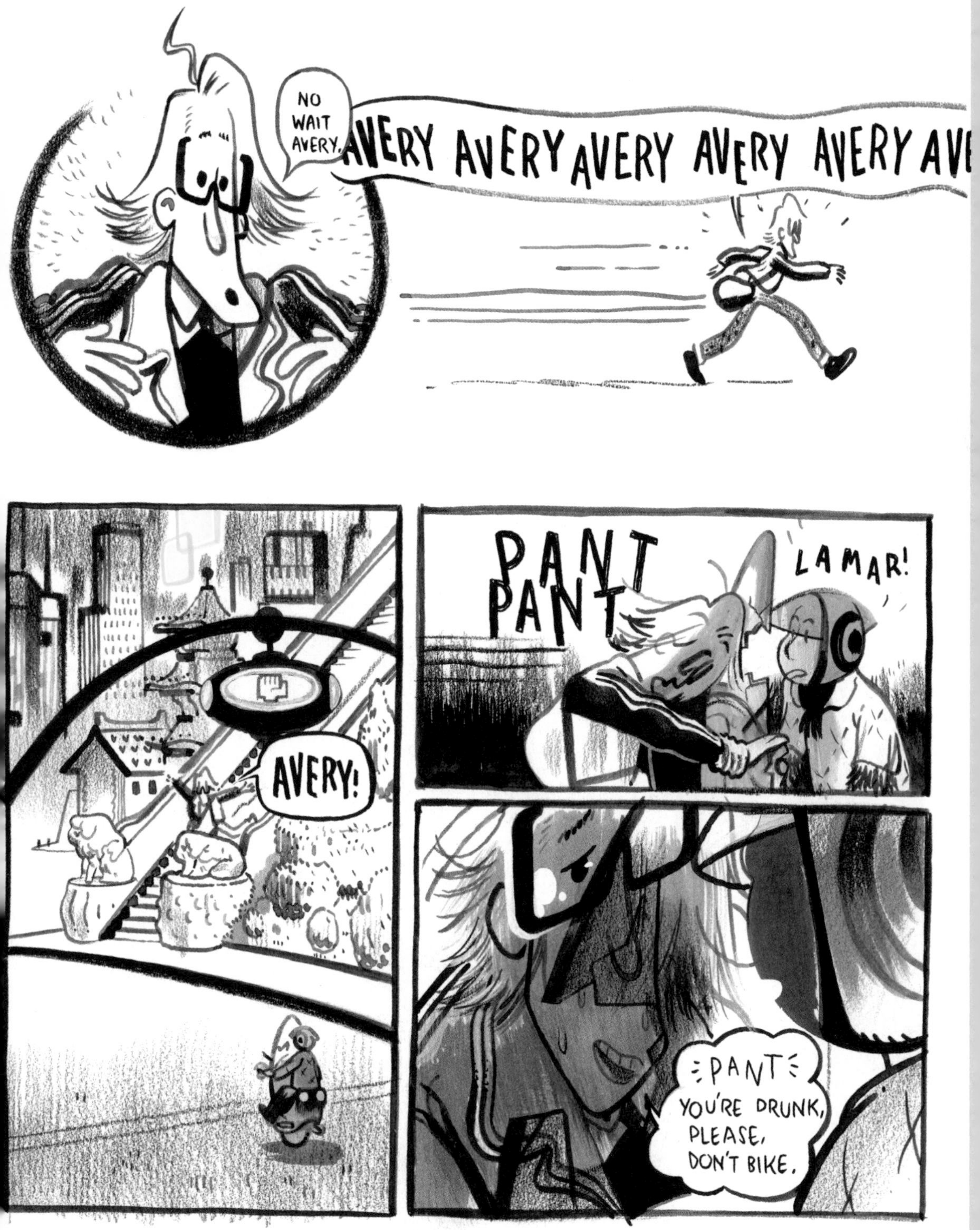
NO WAIT AVERY.
AVERY AVERY AVERY AVERY AVERY
AVERY!
PANT PANT
LAMAR!
PANT
YOU'RE DRUNK, PLEASE, DON'T BIKE.

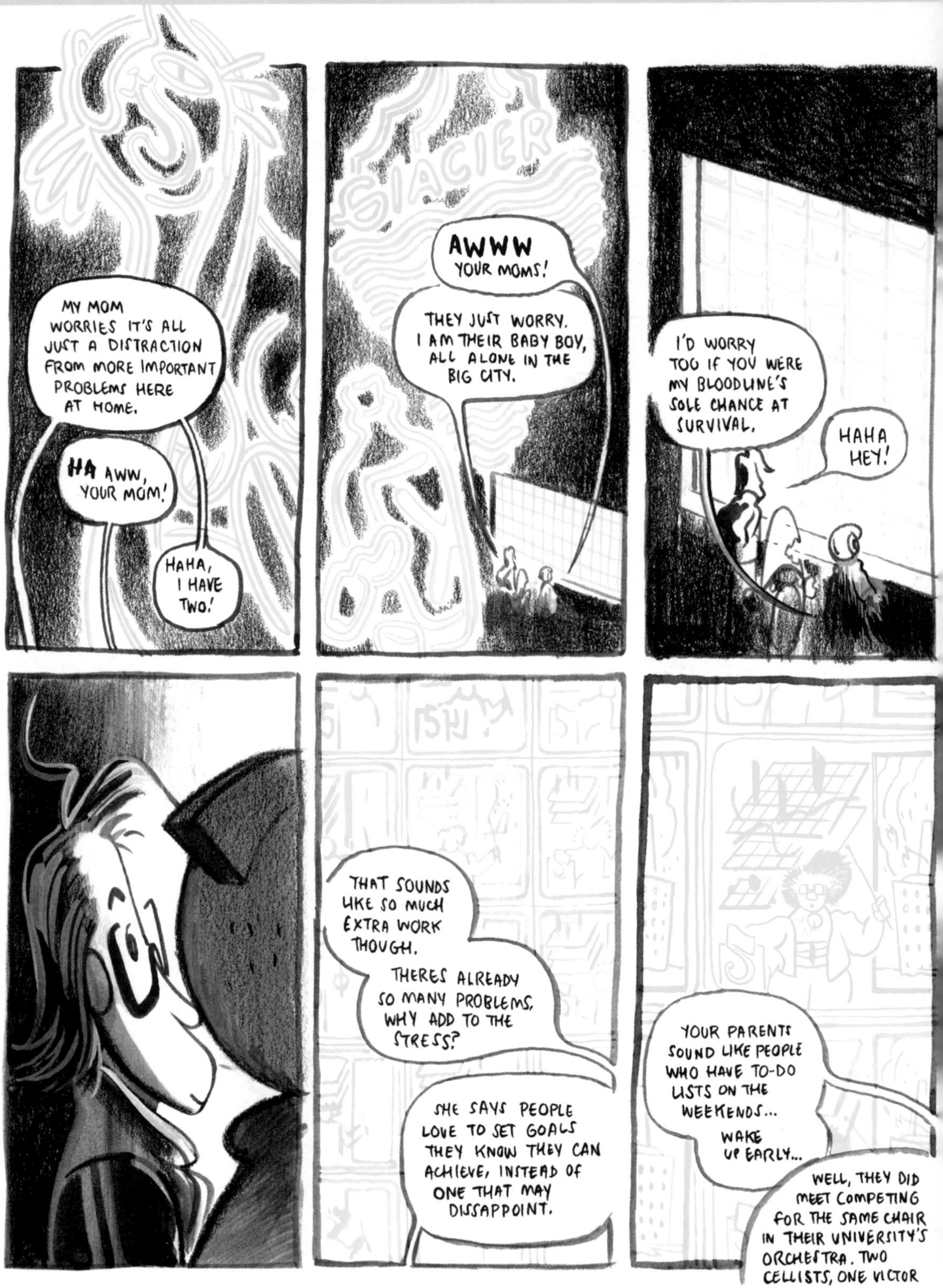
MY MOM WORRIES IT'S ALL JUST A DISTRACTION FROM MORE IMPORTANT PROBLEMS HERE AT HOME.
HA AWW, YOUR MOM!
HAHA, I HAVE TWO!
AWWW YOUR MOMS!
THEY JUST WORRY. I AM THEIR BABY BOY, ALL ALONE IN THE BIG CITY.
I'D WORRY TOO IF YOU WERE MY BLOODLINE'S SOLE CHANCE AT SURVIVAL.
HAHA HEY!
THAT SOUNDS LIKE SO MUCH EXTRA WORK THOUGH.
THERES ALREADY SO MANY PROBLEMS. WHY ADD TO THE STRESS?
SHE SAYS PEOPLE LOVE TO SET GOALS THEY KNOW THEY CAN ACHIEVE, INSTEAD OF ONE THAT MAY DISSAPPOINT.
YOUR PARENTS SOUND LIKE PEOPLE WHO HAVE TO-DO LISTS ON THE WEEKENDS...
WAKE UP EARLY...
WELL, THEY DID MEET COMPETING FOR THE SAME CHAIR IN THEIR UNIVERSITY'S ORCHESTRA. TWO CELLISTS, ONE VICTOR

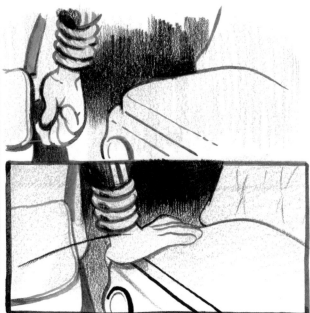

HA HA WAIT, IT'S OVER HERE?!

WHAT IS... OVER...HERE?

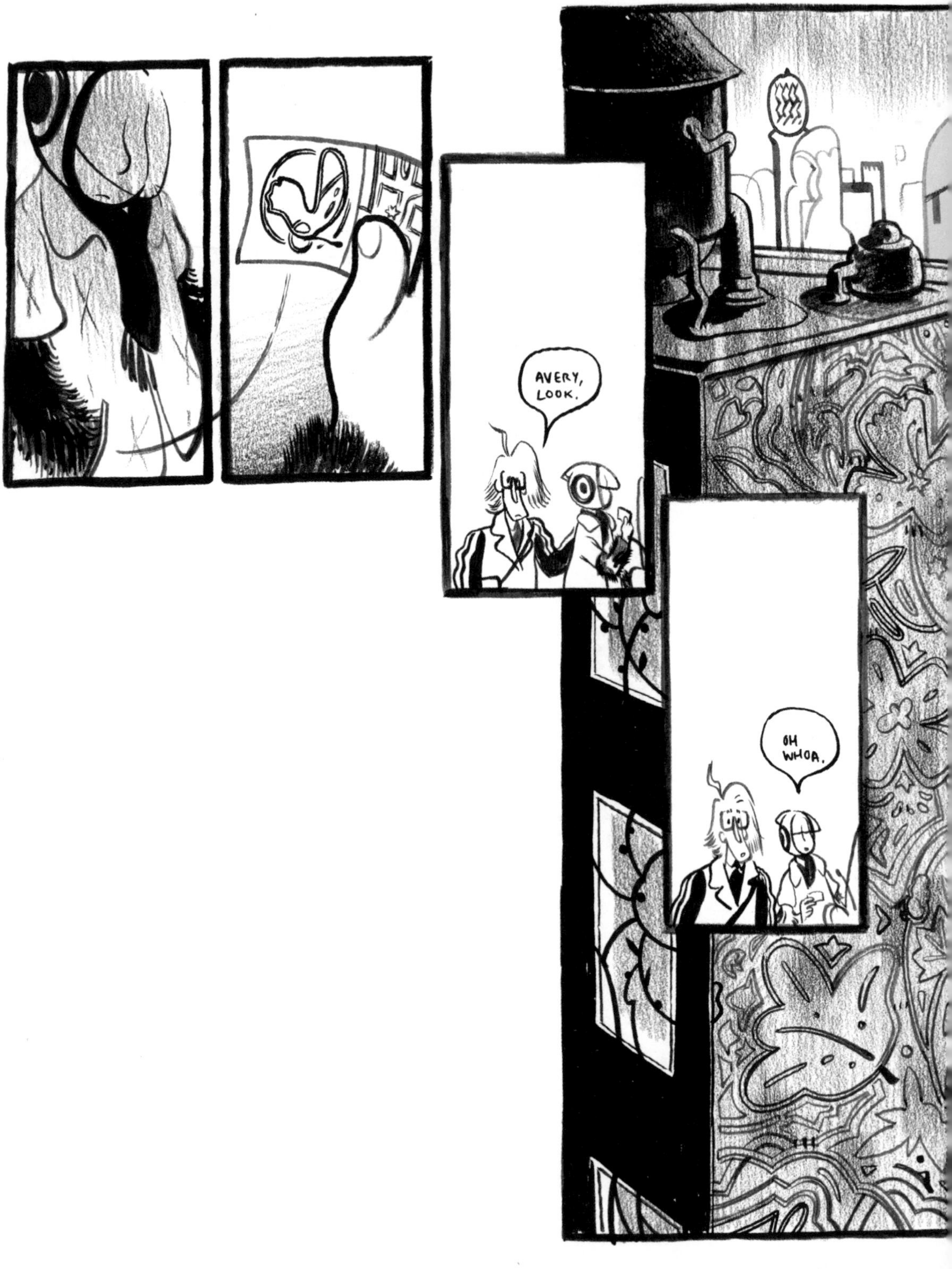
AVERY,
LOOK.
OH
WHOA.

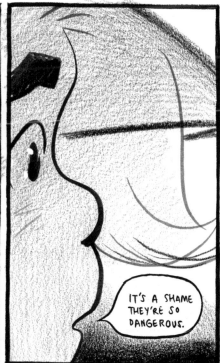

IT'S A SHAME THEY'RE SO DANGEROUS.

FROM THIS DISTANCE, IT'S ALMOST ...LOVELY.

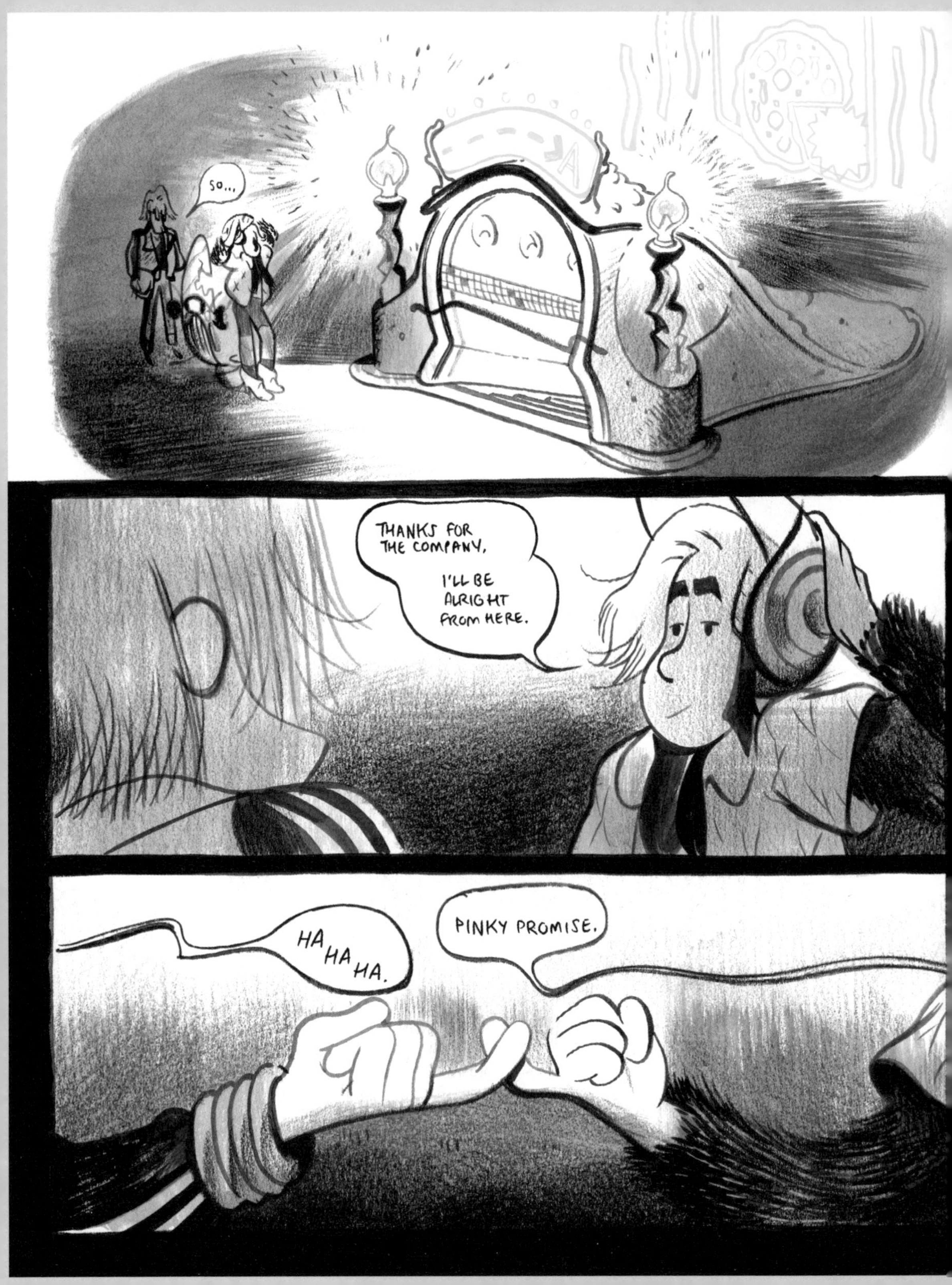
SO...
THANKS FOR THE COMPANY,
I'LL BE ALRIGHT FROM HERE.
HA HA HA.
PINKY PROMISE.

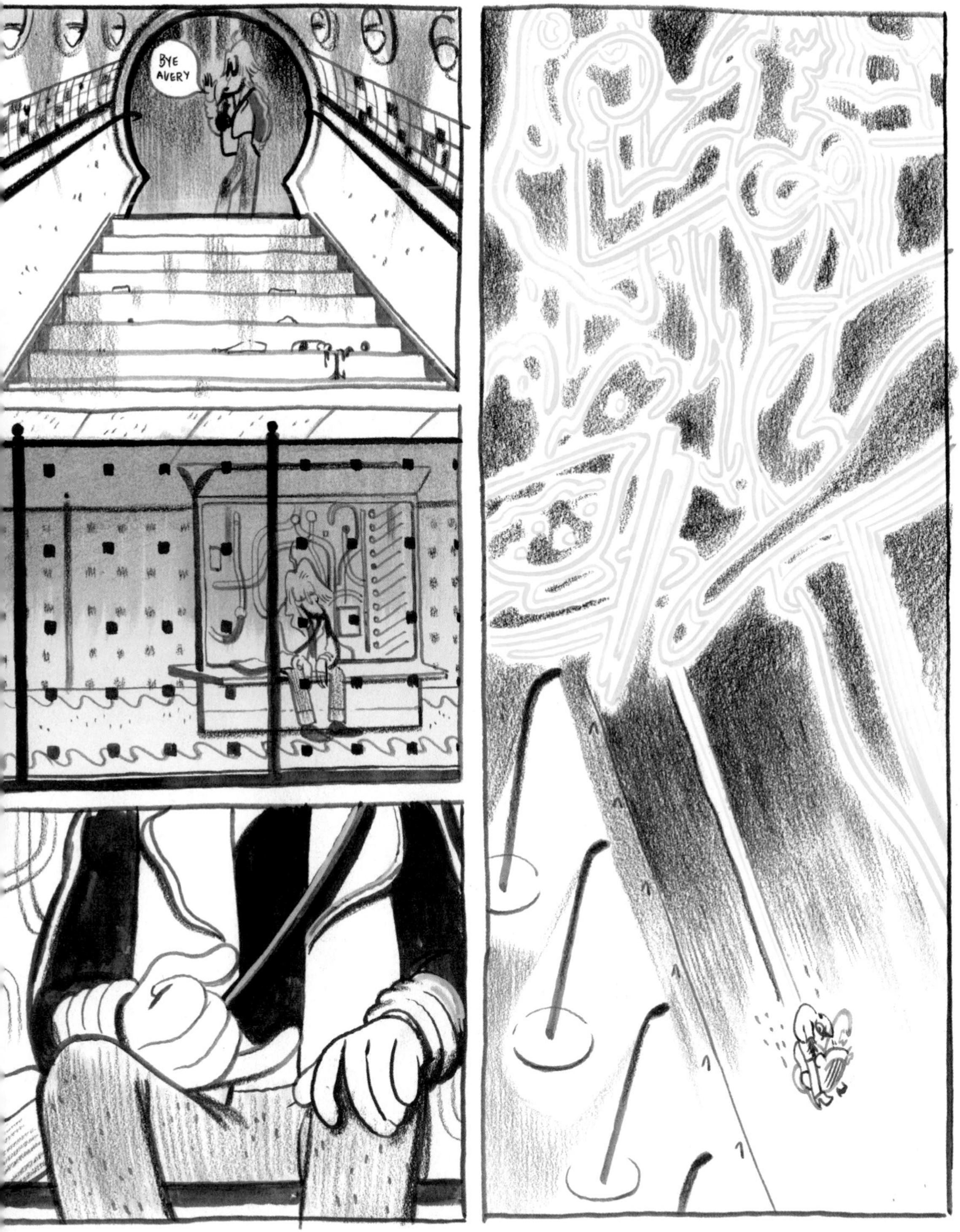
BYE AVERY

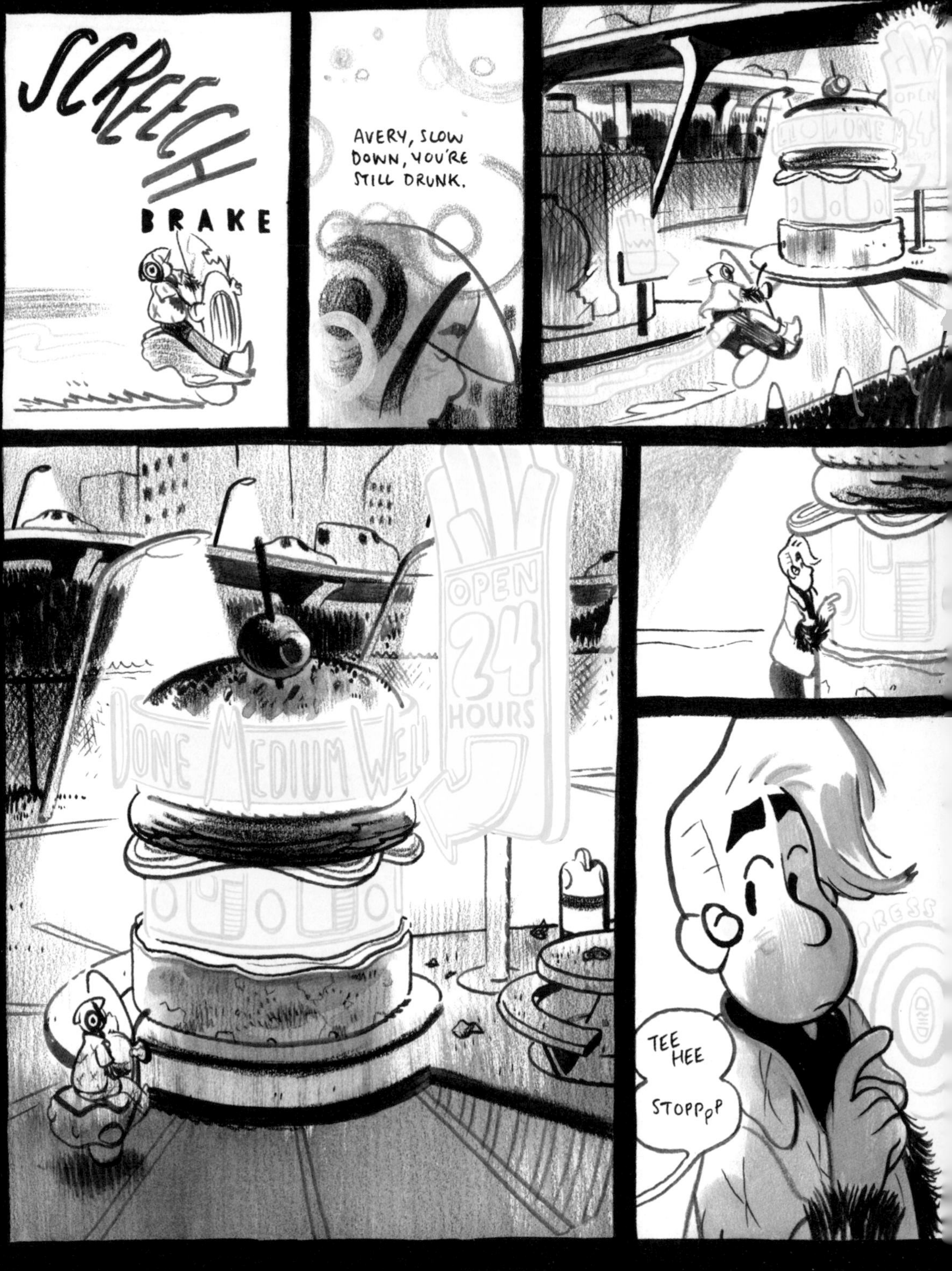
SCREECH
BRAKE
AVERY, SLOW DOWN, YOU'RE STILL DRUNK.
DONE MEDIUM WELL
OPEN 24 HOURS
TEE HEE
STOPPpP
PRESS

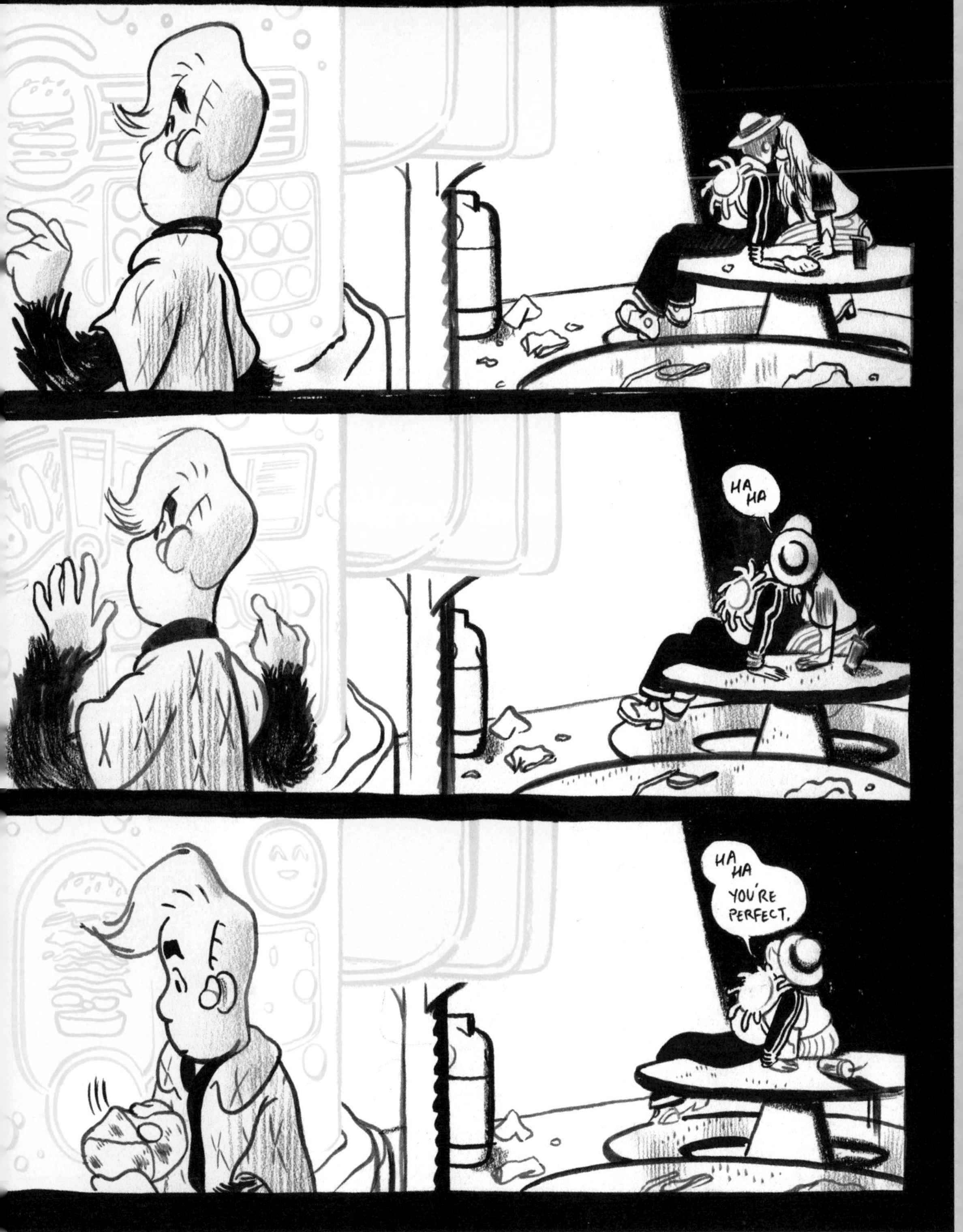
HA HA
HA HA YOU'RE PERFECT.

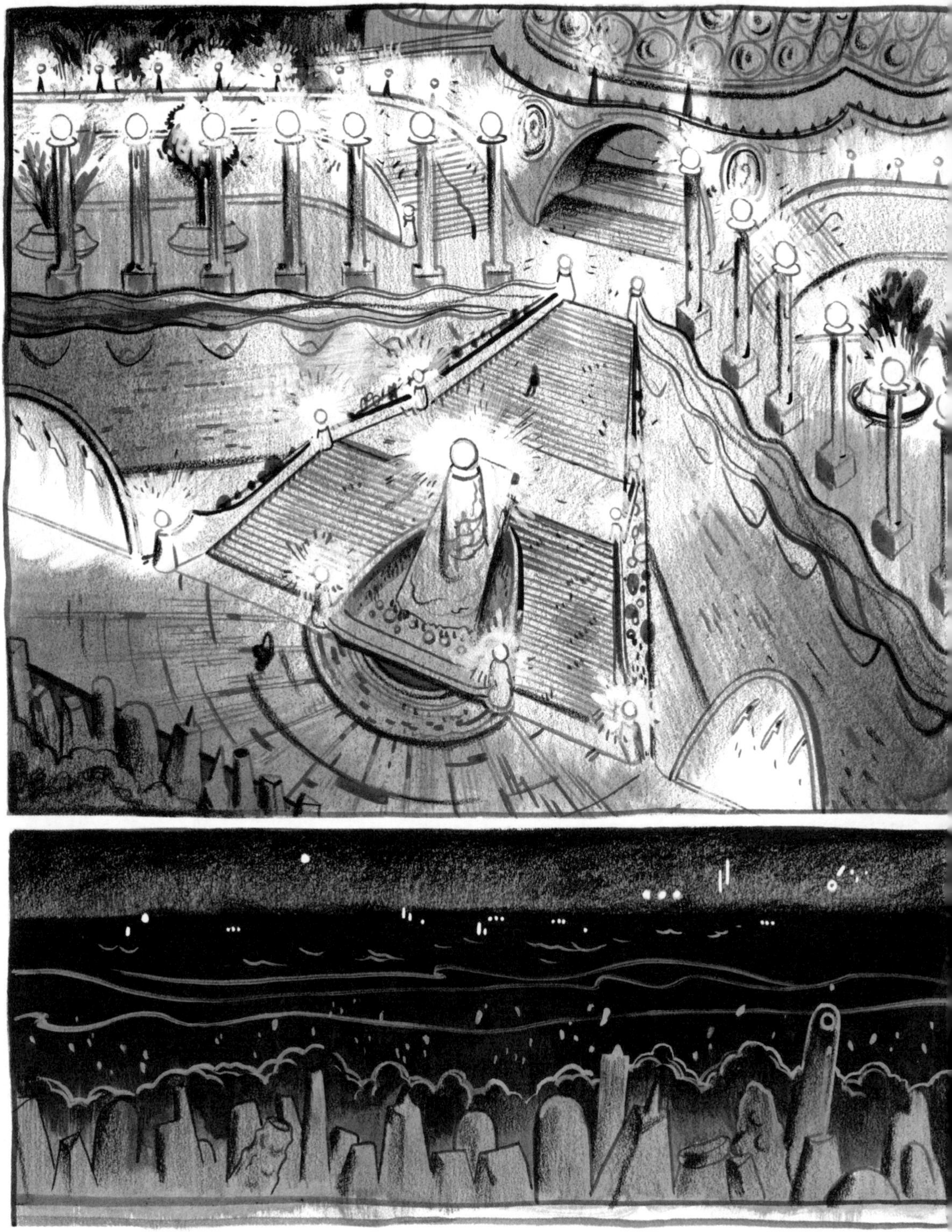

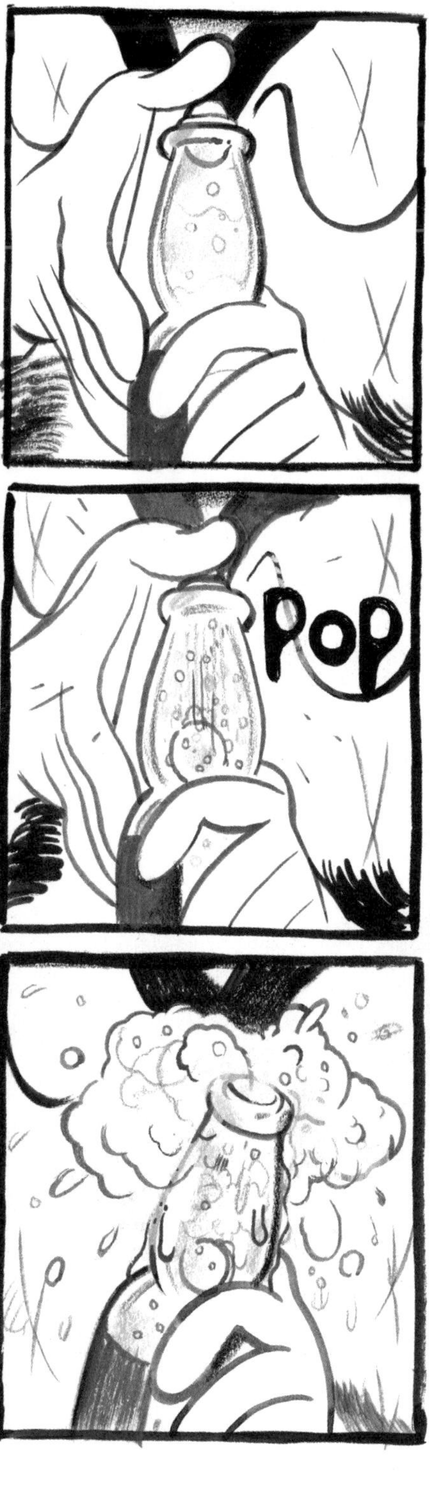
POP

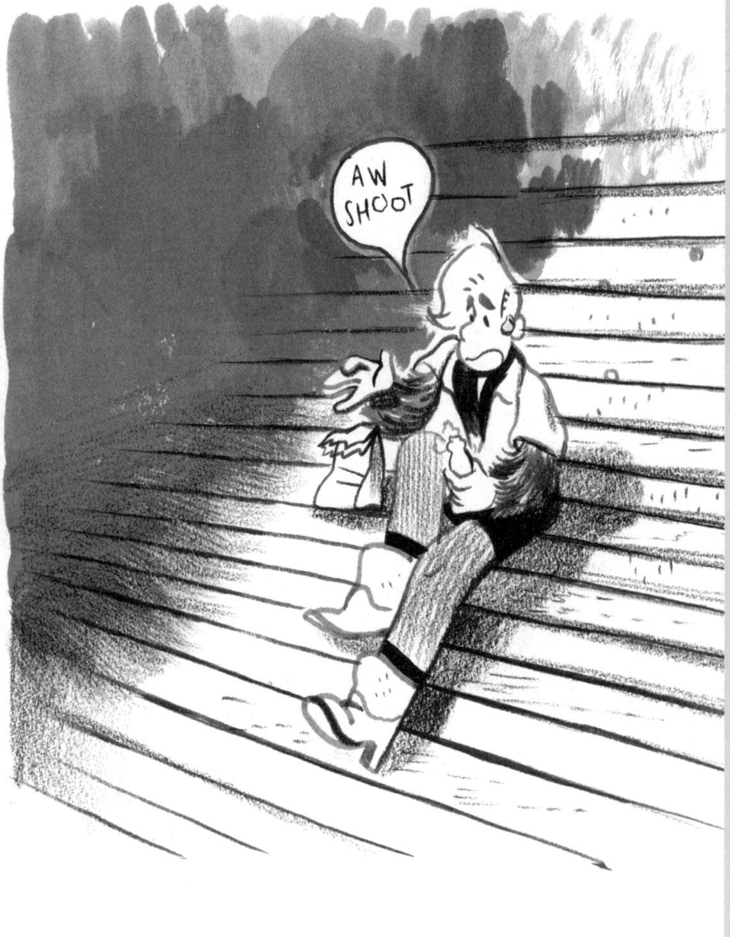
AW SHOOT

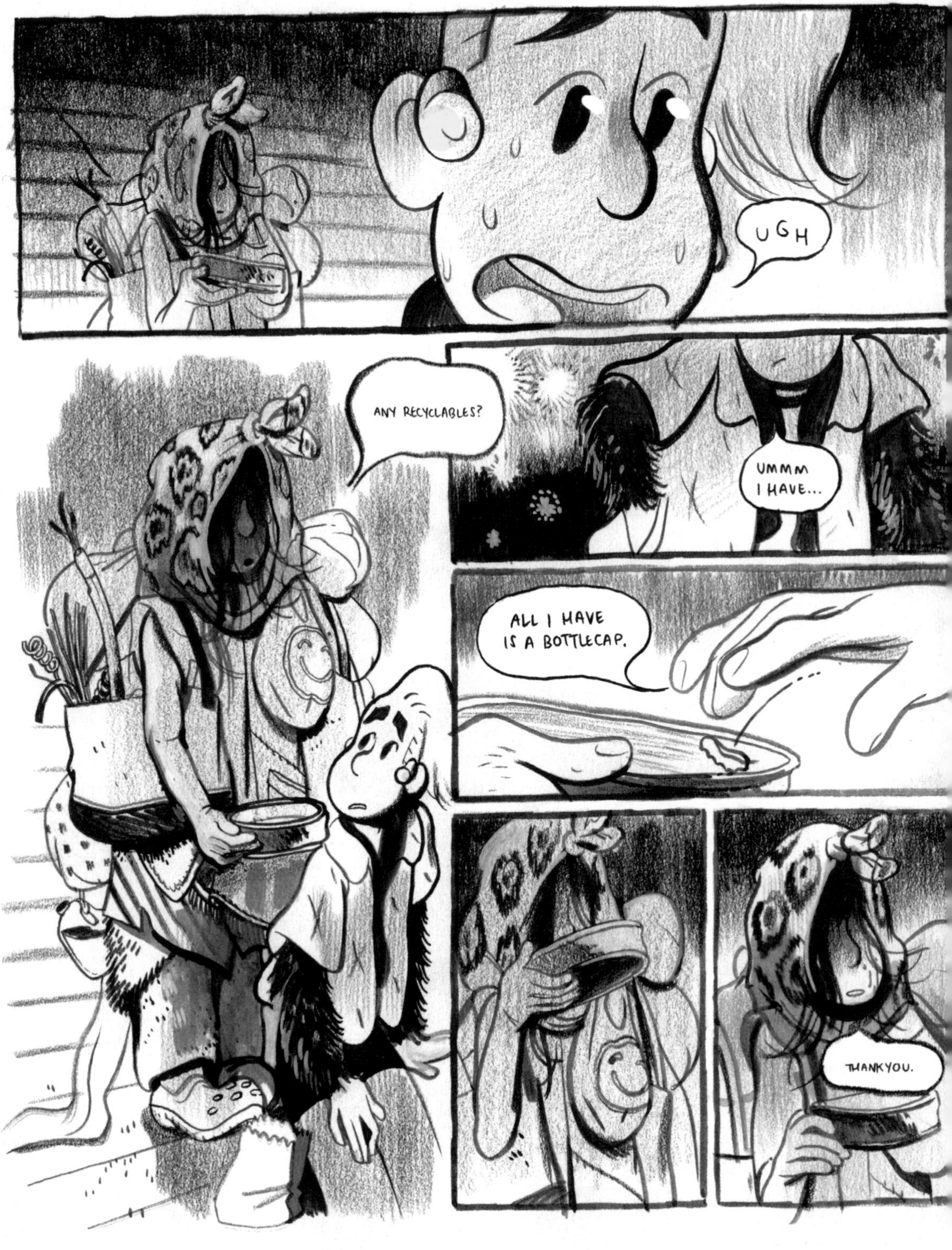
UGH
ANY RECYCLABLES?
UMMM I HAVE...
ALL I HAVE IS A BOTTLECAP.
THANKYOU.

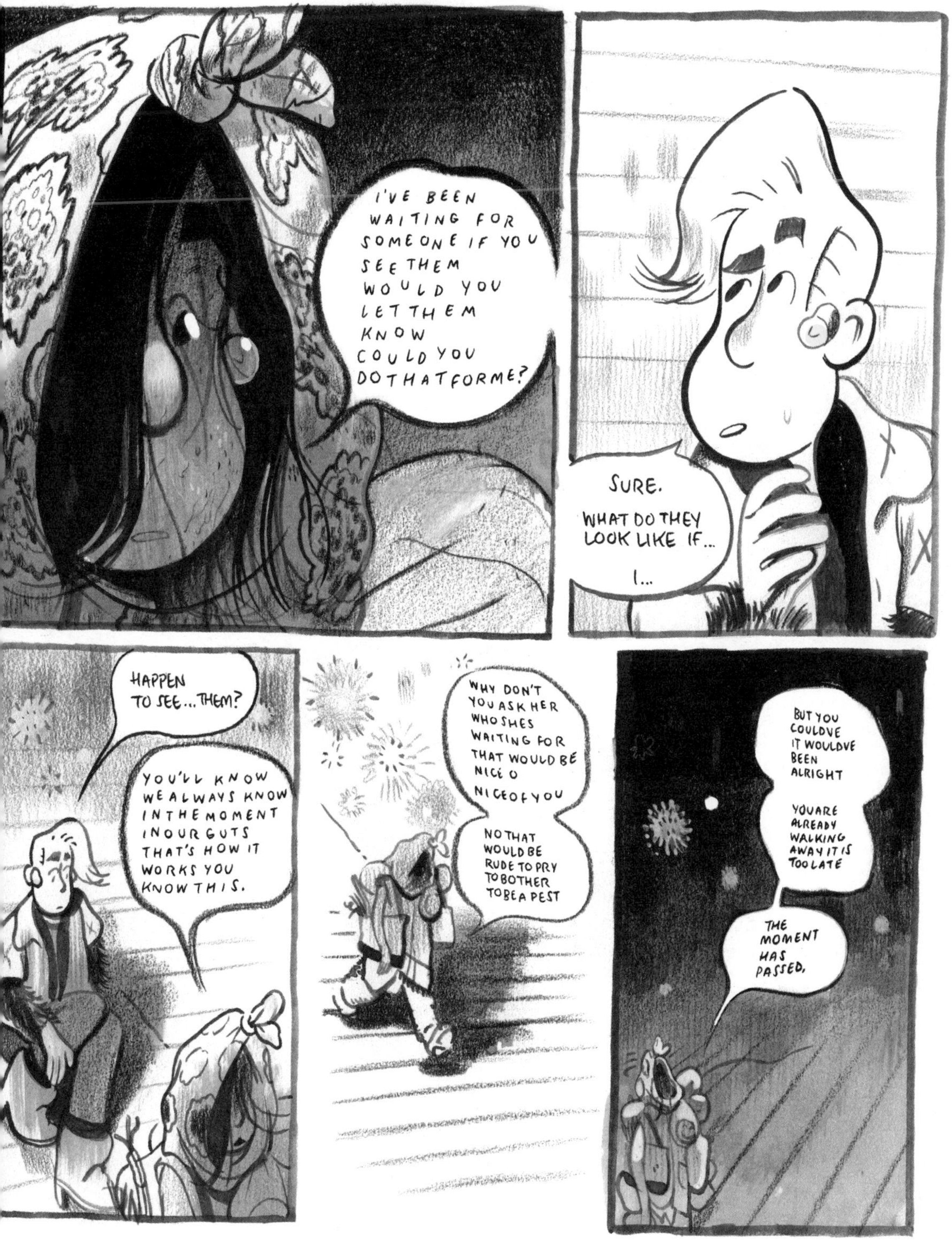
I'VE BEEN WAITING FOR SOMEONE IF YOU SEE THEM WOULD YOU LET THEM KNOW COULD YOU DO THAT FOR ME?
SURE. WHAT DO THEY LOOK LIKE IF... I...
HAPPEN TO SEE... THEM?
YOU'LL KNOW WE ALWAYS KNOW IN THE MOMENT IN OUR GUTS THAT'S HOW IT WORKS YOU KNOW THIS.
WHY DON'T YOU ASK HER WHO SHES WAITING FOR THAT WOULD BE NICE O NICE OF YOU
NO THAT WOULD BE RUDE TO PRY TO BOTHER TO BE A PEST
BUT YOU COULDVE IT WOULDVE BEEN ALRIGHT
YOU ARE ALREADY WALKING AWAY IT IS TOO LATE
THE MOMENT HAS PASSED,

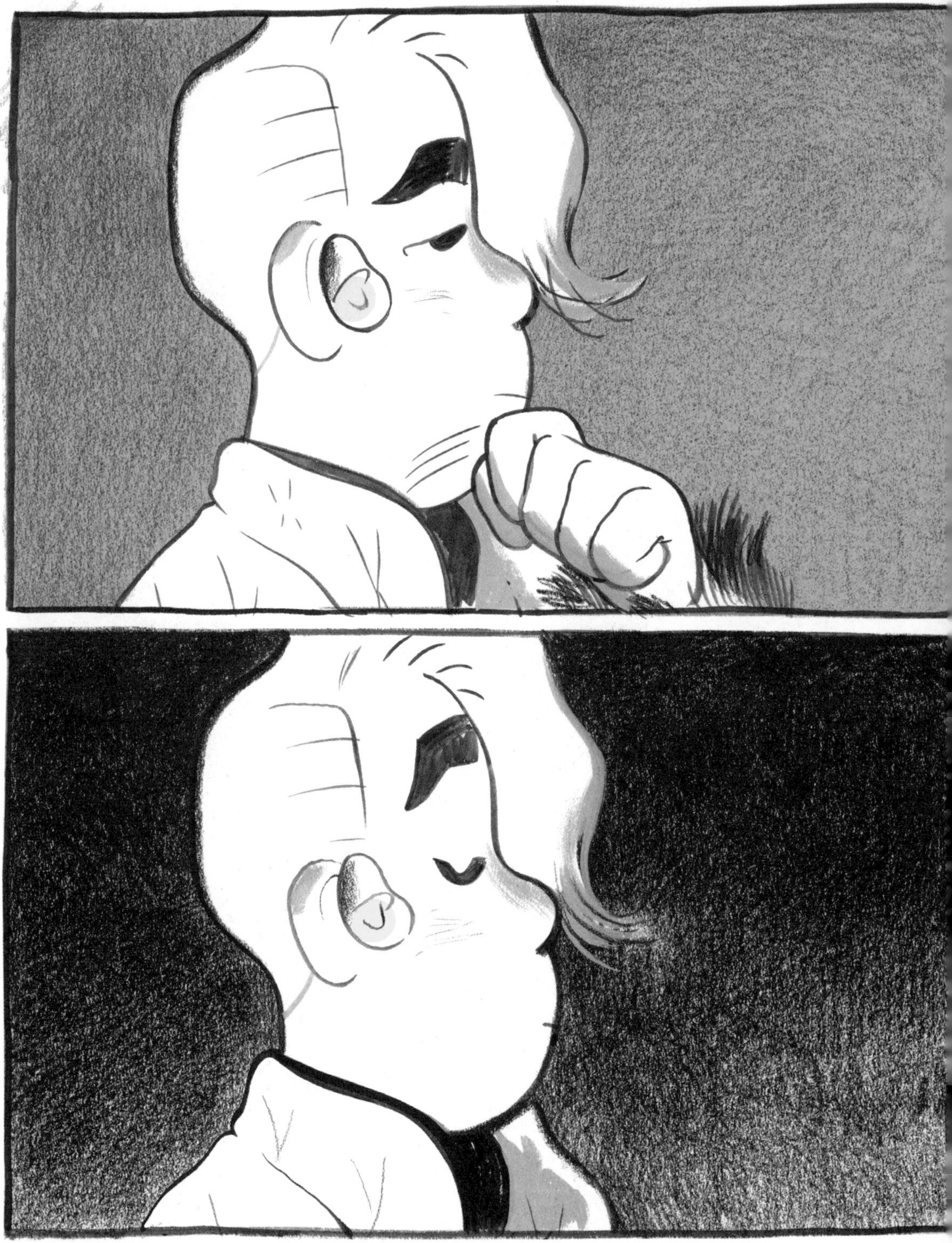

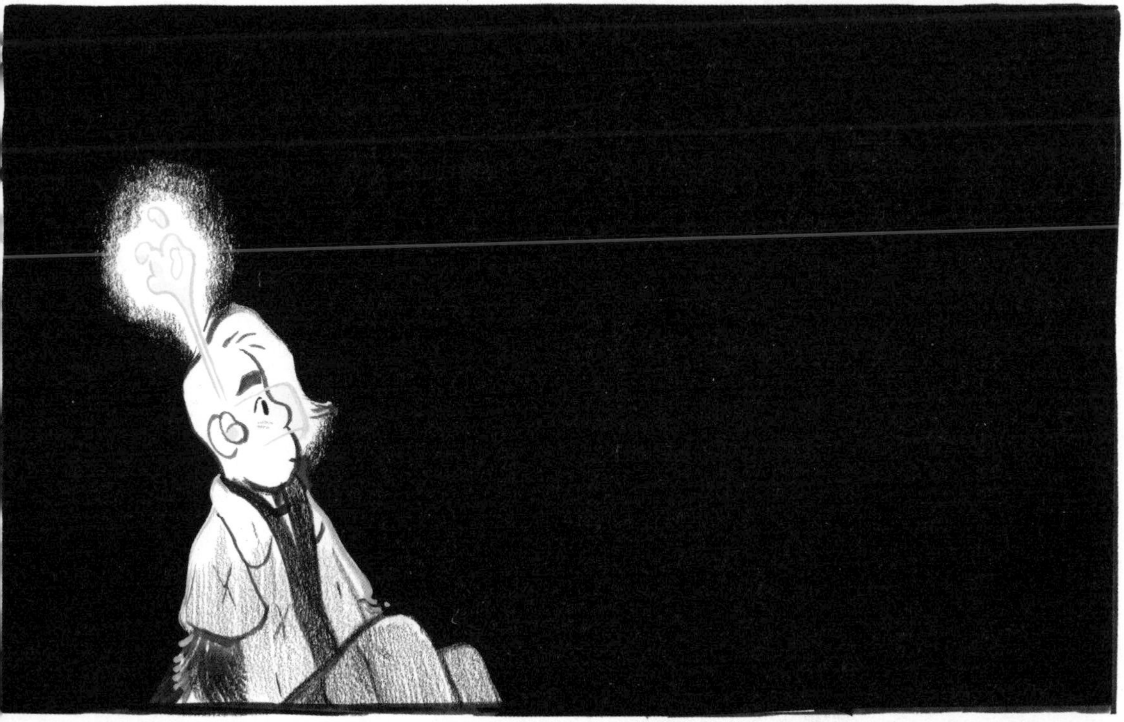

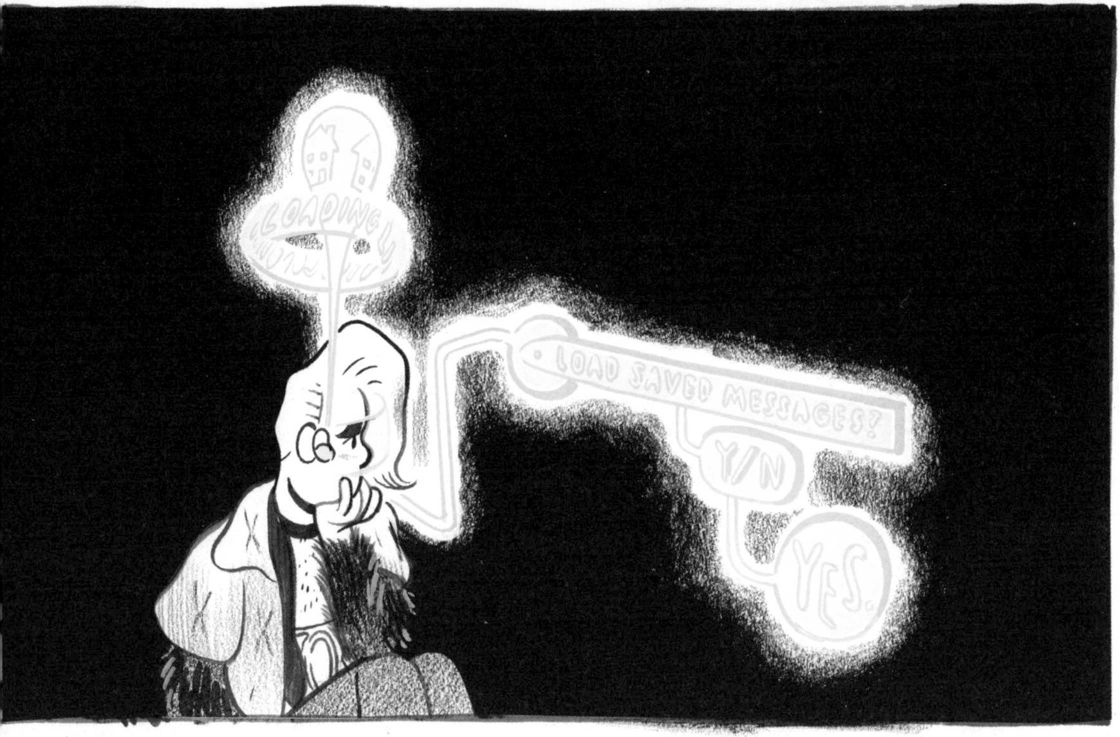
LOADING
LOAD SAVED MESSAGES?
Y/N
YES.

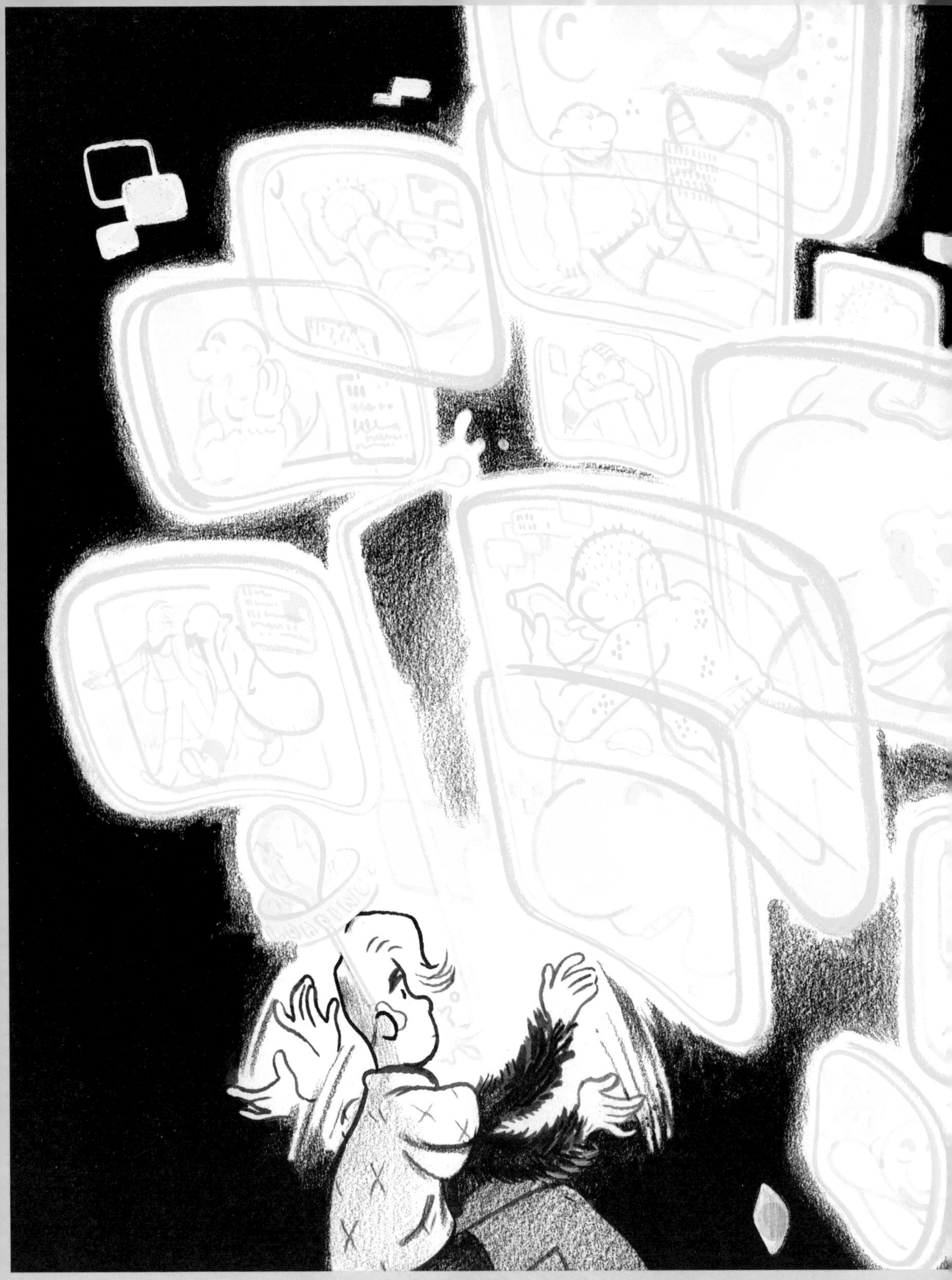

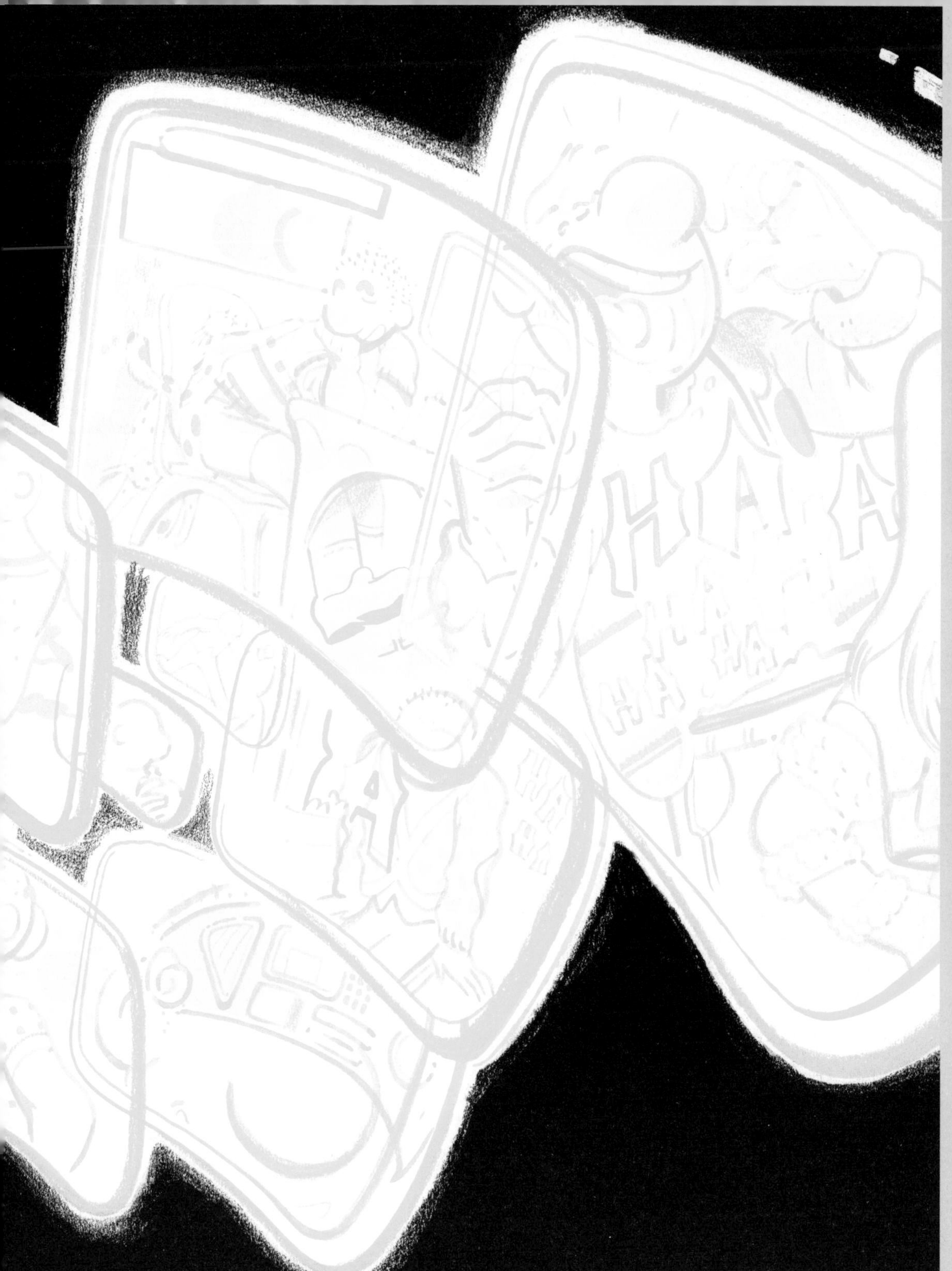

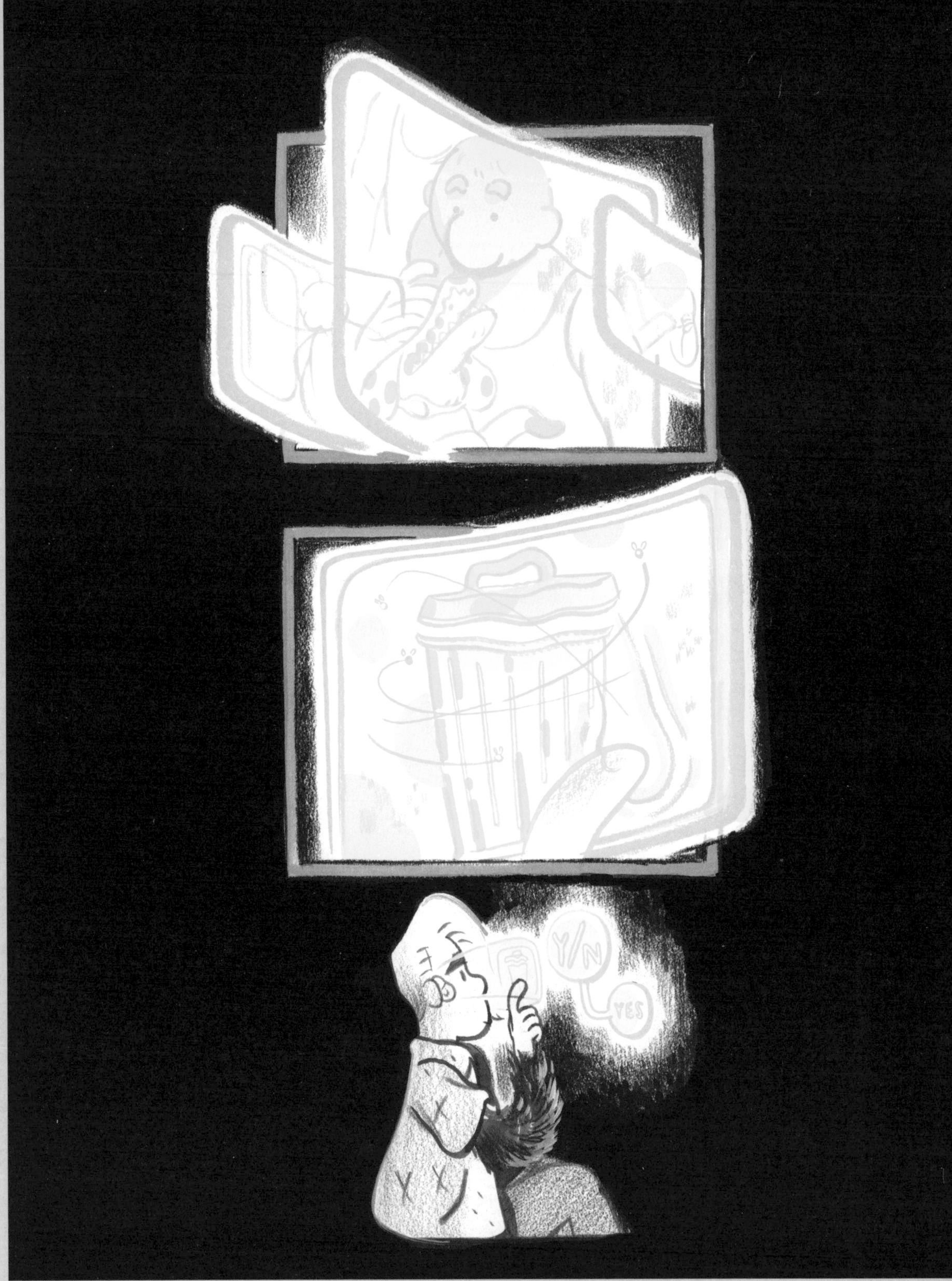
Y/N
YES

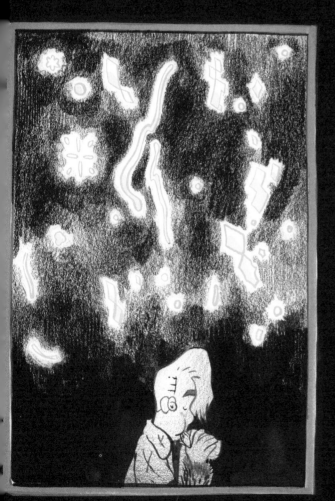

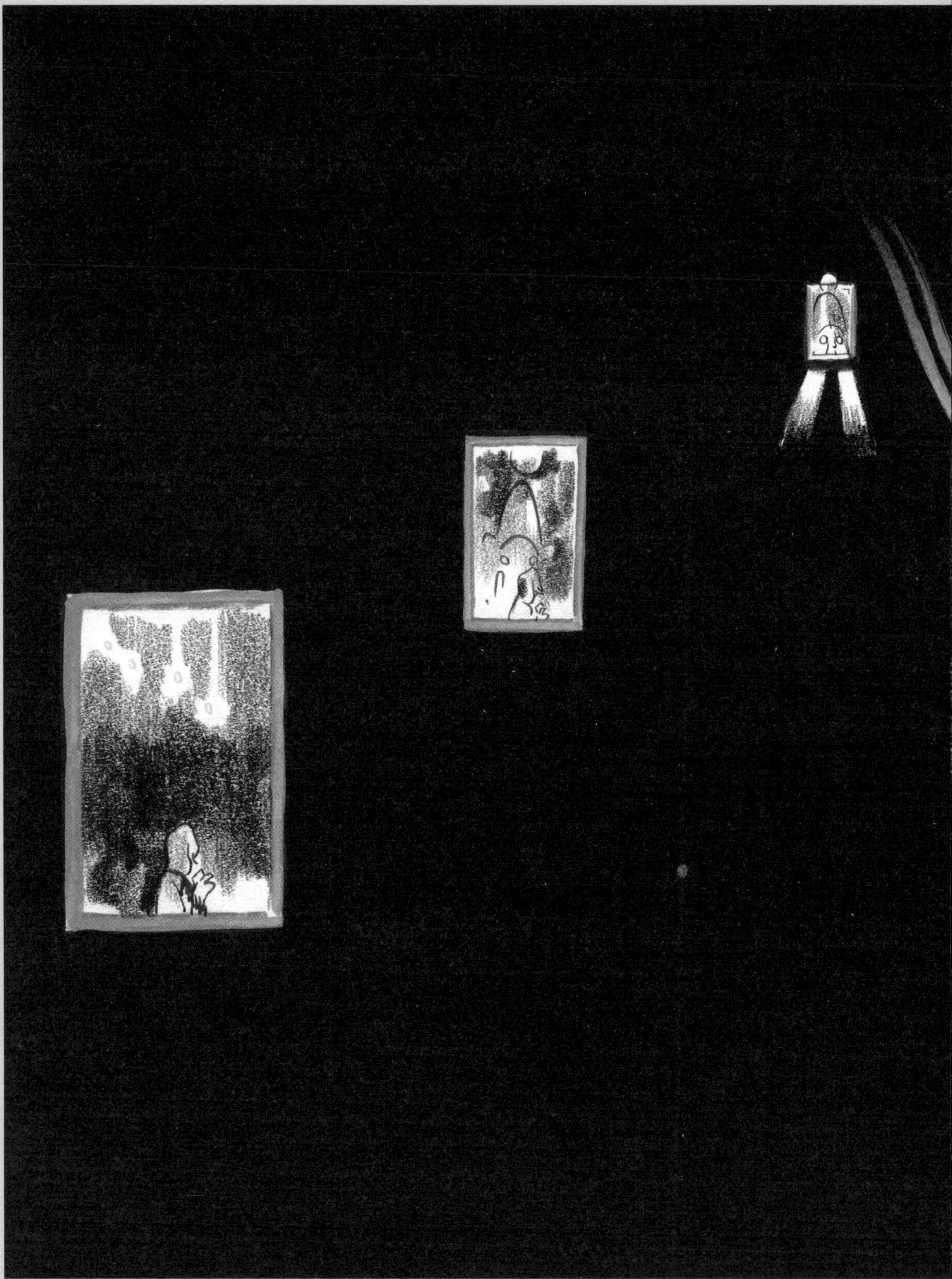

GOOD MORNING Mx. AVERY

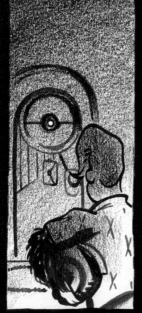

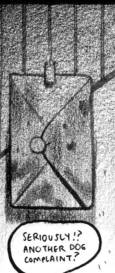

SERIOUSLY!? ANOTHER DOG COMPLAINT?

RIDICULOUS.

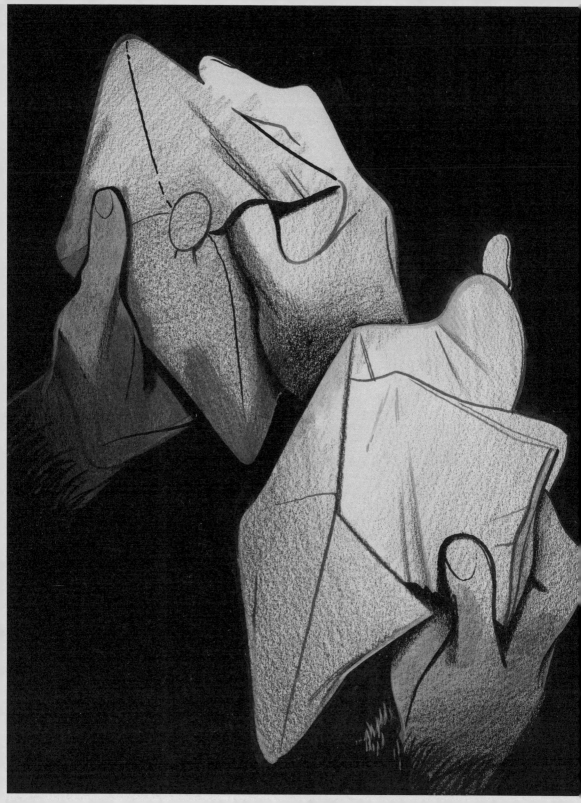

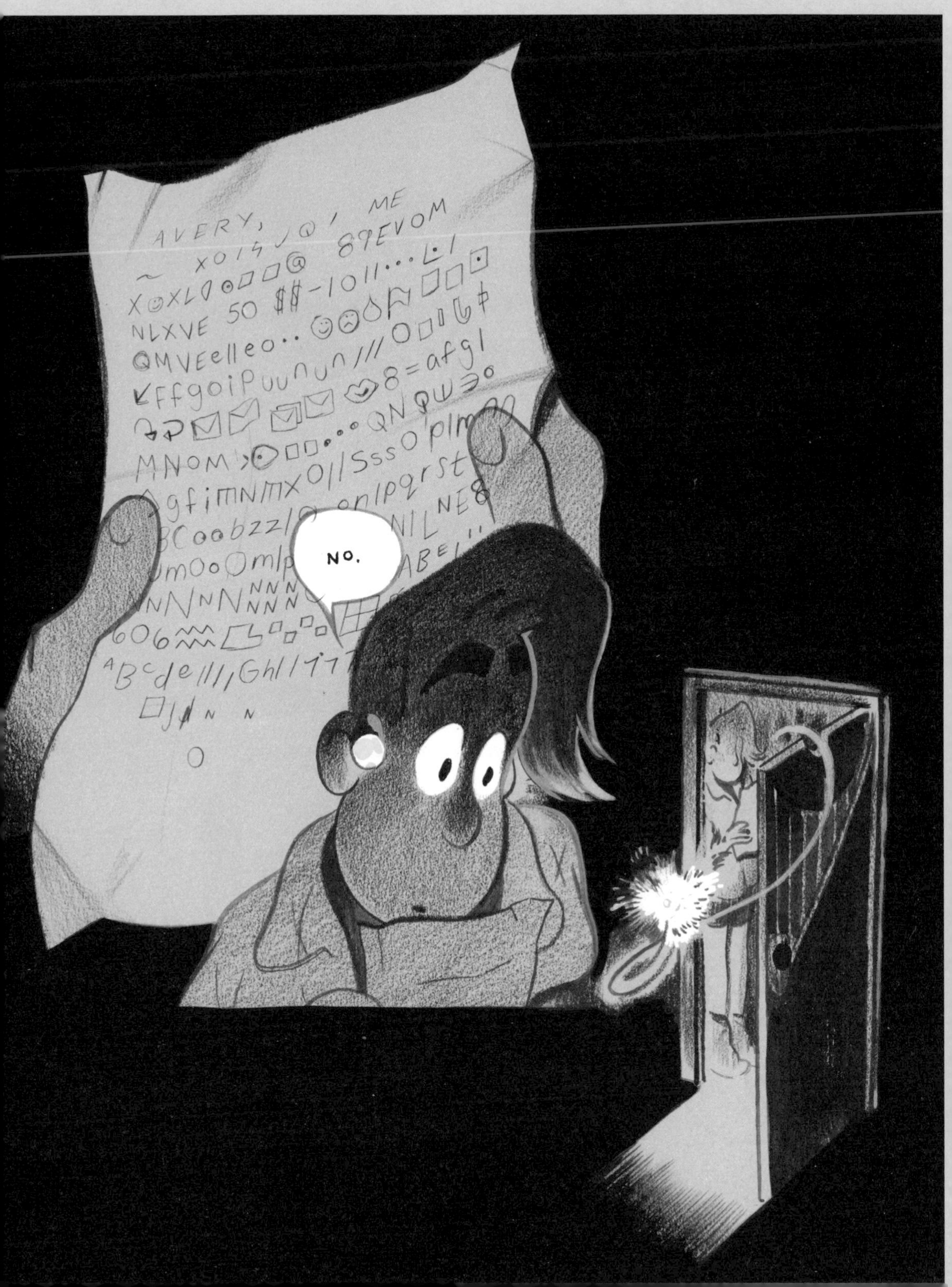
AVERY,
NO.

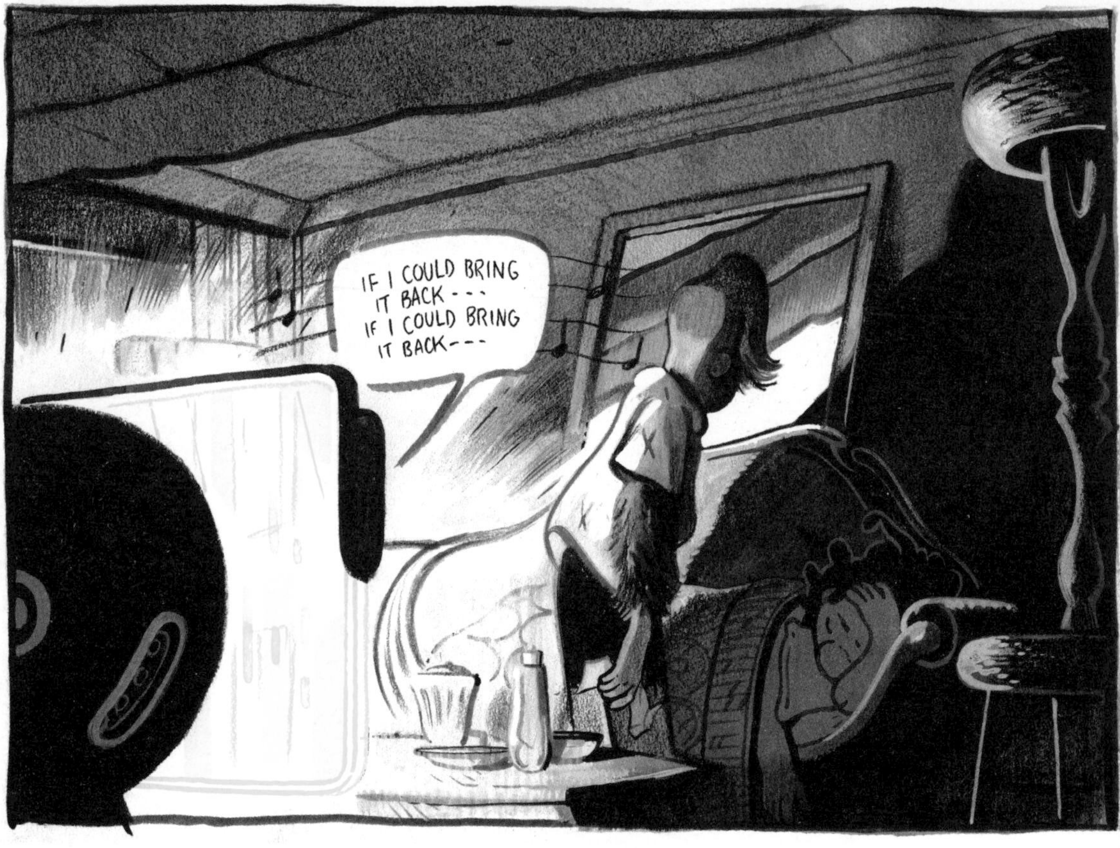
IF I COULD BRING IT BACK--- IF I COULD BRING IT BACK---

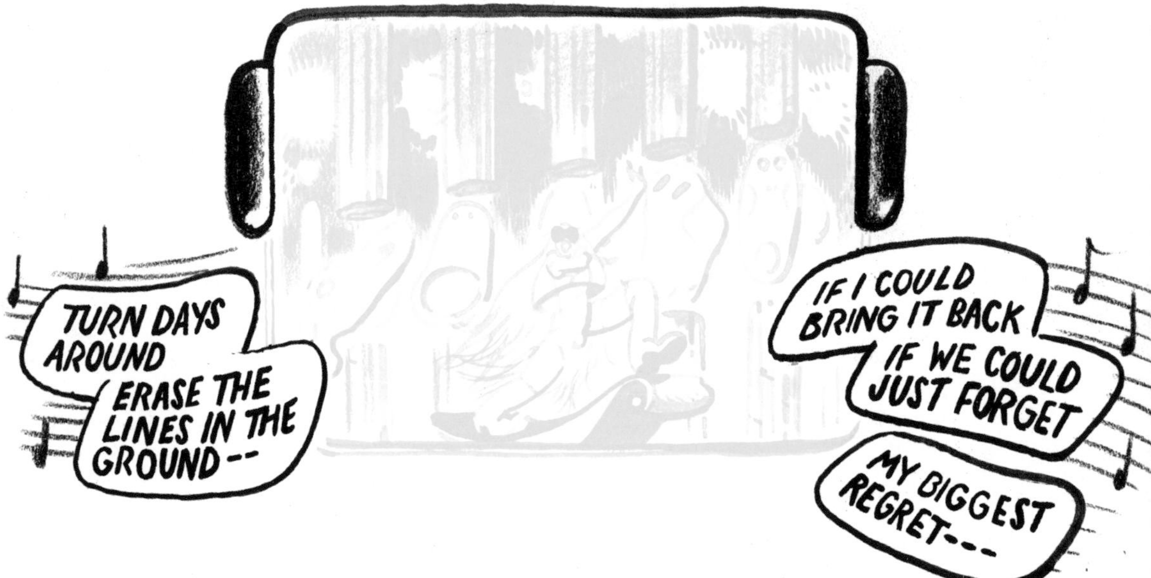
TURN DAYS AROUND
ERASE THE LINES IN THE GROUND--
IF I COULD BRING IT BACK
IF WE COULD JUST FORGET
MY BIGGEST REGRET---

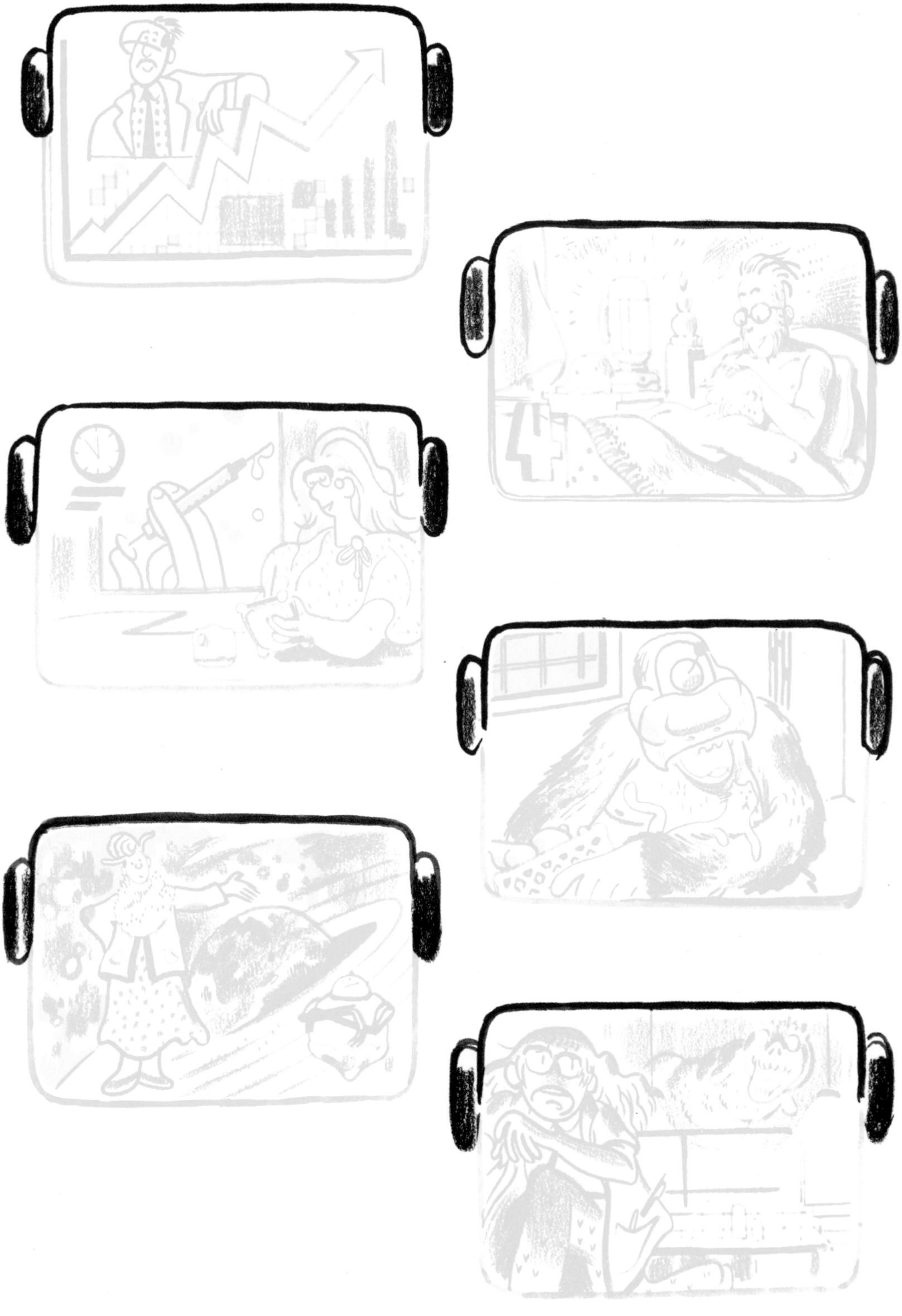

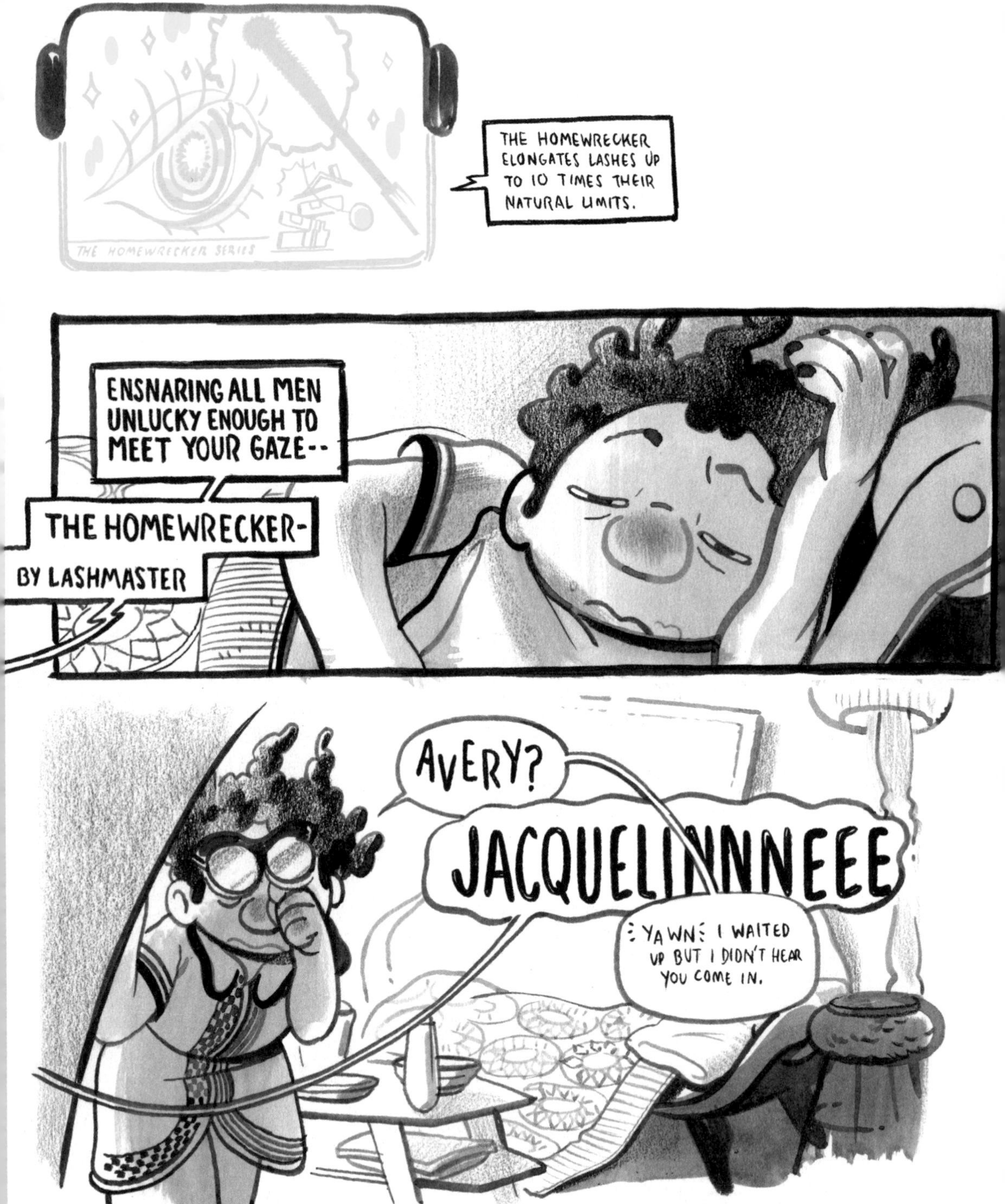
THE HOMEWRECKER SERIES
THE HOMEWRECKER ELONGATES LASHES UP TO 10 TIMES THEIR NATURAL LIMITS.
ENSNARING ALL MEN UNLUCKY ENOUGH TO MEET YOUR GAZE--
THE HOMEWRECKER-
BY LASHMASTER
AVERY?
JACQUELINNNEEE
YAWN I WAITED UP BUT I DIDN'T HEAR YOU COME IN.

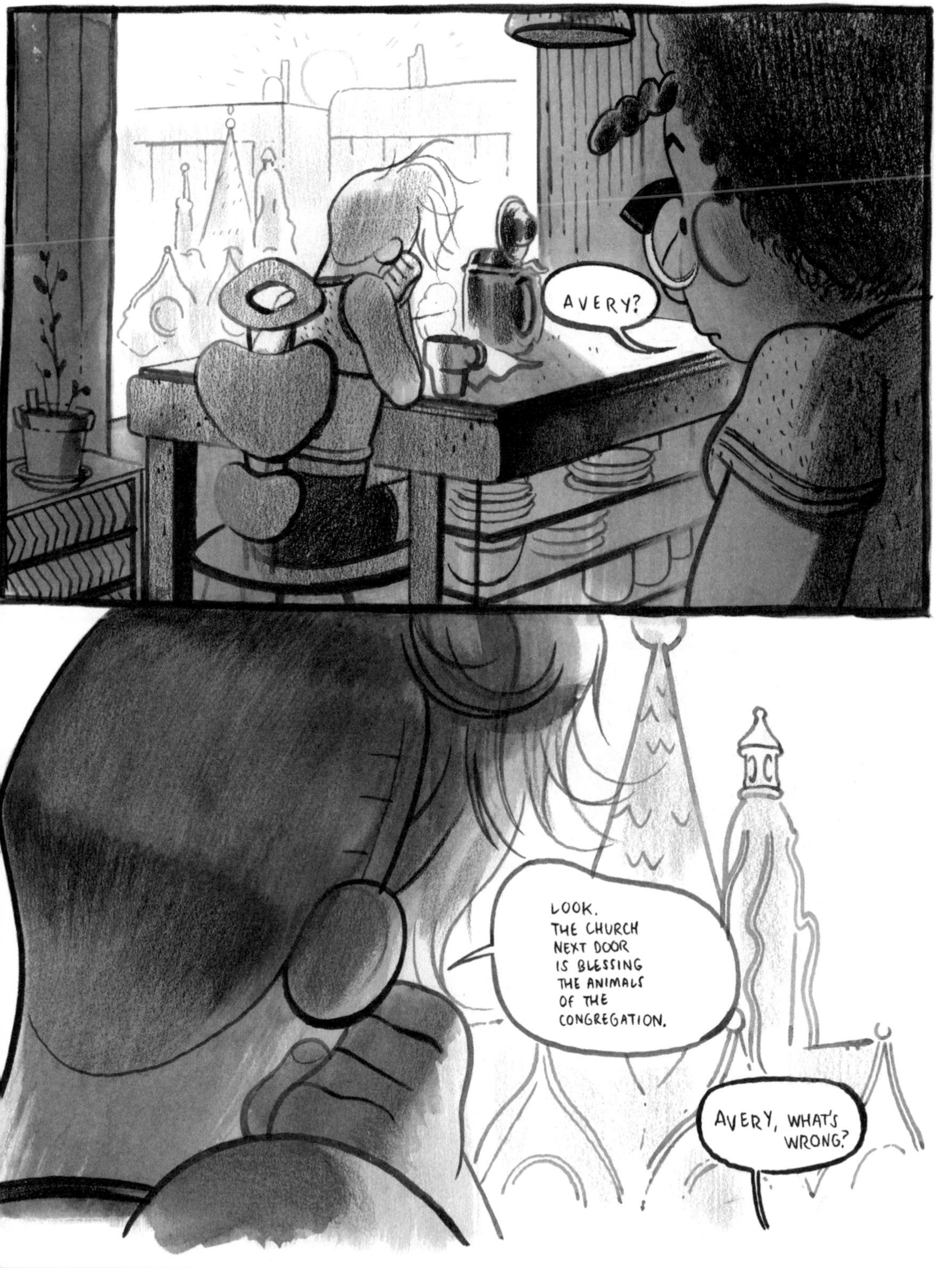
AVERY?
LOOK. THE CHURCH NEXT DOOR IS BLESSING THE ANIMALS OF THE CONGREGATION.
AVERY, WHAT'S WRONG?

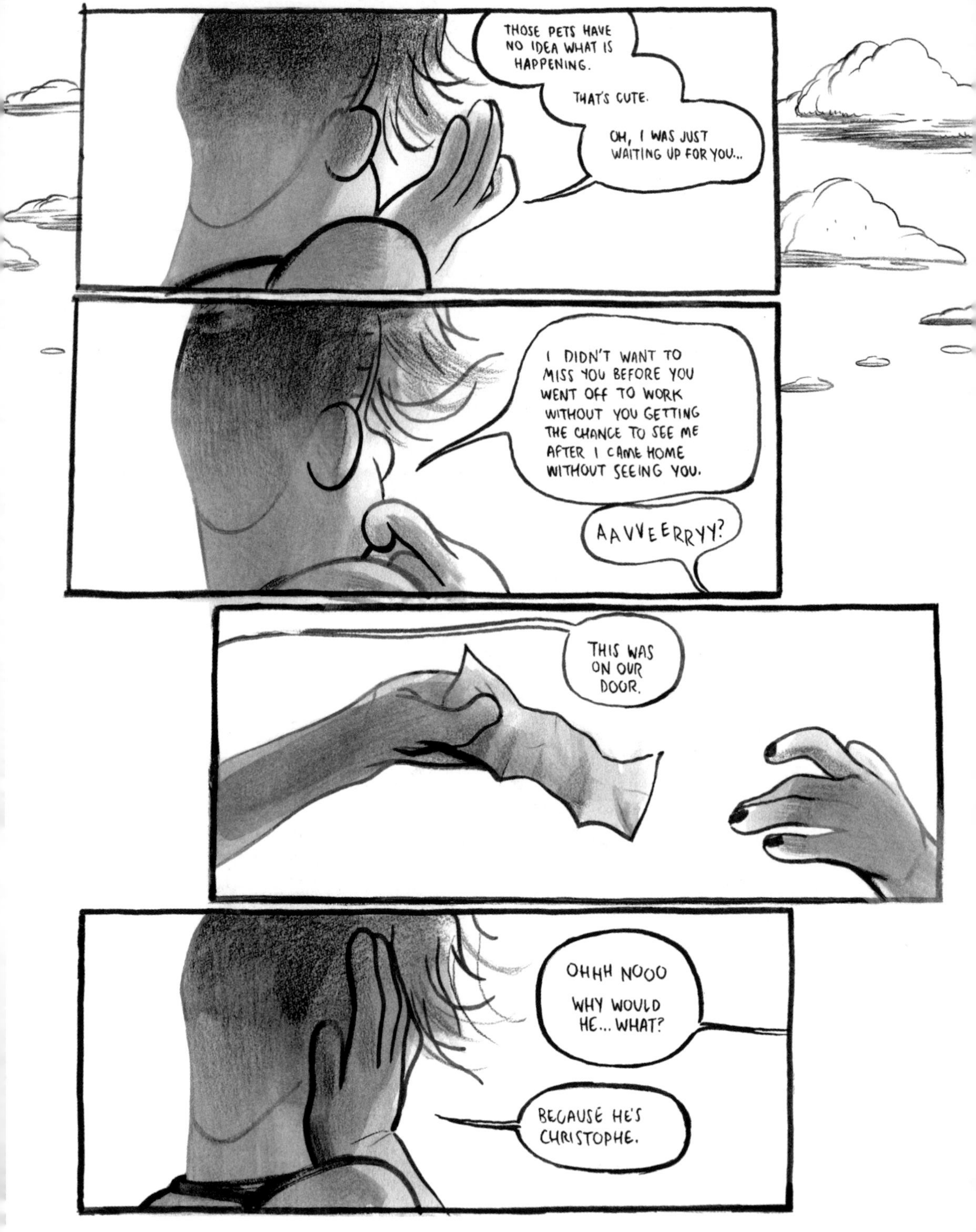
THOSE PETS HAVE NO IDEA WHAT IS HAPPENING.
THAT'S CUTE.
OH, I WAS JUST WAITING UP FOR YOU...
I DIDN'T WANT TO MISS YOU BEFORE YOU WENT OFF TO WORK WITHOUT YOU GETTING THE CHANCE TO SEE ME AFTER I CAME HOME WITHOUT SEEING YOU.
AAVVEERRYY?
THIS WAS ON OUR DOOR.
OHHH NOOO
WHY WOULD HE... WHAT?
BECAUSE HE'S CHRISTOPHE.

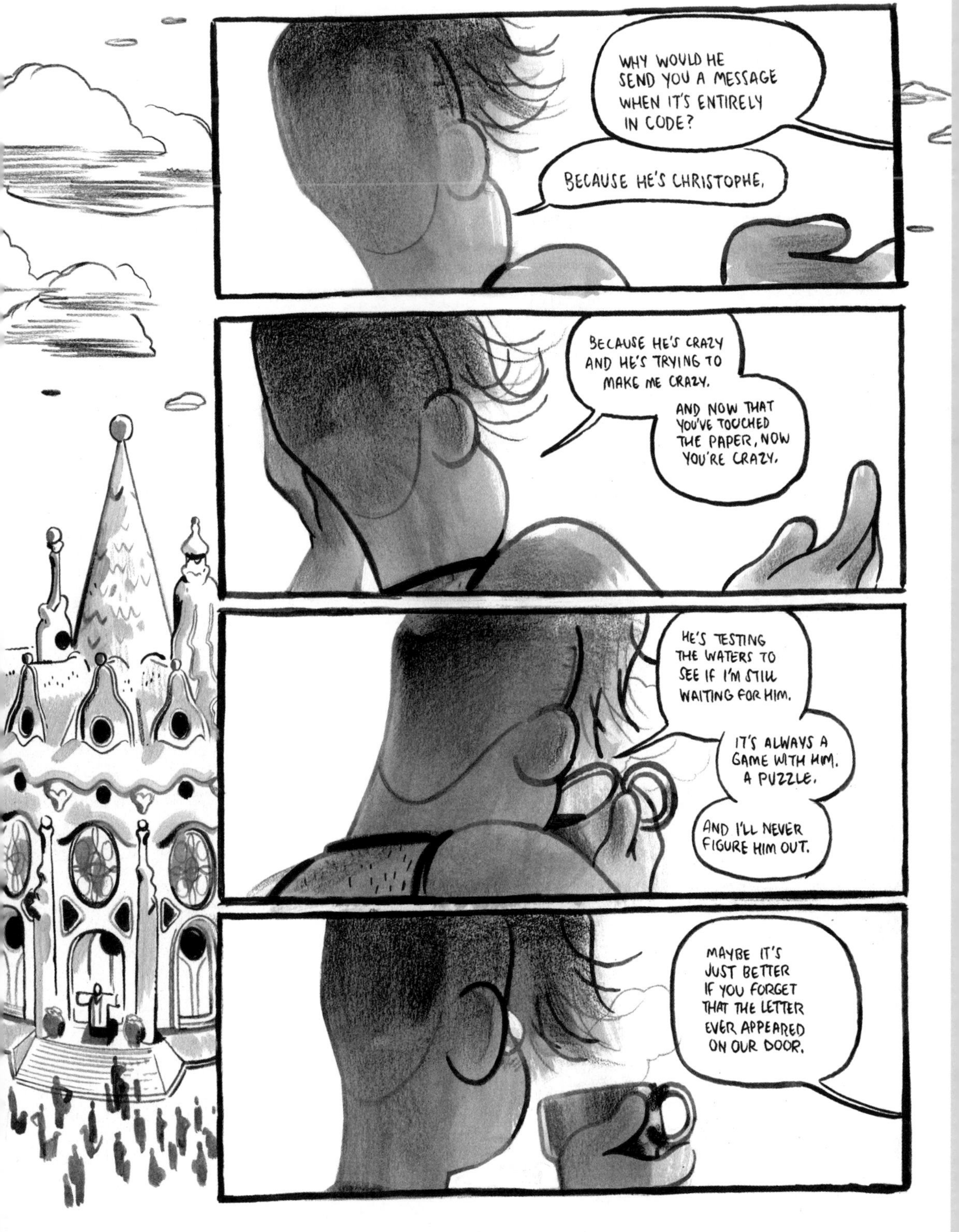
WHY WOULD HE SEND YOU A MESSAGE WHEN IT'S ENTIRELY IN CODE?
BECAUSE HE'S CHRISTOPHE.
BECAUSE HE'S CRAZY AND HE'S TRYING TO MAKE ME CRAZY.
AND NOW THAT YOU'VE TOUCHED THE PAPER, NOW YOU'RE CRAZY.
HE'S TESTING THE WATERS TO SEE IF I'M STILL WAITING FOR HIM.
IT'S ALWAYS A GAME WITH HIM. A PUZZLE.
AND I'LL NEVER FIGURE HIM OUT.
MAYBE IT'S JUST BETTER IF YOU FORGET THAT THE LETTER EVER APPEARED ON OUR DOOR.

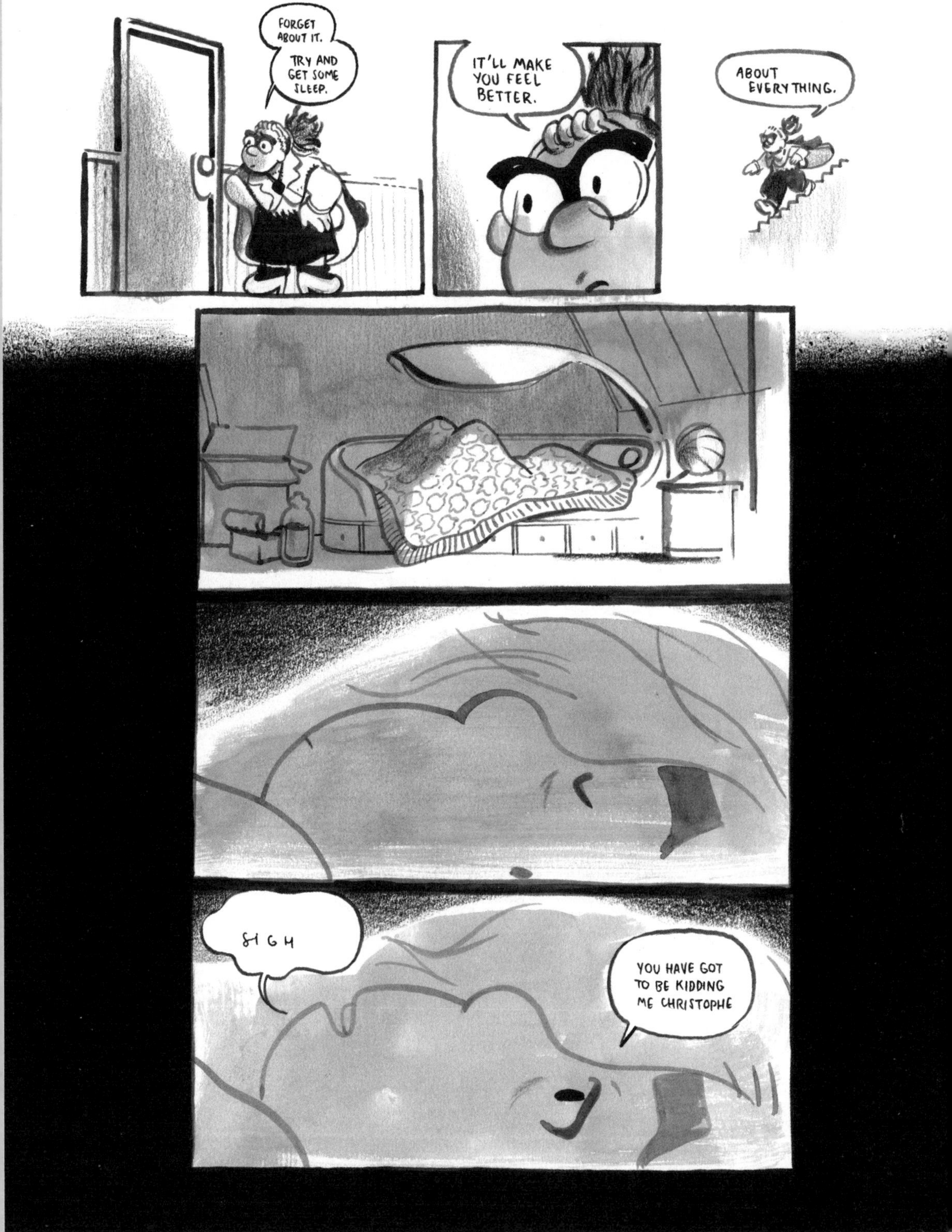
FORGET ABOUT IT.
TRY AND GET SOME SLEEP.
IT'LL MAKE YOU FEEL BETTER.
ABOUT EVERYTHING.
SIGH
YOU HAVE GOT TO BE KIDDING ME CHRISTOPHE

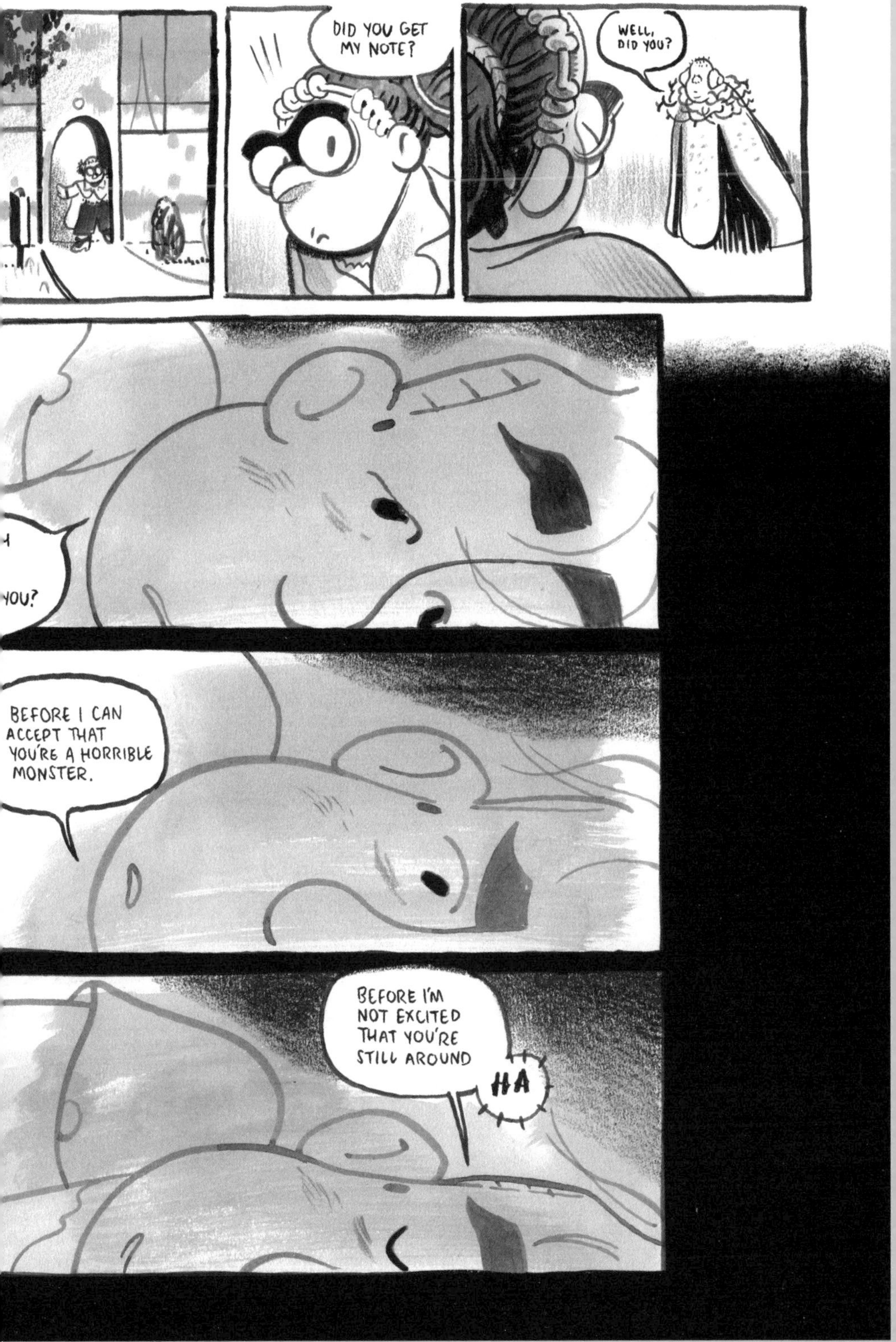
DID YOU GET MY NOTE?
WELL, DID YOU?
BEFORE I CAN ACCEPT THAT YOU'RE A HORRIBLE MONSTER.
BEFORE I'M NOT EXCITED THAT YOU'RE STILL AROUND
HA

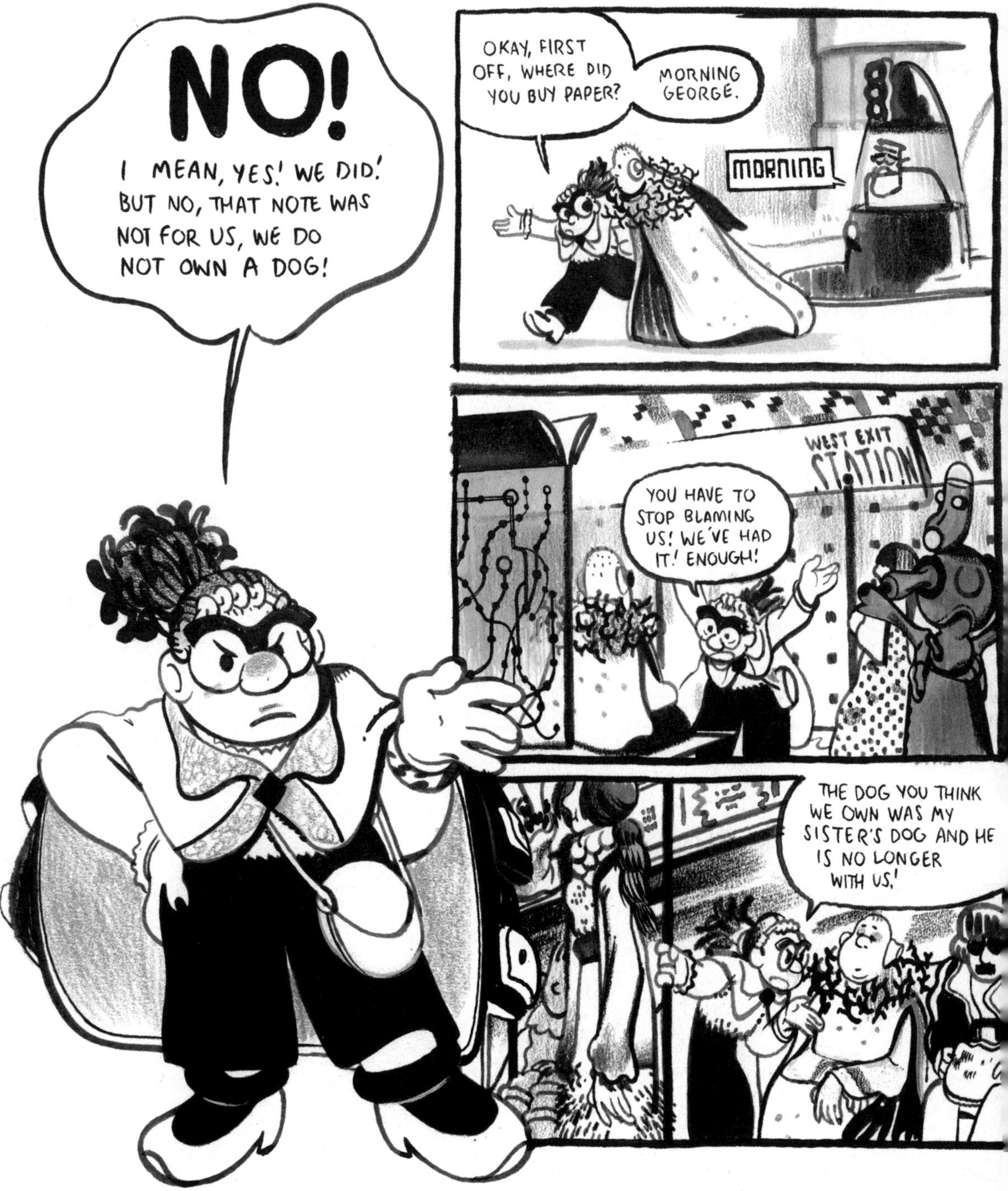
NO!
I MEAN, YES! WE DID! BUT NO, THAT NOTE WAS NOT FOR US, WE DO NOT OWN A DOG!
OKAY, FIRST OFF, WHERE DID YOU BUY PAPER?
MORNING GEORGE.
MORNING
WEST EXIT
STATION
YOU HAVE TO STOP BLAMING US! WE'VE HAD IT! ENOUGH!
THE DOG YOU THINK WE OWN WAS MY SISTER'S DOG AND HE IS NO LONGER WITH US!

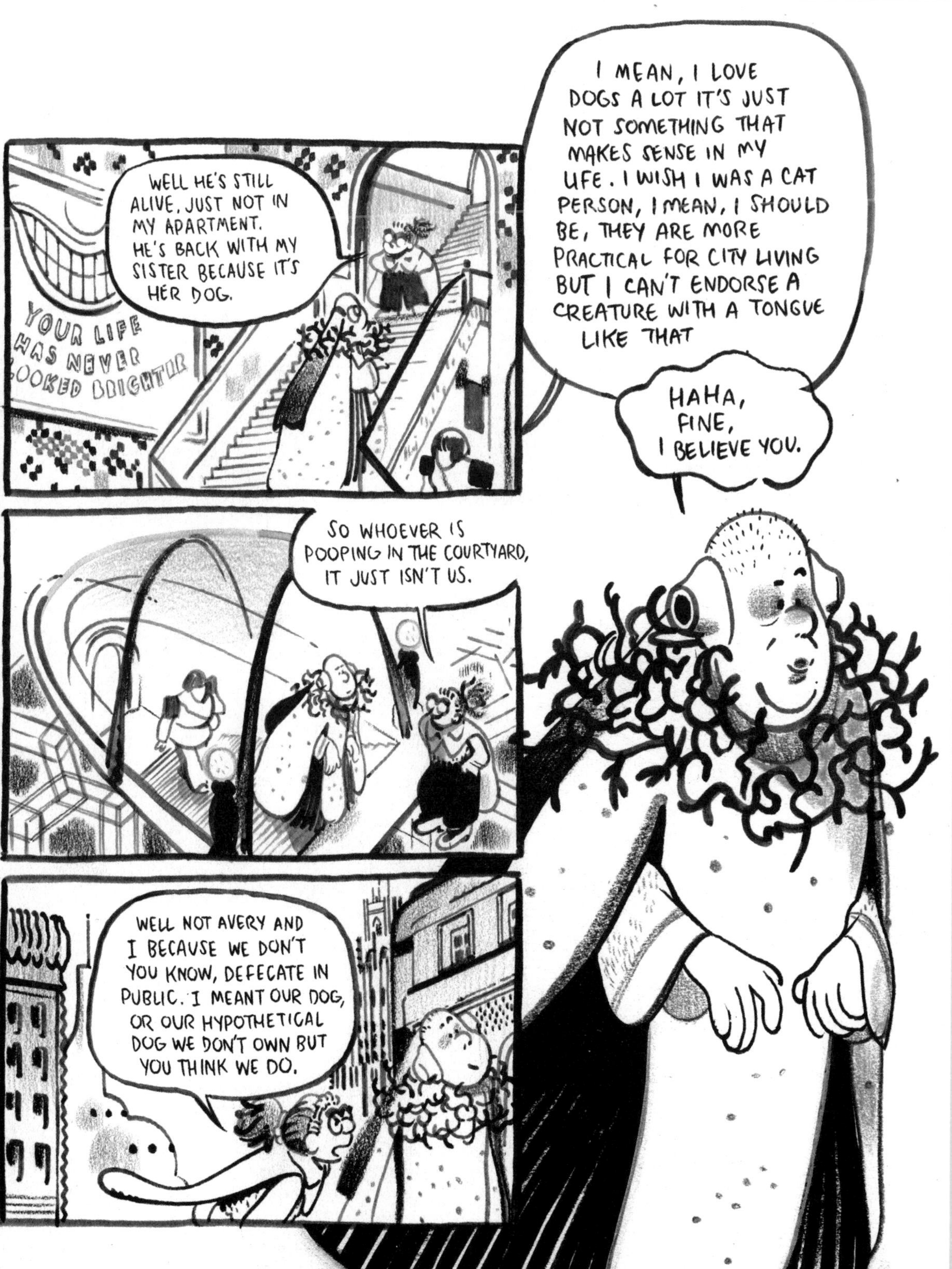
WELL HE'S STILL ALIVE, JUST NOT IN MY APARTMENT. HE'S BACK WITH MY SISTER BECAUSE IT'S HER DOG.
YOUR LIFE HAS NEVER LOOKED BRIGHTER
I MEAN, I LOVE DOGS A LOT IT'S JUST NOT SOMETHING THAT MAKES SENSE IN MY LIFE. I WISH I WAS A CAT PERSON, I MEAN, I SHOULD BE, THEY ARE MORE PRACTICAL FOR CITY LIVING BUT I CAN'T ENDORSE A CREATURE WITH A TONGUE LIKE THAT
HAHA, FINE, I BELIEVE YOU.
SO WHOEVER IS POOPING IN THE COURTYARD, IT JUST ISN'T US.
WELL NOT AVERY AND I BECAUSE WE DON'T YOU KNOW, DEFECATE IN PUBLIC. I MEANT OUR DOG, OR OUR HYPOTHETICAL DOG WE DON'T OWN BUT YOU THINK WE DO.

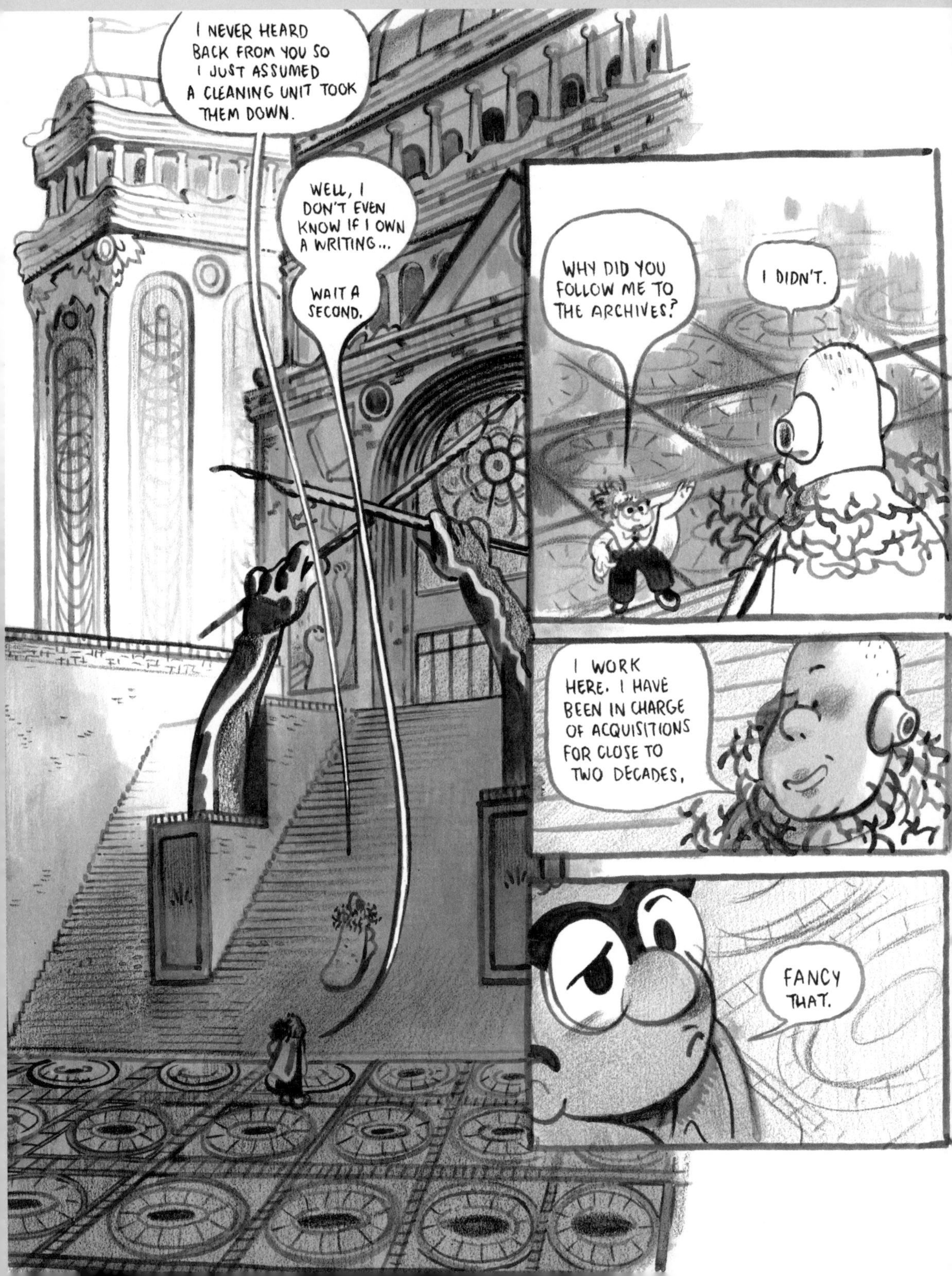

I NEVER HEARD BACK FROM YOU SO I JUST ASSUMED A CLEANING UNIT TOOK THEM DOWN.
WELL, I DON'T EVEN KNOW IF I OWN A WRITING...
WAIT A SECOND.
WHY DID YOU FOLLOW ME TO THE ARCHIVES?
I DIDN'T.
I WORK HERE. I HAVE BEEN IN CHARGE OF ACQUISITIONS FOR CLOSE TO TWO DECADES.
FANCY THAT.

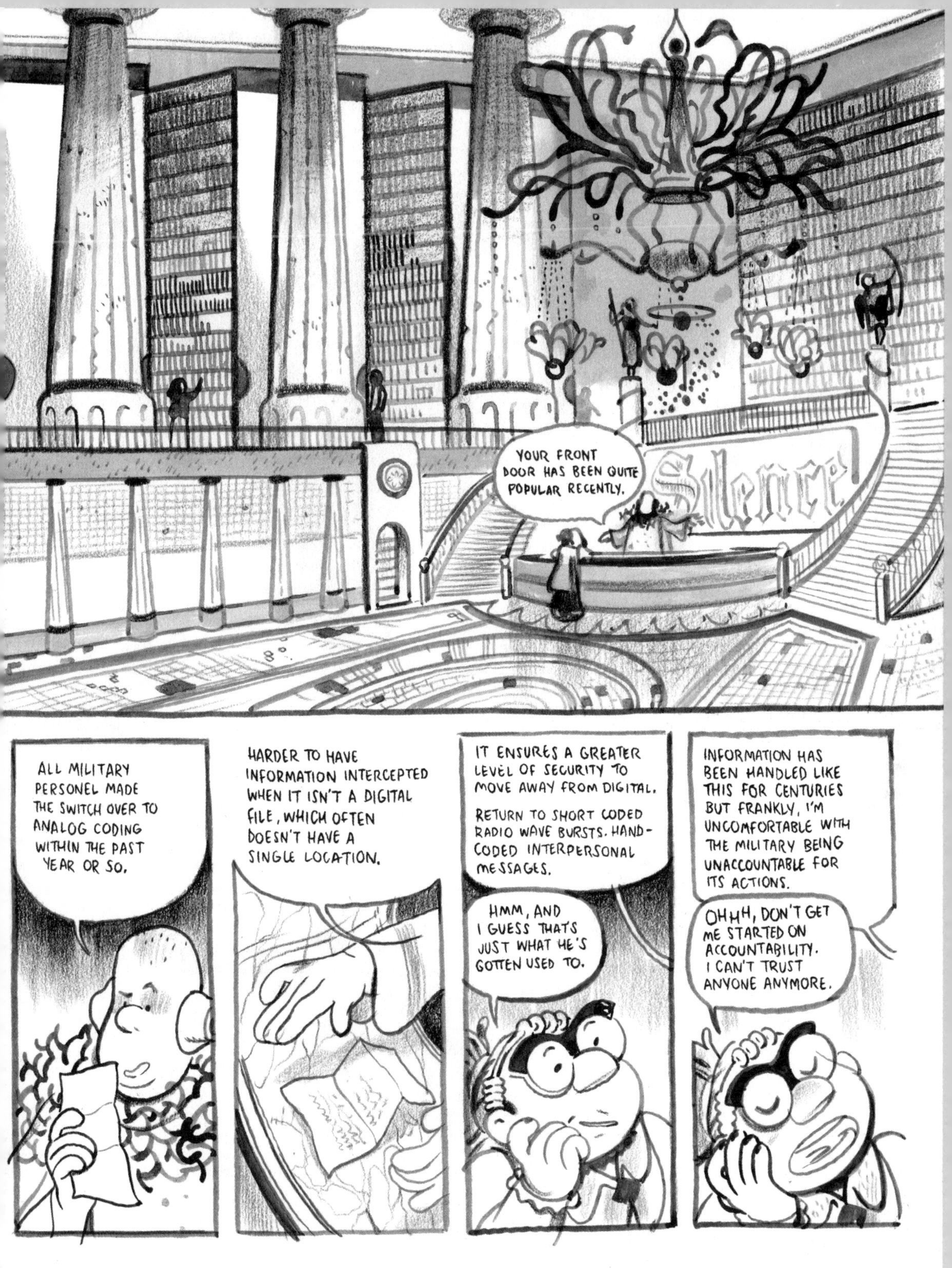
YOUR FRONT DOOR HAS BEEN QUITE POPULAR RECENTLY.
Silence
ALL MILITARY PERSONEL MADE THE SWITCH OVER TO ANALOG CODING WITHIN THE PAST YEAR OR SO.
HARDER TO HAVE INFORMATION INTERCEPTED WHEN IT ISN'T A DIGITAL FILE, WHICH OFTEN DOESN'T HAVE A SINGLE LOCATION.
IT ENSURES A GREATER LEVEL OF SECURITY TO MOVE AWAY FROM DIGITAL.
RETURN TO SHORT CODED RADIO WAVE BURSTS. HAND-CODED INTERPERSONAL MESSAGES.
HMM, AND I GUESS THATS JUST WHAT HE'S GOTTEN USED TO.
INFORMATION HAS BEEN HANDLED LIKE THIS FOR CENTURIES BUT FRANKLY, I'M UNCOMFORTABLE WITH THE MILITARY BEING UNACCOUNTABLE FOR ITS ACTIONS.
OHHH, DON'T GET ME STARTED ON ACCOUNTABILITY. I CAN'T TRUST ANYONE ANYMORE.

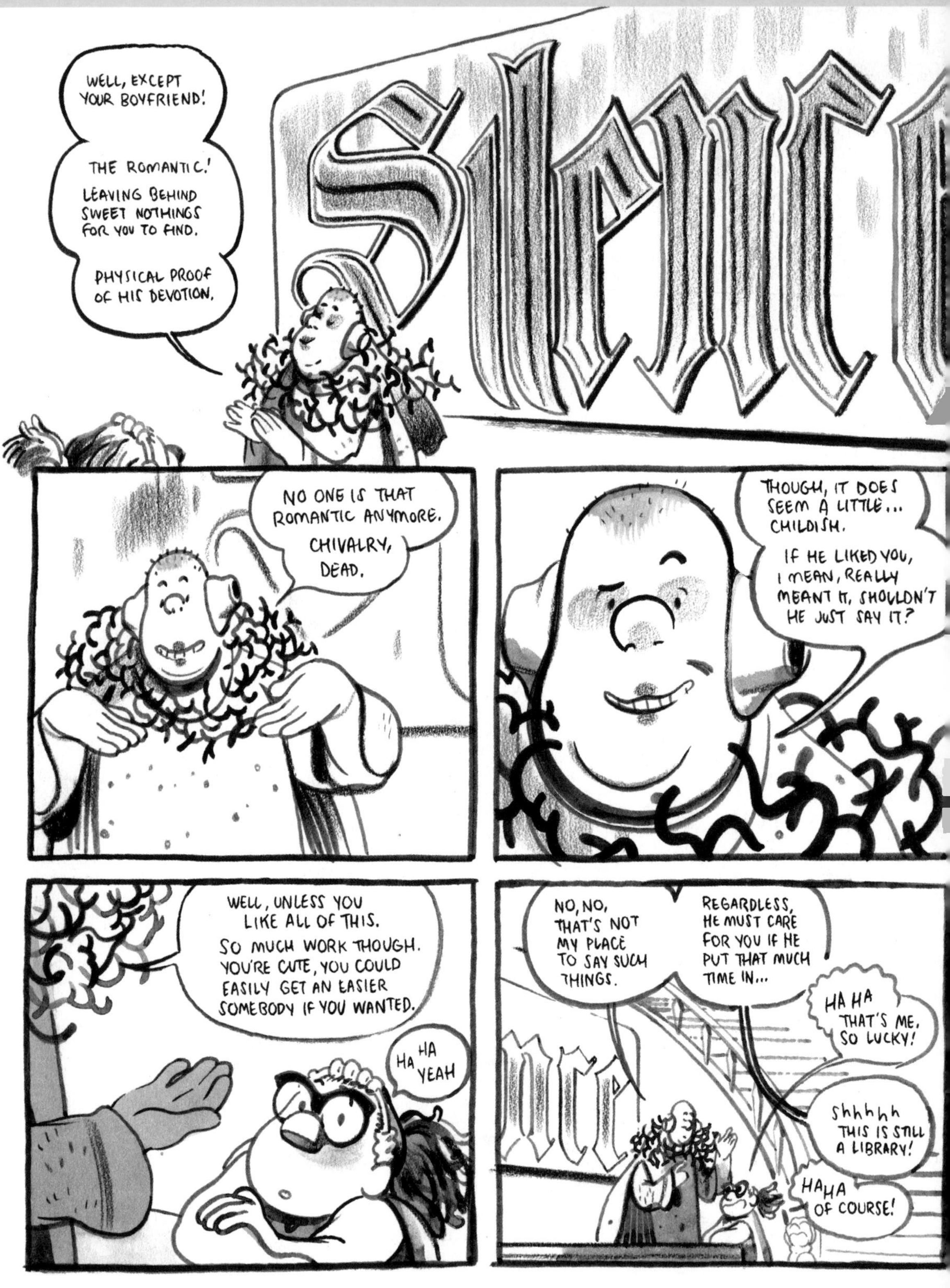
WELL, EXCEPT YOUR BOYFRIEND!
THE ROMANTIC! LEAVING BEHIND SWEET NOTHINGS FOR YOU TO FIND.
PHYSICAL PROOF OF HIS DEVOTION.
NO ONE IS THAT ROMANTIC ANYMORE.
CHIVALRY, DEAD.
THOUGH, IT DOES SEEM A LITTLE... CHILDISH.
IF HE LIKED YOU, I MEAN, REALLY MEANT IT, SHOULDN'T HE JUST SAY IT?
WELL, UNLESS YOU LIKE ALL OF THIS.
SO MUCH WORK THOUGH. YOU'RE CUTE, YOU COULD EASILY GET AN EASIER SOMEBODY IF YOU WANTED.
HA HA YEAH
NO, NO, THAT'S NOT MY PLACE TO SAY SUCH THINGS.
REGARDLESS, HE MUST CARE FOR YOU IF HE PUT THAT MUCH TIME IN...
HA HA THAT'S ME, SO LUCKY!
shhhhh THIS IS STILL A LIBRARY!
HAHA OF COURSE!

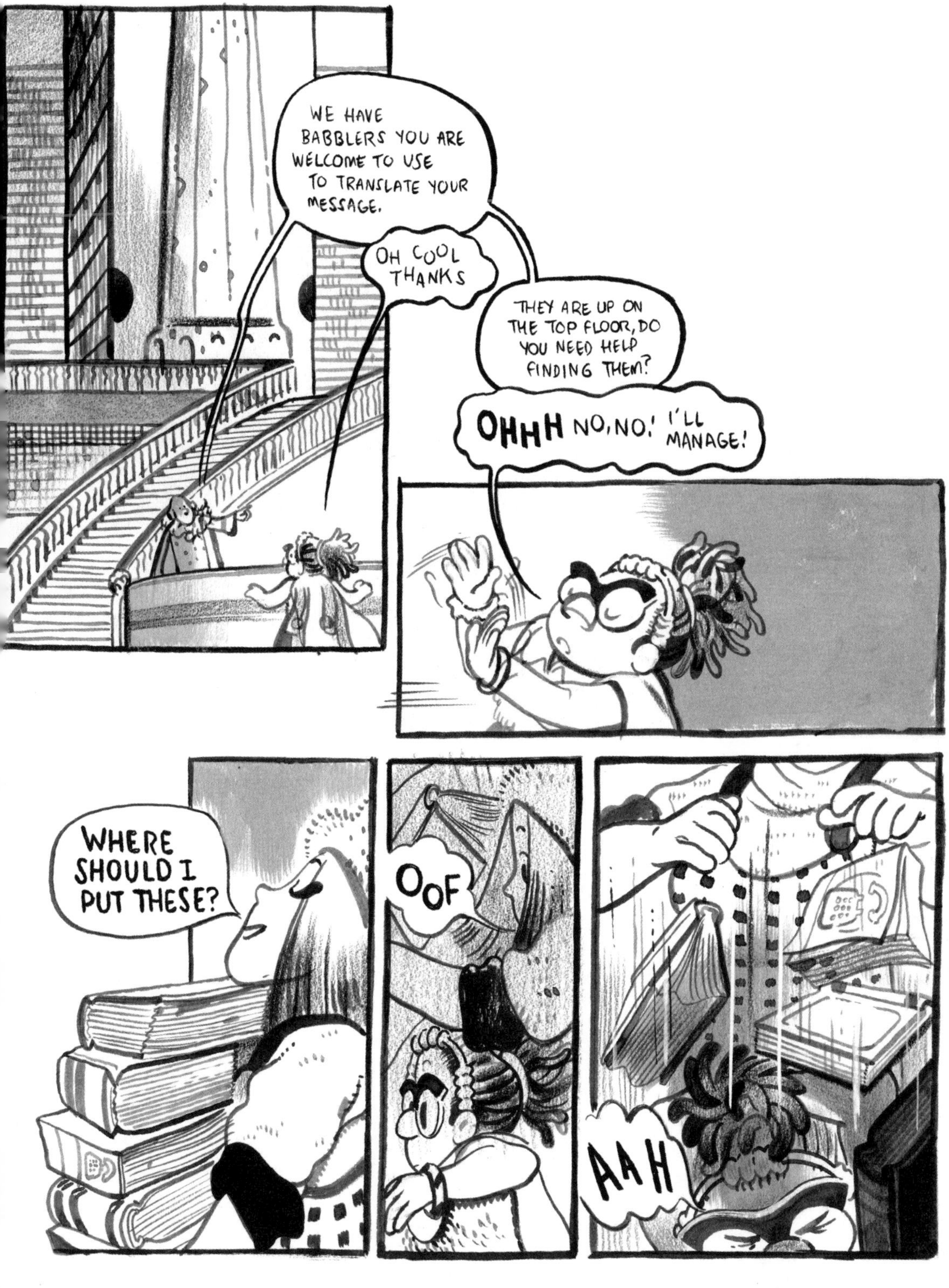
WE HAVE BABBLERS YOU ARE WELCOME TO USE TO TRANSLATE YOUR MESSAGE.
OH COOL THANKS
THEY ARE UP ON THE TOP FLOOR, DO YOU NEED HELP FINDING THEM?
OHHH NO, NO! I'LL MANAGE!
WHERE SHOULD I PUT THESE?
OOF
AAH

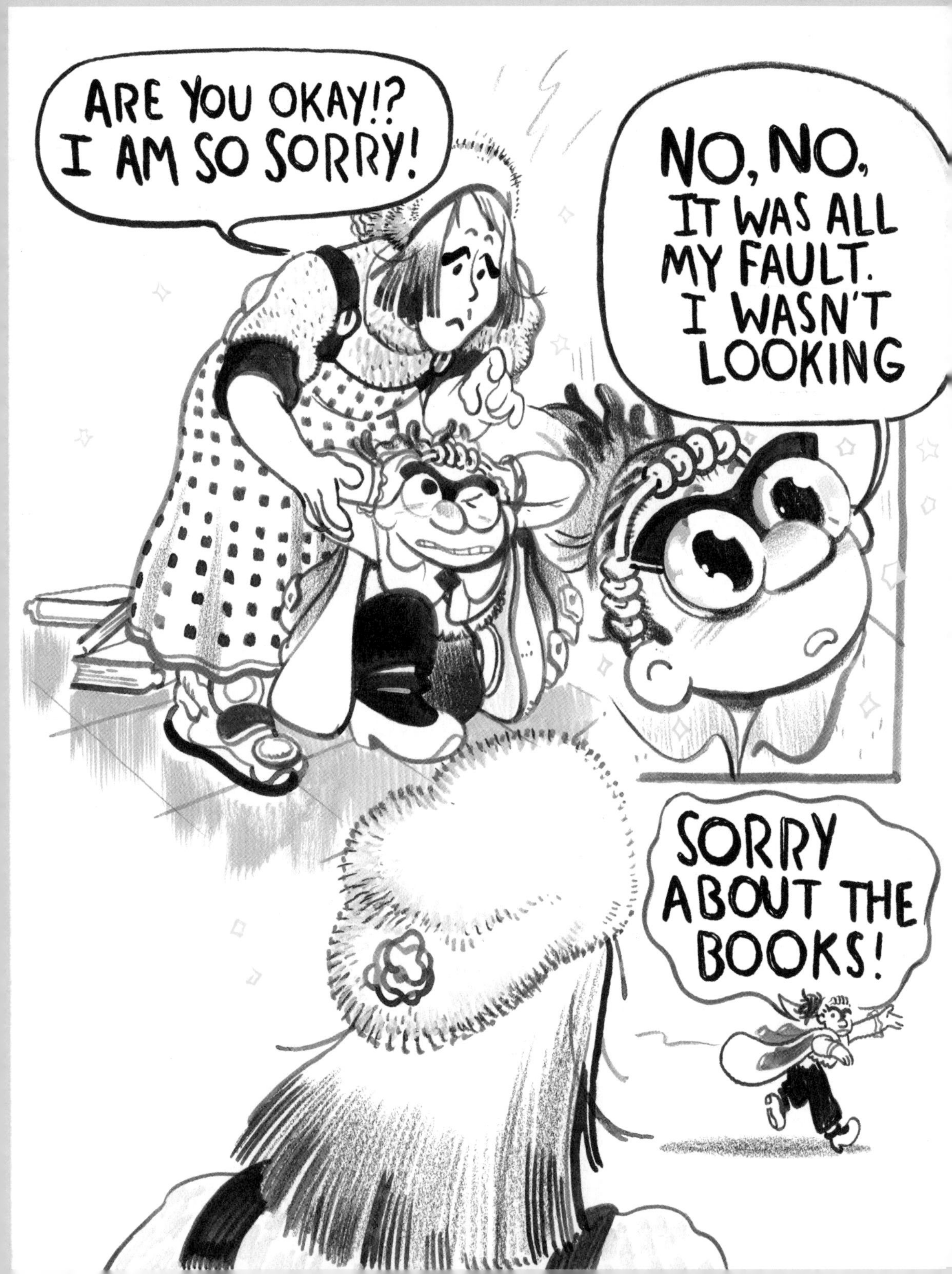
ARE YOU OKAY!? I AM SO SORRY!
NO, NO, IT WAS ALL MY FAULT. I WASN'T LOOKING
SORRY ABOUT THE BOOKS!

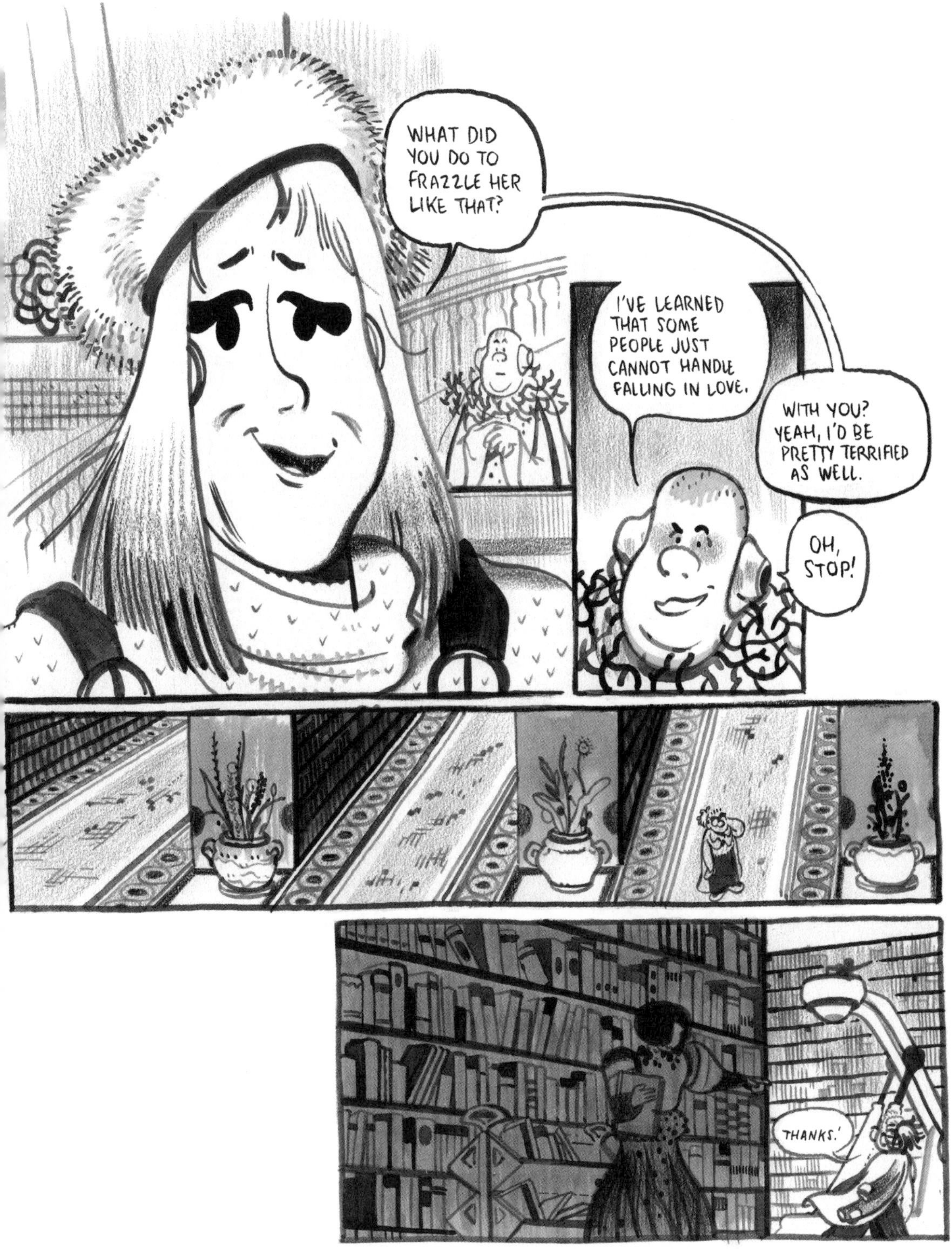
WHAT DID YOU DO TO FRAZZLE HER LIKE THAT?
I'VE LEARNED THAT SOME PEOPLE JUST CANNOT HANDLE FALLING IN LOVE.
WITH YOU? YEAH, I'D BE PRETTY TERRIFIED AS WELL.
OH, STOP!
THANKS.

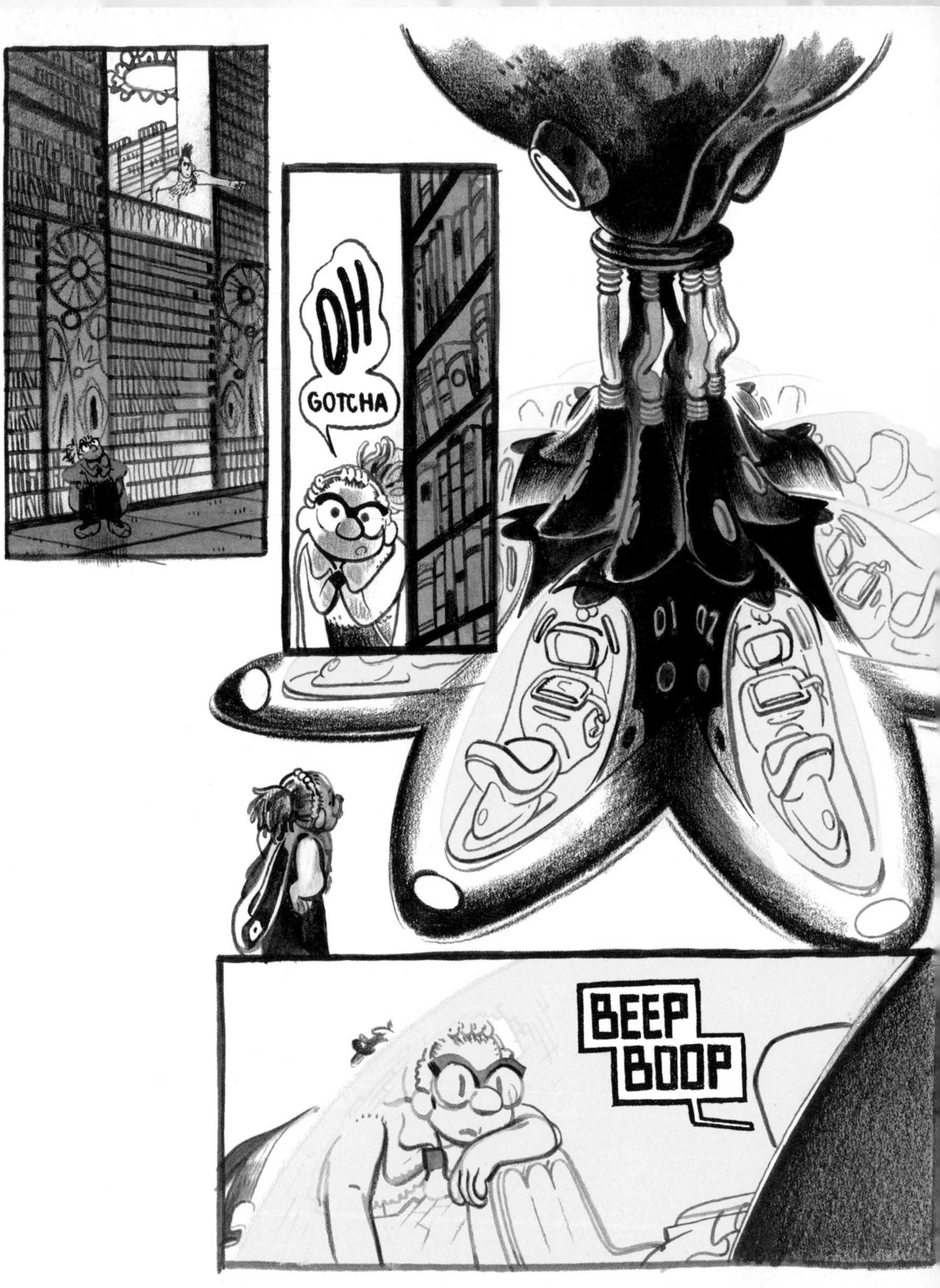
OH
GOTCHA
BEEP
BOOP

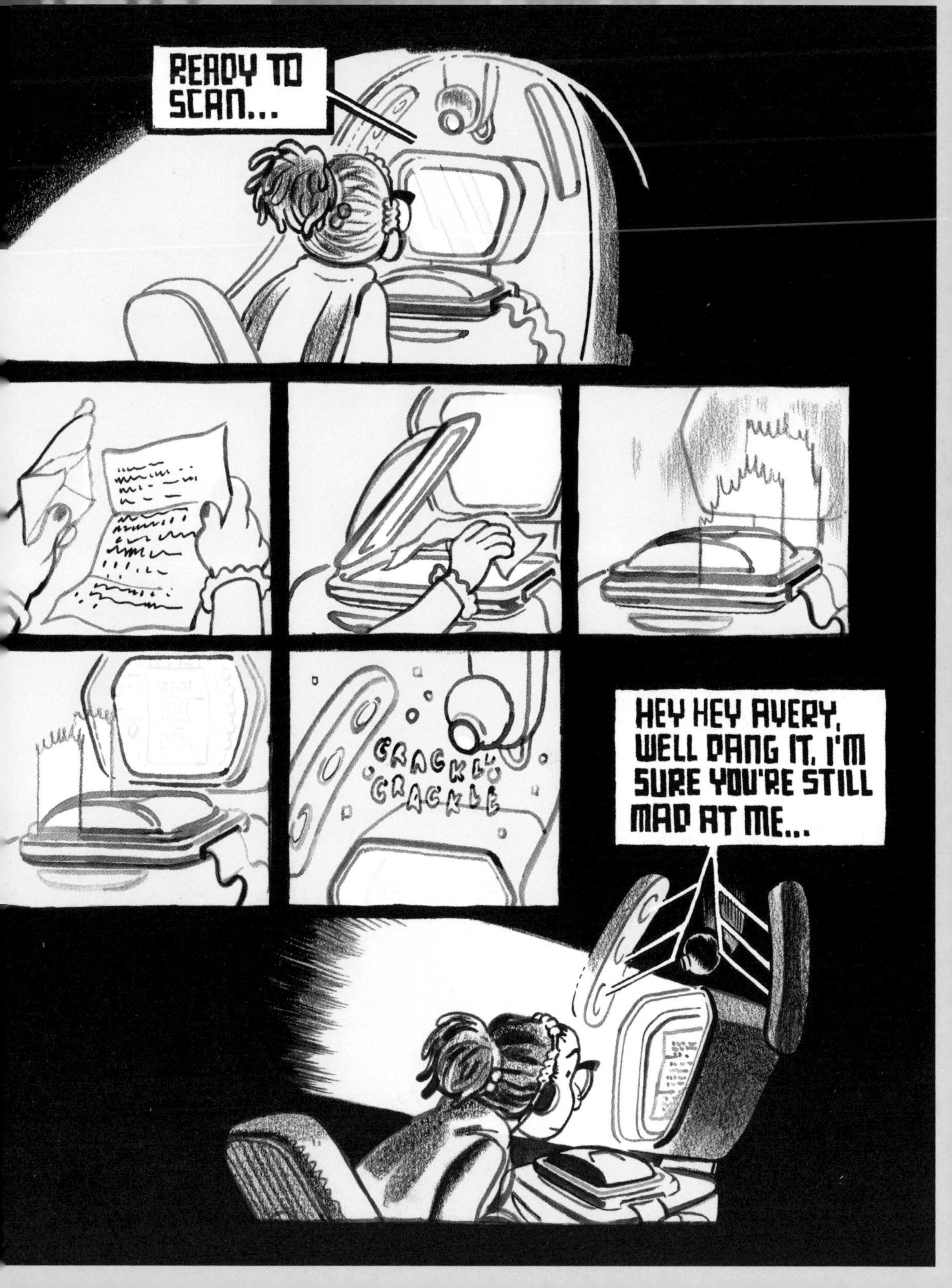
READY TO SCAN...
CRACKLE CRACKLE
HEY HEY AVERY, WELL DANG IT, I'M SURE YOU'RE STILL MAD AT ME...

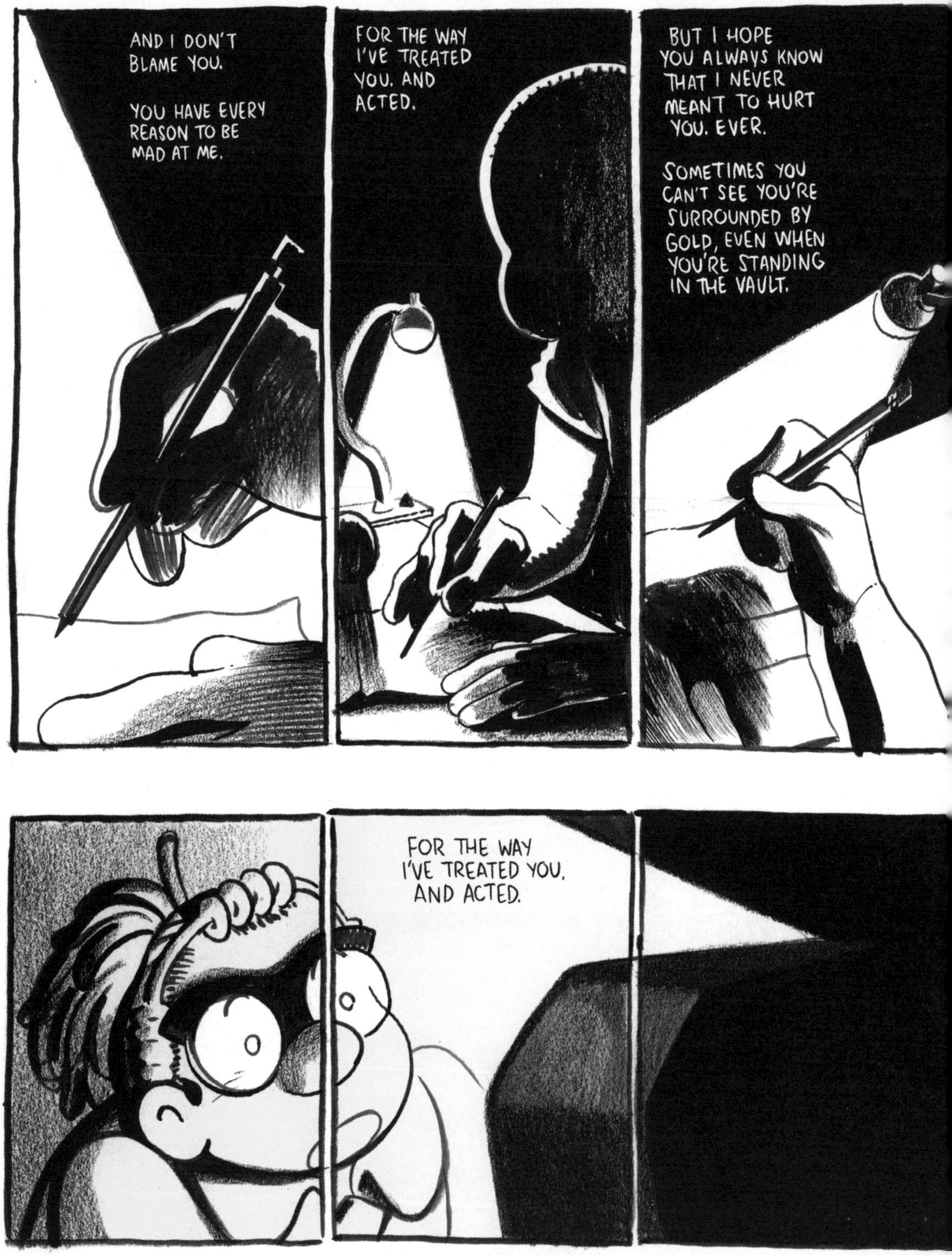
AND I DON'T BLAME YOU.
YOU HAVE EVERY REASON TO BE MAD AT ME.
FOR THE WAY I'VE TREATED YOU. AND ACTED.
BUT I HOPE YOU ALWAYS KNOW THAT I NEVER MEANT TO HURT YOU. EVER.
SOMETIMES YOU CAN'T SEE YOU'RE SURROUNDED BY GOLD, EVEN WHEN YOU'RE STANDING IN THE VAULT.
FOR THE WAY I'VE TREATED YOU. AND ACTED.

SO, BE MAD AT ME.
I UNDERSTAND.
I DON'T BLAME YOU.

JUST KNOW THAT
YOU'LL ALWAYS BE
ON MY MIND.

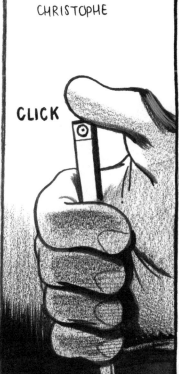

LOVE,
CHRISTOPHE

CLICK

BEEP
BEEP

LA TE

OH
NO!

YOINK

THANKS FOR
THE HELP!

SHE'LL
NEVER
RECOVER

OH,
HUSH!

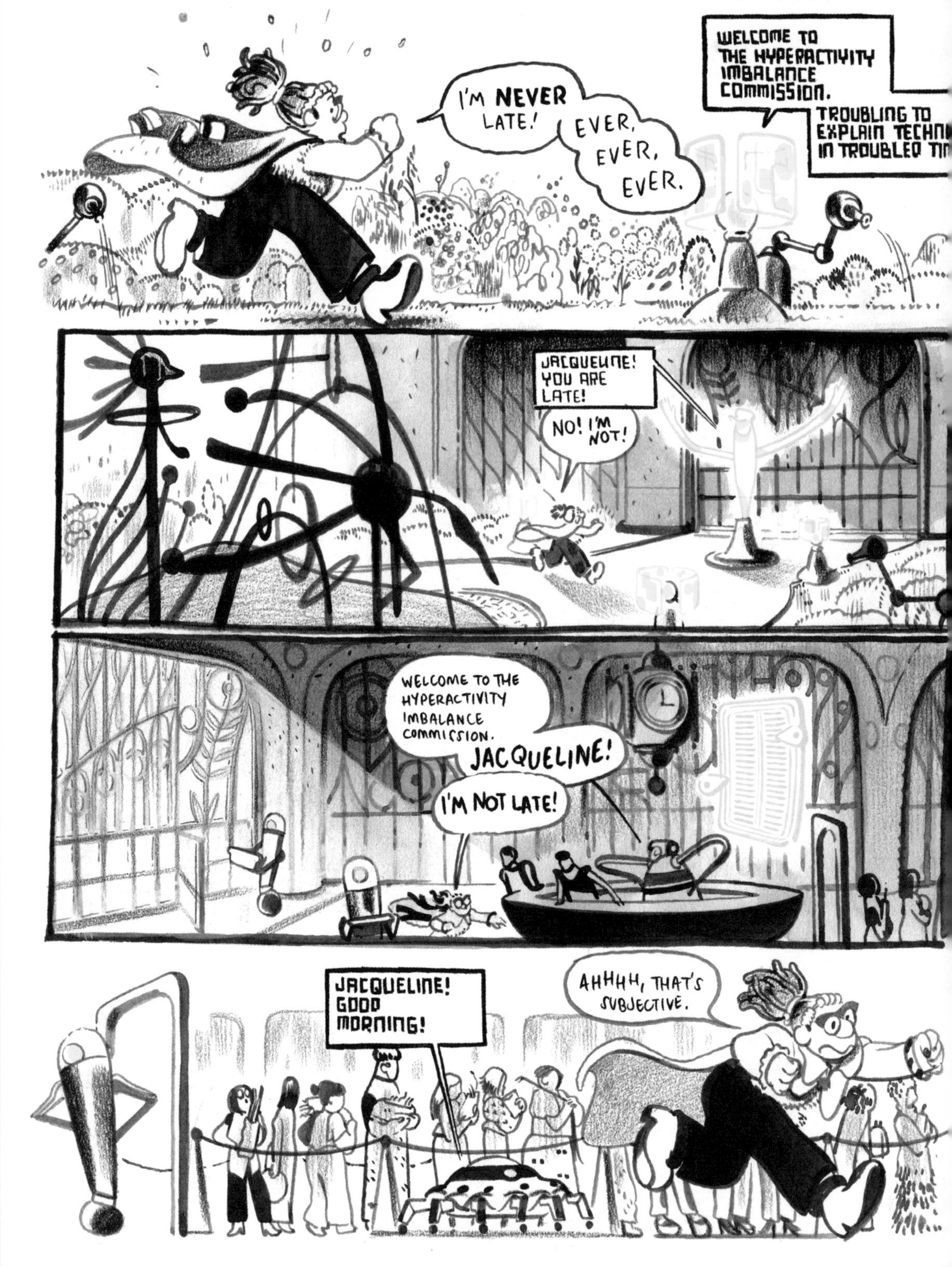
I'M NEVER LATE!
EVER, EVER, EVER.
WELCOME TO THE HYPERACTIVITY IMBALANCE COMMISSION.
TROUBLING TO EXPLAIN TECHN
IN TROUBLED TI
JACQUELINE! YOU ARE LATE!
NO! I'M NOT!
WELCOME TO THE HYPERACTIVITY IMBALANCE COMMISSION.
JACQUELINE!
I'M NOT LATE!
JACQUELINE! GOOD MORNING!
AHHHH, THAT'S SUBJECTIVE.

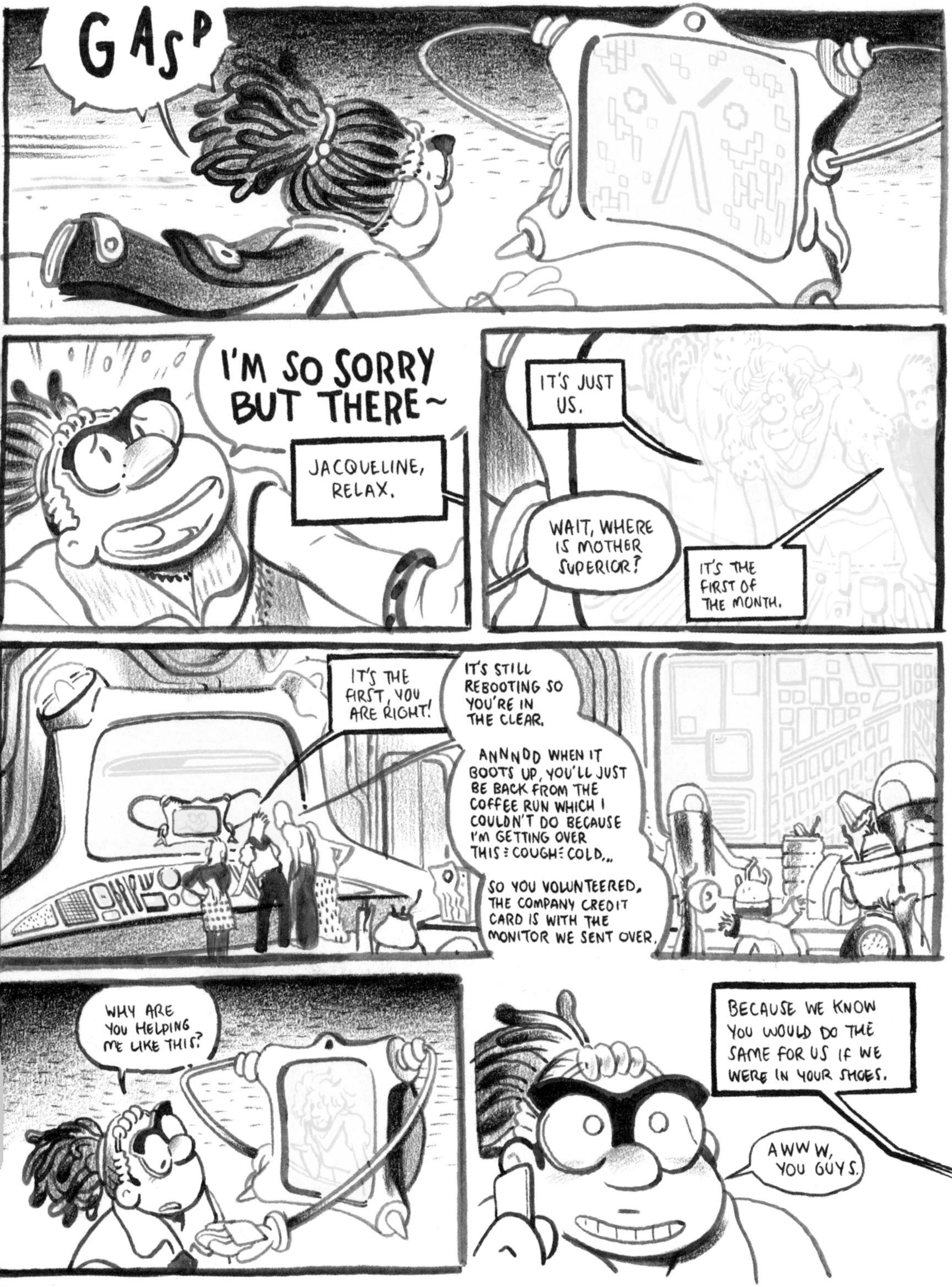
GASP
I'M SO SORRY BUT THERE~
JACQUELINE, RELAX.
IT'S JUST US.
WAIT, WHERE IS MOTHER SUPERIOR?
IT'S THE FIRST OF THE MONTH.
IT'S THE FIRST, YOU ARE RIGHT!
IT'S STILL REBOOTING SO YOU'RE IN THE CLEAR.
ANNNDD WHEN IT BOOTS UP, YOU'LL JUST BE BACK FROM THE COFFEE RUN WHICH I COULDN'T DO BECAUSE I'M GETTING OVER THIS : COUGH : COLD..
SO YOU VOLUNTEERED, THE COMPANY CREDIT CARD IS WITH THE MONITOR WE SENT OVER.
WHY ARE YOU HELPING ME LIKE THIS?
BECAUSE WE KNOW YOU WOULD DO THE SAME FOR US IF WE WERE IN YOUR SHOES.
AWWW, YOU GUYS.

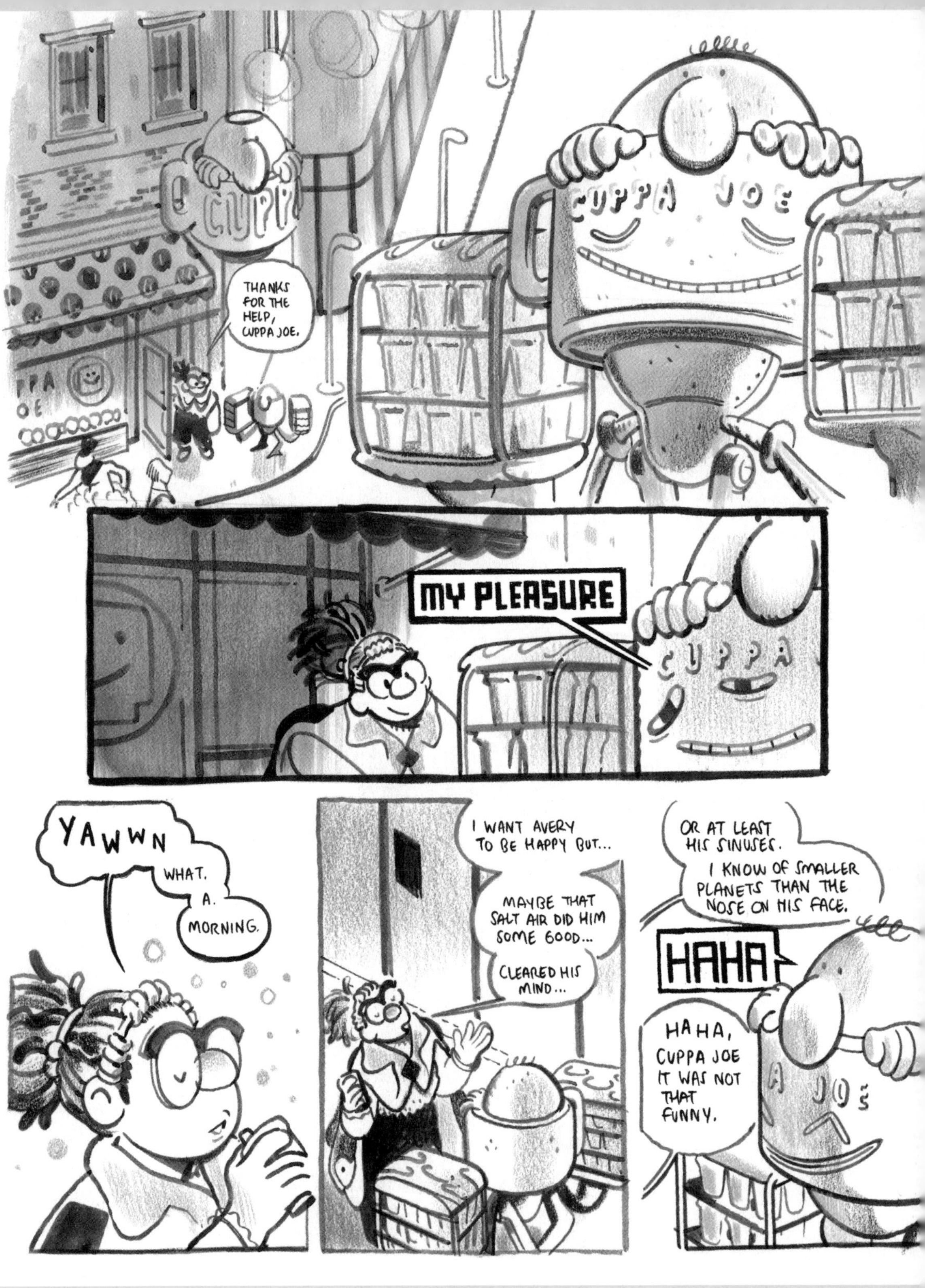

CUPPA JOE
THANKS FOR THE HELP, CUPPA JOE.
CUPPA JOE
MY PLEASURE
CUPPA
YAWWN
WHAT.
A.
MORNING.
I WANT AVERY TO BE HAPPY BUT...
MAYBE THAT SALT AIR DID HIM SOME GOOD...
CLEARED HIS MIND...
OR AT LEAST HIS SINUSES.
I KNOW OF SMALLER PLANETS THAN THE NOSE ON HIS FACE.
HAHA
HAHA, CUPPA JOE IT WAS NOT THAT FUNNY.

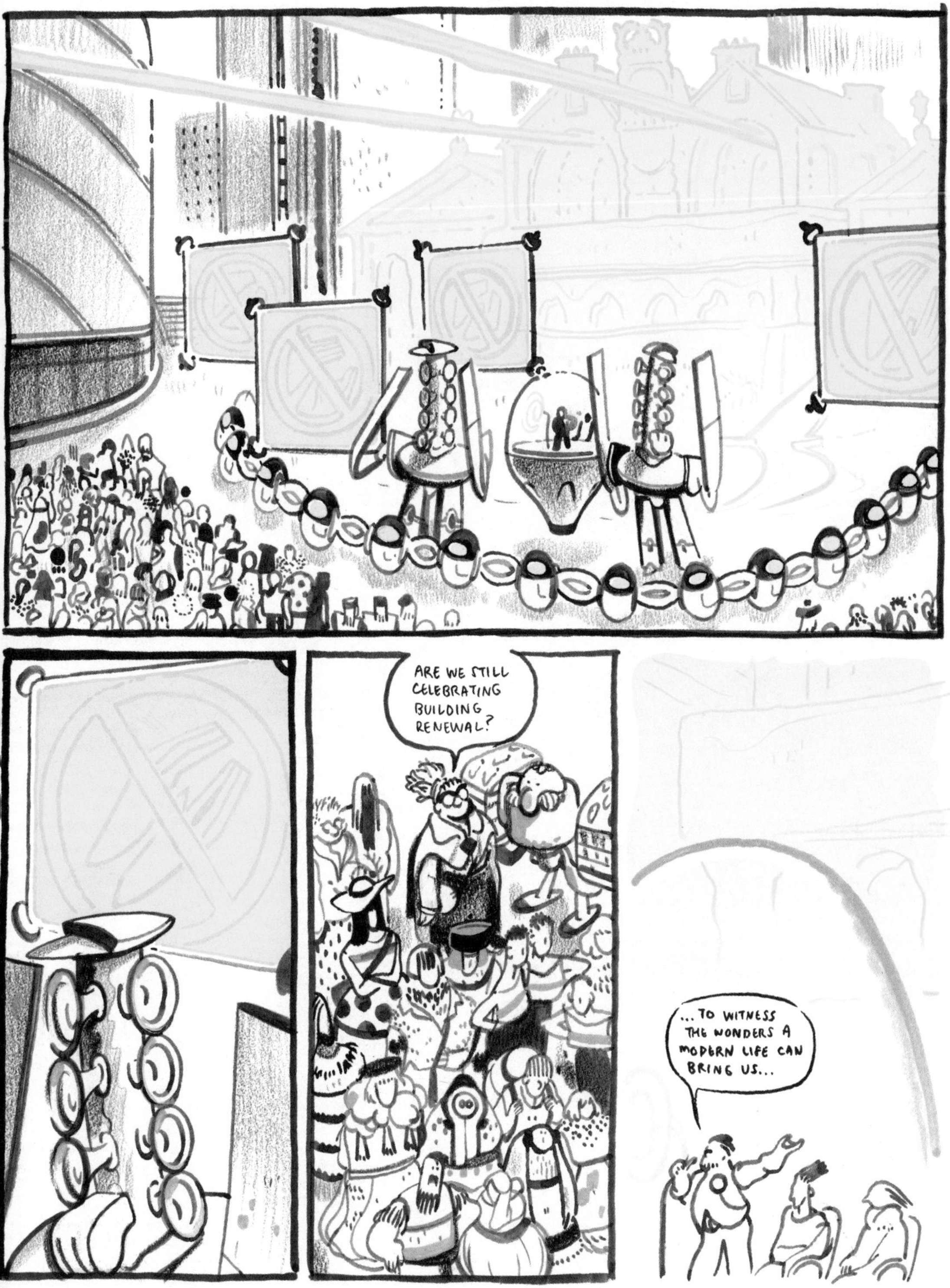
ARE WE STILL CELEBRATING BUILDING RENEWAL?
...TO WITNESS THE WONDERS A MODERN LIFE CAN BRING US...

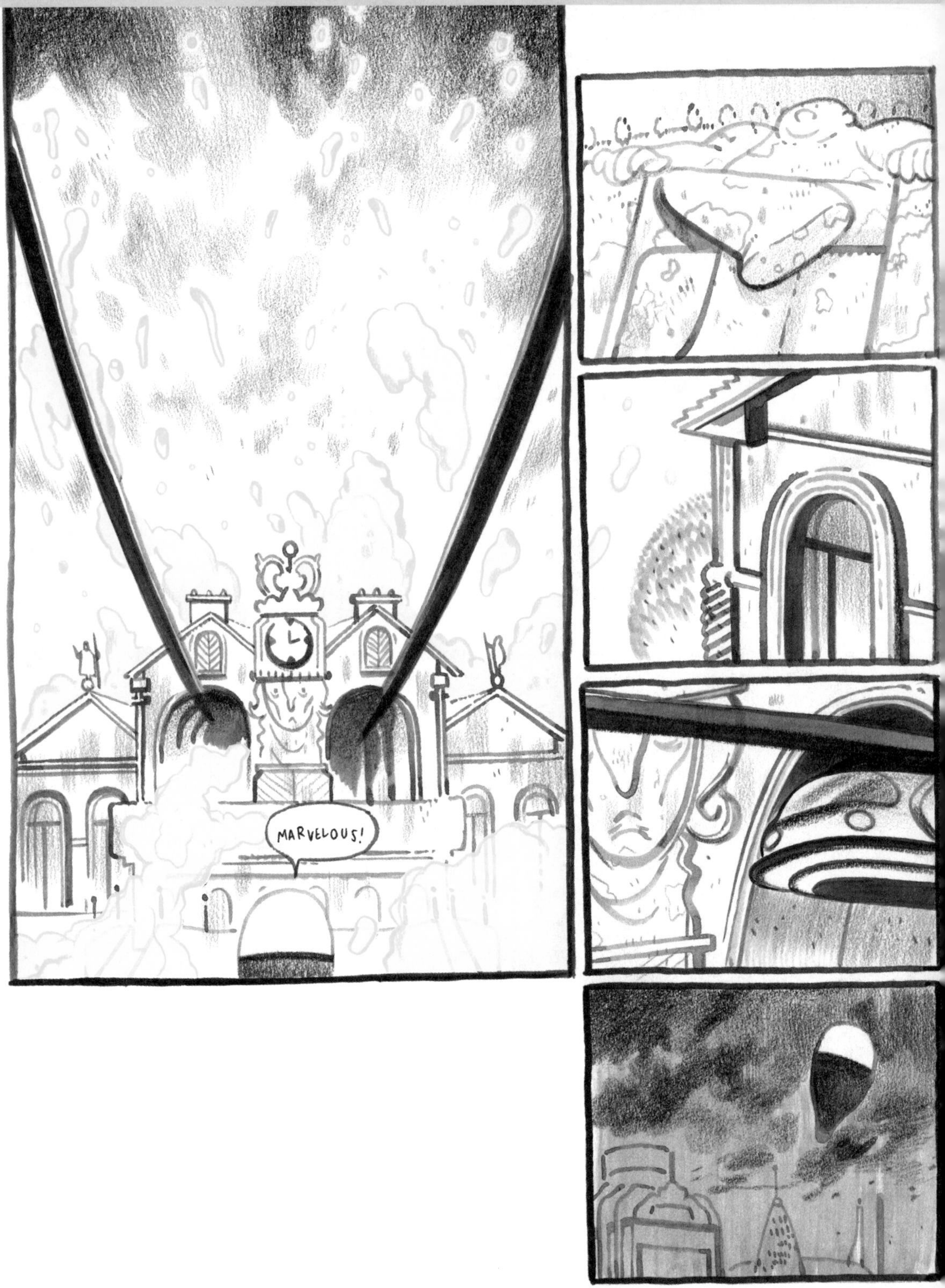
MARVELOUS!

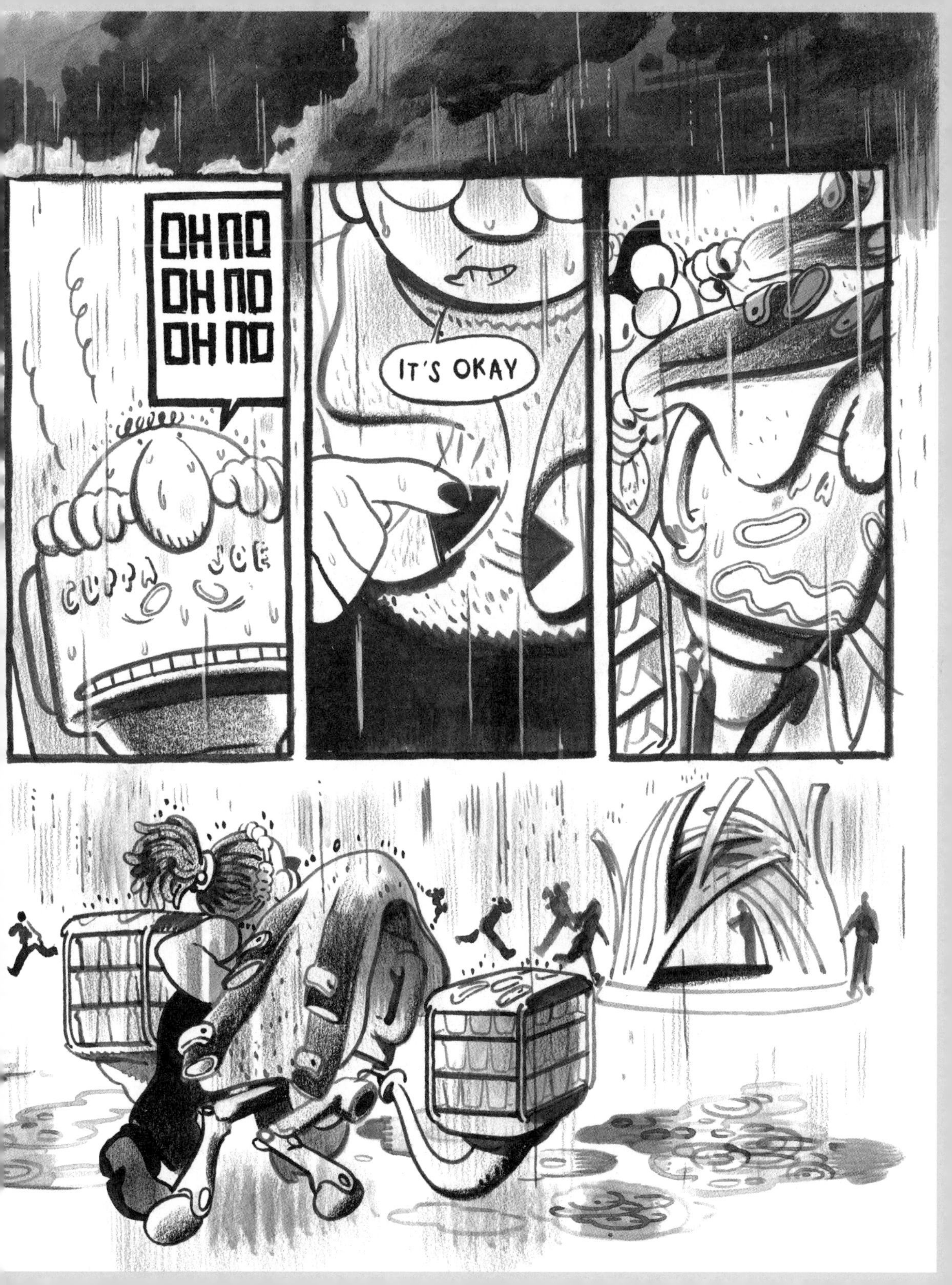
OH NO OH NO OH NO
IT'S OKAY

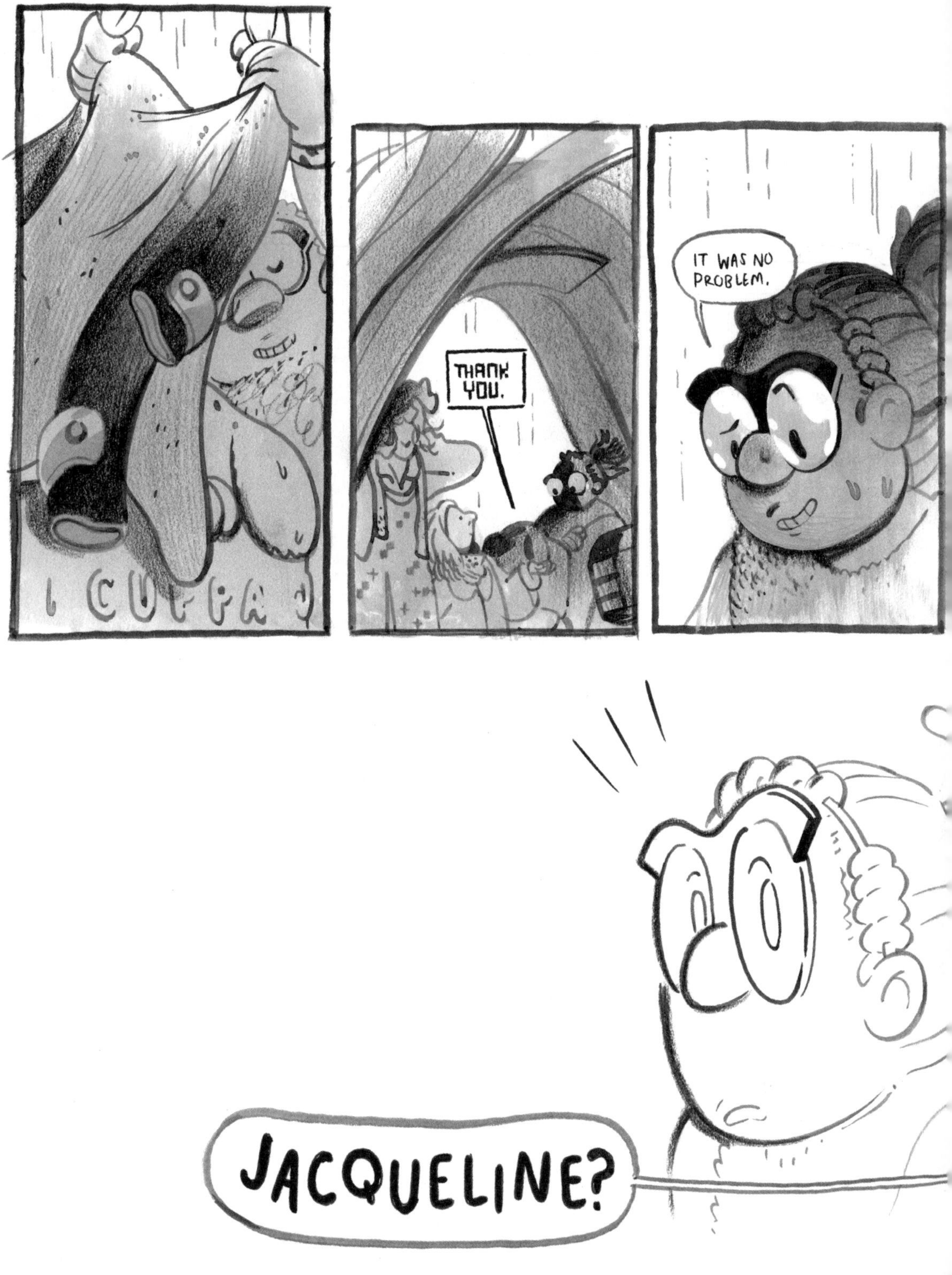
THANK YOU.
IT WAS NO PROBLEM.
JACQUELINE?

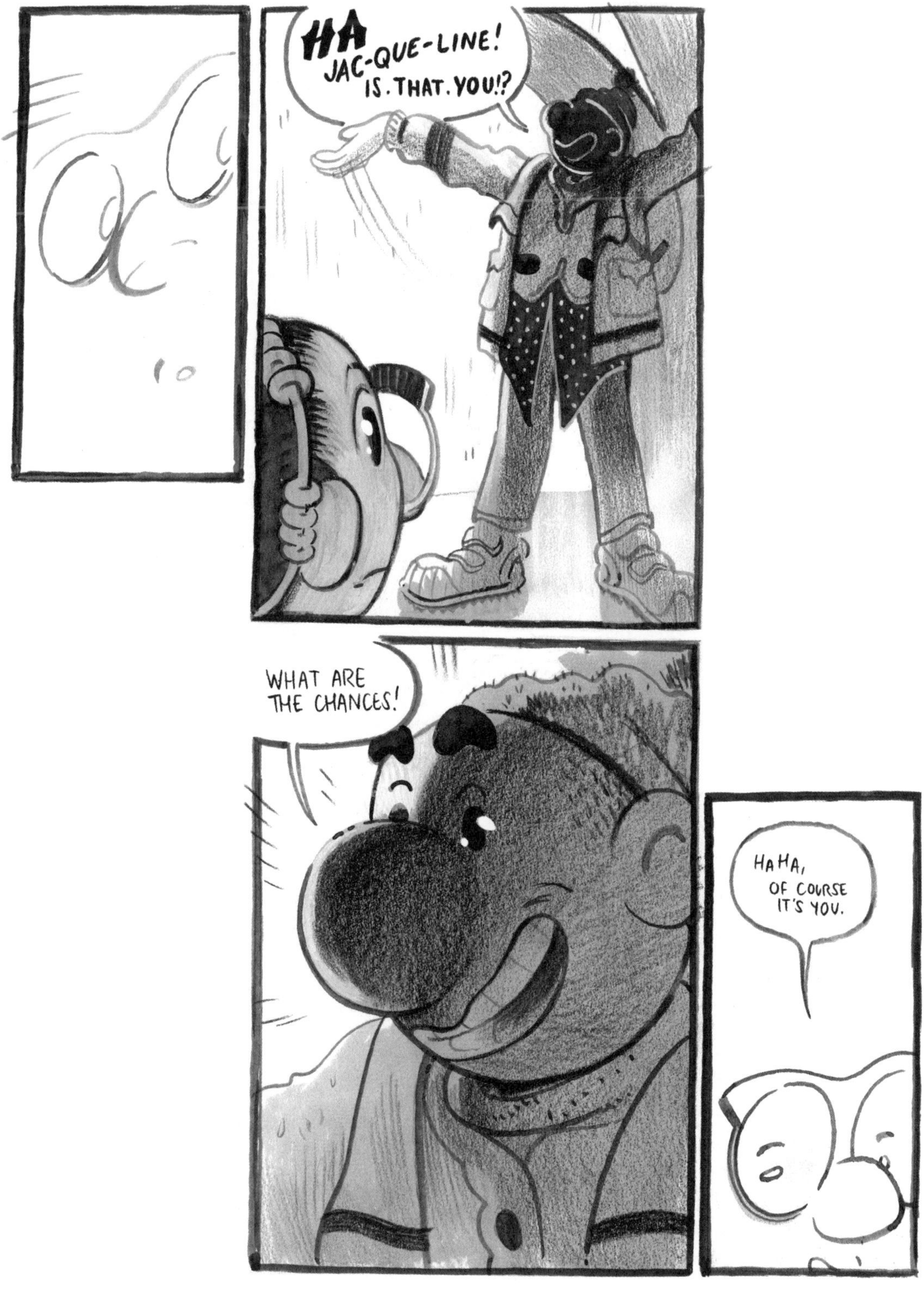
HA
JAC-QUE-LINE! IS. THAT. YOU!?
WHAT ARE THE CHANCES!
HAHA, OF COURSE IT'S YOU.

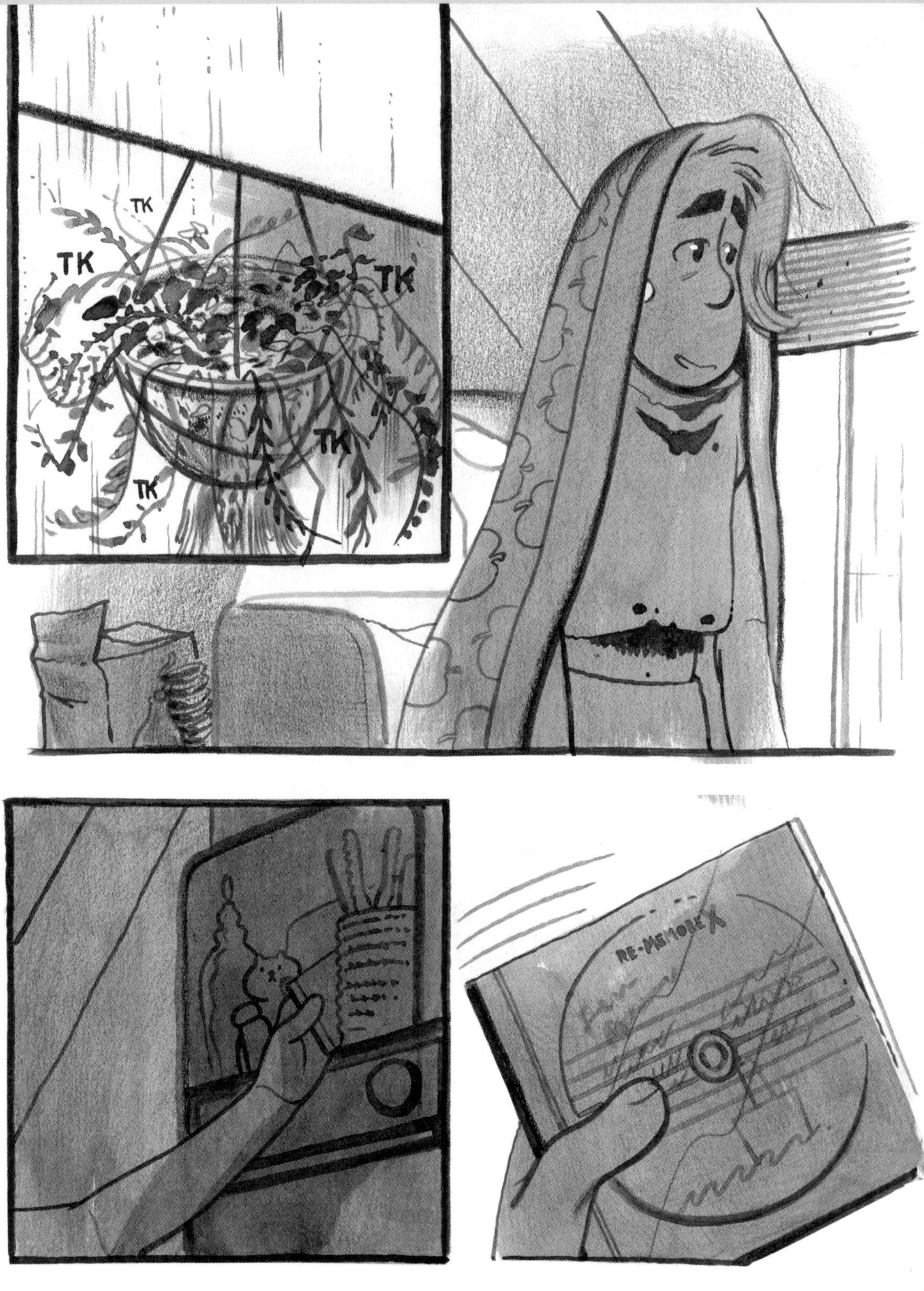
TK
TK
TK
TK
TK
RE-MEMOREX

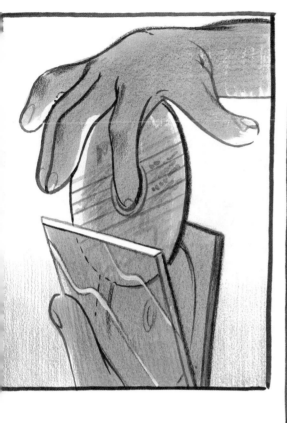

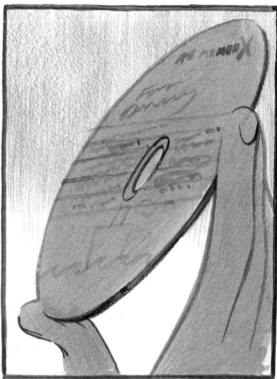

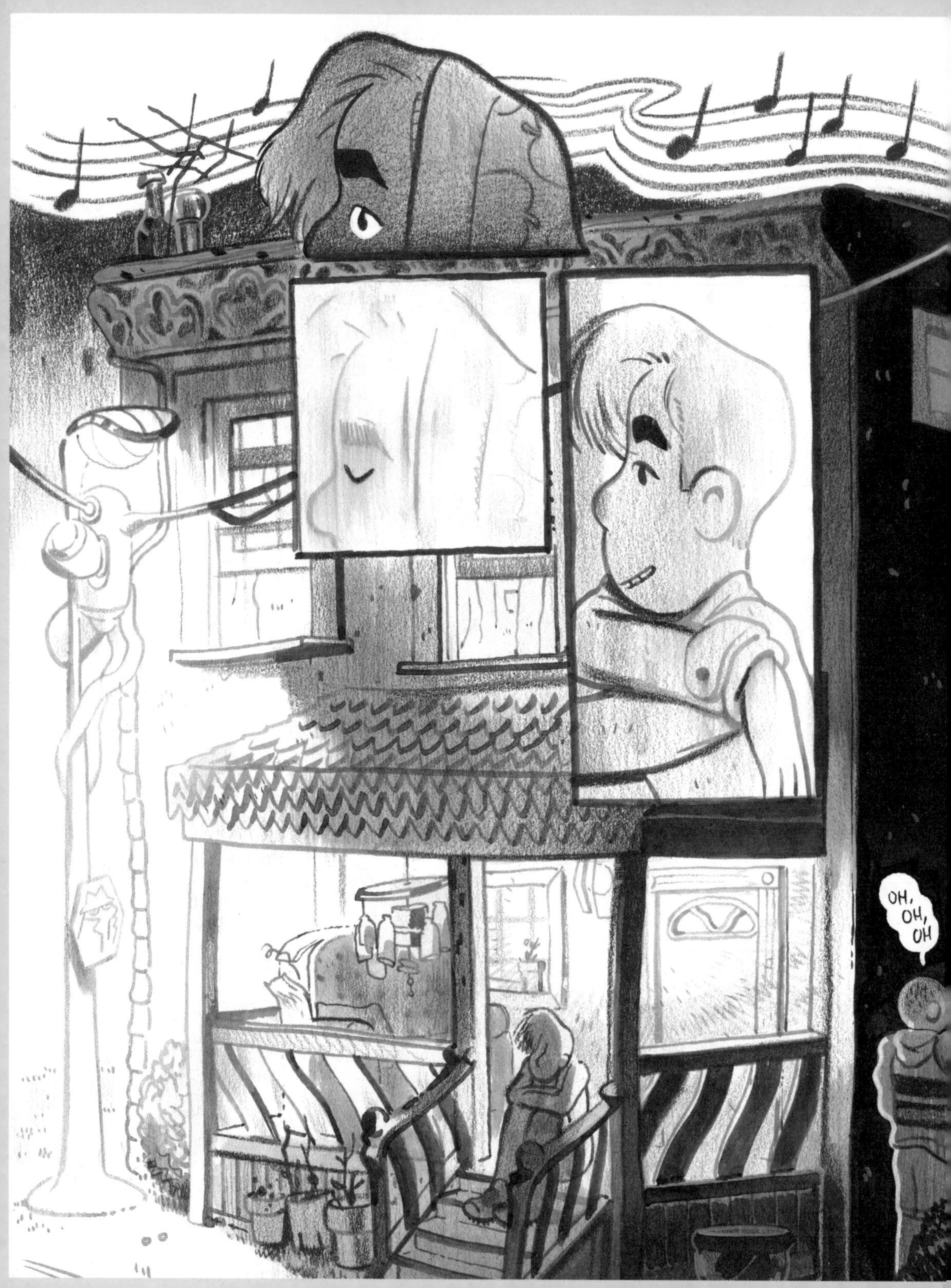
OH, OH, OH

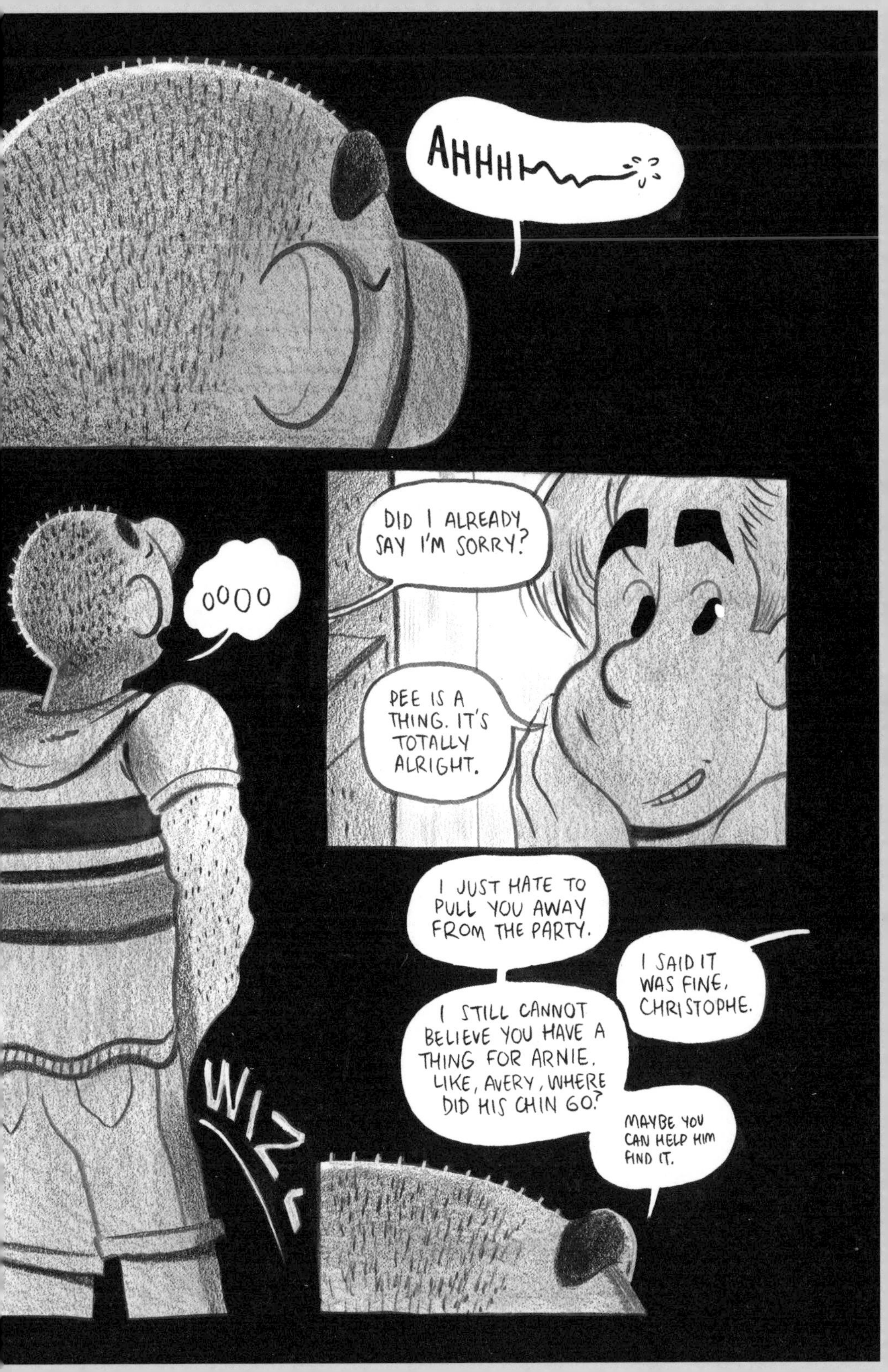
AHHHH
OOOO
DID I ALREADY SAY I'M SORRY?
PEE IS A THING. IT'S TOTALLY ALRIGHT.
I JUST HATE TO PULL YOU AWAY FROM THE PARTY.
I SAID IT WAS FINE, CHRISTOPHE.
I STILL CANNOT BELIEVE YOU HAVE A THING FOR ARNIE. LIKE, AVERY, WHERE DID HIS CHIN GO?
MAYBE YOU CAN HELP HIM FIND IT.
WIZ

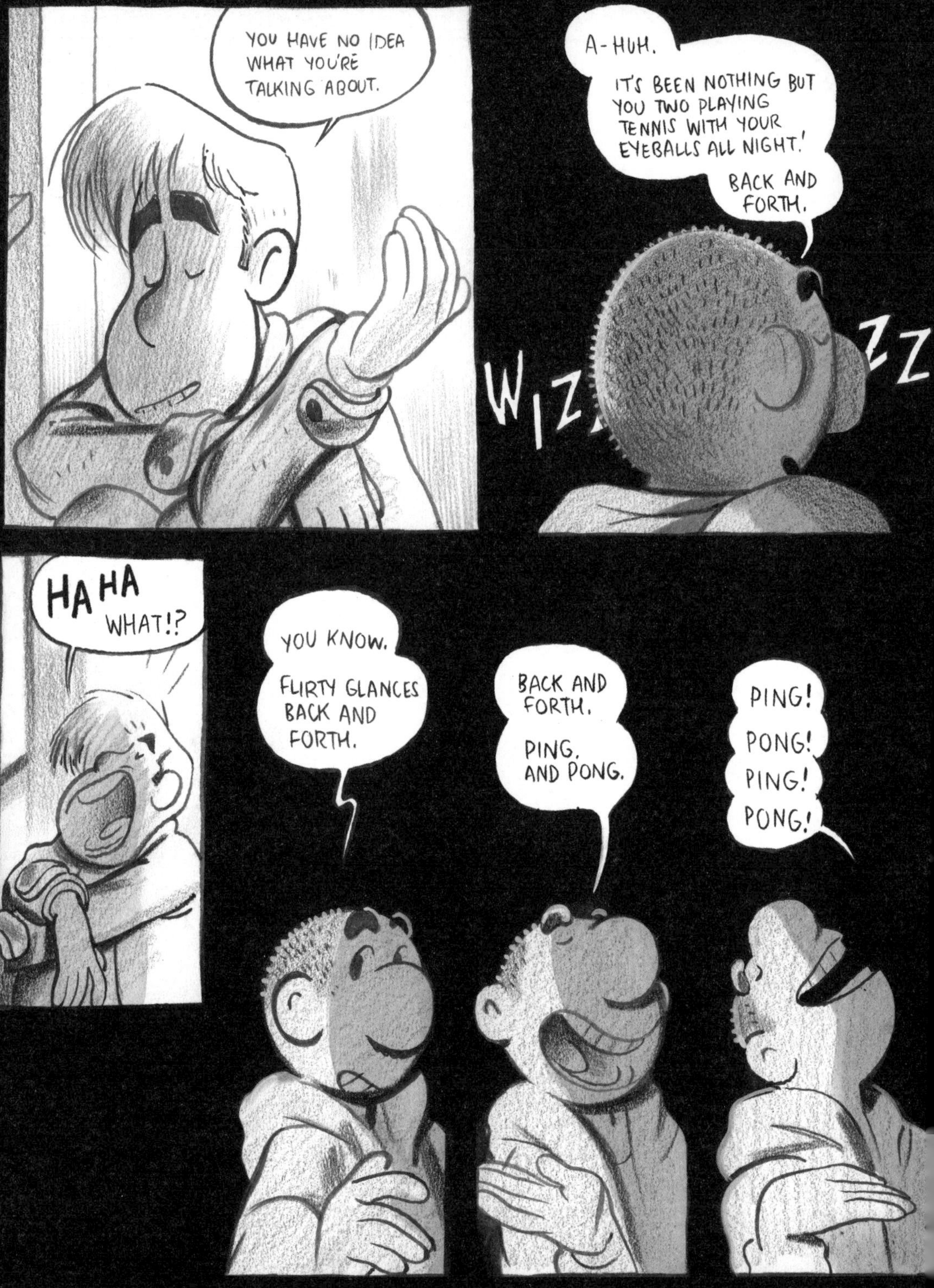

YOU HAVE NO IDEA WHAT YOU'RE TALKING ABOUT.
A-HUH.
IT'S BEEN NOTHING BUT YOU TWO PLAYING TENNIS WITH YOUR EYEBALLS ALL NIGHT!
BACK AND FORTH.
WIZZ ZZ
HAHA WHAT!?
YOU KNOW.
FLIRTY GLANCES BACK AND FORTH.
BACK AND FORTH.
PING, AND PONG.
PING!
PONG!
PING!
PONG!

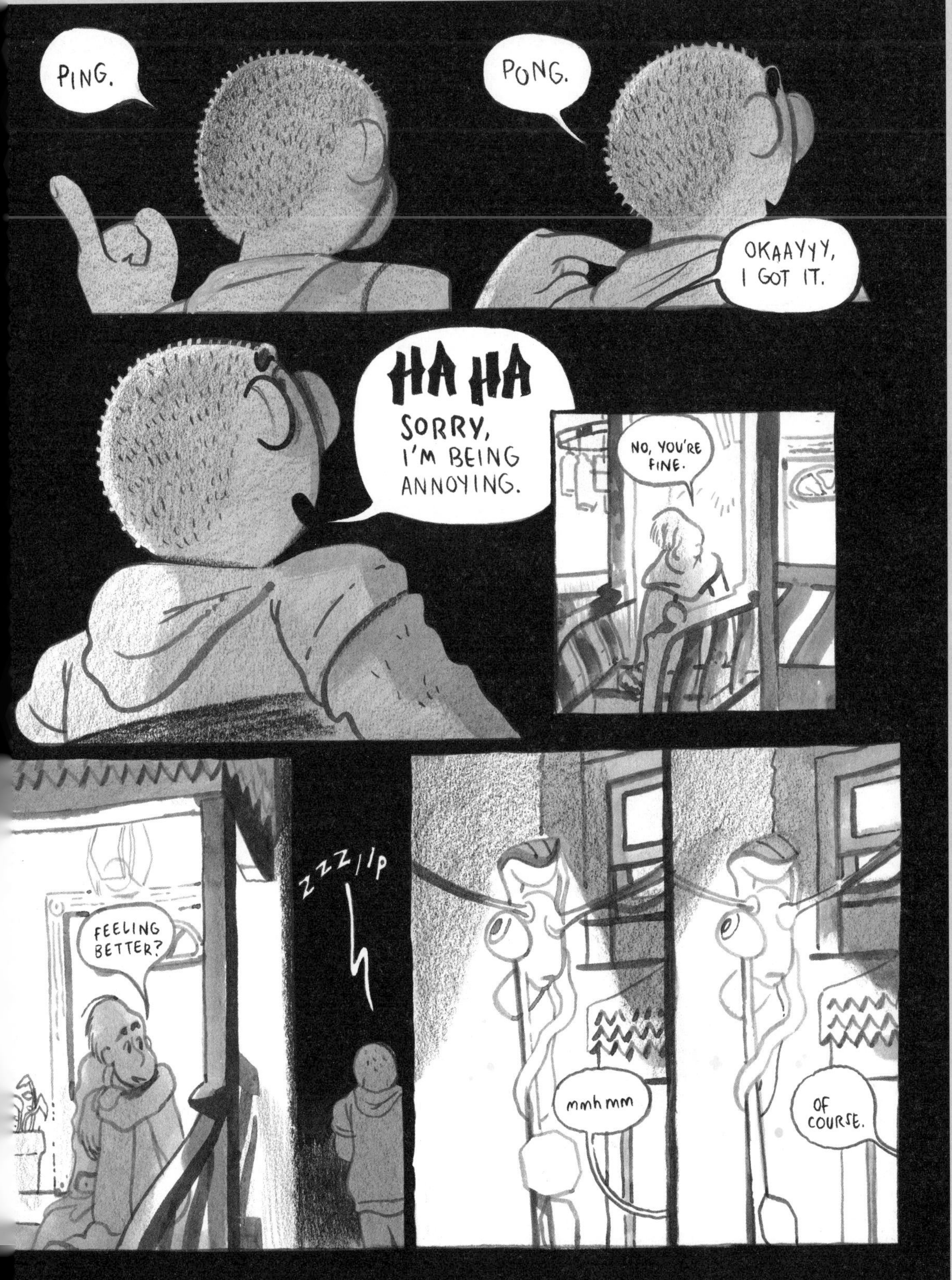
PING.
PONG.
OKAAYYY, I GOT IT.
HA HA
SORRY, I'M BEING ANNOYING.
NO, YOU'RE FINE.
FEELING BETTER?
ZZZIIP
mmhmm
OF COURSE.

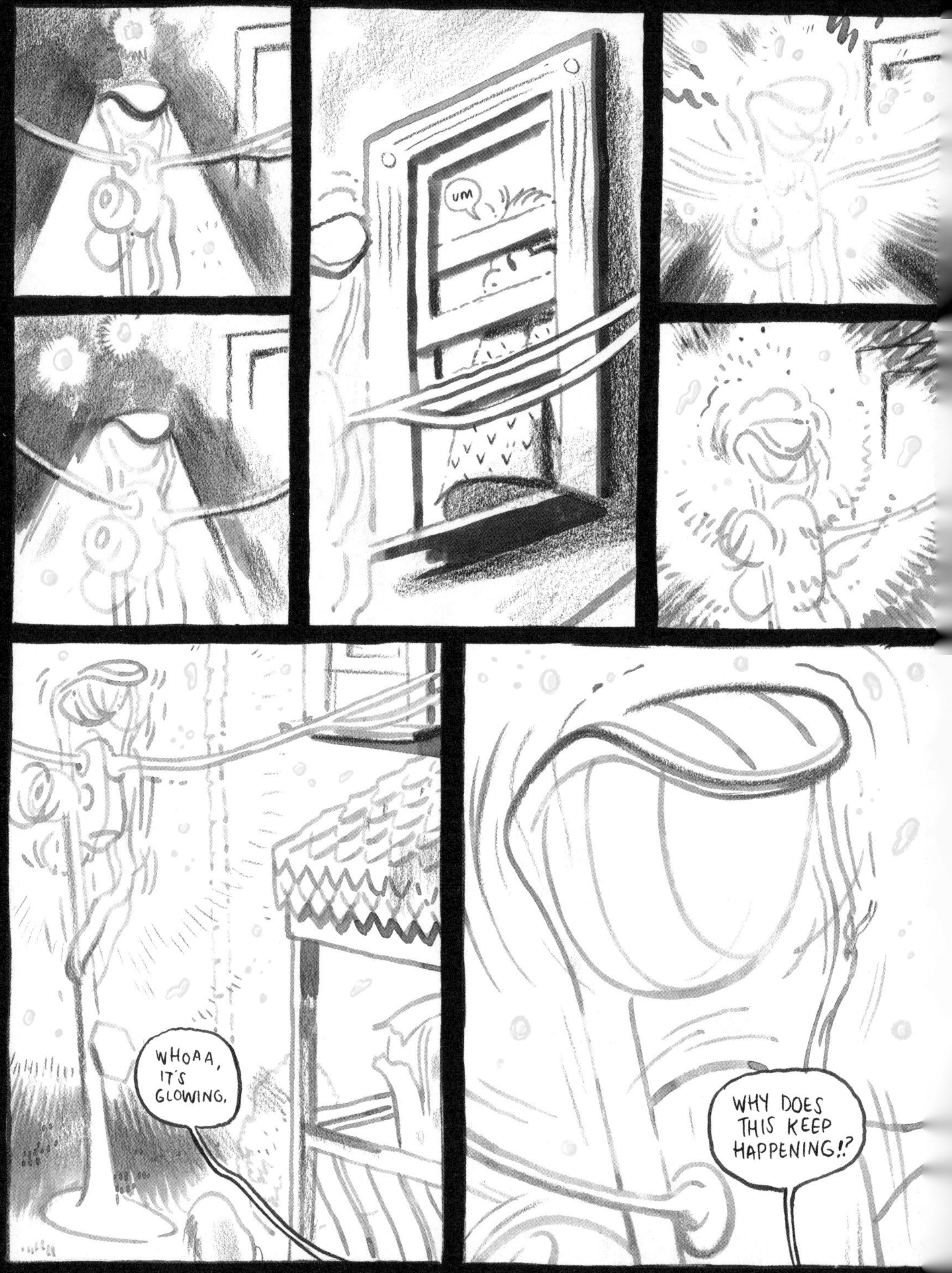
UM
WHOAA, IT'S GLOWING.
WHY DOES THIS KEEP HAPPENING!?

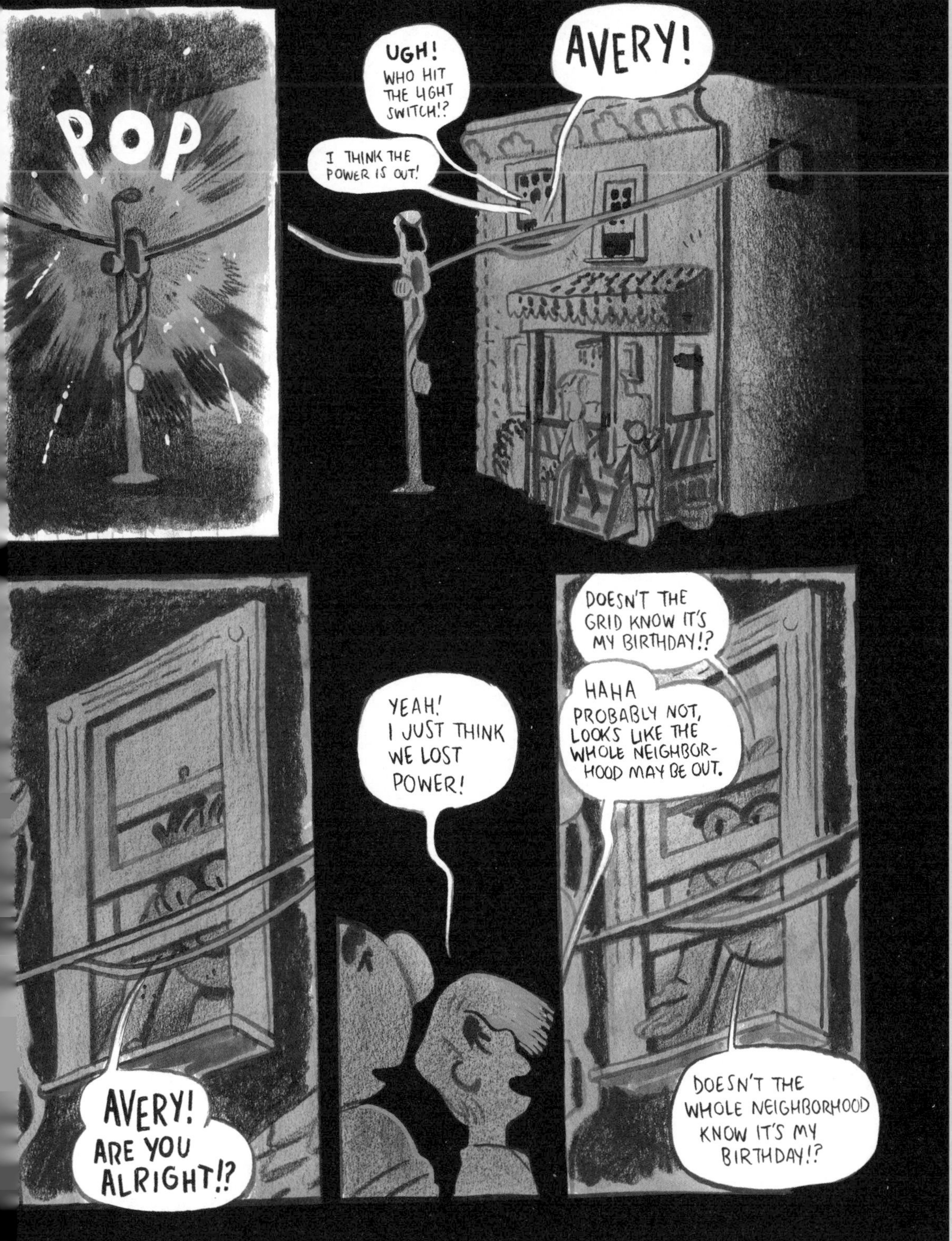
POP
UGH! WHO HIT THE LIGHT SWITCH!?
AVERY!
I THINK THE POWER IS OUT!
AVERY! ARE YOU ALRIGHT!?
YEAH! I JUST THINK WE LOST POWER!
DOESN'T THE GRID KNOW IT'S MY BIRTHDAY!?
HAHA PROBABLY NOT, LOOKS LIKE THE WHOLE NEIGHBOR-HOOD MAY BE OUT.
DOESN'T THE WHOLE NEIGHBORHOOD KNOW IT'S MY BIRTHDAY!?

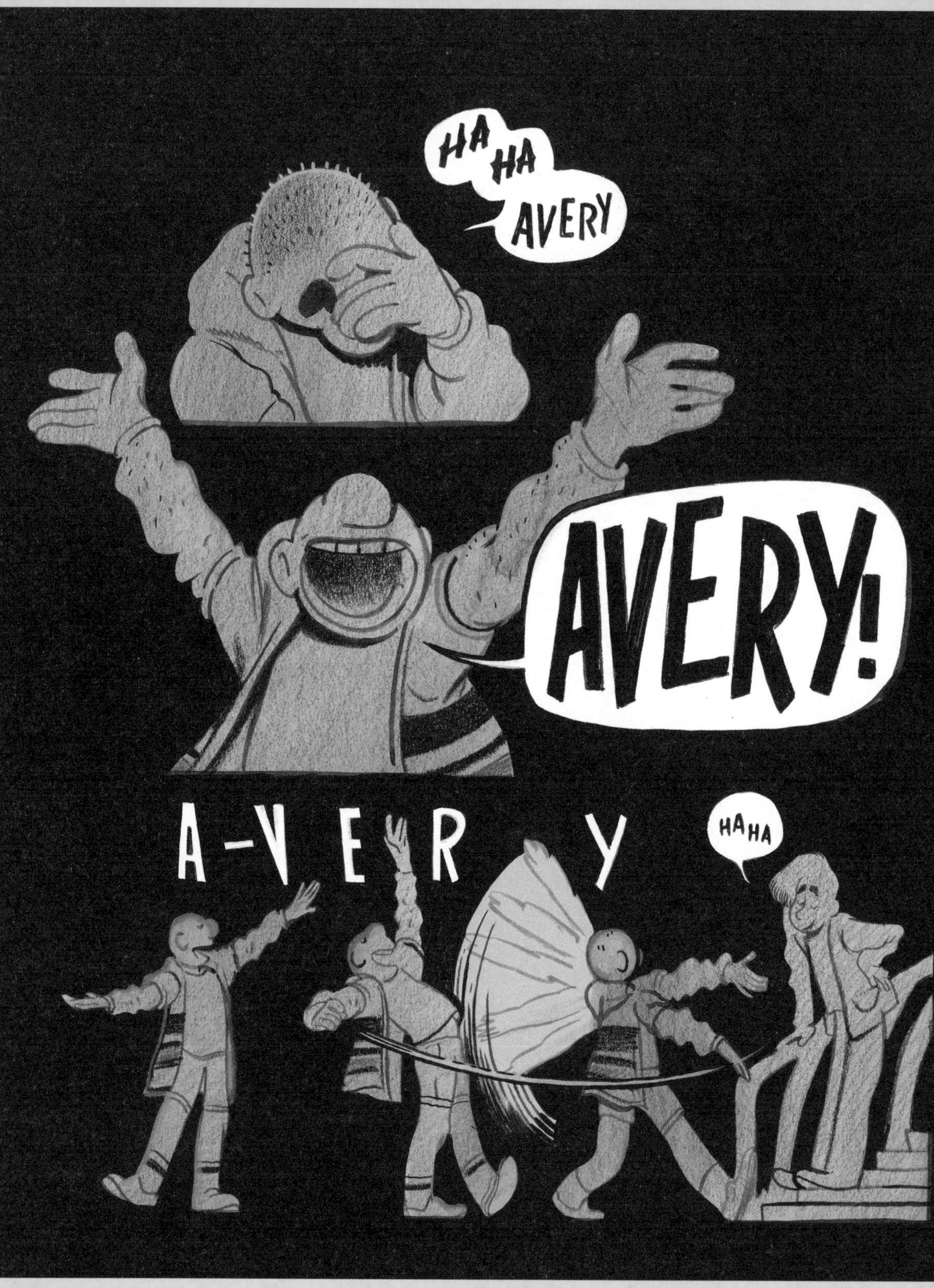
HA HA AVERY
AVERY!
A-V E R Y
HA HA

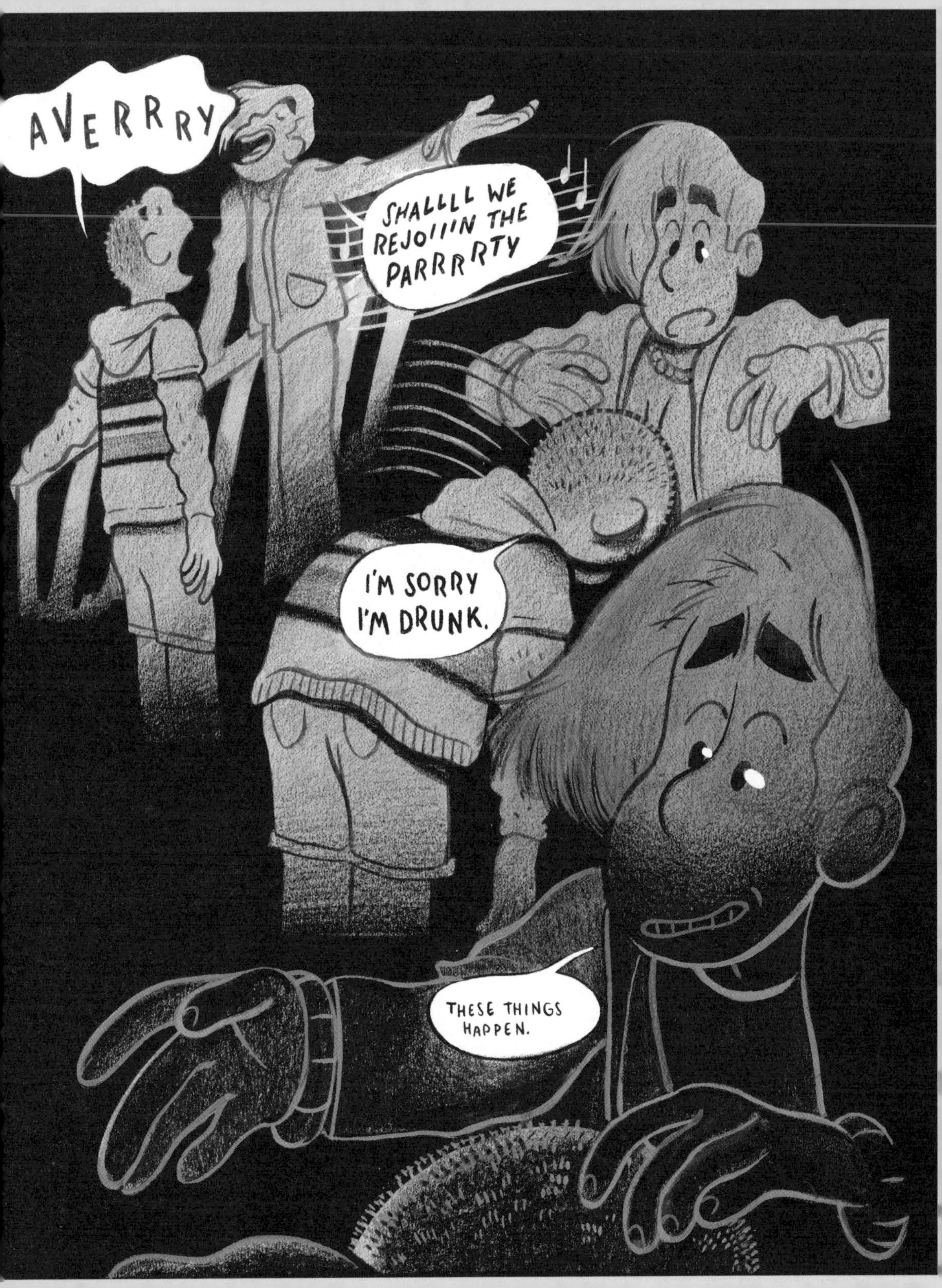
AVERRRY
SHALLLL WE REJOIIIN THE PARRRRTY
I'M SORRY I'M DRUNK.
THESE THINGS HAPPEN.

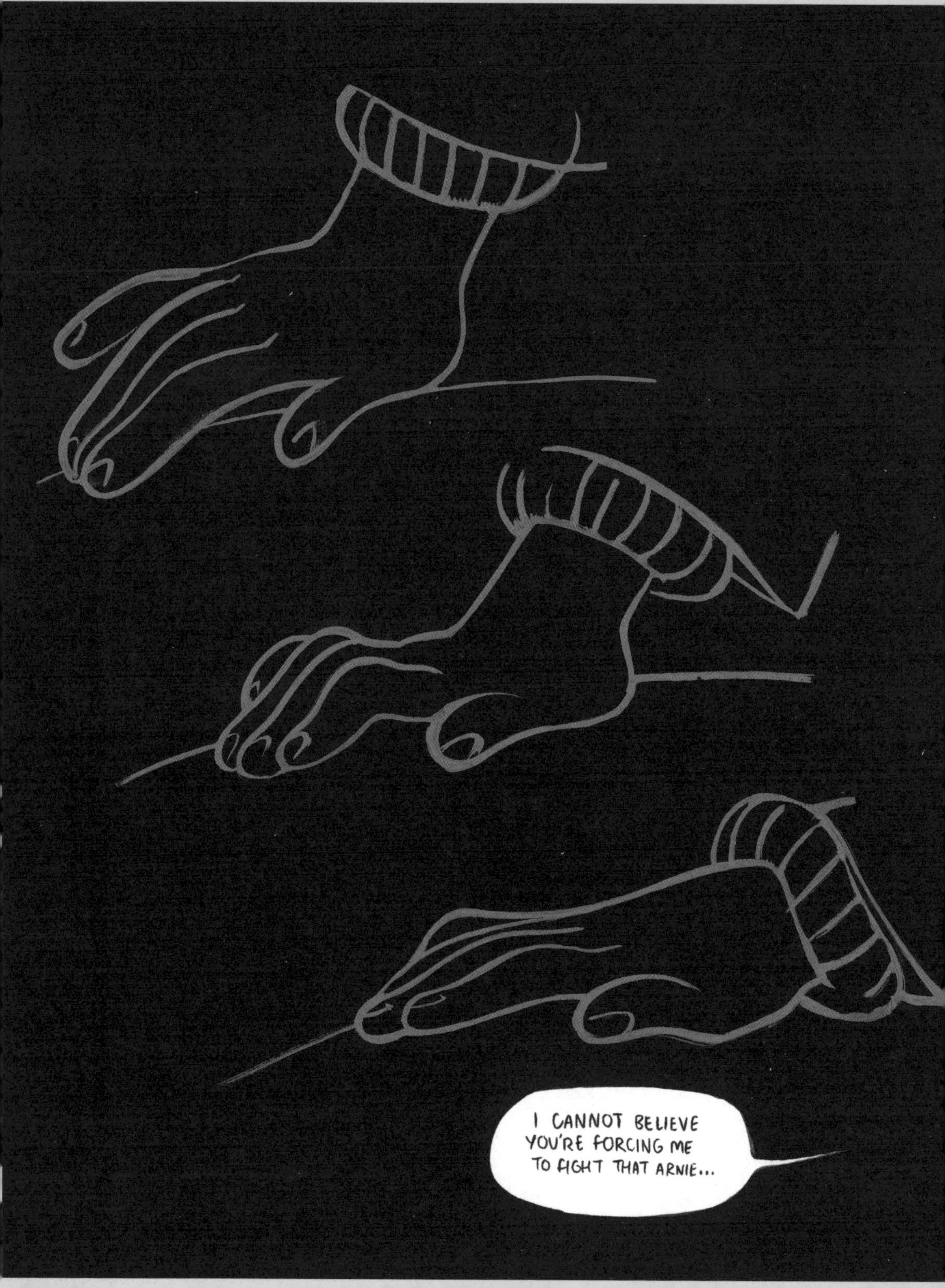
I CANNOT BELIEVE YOU'RE FORCING ME TO FIGHT THAT ARNIE...

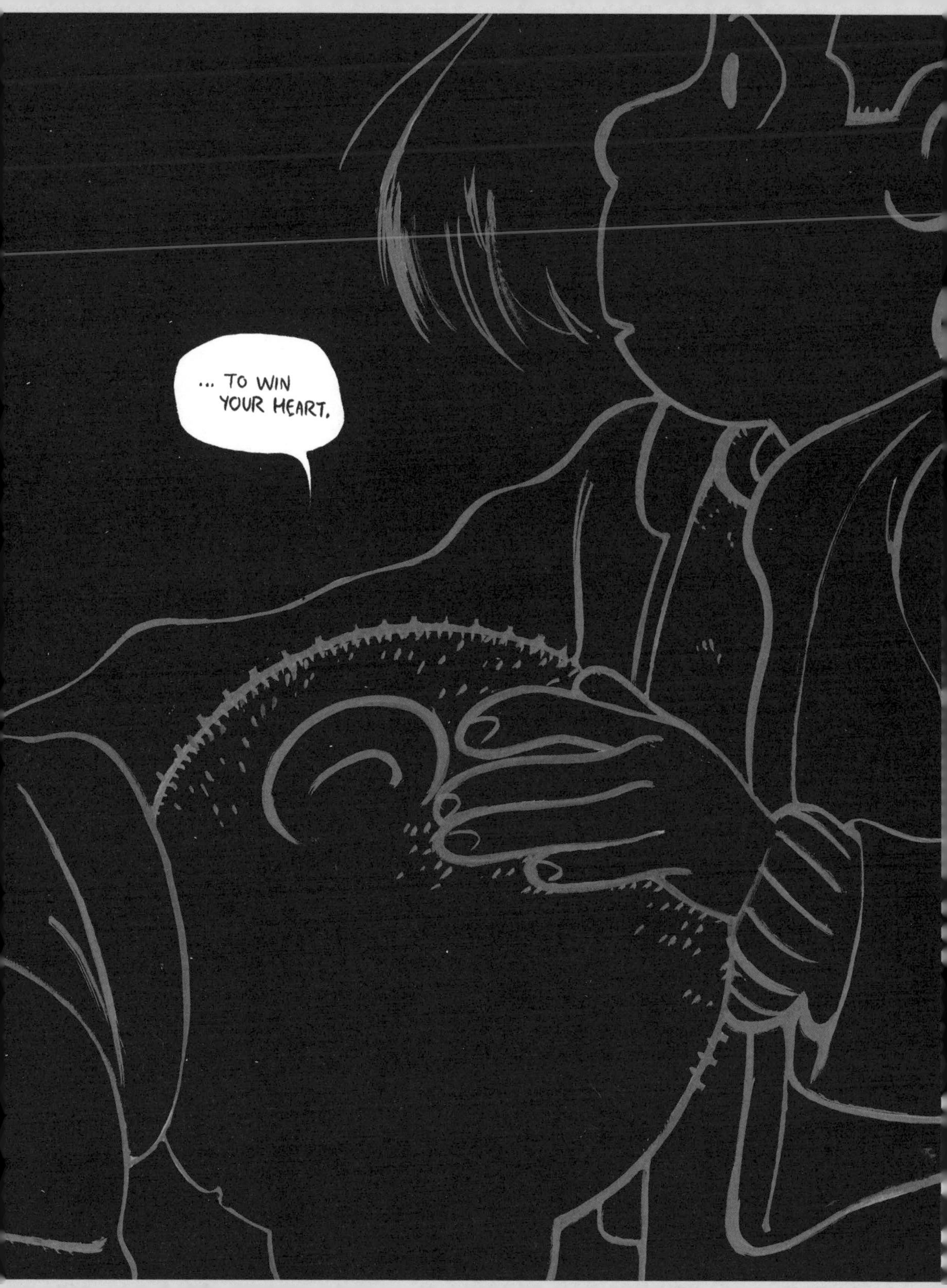
... TO WIN YOUR HEART.

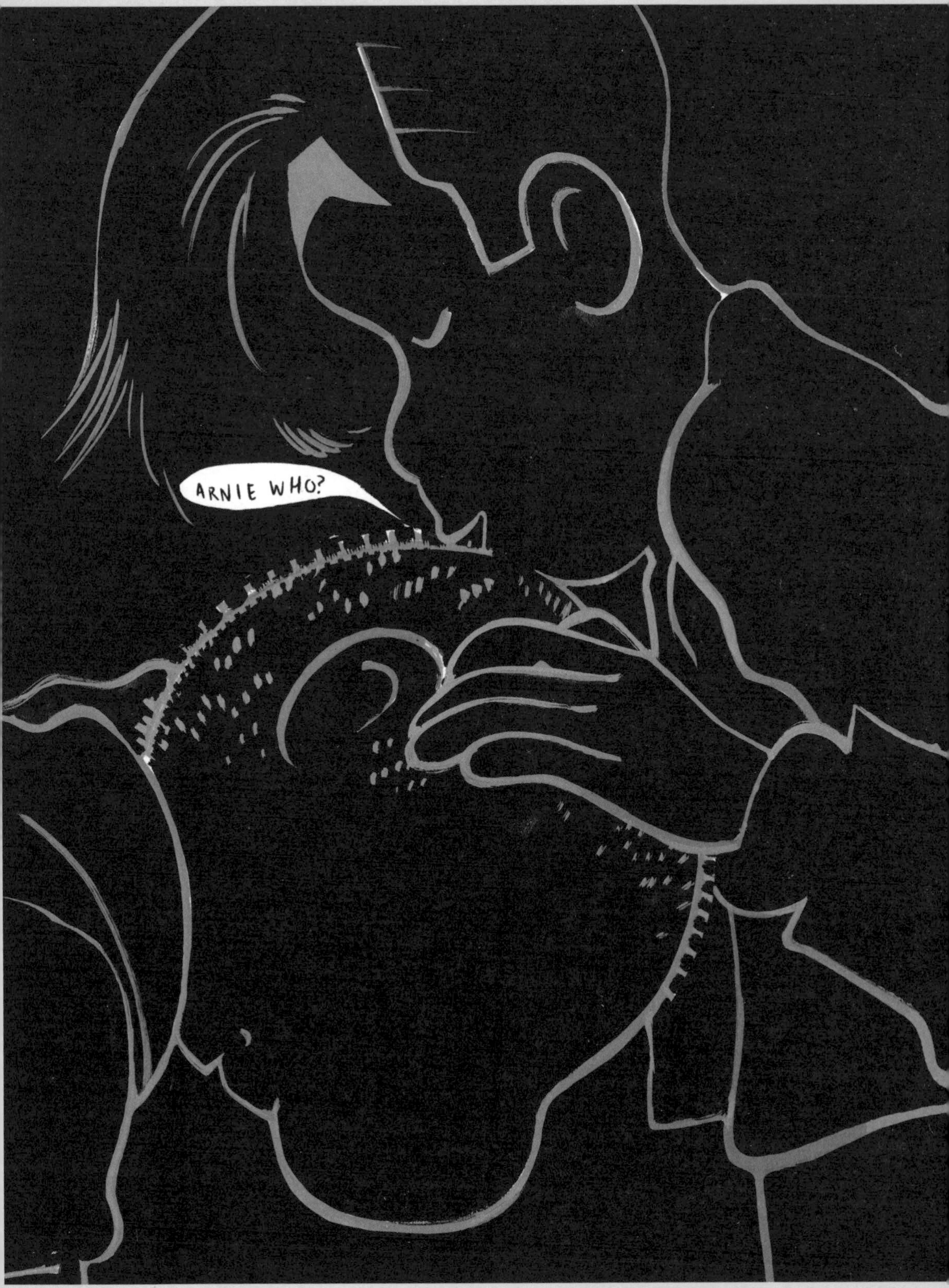
ARNIE WHO?

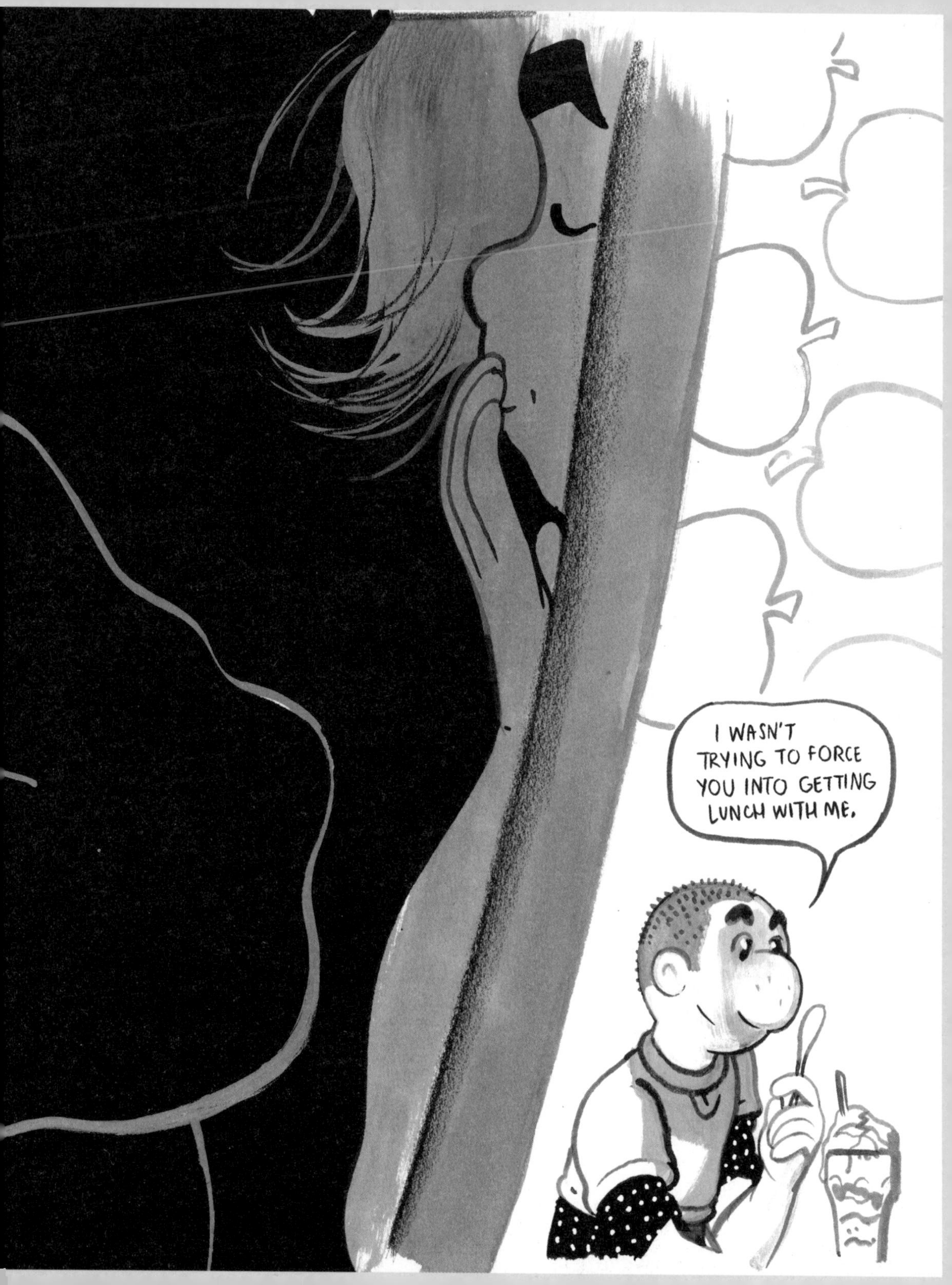
I WASN'T TRYING TO FORCE YOU INTO GETTING LUNCH WITH ME.

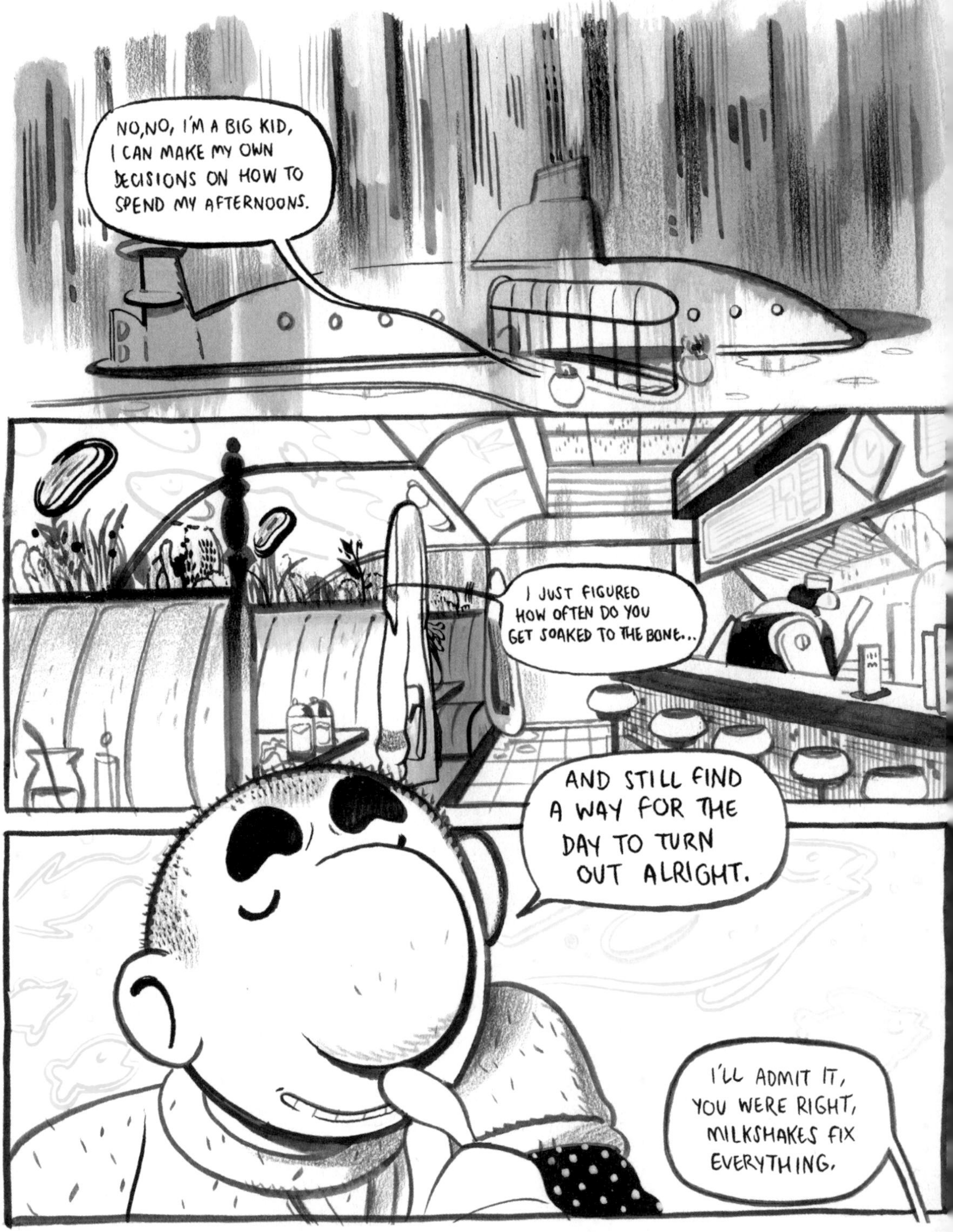
NO,NO, I'M A BIG KID, I CAN MAKE MY OWN DECISIONS ON HOW TO SPEND MY AFTERNOONS.
I JUST FIGURED HOW OFTEN DO YOU GET SOAKED TO THE BONE...
AND STILL FIND A WAY FOR THE DAY TO TURN OUT ALRIGHT.
I'LL ADMIT IT, YOU WERE RIGHT, MILKSHAKES FIX EVERYTHING.

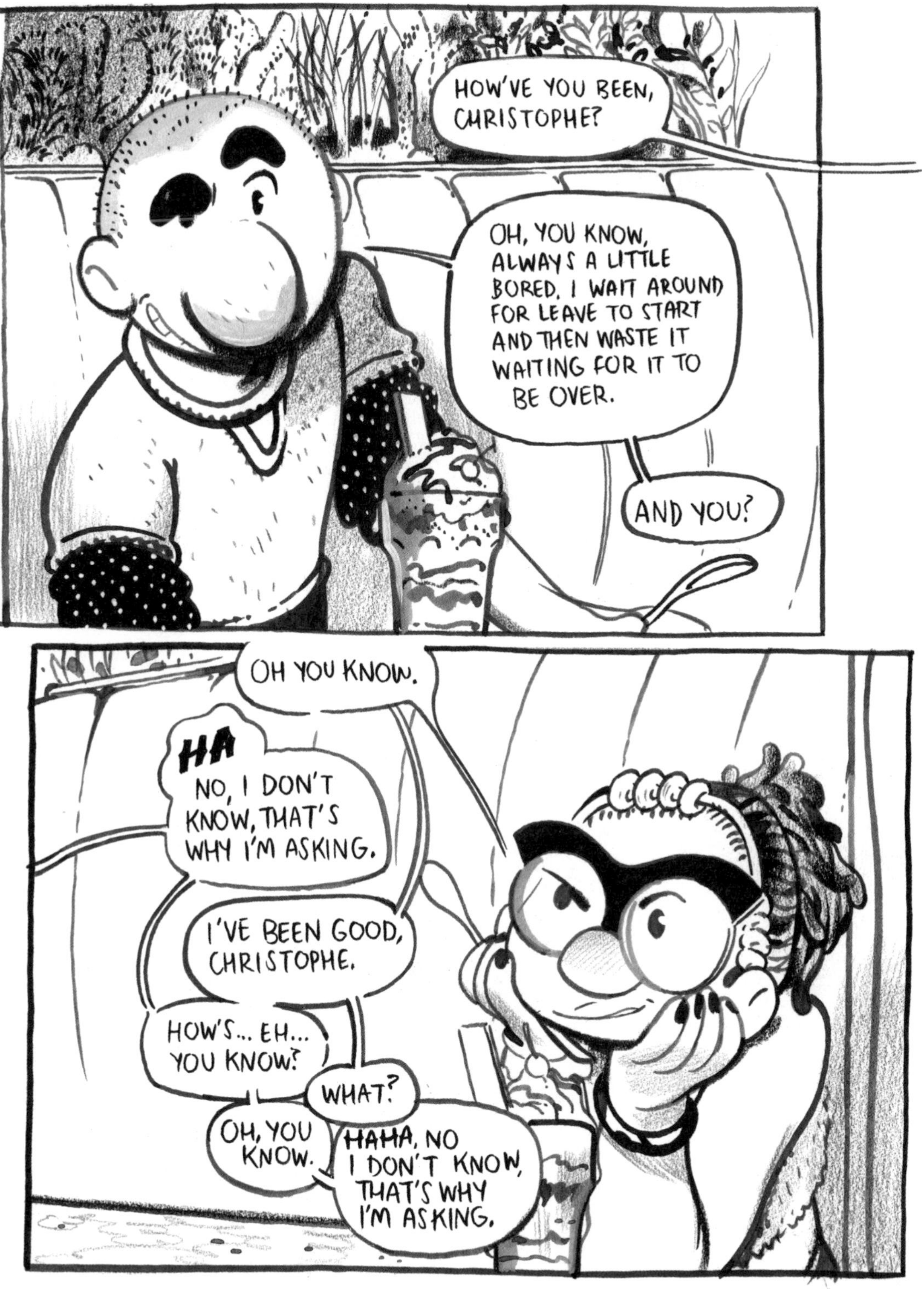
HOW'VE YOU BEEN, CHRISTOPHE?
OH, YOU KNOW, ALWAYS A LITTLE BORED. I WAIT AROUND FOR LEAVE TO START AND THEN WASTE IT WAITING FOR IT TO BE OVER.
AND YOU?
OH YOU KNOW.
HA
NO, I DON'T KNOW, THAT'S WHY I'M ASKING.
I'VE BEEN GOOD, CHRISTOPHE.
HOW'S... EH... YOU KNOW?
WHAT?
OH, YOU KNOW.
HAHA, NO I DON'T KNOW, THAT'S WHY I'M ASKING.

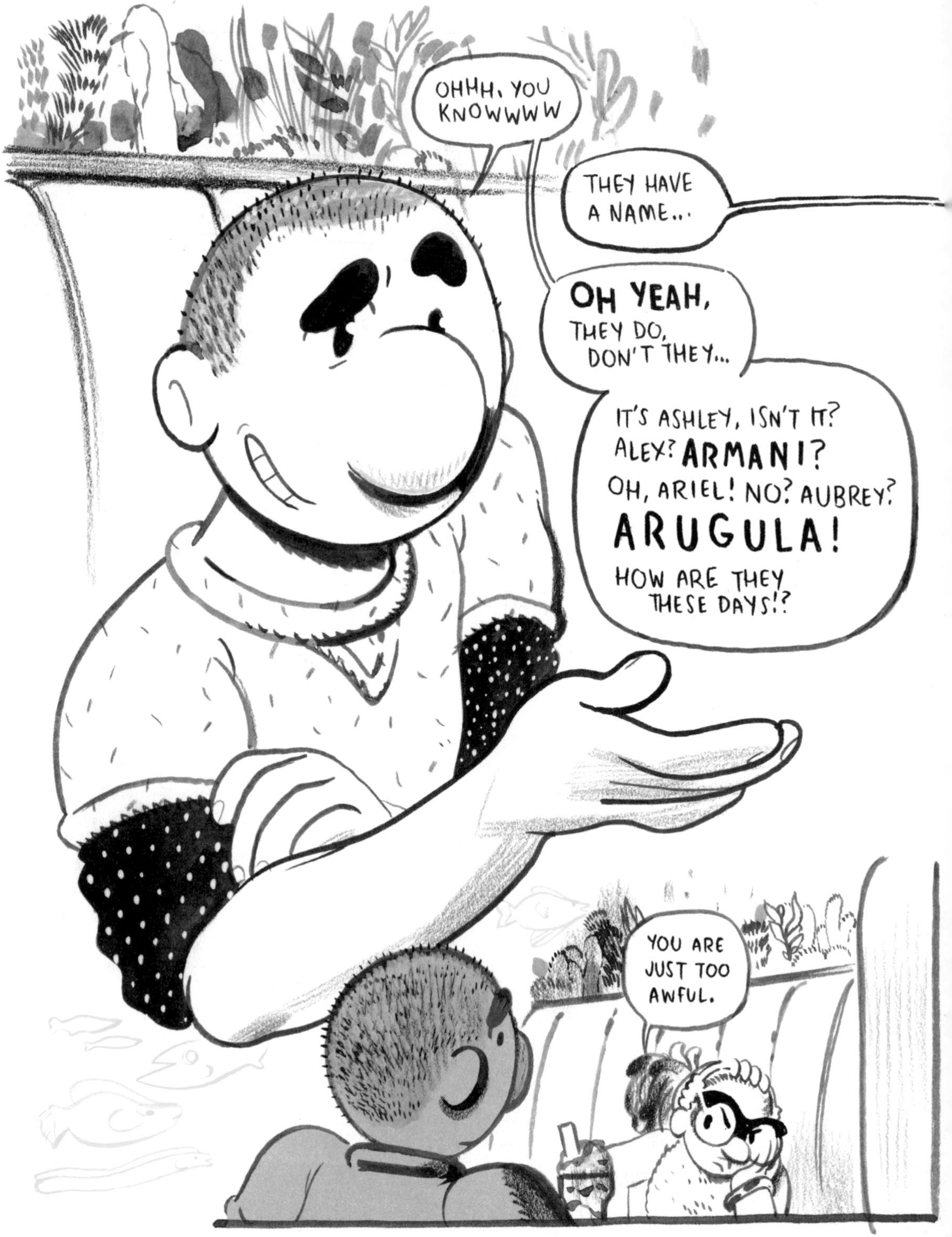
OHHH, YOU KNOWWWW
THEY HAVE A NAME...
OH YEAH, THEY DO, DON'T THEY...
IT'S ASHLEY, ISN'T IT? ALEX? ARMANI? OH, ARIEL! NO? AUBREY? ARUGULA! HOW ARE THEY THESE DAYS!?
YOU ARE JUST TOO AWFUL.

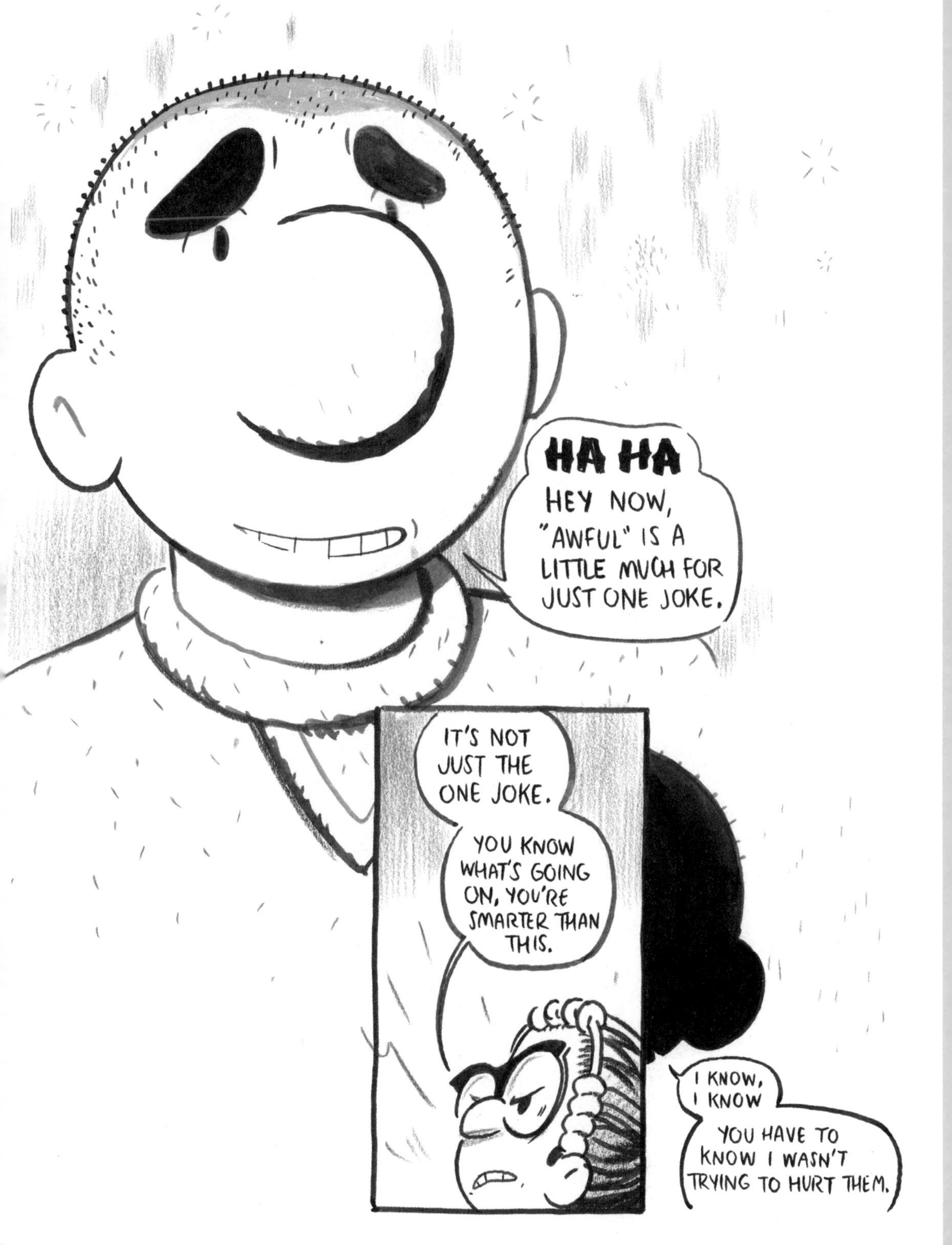

HA HA
HEY NOW, "AWFUL" IS A LITTLE MUCH FOR JUST ONE JOKE.
IT'S NOT JUST THE ONE JOKE.
YOU KNOW WHAT'S GOING ON, YOU'RE SMARTER THAN THIS.
I KNOW, I KNOW
YOU HAVE TO KNOW I WASN'T TRYING TO HURT THEM.

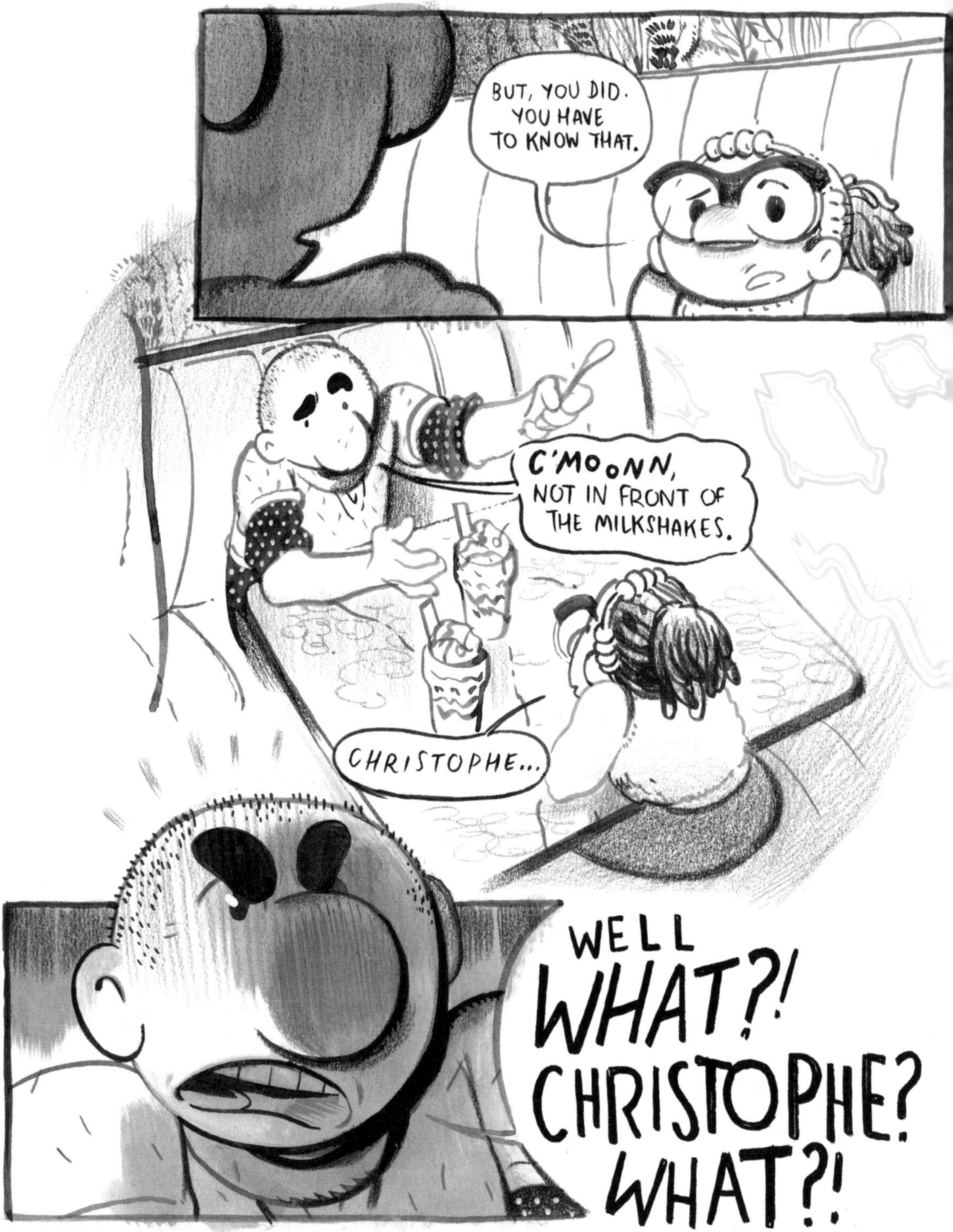
BUT, YOU DID. YOU HAVE TO KNOW THAT.
C'MOONN, NOT IN FRONT OF THE MILKSHAKES.
CHRISTOPHE...
WELL WHAT?! CHRISTOPHE? WHAT?!

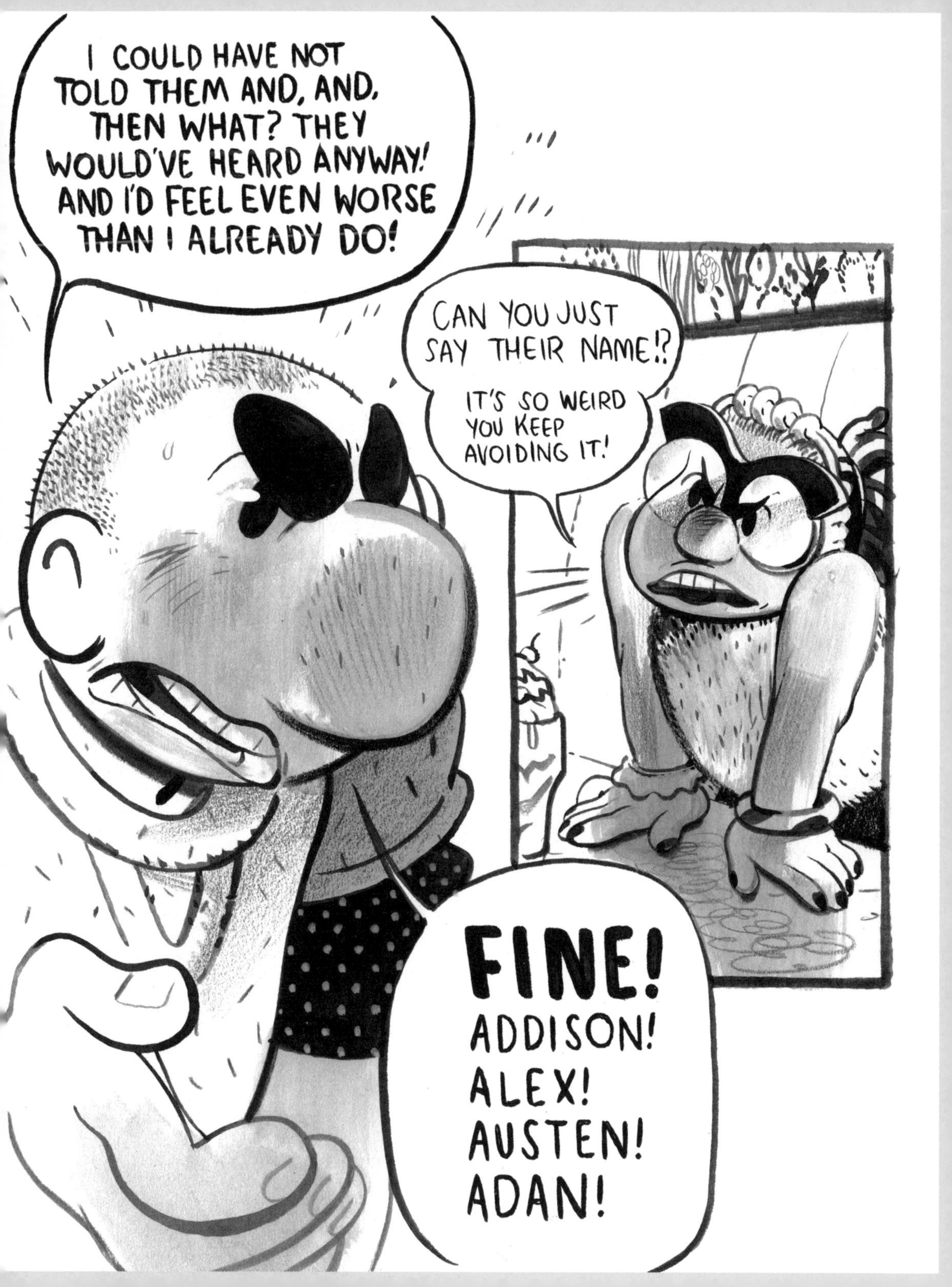
I COULD HAVE NOT TOLD THEM AND, AND, THEN WHAT? THEY WOULD'VE HEARD ANYWAY! AND I'D FEEL EVEN WORSE THAN I ALREADY DO!
CAN YOU JUST SAY THEIR NAME!?
IT'S SO WEIRD YOU KEEP AVOIDING IT!
FINE! ADDISON! ALEX! AUSTEN! ADAN!

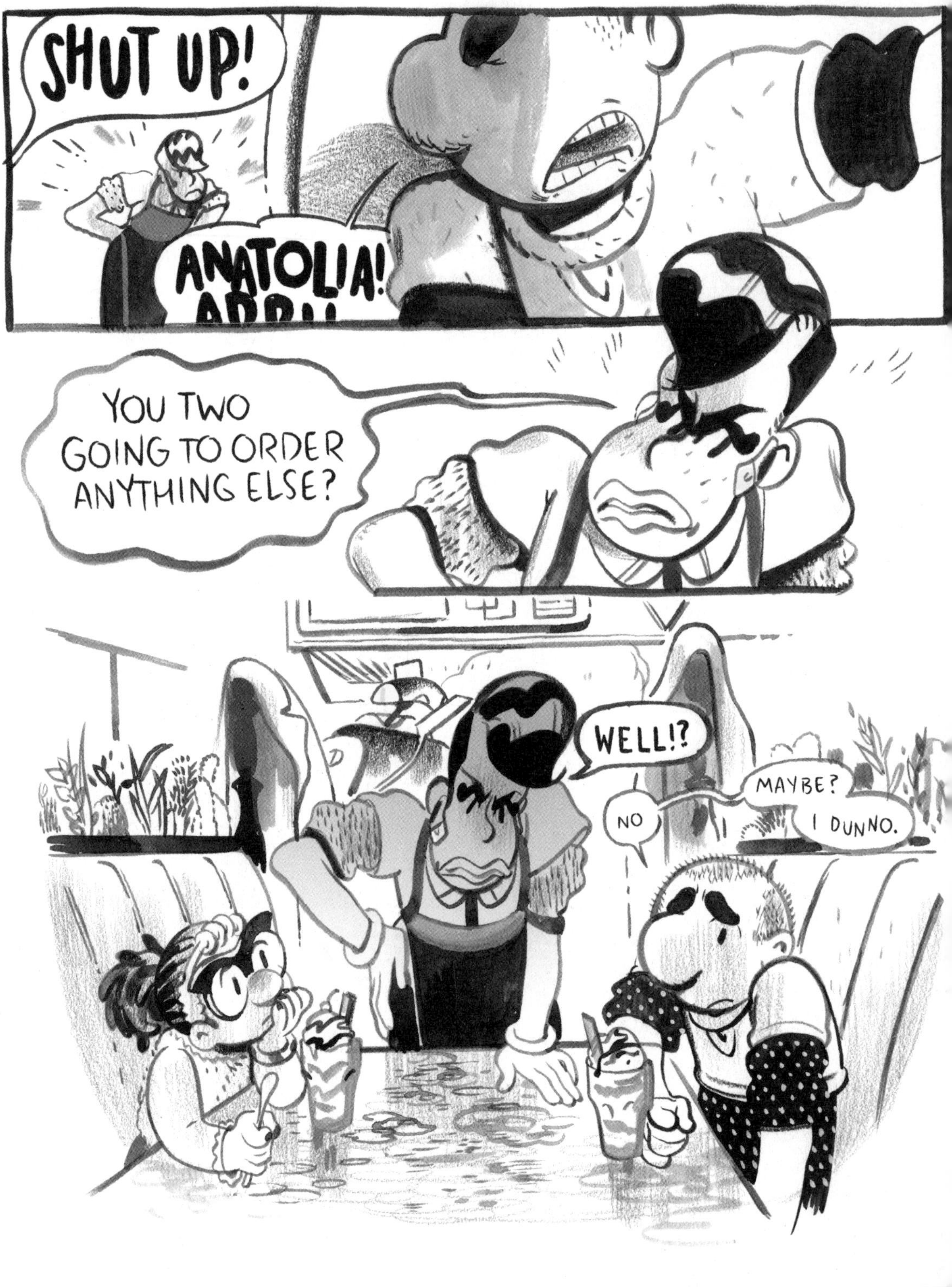
SHUT UP!
ANATOLIA!
YOU TWO GOING TO ORDER ANYTHING ELSE?
WELL!?
NO
MAYBE?
I DUNNO.

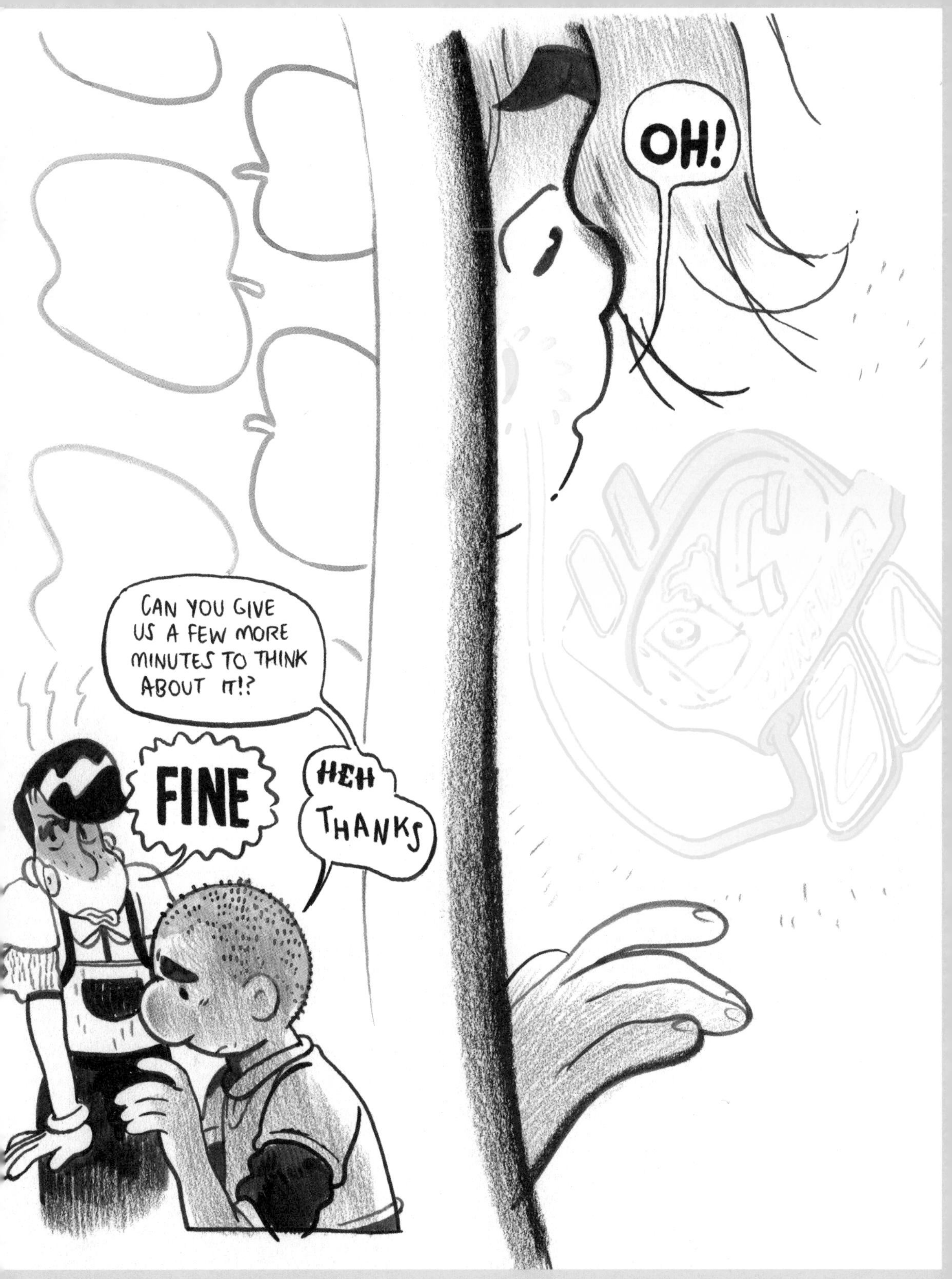
CAN YOU GIVE US A FEW MORE MINUTES TO THINK ABOUT IT!?
FINE
HEH THANKS
OH!

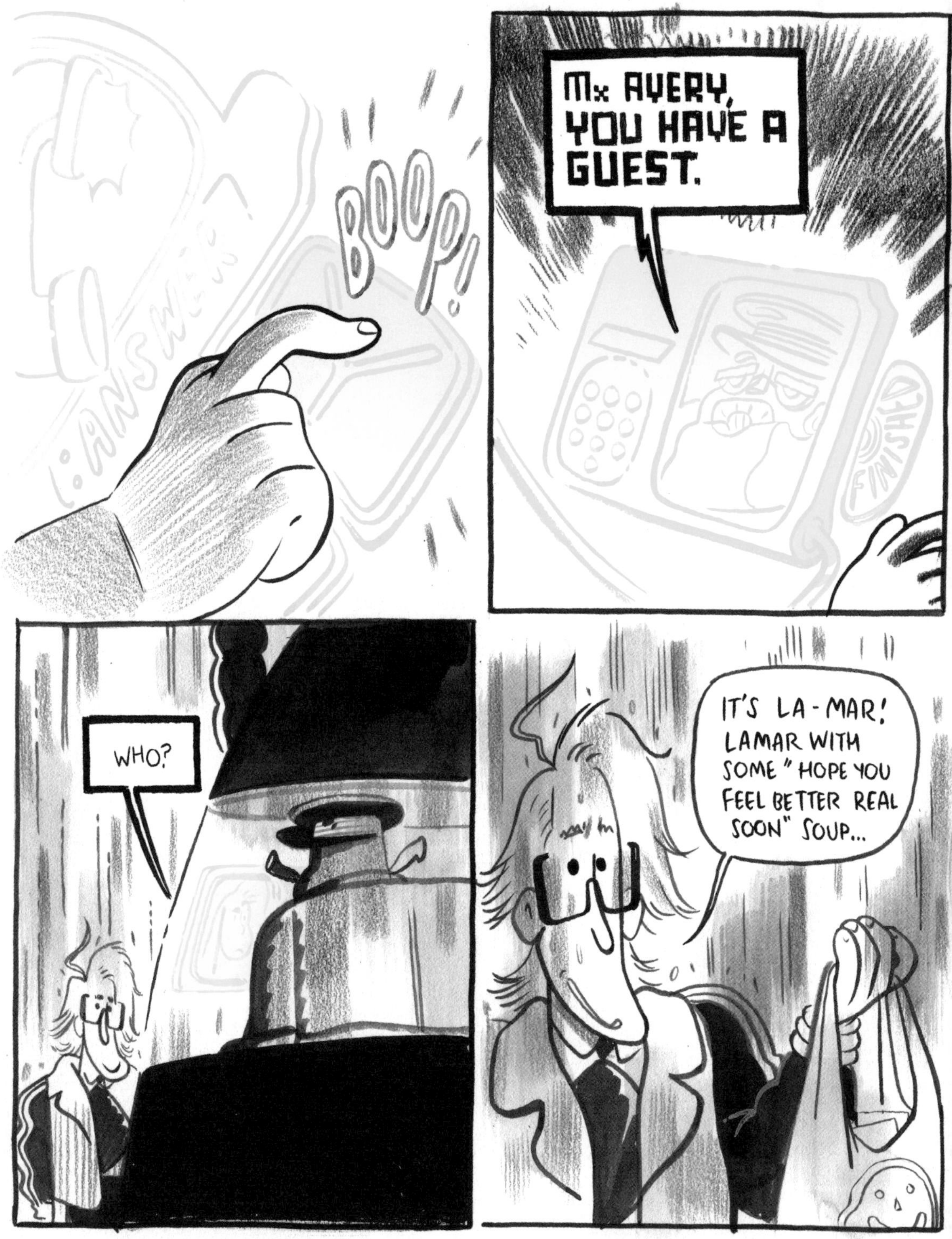

ANSWER
BOOP!
Mx AVERY, YOU HAVE A GUEST.
FINISH
WHO?
IT'S LA-MAR! LAMAR WITH SOME "HOPE YOU FEEL BETTER REAL SOON" SOUP...

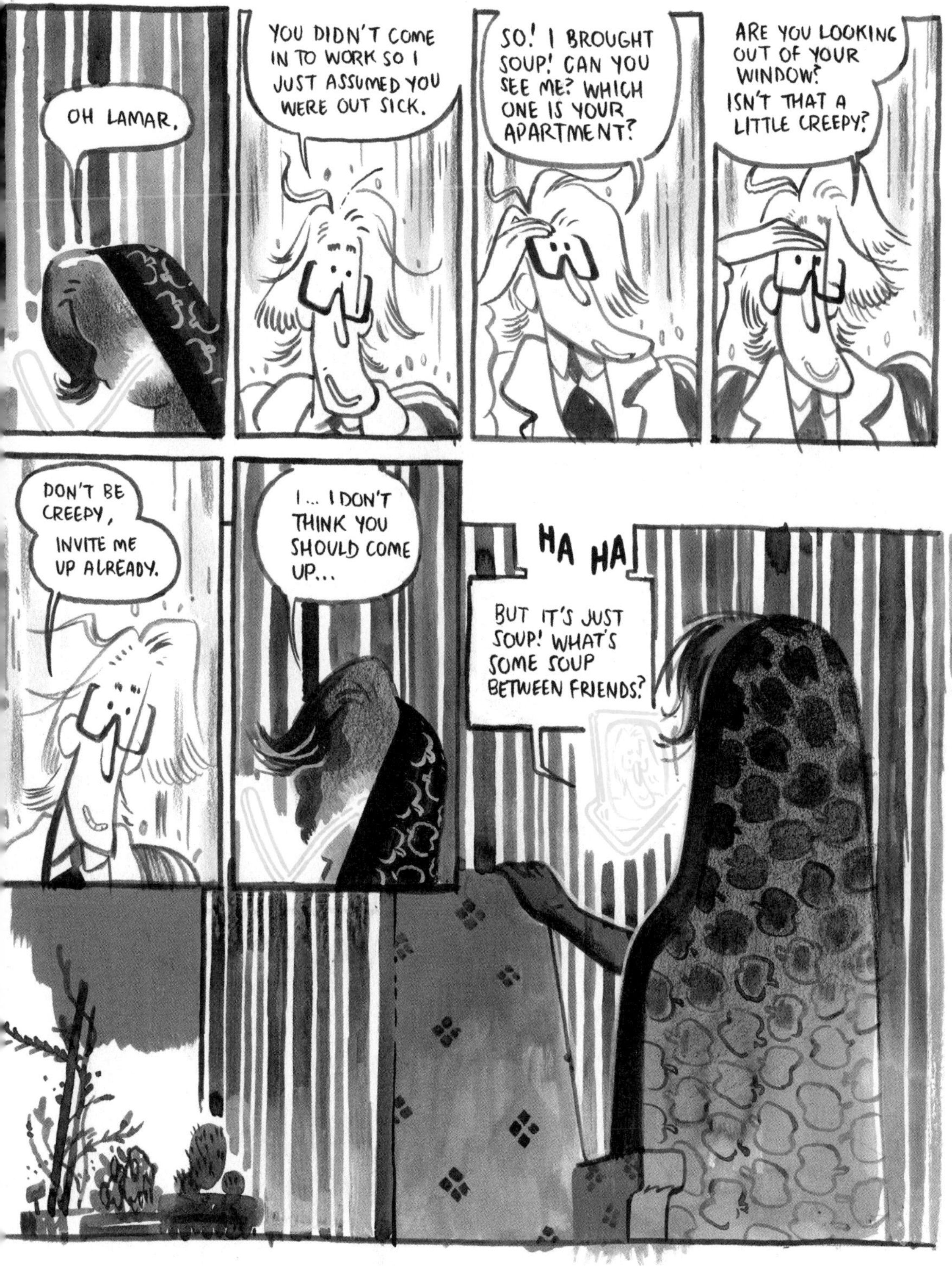
OH LAMAR.
YOU DIDN'T COME IN TO WORK SO I JUST ASSUMED YOU WERE OUT SICK.
SO! I BROUGHT SOUP! CAN YOU SEE ME? WHICH ONE IS YOUR APARTMENT?
ARE YOU LOOKING OUT OF YOUR WINDOW? ISN'T THAT A LITTLE CREEPY?
DON'T BE CREEPY, INVITE ME UP ALREADY.
I... I DON'T THINK YOU SHOULD COME UP...
HA HA
BUT IT'S JUST SOUP! WHAT'S SOME SOUP BETWEEN FRIENDS?

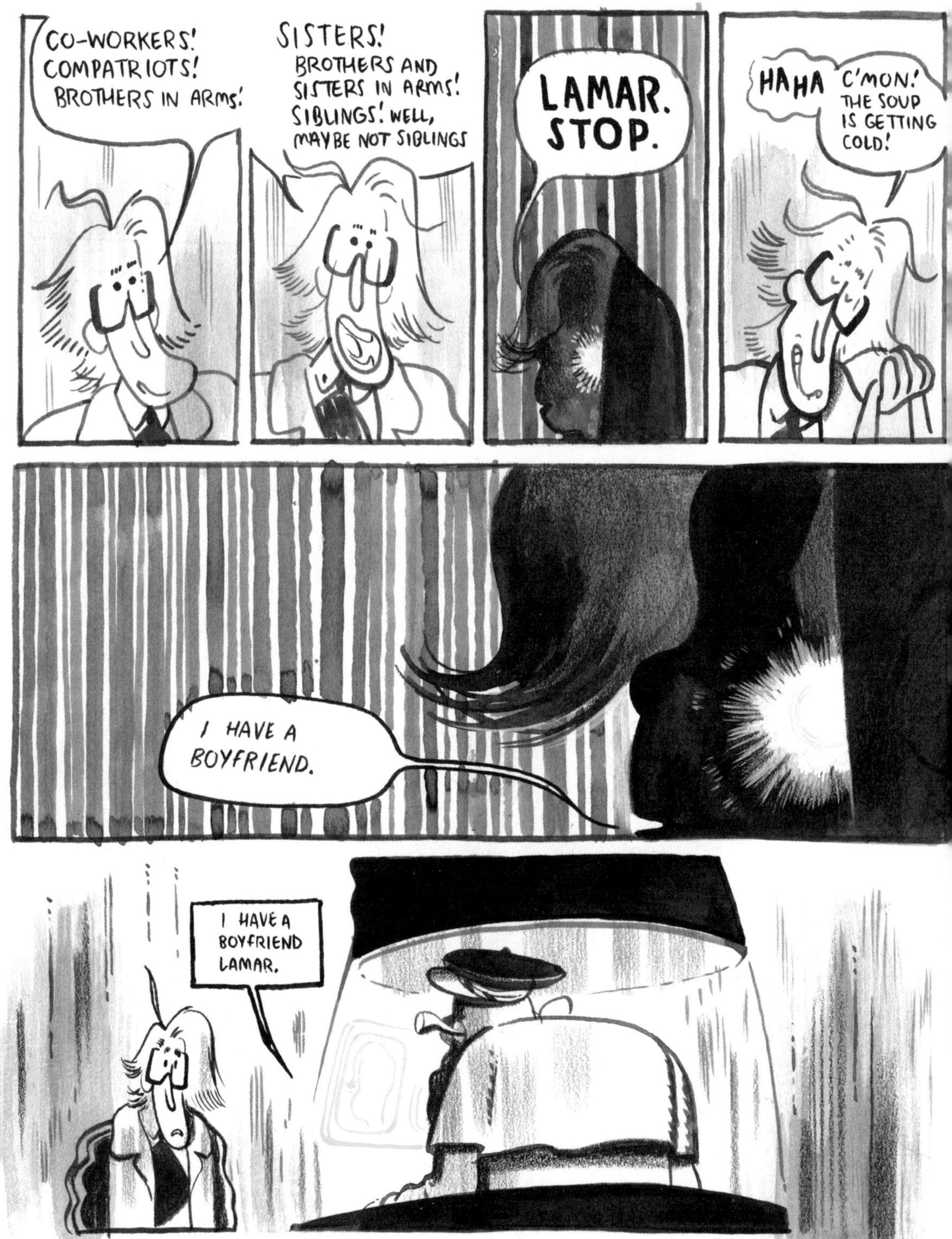
CO-WORKERS! COMPATRIOTS! BROTHERS IN ARMS!
SISTERS! BROTHERS AND SISTERS IN ARMS! SIBLINGS! WELL, MAYBE NOT SIBLINGS
LAMAR. STOP.
HAHA
C'MON! THE SOUP IS GETTING COLD!
I HAVE A BOYFRIEND.
I HAVE A BOYFRIEND LAMAR.

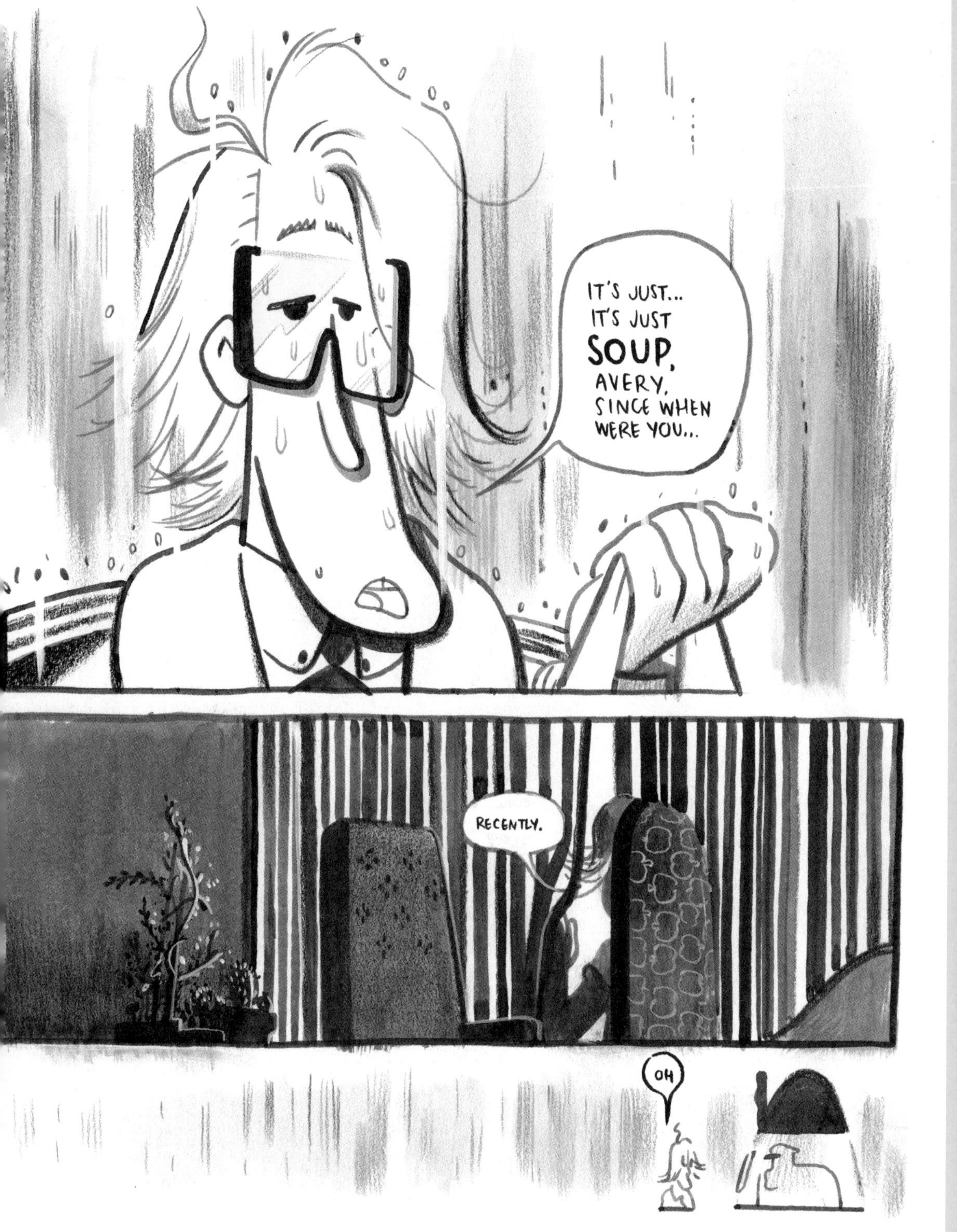
IT'S JUST...
IT'S JUST
SOUP,
AVERY.
SINCE WHEN
WERE YOU...
RECENTLY.
OH

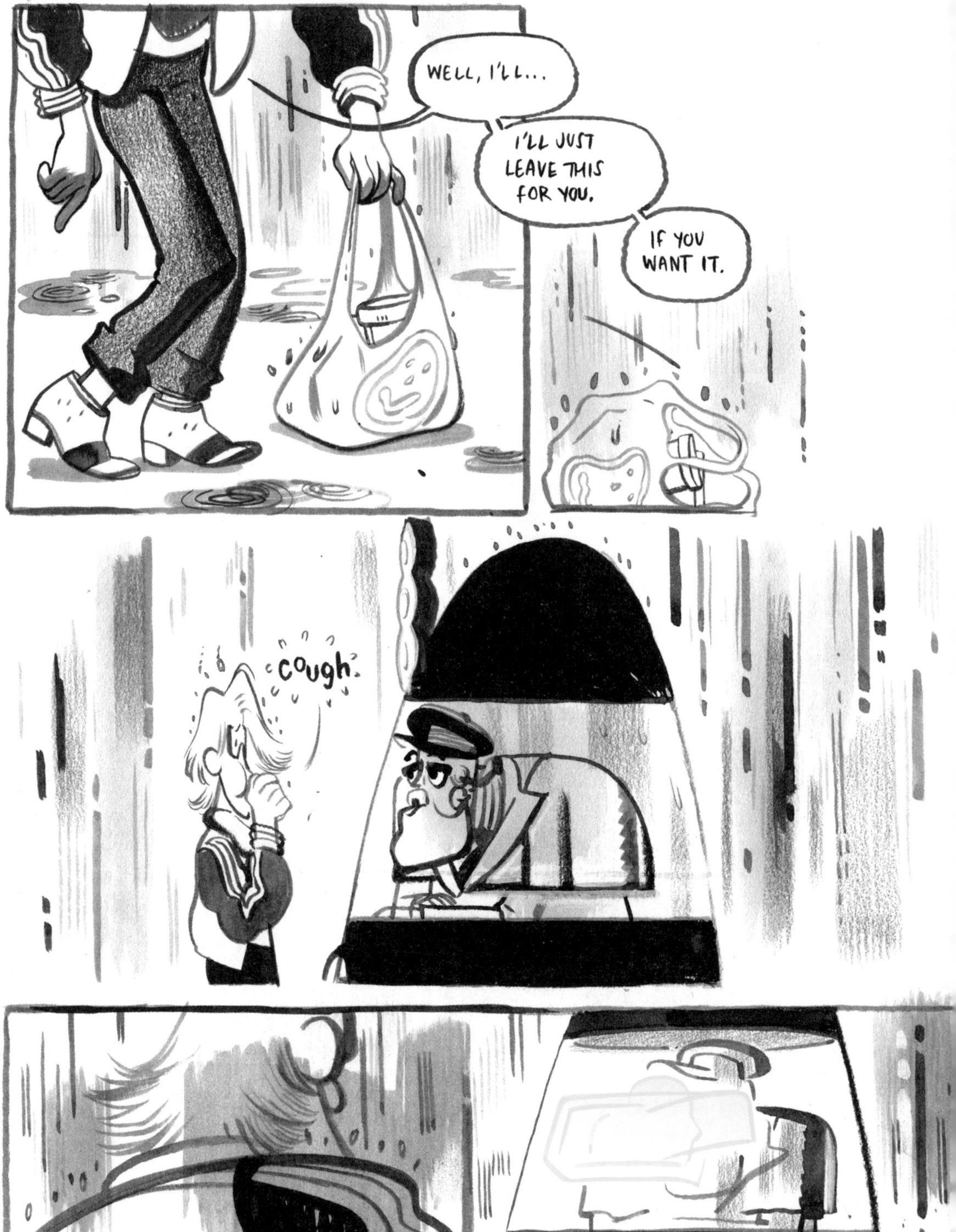
WELL, I'LL...
I'LL JUST LEAVE THIS FOR YOU.
IF YOU WANT IT.
cough

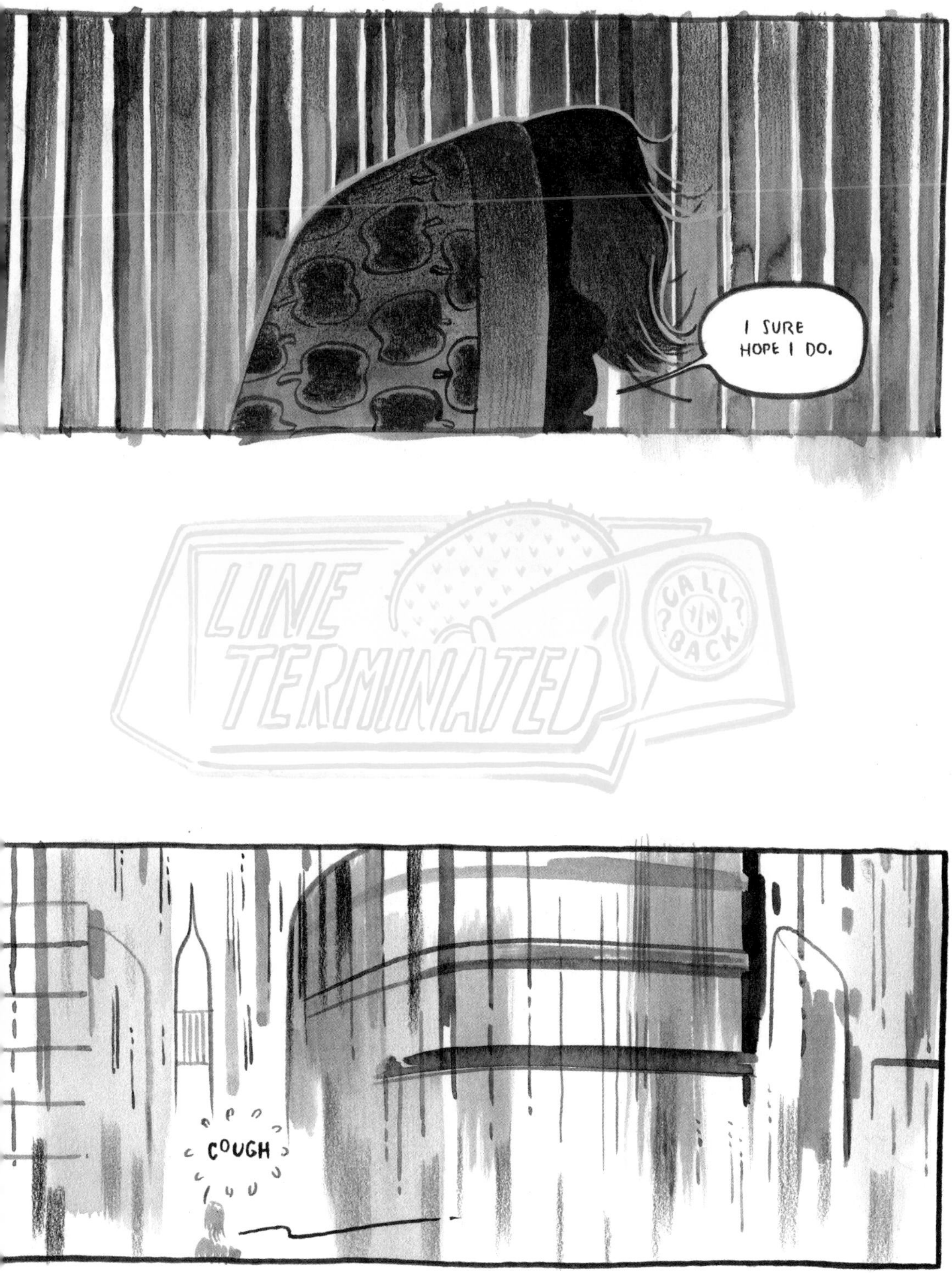
I SURE HOPE I DO.
LINE TERMINATED
CALL BACK? Y/N ?
COUGH

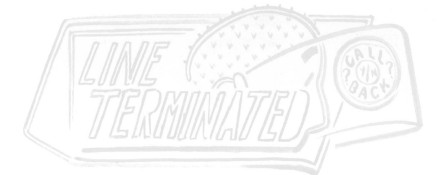

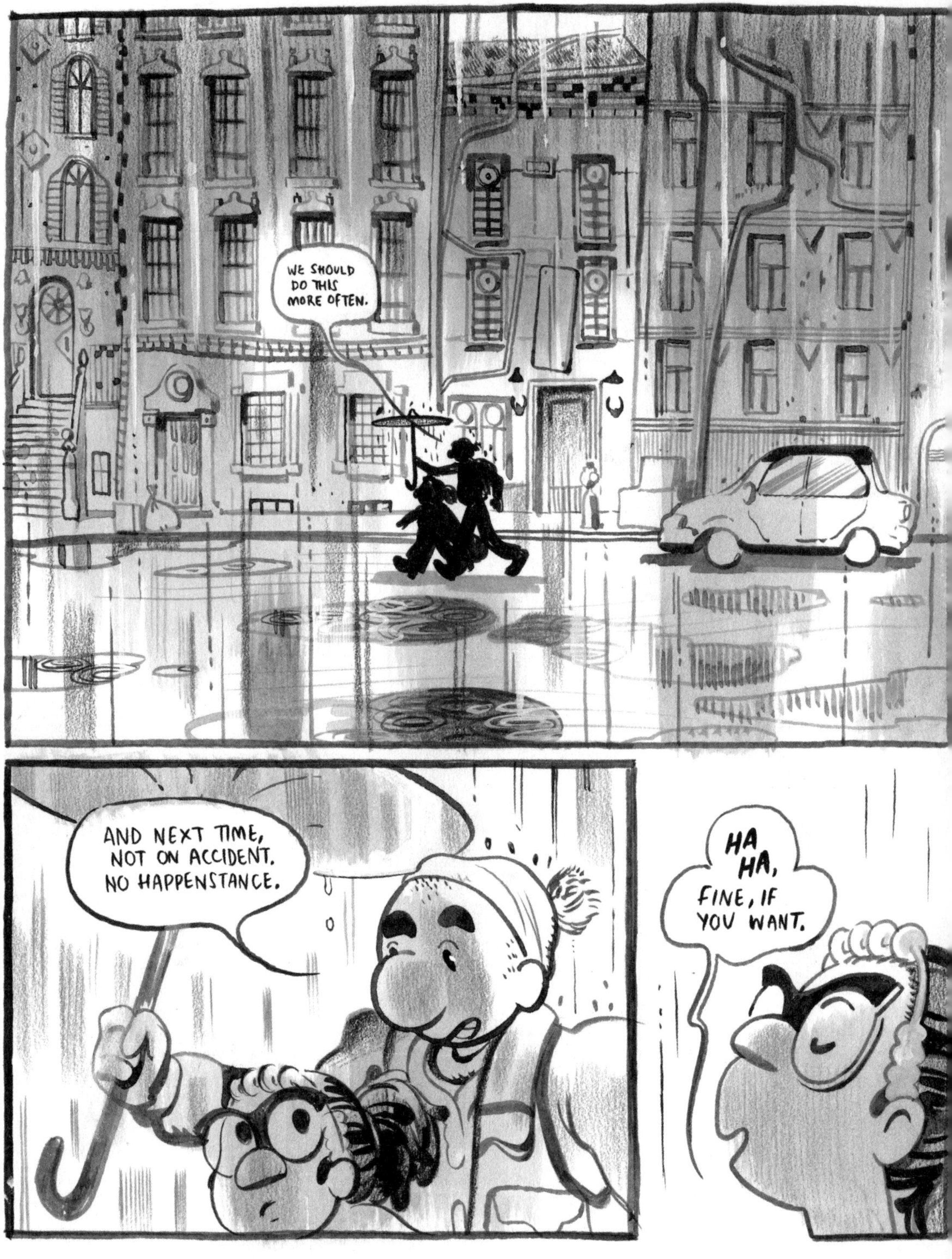
WE SHOULD DO THIS MORE OFTEN.
AND NEXT TIME, NOT ON ACCIDENT. NO HAPPENSTANCE.
HA HA, FINE, IF YOU WANT.

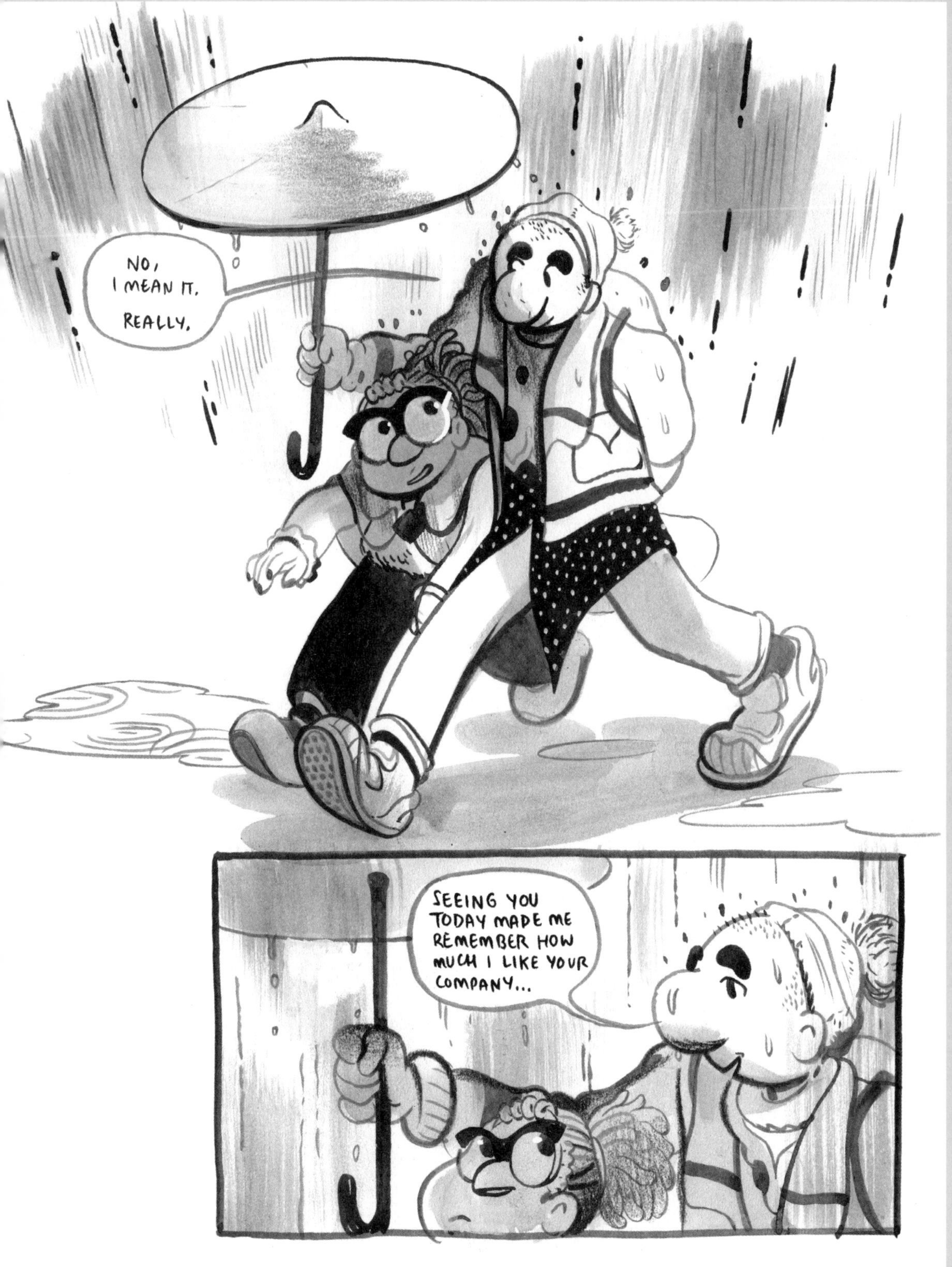
NO, I MEAN IT. REALLY.
SEEING YOU TODAY MADE ME REMEMBER HOW MUCH I LIKE YOUR COMPANY...

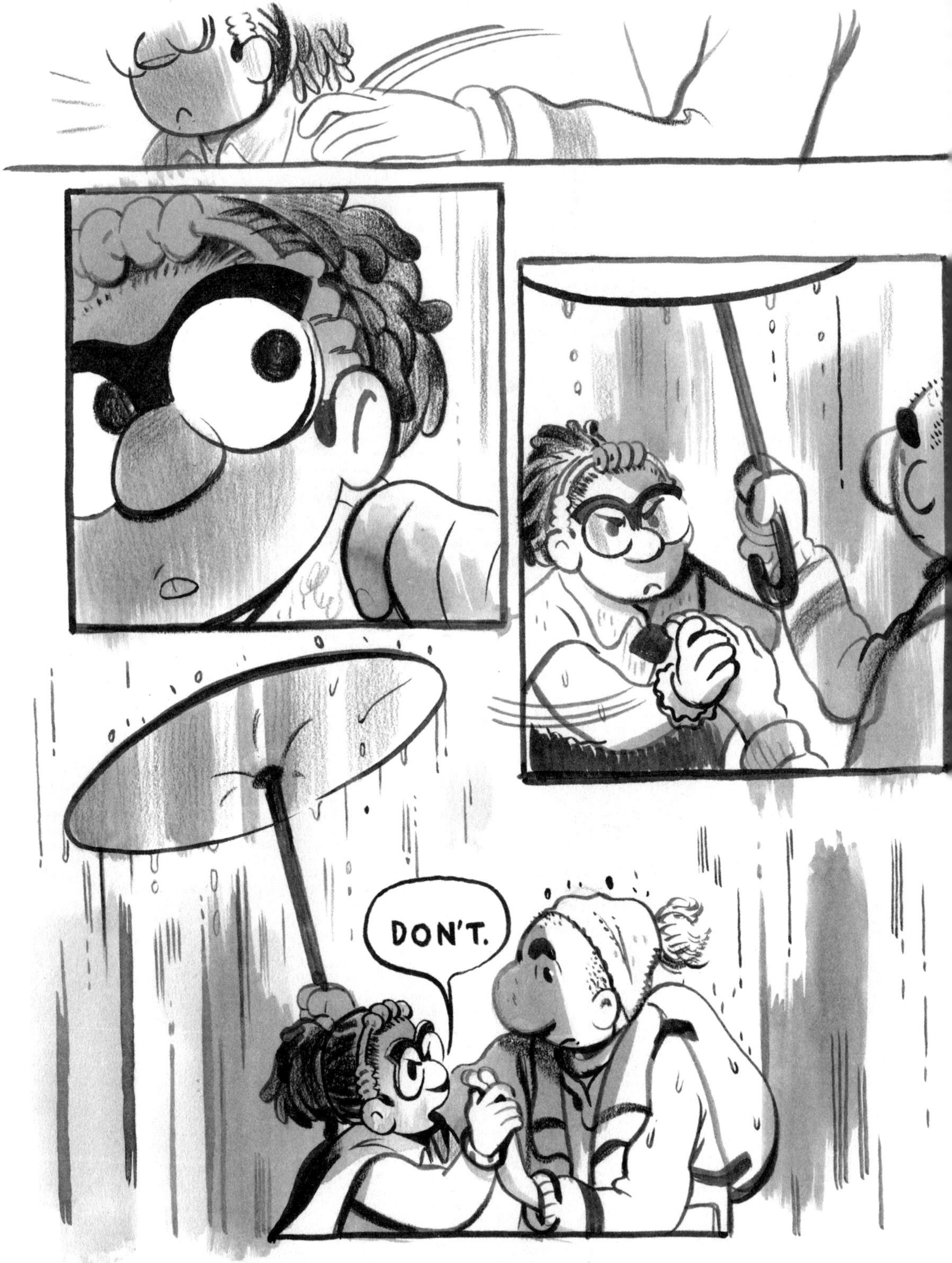
DON'T.

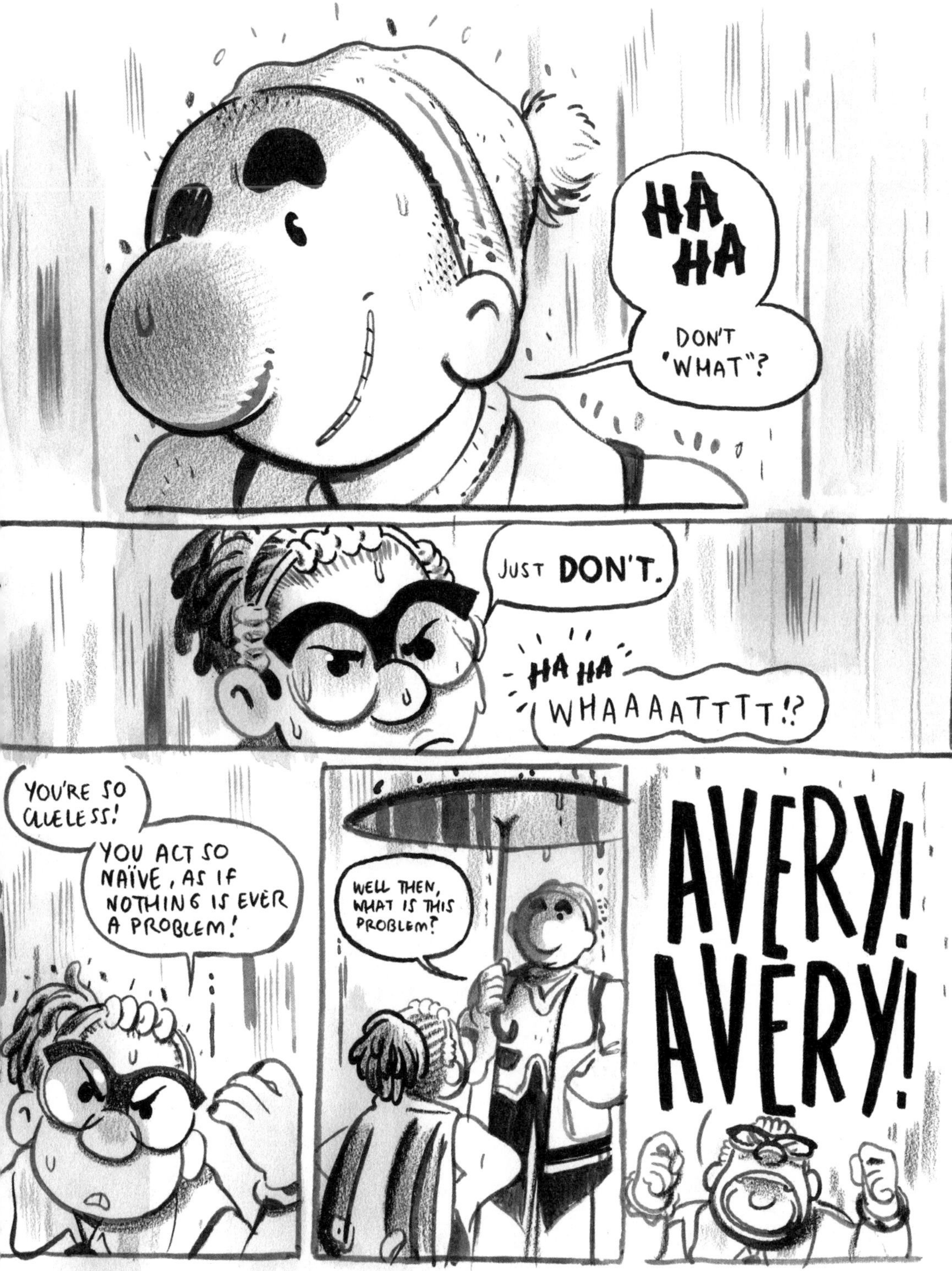
HA HA
DON'T 'WHAT"?
JUST DON'T.
HA HA
WHAAAATTTT!?
YOU'RE SO CLUELESS!
YOU ACT SO NAÏVE, AS IF NOTHING IS EVER A PROBLEM!
WELL THEN, WHAT IS THIS PROBLEM?
AVERY! AVERY!

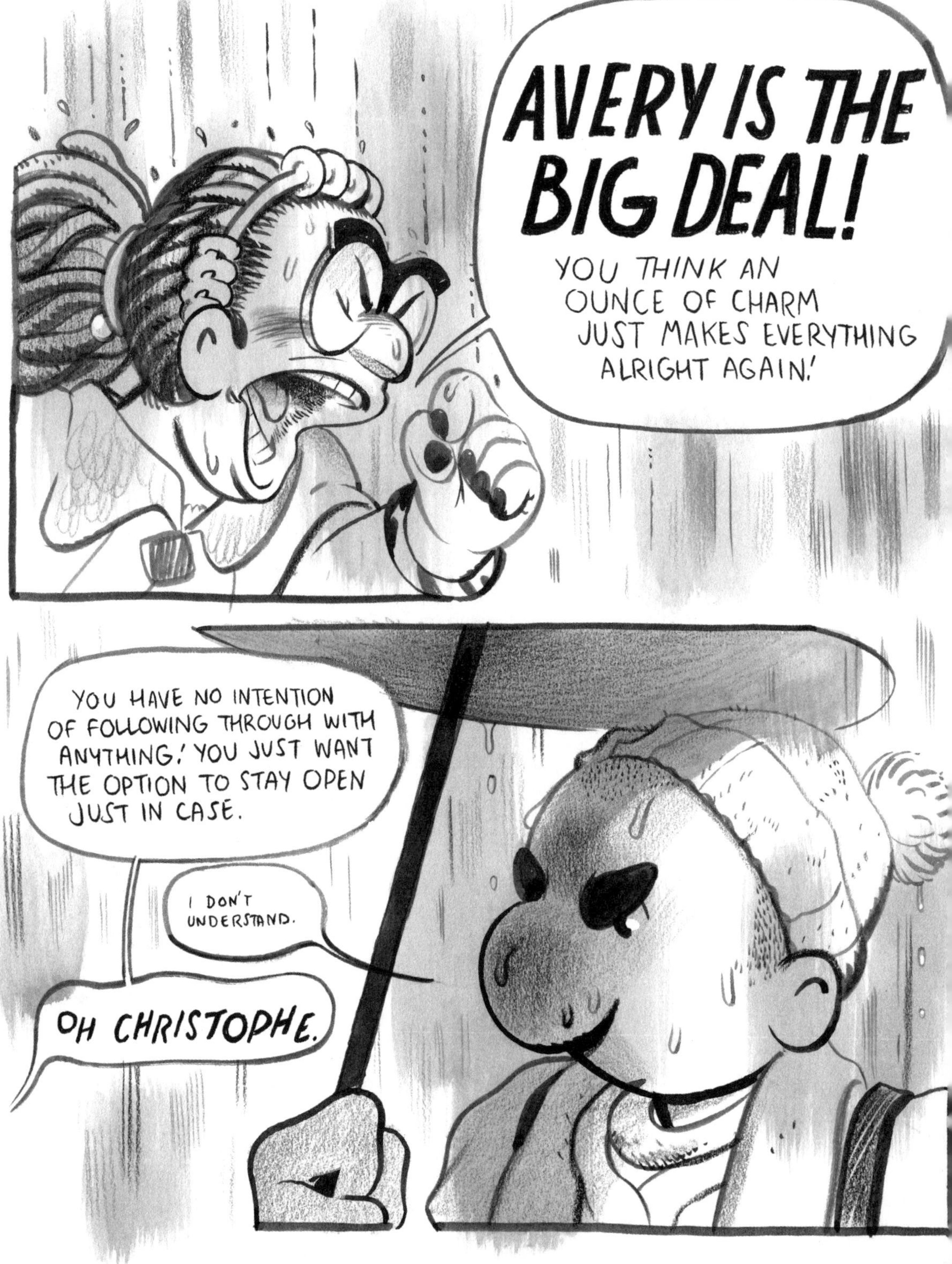
AVERY IS THE BIG DEAL!
YOU THINK AN OUNCE OF CHARM JUST MAKES EVERYTHING ALRIGHT AGAIN!
YOU HAVE NO INTENTION OF FOLLOWING THROUGH WITH ANYTHING! YOU JUST WANT THE OPTION TO STAY OPEN JUST IN CASE.
I DON'T UNDERSTAND.
OH CHRISTOPHE.

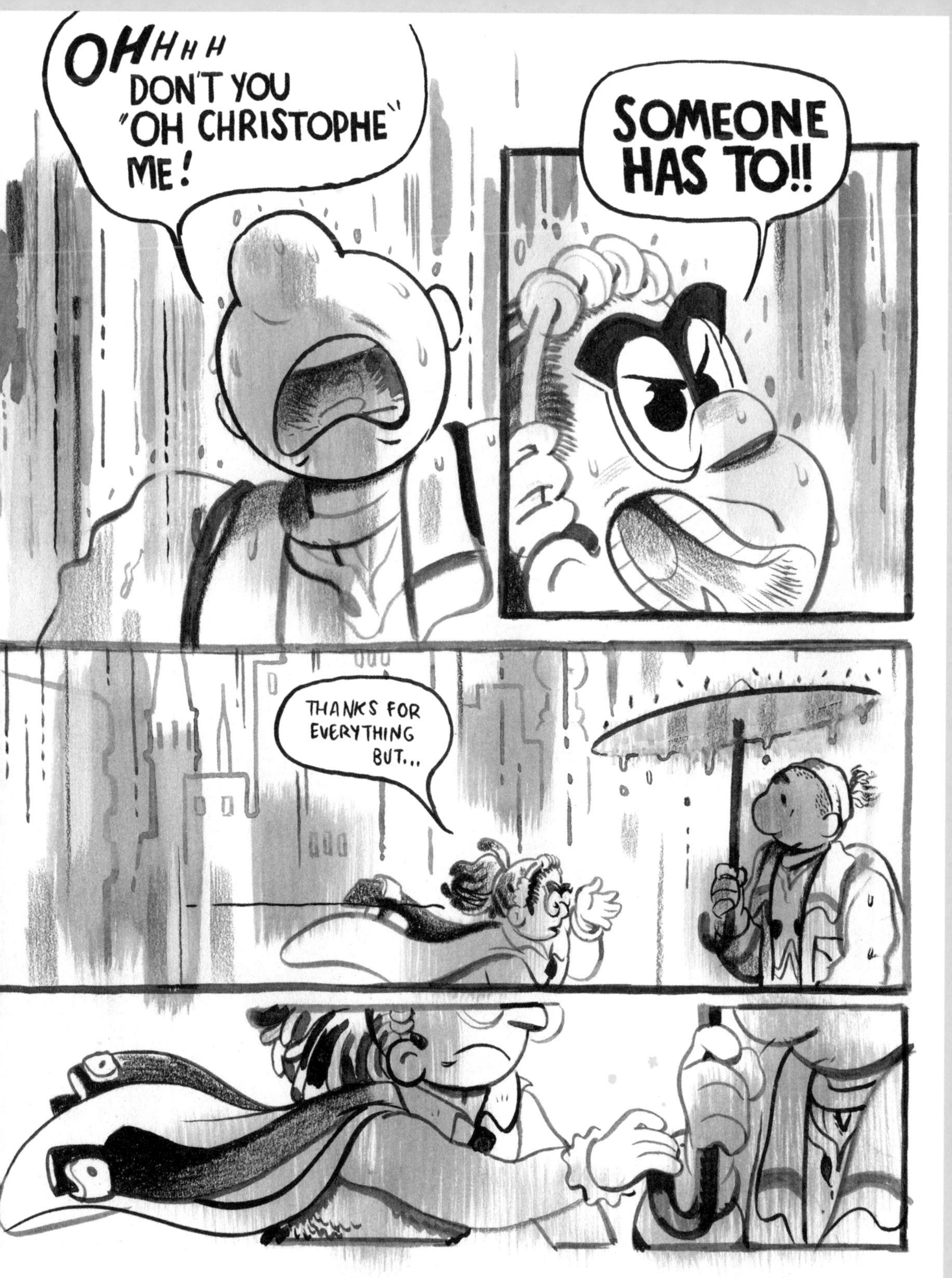
OHHHH DON'T YOU "OH CHRISTOPHE" ME!
SOMEONE HAS TO!!
THANKS FOR EVERYTHING BUT...

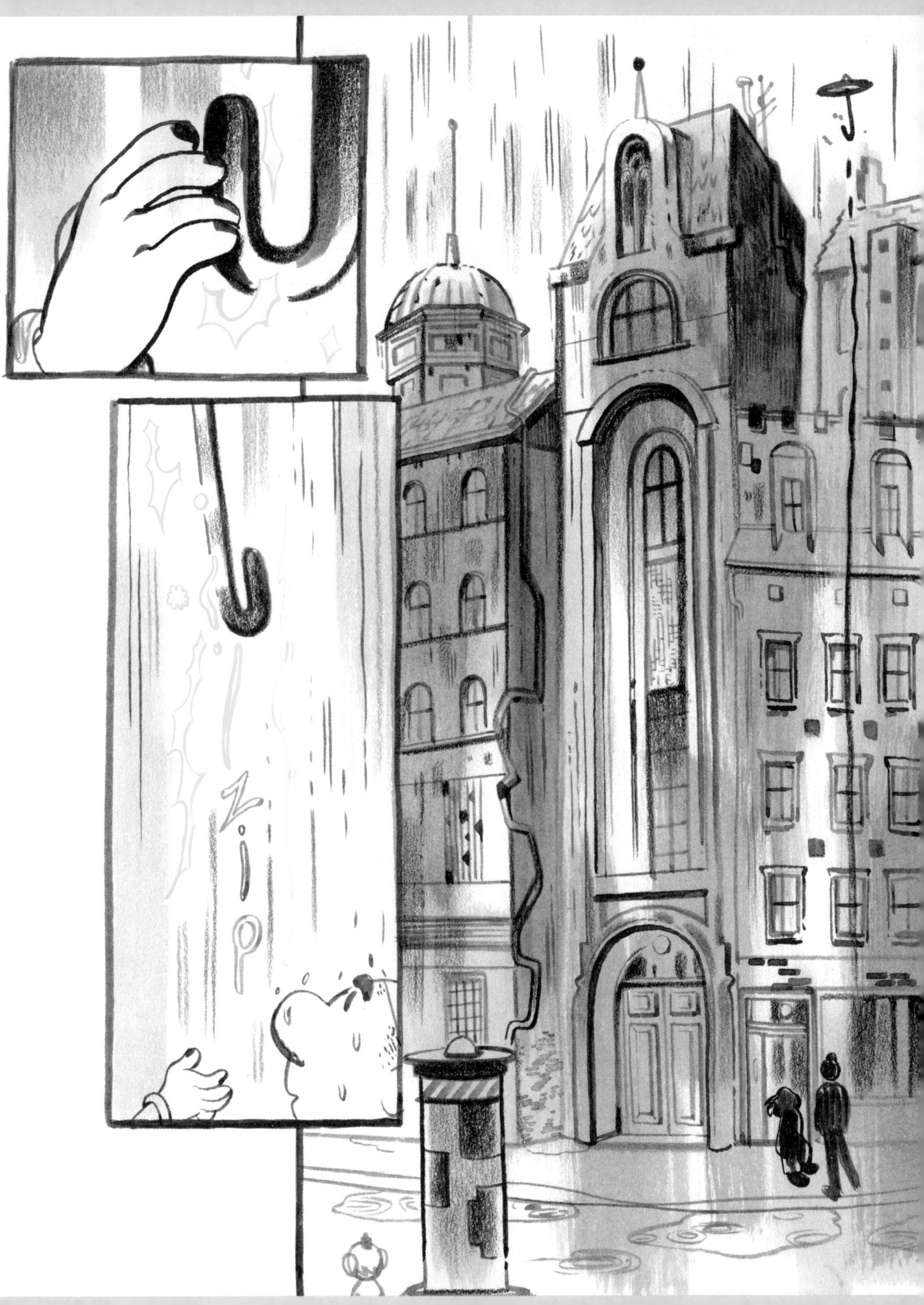
zip

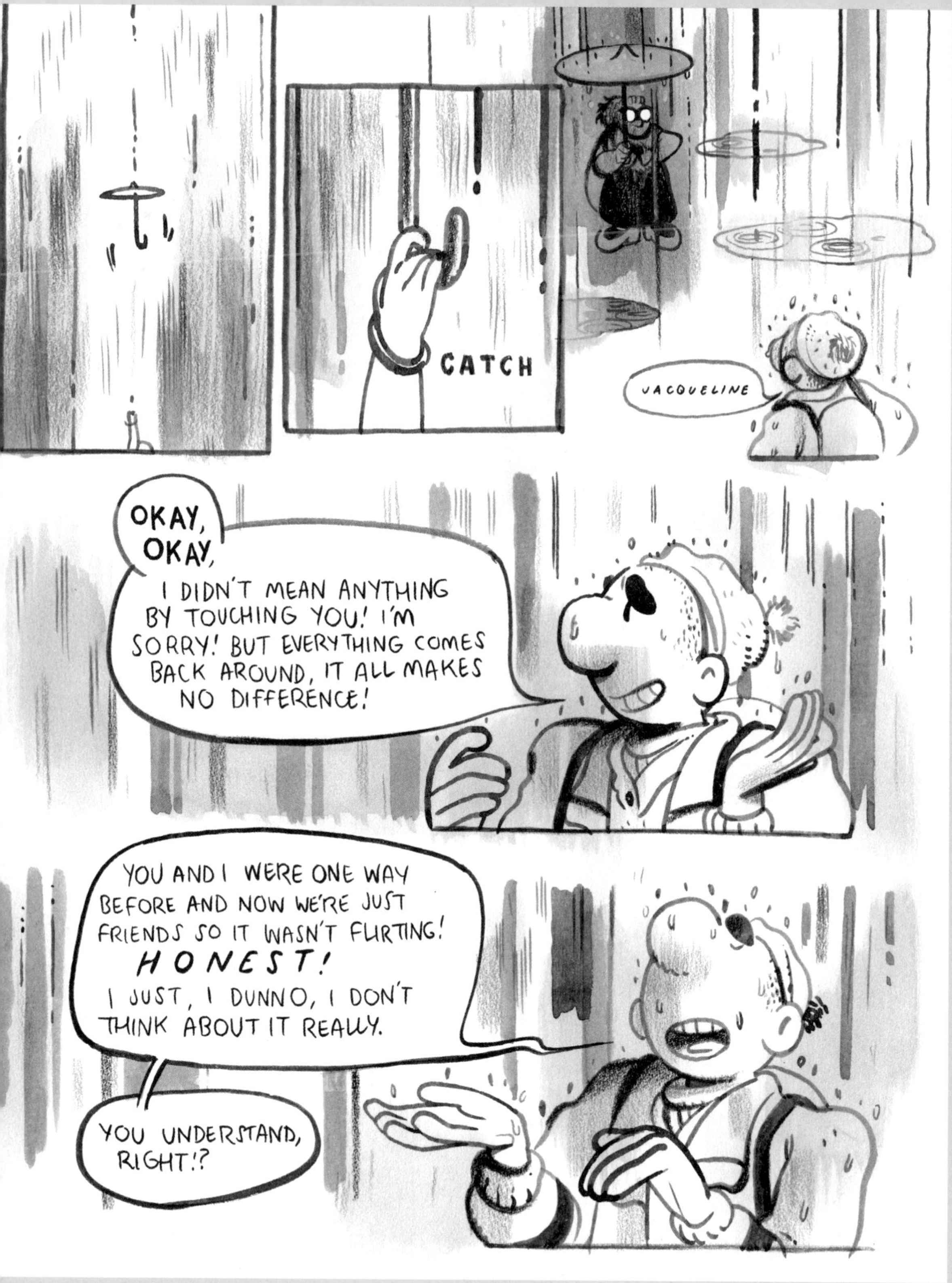
CATCH
JACQUELINE
OKAY, OKAY, I DIDN'T MEAN ANYTHING BY TOUCHING YOU! I'M SORRY! BUT EVERYTHING COMES BACK AROUND, IT ALL MAKES NO DIFFERENCE!
YOU AND I WERE ONE WAY BEFORE AND NOW WE'RE JUST FRIENDS SO IT WASN'T FLIRTING! HONEST! I JUST, I DUNNO, I DON'T THINK ABOUT IT REALLY.
YOU UNDERSTAND, RIGHT!?

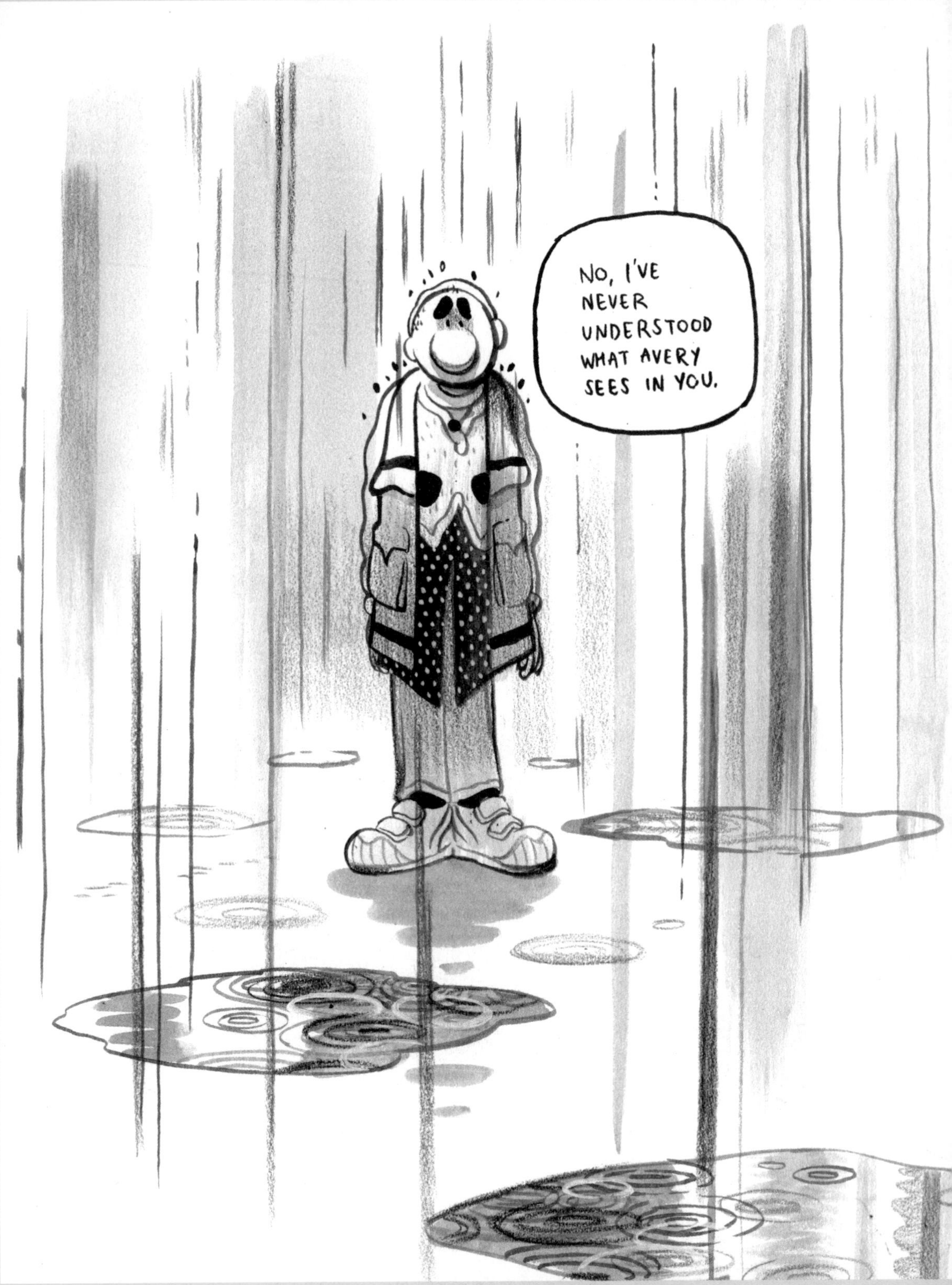
NO, I'VE NEVER UNDERSTOOD WHAT AVERY SEES IN YOU.

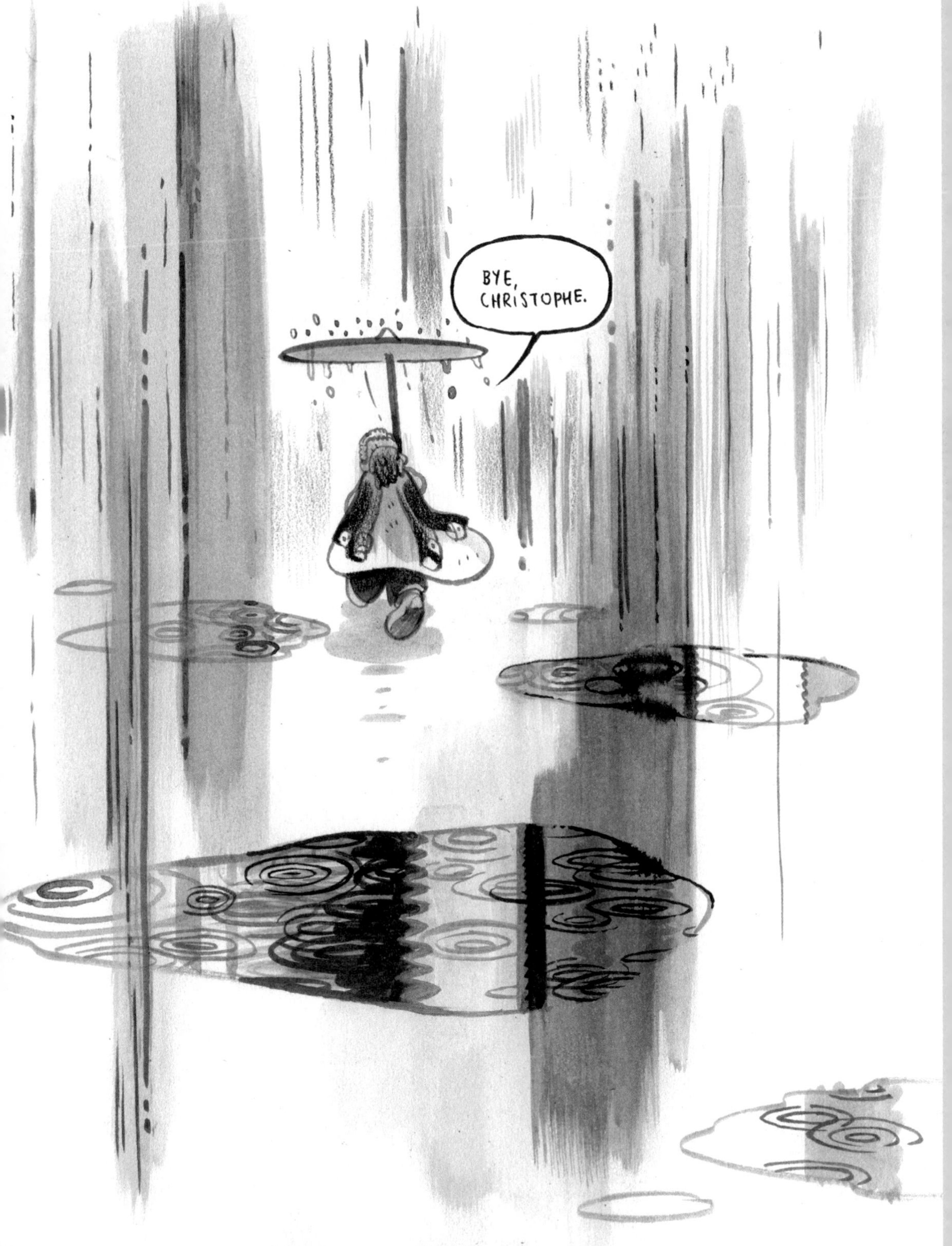
BYE, CHRISTOPHE.

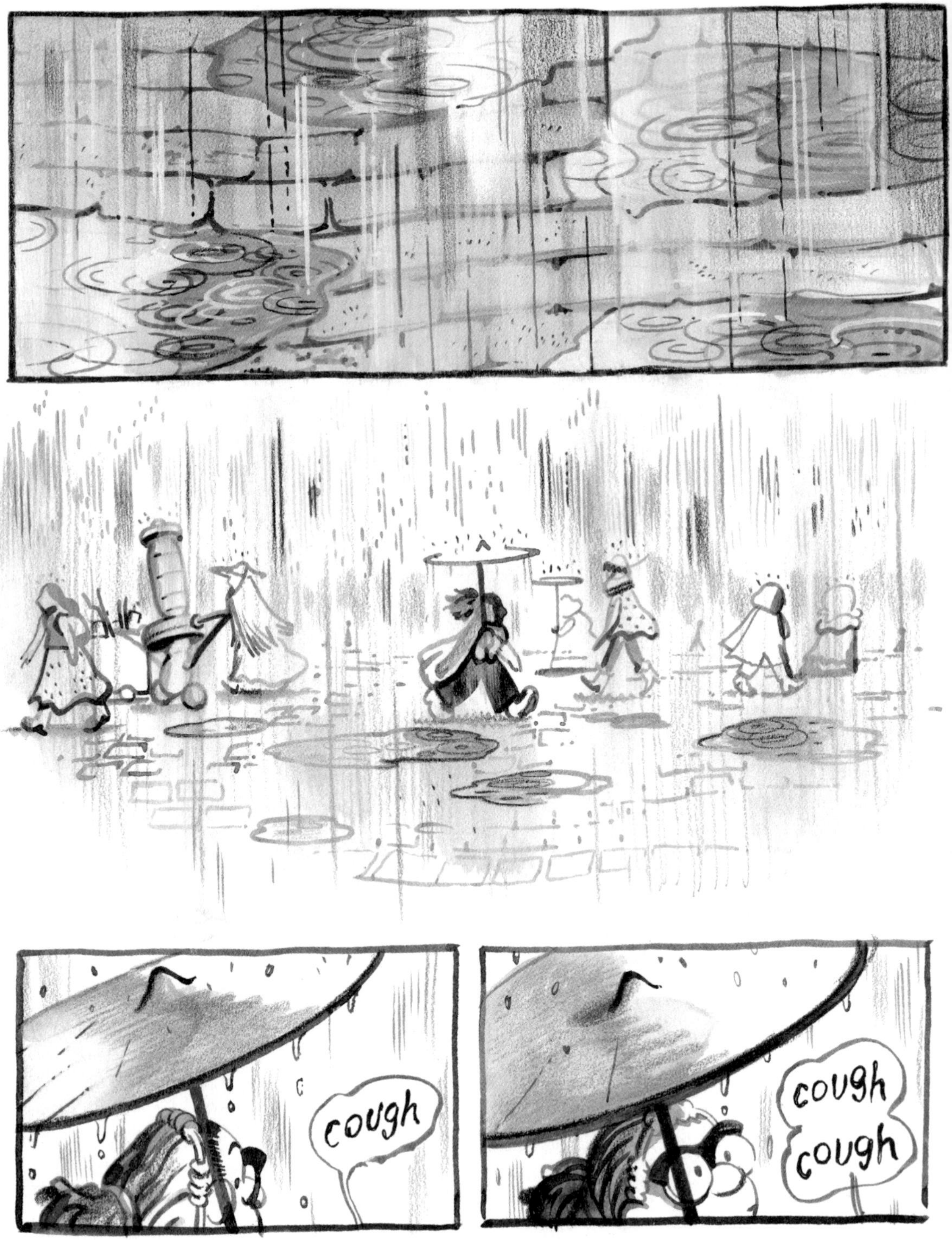
cough
cough
cough

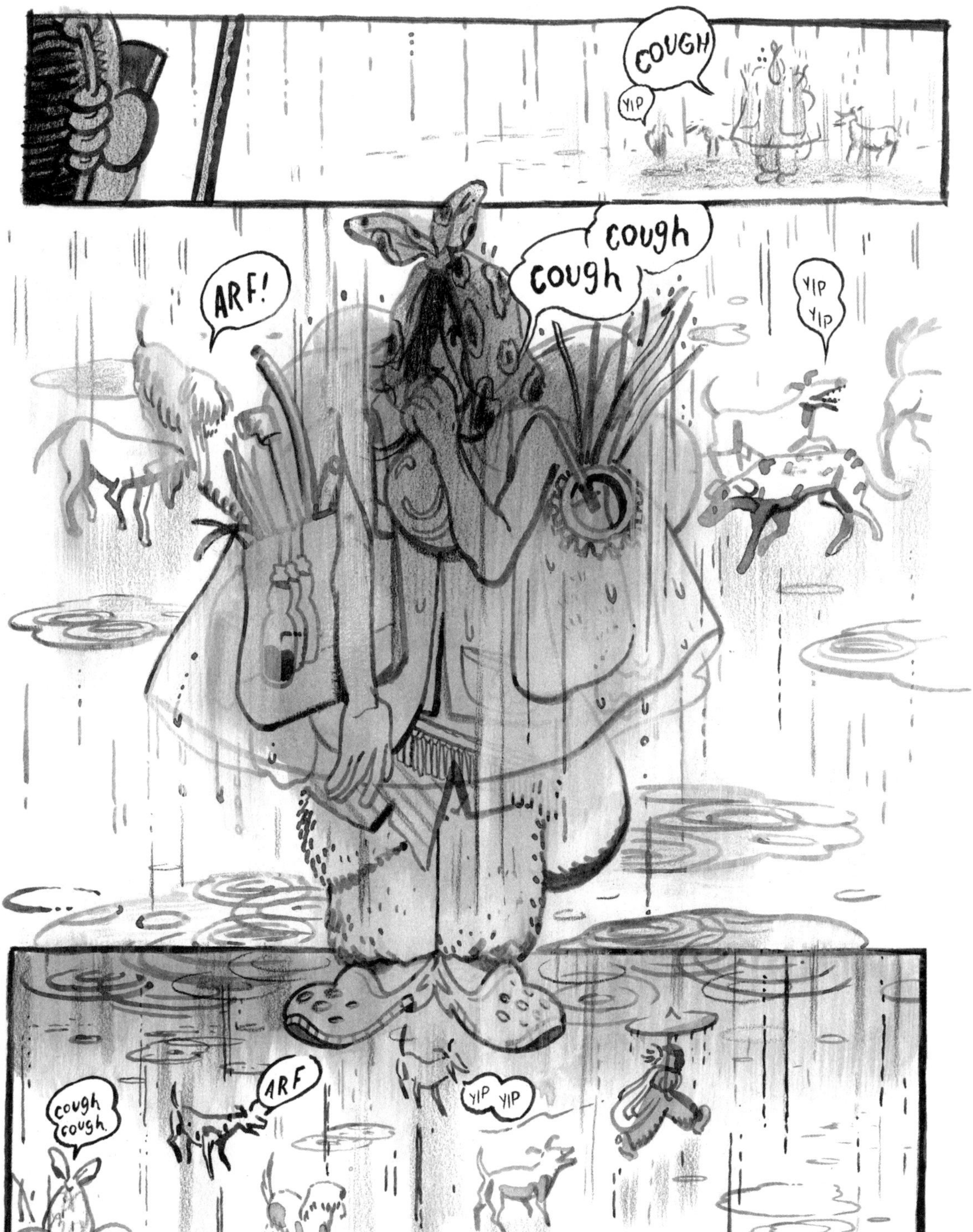
COUGH
YIP
ARF!
cough
cough
YIP
YIP
cough
cough.
ARF
YIP YIP

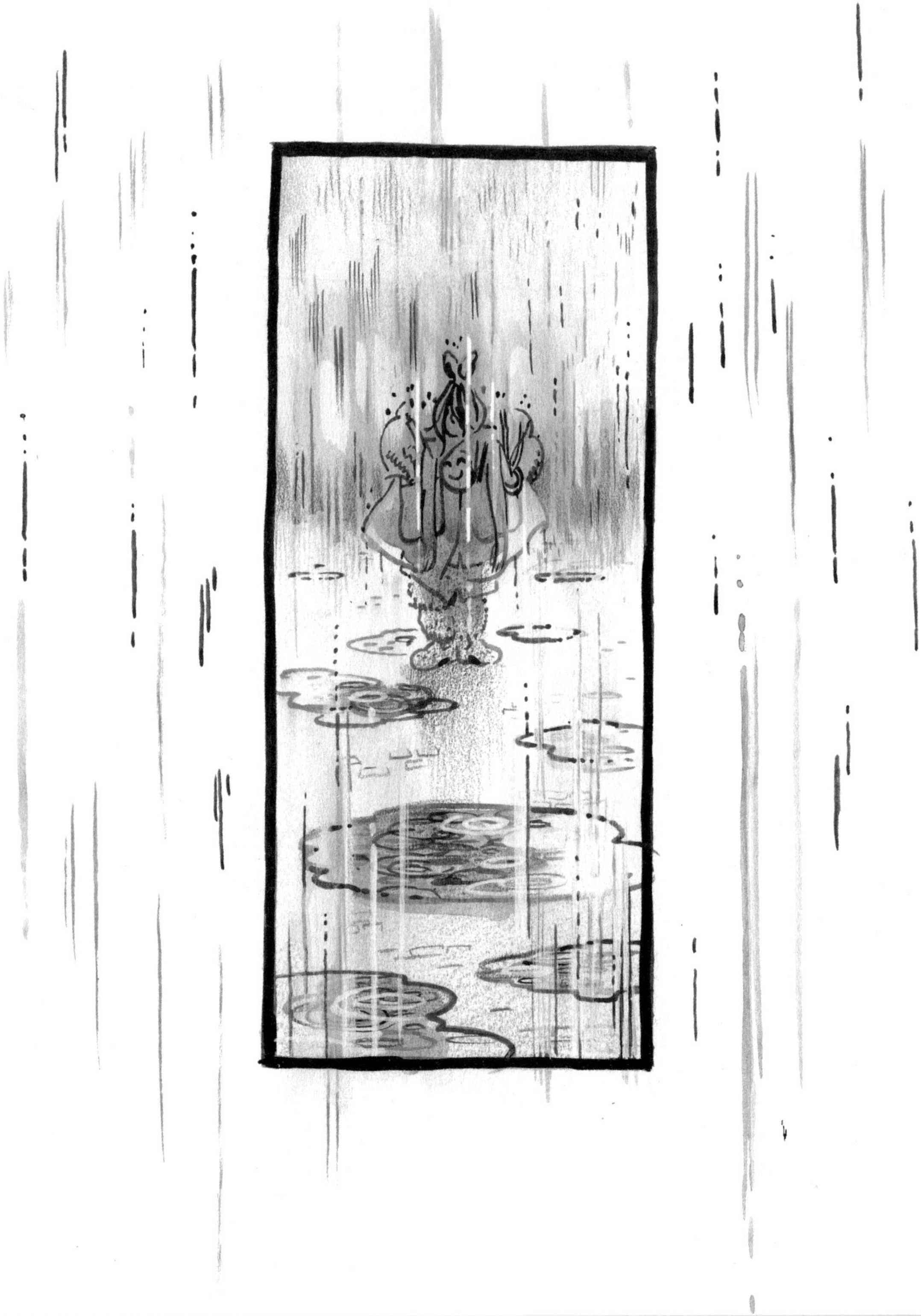

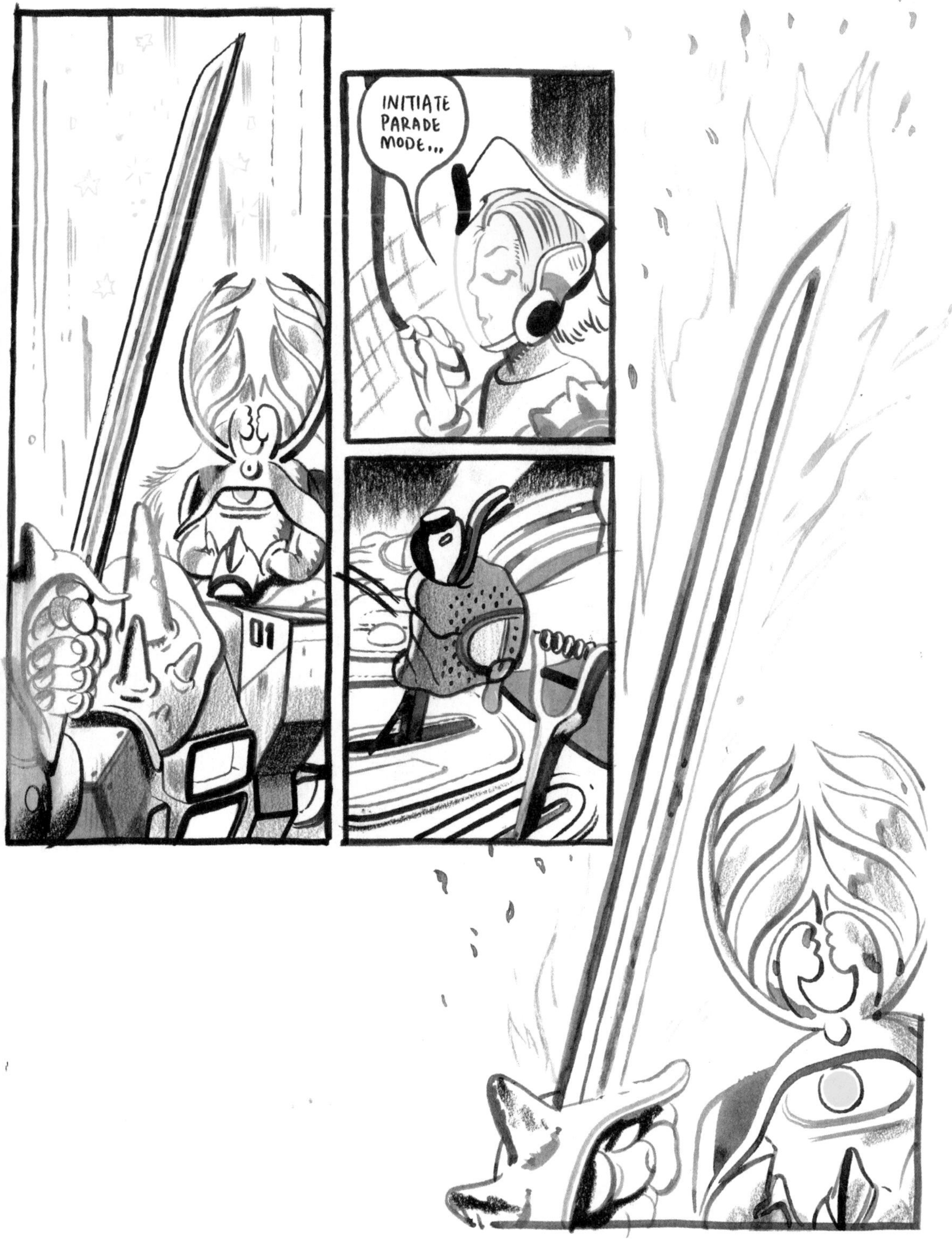
INITIATE PARADE MODE...
01

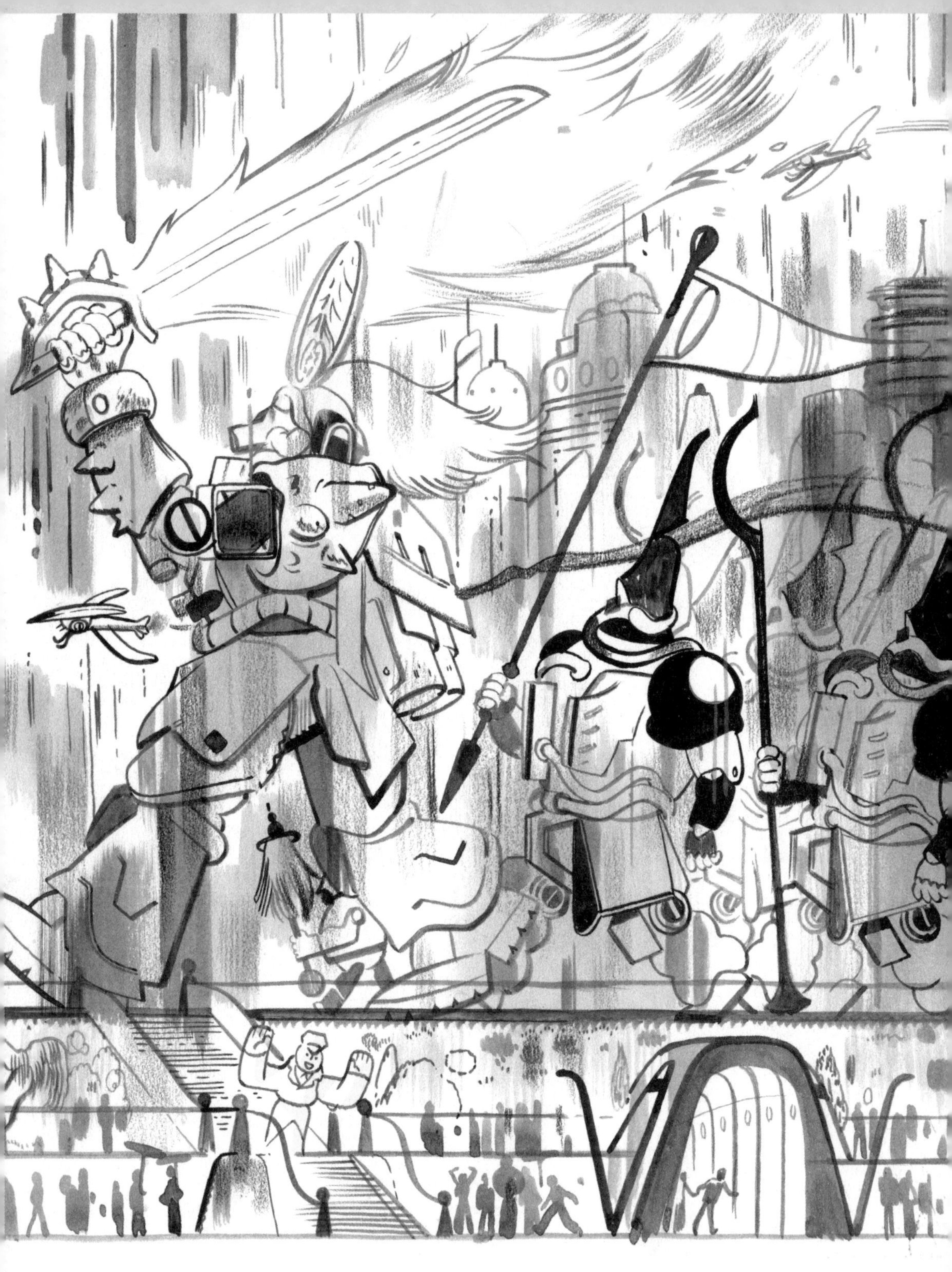

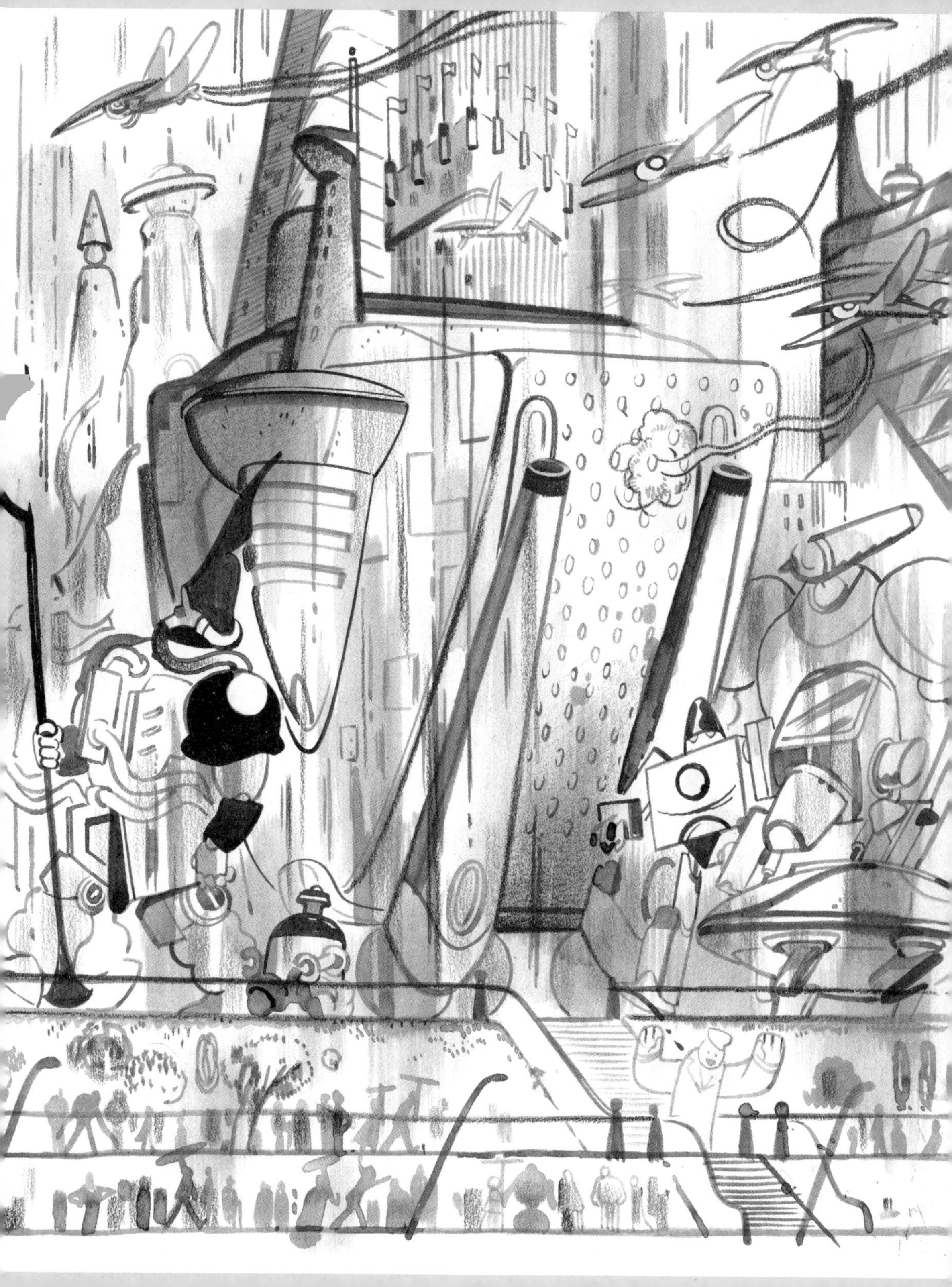

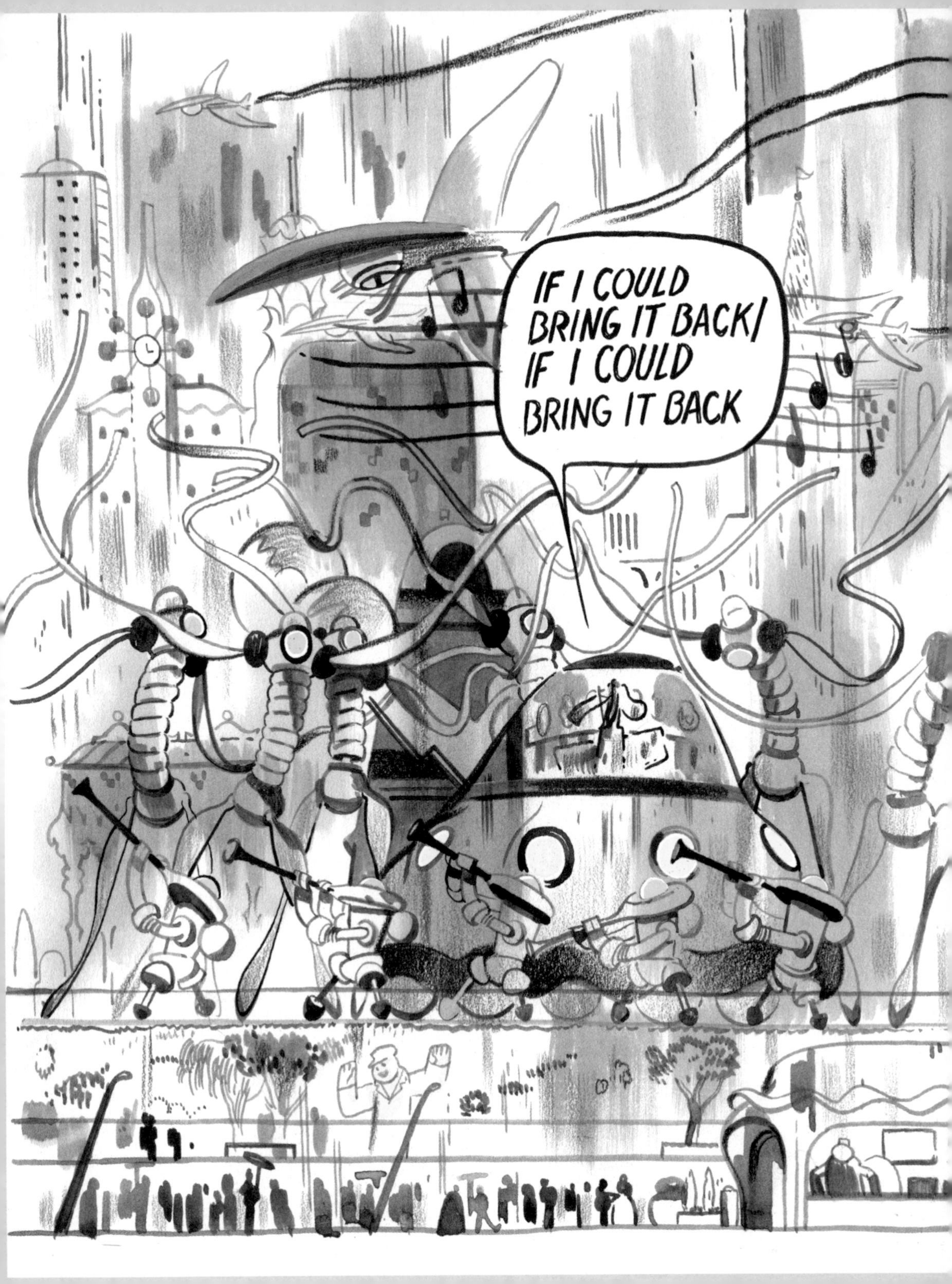
IF I COULD BRING IT BACK/ IF I COULD BRING IT BACK

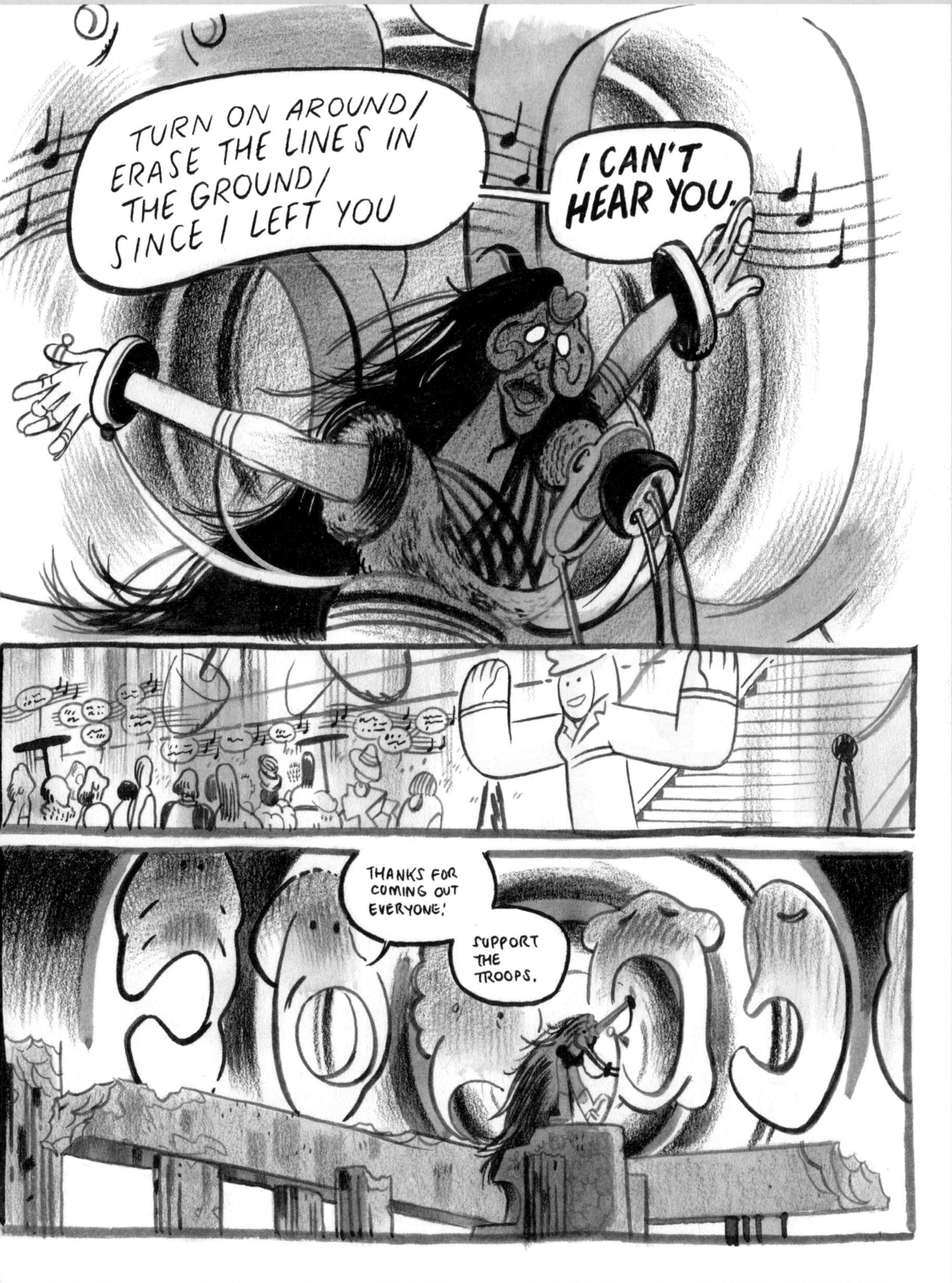
TURN ON AROUND/ ERASE THE LINES IN THE GROUND/ SINCE I LEFT YOU
I CAN'T HEAR YOU.
THANKS FOR COMING OUT EVERYONE!
SUPPORT THE TROOPS.

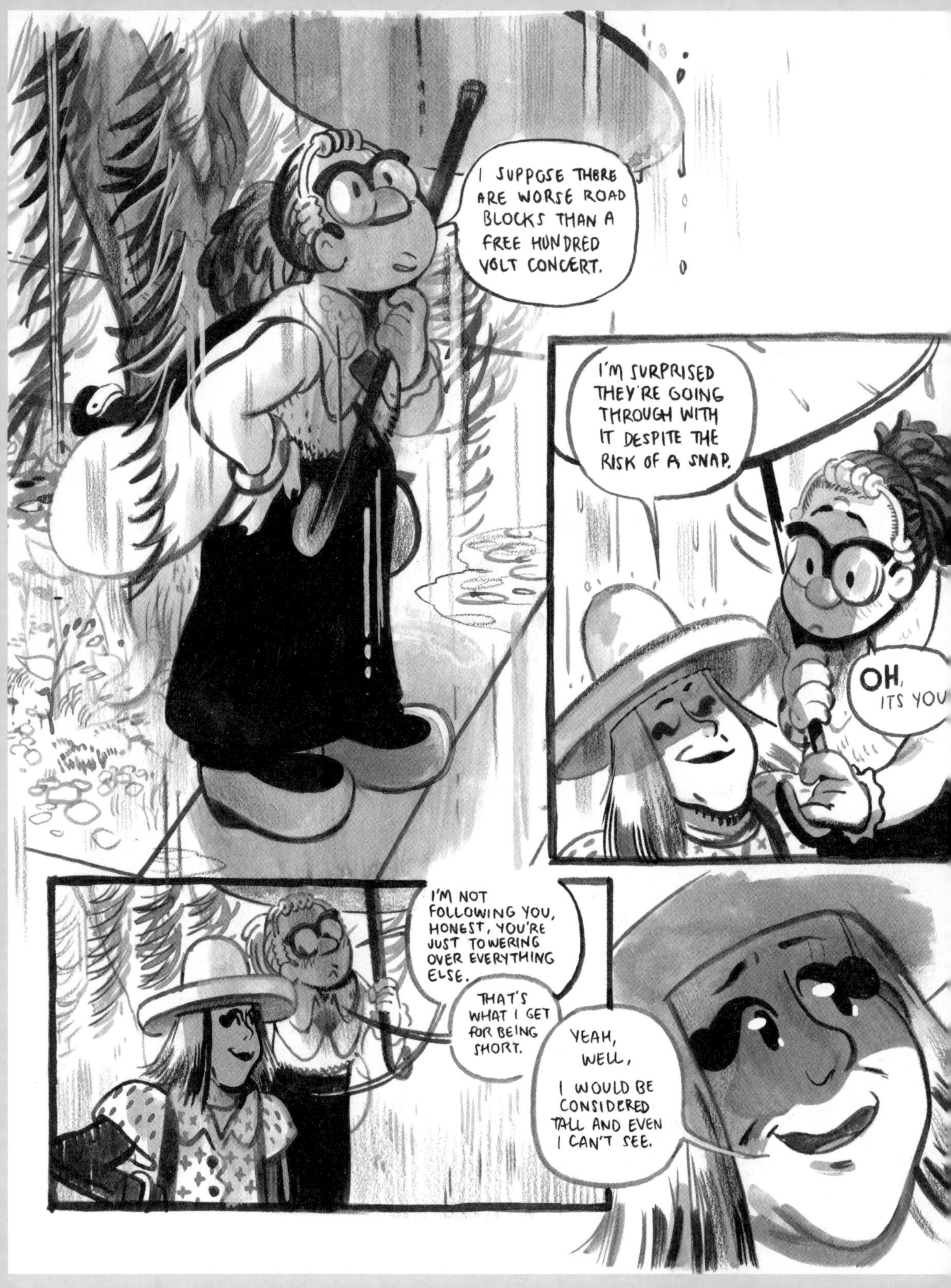
I SUPPOSE THERE ARE WORSE ROAD BLOCKS THAN A FREE HUNDRED VOLT CONCERT.
I'M SURPRISED THEY'RE GOING THROUGH WITH IT DESPITE THE RISK OF A SNAP.
OH, ITS YOU
I'M NOT FOLLOWING YOU, HONEST, YOU'RE JUST TOWERING OVER EVERYTHING ELSE.
THAT'S WHAT I GET FOR BEING SHORT.
YEAH, WELL, I WOULD BE CONSIDERED TALL AND EVEN I CAN'T SEE.

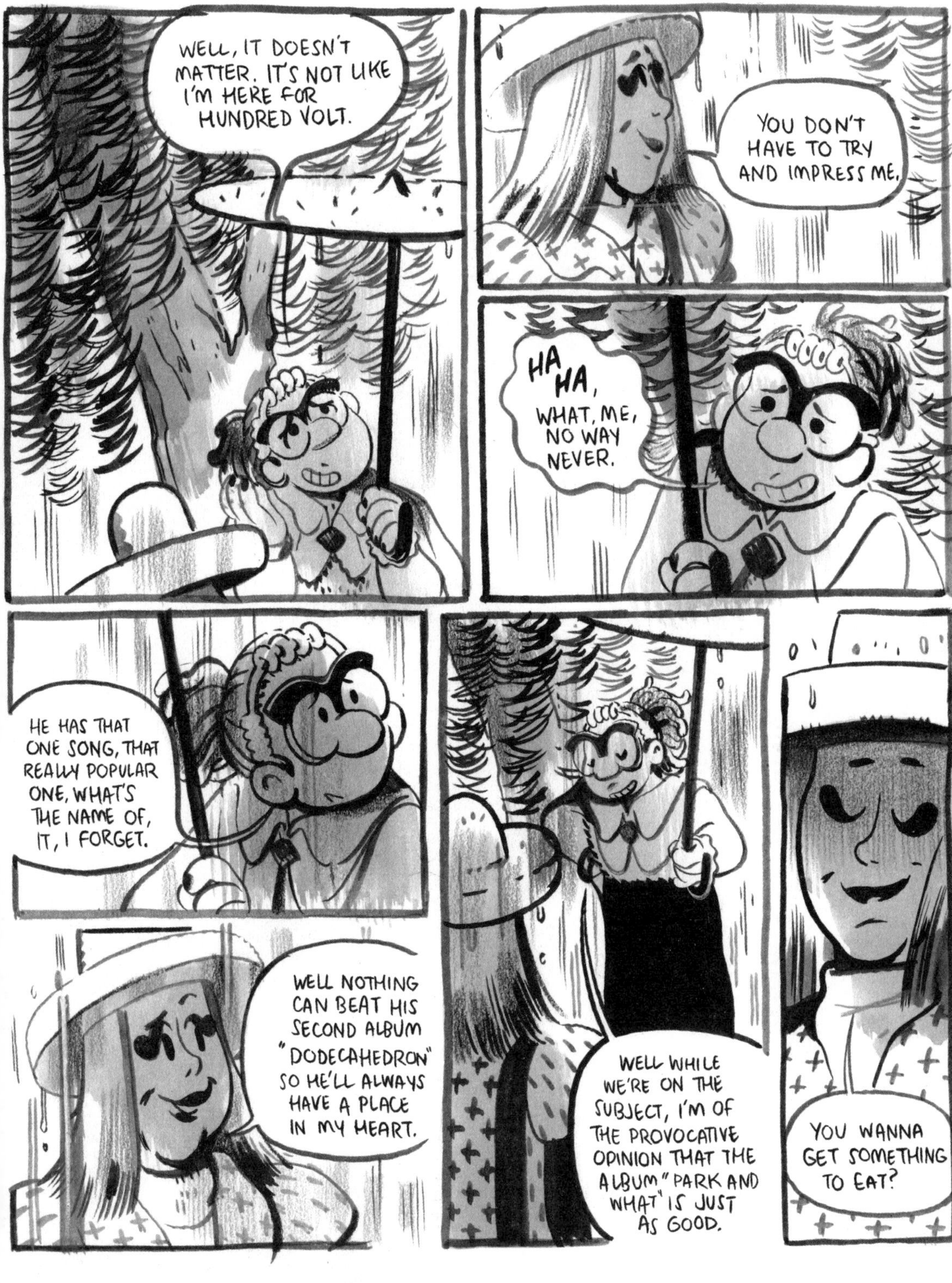
WELL, IT DOESN'T MATTER. IT'S NOT LIKE I'M HERE FOR HUNDRED VOLT.
YOU DON'T HAVE TO TRY AND IMPRESS ME.
HA HA, WHAT, ME, NO WAY NEVER.
HE HAS THAT ONE SONG, THAT REALLY POPULAR ONE, WHAT'S THE NAME OF, IT, I FORGET.
WELL NOTHING CAN BEAT HIS SECOND ALBUM "DODECAHEDRON" SO HE'LL ALWAYS HAVE A PLACE IN MY HEART.
WELL WHILE WE'RE ON THE SUBJECT, I'M OF THE PROVOCATIVE OPINION THAT THE ALBUM "PARK AND WHAT" IS JUST AS GOOD.
YOU WANNA GET SOMETHING TO EAT?

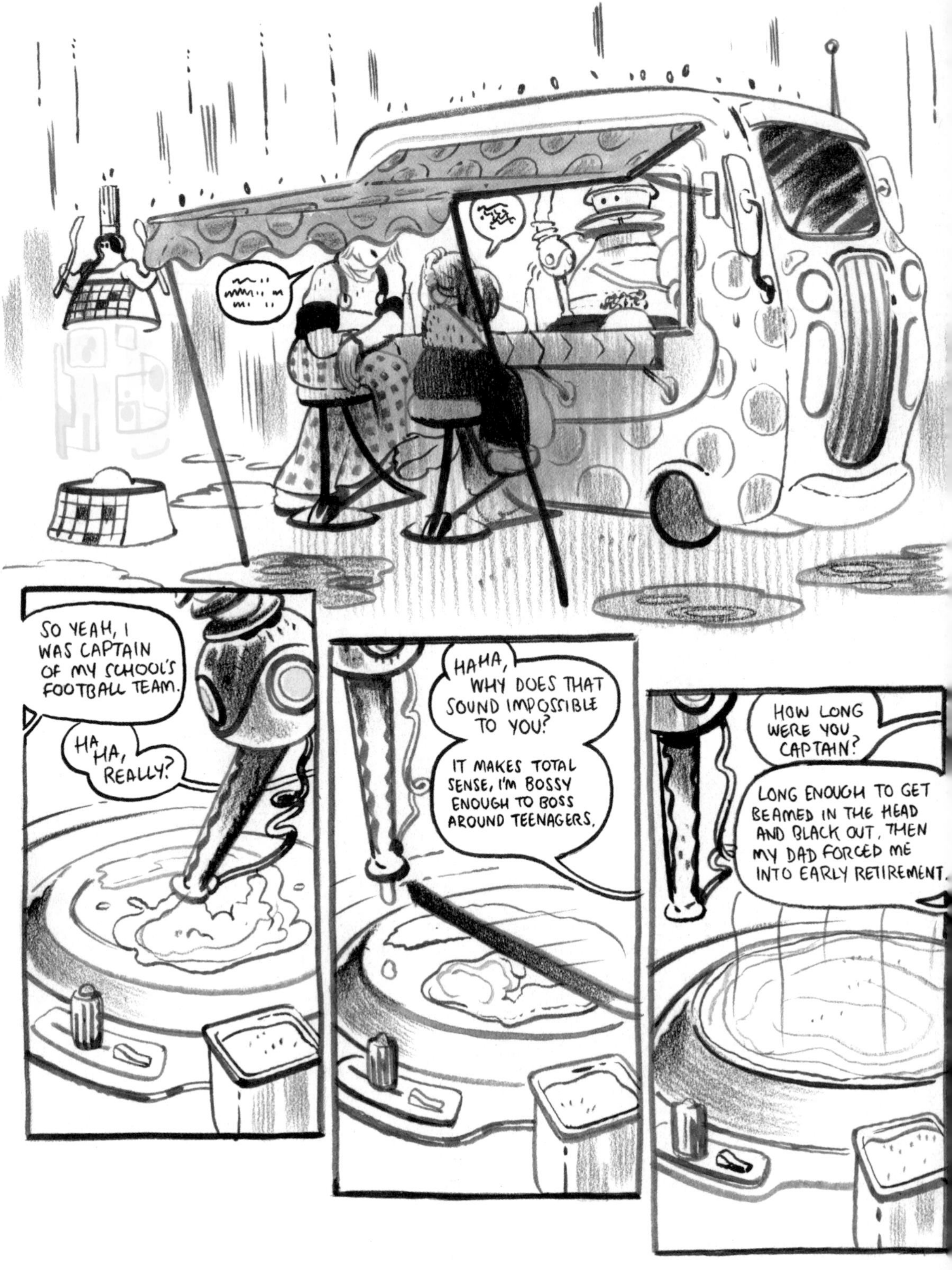

SO YEAH, I WAS CAPTAIN OF MY SCHOOL'S FOOTBALL TEAM.
HA HA, REALLY?
HAHA, WHY DOES THAT SOUND IMPOSSIBLE TO YOU?
IT MAKES TOTAL SENSE, I'M BOSSY ENOUGH TO BOSS AROUND TEENAGERS.
HOW LONG WERE YOU CAPTAIN?
LONG ENOUGH TO GET BEAMED IN THE HEAD AND BLACK OUT, THEN MY DAD FORCED ME INTO EARLY RETIREMENT.

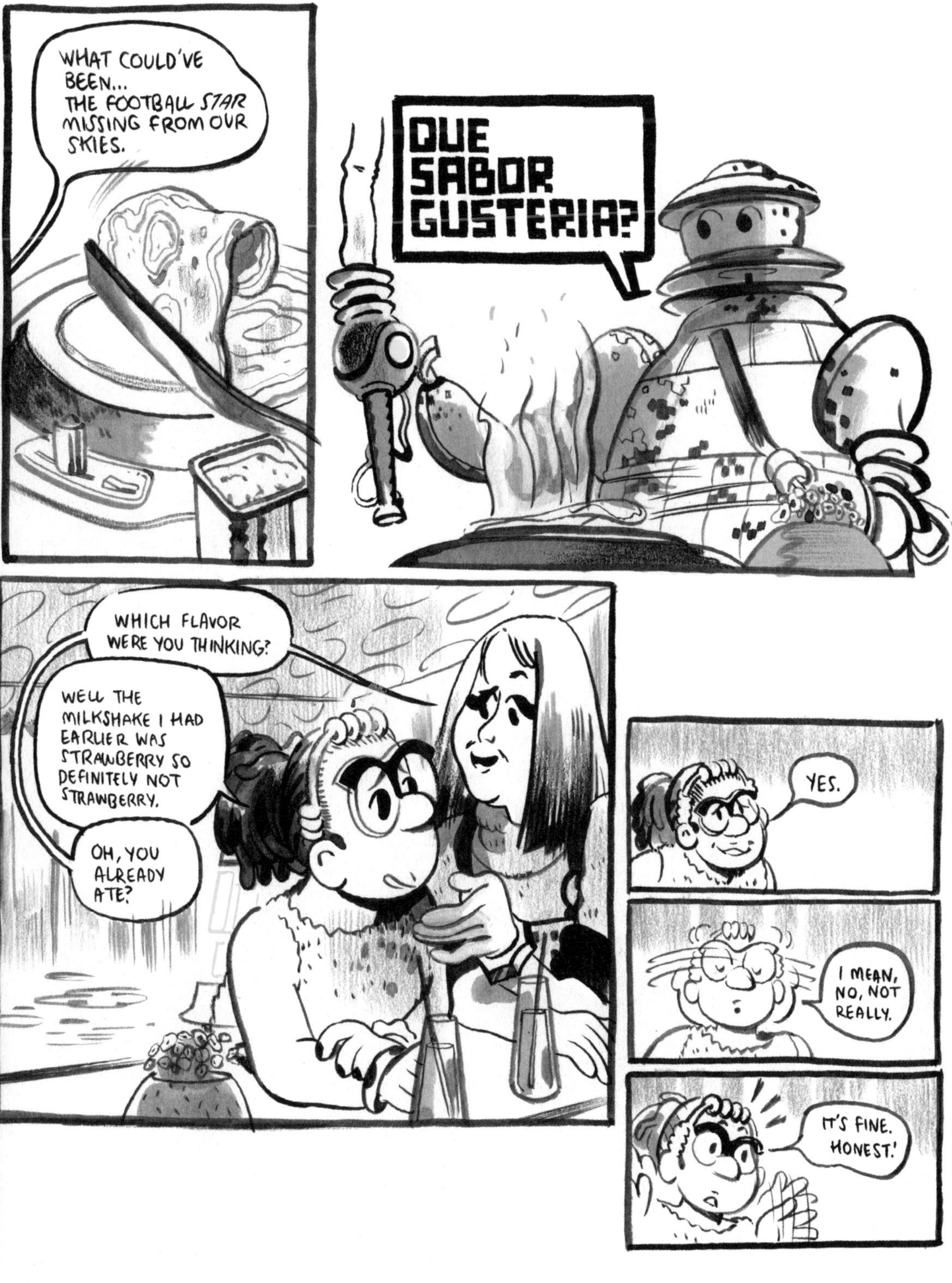
WHAT COULD'VE BEEN... THE FOOTBALL STAR MISSING FROM OUR SKIES.
QUE SABOR GUSTERIA?
WHICH FLAVOR WERE YOU THINKING?
WELL THE MILKSHAKE I HAD EARLIER WAS STRAWBERRY SO DEFINITELY NOT STRAWBERRY.
OH, YOU ALREADY ATE?
YES.
I MEAN, NO, NOT REALLY.
IT'S FINE. HONEST!

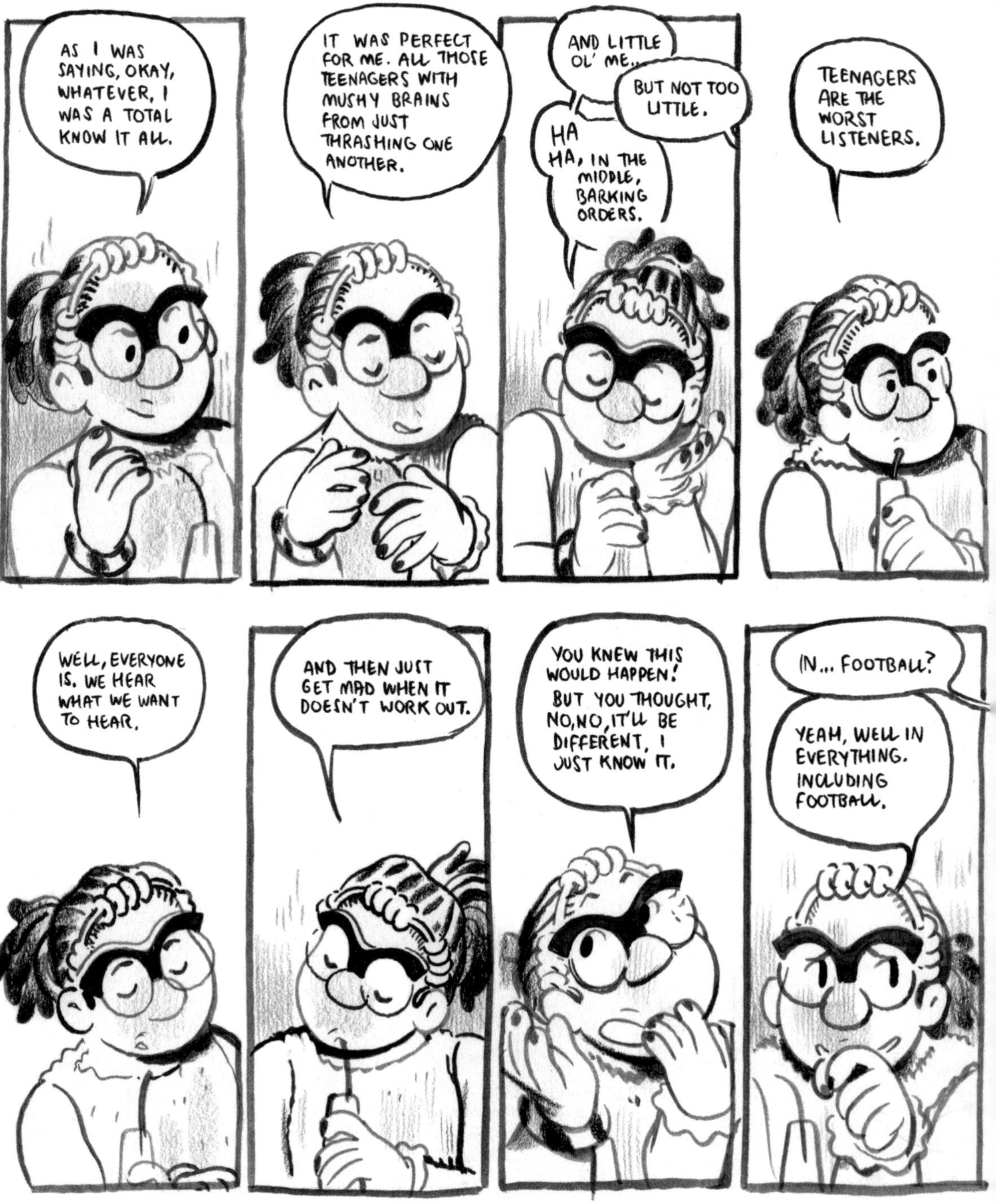
AS I WAS SAYING, OKAY, WHATEVER, I WAS A TOTAL KNOW IT ALL.
IT WAS PERFECT FOR ME. ALL THOSE TEENAGERS WITH MUSHY BRAINS FROM JUST THRASHING ONE ANOTHER.
AND LITTLE OL' ME...
BUT NOT TOO LITTLE.
HA HA, IN THE MIDDLE, BARKING ORDERS.
TEENAGERS ARE THE WORST LISTENERS.
WELL, EVERYONE IS. WE HEAR WHAT WE WANT TO HEAR.
AND THEN JUST GET MAD WHEN IT DOESN'T WORK OUT.
YOU KNEW THIS WOULD HAPPEN!
BUT YOU THOUGHT, NO, NO, IT'LL BE DIFFERENT, I JUST KNOW IT.
IN... FOOTBALL?
YEAH, WELL IN EVERYTHING. INCLUDING FOOTBALL.

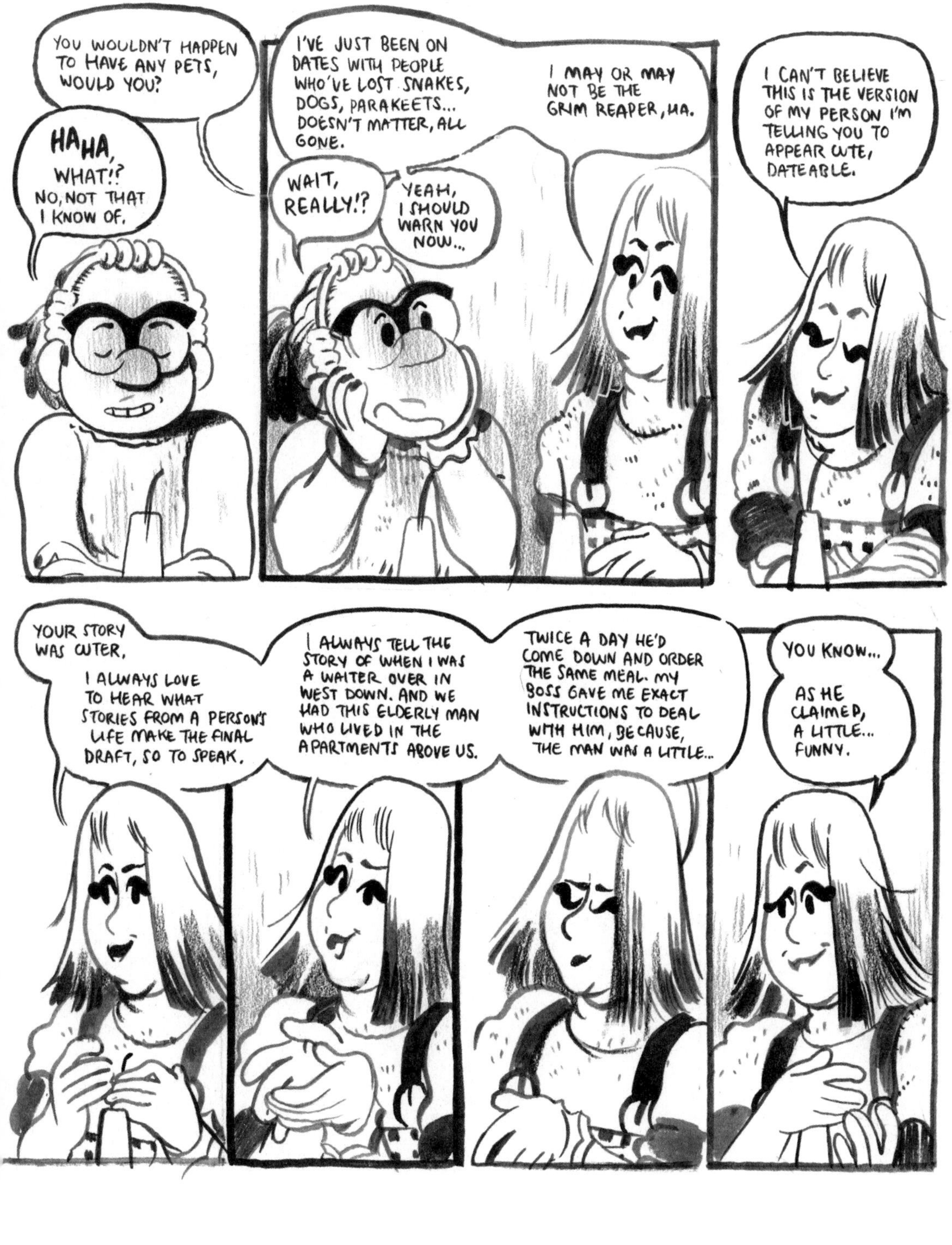
YOU WOULDN'T HAPPEN TO HAVE ANY PETS, WOULD YOU?
HAHA, WHAT!? NO, NOT THAT I KNOW OF.
I'VE JUST BEEN ON DATES WITH PEOPLE WHO'VE LOST SNAKES, DOGS, PARAKEETS... DOESN'T MATTER, ALL GONE.
I MAY OR MAY NOT BE THE GRIM REAPER, HA.
WAIT, REALLY!?
YEAH, I SHOULD WARN YOU NOW...
I CAN'T BELIEVE THIS IS THE VERSION OF MY PERSON I'M TELLING YOU TO APPEAR CUTE, DATEABLE.
YOUR STORY WAS CUTER.
I ALWAYS LOVE TO HEAR WHAT STORIES FROM A PERSON'S LIFE MAKE THE FINAL DRAFT, SO TO SPEAK.
I ALWAYS TELL THE STORY OF WHEN I WAS A WAITER OVER IN WEST DOWN. AND WE HAD THIS ELDERLY MAN WHO LIVED IN THE APARTMENTS ABOVE US.
TWICE A DAY HE'D COME DOWN AND ORDER THE SAME MEAL. MY BOSS GAVE ME EXACT INSTRUCTIONS TO DEAL WITH HIM, BECAUSE, THE MAN WAS A LITTLE...
YOU KNOW...
AS HE CLAIMED, A LITTLE... FUNNY.

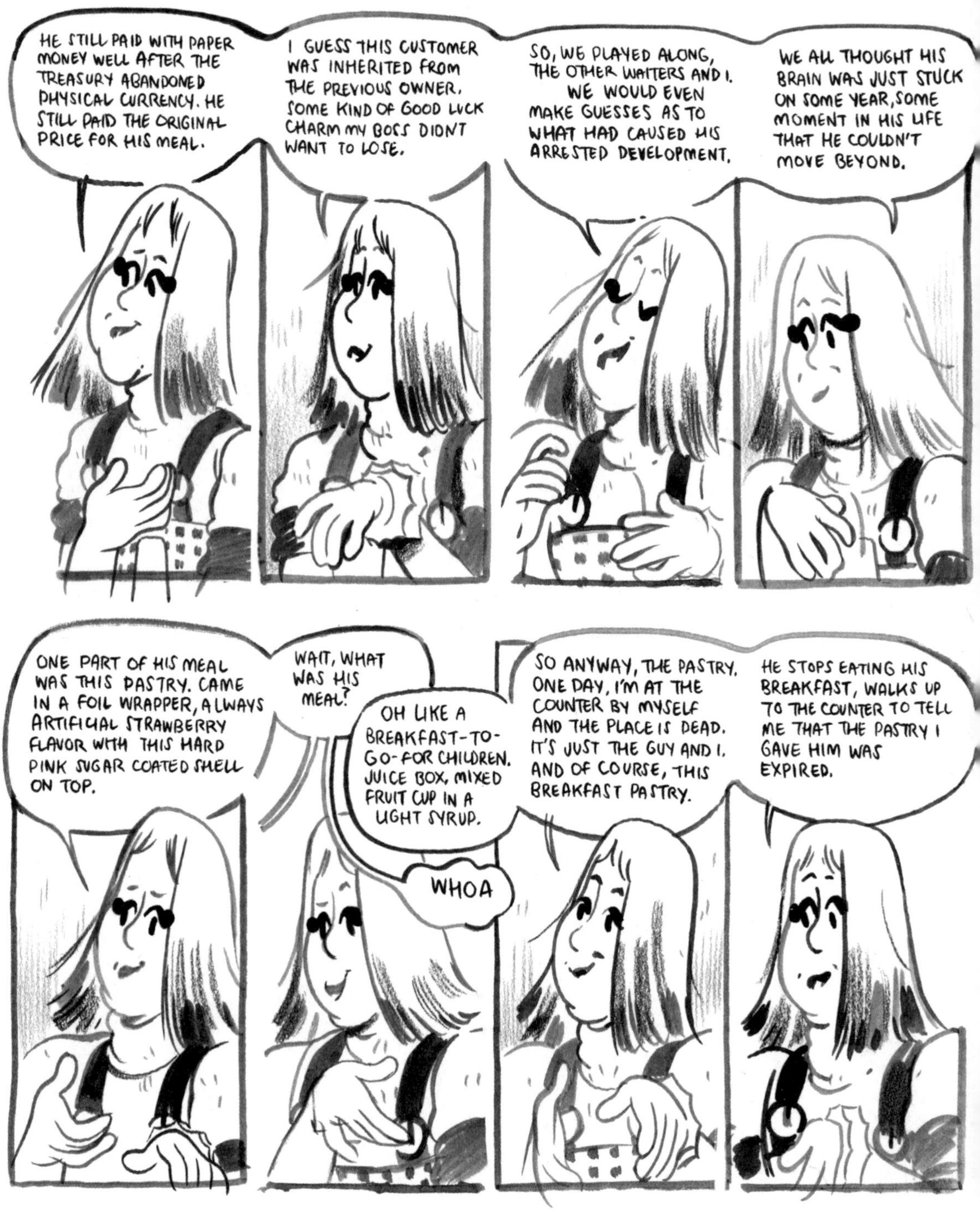

HE STILL PAID WITH PAPER MONEY WELL AFTER THE TREASURY ABANDONED PHYSICAL CURRENCY. HE STILL PAID THE ORIGINAL PRICE FOR HIS MEAL.
I GUESS THIS CUSTOMER WAS INHERITED FROM THE PREVIOUS OWNER. SOME KIND OF GOOD LUCK CHARM MY BOSS DIDNT WANT TO LOSE.
SO, WE PLAYED ALONG, THE OTHER WAITERS AND I. WE WOULD EVEN MAKE GUESSES AS TO WHAT HAD CAUSED HIS ARRESTED DEVELOPMENT.
WE ALL THOUGHT HIS BRAIN WAS JUST STUCK ON SOME YEAR, SOME MOMENT IN HIS LIFE THAT HE COULDN'T MOVE BEYOND.
ONE PART OF HIS MEAL WAS THIS PASTRY. CAME IN A FOIL WRAPPER, ALWAYS ARTIFICIAL STRAWBERRY FLAVOR WITH THIS HARD PINK SUGAR COATED SHELL ON TOP.
WAIT, WHAT WAS HIS MEAL?
OH LIKE A BREAKFAST-TO-GO-FOR CHILDREN. JUICE BOX, MIXED FRUIT CUP IN A LIGHT SYRUP.
WHOA
SO ANYWAY, THE PASTRY. ONE DAY, I'M AT THE COUNTER BY MYSELF AND THE PLACE IS DEAD. IT'S JUST THE GUY AND I. AND OF COURSE, THIS BREAKFAST PASTRY.
HE STOPS EATING HIS BREAKFAST, WALKS UP TO THE COUNTER TO TELL ME THAT THE PASTRY I GAVE HIM WAS EXPIRED.

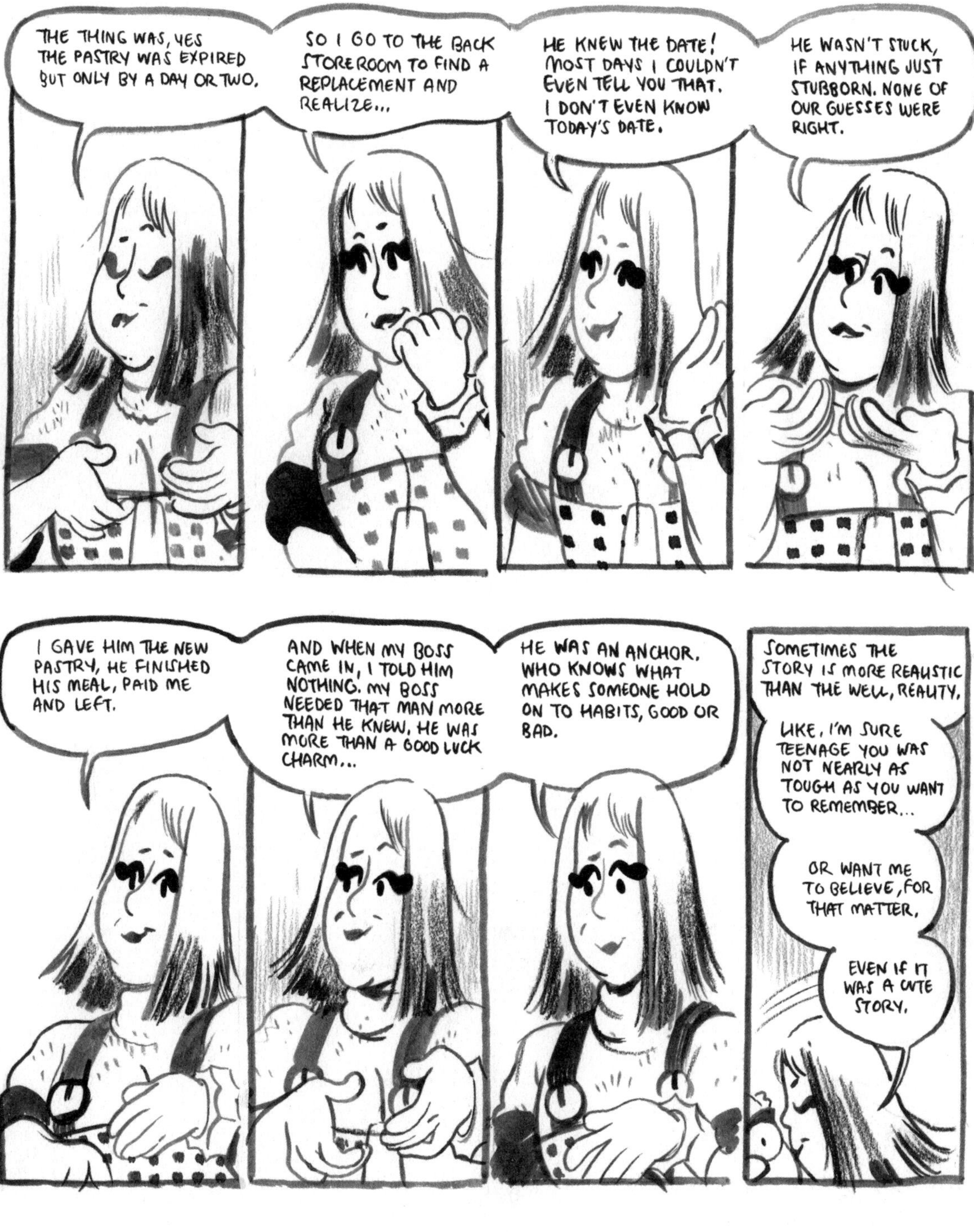
THE THING WAS, YES THE PASTRY WAS EXPIRED BUT ONLY BY A DAY OR TWO.
SO I GO TO THE BACK STOREROOM TO FIND A REPLACEMENT AND REALIZE...
HE KNEW THE DATE! MOST DAYS I COULDN'T EVEN TELL YOU THAT. I DON'T EVEN KNOW TODAY'S DATE.
HE WASN'T STUCK, IF ANYTHING JUST STUBBORN. NONE OF OUR GUESSES WERE RIGHT.
I GAVE HIM THE NEW PASTRY, HE FINISHED HIS MEAL, PAID ME AND LEFT.
AND WHEN MY BOSS CAME IN, I TOLD HIM NOTHING. MY BOSS NEEDED THAT MAN MORE THAN HE KNEW, HE WAS MORE THAN A GOOD LUCK CHARM...
HE WAS AN ANCHOR. WHO KNOWS WHAT MAKES SOMEONE HOLD ON TO HABITS, GOOD OR BAD.
SOMETIMES THE STORY IS MORE REALISTIC THAN THE WELL, REALITY.
LIKE, I'M SURE TEENAGE YOU WAS NOT NEARLY AS TOUGH AS YOU WANT TO REMEMBER...
OR WANT ME TO BELIEVE, FOR THAT MATTER,
EVEN IF IT WAS A CUTE STORY.

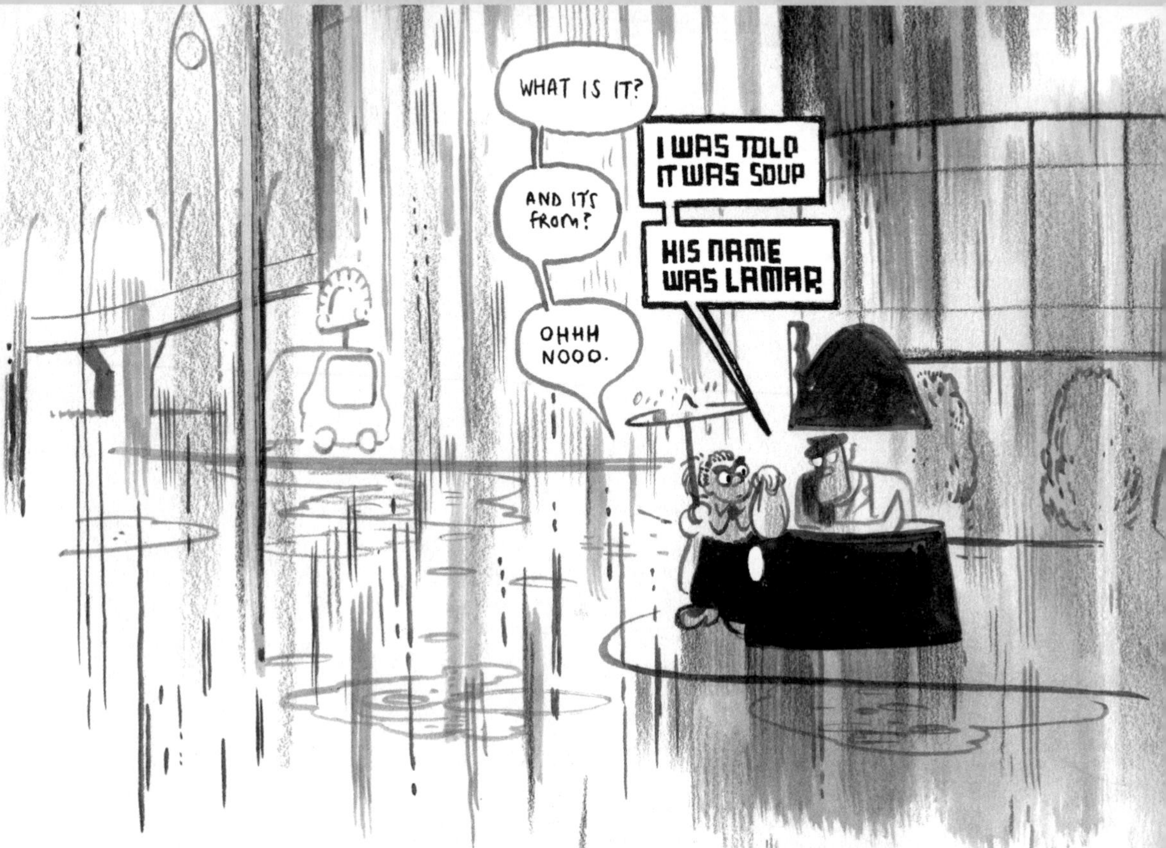
WHAT IS IT?
I WAS TOLD IT WAS SOUP
AND IT'S FROM?
HIS NAME WAS LAMAR
OHHH NOOO.

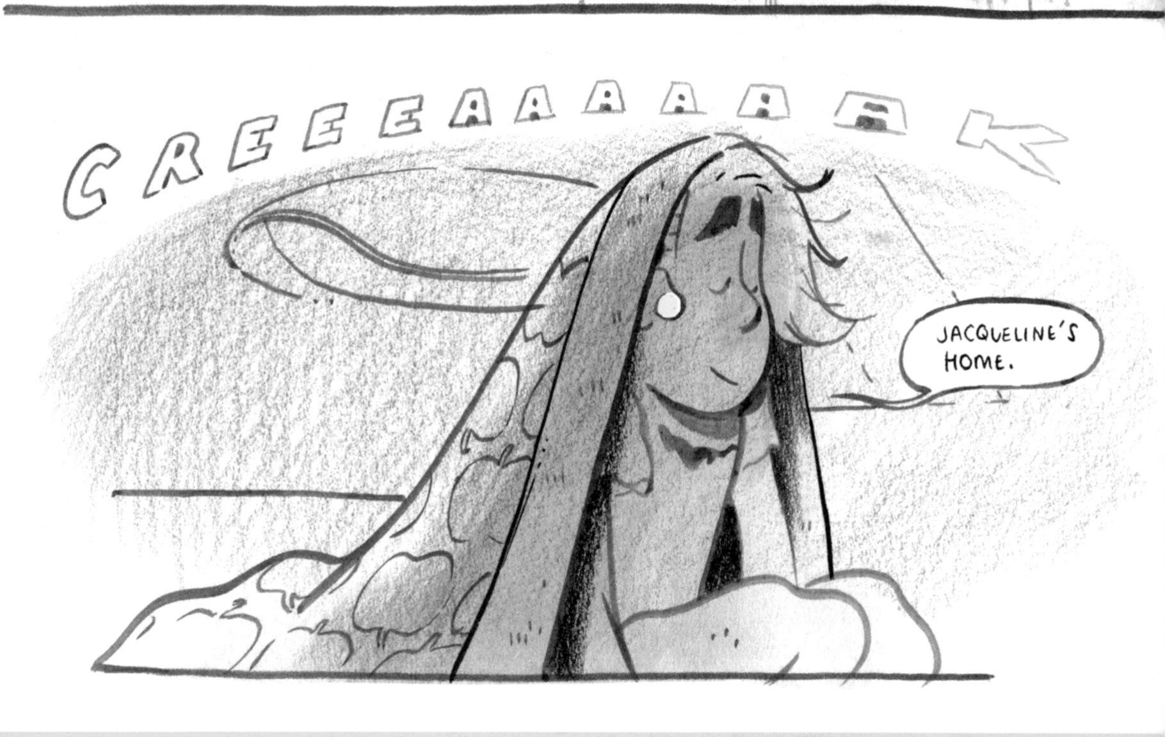
CREEEAAAAAAK
JACQUELINE'S HOME.

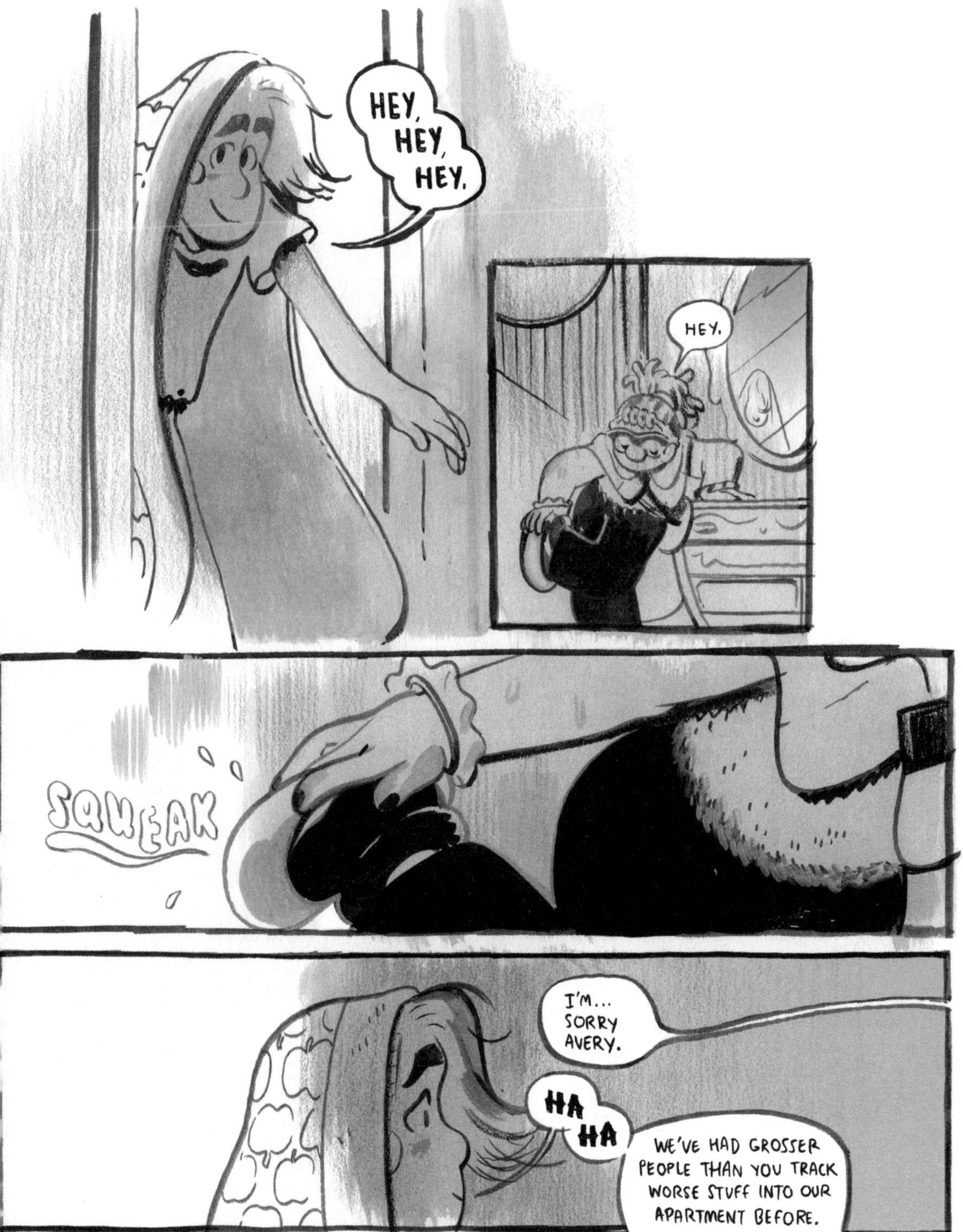
HEY, HEY, HEY.
HEY.
SQUEAK
I'M... SORRY AVERY.
HA HA
WE'VE HAD GROSSER PEOPLE THAN YOU TRACK WORSE STUFF INTO OUR APARTMENT BEFORE.

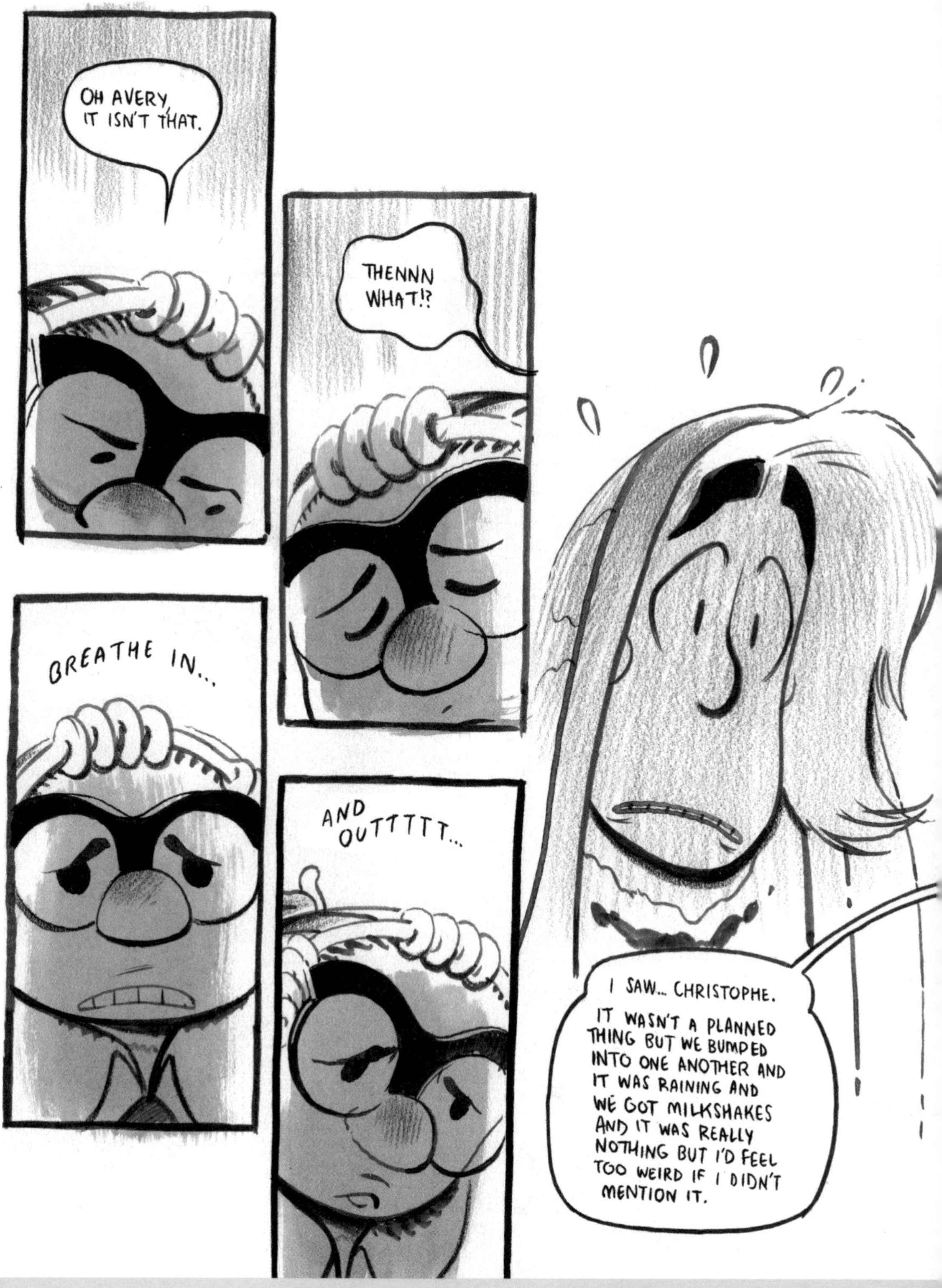

OH AVERY, IT ISN'T THAT.
THENNN WHAT!?
BREATHE IN...
AND OUTTTTTT...
I SAW... CHRISTOPHE.
IT WASN'T A PLANNED THING BUT WE BUMPED INTO ONE ANOTHER AND IT WAS RAINING AND WE GOT MILKSHAKES AND IT WAS REALLY NOTHING BUT I'D FEEL TOO WEIRD IF I DIDN'T MENTION IT.

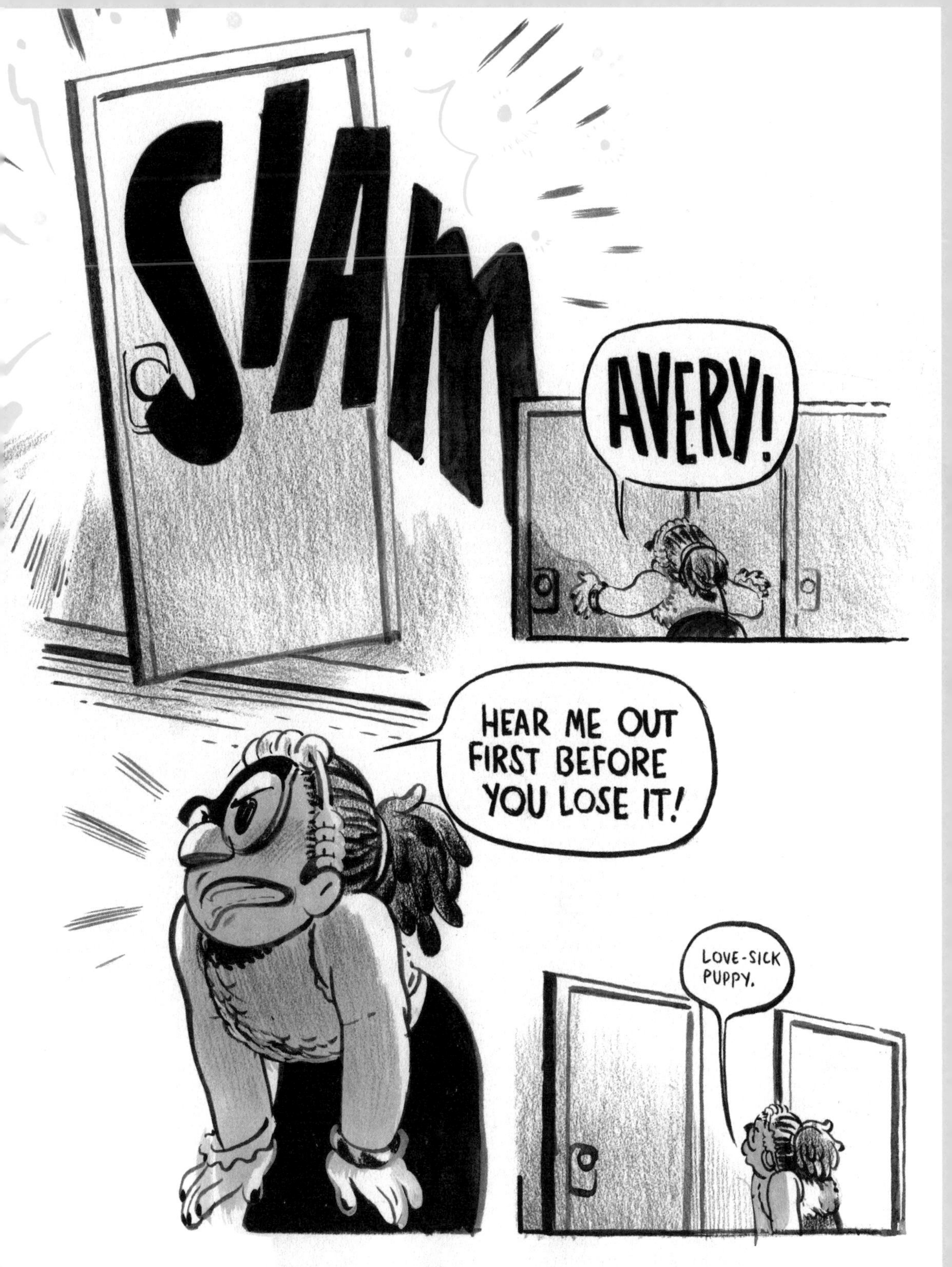
SLAM
AVERY!
HEAR ME OUT FIRST BEFORE YOU LOSE IT!
LOVE-SICK PUPPY.

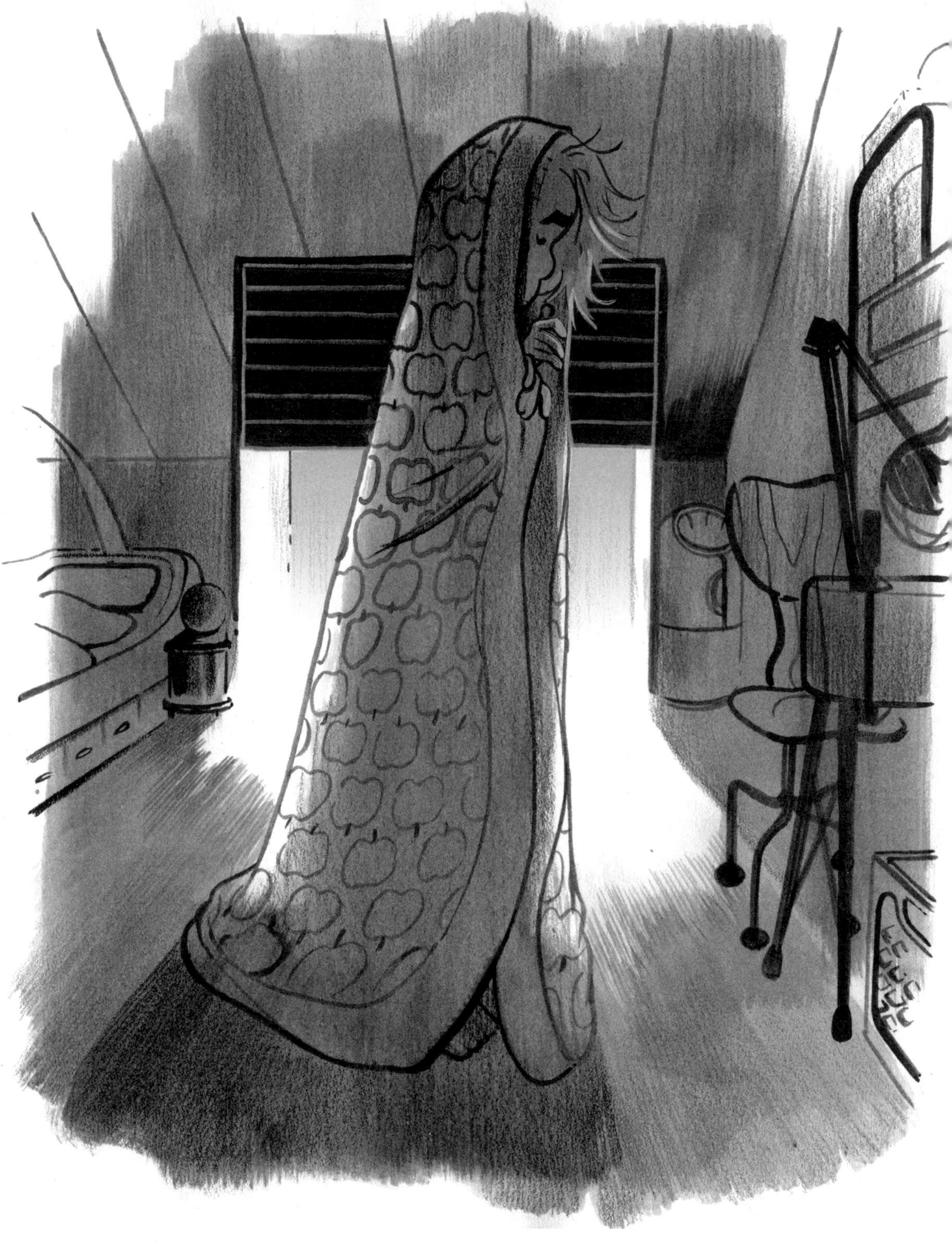

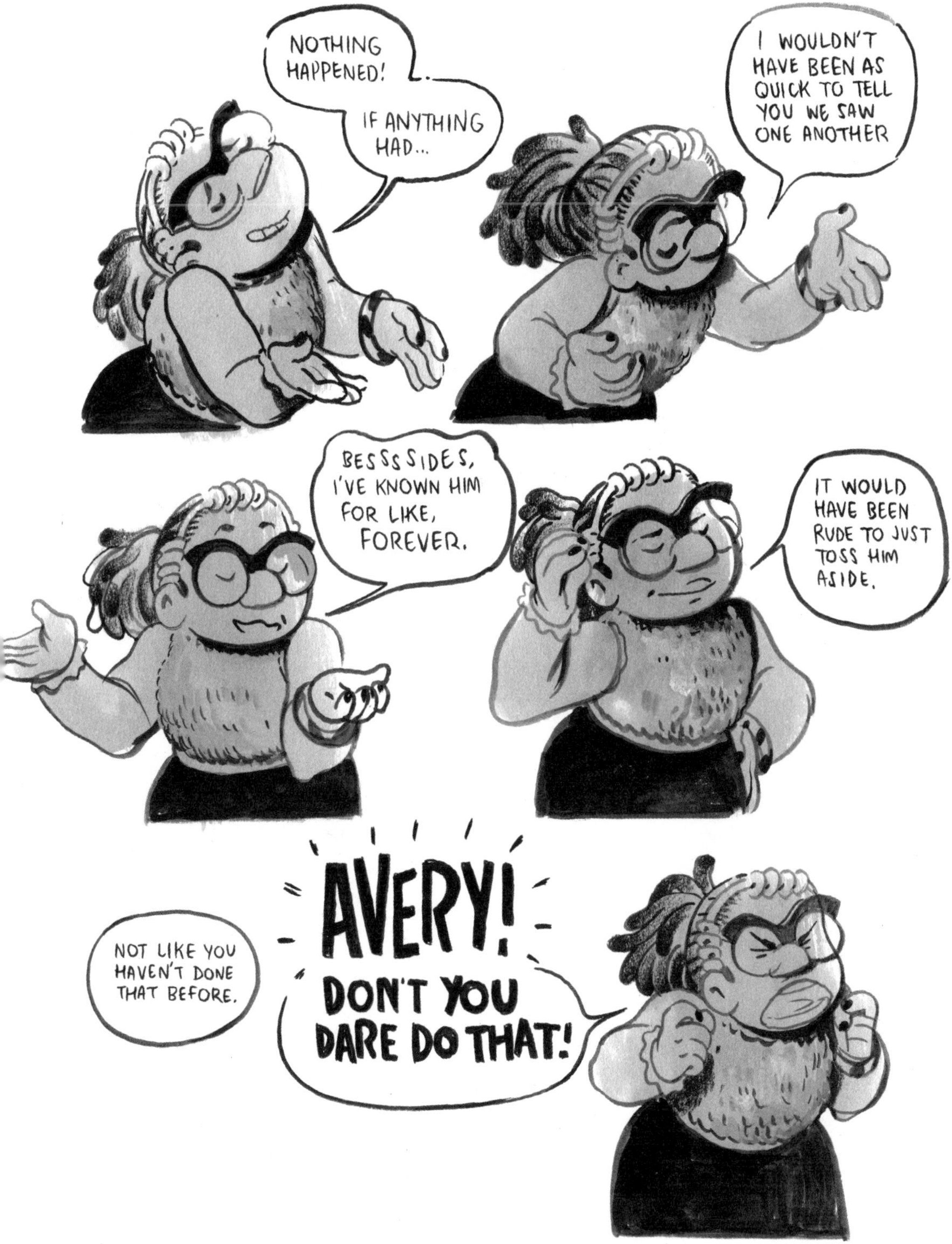
NOTHING HAPPENED!
IF ANYTHING HAD...
I WOULDN'T HAVE BEEN AS QUICK TO TELL YOU WE SAW ONE ANOTHER
BESSSSIDES, I'VE KNOWN HIM FOR LIKE, FOREVER.
IT WOULD HAVE BEEN RUDE TO JUST TOSS HIM ASIDE.
NOT LIKE YOU HAVEN'T DONE THAT BEFORE.
AVERY! DON'T YOU DARE DO THAT!

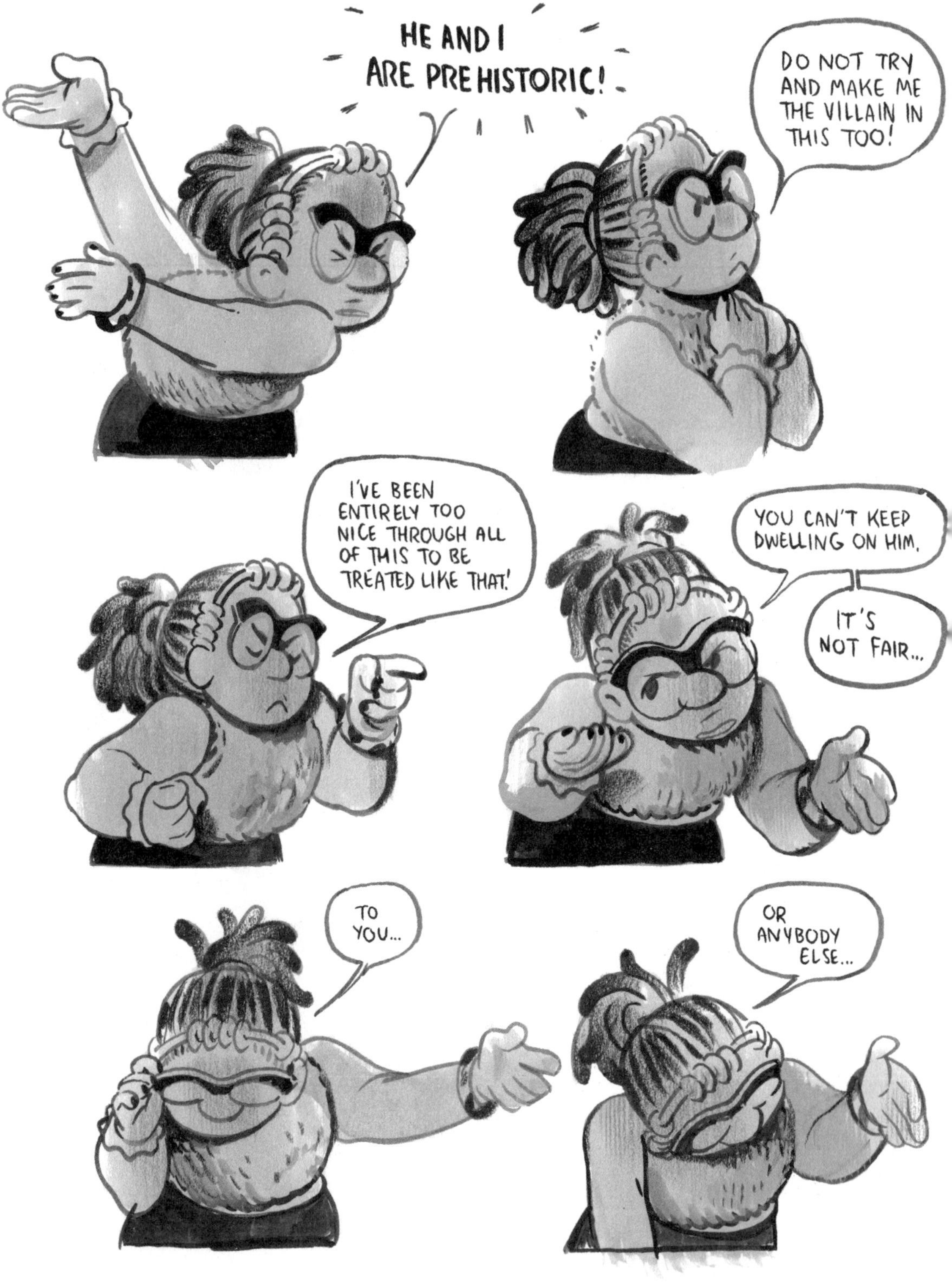
HE AND I ARE PREHISTORIC!
DO NOT TRY AND MAKE ME THE VILLAIN IN THIS TOO!
I'VE BEEN ENTIRELY TOO NICE THROUGH ALL OF THIS TO BE TREATED LIKE THAT!
YOU CAN'T KEEP DWELLING ON HIM.
IT'S NOT FAIR...
TO YOU...
OR ANYBODY ELSE...

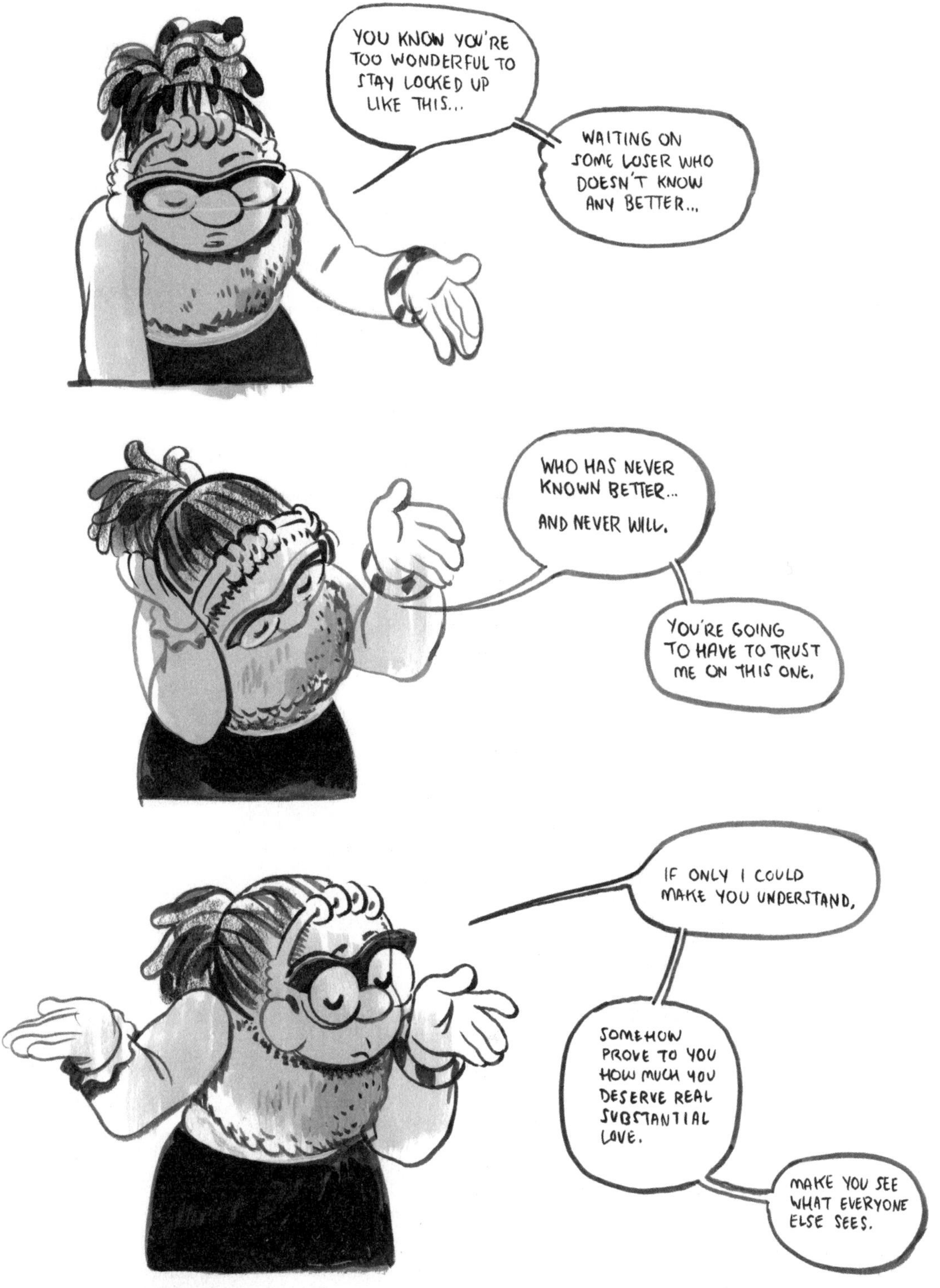
YOU KNOW YOU'RE TOO WONDERFUL TO STAY LOCKED UP LIKE THIS...
WAITING ON SOME LOSER WHO DOESN'T KNOW ANY BETTER...
WHO HAS NEVER KNOWN BETTER...
AND NEVER WILL.
YOU'RE GOING TO HAVE TO TRUST ME ON THIS ONE.
IF ONLY I COULD MAKE YOU UNDERSTAND,
SOMEHOW PROVE TO YOU HOW MUCH YOU DESERVE REAL SUBSTANTIAL LOVE.
MAKE YOU SEE WHAT EVERYONE ELSE SEES.

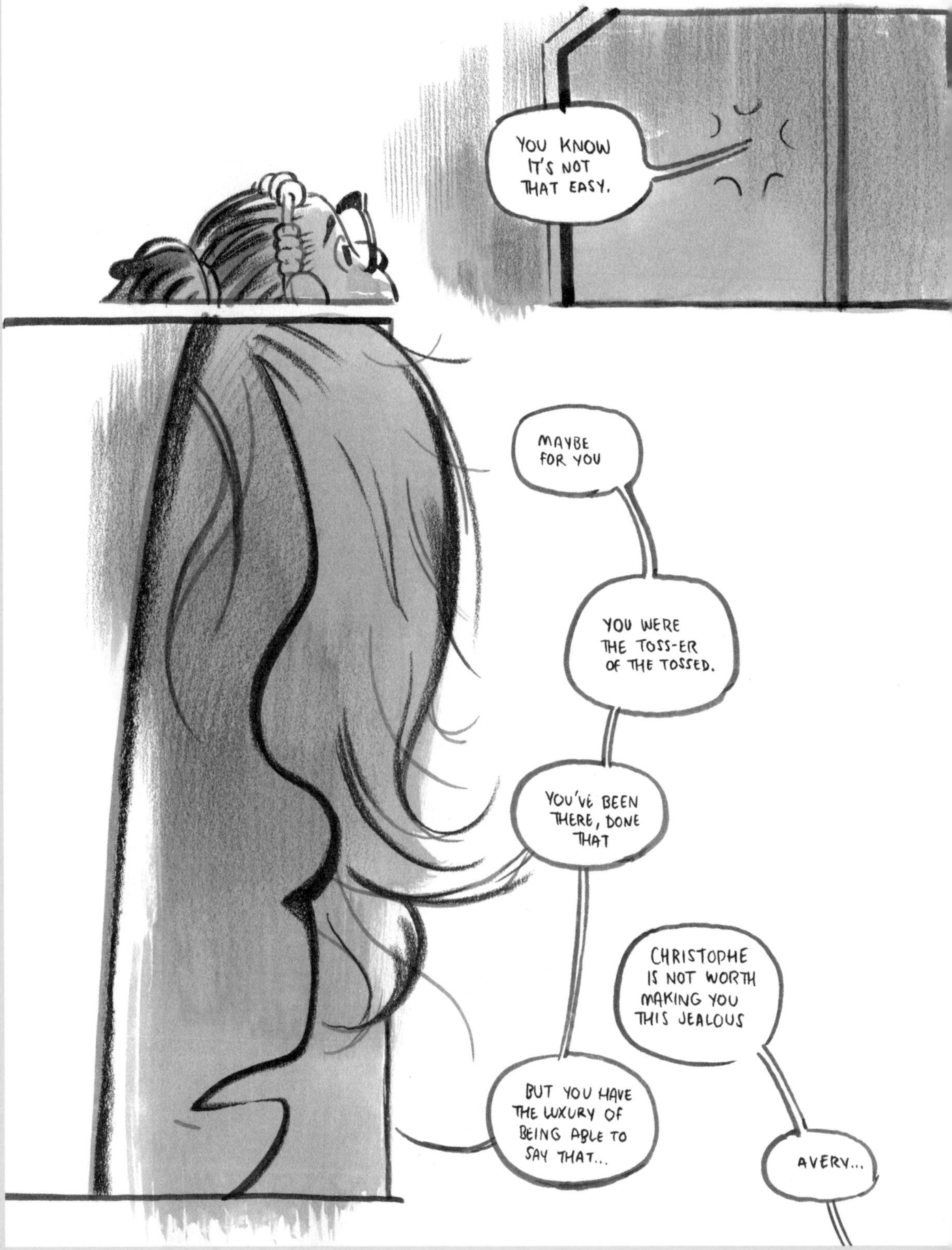
YOU KNOW IT'S NOT THAT EASY.
MAYBE FOR YOU
YOU WERE THE TOSS-ER OF THE TOSSED.
YOU'VE BEEN THERE, DONE THAT
BUT YOU HAVE THE LUXURY OF BEING ABLE TO SAY THAT...
CHRISTOPHE IS NOT WORTH MAKING YOU THIS JEALOUS
AVERY...

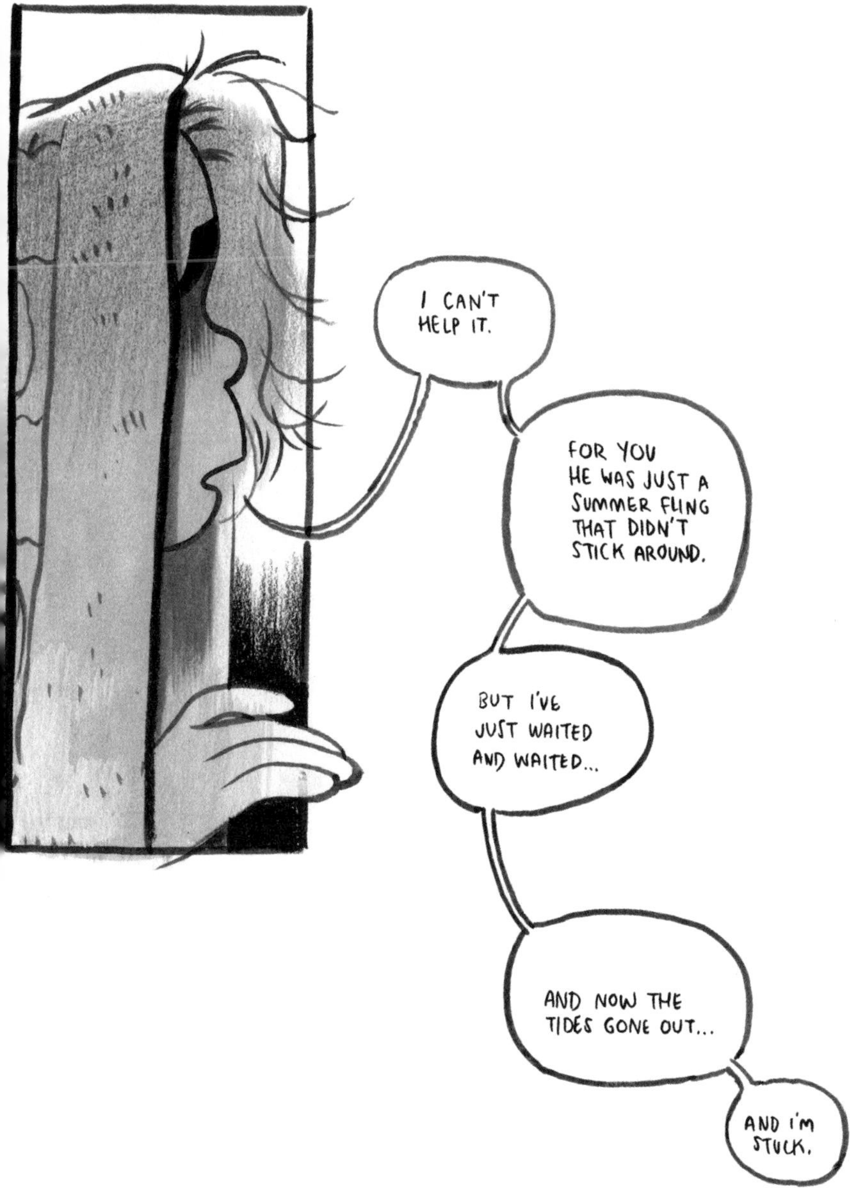
I CAN'T HELP IT.
FOR YOU HE WAS JUST A SUMMER FLING THAT DIDN'T STICK AROUND.
BUT I'VE JUST WAITED AND WAITED...
AND NOW THE TIDES GONE OUT...
AND I'M STUCK.

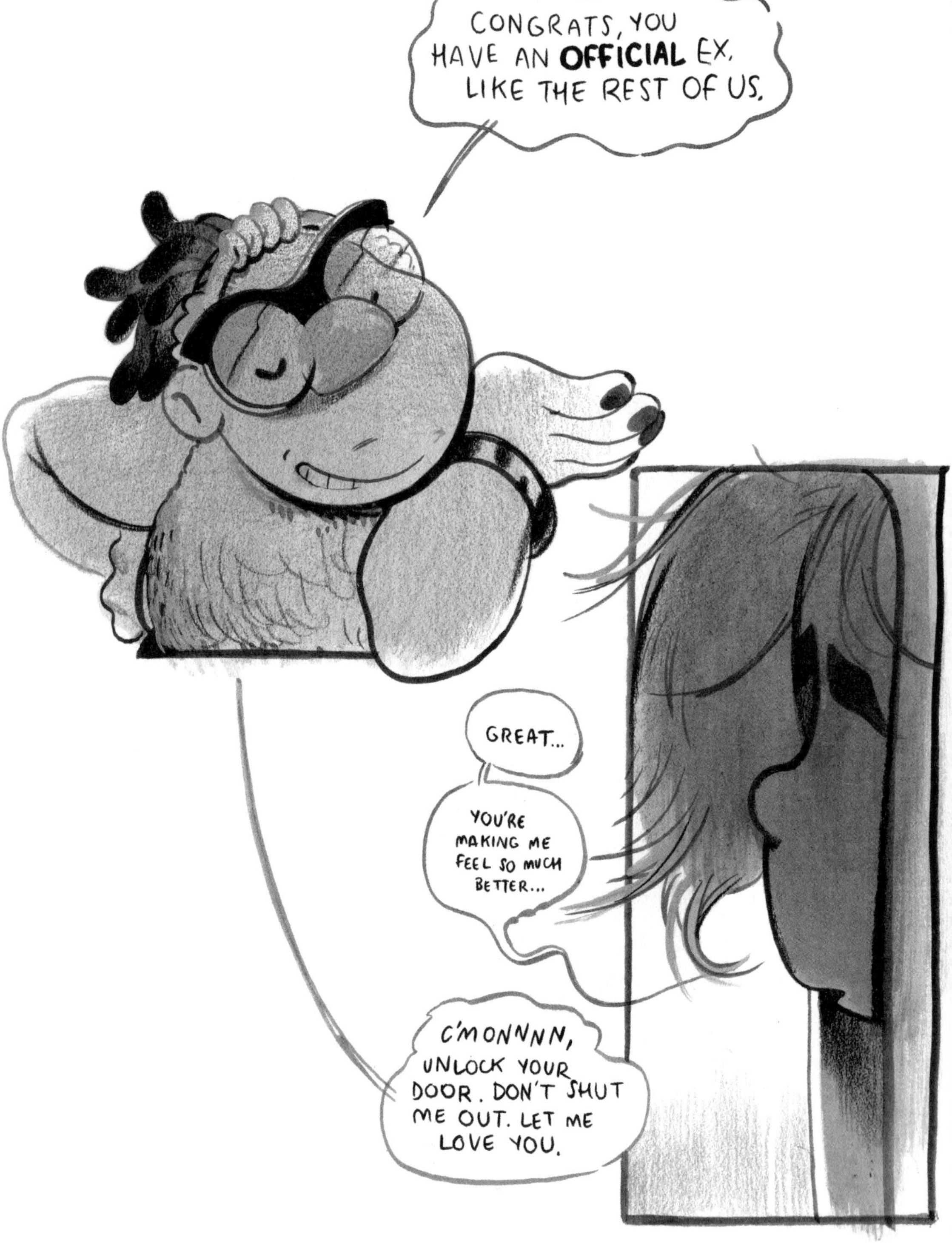
CONGRATS, YOU HAVE AN **OFFICIAL** EX, LIKE THE REST OF US.
GREAT...
YOU'RE MAKING ME FEEL SO MUCH BETTER...
C'MONNNN, UNLOCK YOUR DOOR. DON'T SHUT ME OUT. LET ME LOVE YOU.

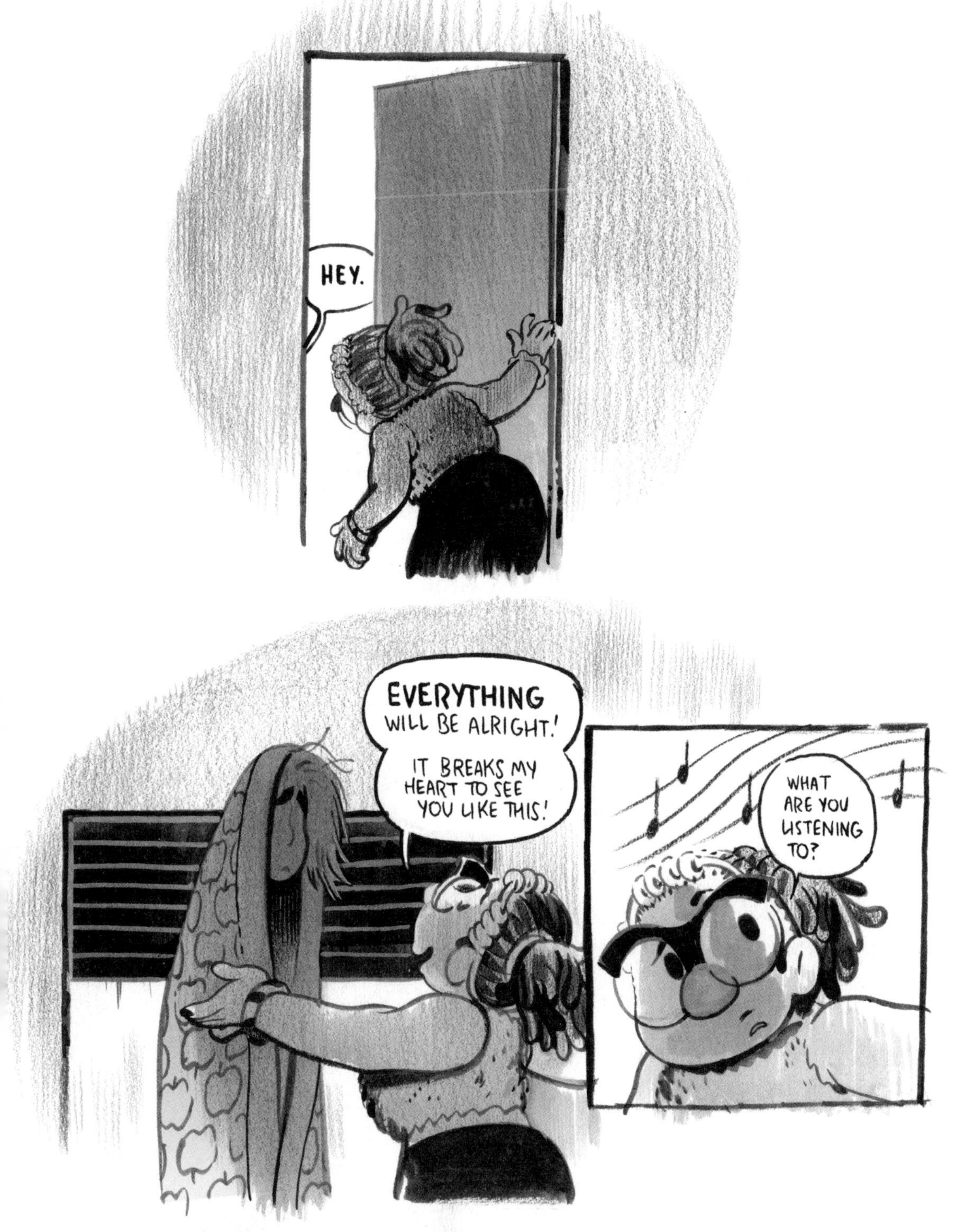
HEY.
EVERYTHING WILL BE ALRIGHT!
IT BREAKS MY HEART TO SEE YOU LIKE THIS!
WHAT ARE YOU LISTENING TO?

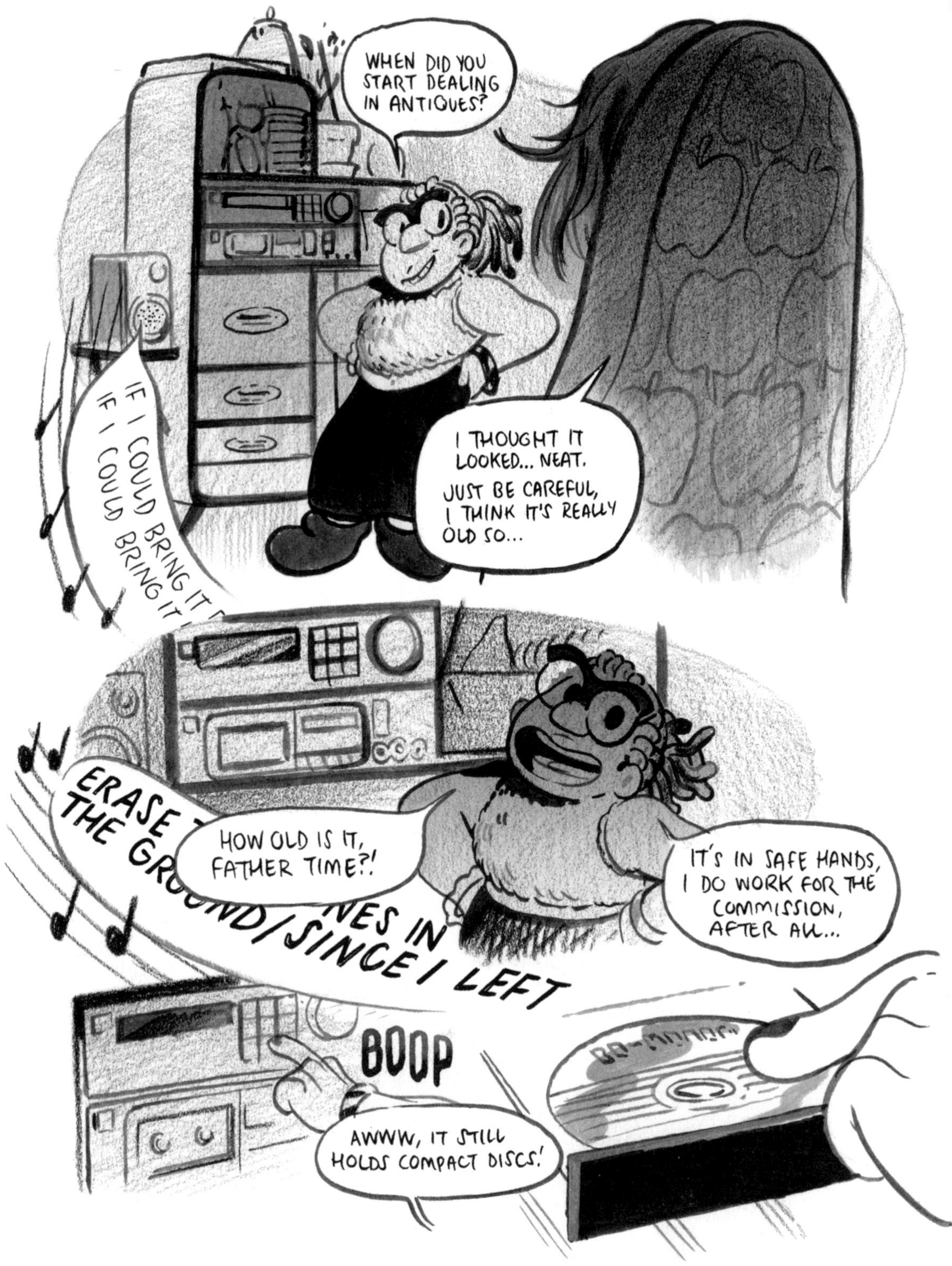
WHEN DID YOU START DEALING IN ANTIQUES?
I THOUGHT IT LOOKED... NEAT.
JUST BE CAREFUL, I THINK IT'S REALLY OLD SO...
IF I COULD BRING IT
IF I COULD BRING IT
ERASE T
NES IN
THE GROUND/SINCE I LEFT
HOW OLD IS IT, FATHER TIME?!
IT'S IN SAFE HANDS, I DO WORK FOR THE COMMISSION, AFTER ALL...
BOOP
AWWW, IT STILL HOLDS COMPACT DISCS!

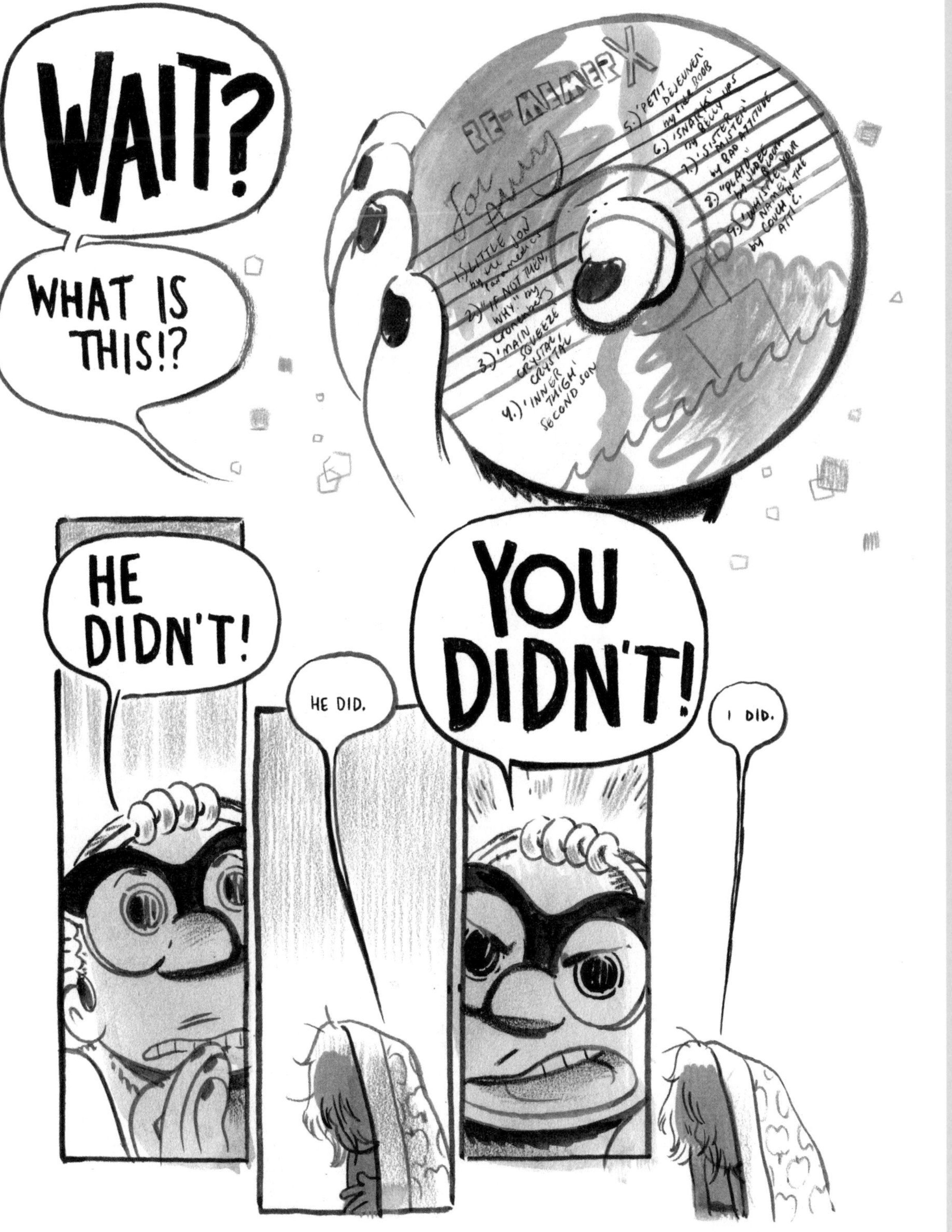
WAIT?
WHAT IS THIS!?
HE DIDN'T!
HE DID.
YOU DIDN'T!
I DID.

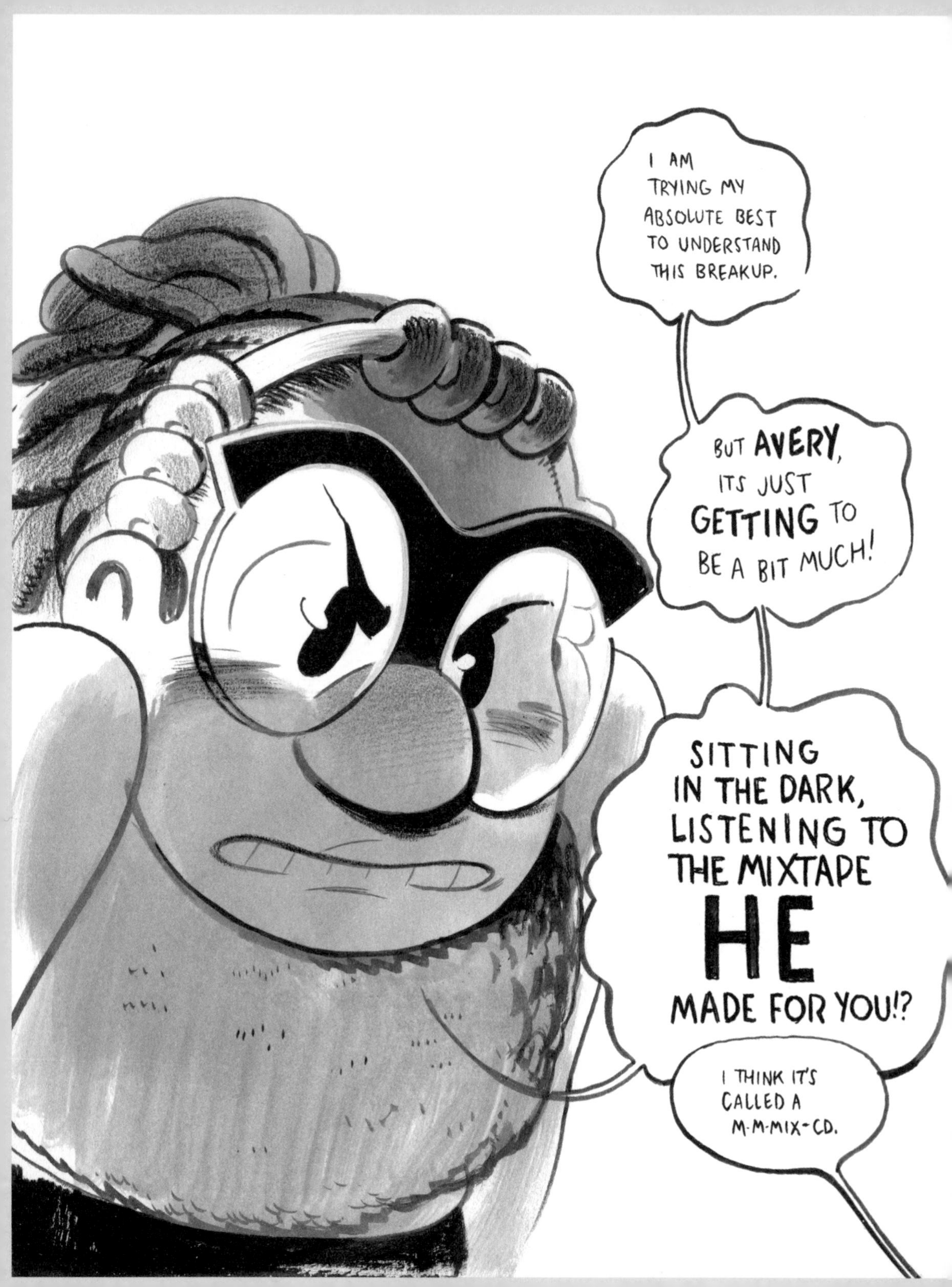
I AM TRYING MY ABSOLUTE BEST TO UNDERSTAND THIS BREAKUP.
BUT AVERY, ITS JUST GETTING TO BE A BIT MUCH!
SITTING IN THE DARK, LISTENING TO THE MIXTAPE HE MADE FOR YOU!?
I THINK IT'S CALLED A M-M-MIX-CD.

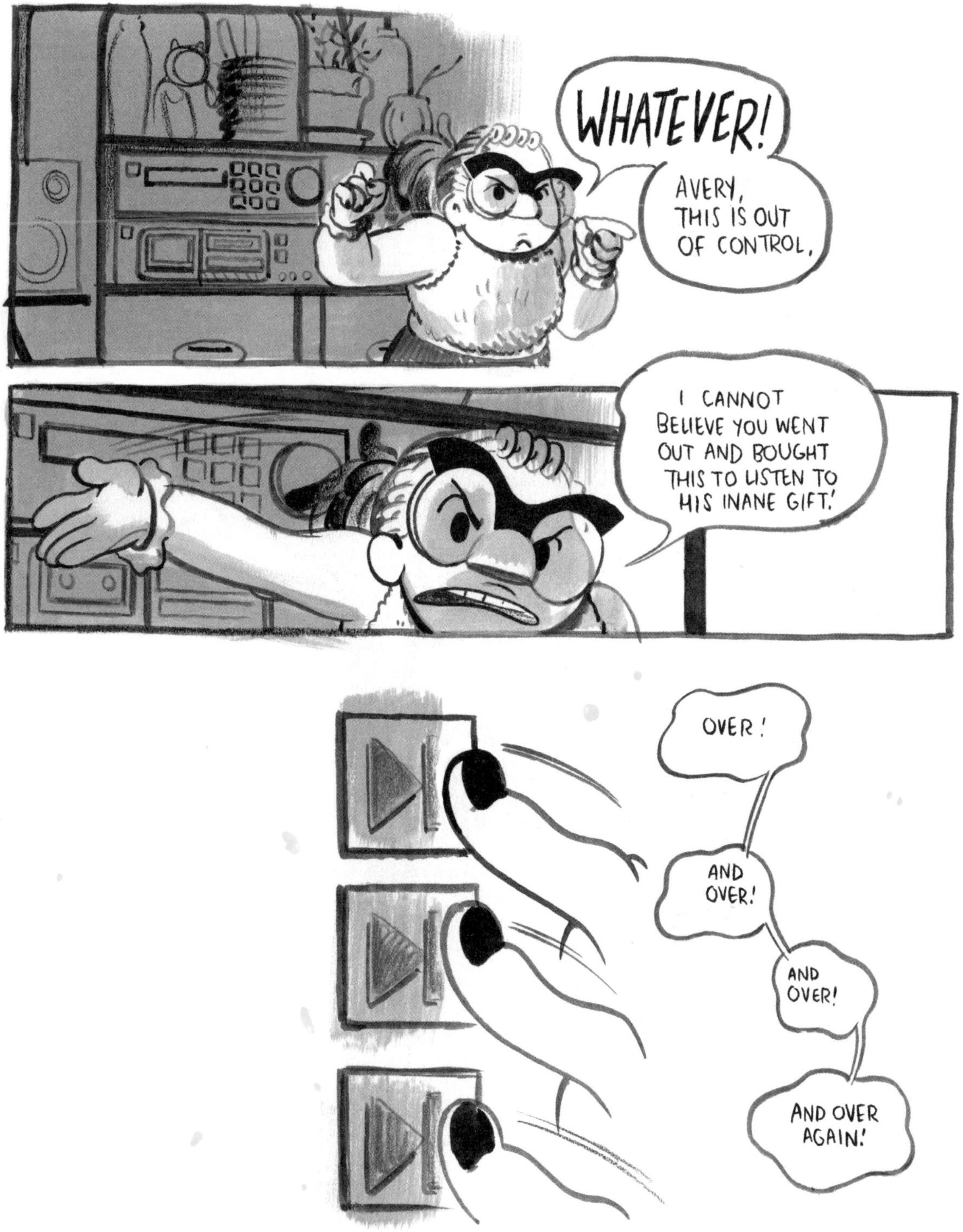
WHATEVER!
AVERY, THIS IS OUT OF CONTROL,
I CANNOT BELIEVE YOU WENT OUT AND BOUGHT THIS TO LISTEN TO HIS INANE GIFT!
OVER!
AND OVER!
AND OVER!
AND OVER AGAIN!

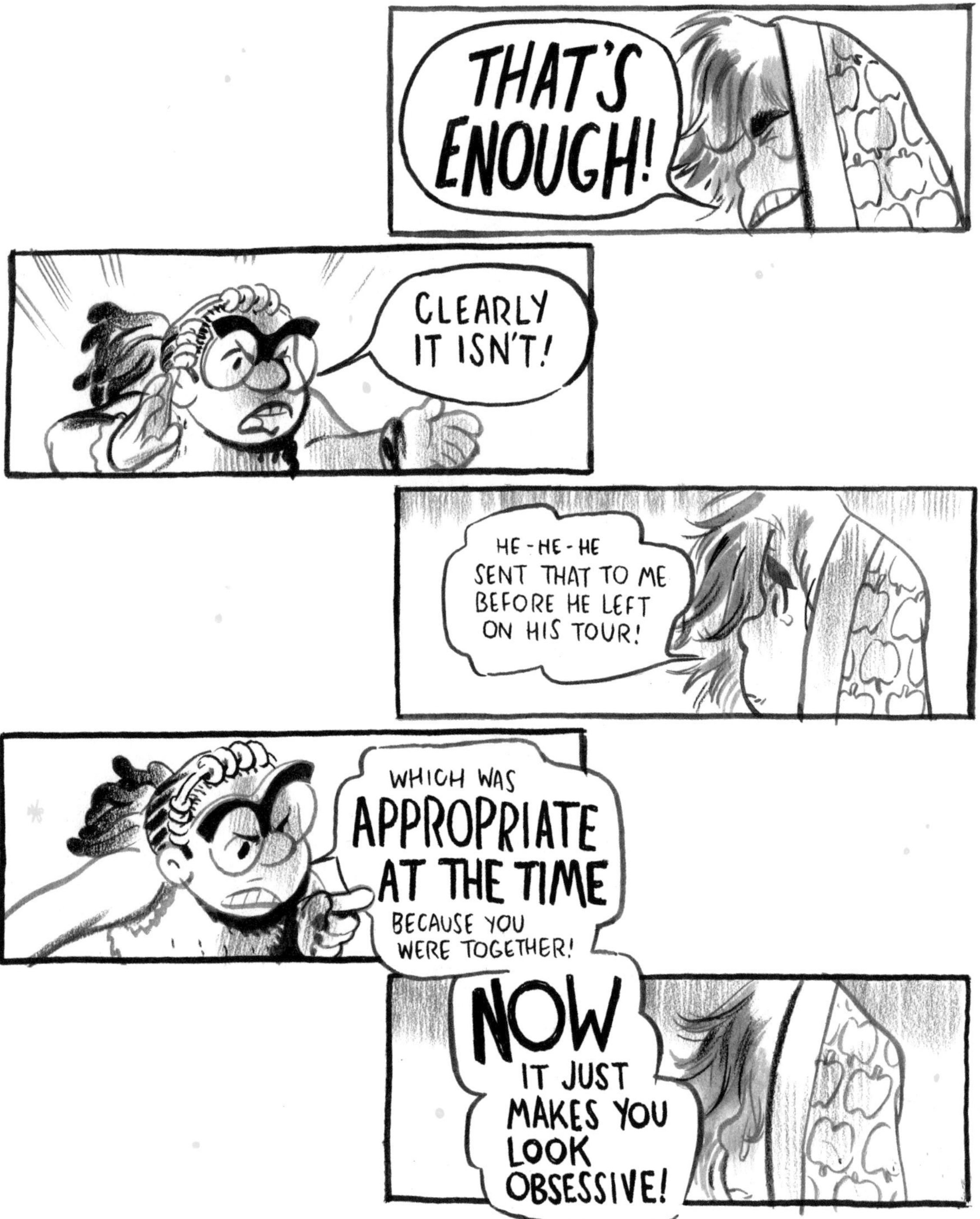
THAT'S ENOUGH!
CLEARLY IT ISN'T!
HE-HE-HE SENT THAT TO ME BEFORE HE LEFT ON HIS TOUR!
WHICH WAS APPROPRIATE AT THE TIME BECAUSE YOU WERE TOGETHER!
NOW IT JUST MAKES YOU LOOK OBSESSIVE!

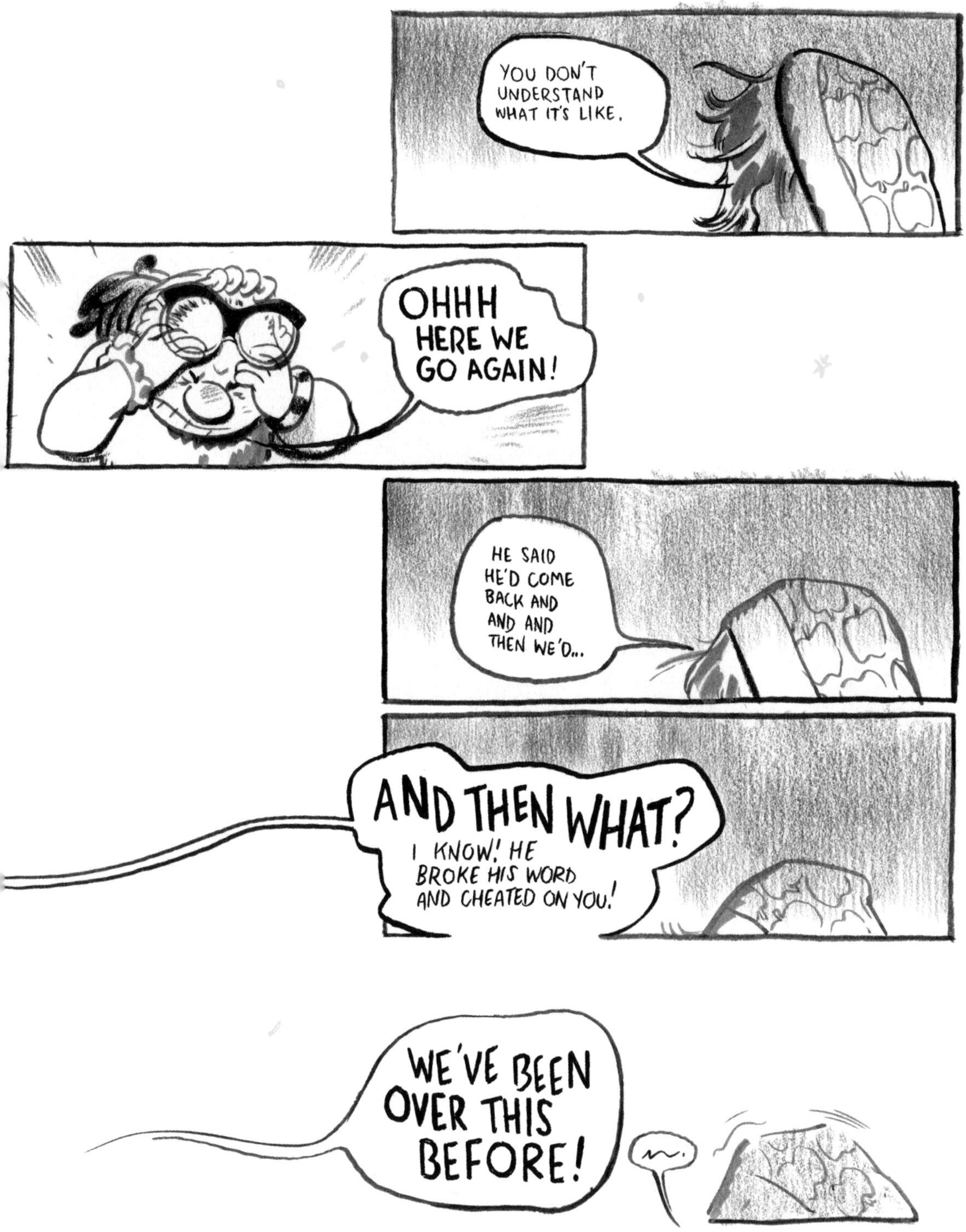
YOU DON'T UNDERSTAND WHAT IT'S LIKE.
OHHH HERE WE GO AGAIN!
HE SAID HE'D COME BACK AND AND AND THEN WE'D...
AND THEN WHAT? I KNOW! HE BROKE HIS WORD AND CHEATED ON YOU!
WE'VE BEEN OVER THIS BEFORE!

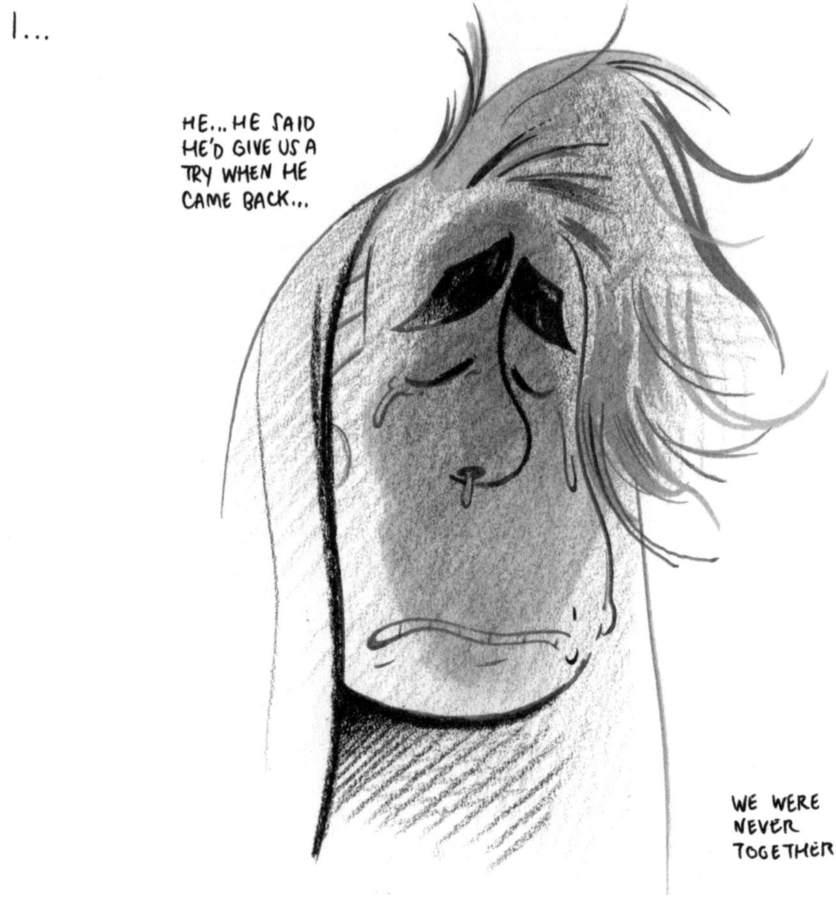
I...
HE... HE SAID HE'D GIVE US A TRY WHEN HE CAME BACK...
WE WERE NEVER TOGETHER,

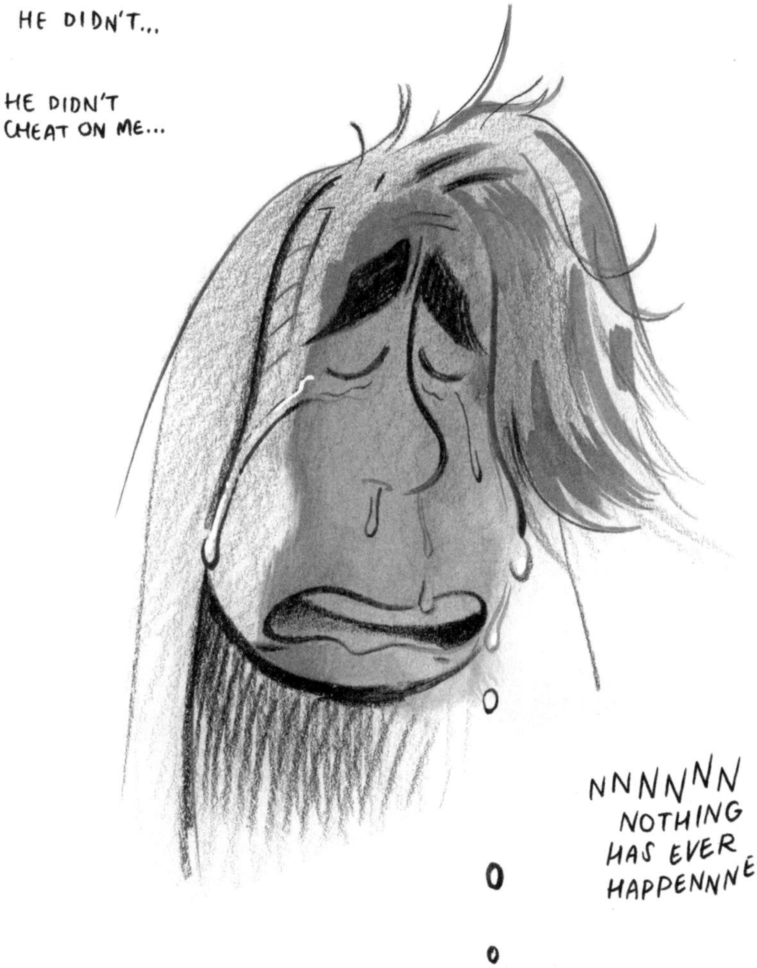
HE DIDN'T...
HE DIDN'T CHEAT ON ME...
NNNNNN NOTHING HAS EVER HAPPENNNED.

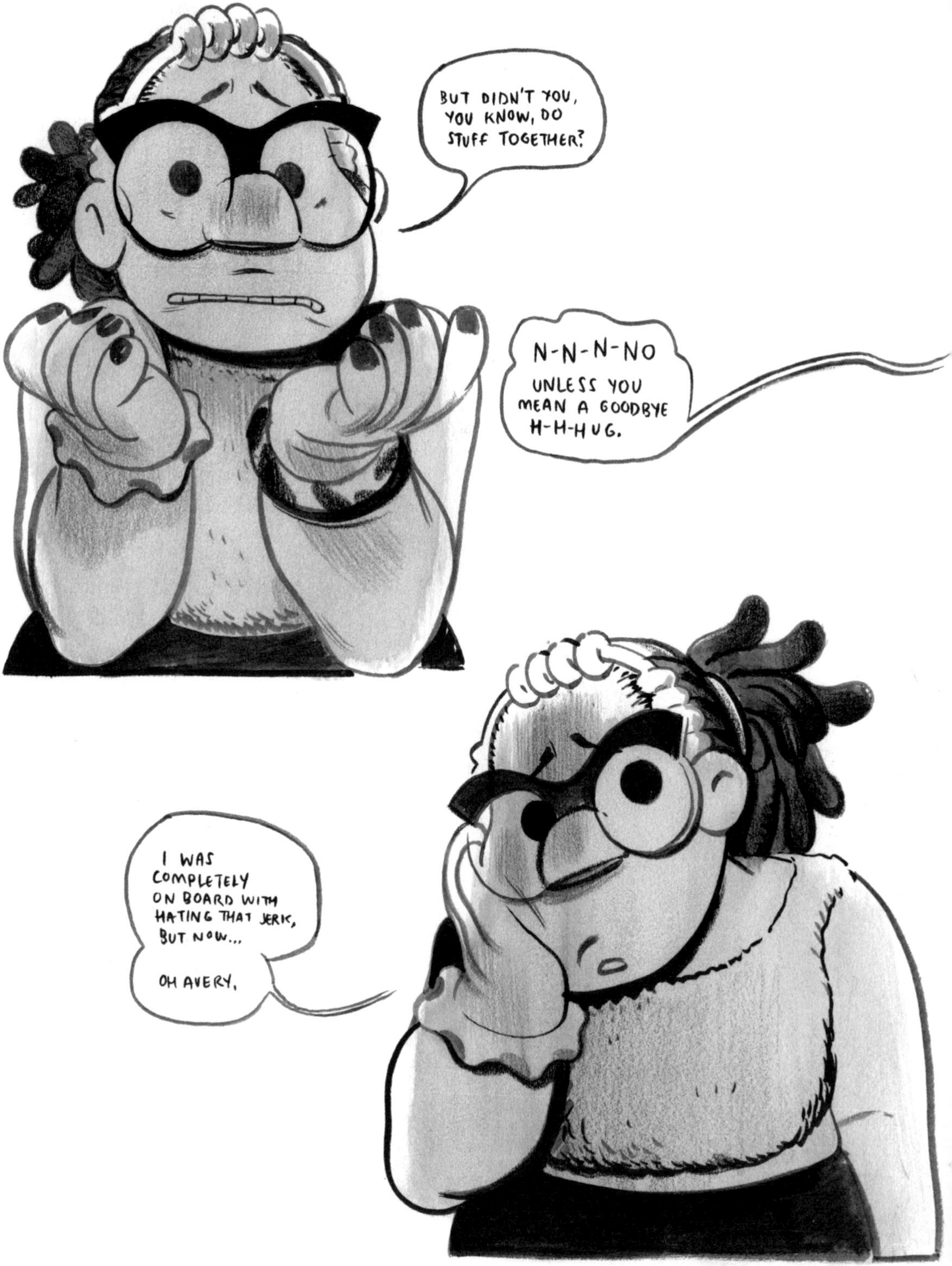
BUT DIDN'T YOU, YOU KNOW, DO STUFF TOGETHER?
N-N-N-NO UNLESS YOU MEAN A GOODBYE H-H-HUG.
I WAS COMPLETELY ON BOARD WITH HATING THAT JERK, BUT NOW...
OH AVERY.

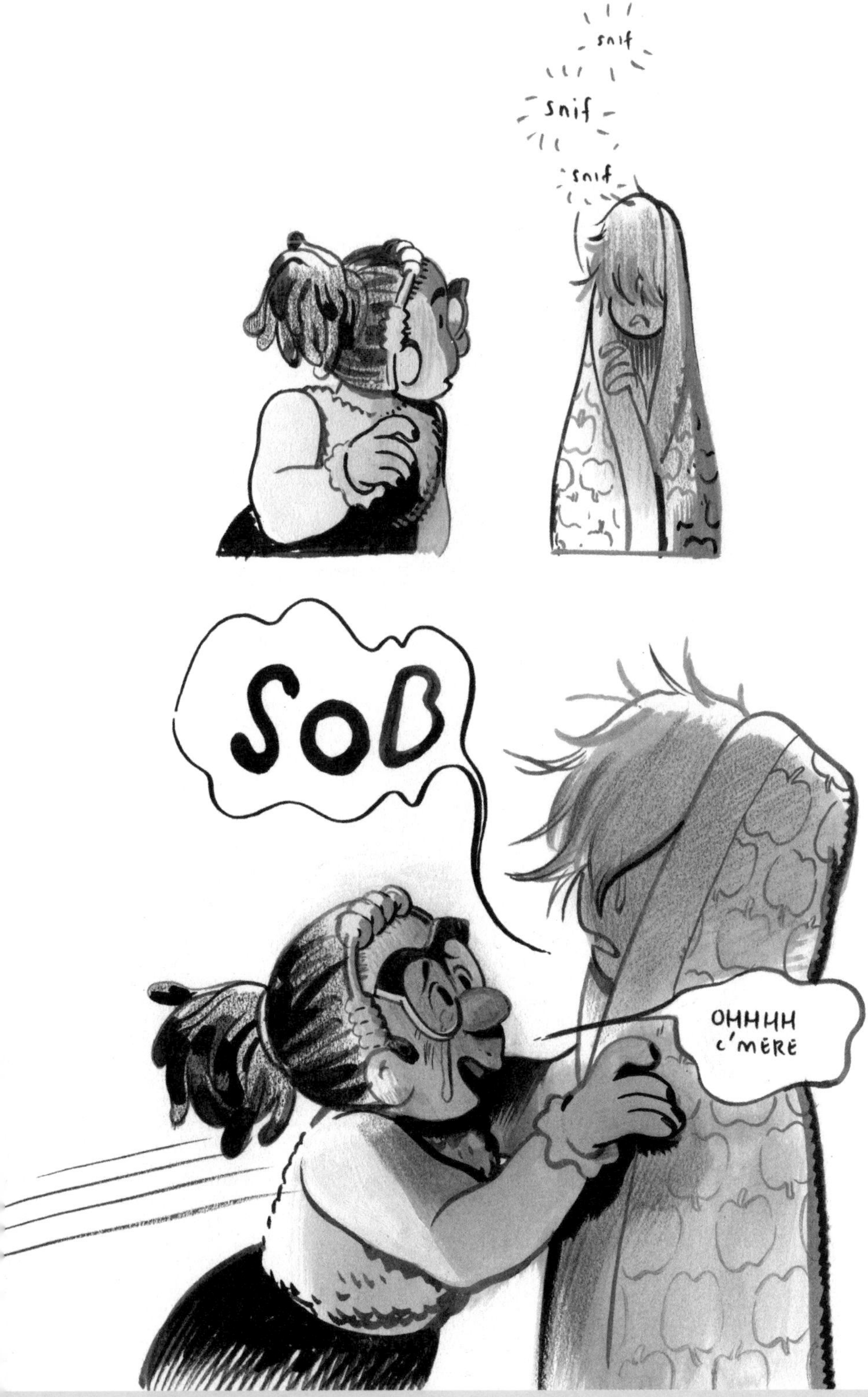
snif
snif
snif
SOB
OHHHH C'MERE

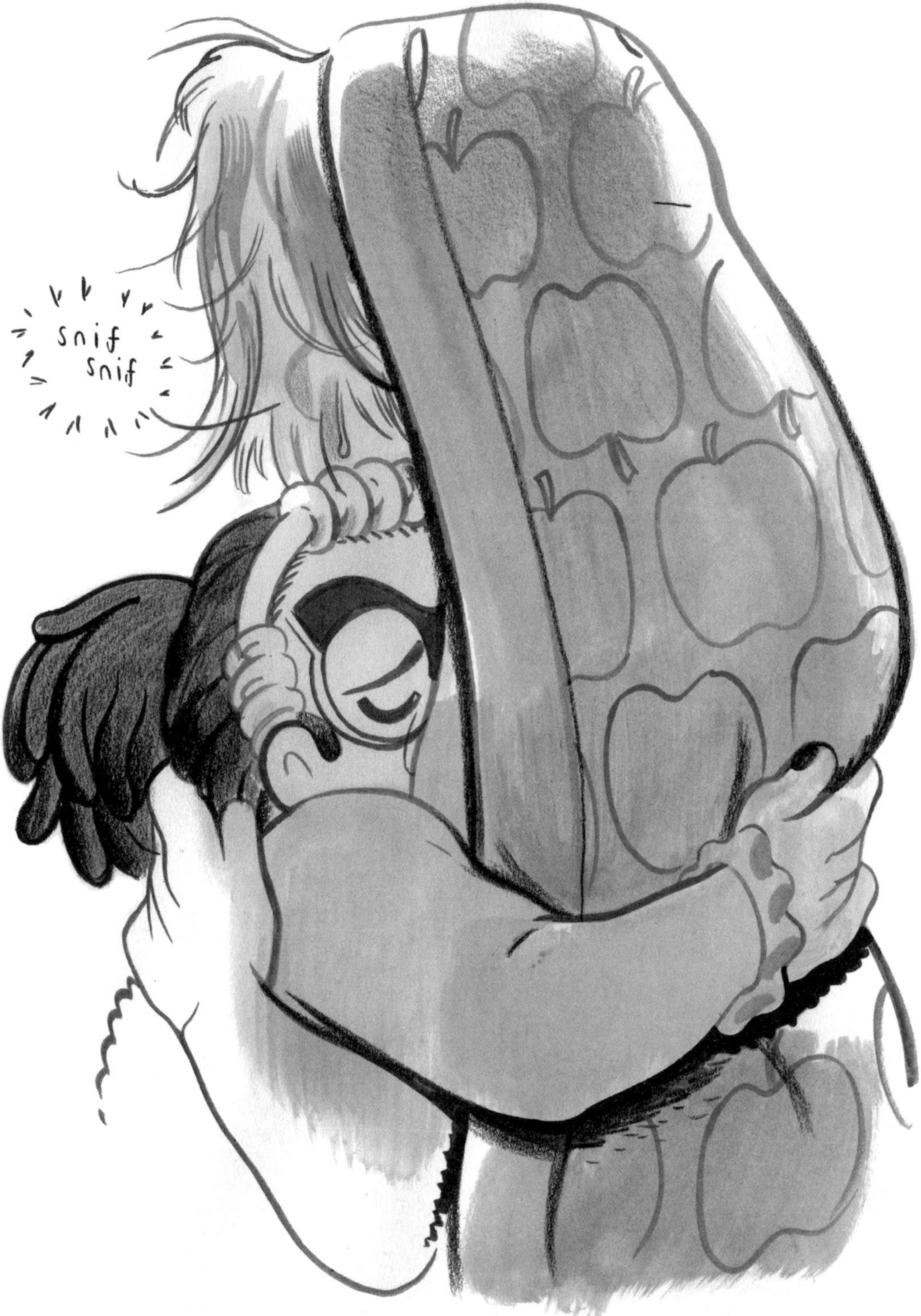
snif
snif

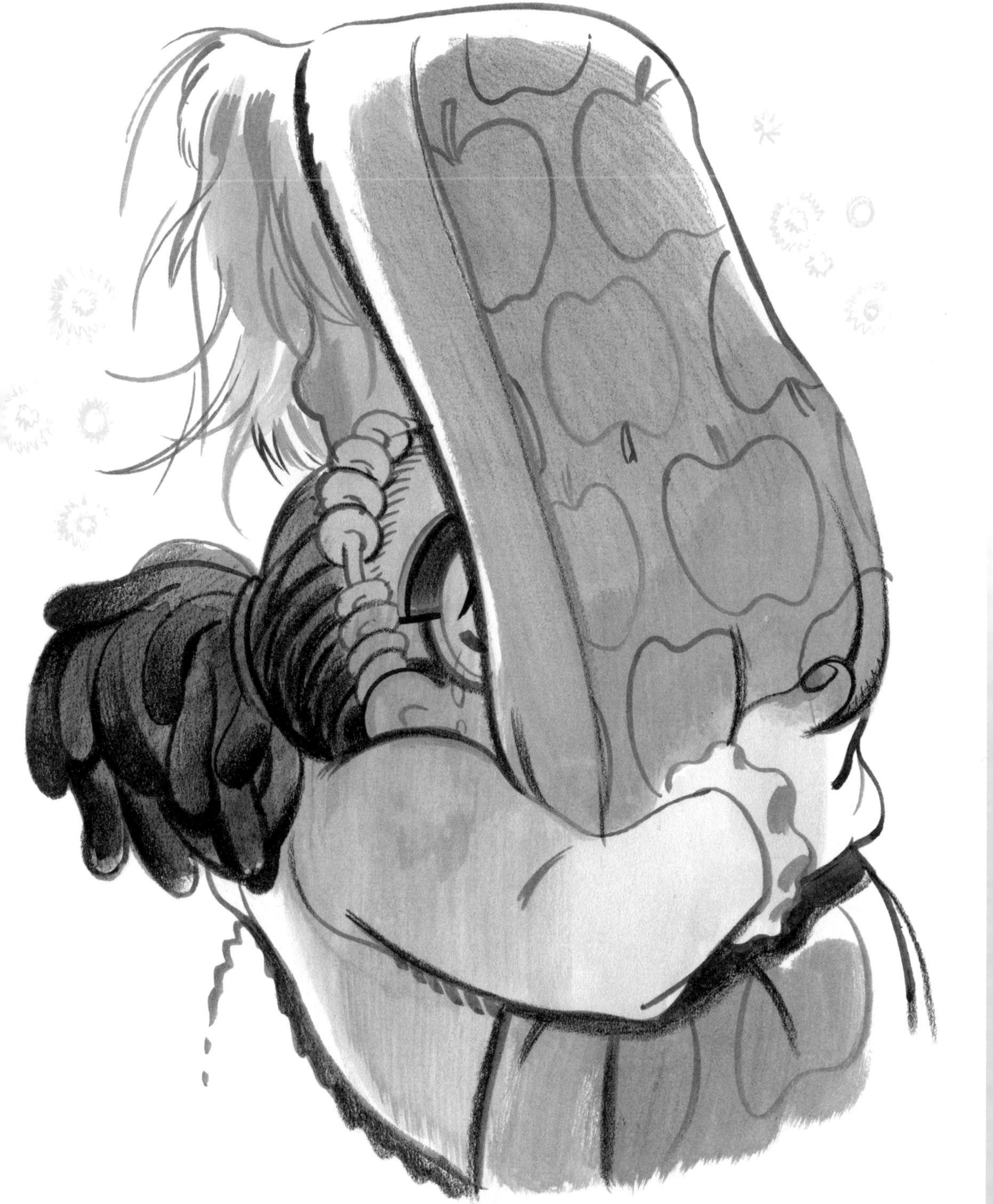

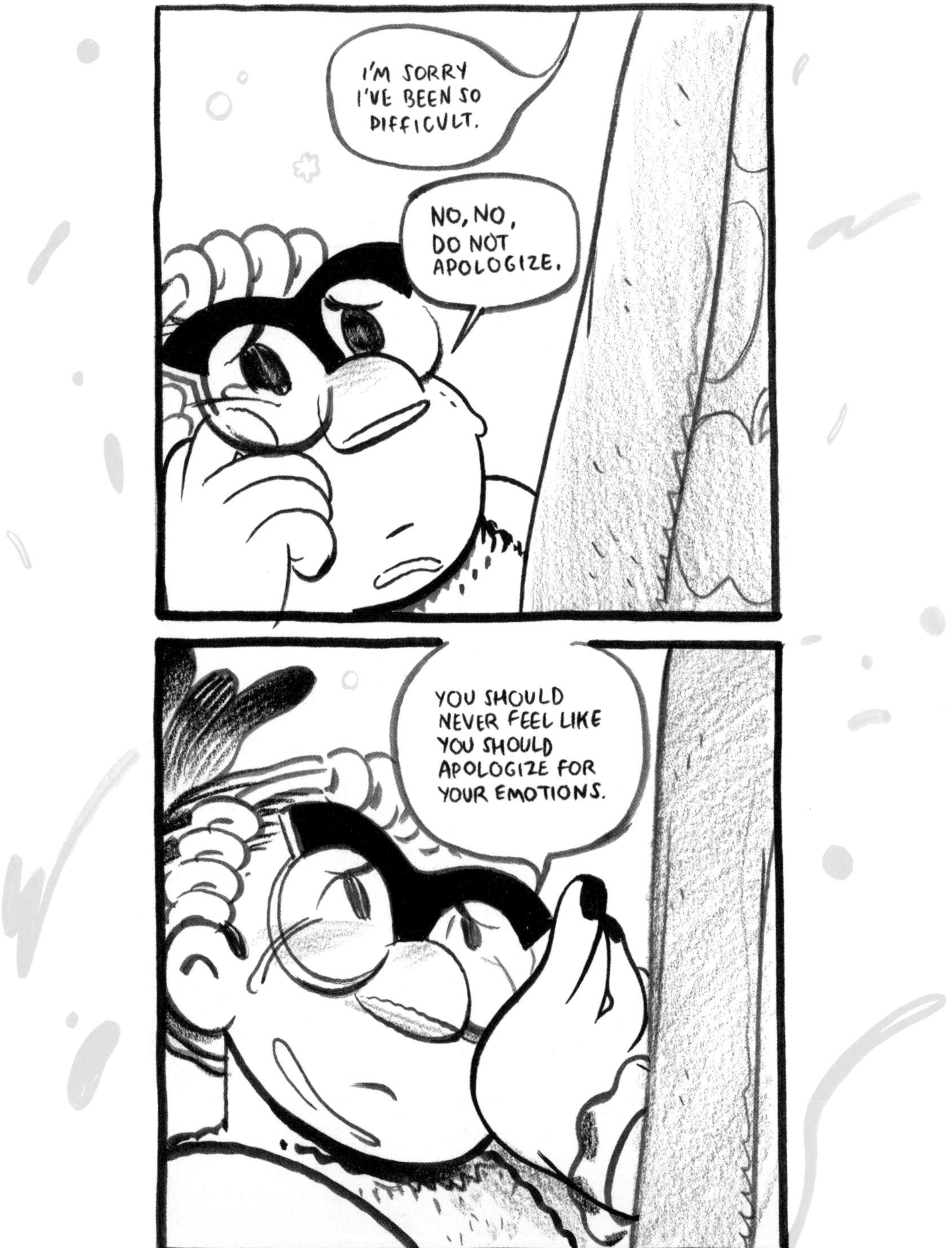
I'M SORRY I'VE BEEN SO DIFFICULT.
NO, NO, DO NOT APOLOGIZE.
YOU SHOULD NEVER FEEL LIKE YOU SHOULD APOLOGIZE FOR YOUR EMOTIONS.

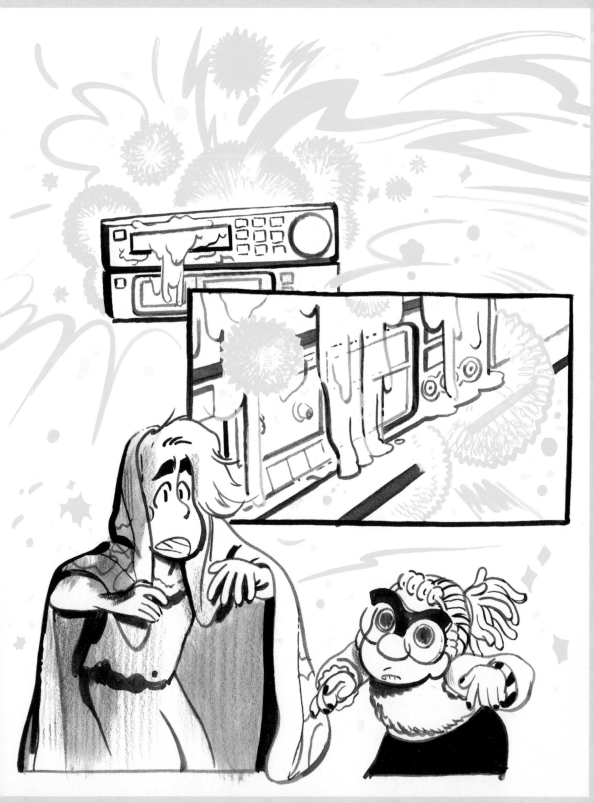

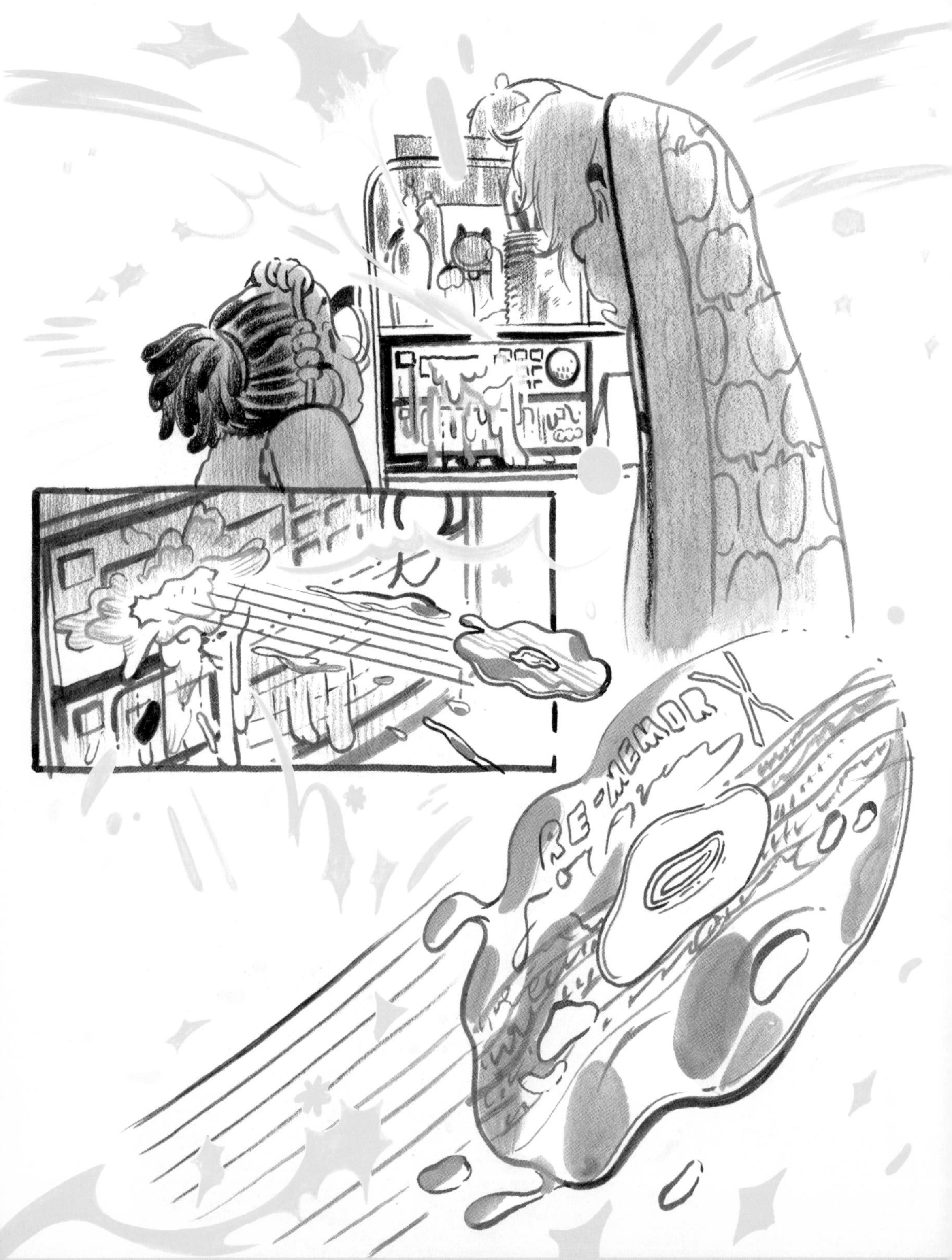
RE-MEMOR

ZIIIPP

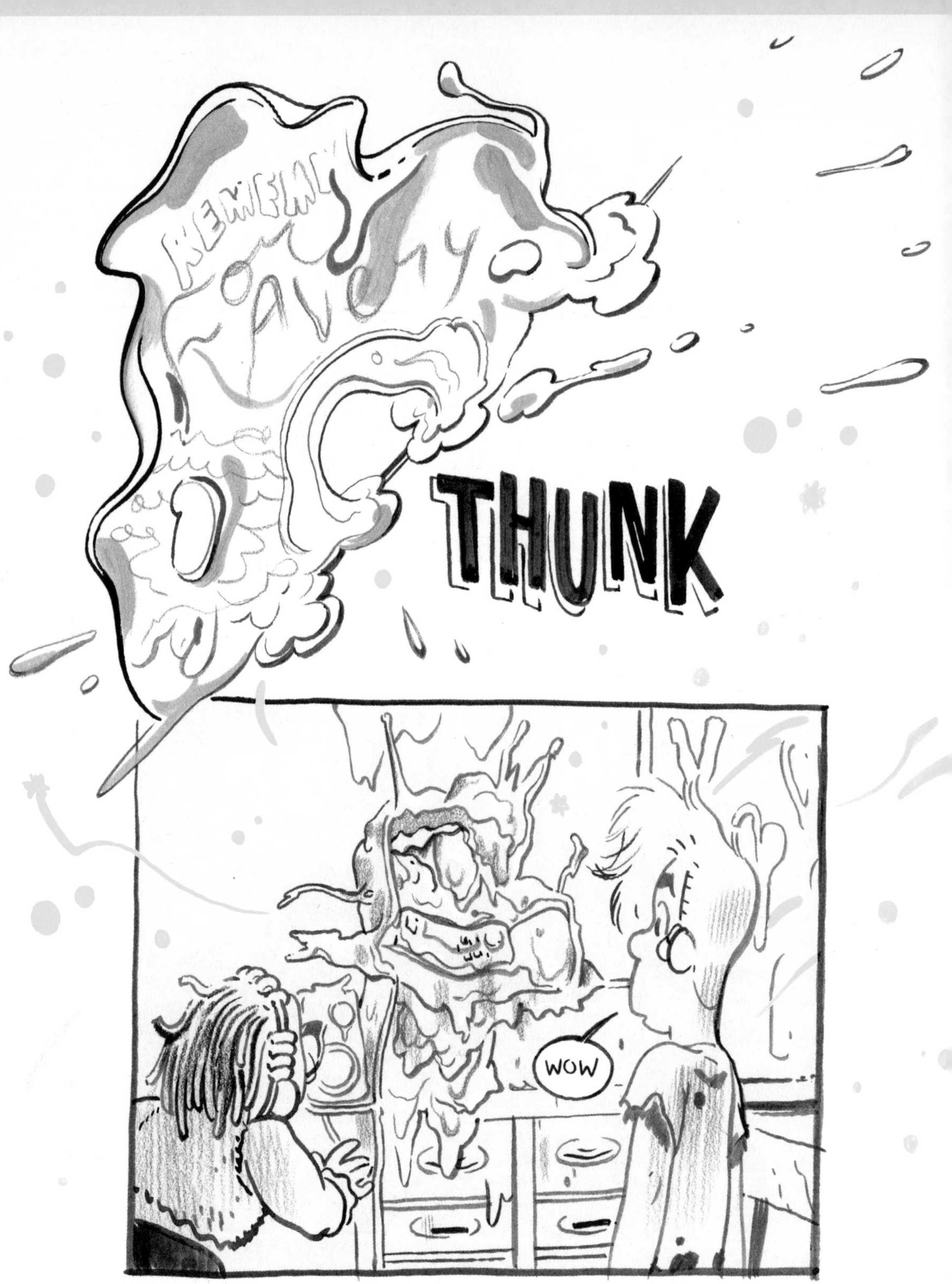
THUNK
WOW

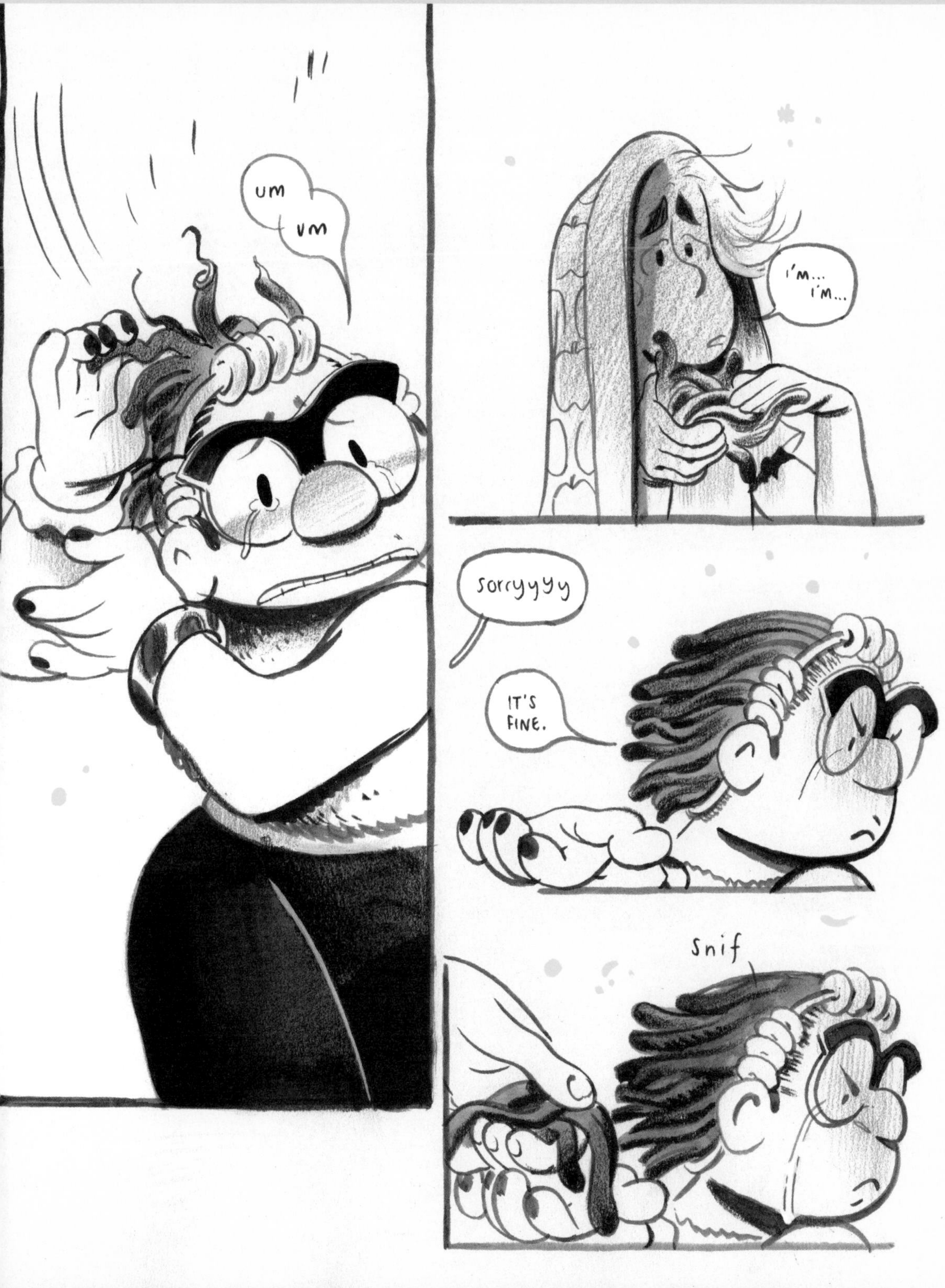
um
um
I'M...
I'M...
sorryyyy
IT'S FINE.
snif

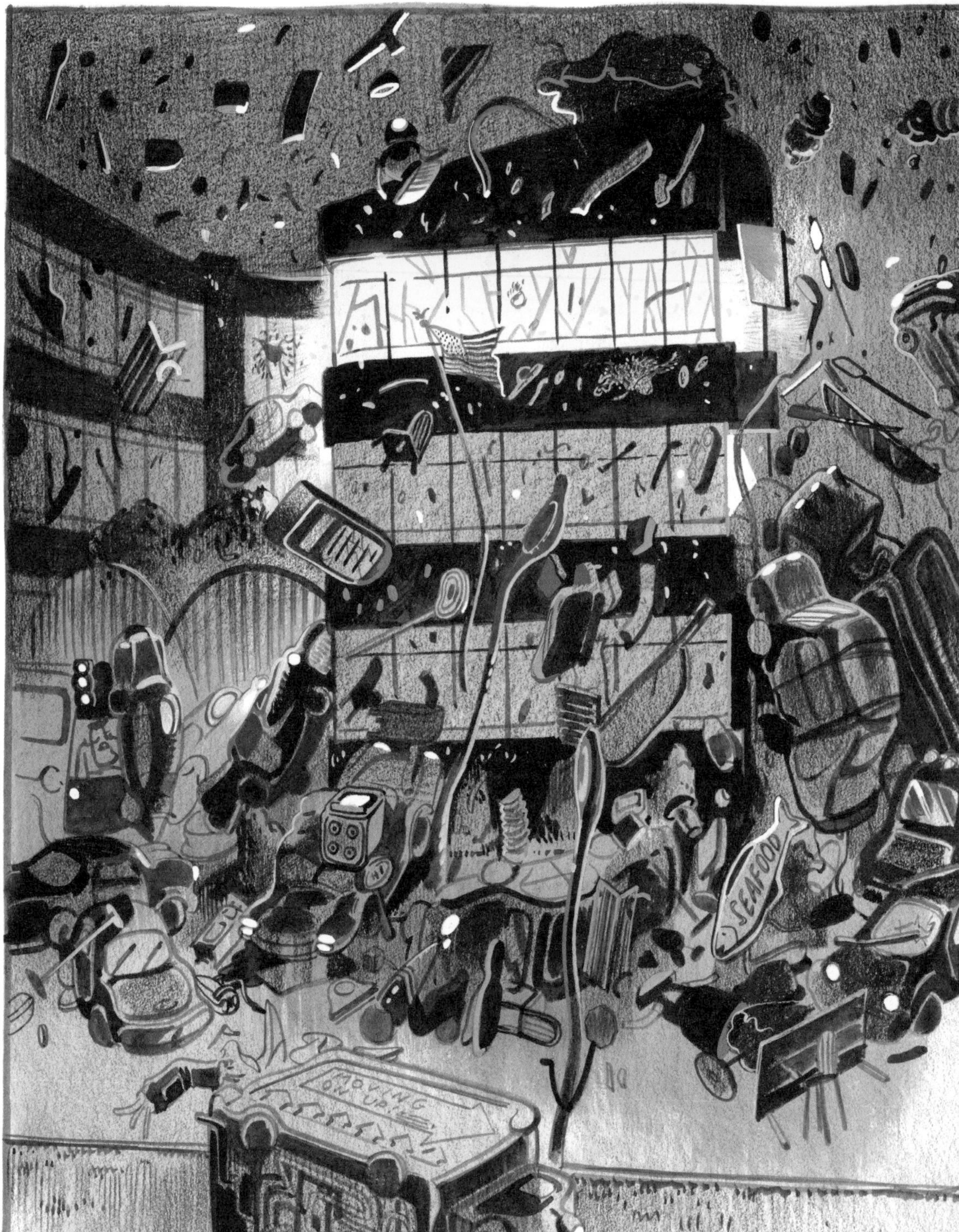
SEAFOOD
MOVING ON UP

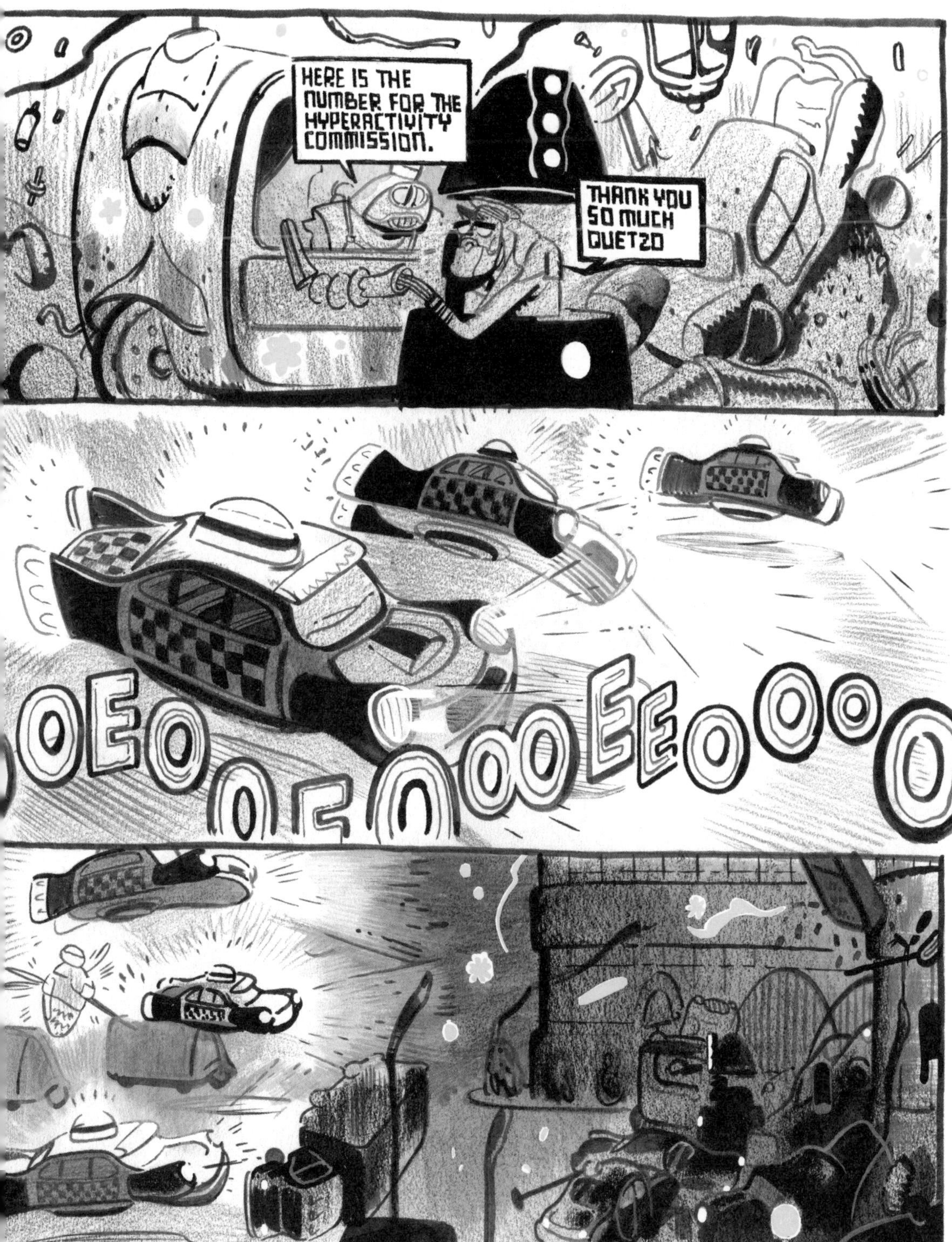
HERE IS THE NUMBER FOR THE HYPERACTIVITY COMMISSION.
THANK YOU SO MUCH QUETZO
OEOOEOOOOEEOOOO

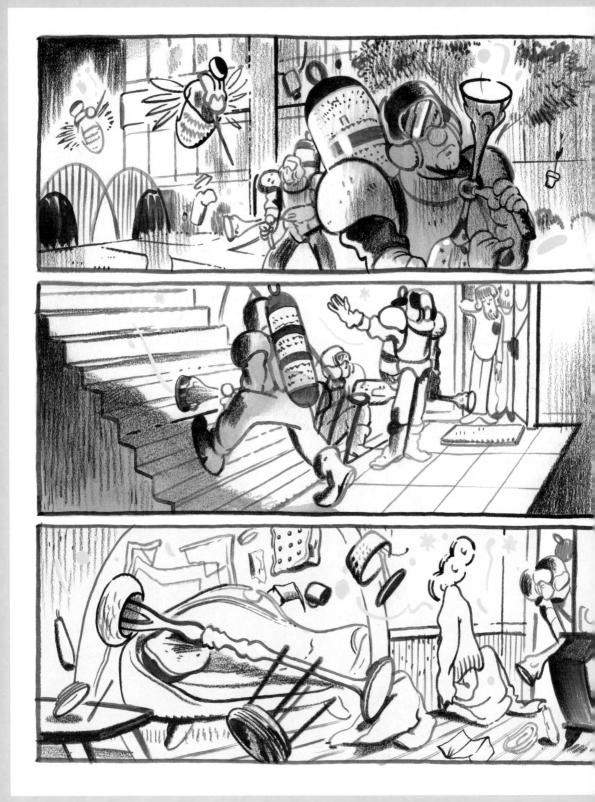

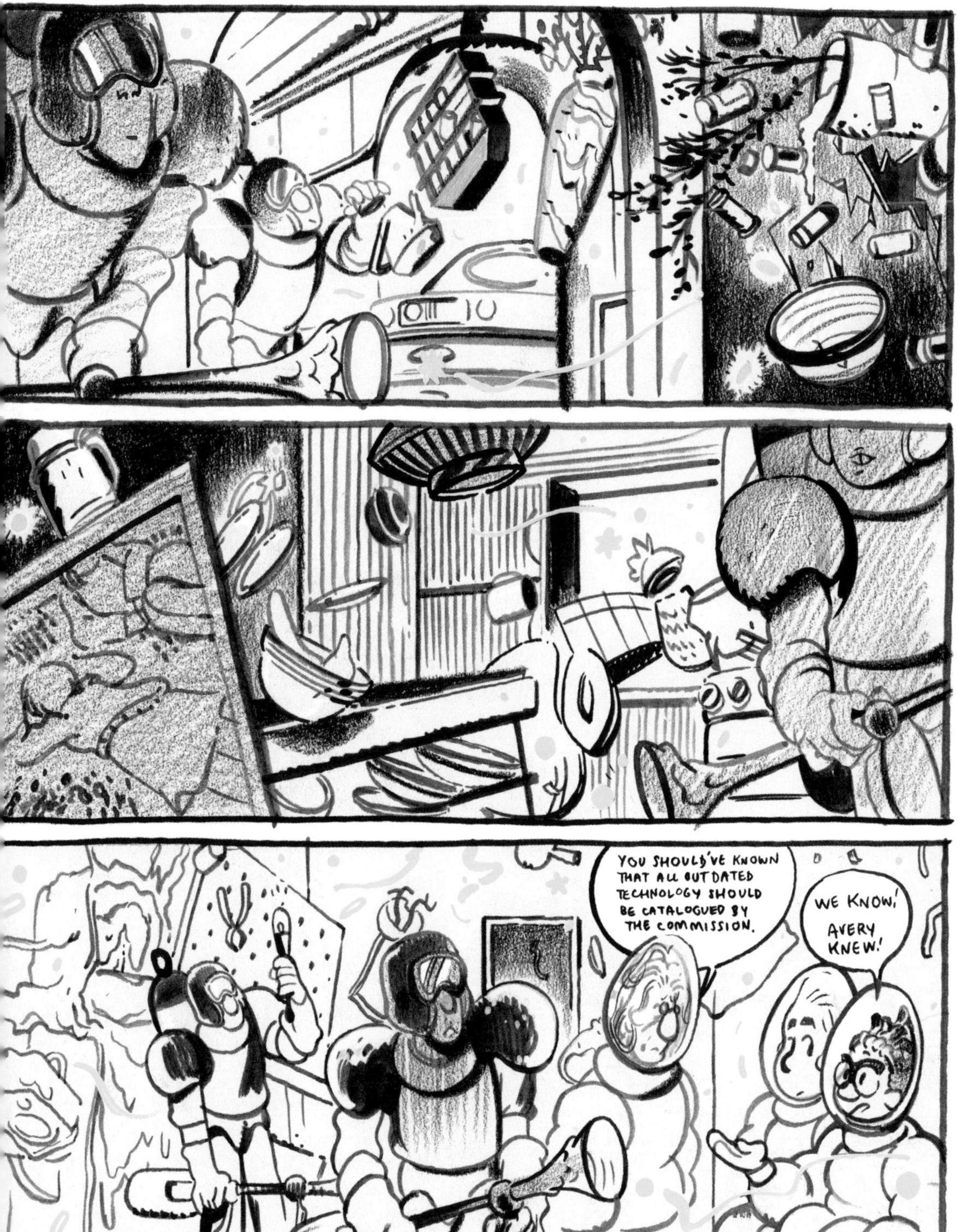
YOU SHOULD'VE KNOWN THAT ALL OUTDATED TECHNOLOGY SHOULD BE CATALOGUED BY THE COMMISSION.
WE KNOW!
AVERY KNEW!

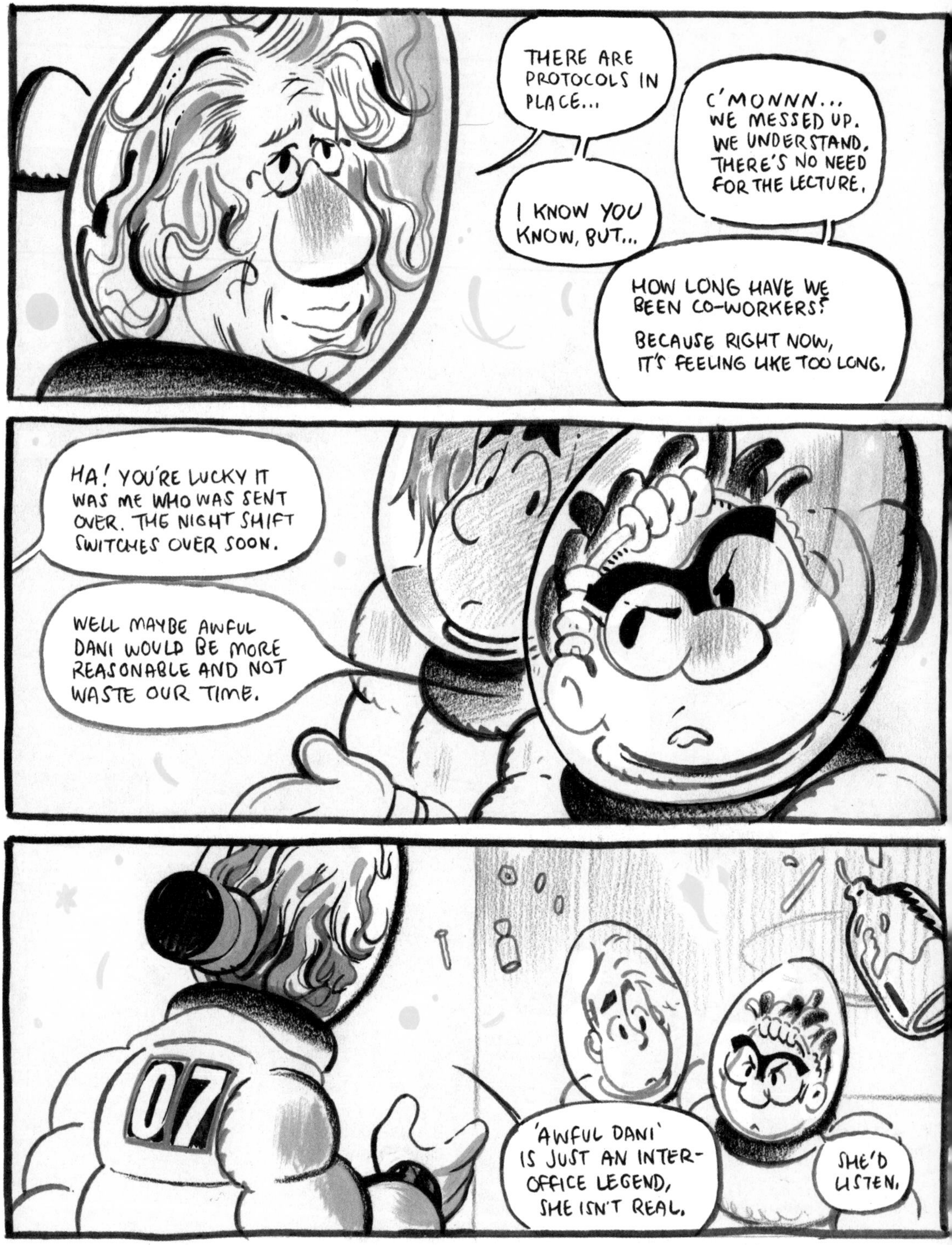
THERE ARE PROTOCOLS IN PLACE...
I KNOW YOU KNOW, BUT...
C'MONNN... WE MESSED UP. WE UNDERSTAND. THERE'S NO NEED FOR THE LECTURE.
HOW LONG HAVE WE BEEN CO-WORKERS?
BECAUSE RIGHT NOW, IT'S FEELING LIKE TOO LONG.
HA! YOU'RE LUCKY IT WAS ME WHO WAS SENT OVER. THE NIGHT SHIFT SWITCHES OVER SOON.
WELL MAYBE AWFUL DANI WOULD BE MORE REASONABLE AND NOT WASTE OUR TIME.
07
'AWFUL DANI' IS JUST AN INTER-OFFICE LEGEND, SHE ISN'T REAL.
SHE'D LISTEN.

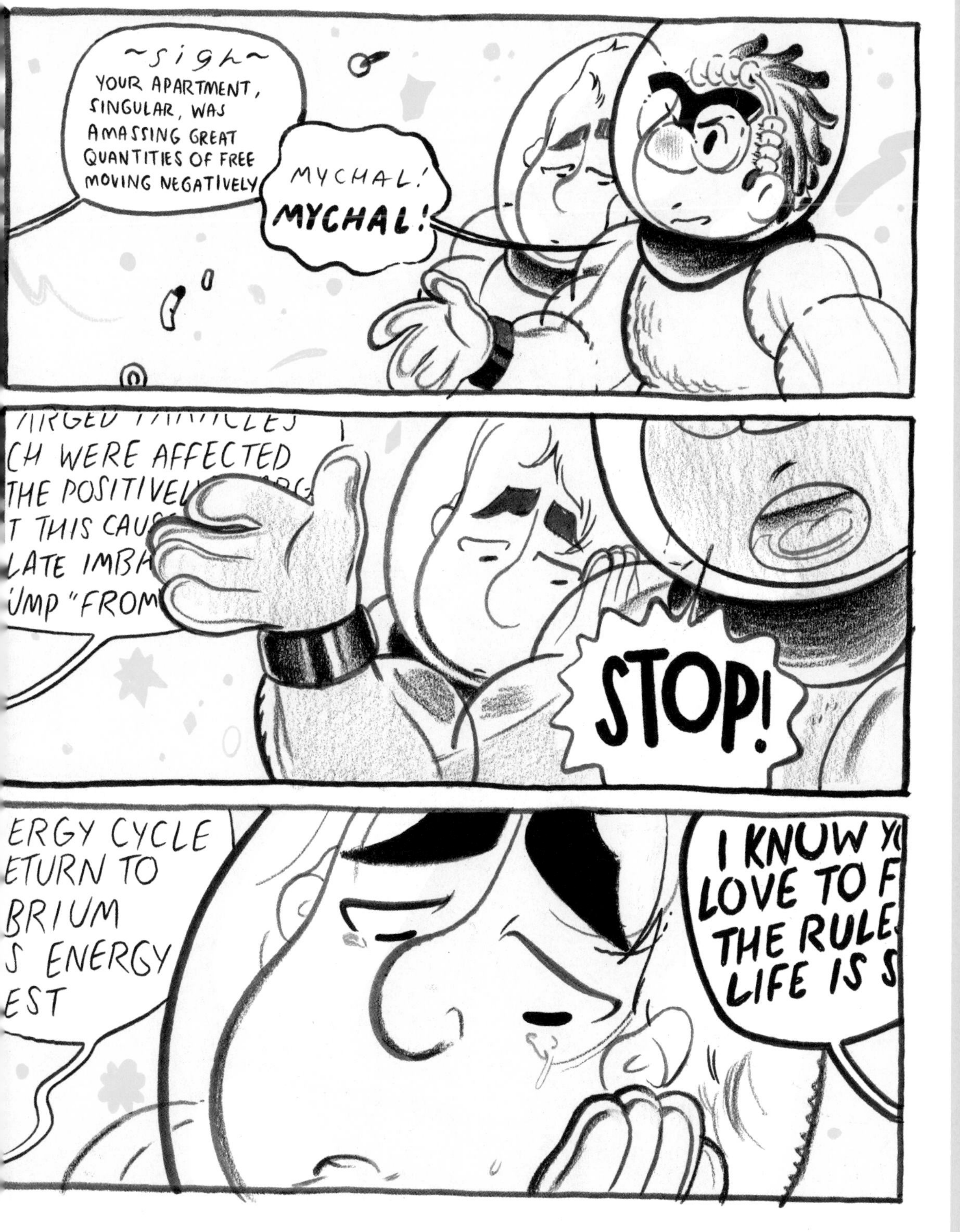
~sigh~
YOUR APARTMENT, SINGULAR, WAS AMASSING GREAT QUANTITIES OF FREE MOVING NEGATIVELY
MYCHAL! MYCHAL!
ARGED PARTICLES
CH WERE AFFECTED
THE POSITIVEL
T THIS CAUS
LATE IMBA
UMP "FROM
STOP!
ERGY CYCLE
ETURN TO
BRIUM
S ENERGY
EST
I KNOW YO
LOVE TO F
THE RULE
LIFE IS S

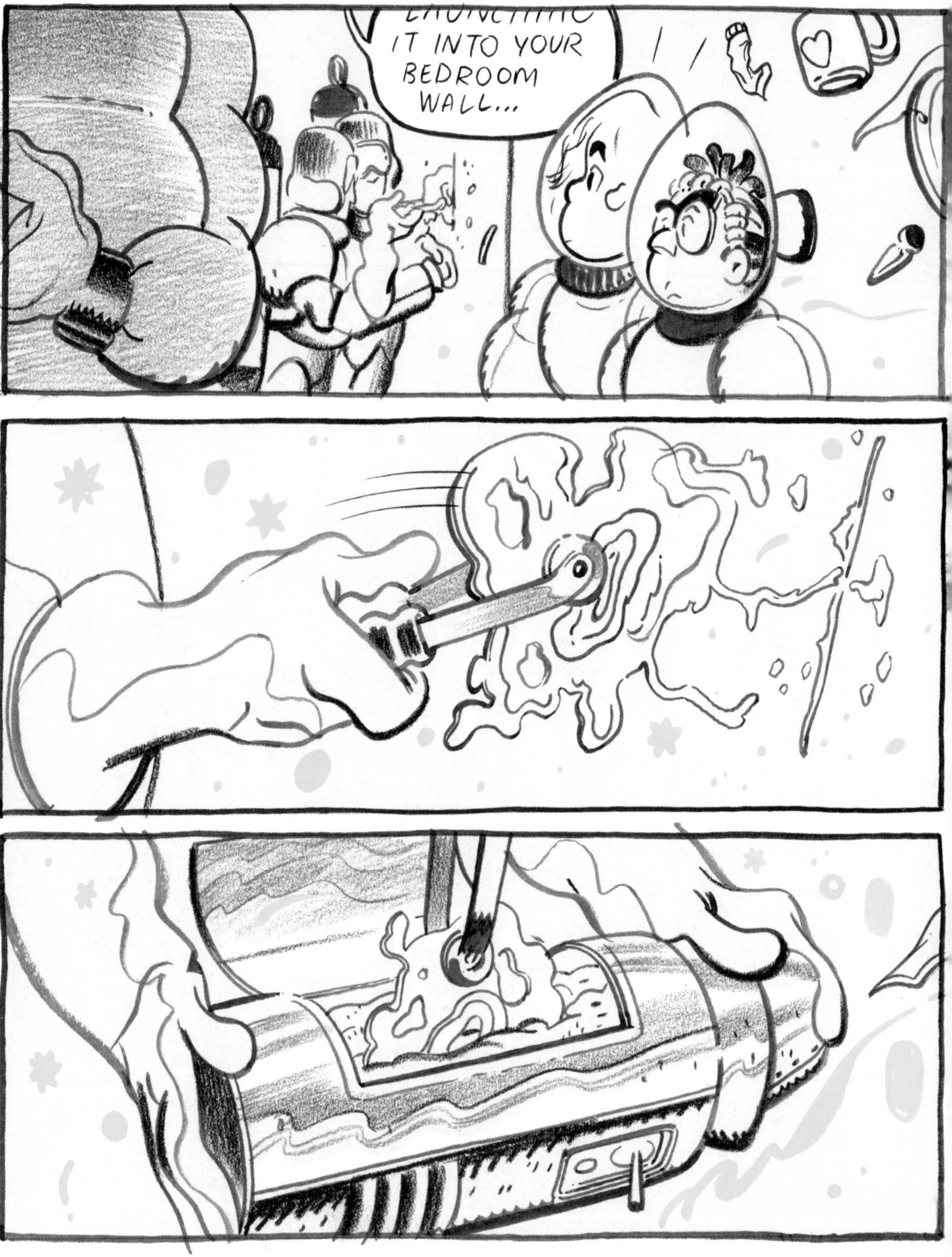
IT INTO YOUR BEDROOM WALL...

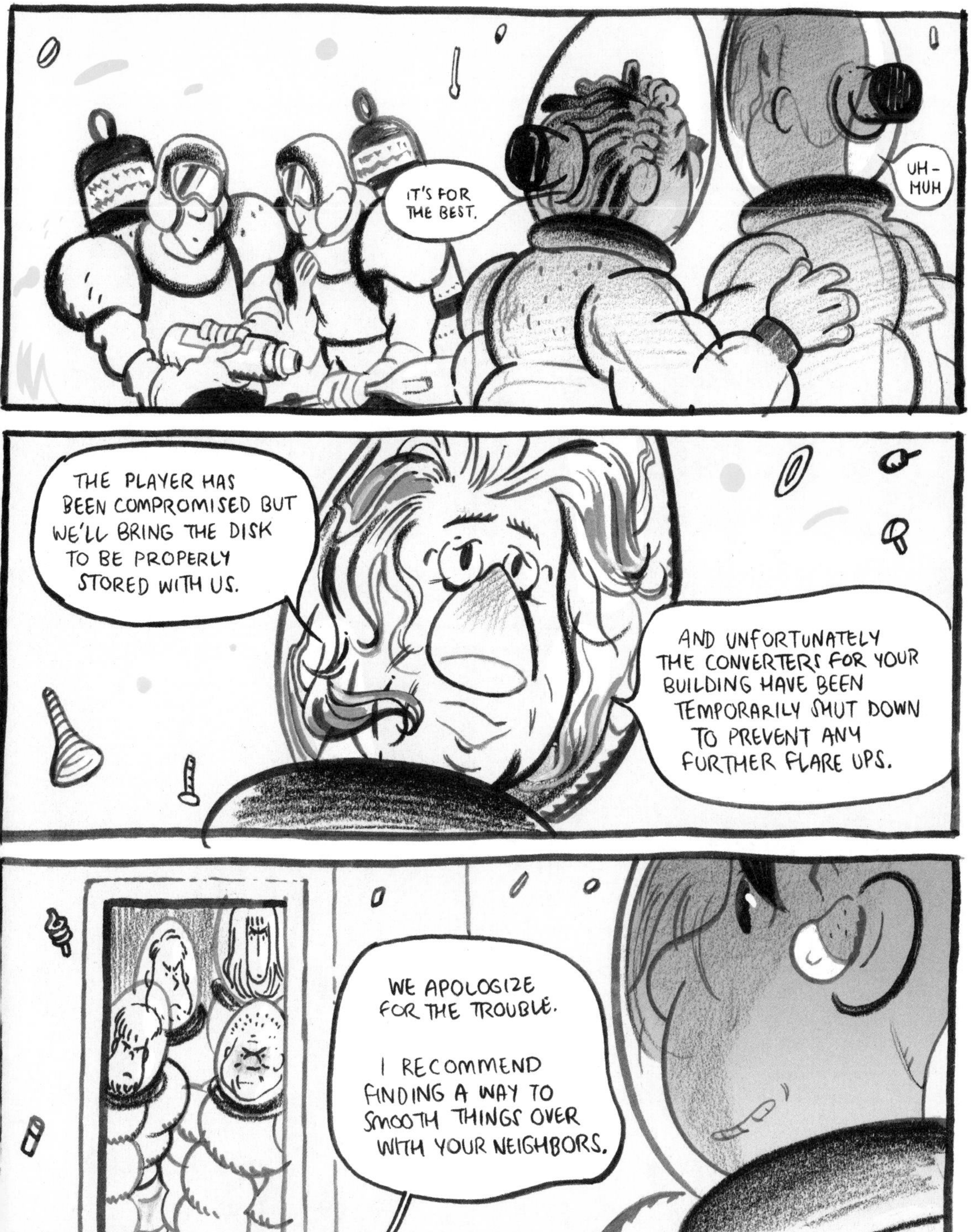
IT'S FOR THE BEST.
UH-MUH
THE PLAYER HAS BEEN COMPROMISED BUT WE'LL BRING THE DISK TO BE PROPERLY STORED WITH US.
AND UNFORTUNATELY THE CONVERTERS FOR YOUR BUILDING HAVE BEEN TEMPORARILY SHUT DOWN TO PREVENT ANY FURTHER FLARE UPS.
WE APOLOGIZE FOR THE TROUBLE.
I RECOMMEND FINDING A WAY TO SMOOTH THINGS OVER WITH YOUR NEIGHBORS.

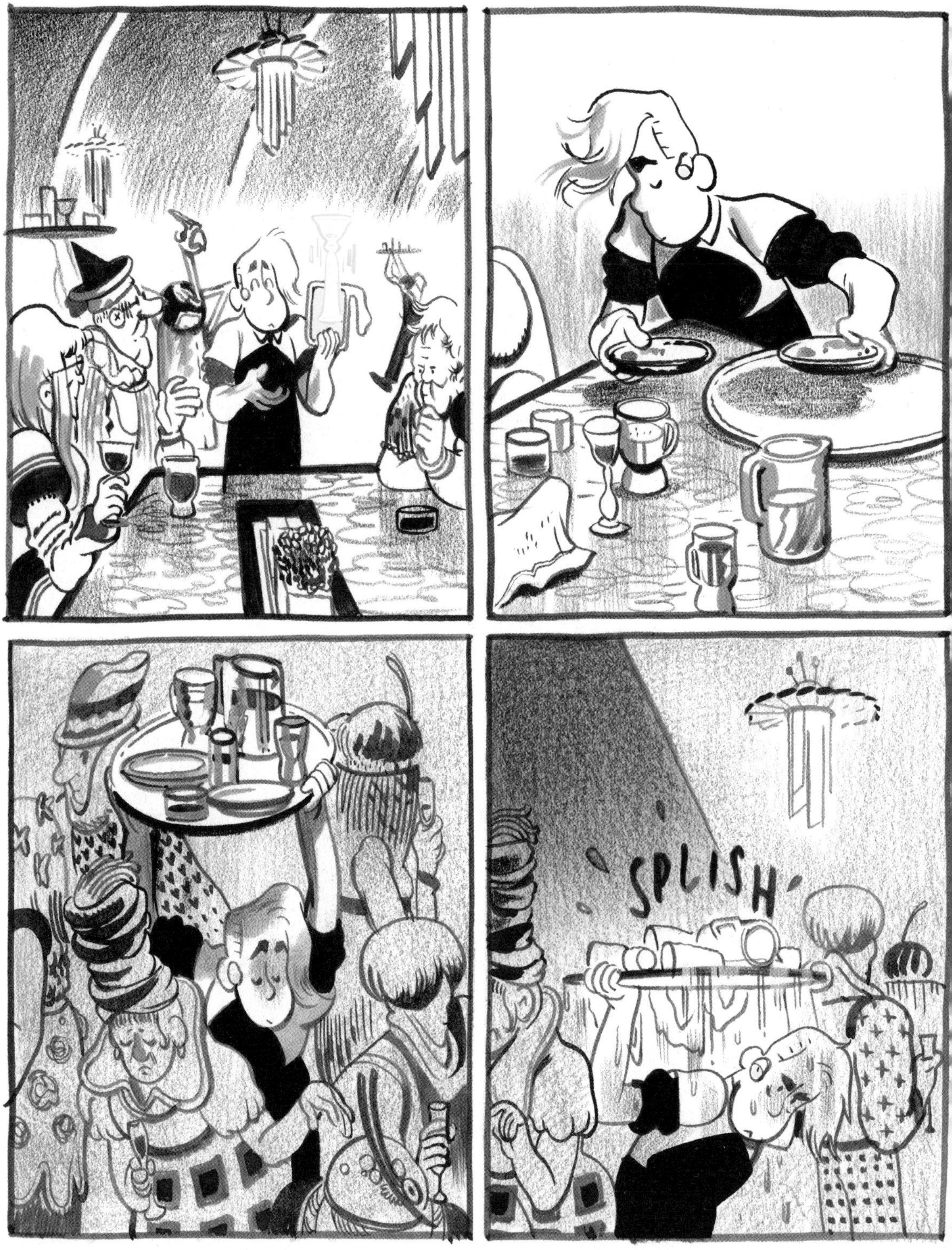
SPLISH

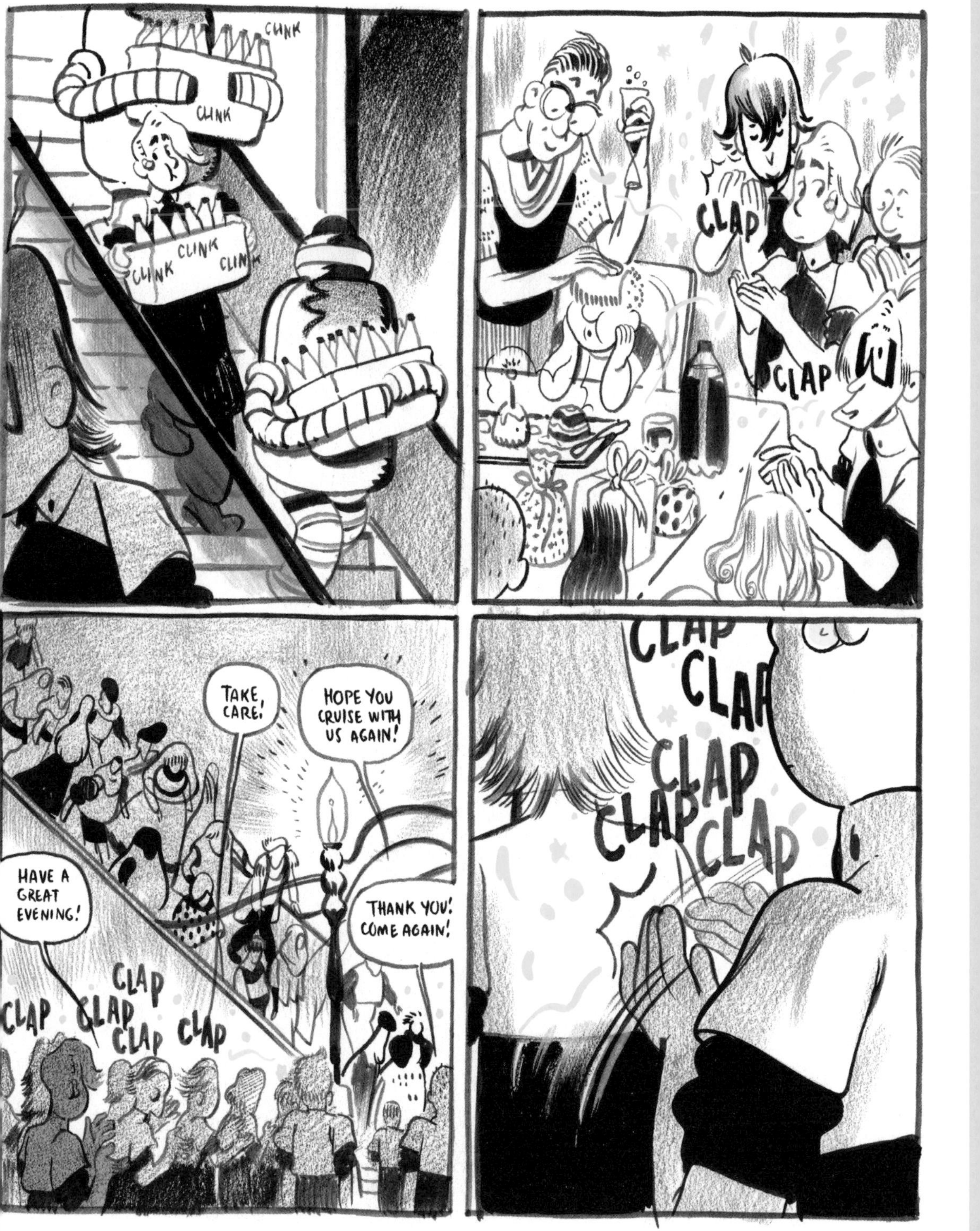
CLINK
CLINK
CLINK
CLINK
CLINK
CLAP
CLAP
TAKE CARE!
HOPE YOU CRUISE WITH US AGAIN!
HAVE A GREAT EVENING!
THANK YOU! COME AGAIN!
CLAP
CLAP
CLAP
CLAP
CLAP
CLAP
CLAP
CLAP
CLAP
CLAP

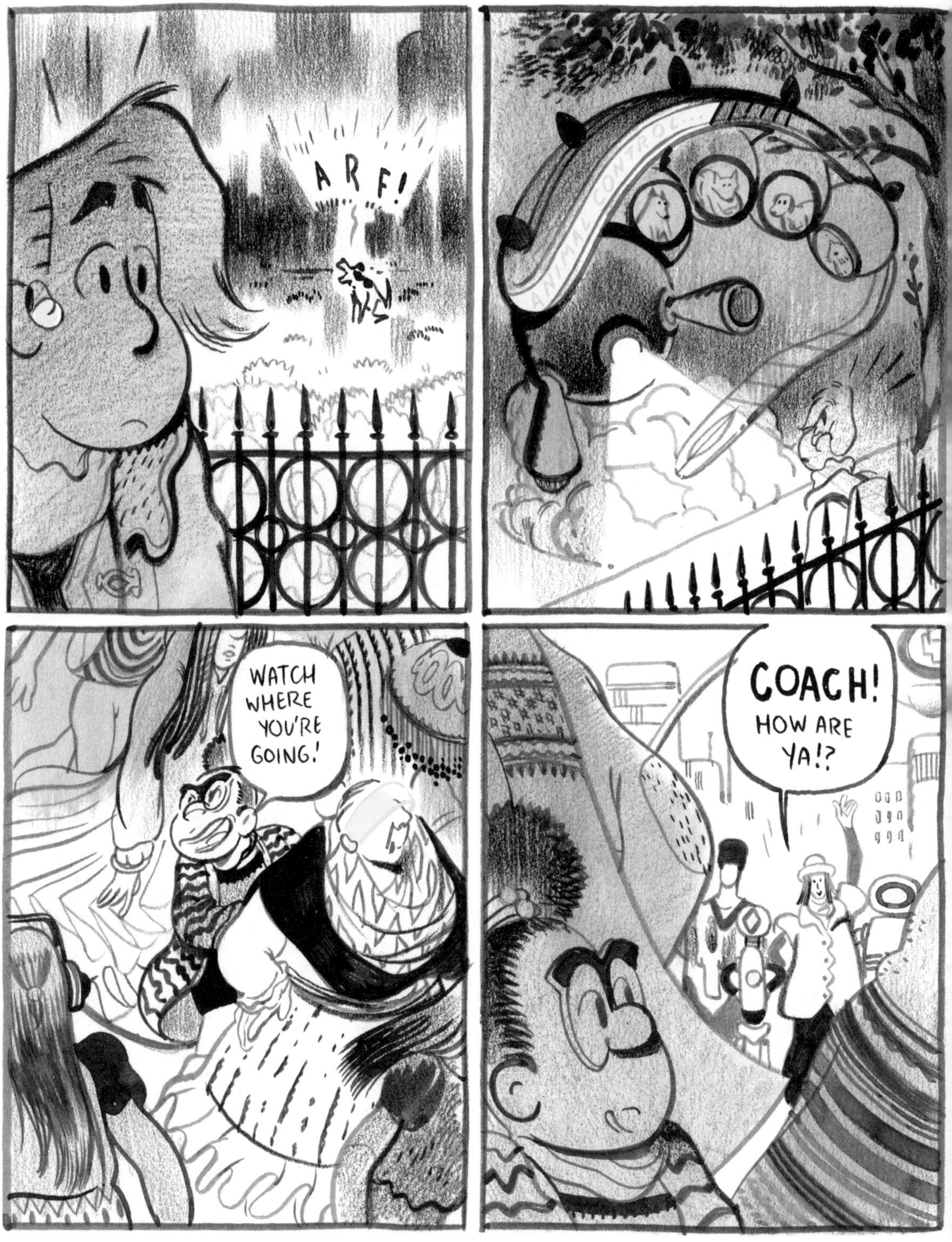
ARF!
ANIMAL CONTROL...
WATCH WHERE YOU'RE GOING!
COACH! HOW ARE YA!?

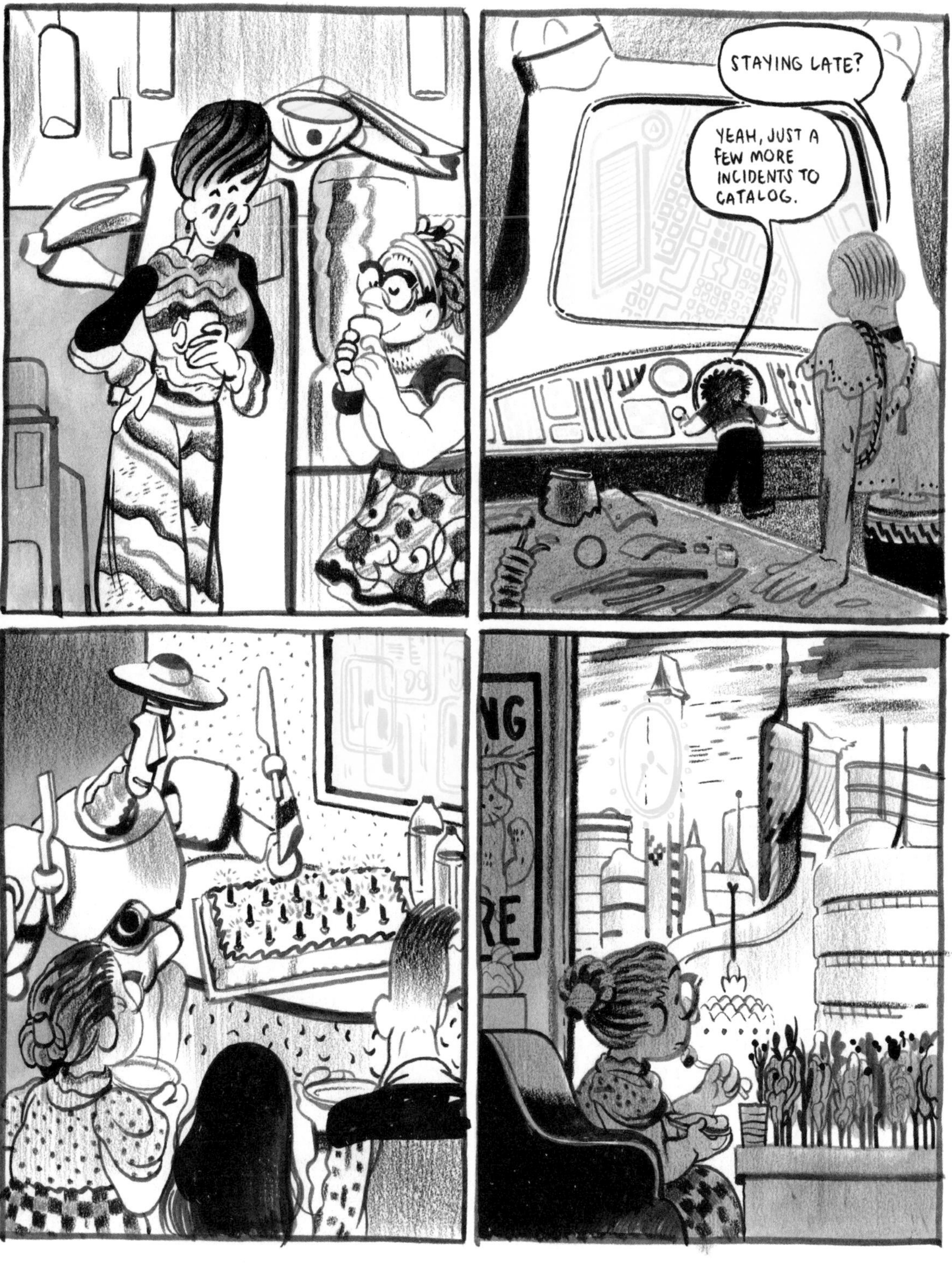
STAYING LATE?
YEAH, JUST A FEW MORE INCIDENTS TO CATALOG.

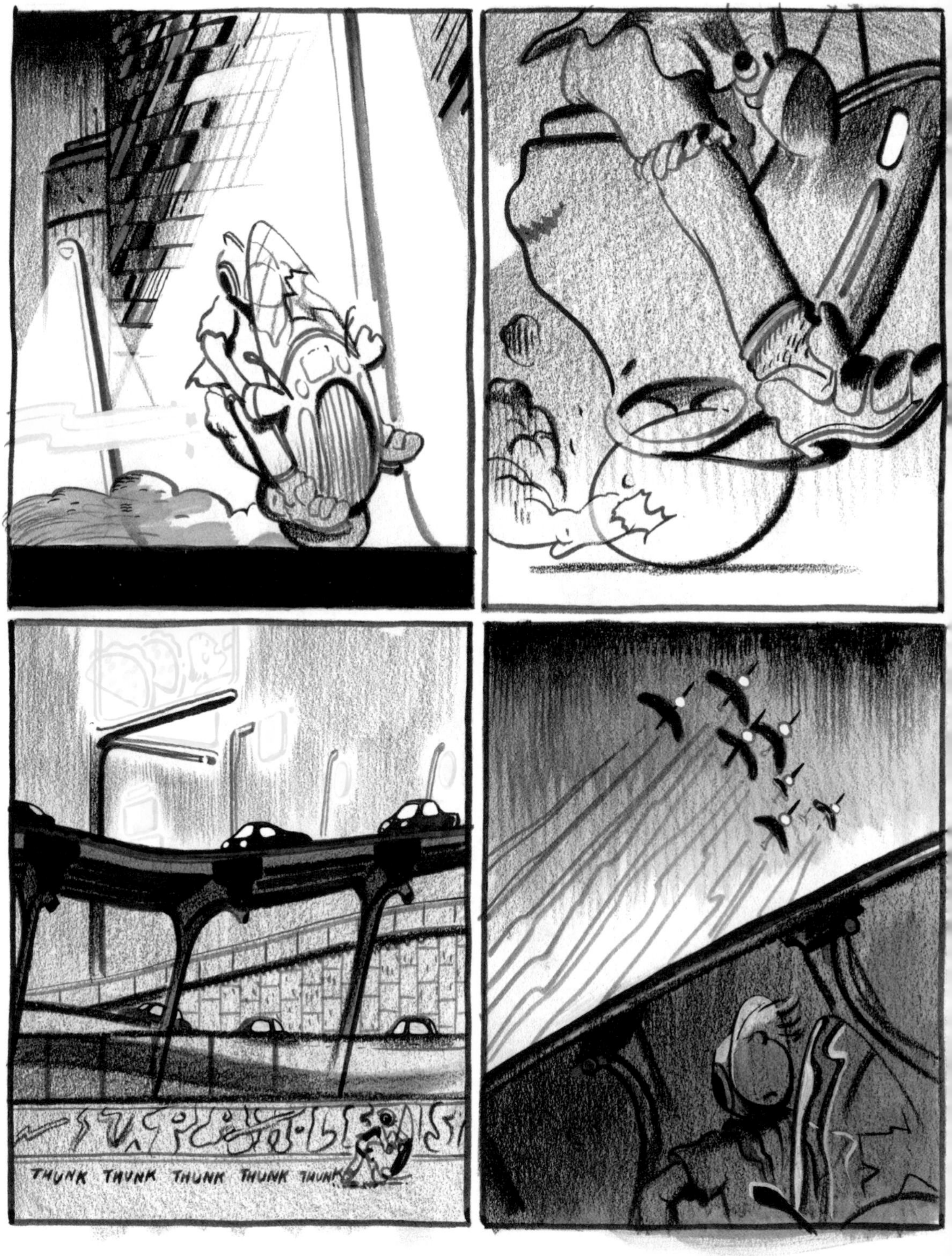
THUNK THUNK THUNK THUNK THUNK

VRRRR
I HATE THIS.
TARGET HAS BEEN TERMINATED.

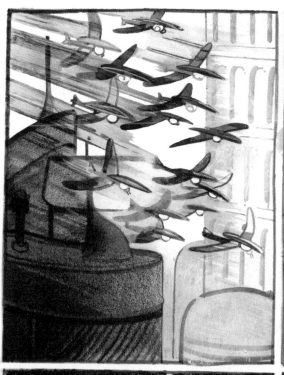

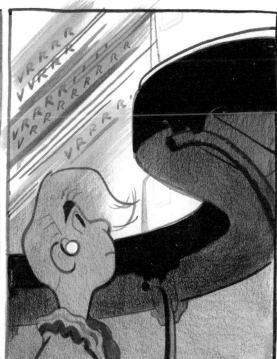

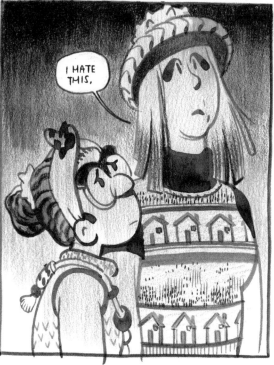

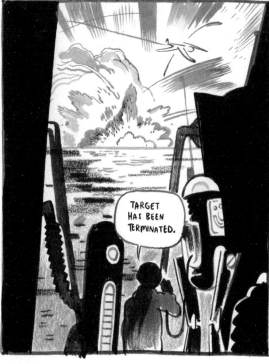

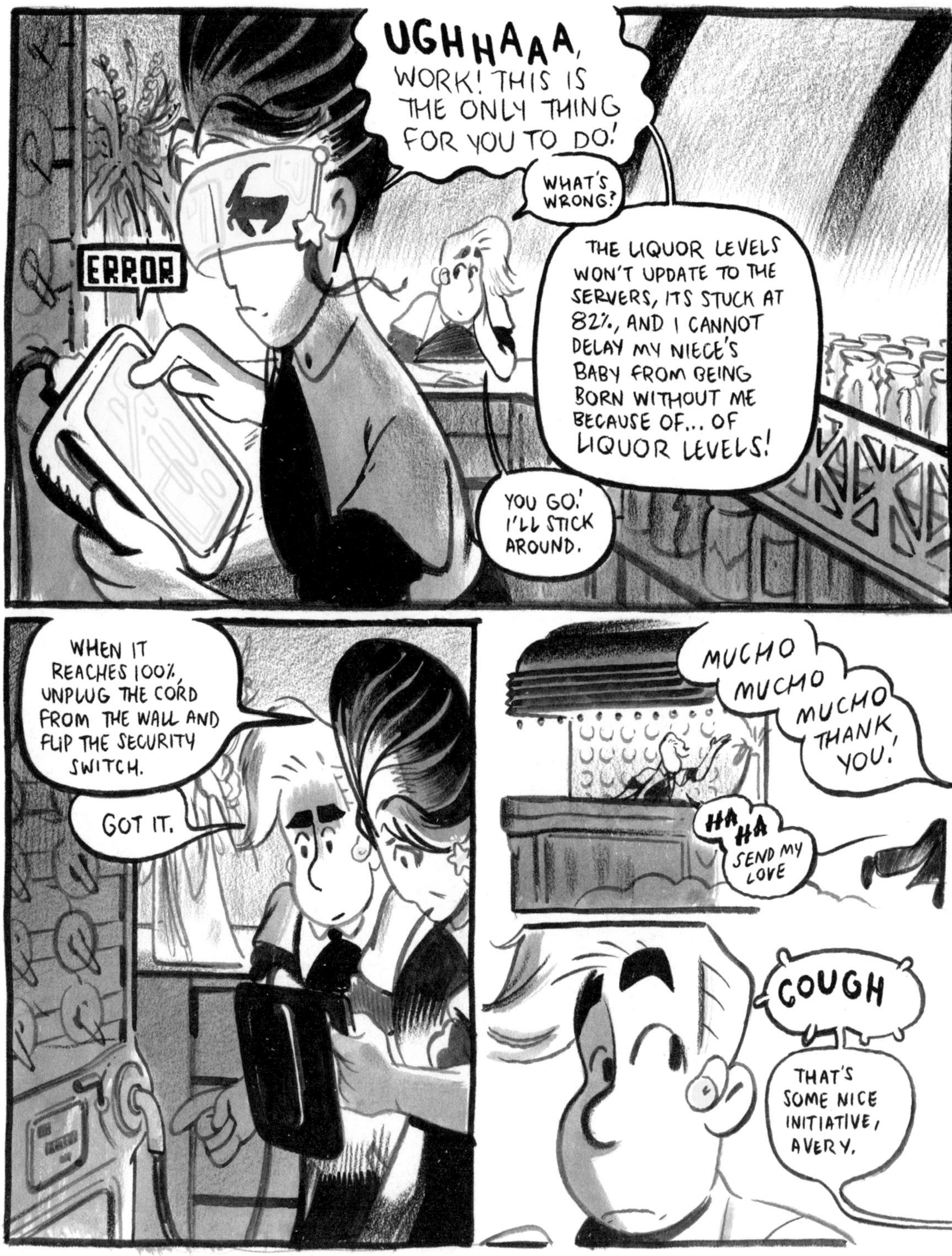
UGHHAAA, WORK! THIS IS THE ONLY THING FOR YOU TO DO!
ERROR
WHAT'S WRONG?
THE LIQUOR LEVELS WON'T UPDATE TO THE SERVERS, ITS STUCK AT 82%, AND I CANNOT DELAY MY NIECE'S BABY FROM BEING BORN WITHOUT ME BECAUSE OF... OF LIQUOR LEVELS!
YOU GO! I'LL STICK AROUND.
WHEN IT REACHES 100%, UNPLUG THE CORD FROM THE WALL AND FLIP THE SECURITY SWITCH.
GOT IT.
MUCHO MUCHO MUCHO THANK YOU!
HA HA SEND MY LOVE
COUGH
THAT'S SOME NICE INITIATIVE, AVERY.

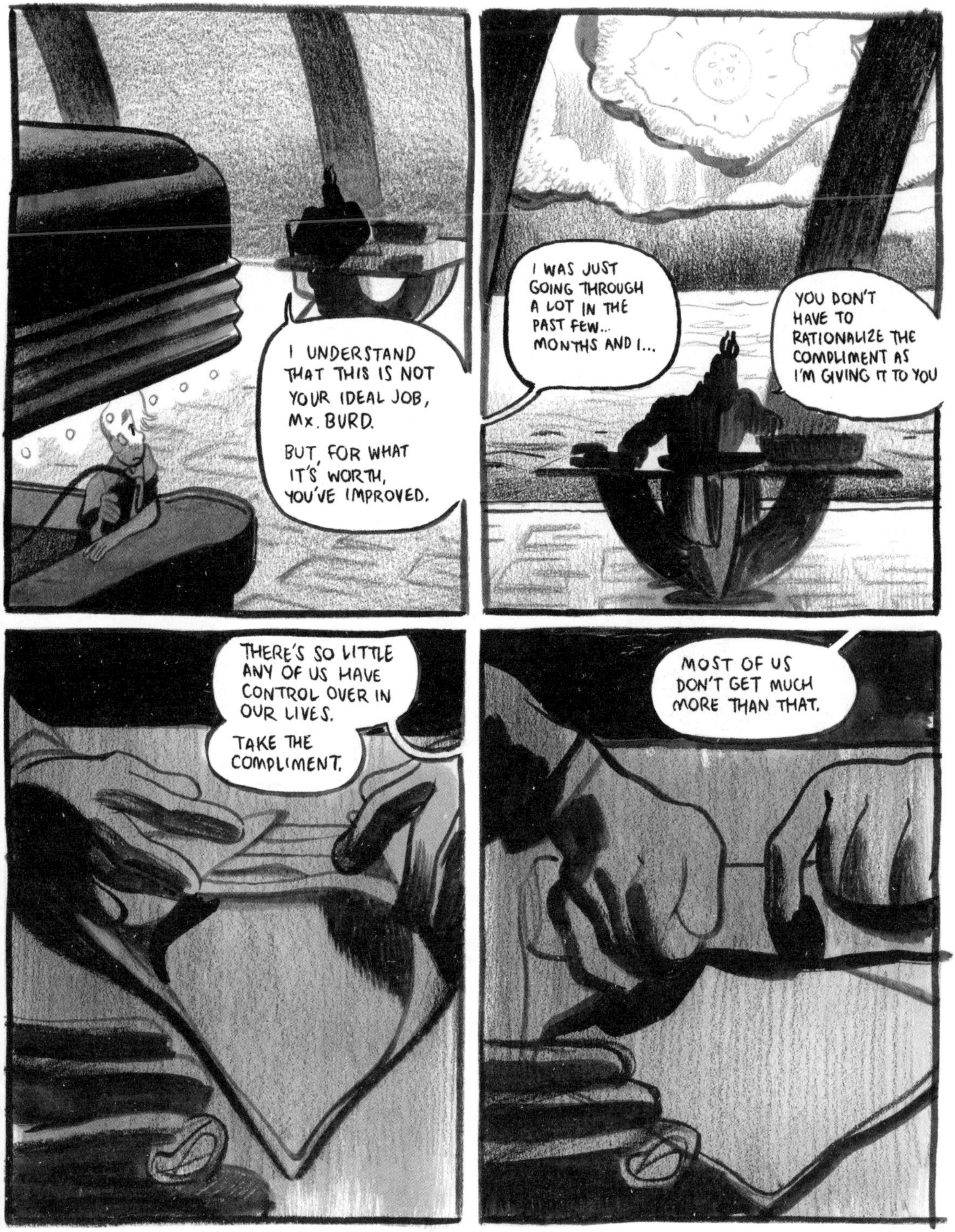
I UNDERSTAND THAT THIS IS NOT YOUR IDEAL JOB, Mx. BURD.
BUT, FOR WHAT IT'S WORTH, YOU'VE IMPROVED.
I WAS JUST GOING THROUGH A LOT IN THE PAST FEW... MONTHS AND I...
YOU DON'T HAVE TO RATIONALIZE THE COMPLIMENT AS I'M GIVING IT TO YOU
THERE'S SO LITTLE ANY OF US HAVE CONTROL OVER IN OUR LIVES.
TAKE THE COMPLIMENT.
MOST OF US DON'T GET MUCH MORE THAN THAT.

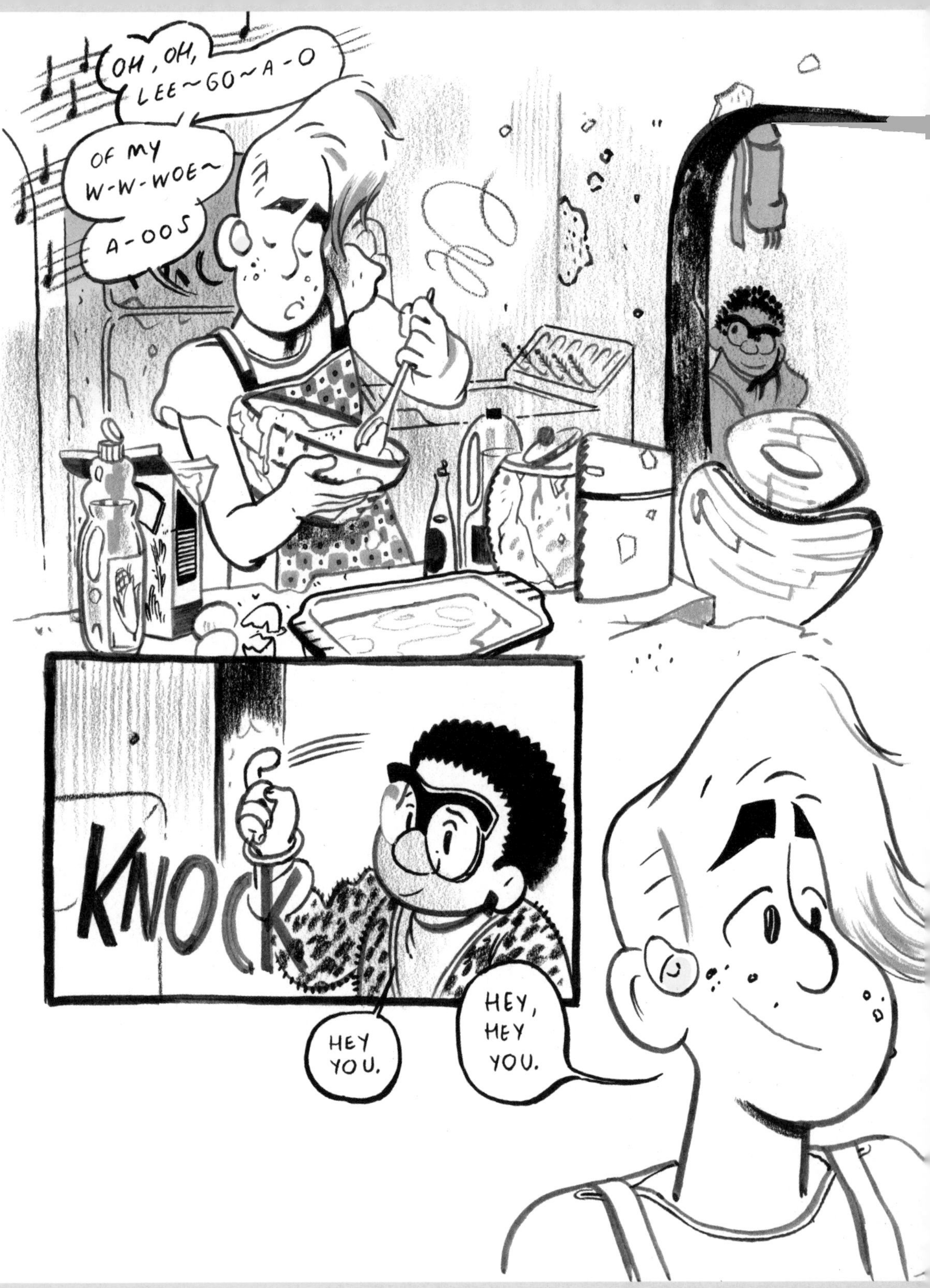
OH, OH, LEE~GO~A-O
OF MY W-W-WOE~
A-OOS
KNOCK
HEY YOU.
HEY, HEY YOU.

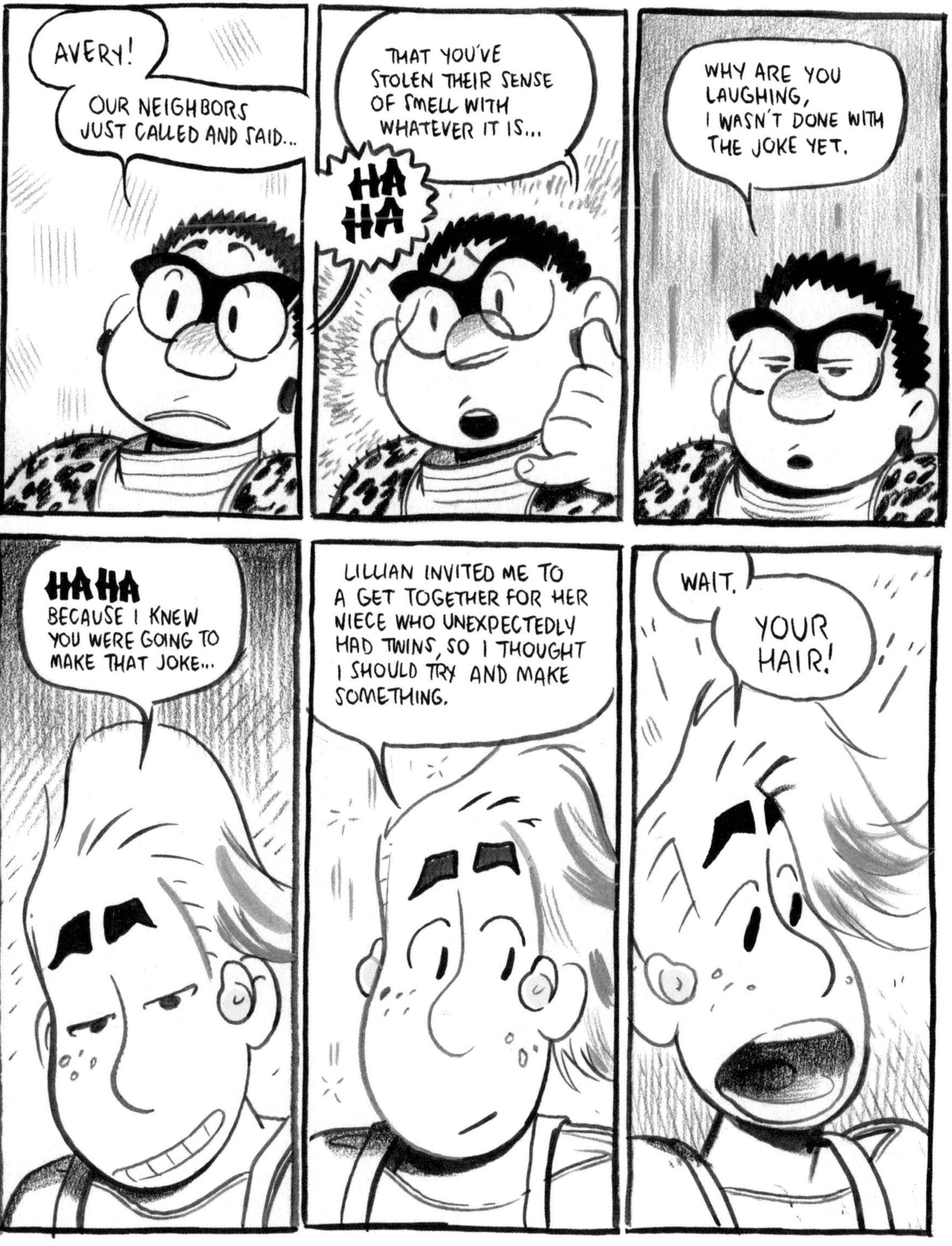
AVERY!
OUR NEIGHBORS JUST CALLED AND SAID...
THAT YOU'VE STOLEN THEIR SENSE OF SMELL WITH WHATEVER IT IS...
HA HA
WHY ARE YOU LAUGHING, I WASN'T DONE WITH THE JOKE YET.
HAHA BECAUSE I KNEW YOU WERE GOING TO MAKE THAT JOKE...
LILLIAN INVITED ME TO A GET TOGETHER FOR HER NIECE WHO UNEXPECTEDLY HAD TWINS, SO I THOUGHT I SHOULD TRY AND MAKE SOMETHING.
WAIT.
YOUR HAIR!

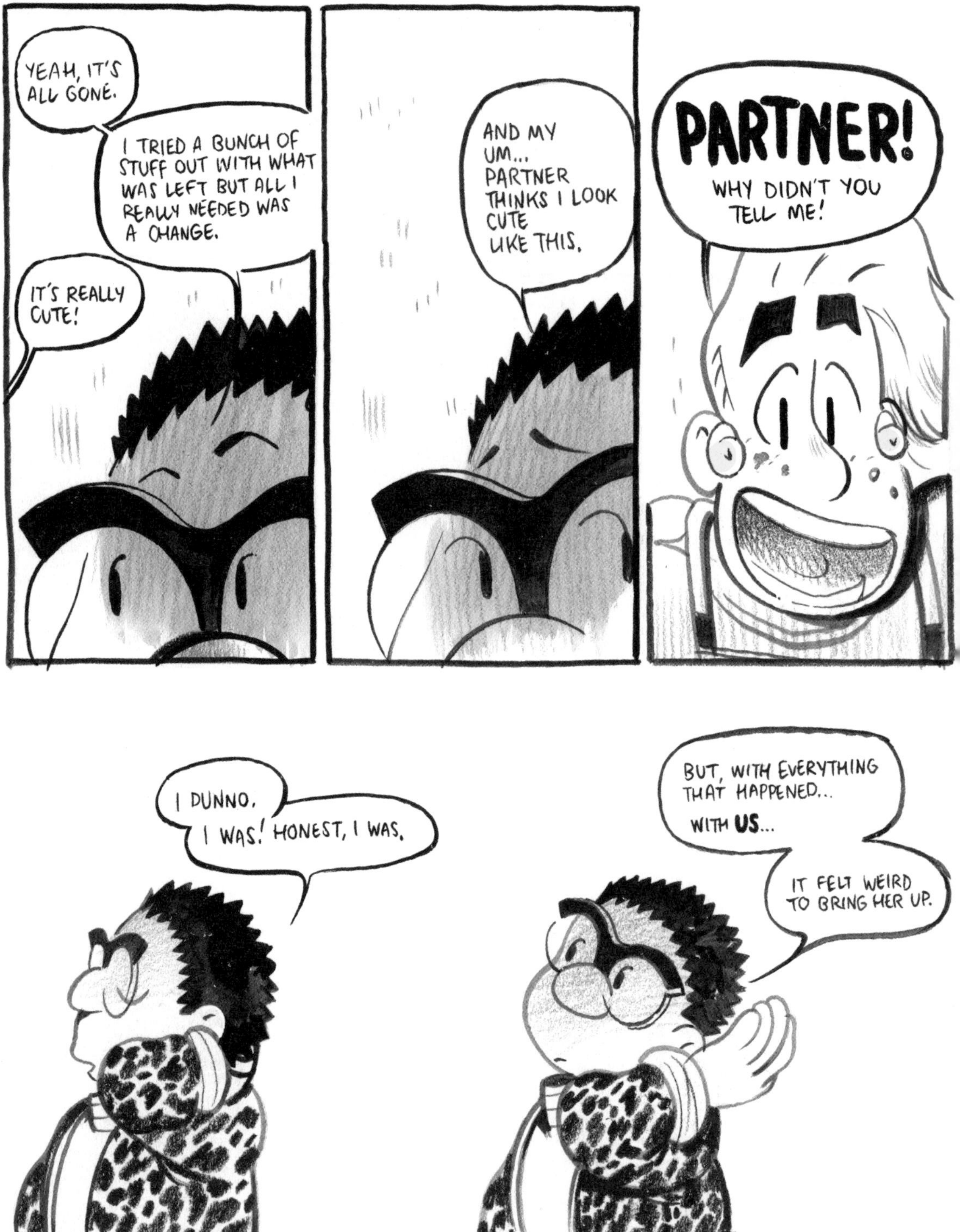
YEAH, IT'S ALL GONE.
I TRIED A BUNCH OF STUFF OUT WITH WHAT WAS LEFT BUT ALL I REALLY NEEDED WAS A CHANGE.
IT'S REALLY CUTE!
AND MY UM... PARTNER THINKS I LOOK CUTE LIKE THIS.
PARTNER!
WHY DIDN'T YOU TELL ME!
I DUNNO.
I WAS! HONEST, I WAS.
BUT, WITH EVERYTHING THAT HAPPENED...
WITH US...
IT FELT WEIRD TO BRING HER UP.

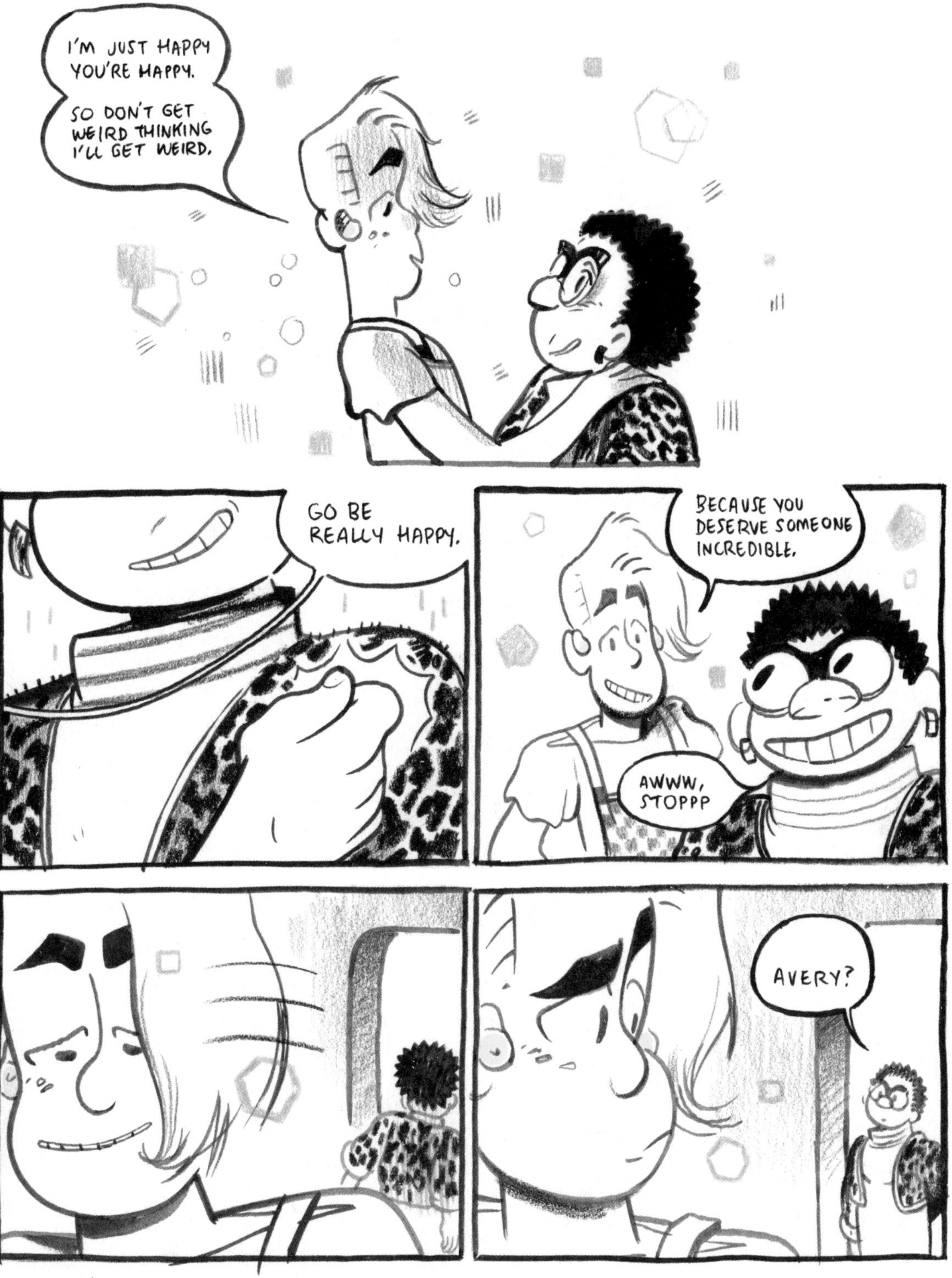
I'M JUST HAPPY YOU'RE HAPPY.
SO DON'T GET WEIRD THINKING I'LL GET WEIRD.
GO BE REALLY HAPPY.
BECAUSE YOU DESERVE SOMEONE INCREDIBLE.
AWWW, STOPPP
AVERY?

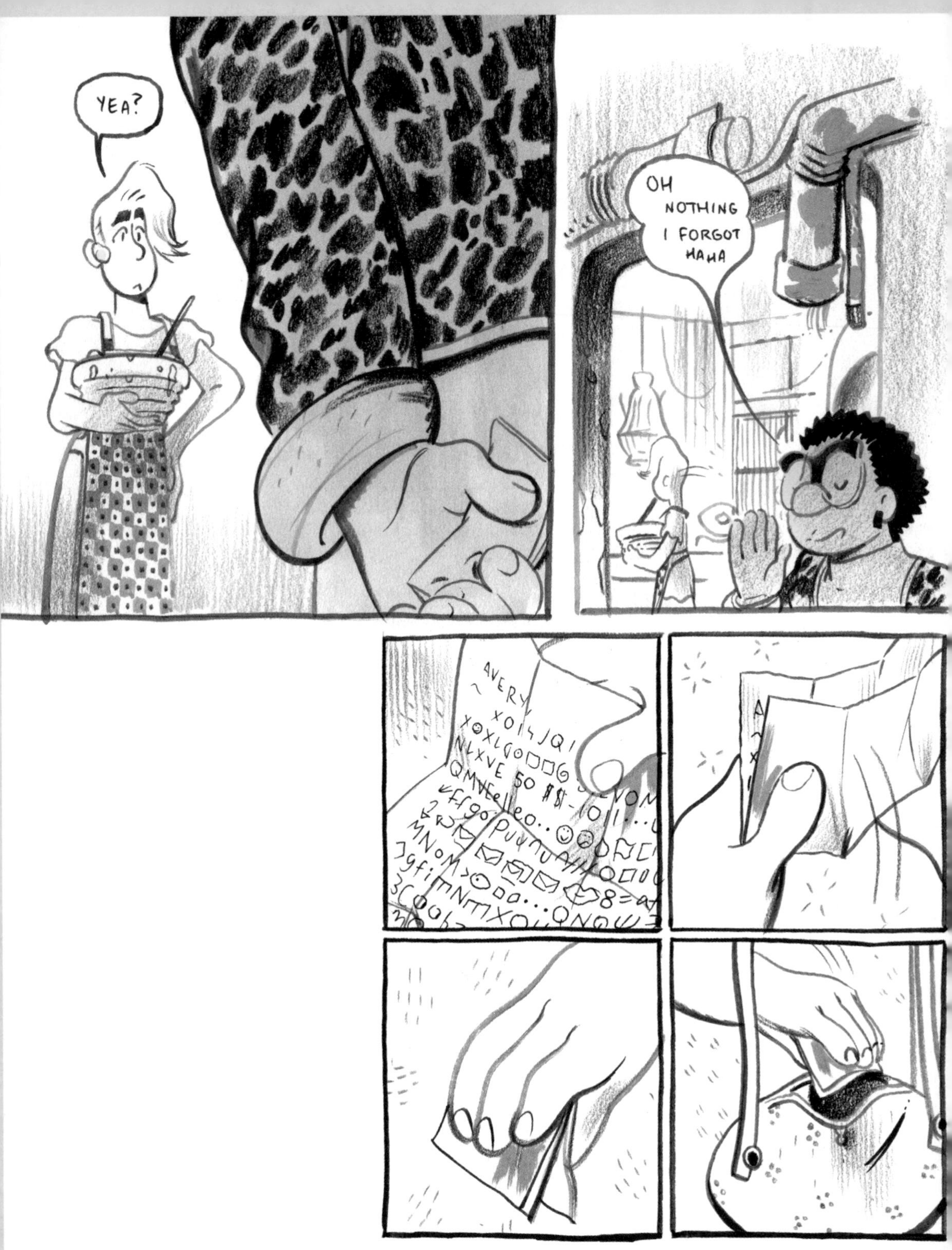
YEA?
OH NOTHING I FORGOT HAHA
AVERY

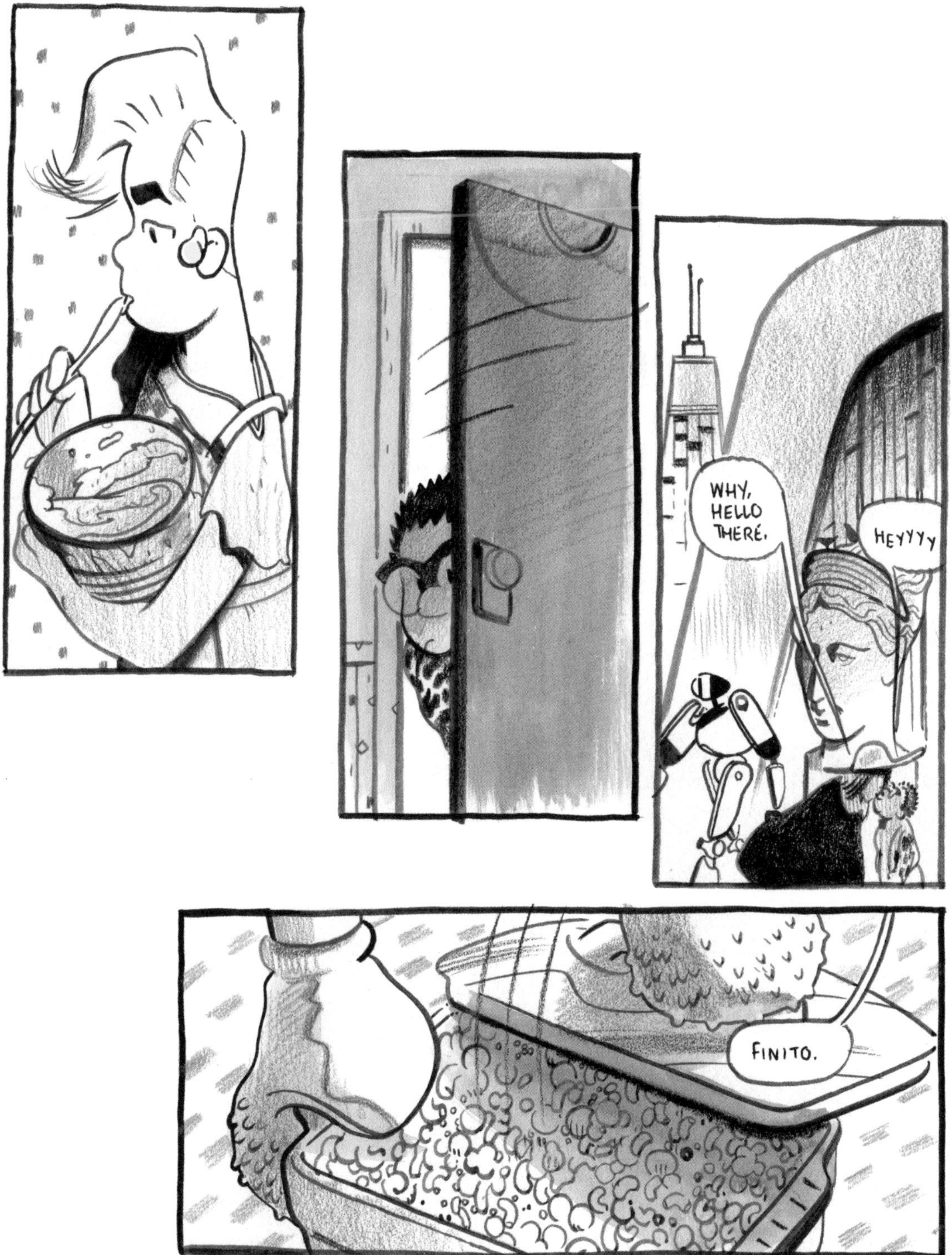
WHY, HELLO THERE.
HEYYYY
FINITO.

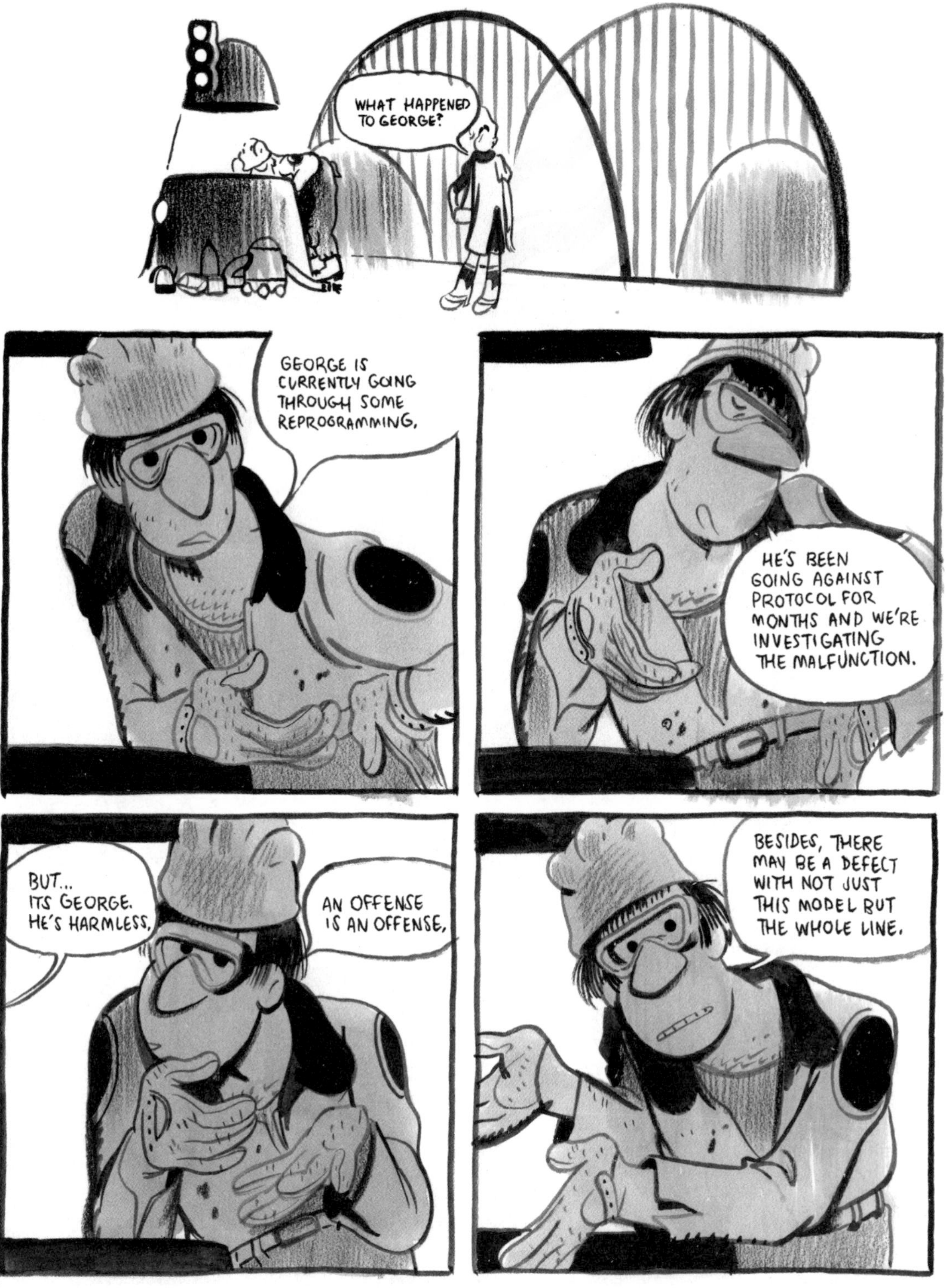
WHAT HAPPENED TO GEORGE?
GEORGE IS CURRENTLY GOING THROUGH SOME REPROGRAMMING.
HE'S BEEN GOING AGAINST PROTOCOL FOR MONTHS AND WE'RE INVESTIGATING THE MALFUNCTION.
BUT... ITS GEORGE. HE'S HARMLESS.
AN OFFENSE IS AN OFFENSE.
BESIDES, THERE MAY BE A DEFECT WITH NOT JUST THIS MODEL BUT THE WHOLE LINE.

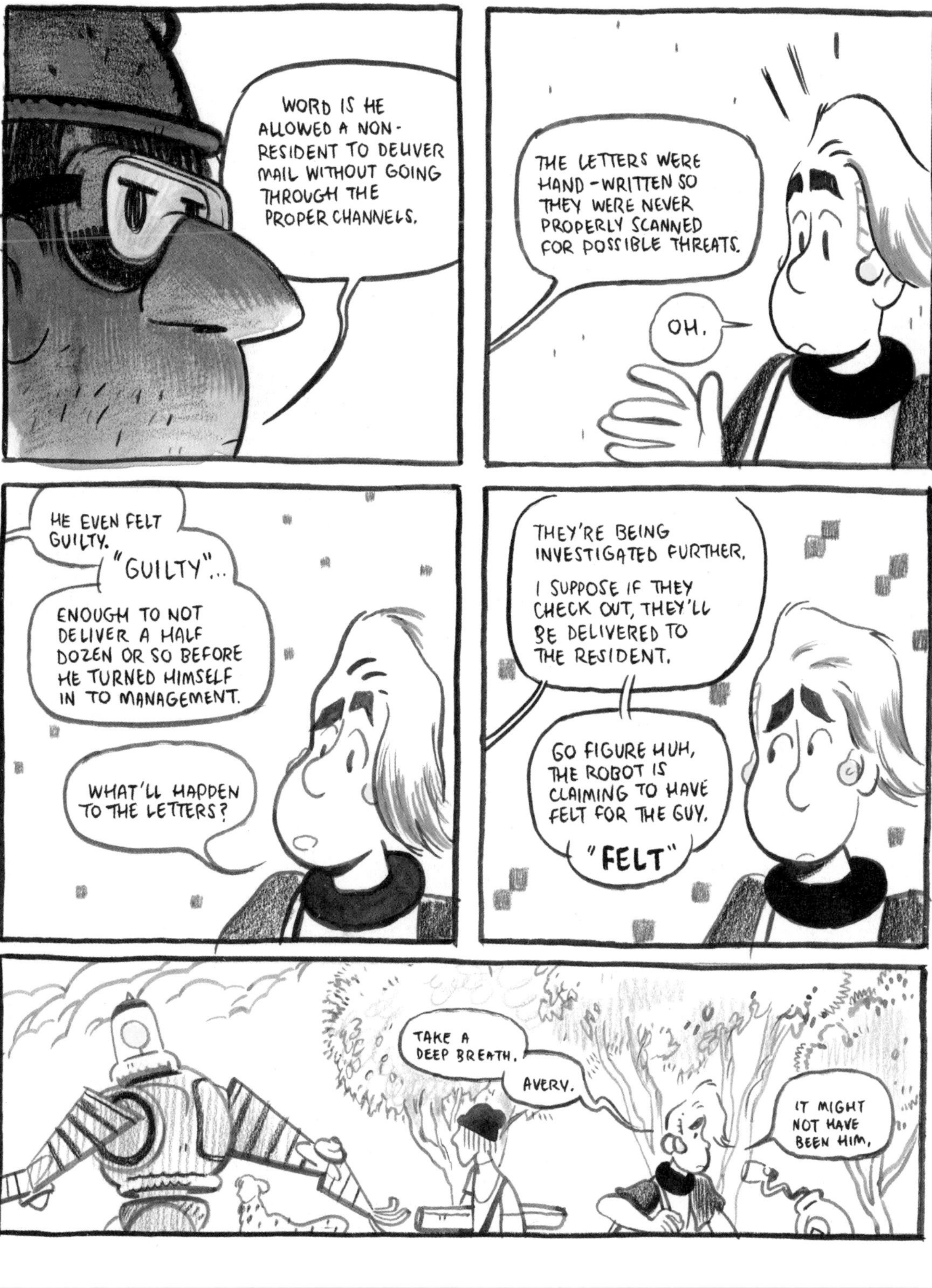
WORD IS HE ALLOWED A NON-RESIDENT TO DELIVER MAIL WITHOUT GOING THROUGH THE PROPER CHANNELS.
THE LETTERS WERE HAND-WRITTEN SO THEY WERE NEVER PROPERLY SCANNED FOR POSSIBLE THREATS.
OH.
HE EVEN FELT GUILTY.
"GUILTY"...
ENOUGH TO NOT DELIVER A HALF DOZEN OR SO BEFORE HE TURNED HIMSELF IN TO MANAGEMENT.
WHAT'LL HAPPEN TO THE LETTERS?
THEY'RE BEING INVESTIGATED FURTHER.
I SUPPOSE IF THEY CHECK OUT, THEY'LL BE DELIVERED TO THE RESIDENT.
GO FIGURE HUH, THE ROBOT IS CLAIMING TO HAVE FELT FOR THE GUY.
"FELT"
TAKE A DEEP BREATH.
AVERY.
IT MIGHT NOT HAVE BEEN HIM.

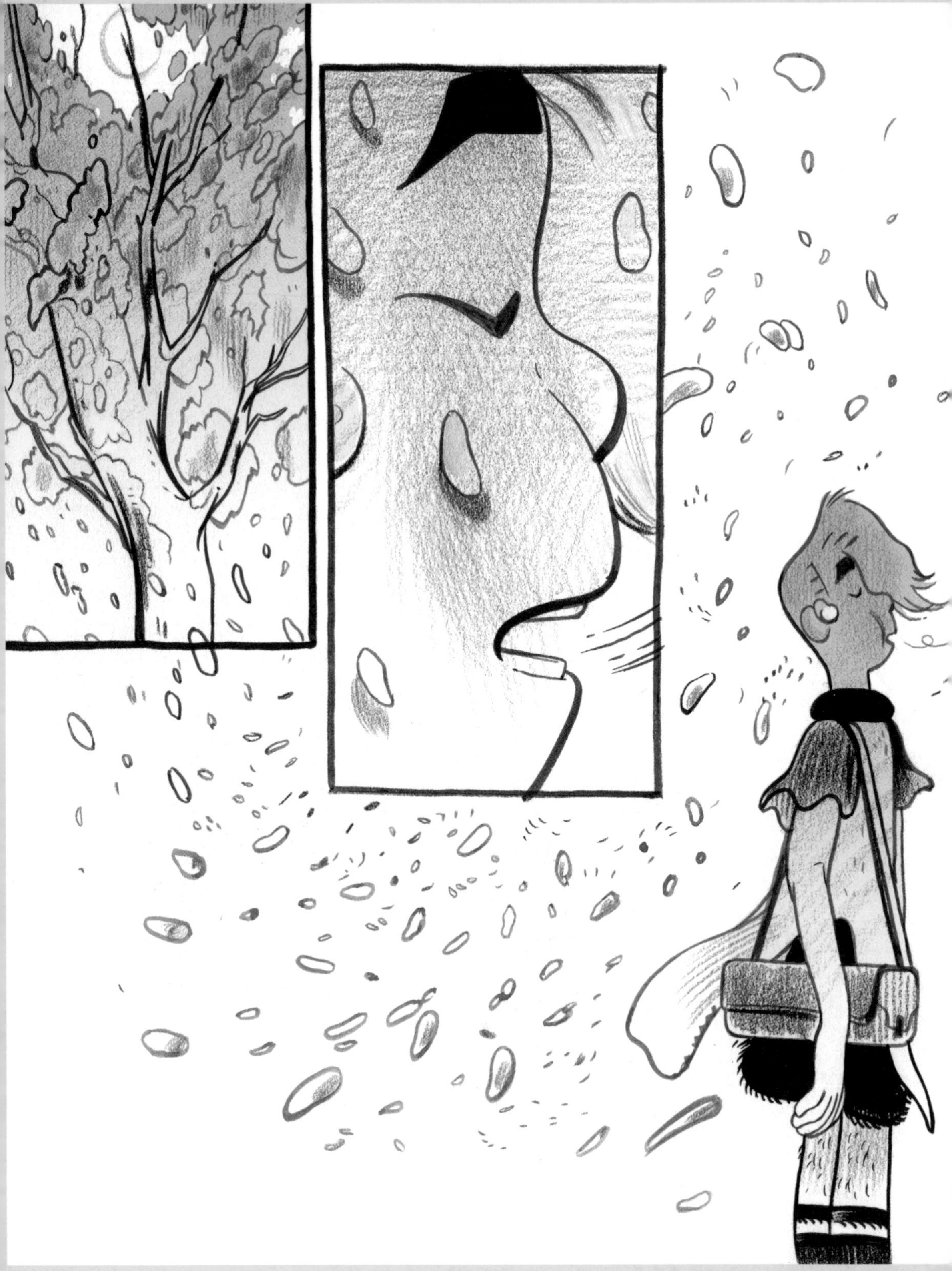

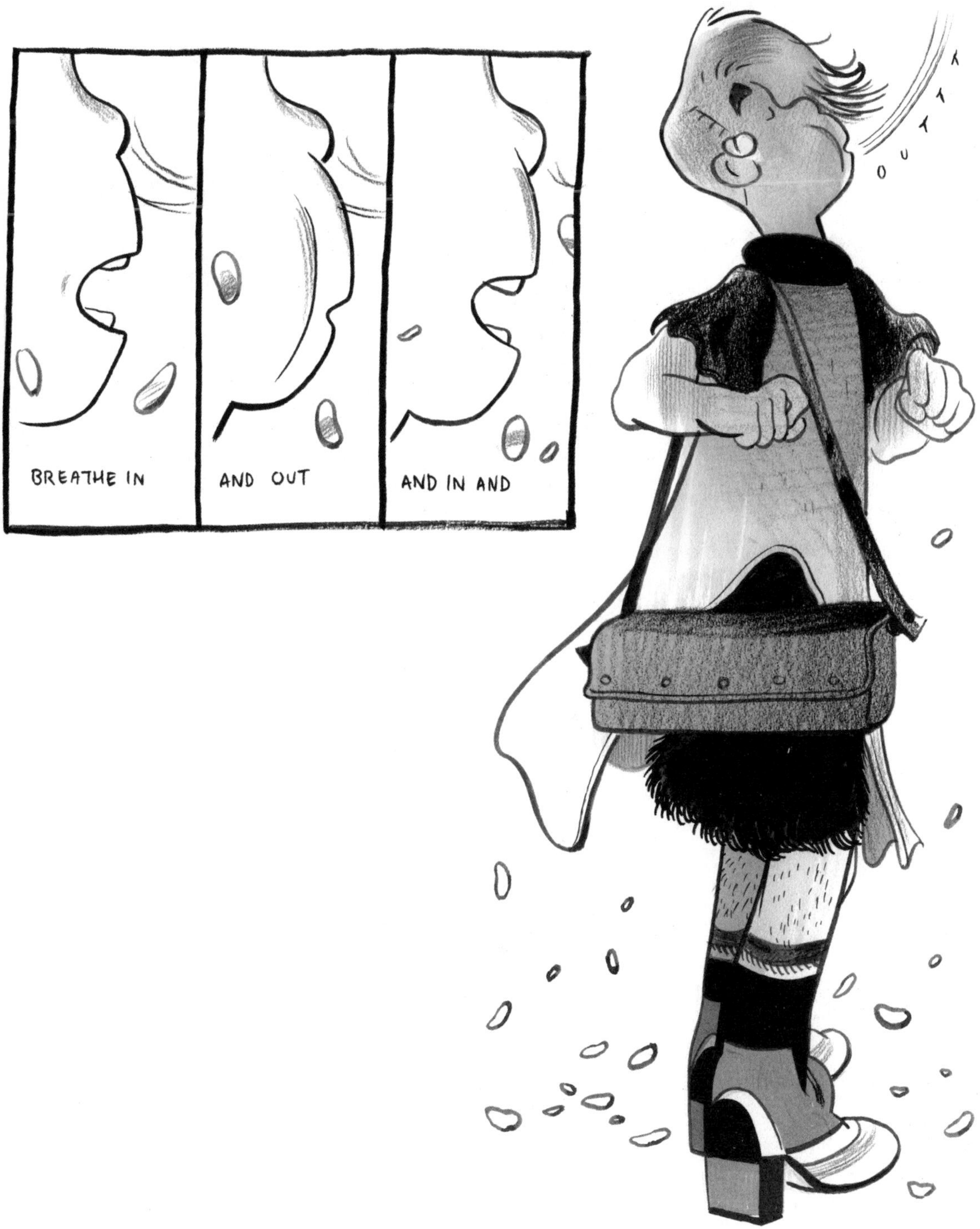
BREATHE IN
AND OUT
AND IN AND
OUTTT

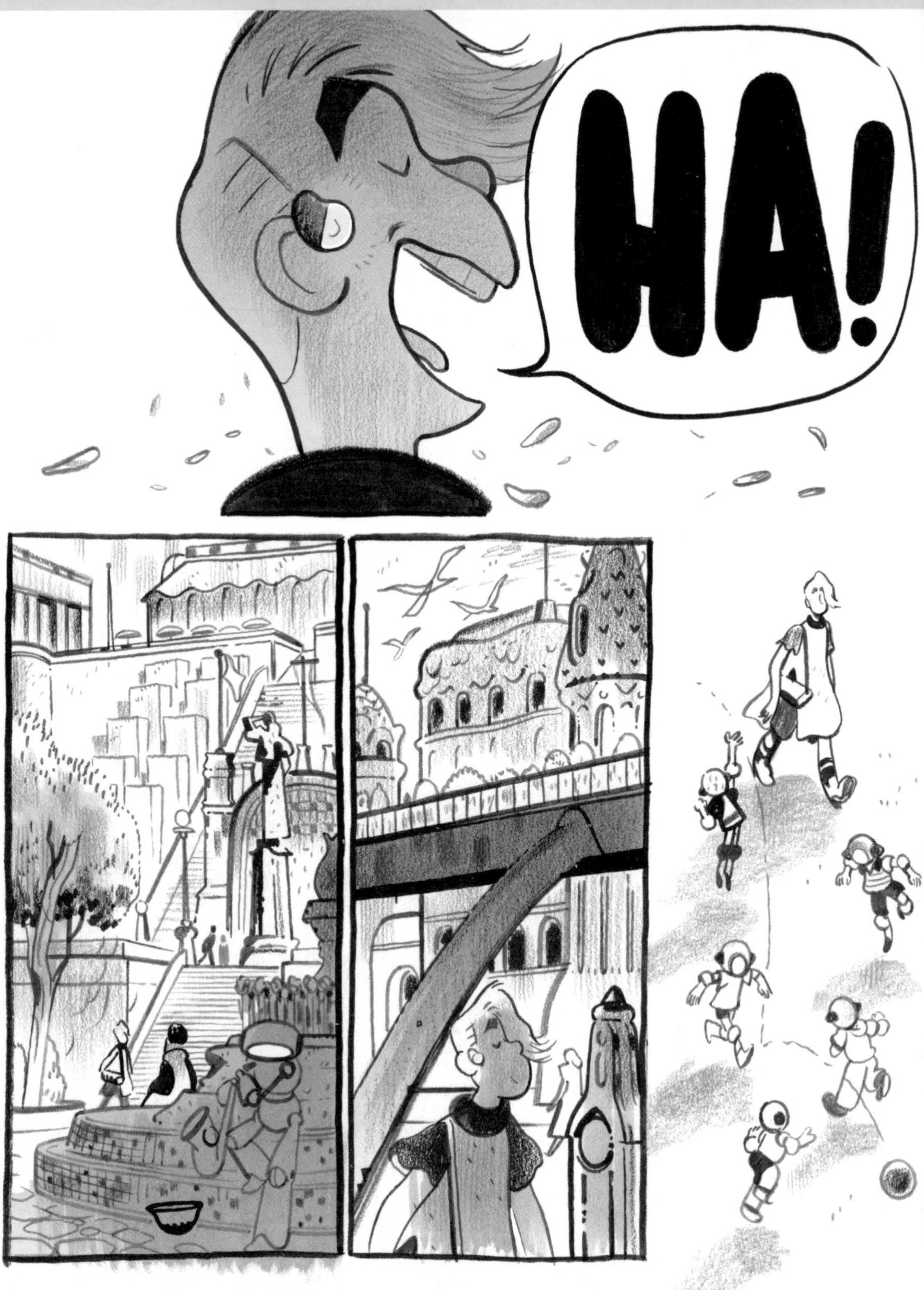
HA!

VROOOMMMM

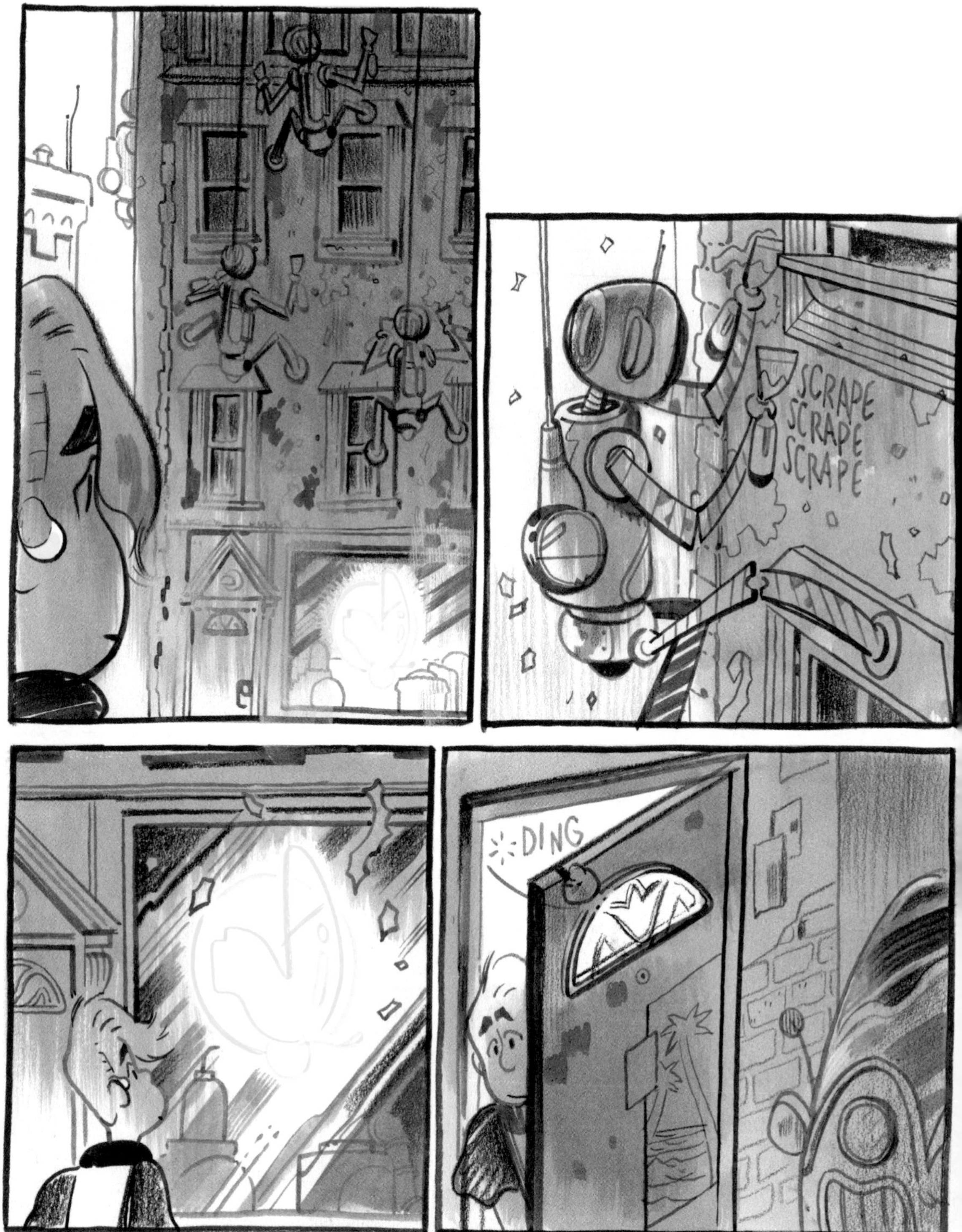
SCRAPE
SCRAPE
SCRAPE
DING

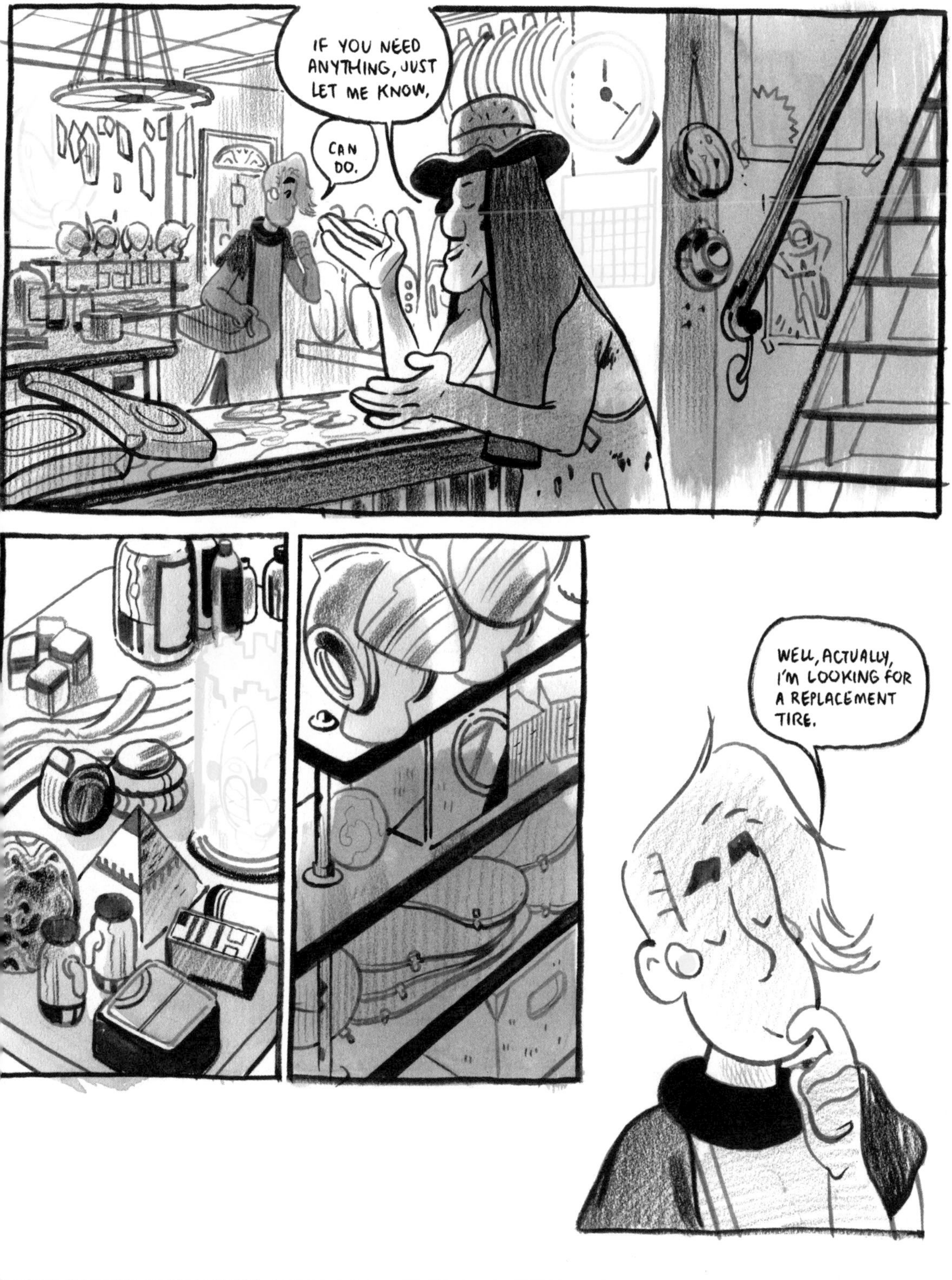
IF YOU NEED ANYTHING, JUST LET ME KNOW,
CAN DO.
WELL, ACTUALLY, I'M LOOKING FOR A REPLACEMENT TIRE.

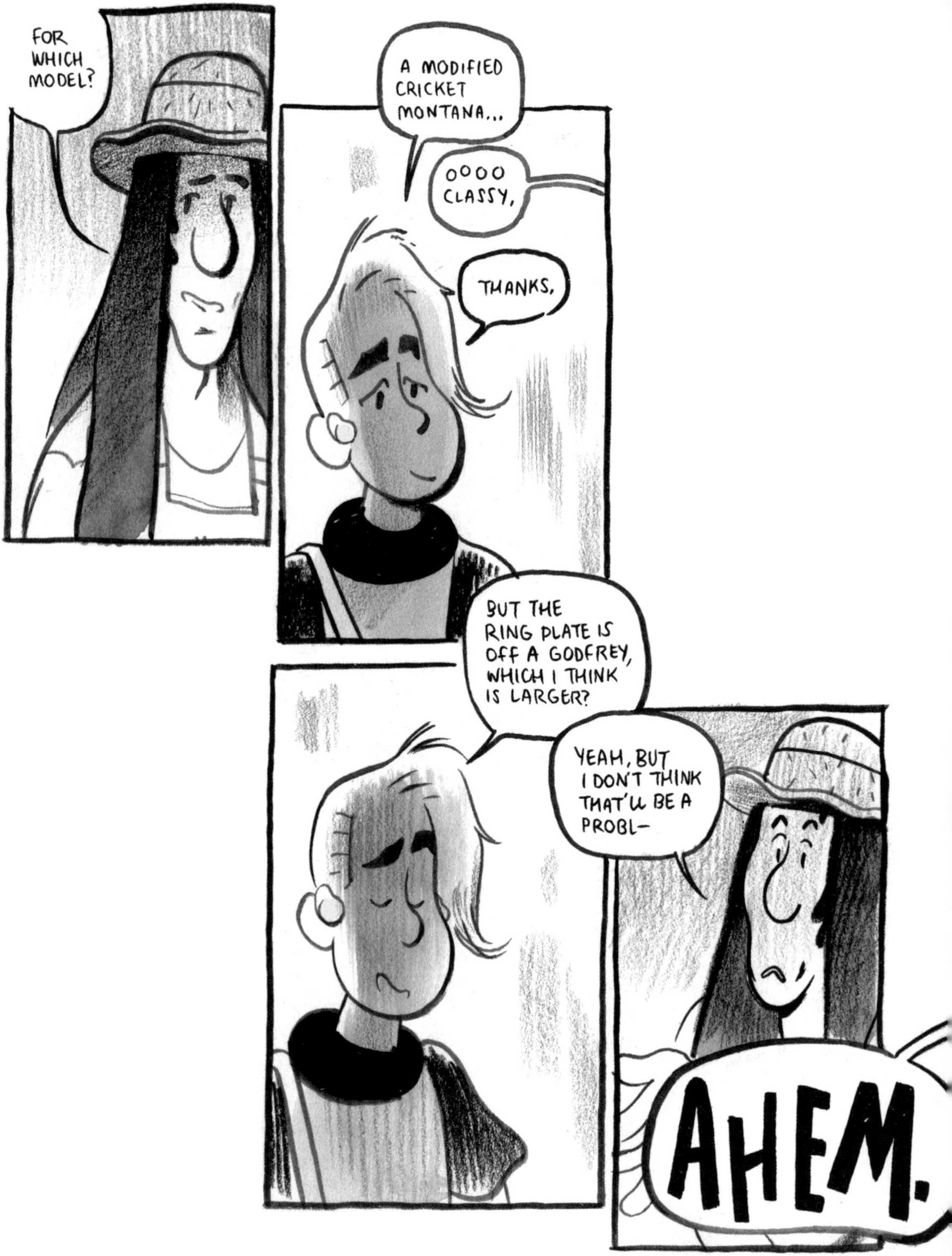
FOR WHICH MODEL?
A MODIFIED CRICKET MONTANA...
OOOO CLASSY,
THANKS,
BUT THE RING PLATE IS OFF A GODFREY, WHICH I THINK IS LARGER?
YEAH, BUT I DON'T THINK THAT'LL BE A PROBL-
AHEM.

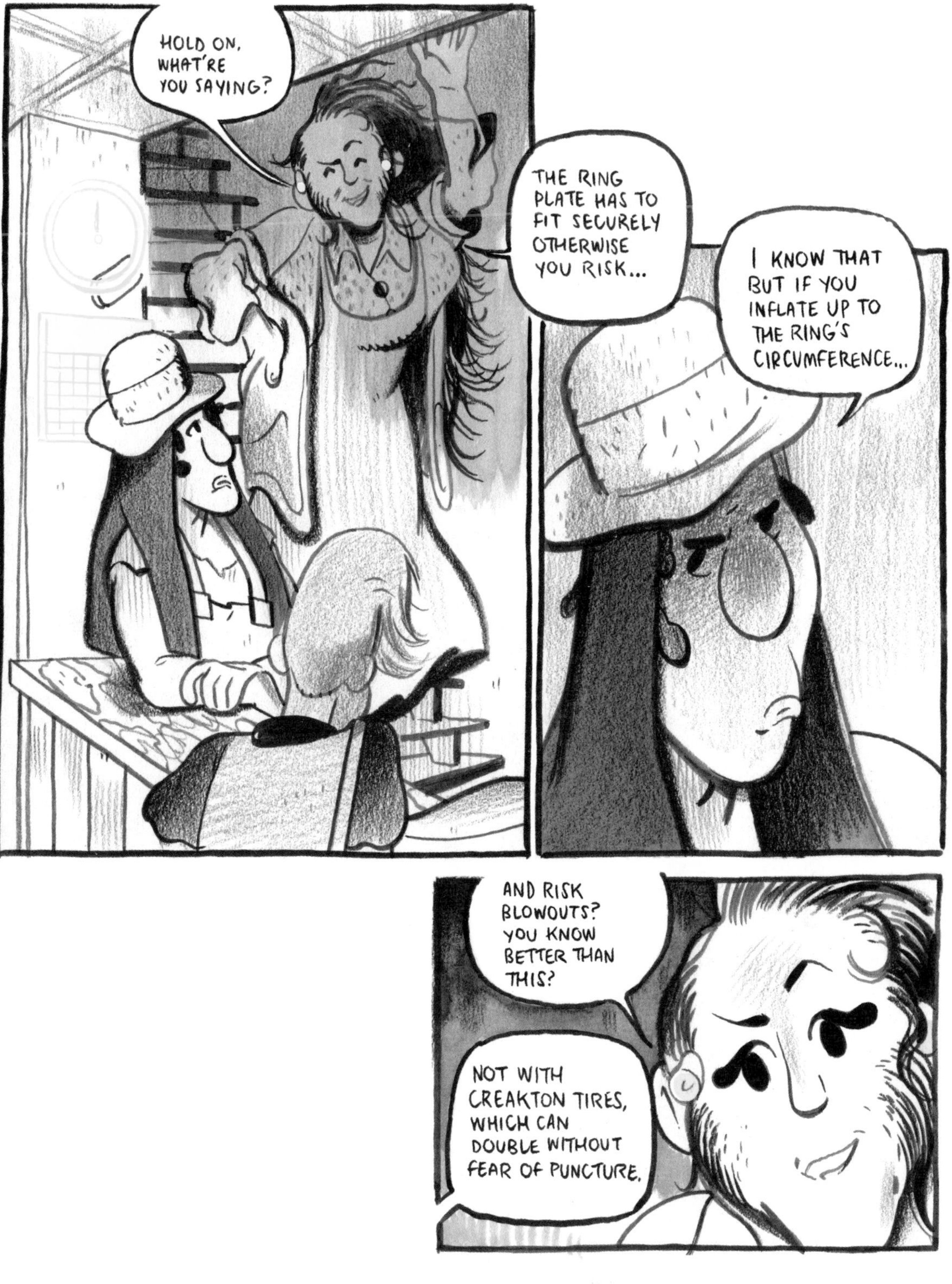
HOLD ON, WHAT'RE YOU SAYING?
THE RING PLATE HAS TO FIT SECURELY OTHERWISE YOU RISK...
I KNOW THAT BUT IF YOU INFLATE UP TO THE RING'S CIRCUMFERENCE...
AND RISK BLOWOUTS? YOU KNOW BETTER THAN THIS?
NOT WITH CREAKTON TIRES, WHICH CAN DOUBLE WITHOUT FEAR OF PUNCTURE.

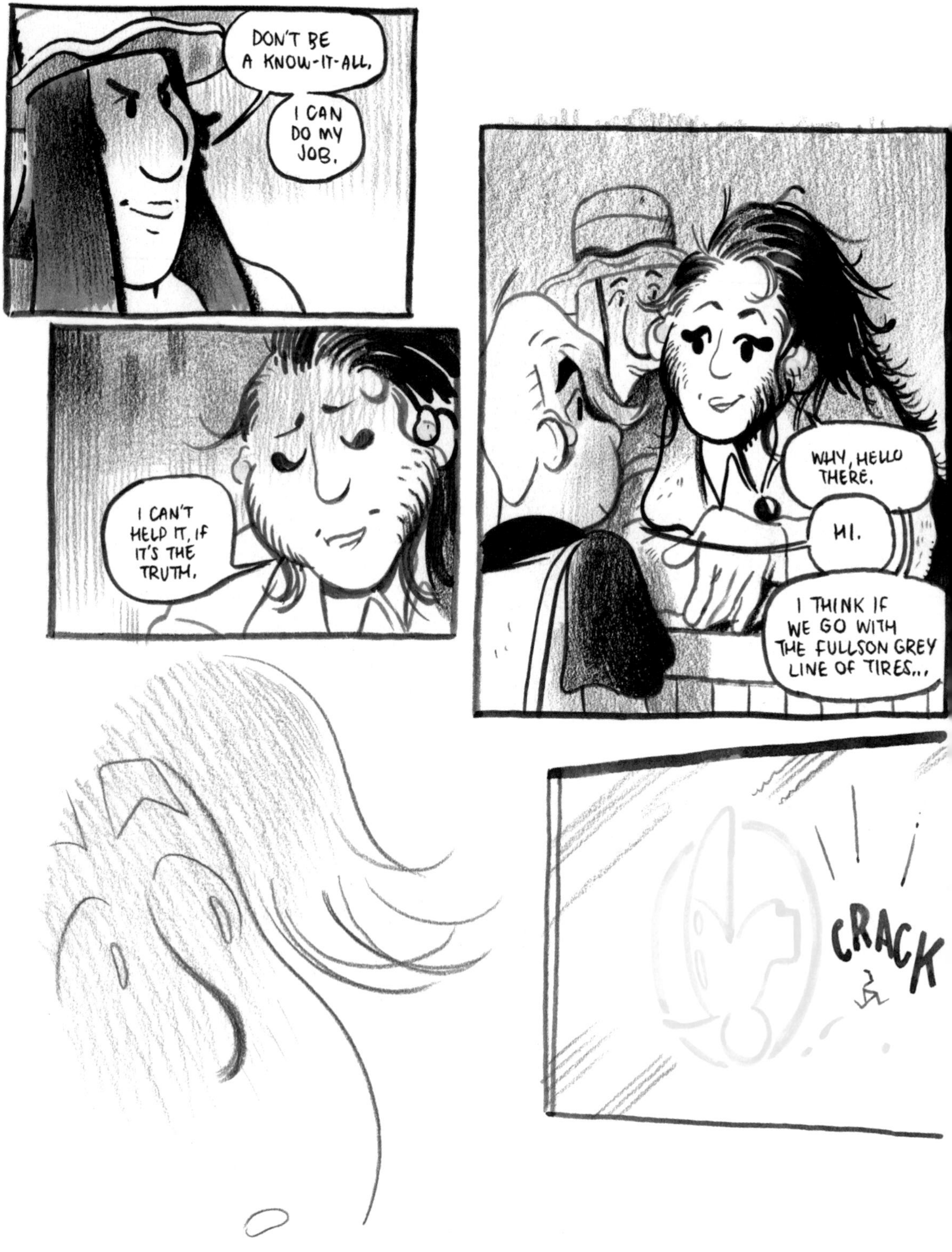
DON'T BE A KNOW-IT-ALL.
I CAN DO MY JOB.
I CAN'T HELP IT, IF IT'S THE TRUTH.
WHY, HELLO THERE.
HI.
I THINK IF WE GO WITH THE FULLSON GREY LINE OF TIRES...
CRACK

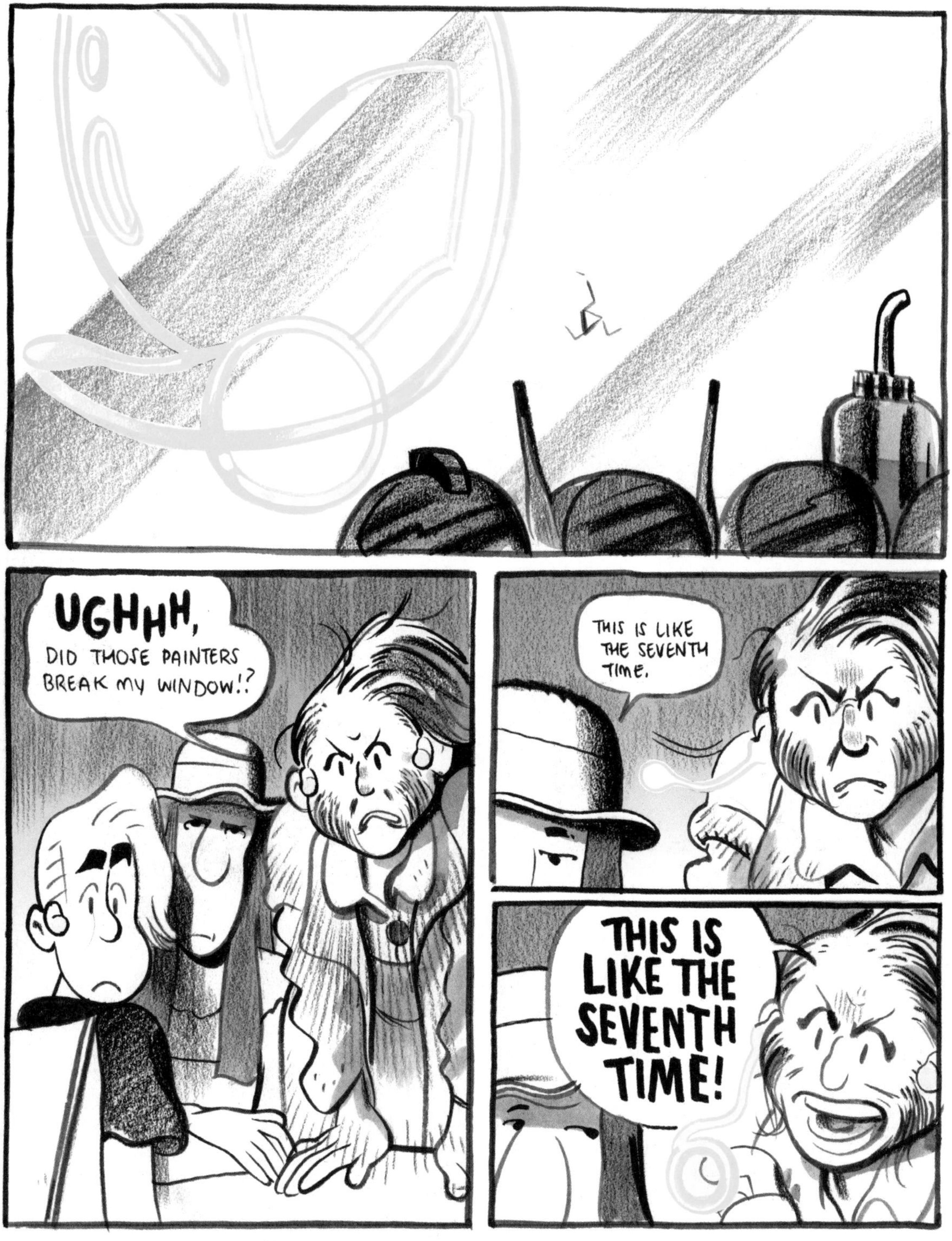
UGHHH,
DID THOSE PAINTERS BREAK MY WINDOW!?
THIS IS LIKE THE SEVENTH TIME.
THIS IS LIKE THE SEVENTH TIME!

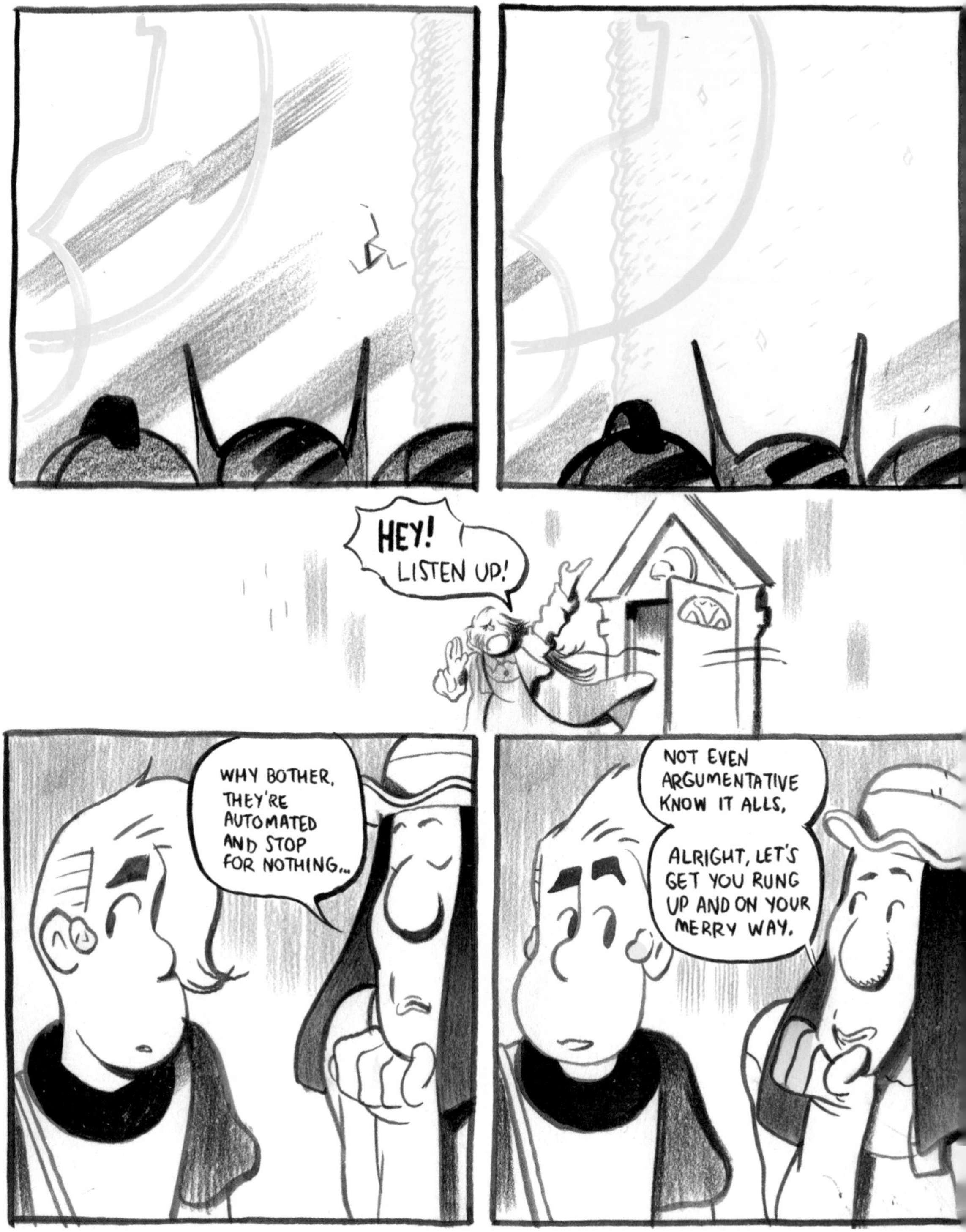
HEY! LISTEN UP!
WHY BOTHER, THEY'RE AUTOMATED AND STOP FOR NOTHING...
NOT EVEN ARGUMENTATIVE KNOW IT ALLS.
ALRIGHT, LET'S GET YOU RUNG UP AND ON YOUR MERRY WAY.

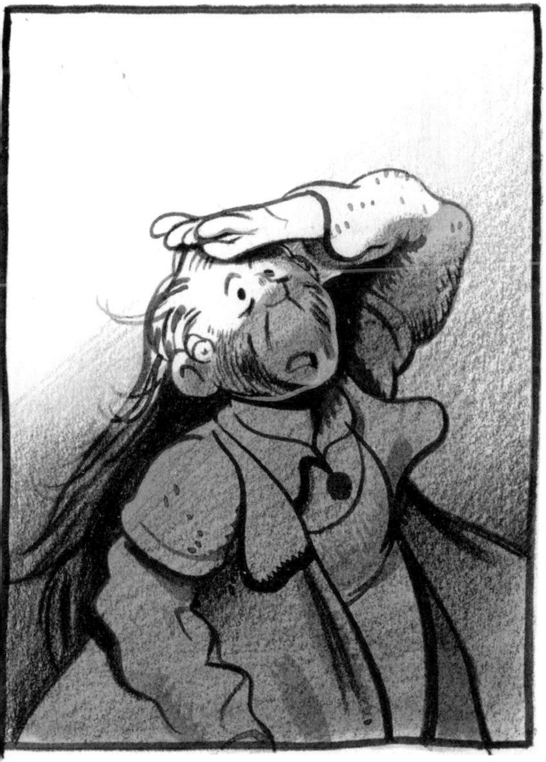

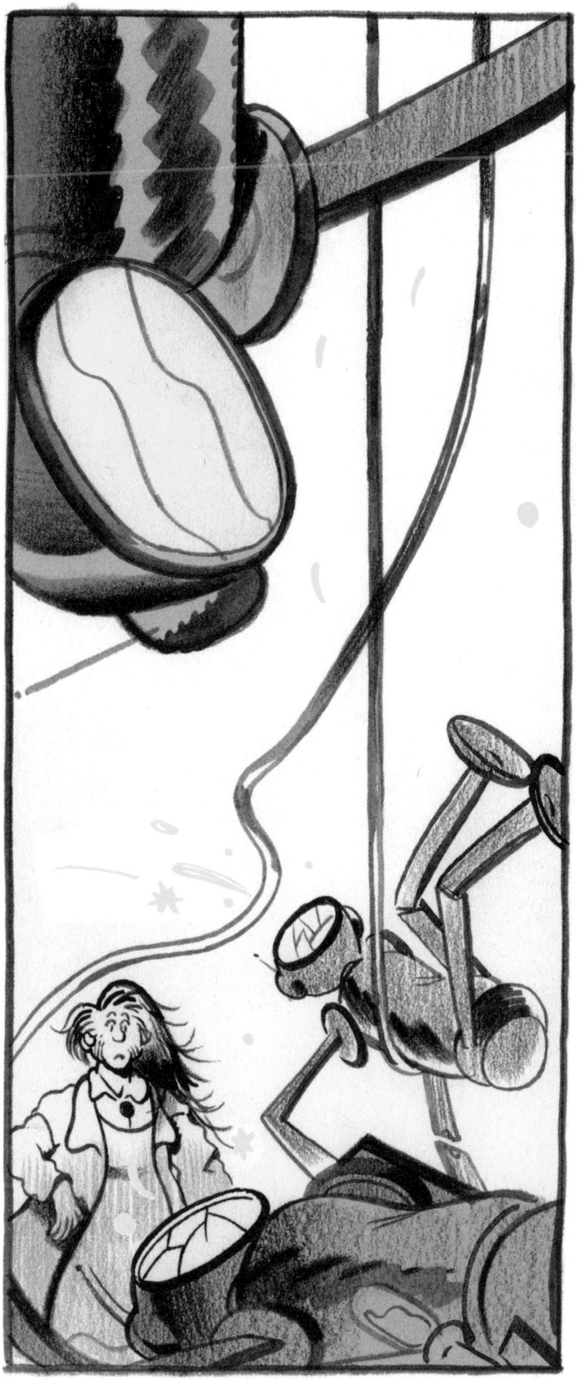

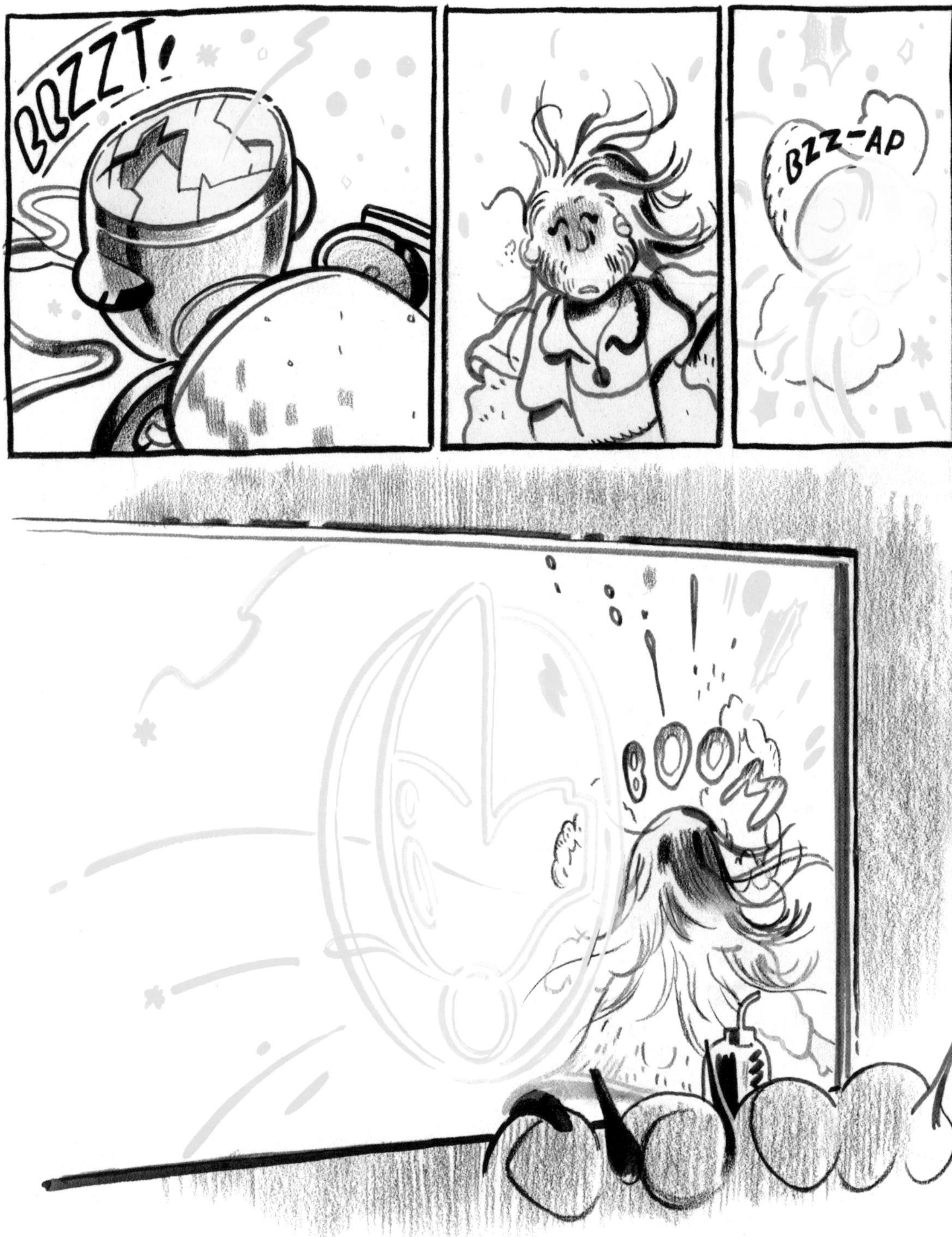
BBZZZT!
BZZ-AP
BOOM

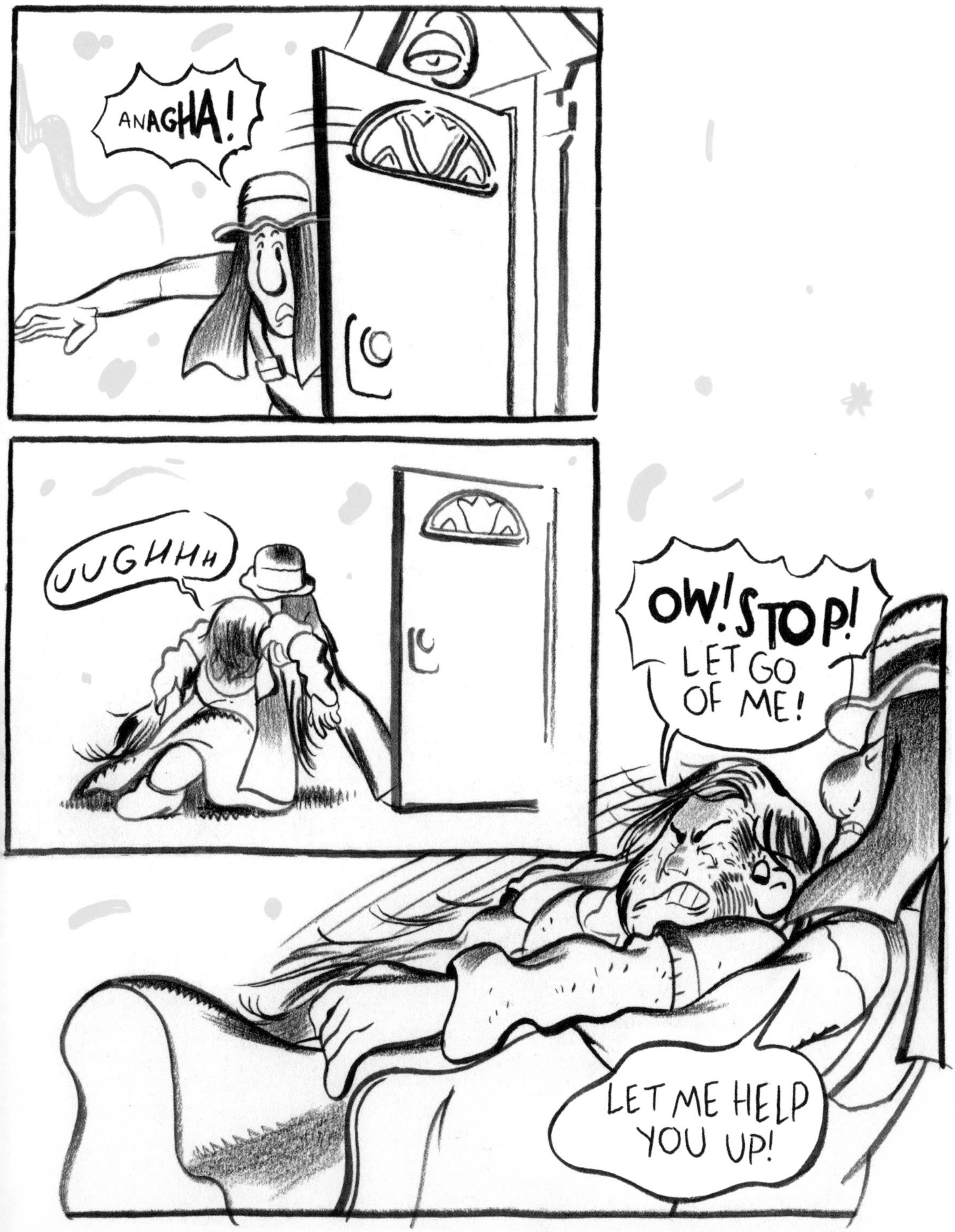
ANAGHA!
UUGHHH
OW! STOP! LET GO OF ME!
LET ME HELP YOU UP!

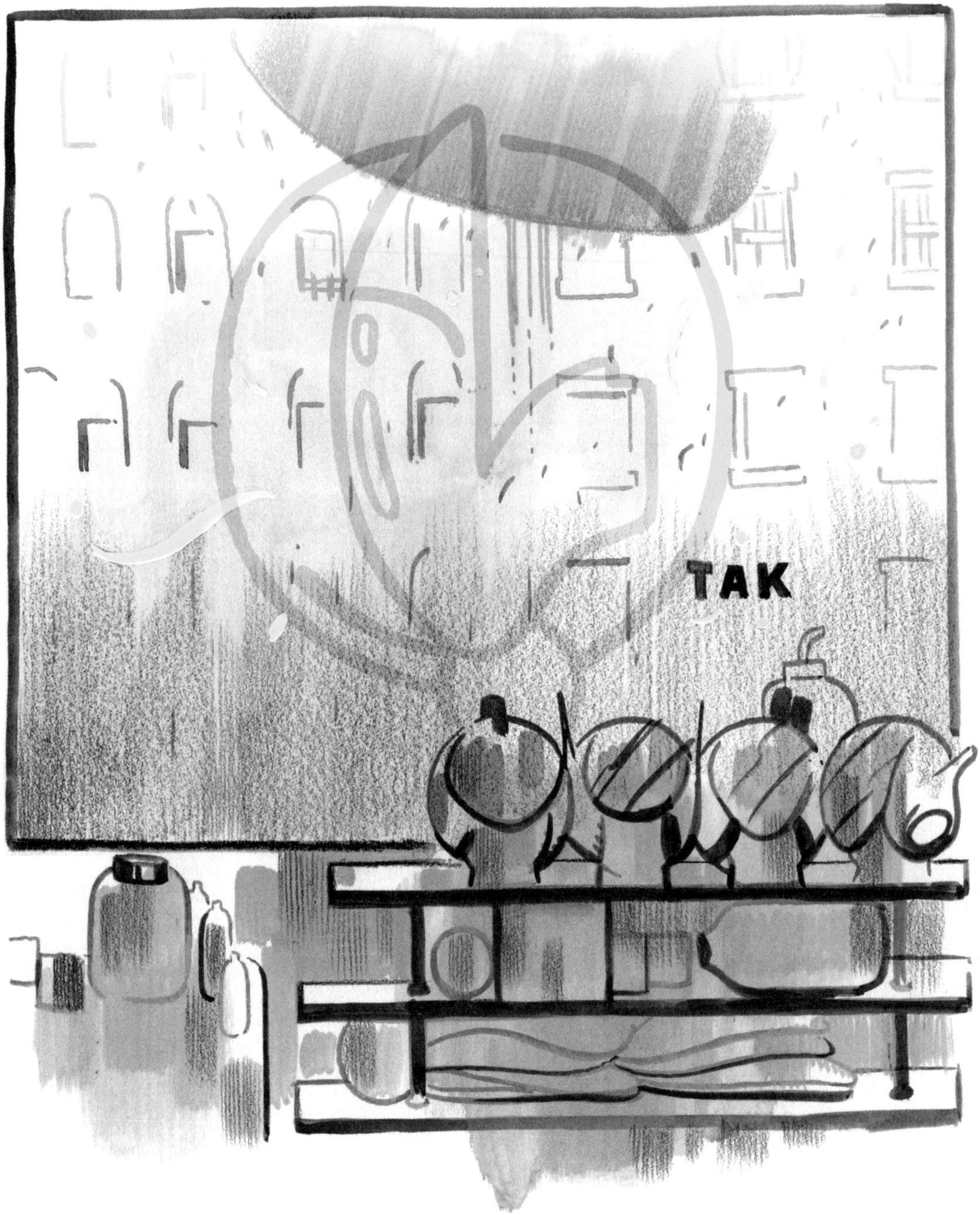
TAK

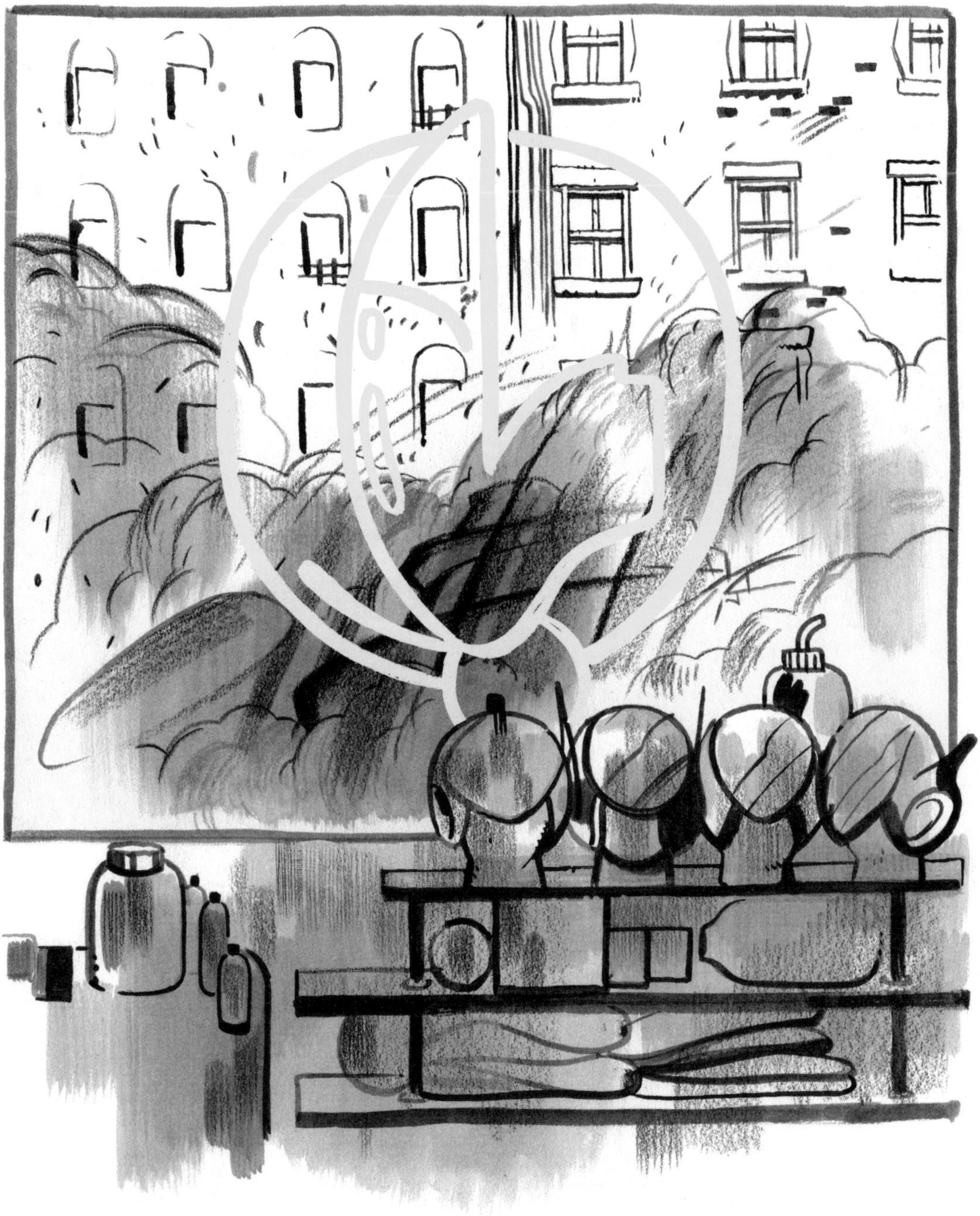

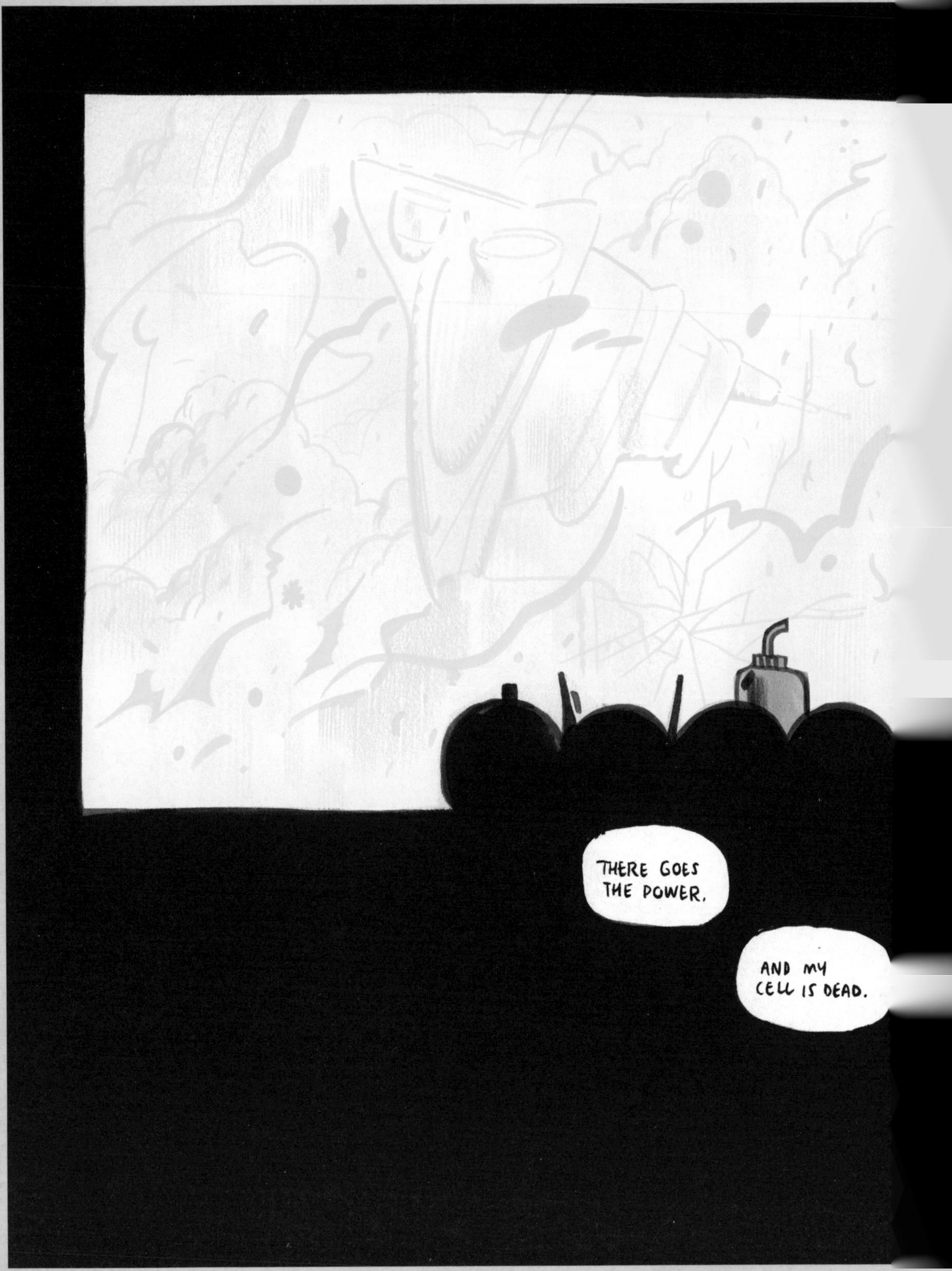
THERE GOES THE POWER.
AND MY CELL IS DEAD.

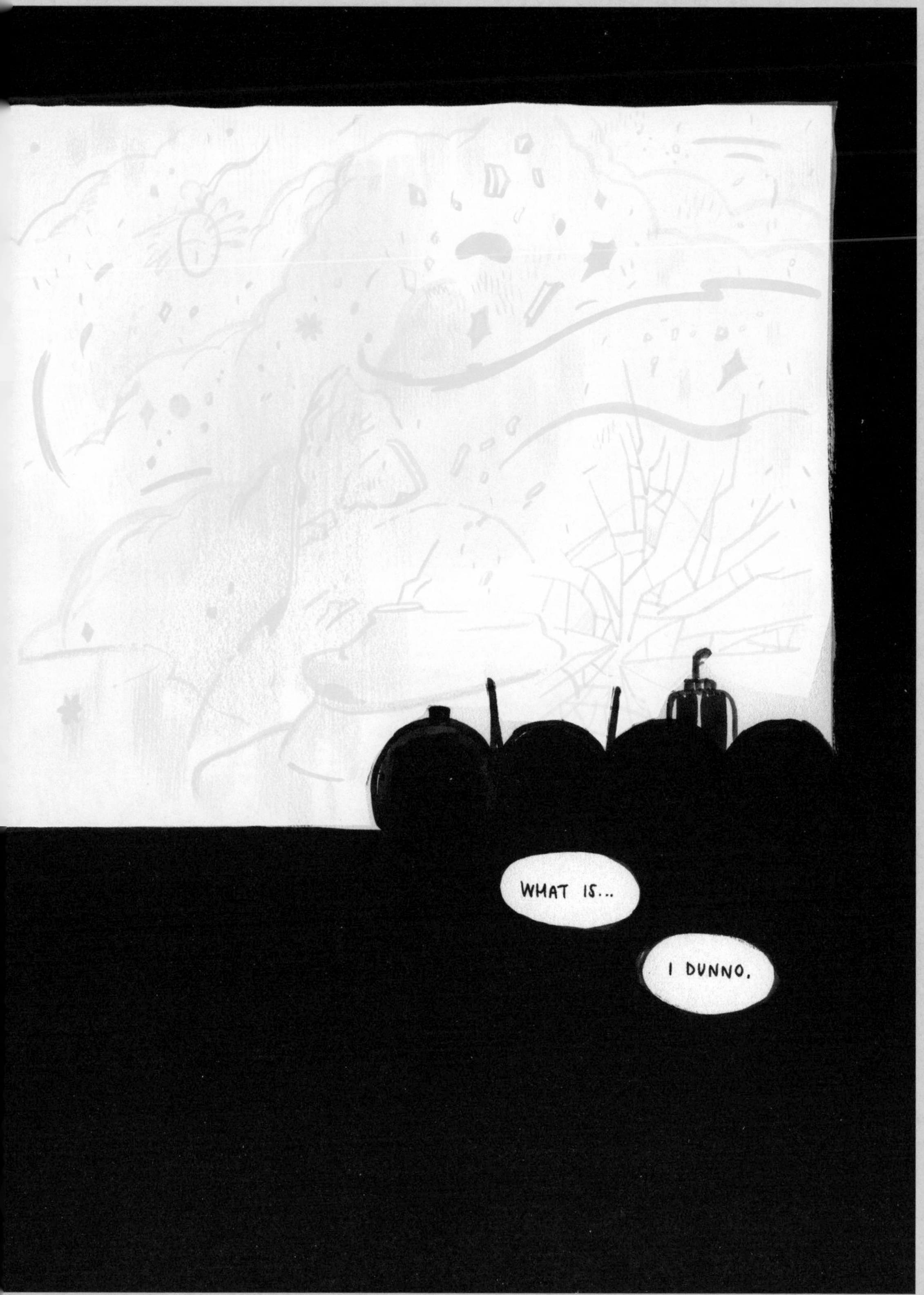
WHAT IS...
I DUNNO.

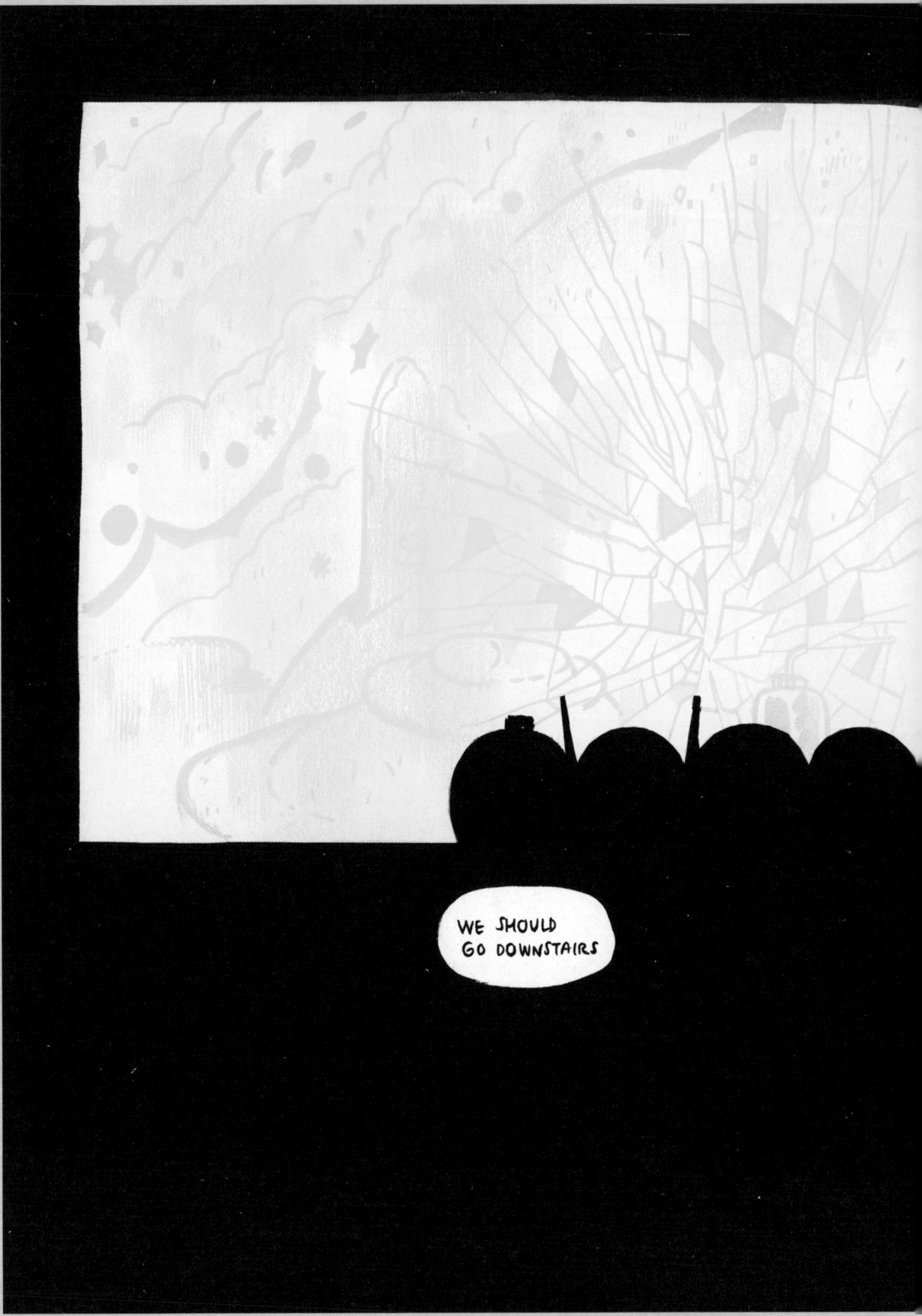
WE SHOULD GO DOWNSTAIRS

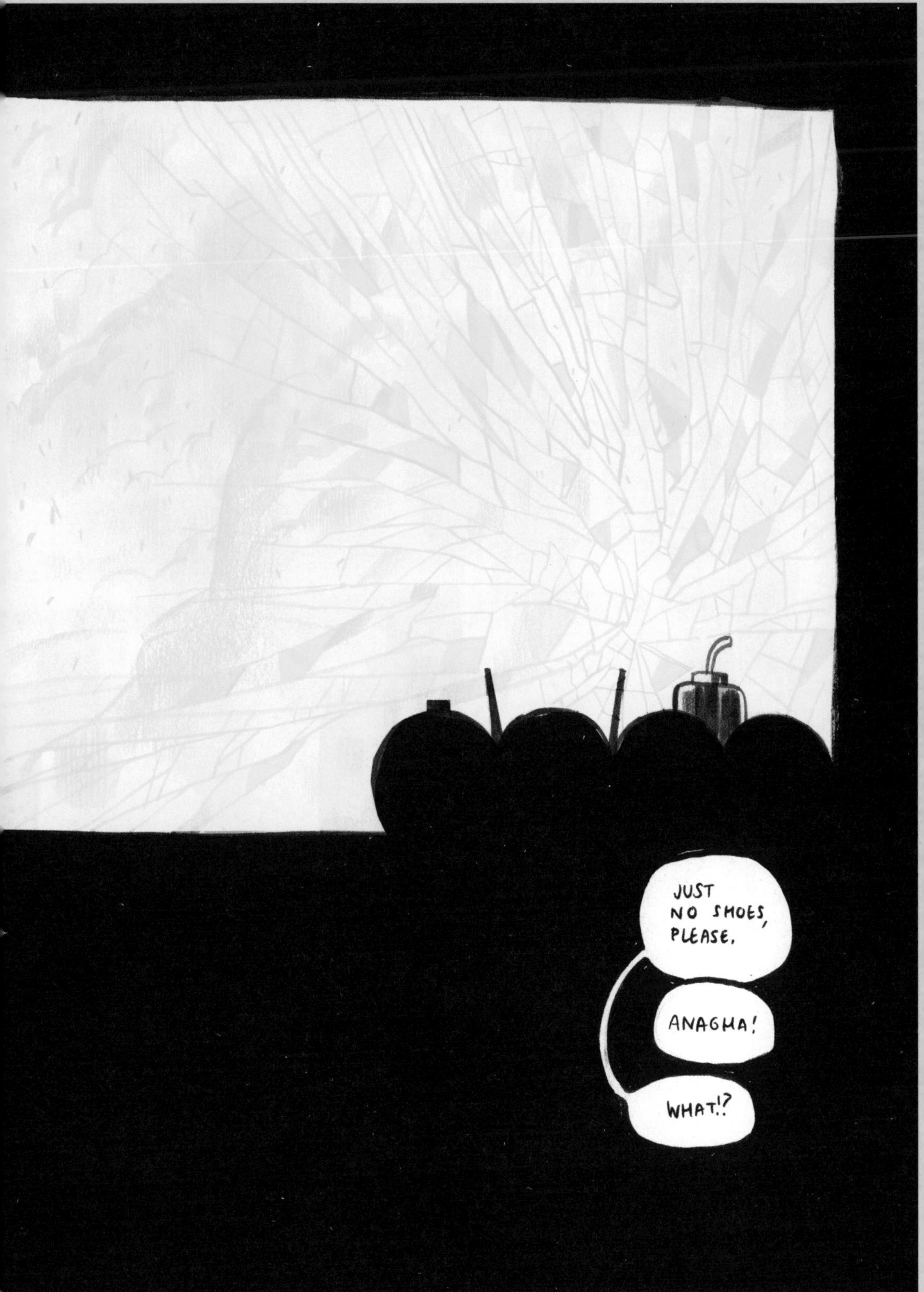
JUST NO SHOES, PLEASE.
ANAGHA!
WHAT!?

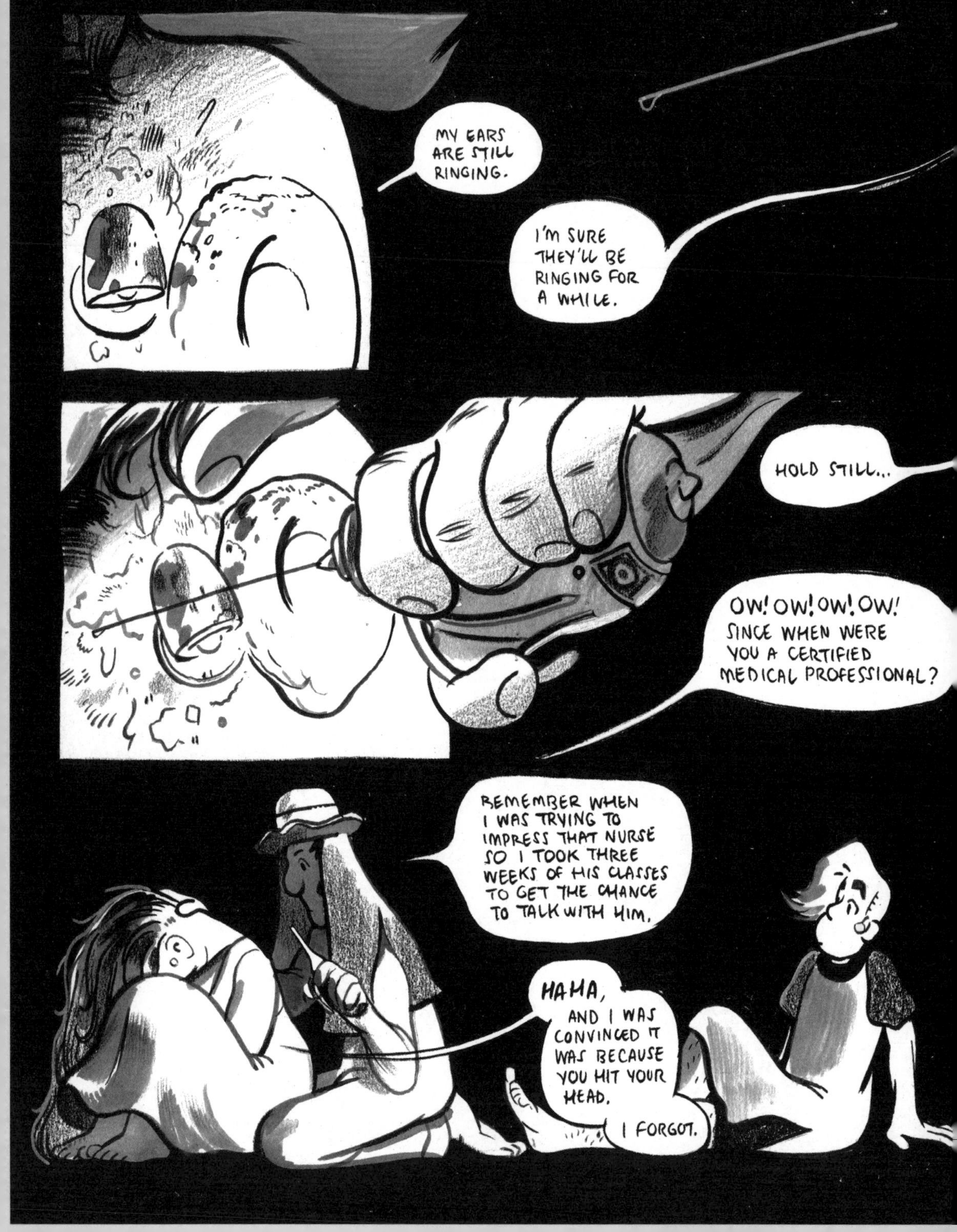
MY EARS ARE STILL RINGING.
I'M SURE THEY'LL BE RINGING FOR A WHILE.
HOLD STILL...
OW! OW! OW! OW! SINCE WHEN WERE YOU A CERTIFIED MEDICAL PROFESSIONAL?
REMEMBER WHEN I WAS TRYING TO IMPRESS THAT NURSE SO I TOOK THREE WEEKS OF HIS CLASSES TO GET THE CHANCE TO TALK WITH HIM.
HAHA,
AND I WAS CONVINCED IT WAS BECAUSE YOU HIT YOUR HEAD.
I FORGOT.

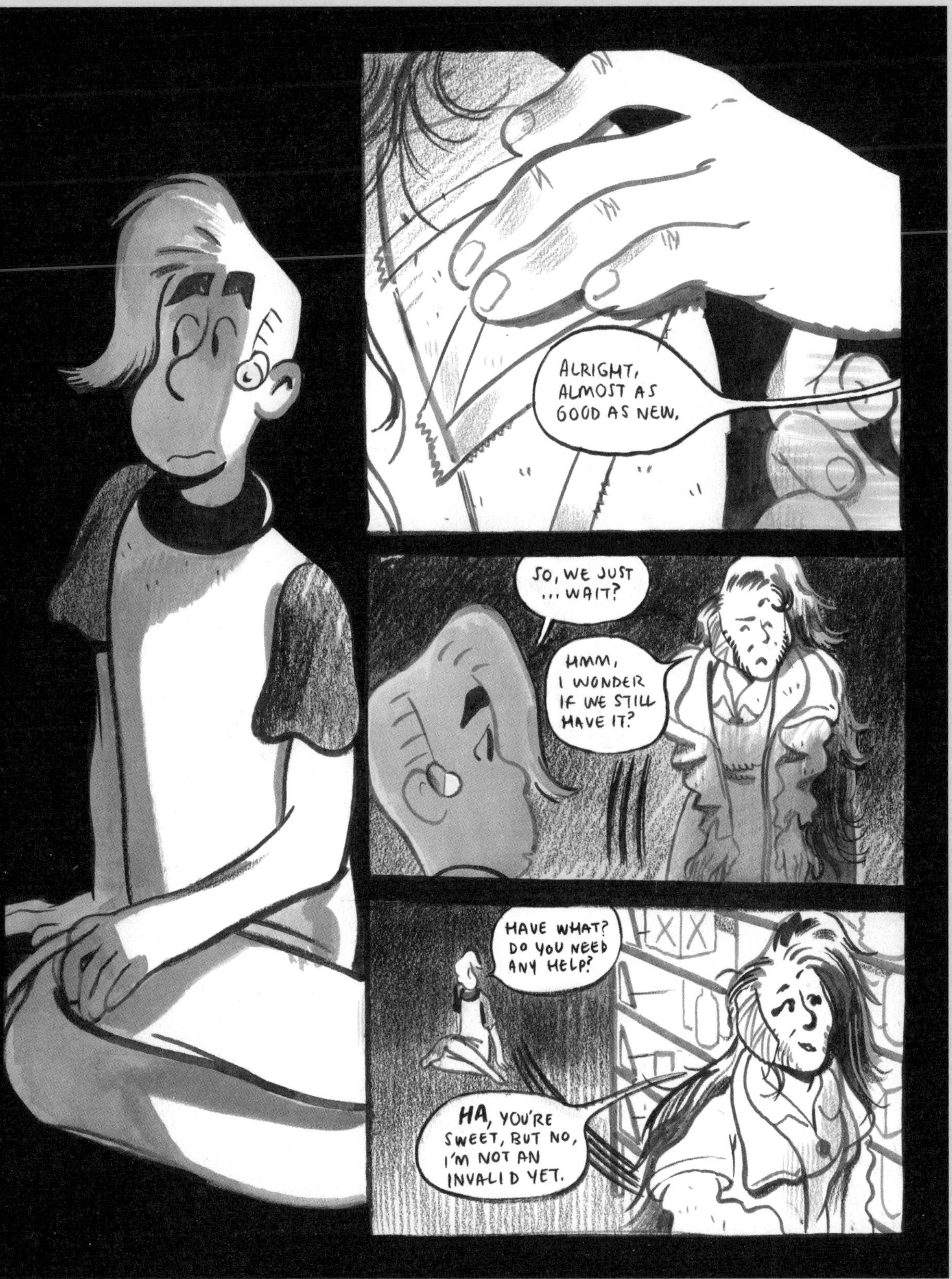
ALRIGHT, ALMOST AS GOOD AS NEW.
SO, WE JUST ... WAIT?
HMM, I WONDER IF WE STILL HAVE IT?
HAVE WHAT? DO YOU NEED ANY HELP?
HA, YOU'RE SWEET, BUT NO, I'M NOT AN INVALID YET.

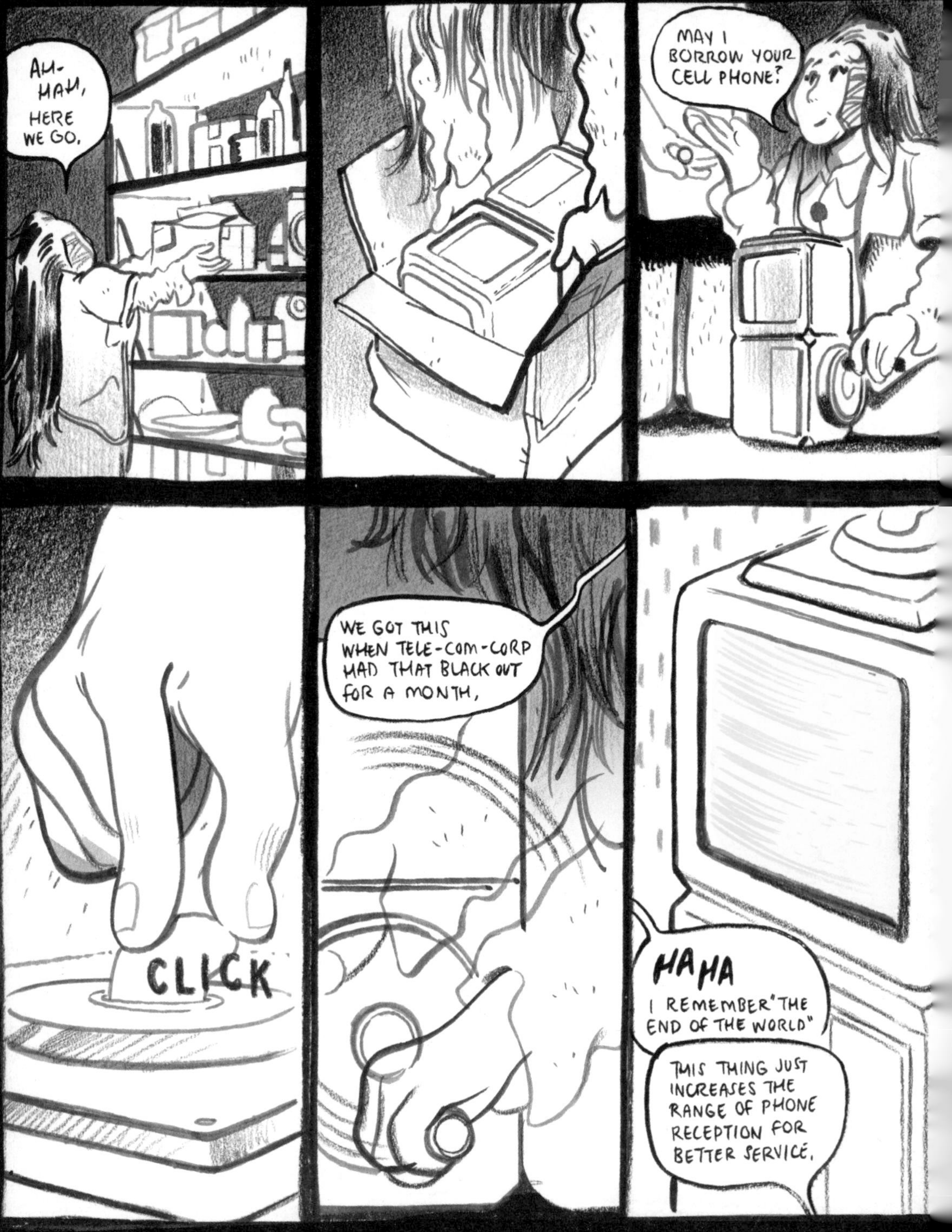
AH-HAH, HERE WE GO.
MAY I BORROW YOUR CELL PHONE?
CLICK
WE GOT THIS WHEN TELE-COM-CORP HAD THAT BLACK OUT FOR A MONTH.
HAHA
I REMEMBER "THE END OF THE WORLD"
THIS THING JUST INCREASES THE RANGE OF PHONE RECEPTION FOR BETTER SERVICE.

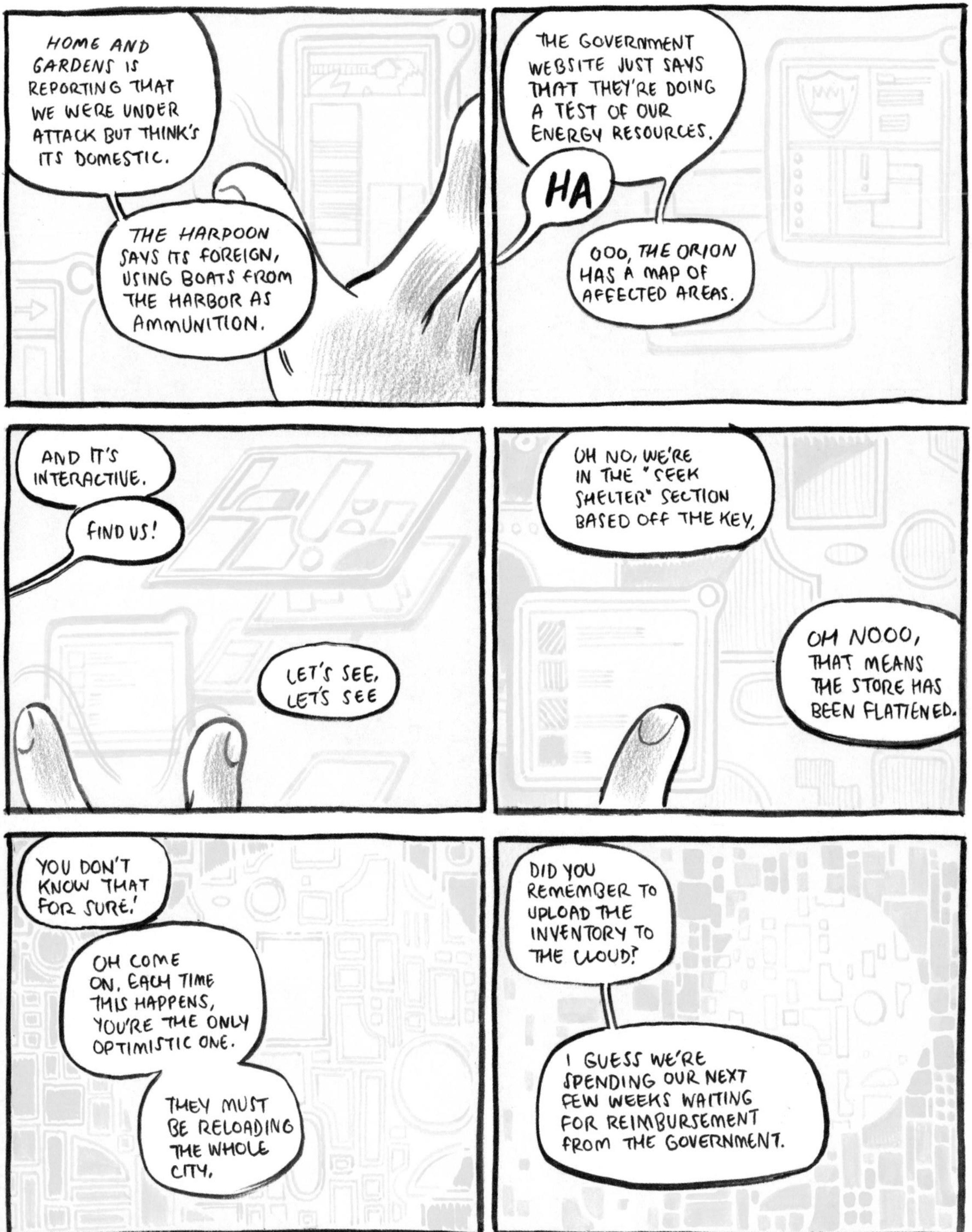
HOME AND GARDENS IS REPORTING THAT WE WERE UNDER ATTACK BUT THINK'S ITS DOMESTIC.
THE HARPOON SAYS ITS FOREIGN, USING BOATS FROM THE HARBOR AS AMMUNITION.
THE GOVERNMENT WEBSITE JUST SAYS THAT THEY'RE DOING A TEST OF OUR ENERGY RESOURCES.
HA
OOO, THE ORION HAS A MAP OF AFFECTED AREAS.
AND IT'S INTERACTIVE.
FIND US!
LET'S SEE, LET'S SEE
OH NO, WE'RE IN THE "SEEK SHELTER" SECTION BASED OFF THE KEY,
OH NOOO, THAT MEANS THE STORE HAS BEEN FLATTENED.
YOU DON'T KNOW THAT FOR SURE!
OH COME ON, EACH TIME THIS HAPPENS, YOU'RE THE ONLY OPTIMISTIC ONE.
THEY MUST BE RELOADING THE WHOLE CITY.
DID YOU REMEMBER TO UPLOAD THE INVENTORY TO THE CLOUD?
I GUESS WE'RE SPENDING OUR NEXT FEW WEEKS WAITING FOR REIMBURSEMENT FROM THE GOVERNMENT.

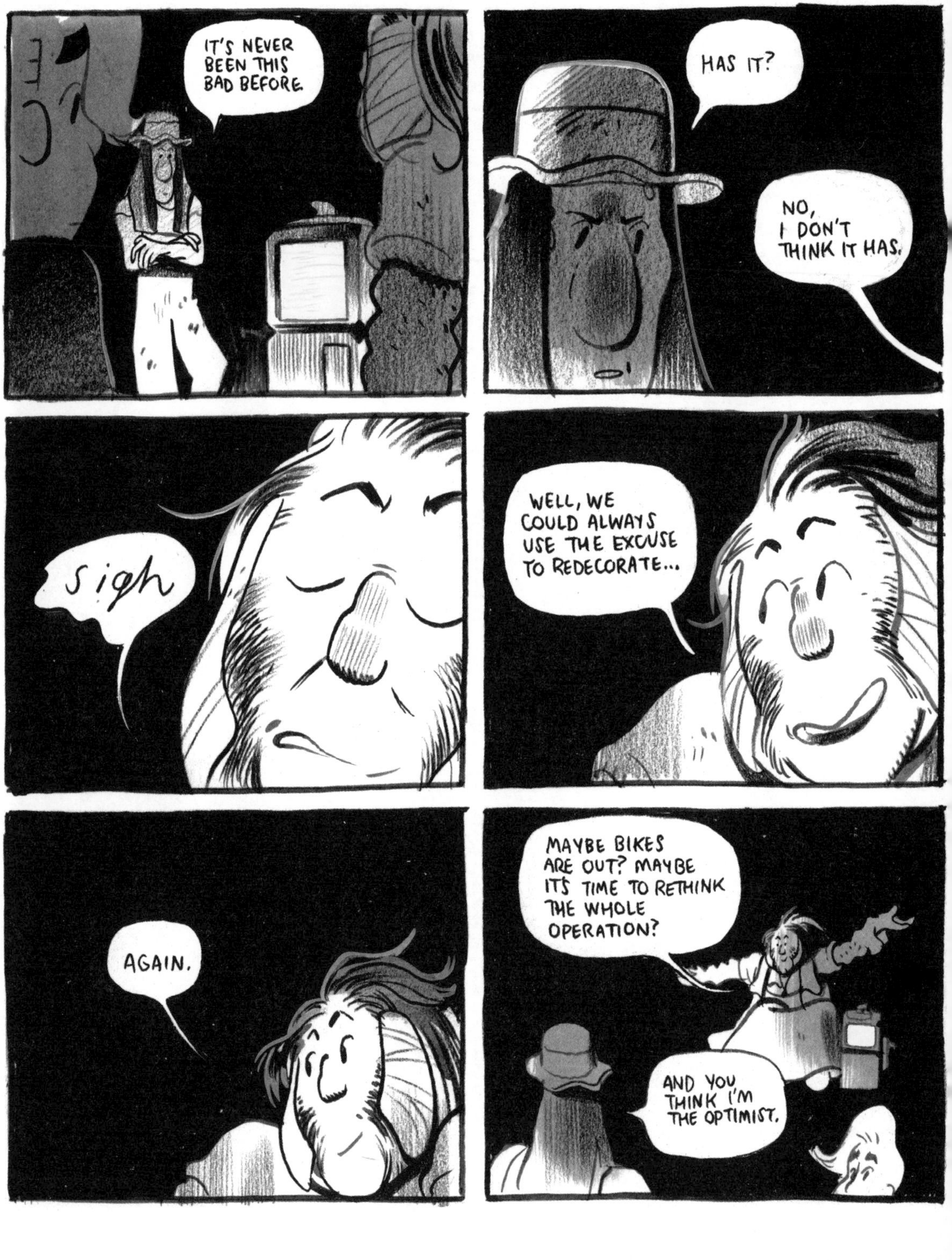
IT'S NEVER BEEN THIS BAD BEFORE.
HAS IT?
NO, I DON'T THINK IT HAS.
sigh
WELL, WE COULD ALWAYS USE THE EXCUSE TO REDECORATE...
AGAIN.
MAYBE BIKES ARE OUT? MAYBE IT'S TIME TO RETHINK THE WHOLE OPERATION?
AND YOU THINK I'M THE OPTIMIST.

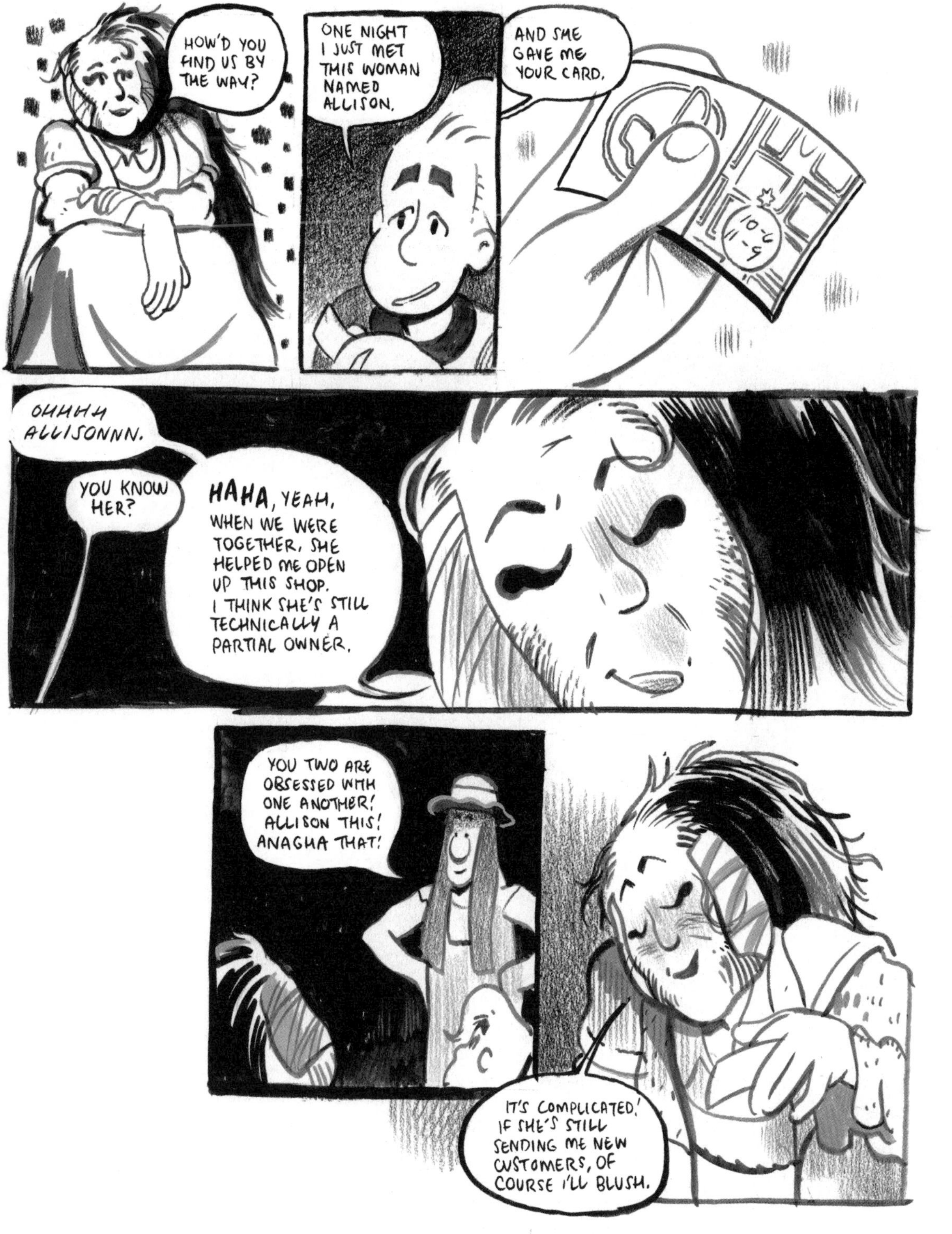
HOW'D YOU FIND US BY THE WAY?
ONE NIGHT I JUST MET THIS WOMAN NAMED ALLISON.
AND SHE GAVE ME YOUR CARD.
OHHHH ALLISONNN.
YOU KNOW HER?
HAHA, YEAH, WHEN WE WERE TOGETHER, SHE HELPED ME OPEN UP THIS SHOP. I THINK SHE'S STILL TECHNICALLY A PARTIAL OWNER.
YOU TWO ARE OBSESSED WITH ONE ANOTHER! ALLISON THIS! ANAGHA THAT!
IT'S COMPLICATED! IF SHE'S STILL SENDING ME NEW CUSTOMERS, OF COURSE I'LL BLUSH.

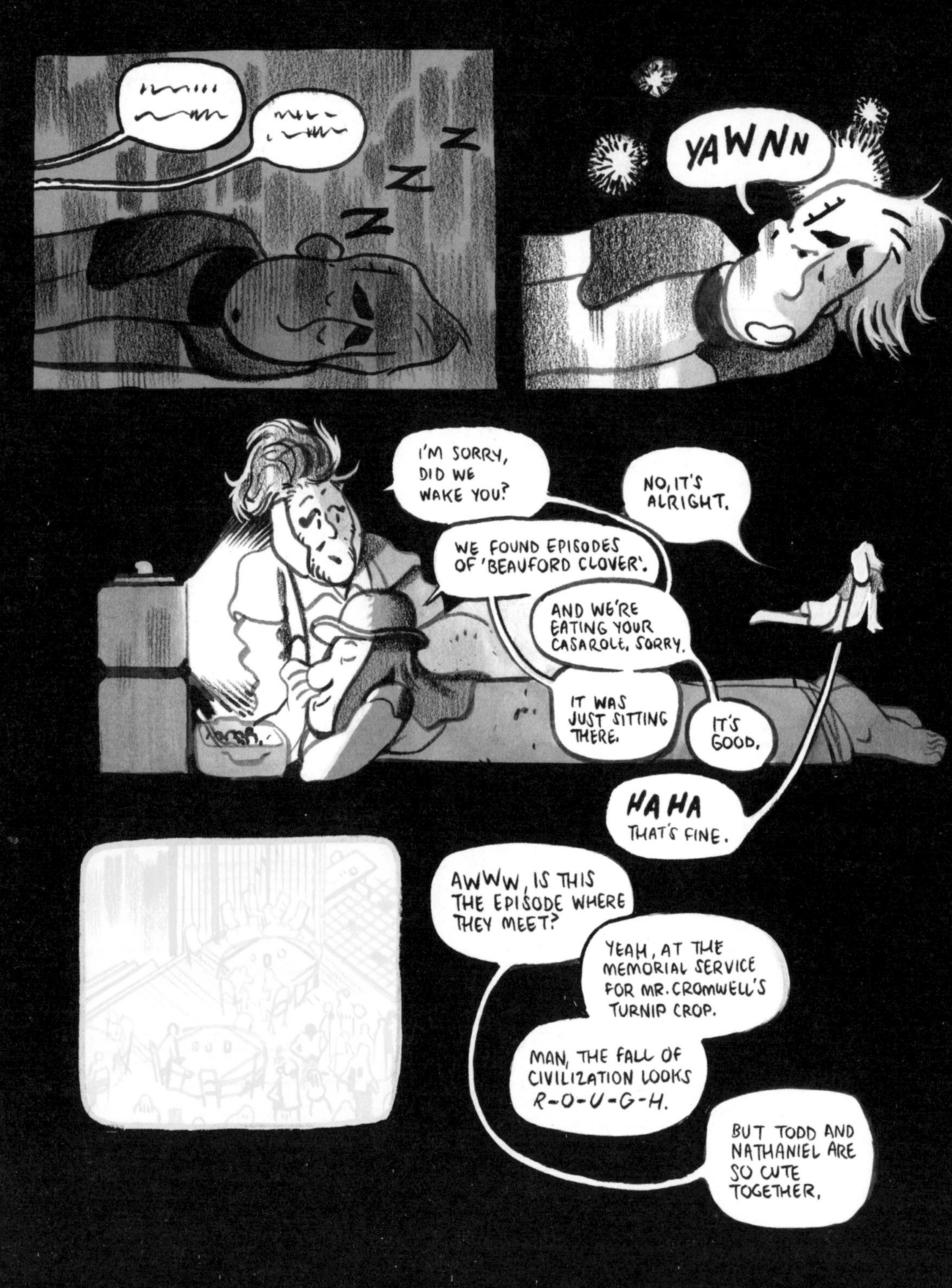
YAWNN
I'M SORRY, DID WE WAKE YOU?
NO, IT'S ALRIGHT.
WE FOUND EPISODES OF 'BEAUFORD CLOVER'.
AND WE'RE EATING YOUR CASAROLE, SORRY.
IT WAS JUST SITTING THERE.
IT'S GOOD.
HAHA THAT'S FINE.
AWWW, IS THIS THE EPISODE WHERE THEY MEET?
YEAH, AT THE MEMORIAL SERVICE FOR MR. CROMWELL'S TURNIP CROP.
MAN, THE FALL OF CIVILIZATION LOOKS R-O-U-G-H.
BUT TODD AND NATHANIEL ARE SO CUTE TOGETHER.

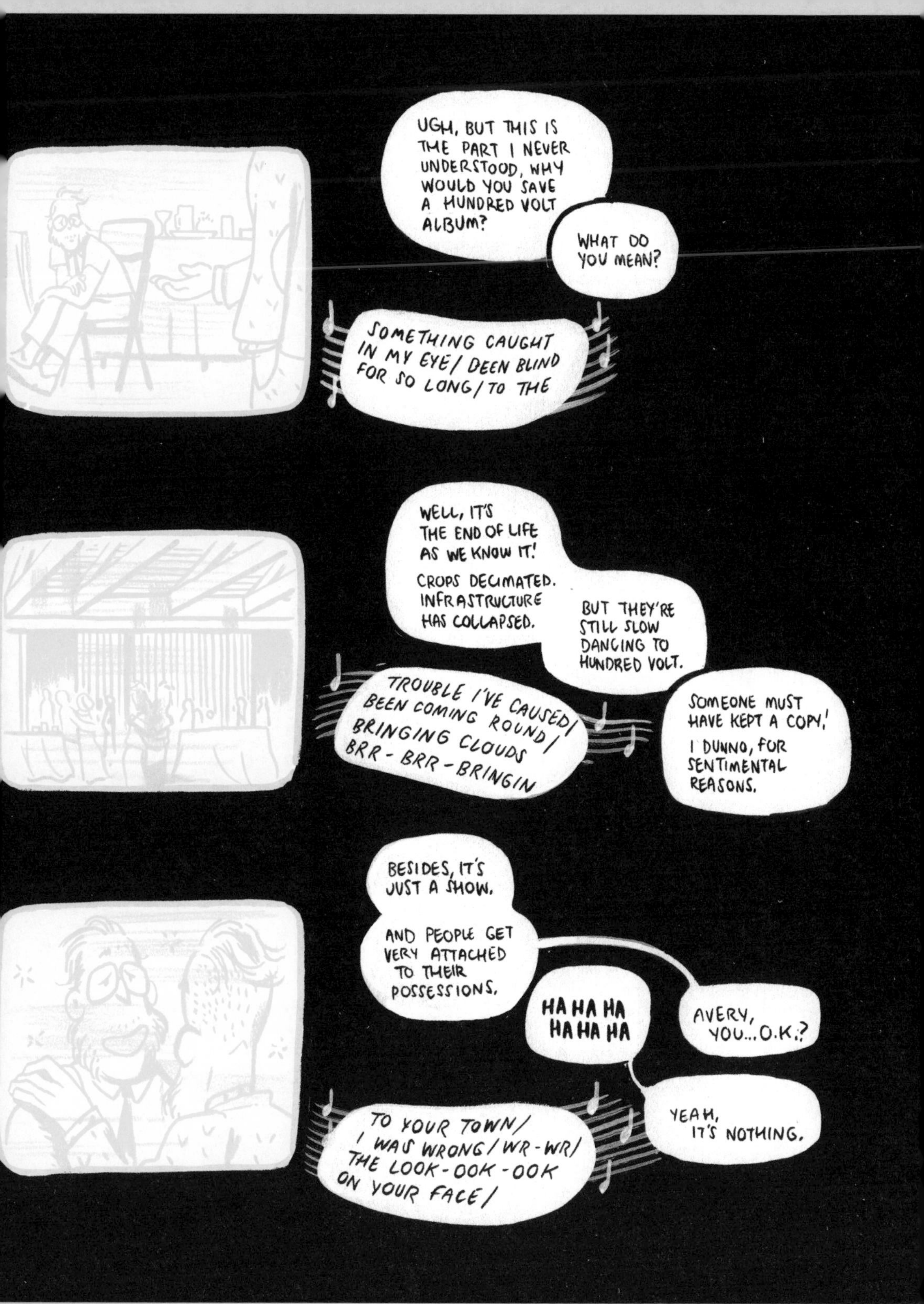

UGH, BUT THIS IS THE PART I NEVER UNDERSTOOD, WHY WOULD YOU SAVE A HUNDRED VOLT ALBUM?
WHAT DO YOU MEAN?
SOMETHING CAUGHT IN MY EYE/ DEEN BLIND FOR SO LONG/ TO THE
WELL, IT'S THE END OF LIFE AS WE KNOW IT!
CROPS DECIMATED. INFRASTRUCTURE HAS COLLAPSED.
BUT THEY'RE STILL SLOW DANCING TO HUNDRED VOLT.
TROUBLE I'VE CAUSED/ BEEN COMING ROUND/ BRINGING CLOUDS BRR - BRR - BRINGIN
SOMEONE MUST HAVE KEPT A COPY!
I DUNNO, FOR SENTIMENTAL REASONS.
BESIDES, IT'S JUST A SHOW.
AND PEOPLE GET VERY ATTACHED TO THEIR POSSESSIONS.
HA HA HA HA HA HA
AVERY, YOU... O.K.?
YEAH, IT'S NOTHING.
TO YOUR TOWN/ I WAS WRONG/ WR - WR/ THE LOOK - OOK - OOK ON YOUR FACE/

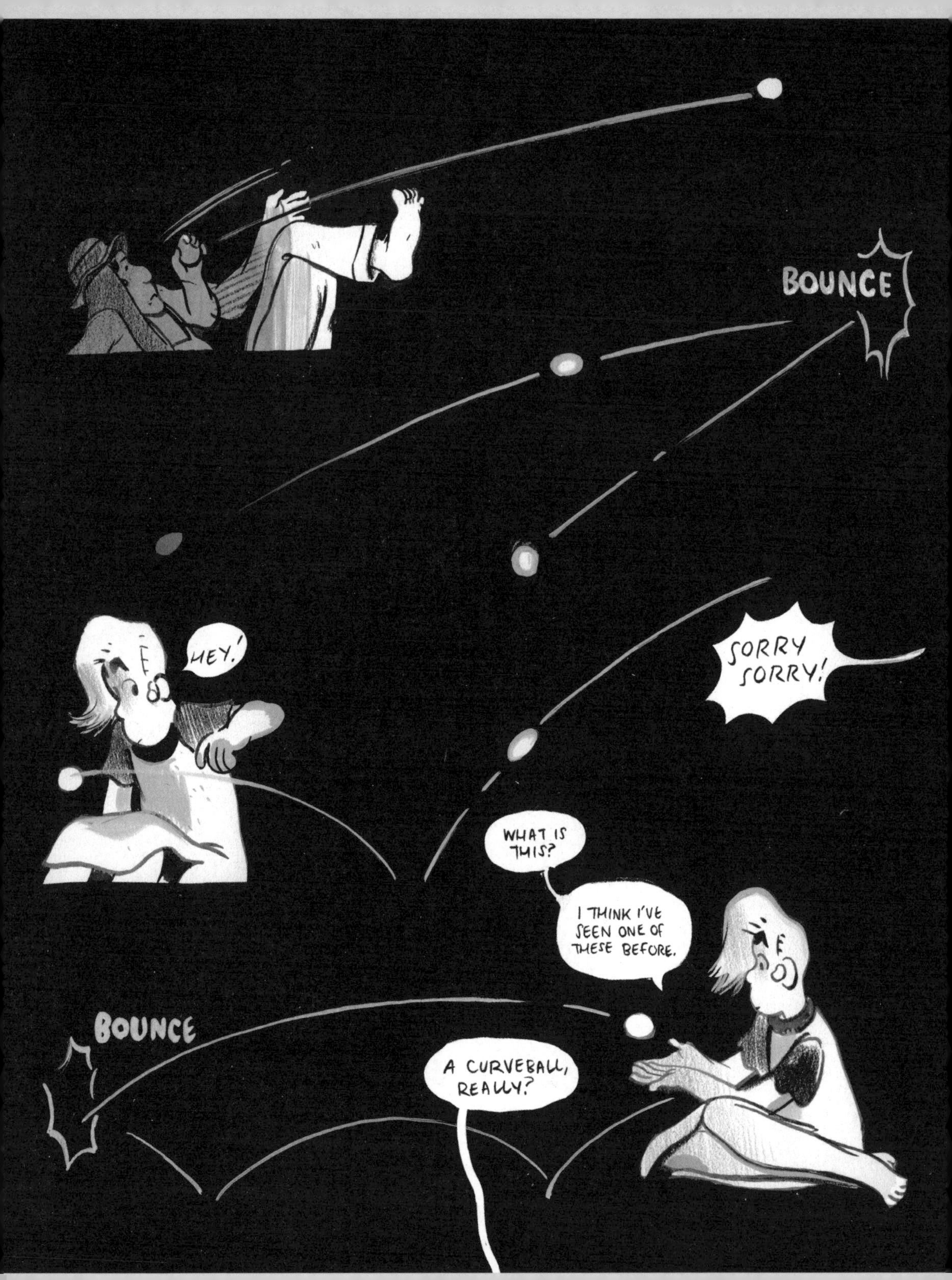
BOUNCE
HEY!
SORRY SORRY!
WHAT IS THIS?
I THINK I'VE SEEN ONE OF THESE BEFORE.
BOUNCE
A CURVEBALL, REALLY?

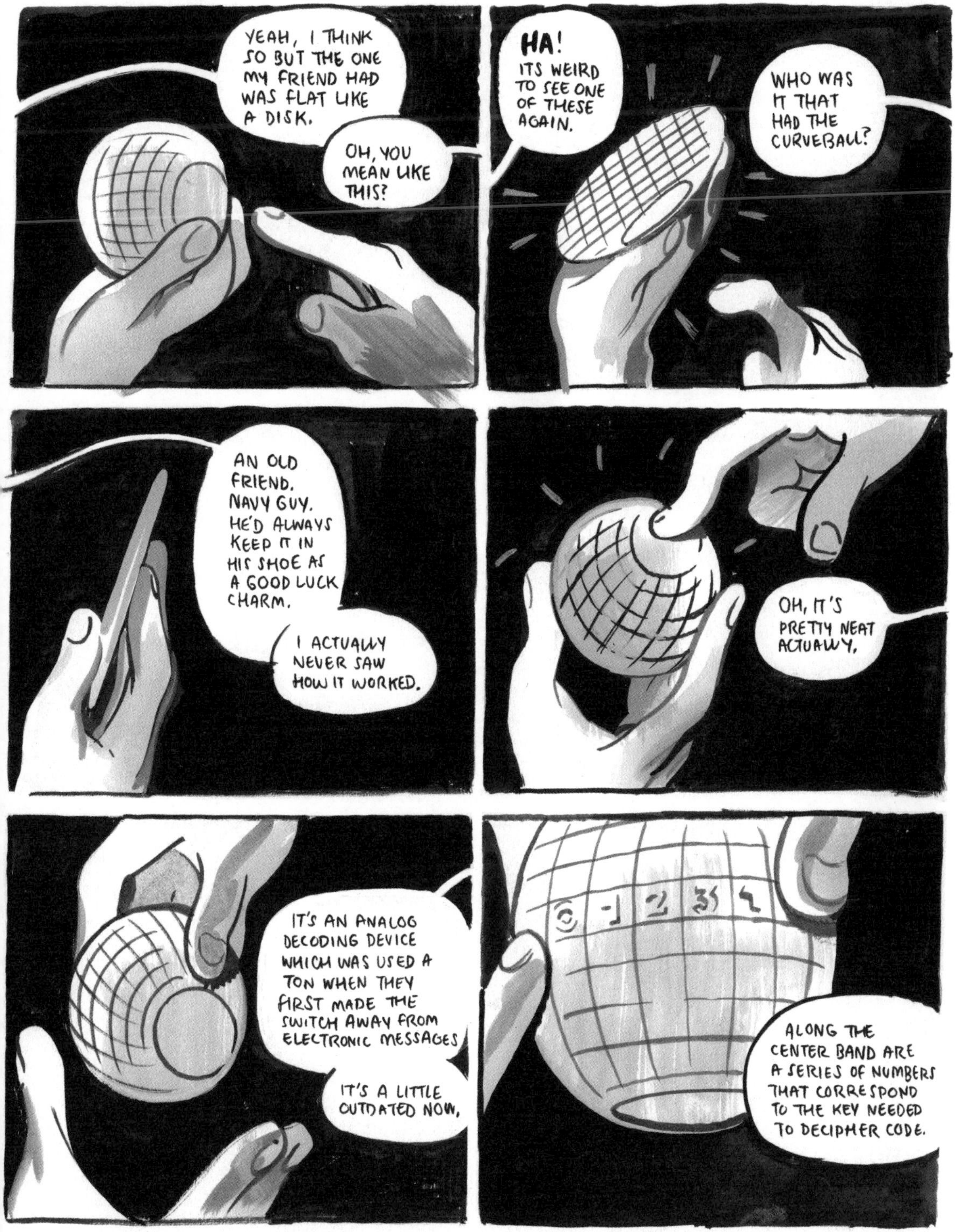

YEAH, I THINK SO BUT THE ONE MY FRIEND HAD WAS FLAT LIKE A DISK.
OH, YOU MEAN LIKE THIS?
HA! ITS WEIRD TO SEE ONE OF THESE AGAIN.
WHO WAS IT THAT HAD THE CURVEBALL?
AN OLD FRIEND. NAVY GUY. HE'D ALWAYS KEEP IT IN HIS SHOE AS A GOOD LUCK CHARM.
I ACTUALLY NEVER SAW HOW IT WORKED.
OH, IT'S PRETTY NEAT ACTUALLY.
IT'S AN ANALOG DECODING DEVICE WHICH WAS USED A TON WHEN THEY FIRST MADE THE SWITCH AWAY FROM ELECTRONIC MESSAGES
IT'S A LITTLE OUTDATED NOW.
ALONG THE CENTER BAND ARE A SERIES OF NUMBERS THAT CORRESPOND TO THE KEY NEEDED TO DECIPHER CODE.

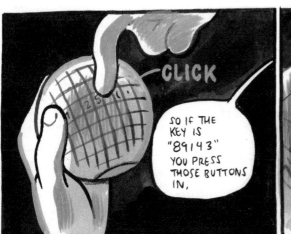

CLICK

SO IF THE KEY IS "89143" YOU PRESS THOSE BUTTONS IN,

WHICH BRINGS UP A WHOLE KEY SPECIFIC ALPHABET TO DECIPHER THE MESSAGE YOU'VE BEEN GIVEN,

AS YOU PRESS THE CORRESPONDING KEYS LIKE SO...

IT PRINTS OUT YOUR DECODED MESSAGE, IF I WAS DECODING AN ACTUAL CODED MESSAGE, THIS WOULD SAY SOMETHING COHERENT.

TIK TIK TIK

WHEN YOU'RE DONE, YOU CAN TEAR THE STRIP OF PAPER OFF, WHICH DISSOLVES AFTER A LITTLE WHILE ANYWAY,

WHEN YOU TEAR THAT STRIP OFF, THE CURVEBALL SENSES YOU'RE DONE AND SCRAMBLES ITSELF.

THIS WAY IT CAN'T FALL INTO THE WRONG HANDS AND USE THE SAME KEY TO DECODE MESSAGES.

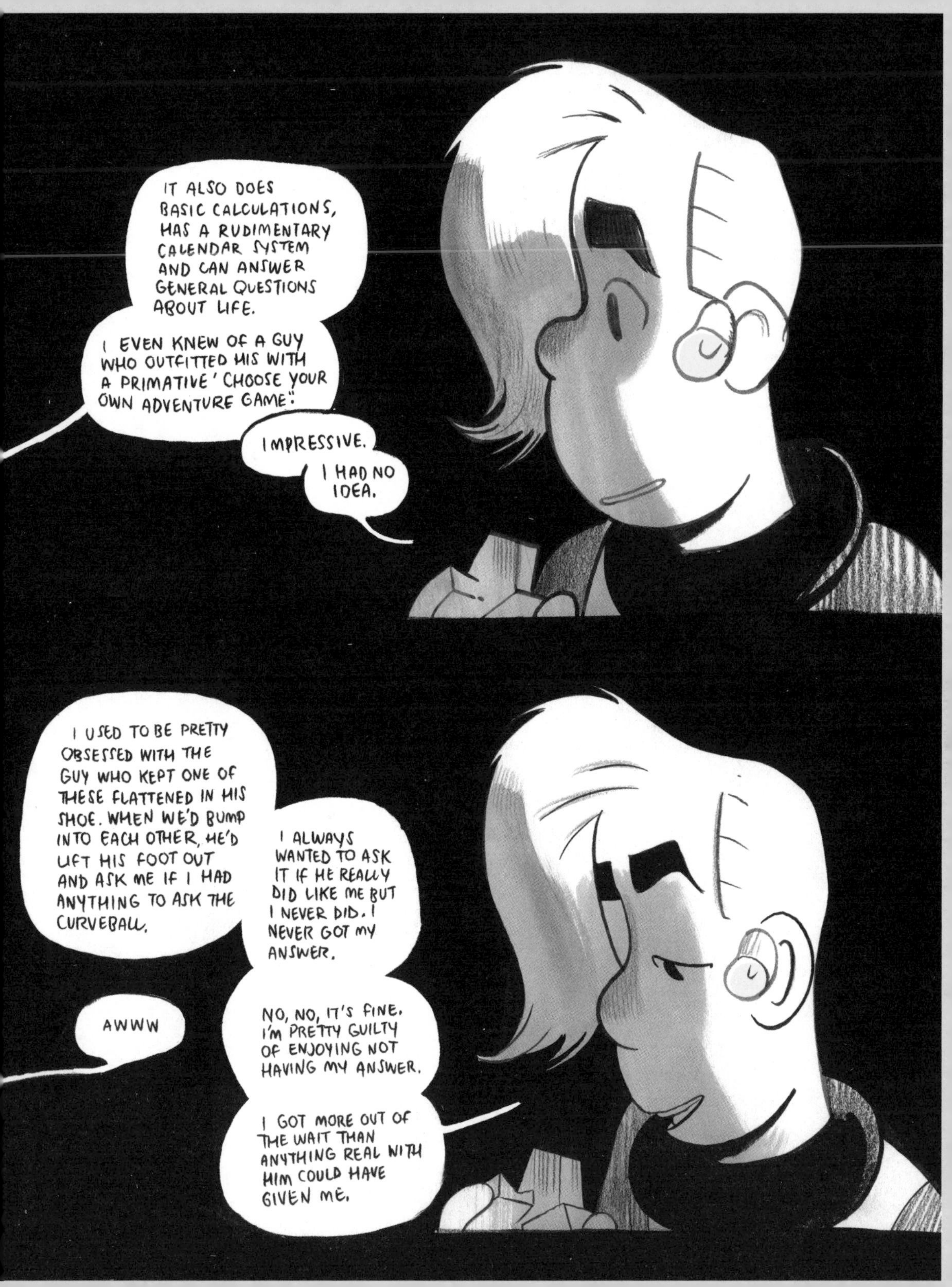
IT ALSO DOES BASIC CALCULATIONS, HAS A RUDIMENTARY CALENDAR SYSTEM AND CAN ANSWER GENERAL QUESTIONS ABOUT LIFE.
I EVEN KNEW OF A GUY WHO OUTFITTED HIS WITH A PRIMATIVE 'CHOOSE YOUR OWN ADVENTURE GAME".
IMPRESSIVE.
I HAD NO IDEA.
I USED TO BE PRETTY OBSESSED WITH THE GUY WHO KEPT ONE OF THESE FLATTENED IN HIS SHOE. WHEN WE'D BUMP INTO EACH OTHER, HE'D LIFT HIS FOOT OUT AND ASK ME IF I HAD ANYTHING TO ASK THE CURVEBALL.
I ALWAYS WANTED TO ASK IT IF HE REALLY DID LIKE ME BUT I NEVER DID. I NEVER GOT MY ANSWER.
AWWW
NO, NO, IT'S FINE. I'M PRETTY GUILTY OF ENJOYING NOT HAVING MY ANSWER.
I GOT MORE OUT OF THE WAIT THAN ANYTHING REAL WITH HIM COULD HAVE GIVEN ME.

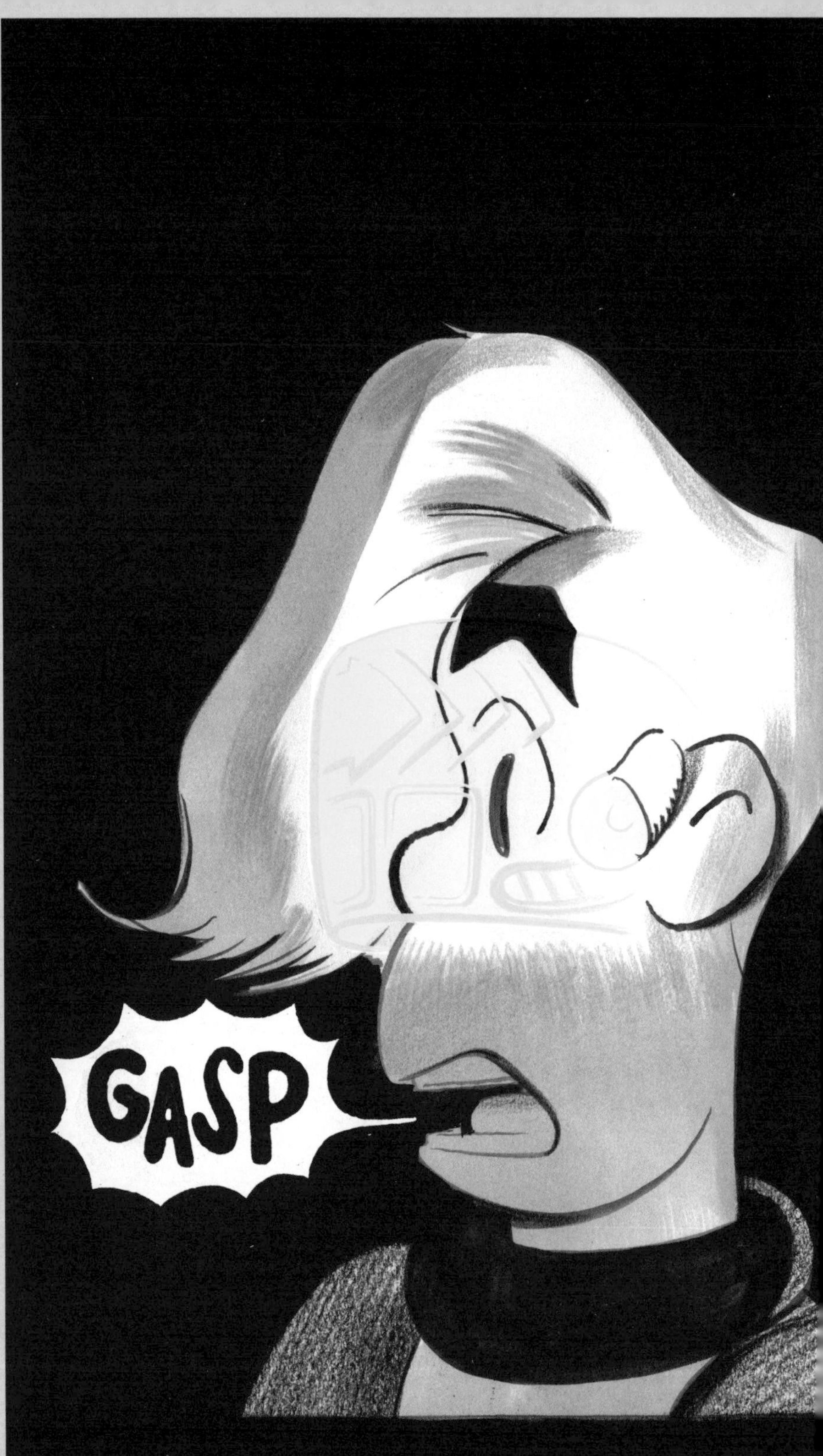
GASP

THEY'RE DIRECTING US TO THE NEAREST SHELTER.

Shhh hh

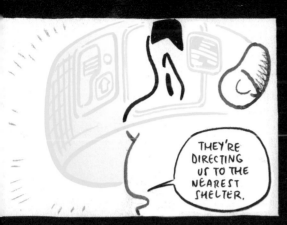

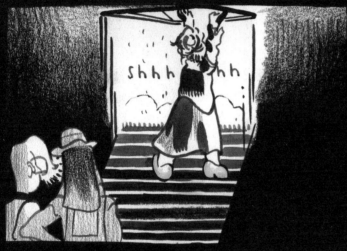

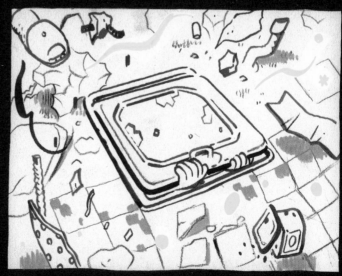

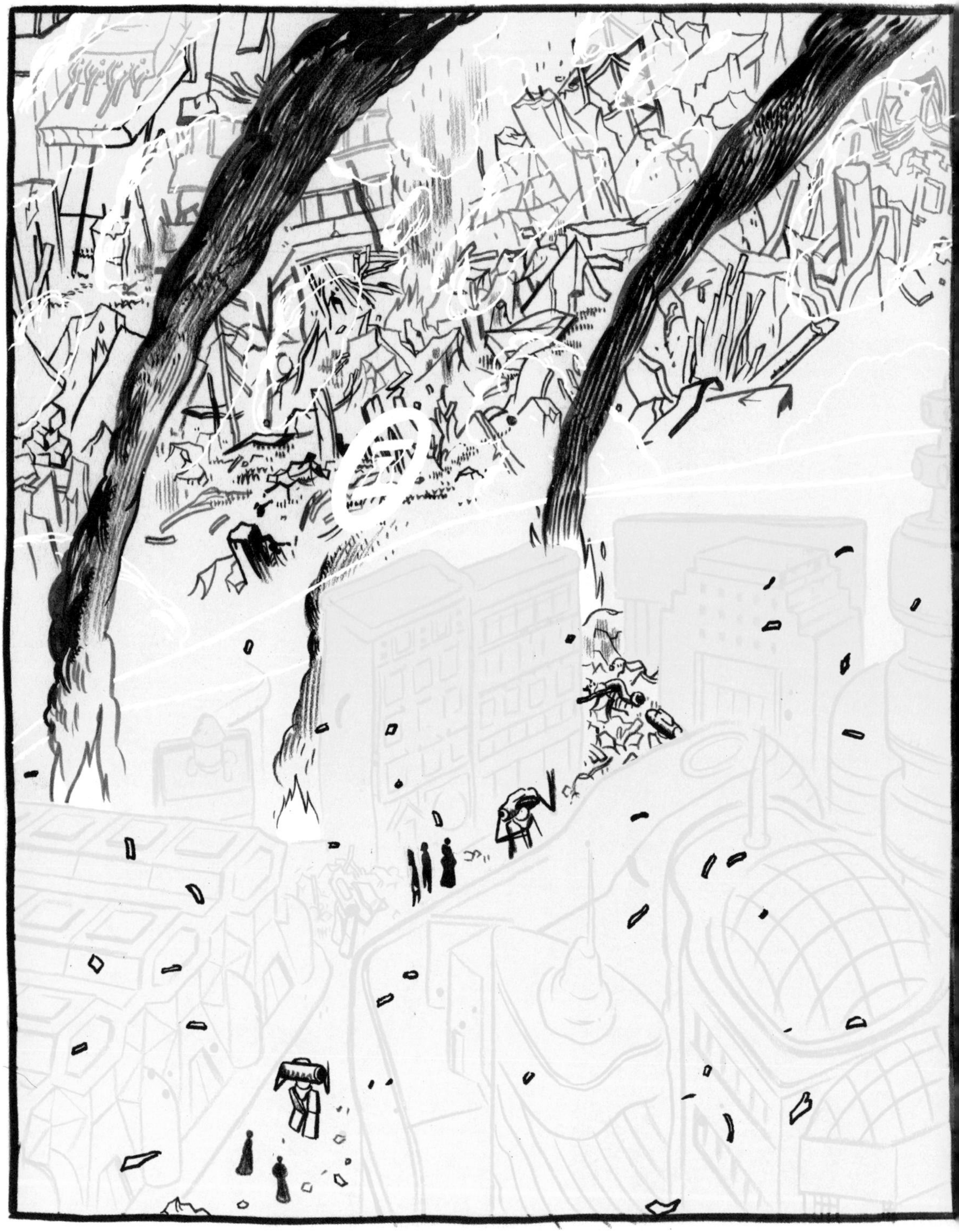

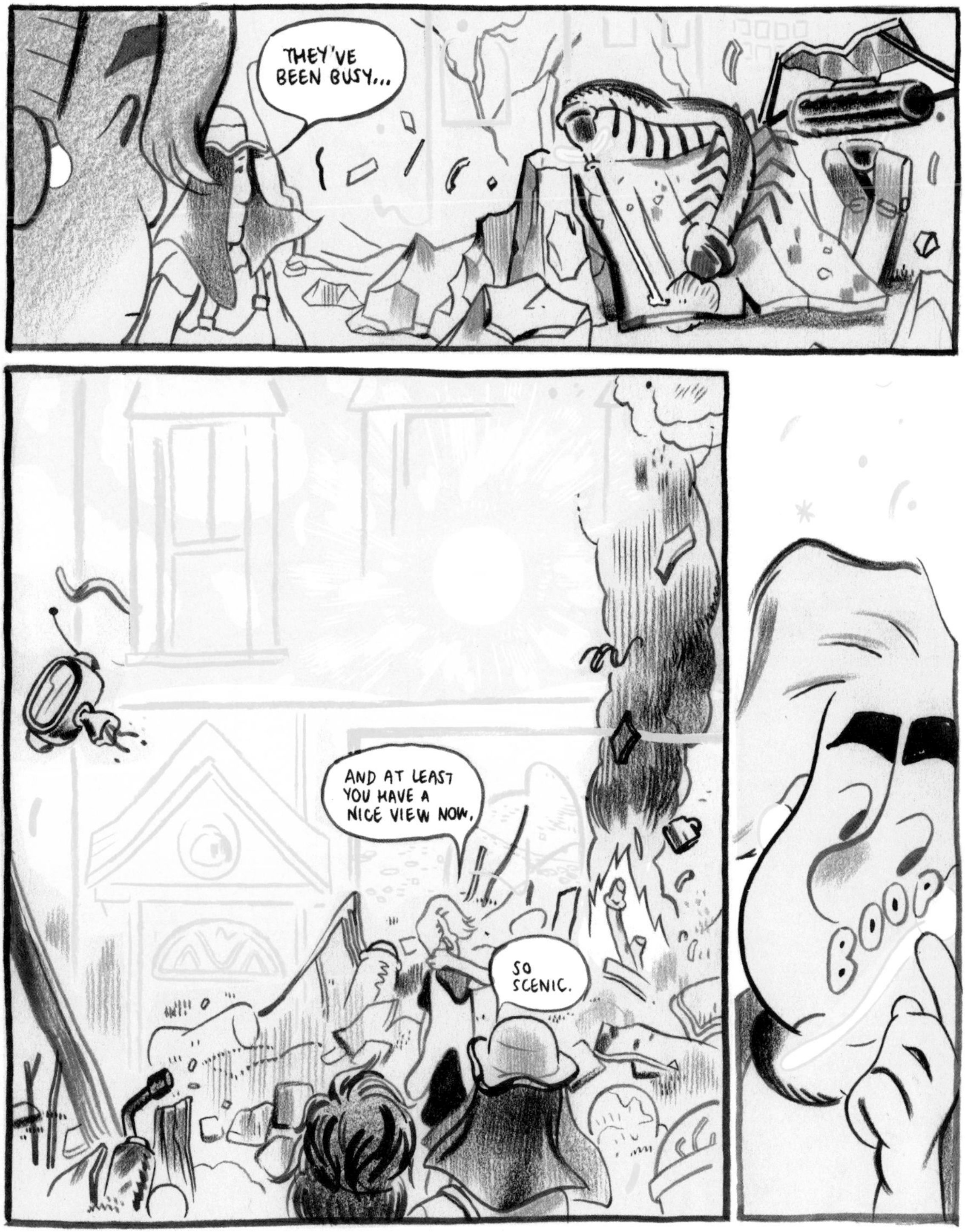
THEY'VE BEEN BUSY...
AND AT LEAST YOU HAVE A NICE VIEW NOW.
SO SCENIC.
BOOP

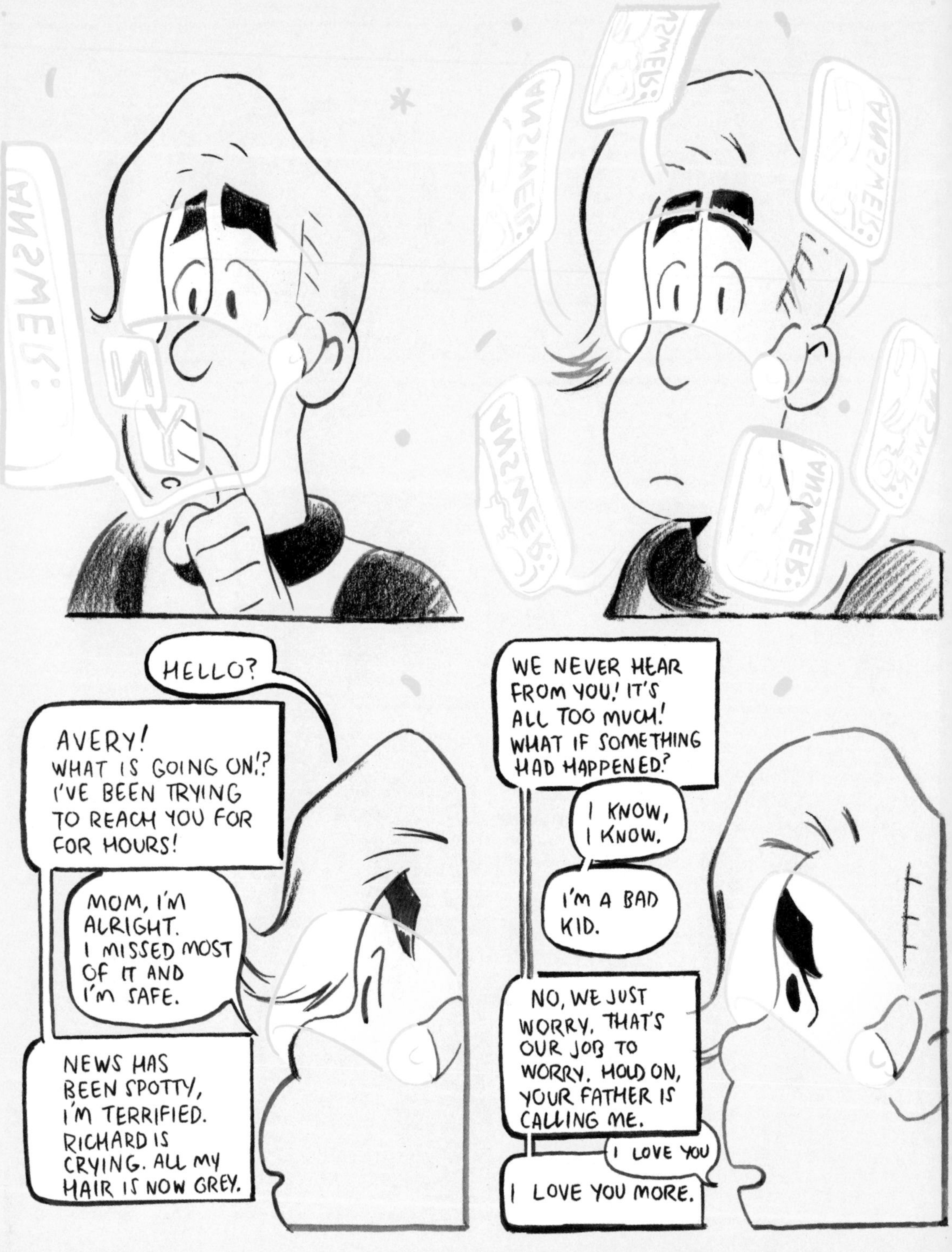
HELLO?
AVERY! WHAT IS GOING ON!? I'VE BEEN TRYING TO REACH YOU FOR FOR HOURS!
MOM, I'M ALRIGHT. I MISSED MOST OF IT AND I'M SAFE.
NEWS HAS BEEN SPOTTY, I'M TERRIFIED. RICHARD IS CRYING. ALL MY HAIR IS NOW GREY.
WE NEVER HEAR FROM YOU! IT'S ALL TOO MUCH! WHAT IF SOMETHING HAD HAPPENED?
I KNOW, I KNOW.
I'M A BAD KID.
NO, WE JUST WORRY. THAT'S OUR JOB TO WORRY. HOLD ON, YOUR FATHER IS CALLING ME.
I LOVE YOU
I LOVE YOU MORE.

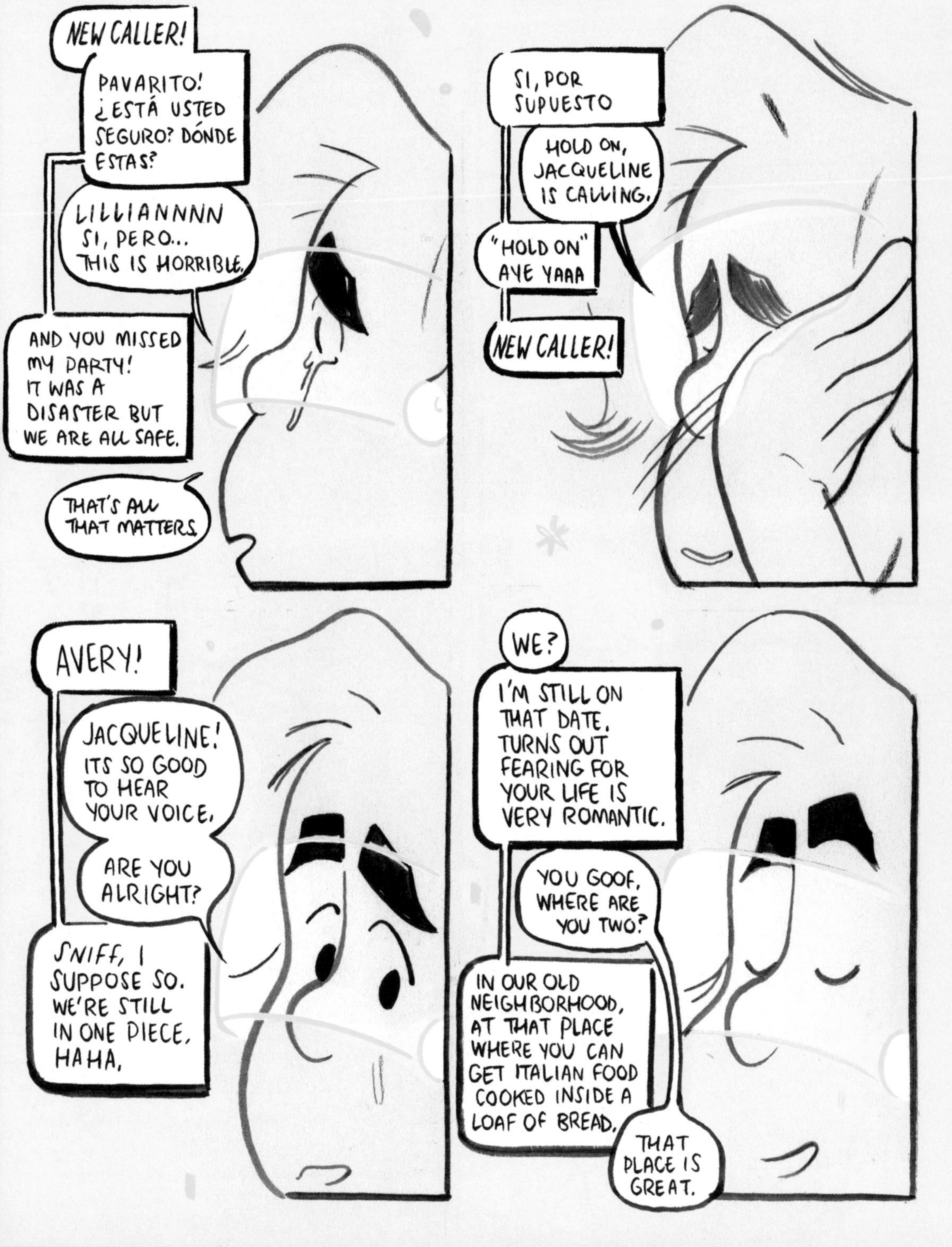
NEW CALLER!
PAVARITO! ¿ESTÁ USTED SEGURO? DÓNDE ESTAS?
LILLIANNNN SI, PERO... THIS IS HORRIBLE.
AND YOU MISSED MY PARTY! IT WAS A DISASTER BUT WE ARE ALL SAFE.
THAT'S ALL THAT MATTERS.
SI, POR SUPUESTO
HOLD ON, JACQUELINE IS CALLING.
"HOLD ON" AYE YAAA
NEW CALLER!
AVERY!
JACQUELINE! ITS SO GOOD TO HEAR YOUR VOICE.
ARE YOU ALRIGHT?
SNIFF, I SUPPOSE SO. WE'RE STILL IN ONE PIECE, HAHA.
WE?
I'M STILL ON THAT DATE. TURNS OUT FEARING FOR YOUR LIFE IS VERY ROMANTIC.
YOU GOOF, WHERE ARE YOU TWO?
IN OUR OLD NEIGHBORHOOD, AT THAT PLACE WHERE YOU CAN GET ITALIAN FOOD COOKED INSIDE A LOAF OF BREAD.
THAT PLACE IS GREAT.

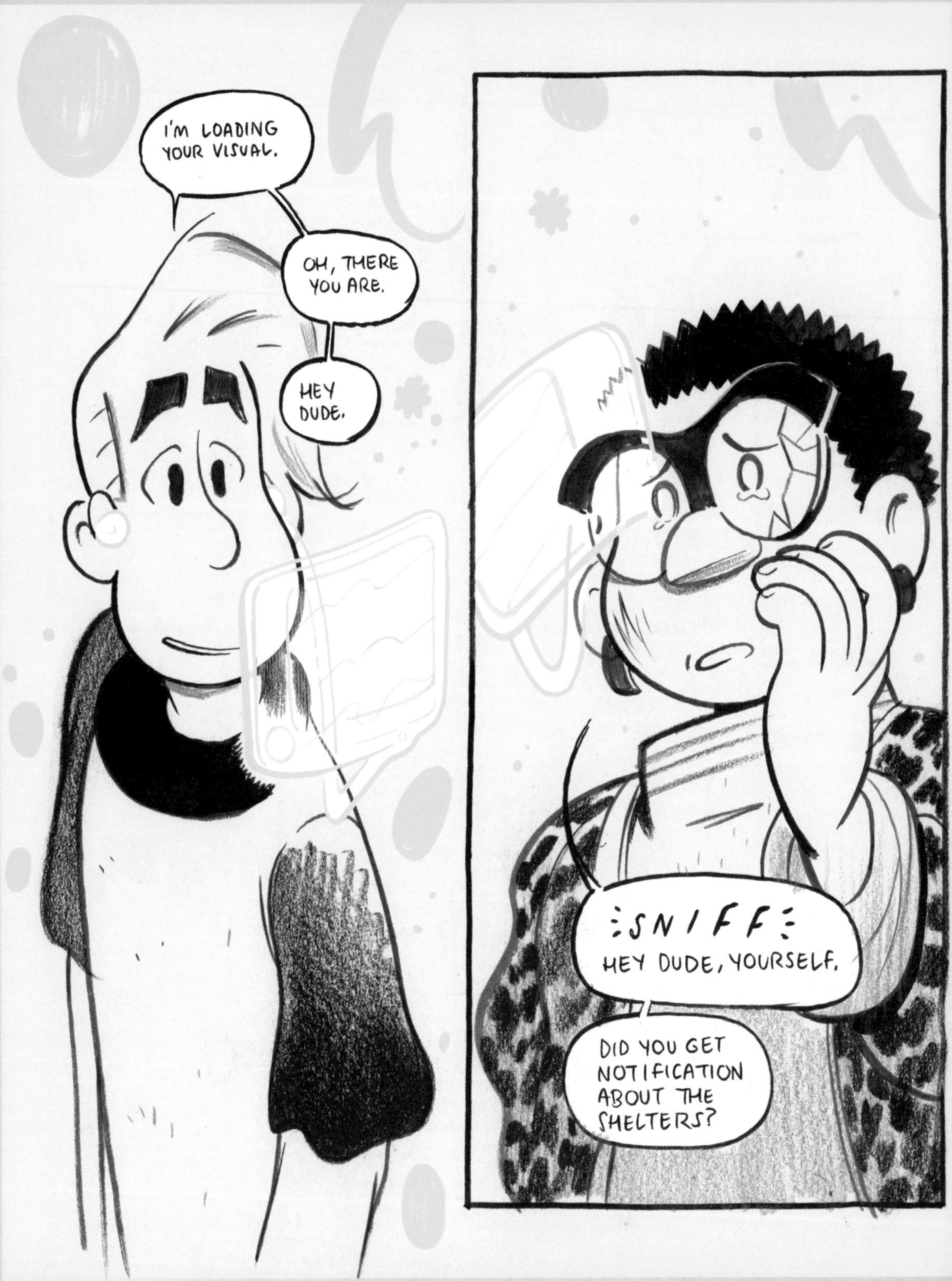
I'M LOADING YOUR VISUAL.
OH, THERE YOU ARE.
HEY DUDE.
SNIFF
HEY DUDE, YOURSELF.
DID YOU GET NOTIFICATION ABOUT THE SHELTERS?

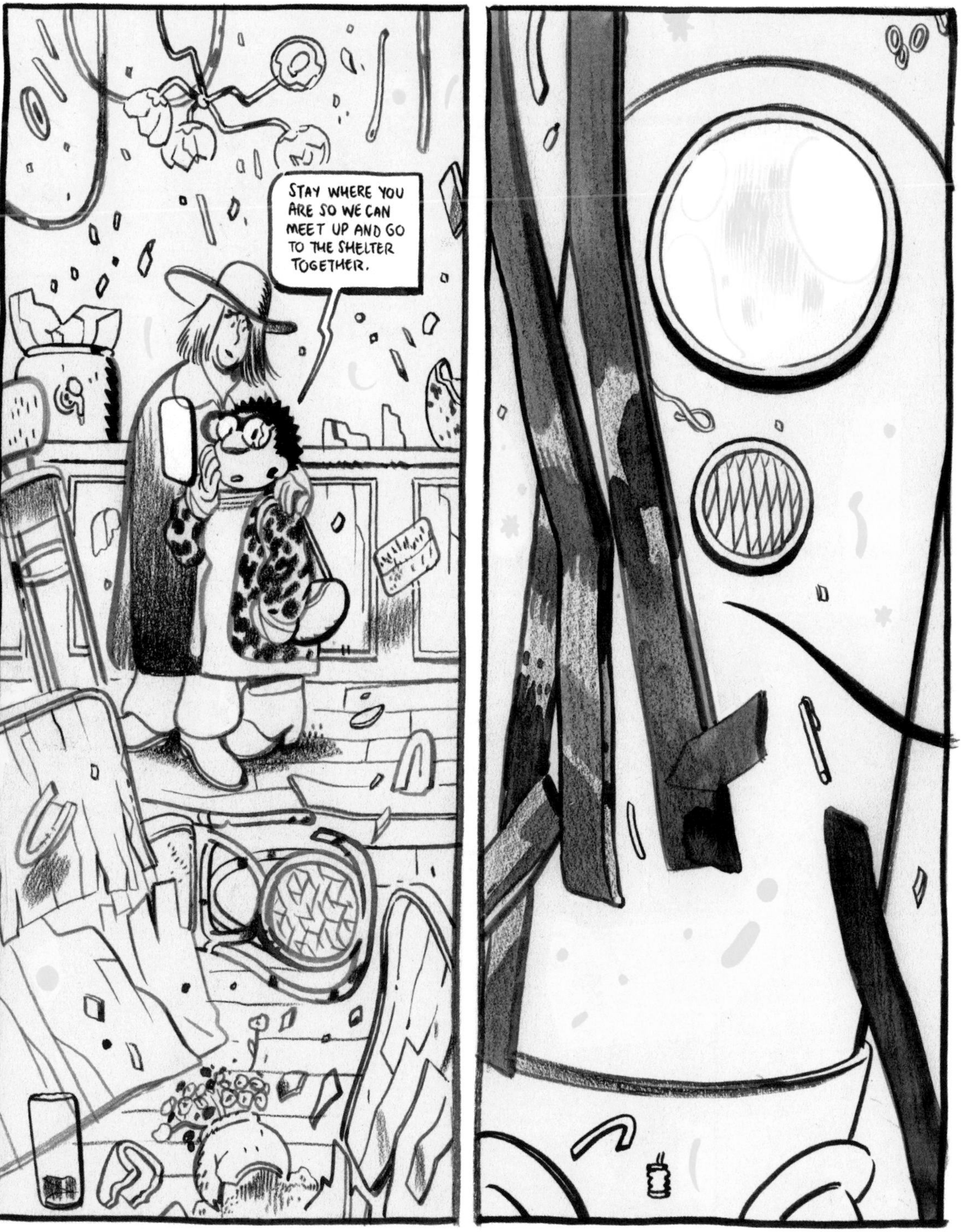
STAY WHERE YOU ARE SO WE CAN MEET UP AND GO TO THE SHELTER TOGETHER.

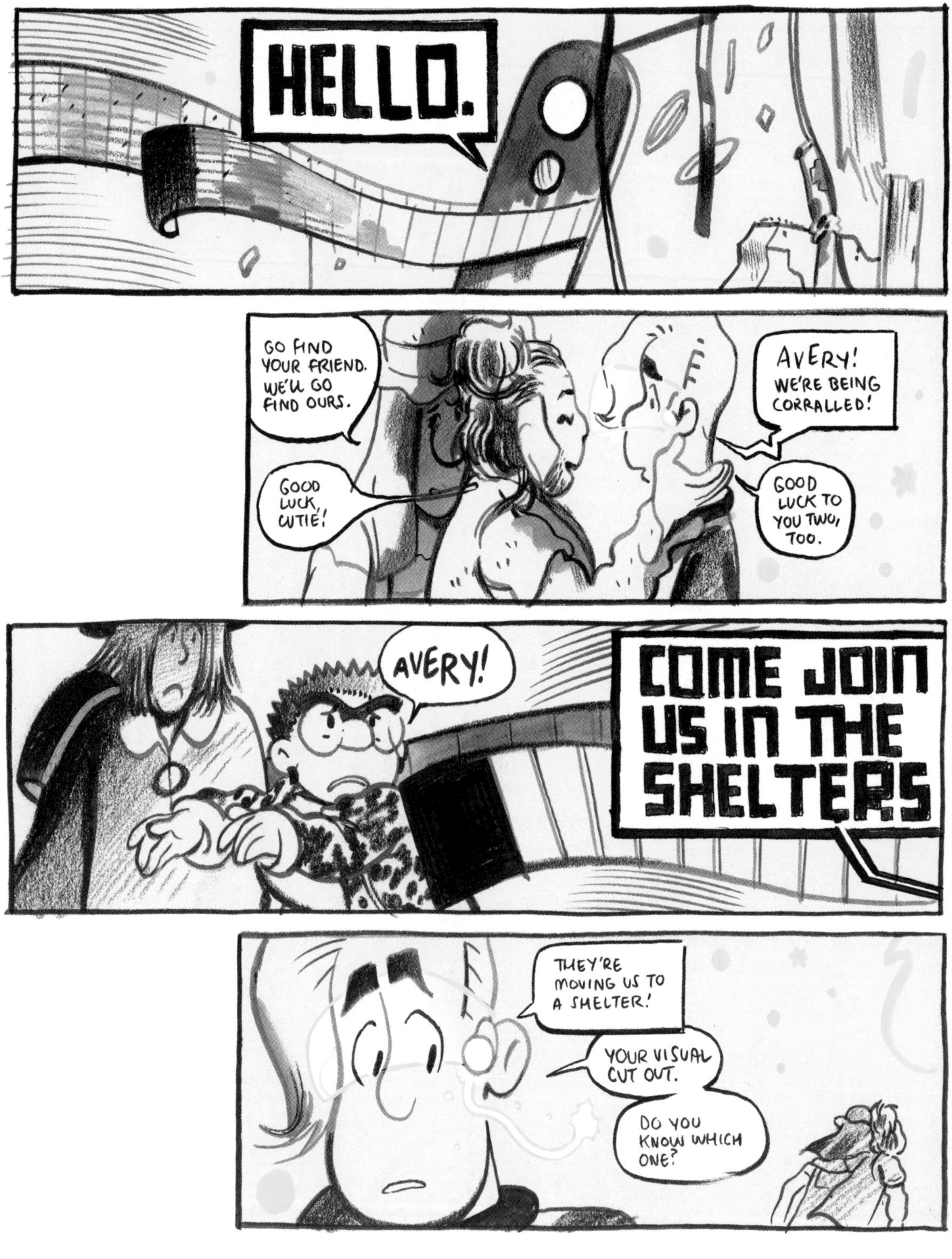
HELLO.
GO FIND YOUR FRIEND. WE'LL GO FIND OURS.
GOOD LUCK, CUTIE!
AVERY! WE'RE BEING CORRALLED!
GOOD LUCK TO YOU TWO, TOO.
AVERY!
COME JOIN US IN THE SHELTERS
THEY'RE MOVING US TO A SHELTER!
YOUR VISUAL CUT OUT.
DO YOU KNOW WHICH ONE?

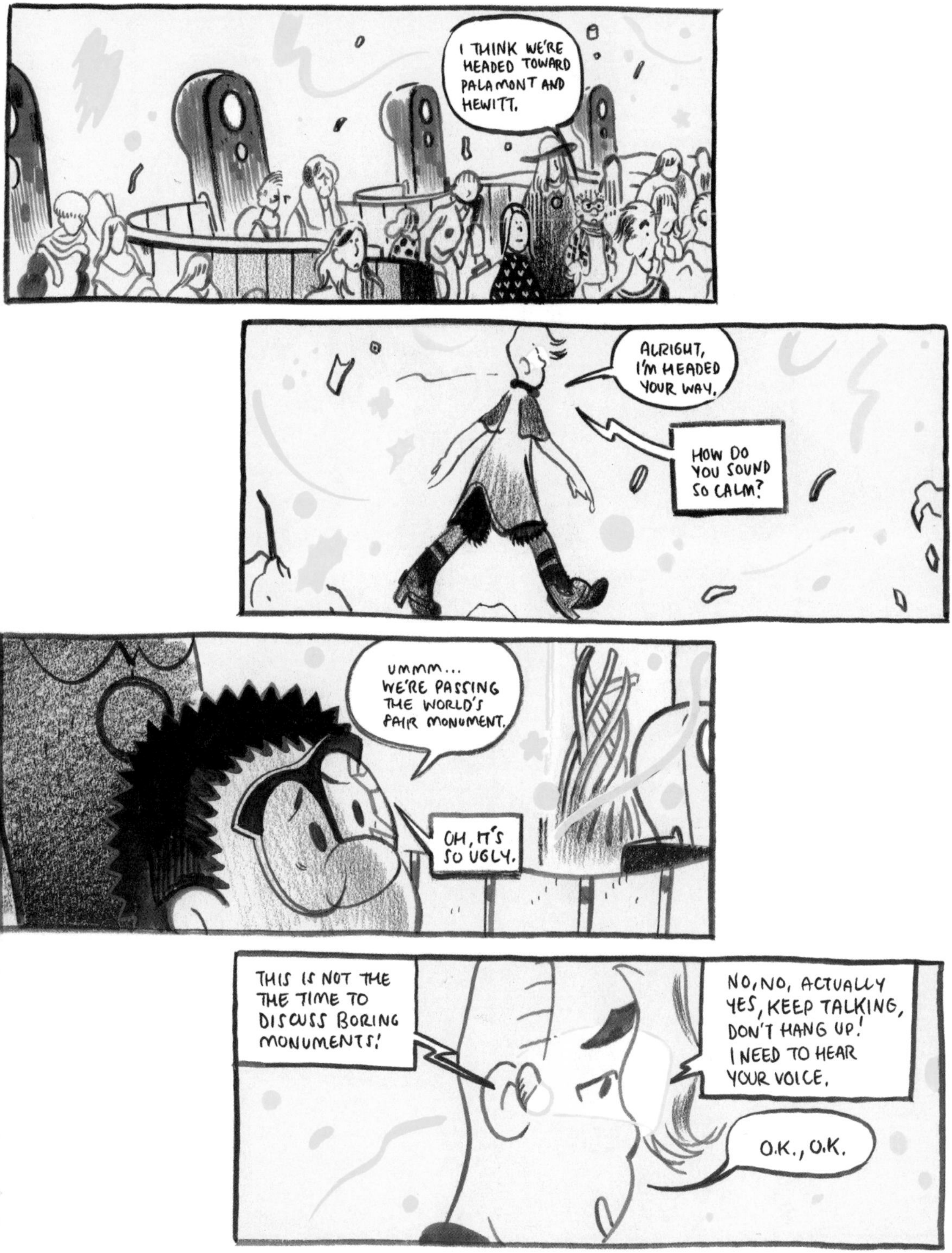
I THINK WE'RE HEADED TOWARD PALAMONT AND HEWITT.
ALRIGHT, I'M HEADED YOUR WAY.
HOW DO YOU SOUND SO CALM?
UMMM... WE'RE PASSING THE WORLD'S FAIR MONUMENT.
OH, IT'S SO UGLY.
THIS IS NOT THE THE TIME TO DISCUSS BORING MONUMENTS!
NO, NO, ACTUALLY YES, KEEP TALKING, DON'T HANG UP! I NEED TO HEAR YOUR VOICE.
O.K., O.K.

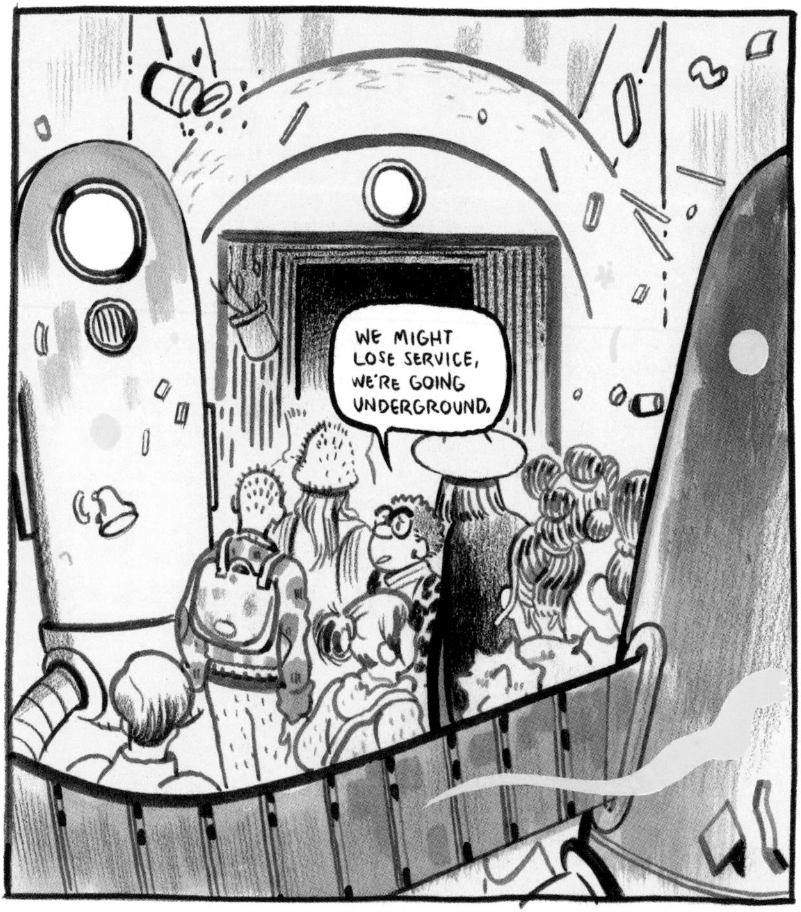
WE MIGHT LOSE SERVICE, WE'RE GOING UNDERGROUND.

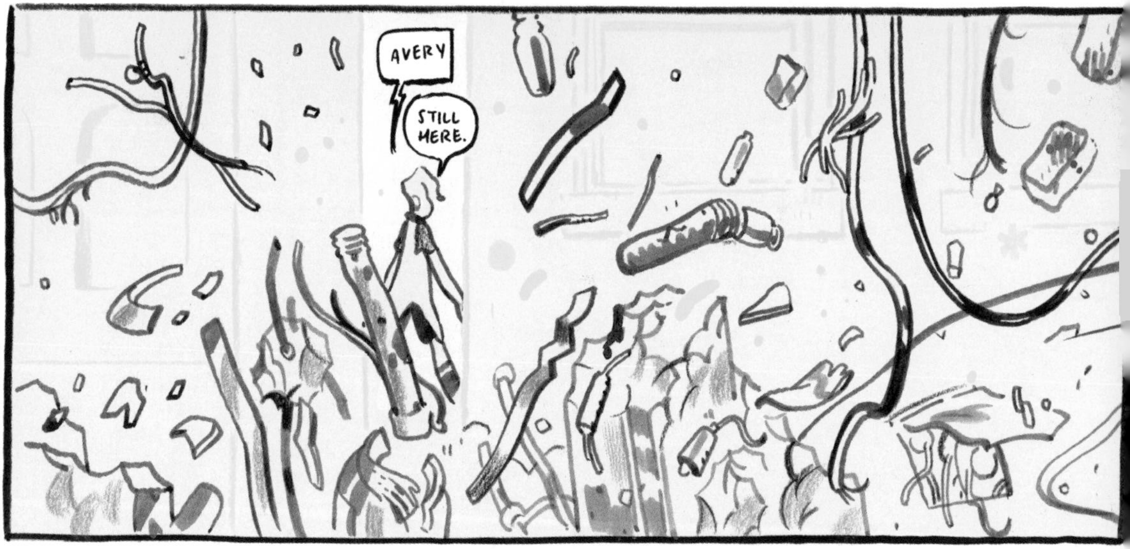
AVERY
STILL HERE.

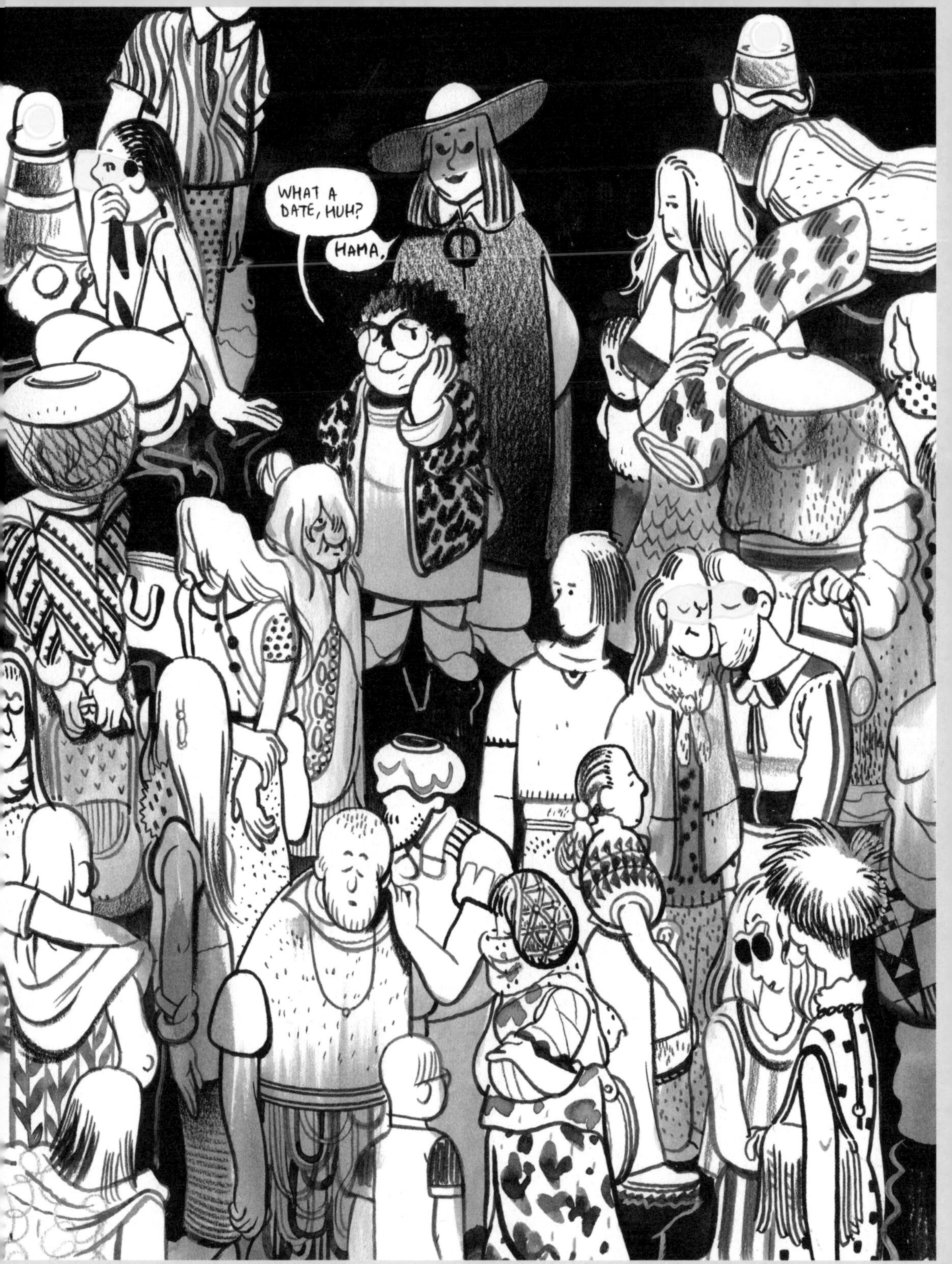
WHAT A DATE, HUH?
HAMA.

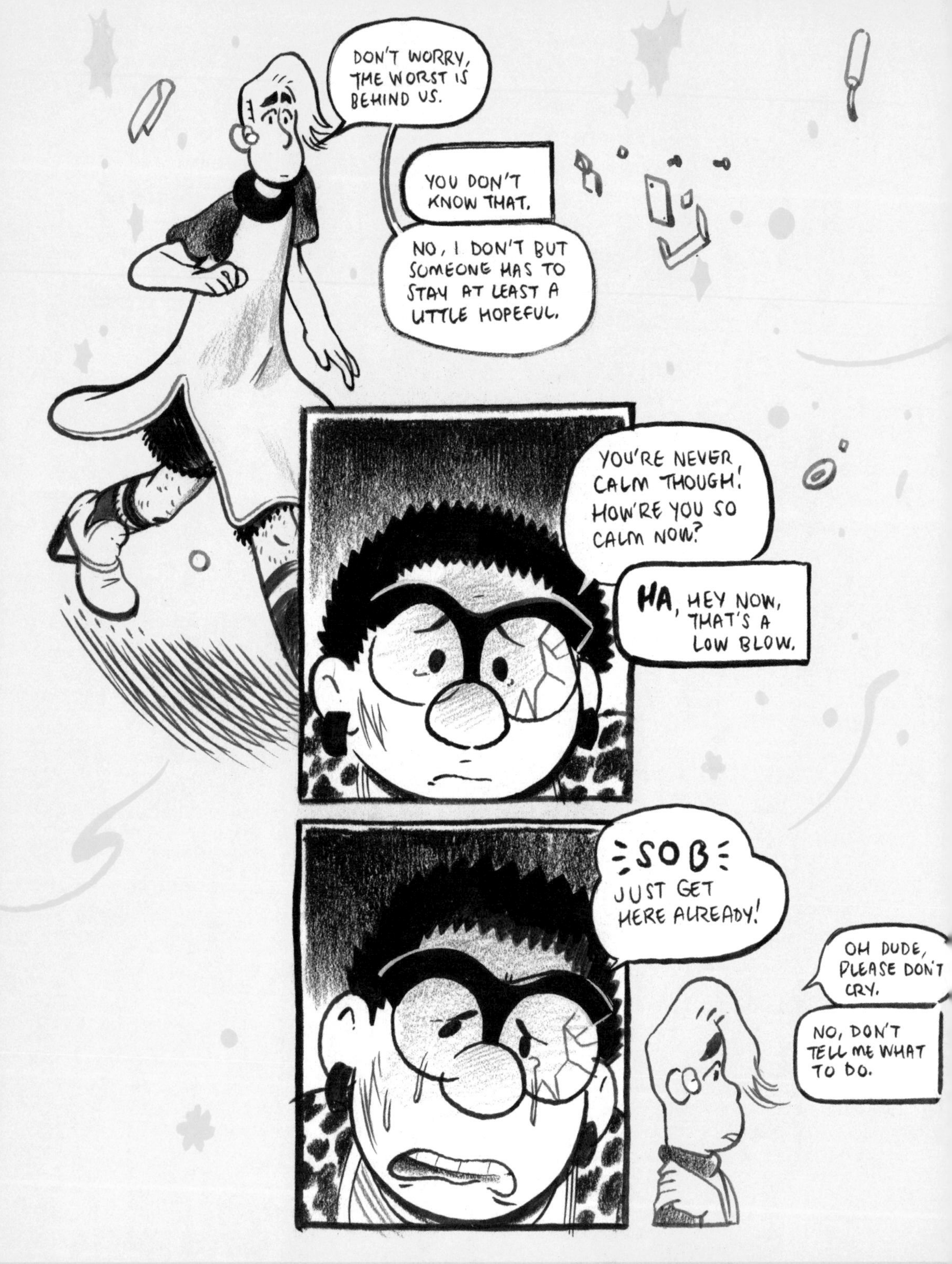
DON'T WORRY, THE WORST IS BEHIND US.
YOU DON'T KNOW THAT.
NO, I DON'T BUT SOMEONE HAS TO STAY AT LEAST A LITTLE HOPEFUL.
YOU'RE NEVER CALM THOUGH! HOW'RE YOU SO CALM NOW?
HA, HEY NOW, THAT'S A LOW BLOW.
SOB
JUST GET HERE ALREADY!
OH DUDE, PLEASE DON'T CRY.
NO, DON'T TELL ME WHAT TO DO.

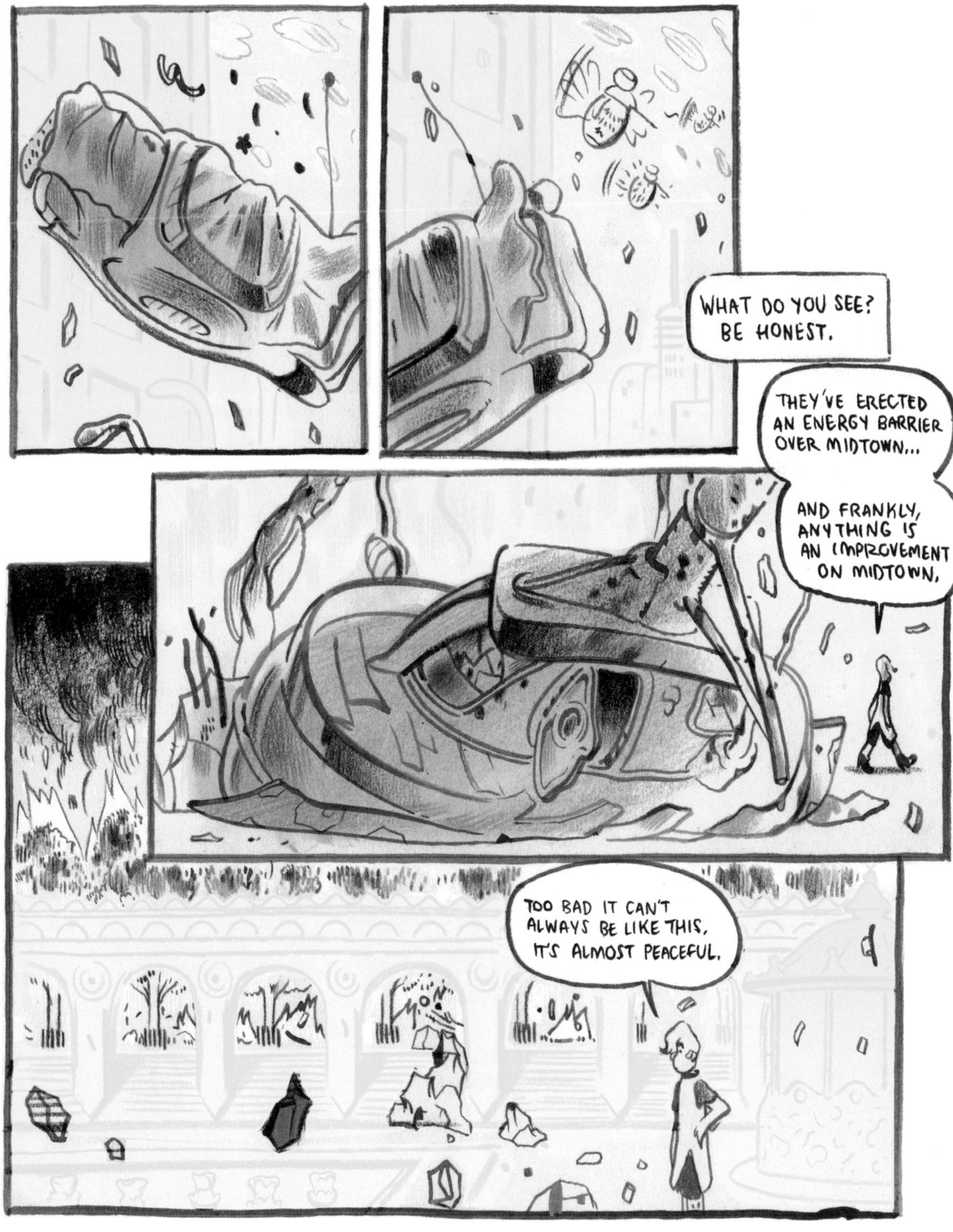
WHAT DO YOU SEE? BE HONEST.
THEY'VE ERECTED AN ENERGY BARRIER OVER MIDTOWN...
AND FRANKLY, ANYTHING IS AN IMPROVEMENT ON MIDTOWN.
TOO BAD IT CAN'T ALWAYS BE LIKE THIS. IT'S ALMOST PEACEFUL.

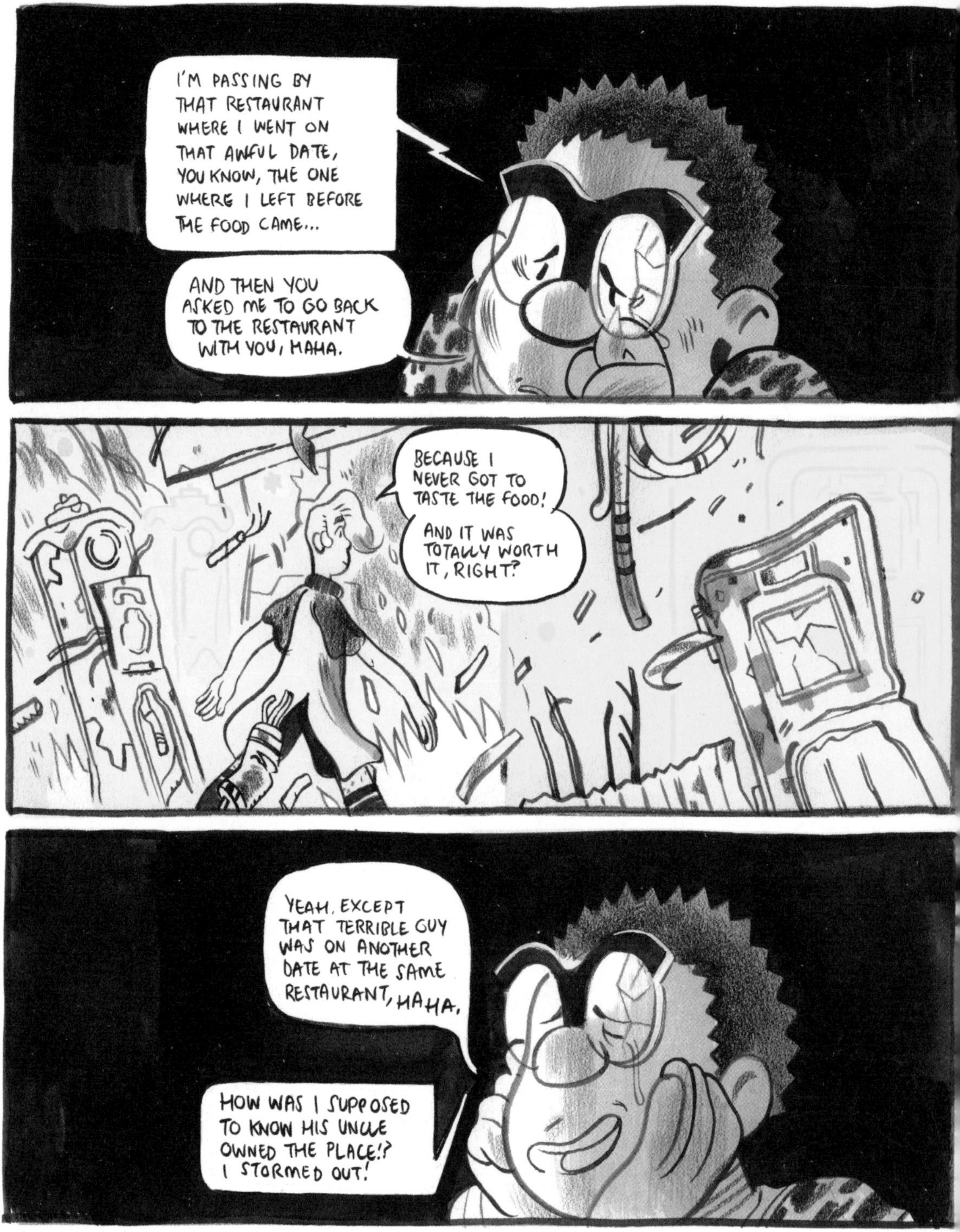
I'M PASSING BY THAT RESTAURANT WHERE I WENT ON THAT AWFUL DATE, YOU KNOW, THE ONE WHERE I LEFT BEFORE THE FOOD CAME...
AND THEN YOU ASKED ME TO GO BACK TO THE RESTAURANT WITH YOU, HAHA.
BECAUSE I NEVER GOT TO TASTE THE FOOD!
AND IT WAS TOTALLY WORTH IT, RIGHT?
YEAH, EXCEPT THAT TERRIBLE GUY WAS ON ANOTHER DATE AT THE SAME RESTAURANT, HAHA.
HOW WAS I SUPPOSED TO KNOW HIS UNCLE OWNED THE PLACE!? I STORMED OUT!

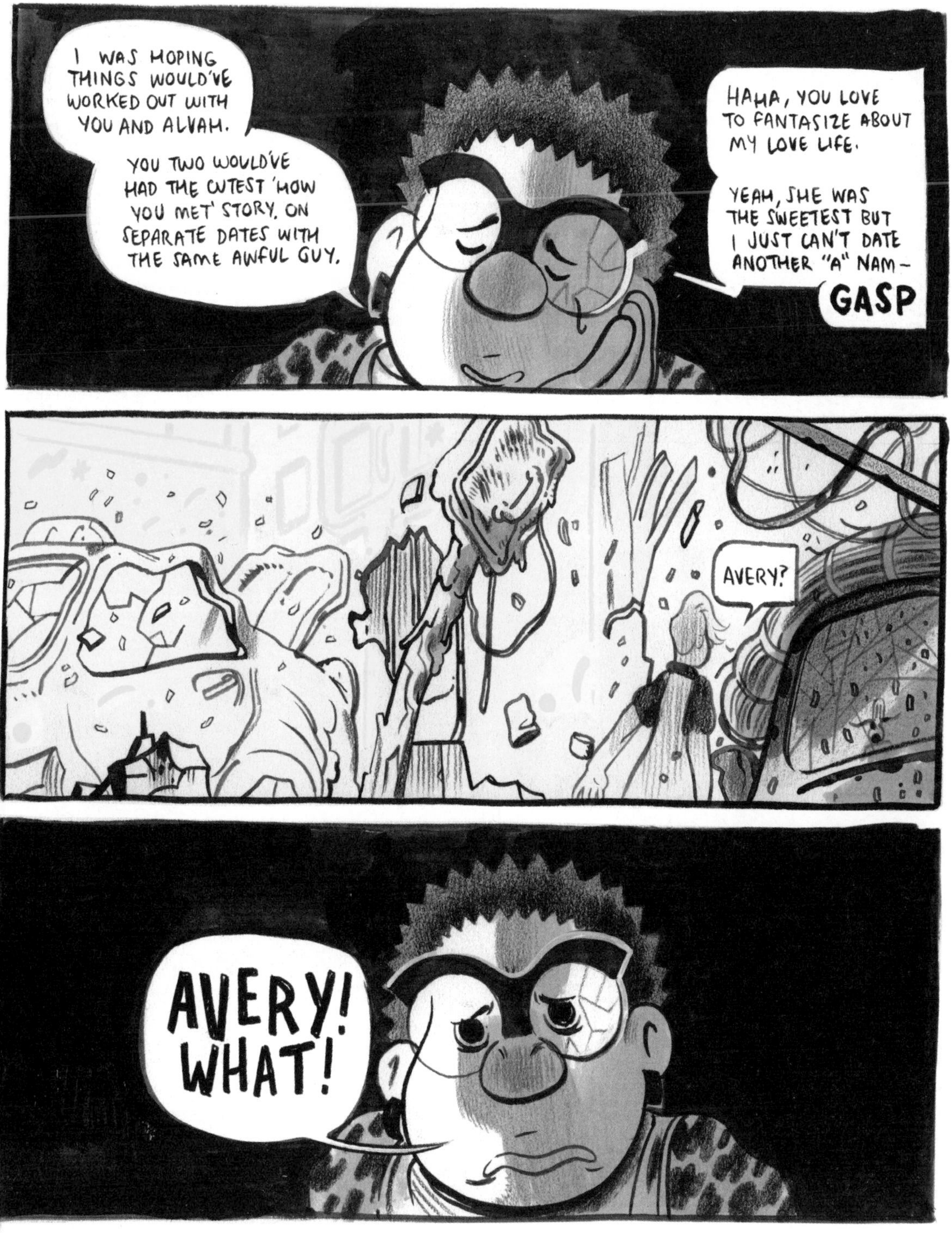
I WAS HOPING THINGS WOULD'VE WORKED OUT WITH YOU AND ALVAH.
YOU TWO WOULD'VE HAD THE CUTEST 'HOW YOU MET' STORY. ON SEPARATE DATES WITH THE SAME AWFUL GUY.
HAHA, YOU LOVE TO FANTASIZE ABOUT MY LOVE LIFE.
YEAH, SHE WAS THE SWEETEST BUT I JUST CAN'T DATE ANOTHER "A" NAM–
GASP
AVERY?
AVERY! WHAT!

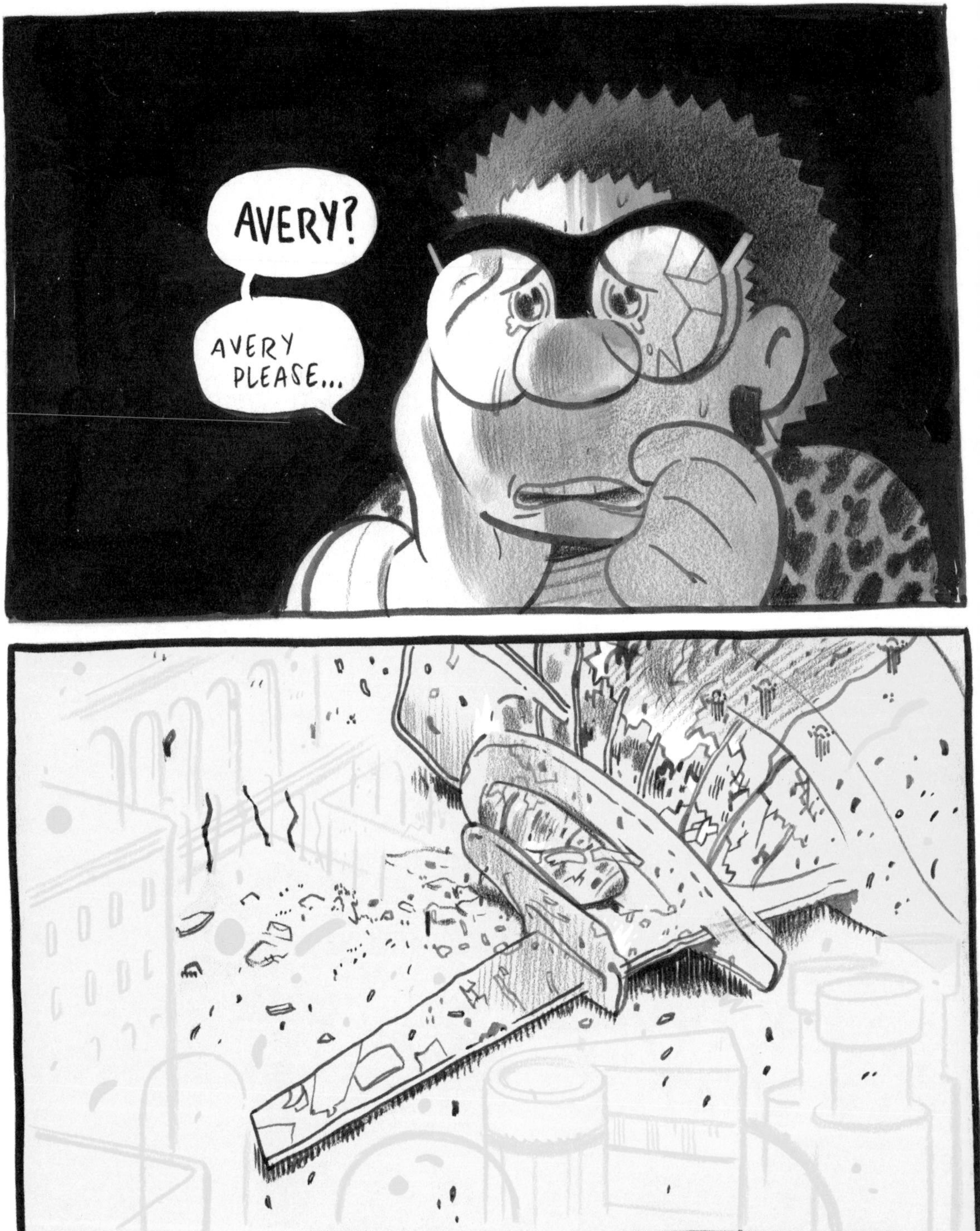
AVERY?
AVERY PLEASE...

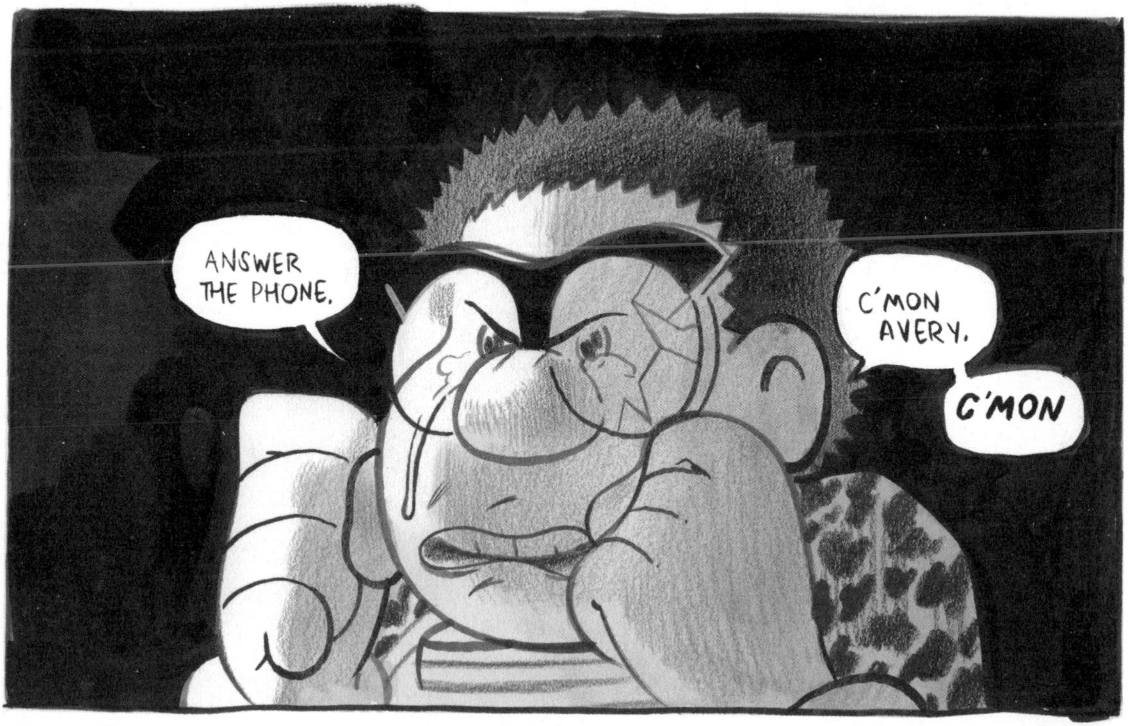
ANSWER THE PHONE.
C'MON AVERY.
C'MON

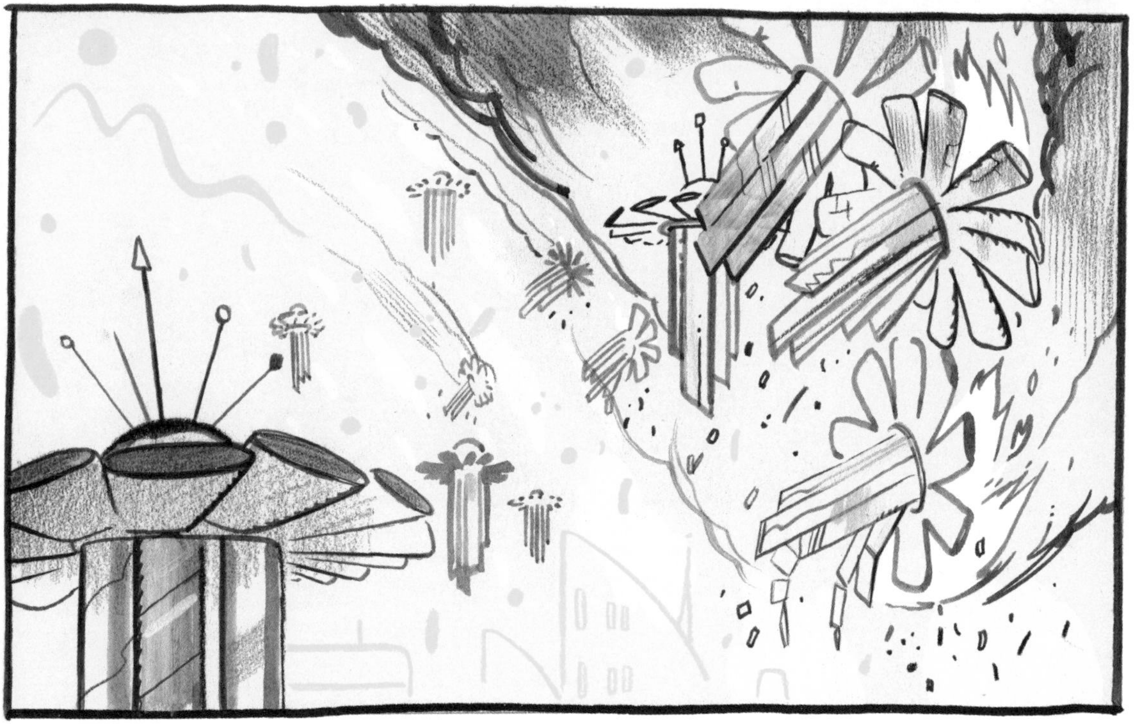

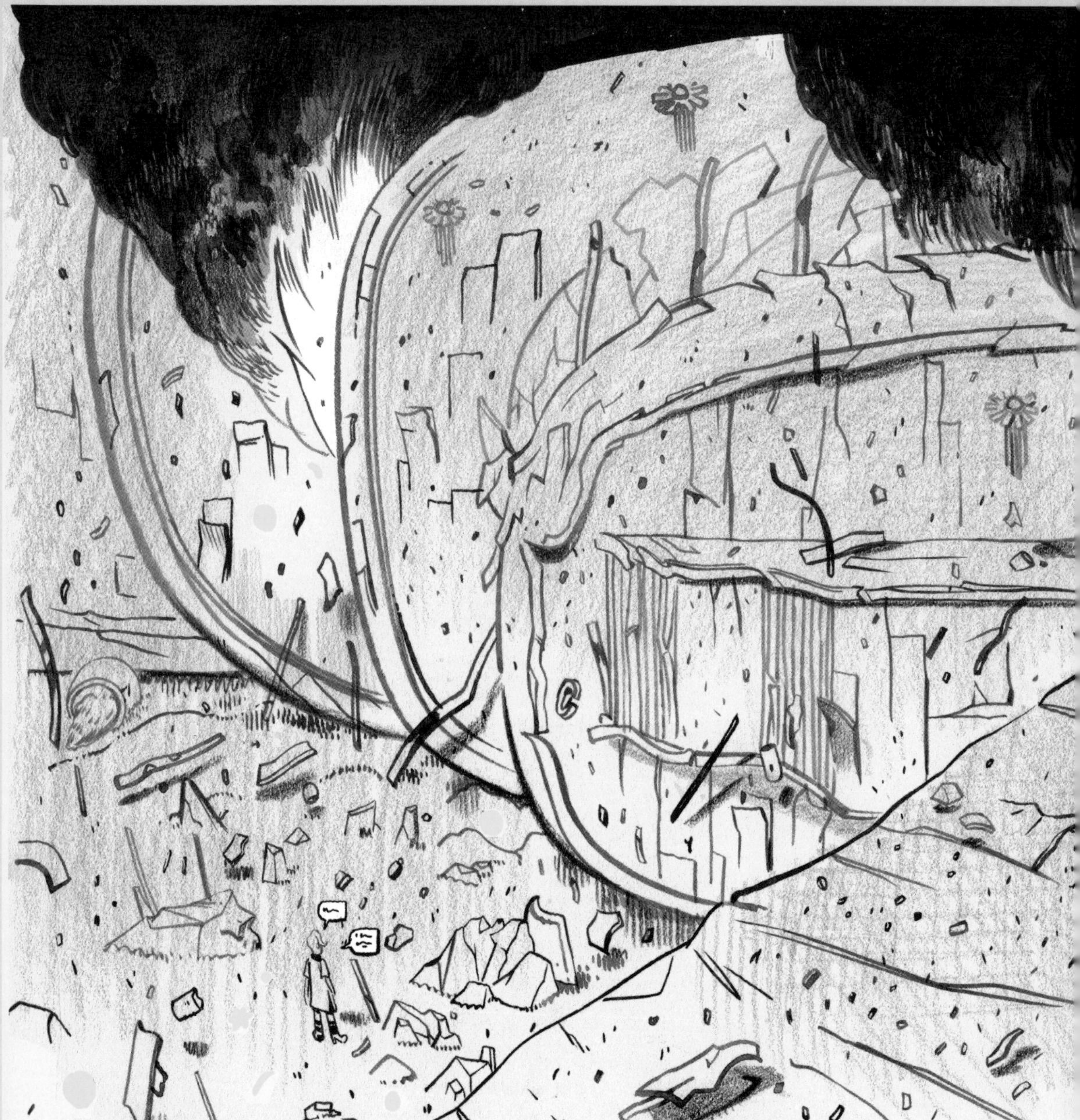

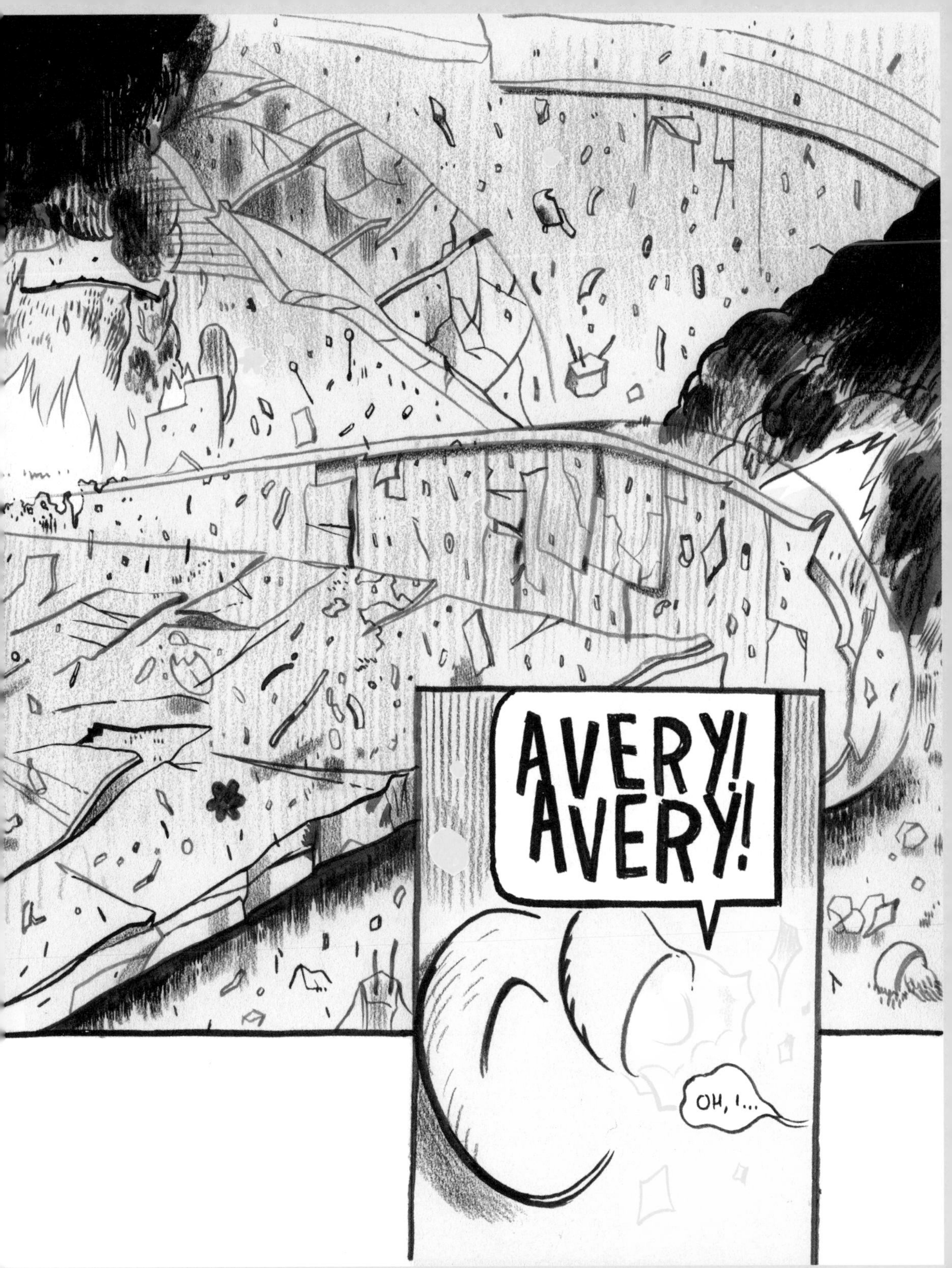
AVERY! AVERY!
OH, I...

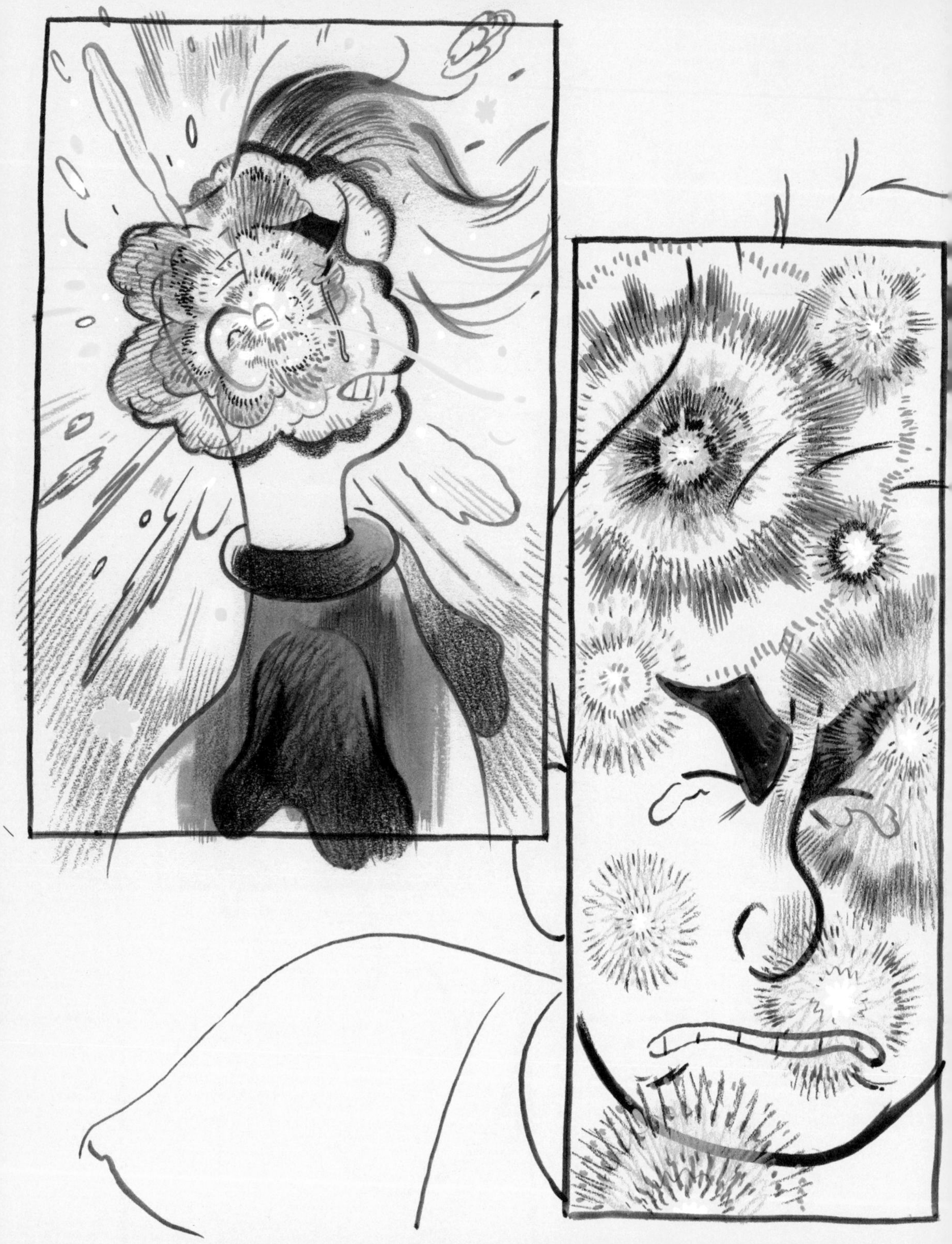

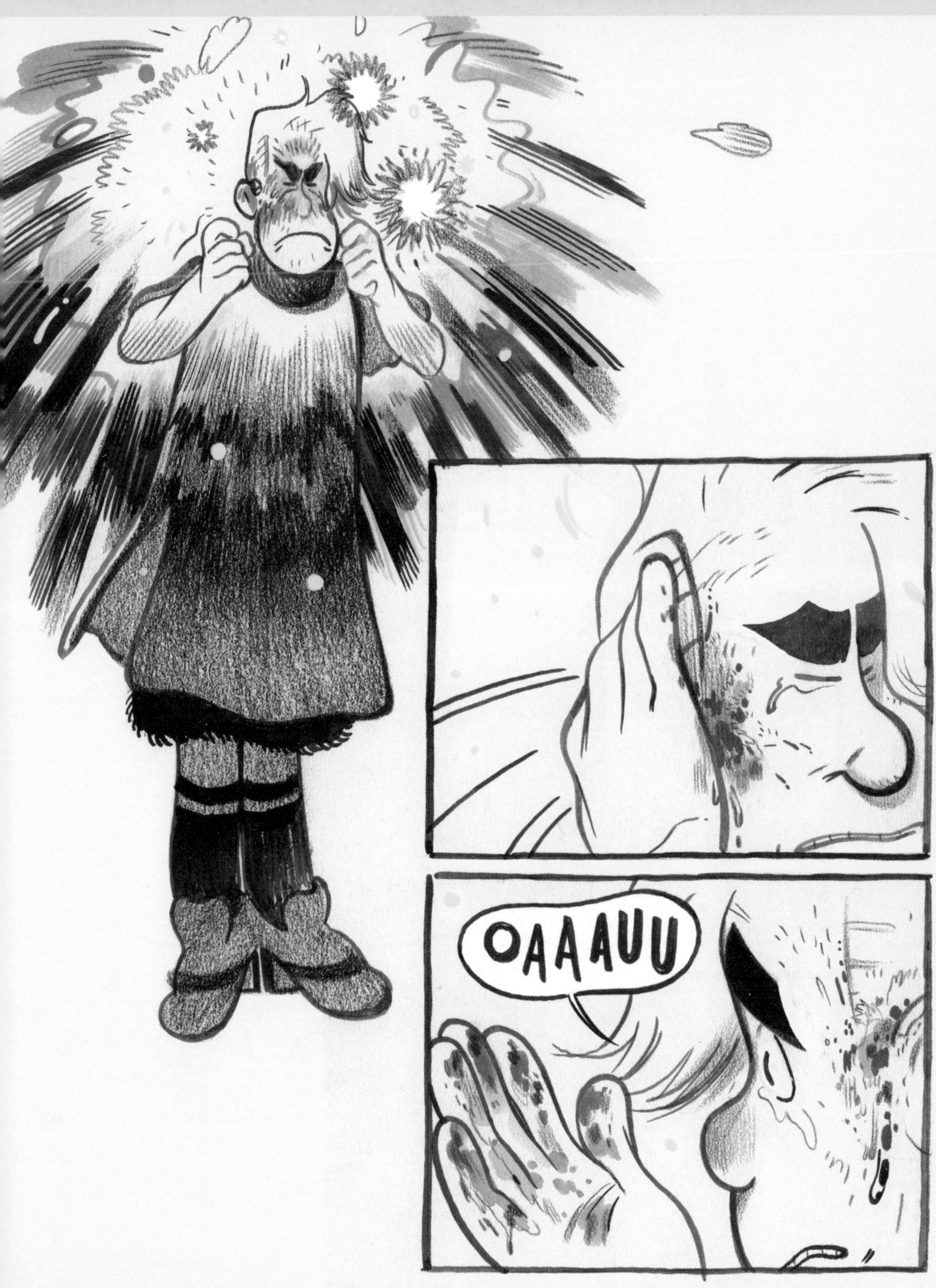
OAAAUU

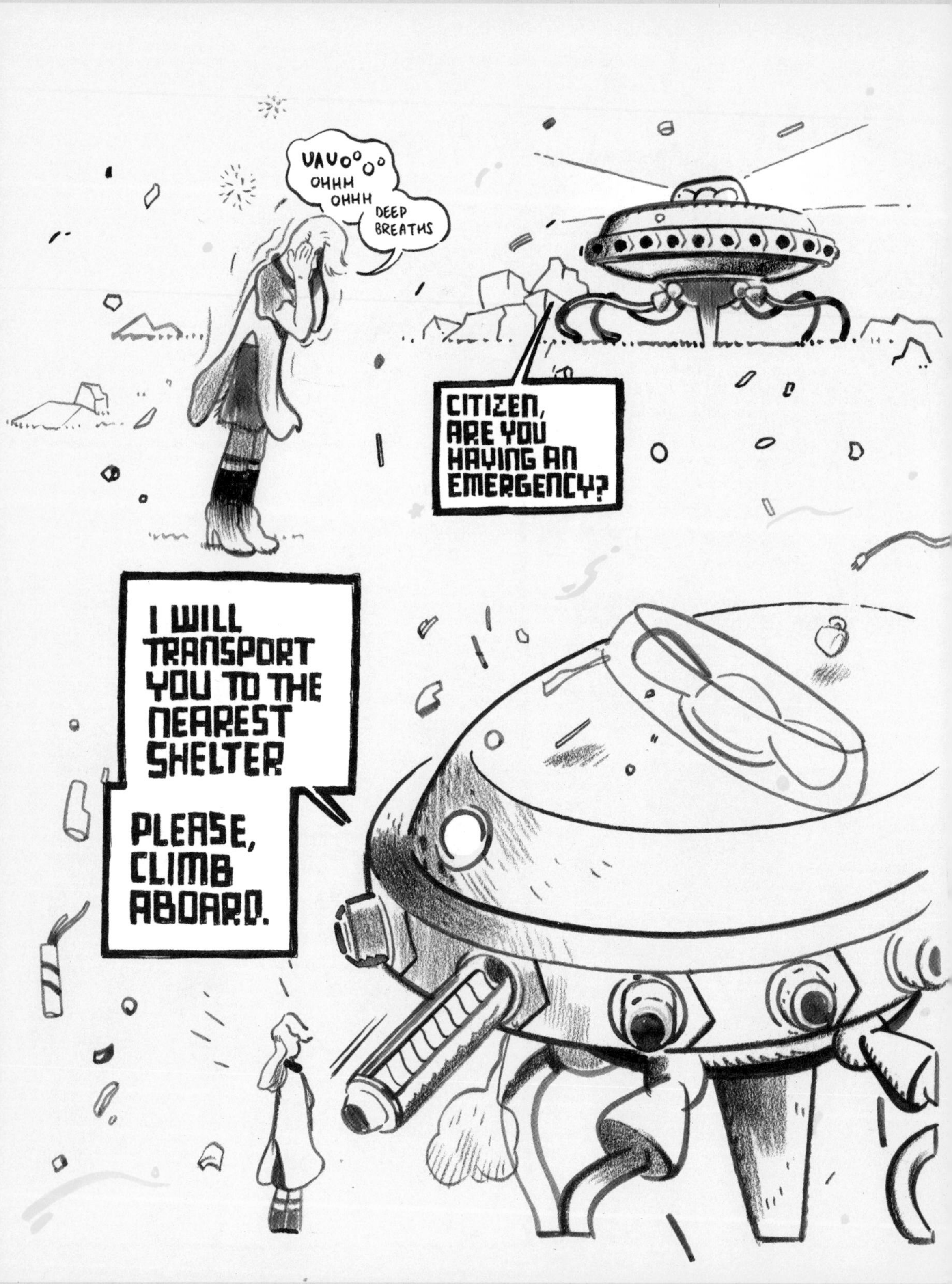
UAUOooo
OHHH
OHHH
DEEP BREATHS
CITIZEN, ARE YOU HAVING AN EMERGENCY?
I WILL TRANSPORT YOU TO THE NEAREST SHELTER
PLEASE, CLIMB ABOARD.

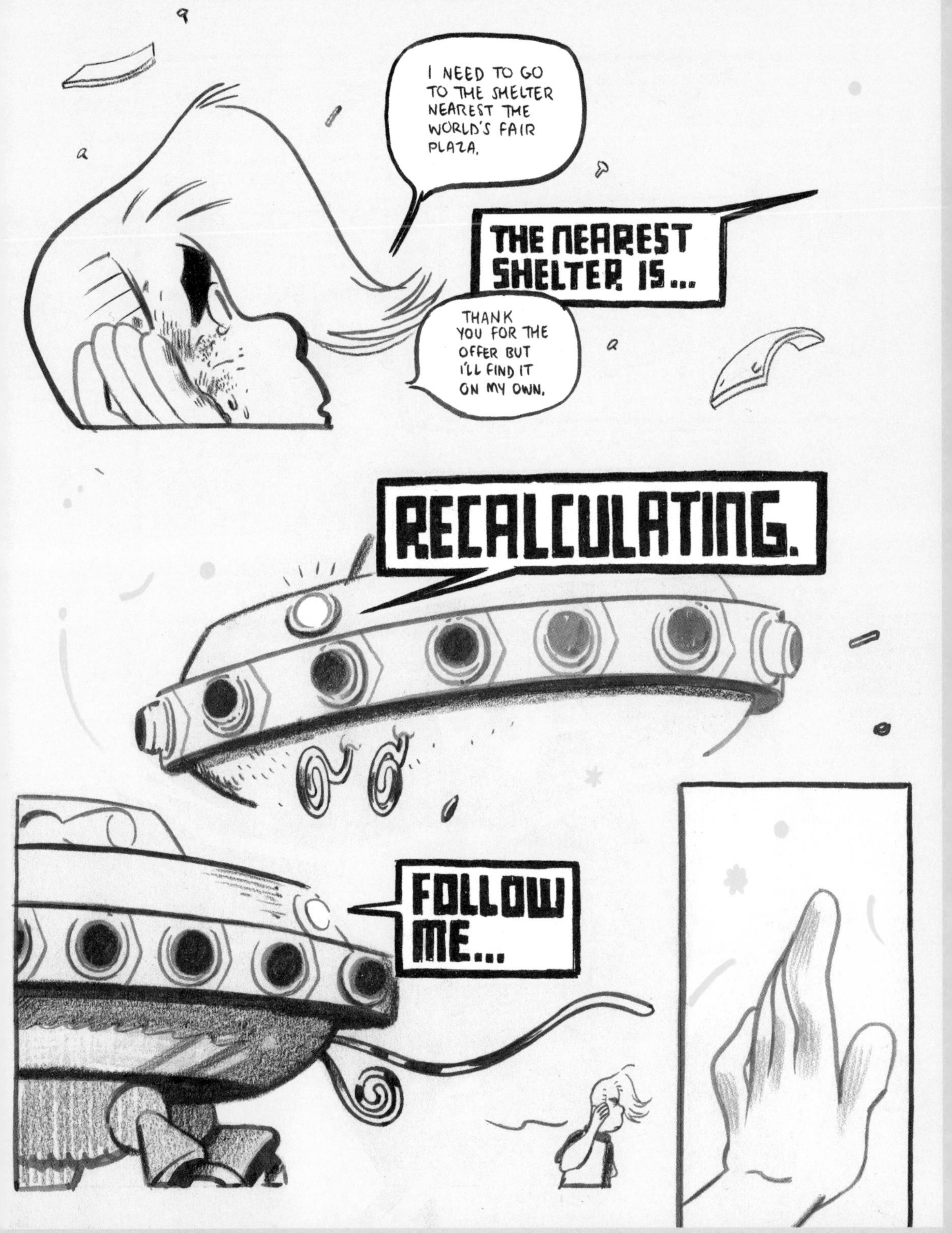
I NEED TO GO TO THE SHELTER NEAREST THE WORLD'S FAIR PLAZA.
THE NEAREST SHELTER IS...
THANK YOU FOR THE OFFER BUT I'LL FIND IT ON MY OWN.
RECALCULATING.
FOLLOW ME...

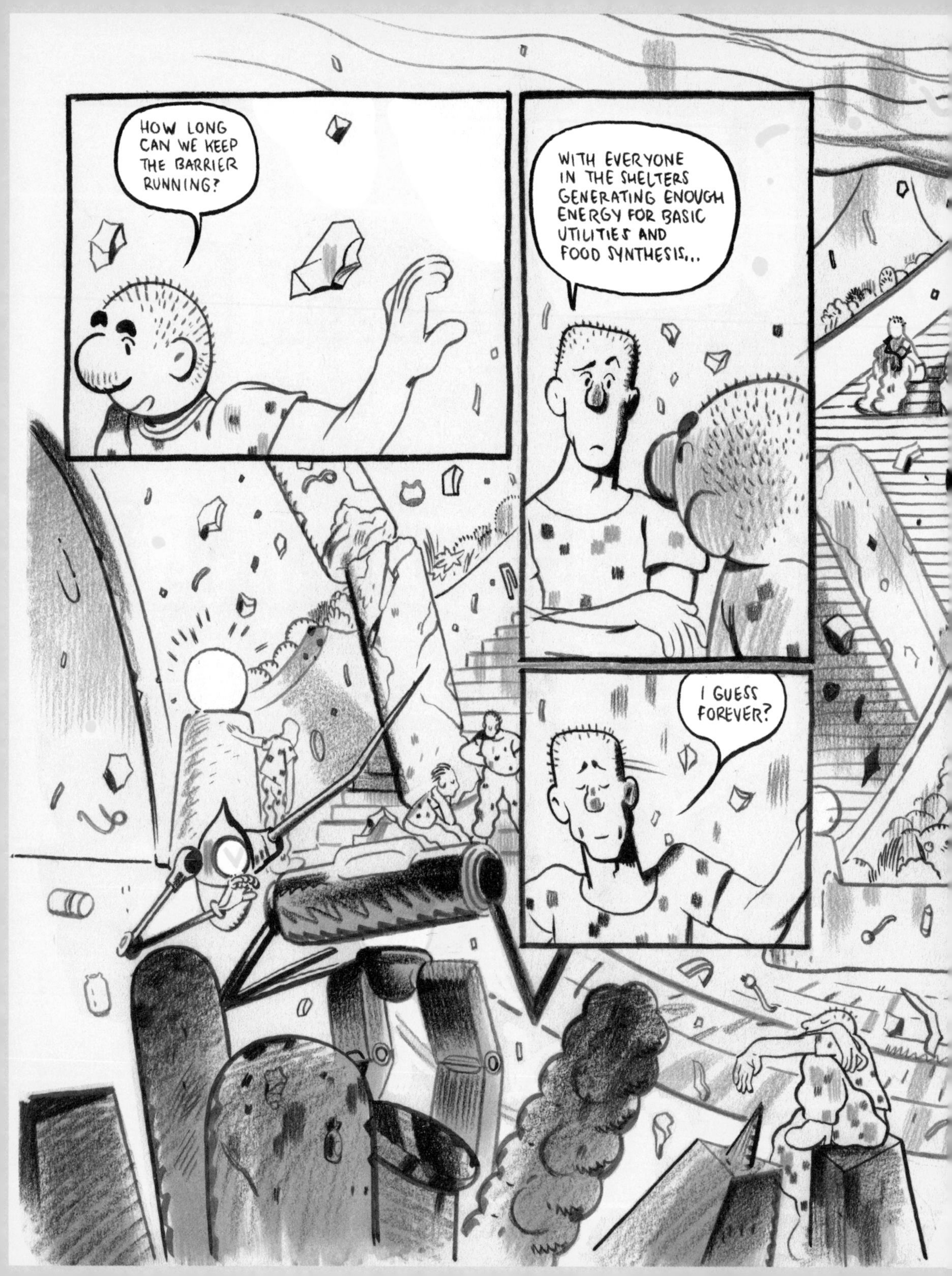
HOW LONG CAN WE KEEP THE BARRIER RUNNING?
WITH EVERYONE IN THE SHELTERS GENERATING ENOUGH ENERGY FOR BASIC UTILITIES AND FOOD SYNTHESIS...
I GUESS FOREVER?

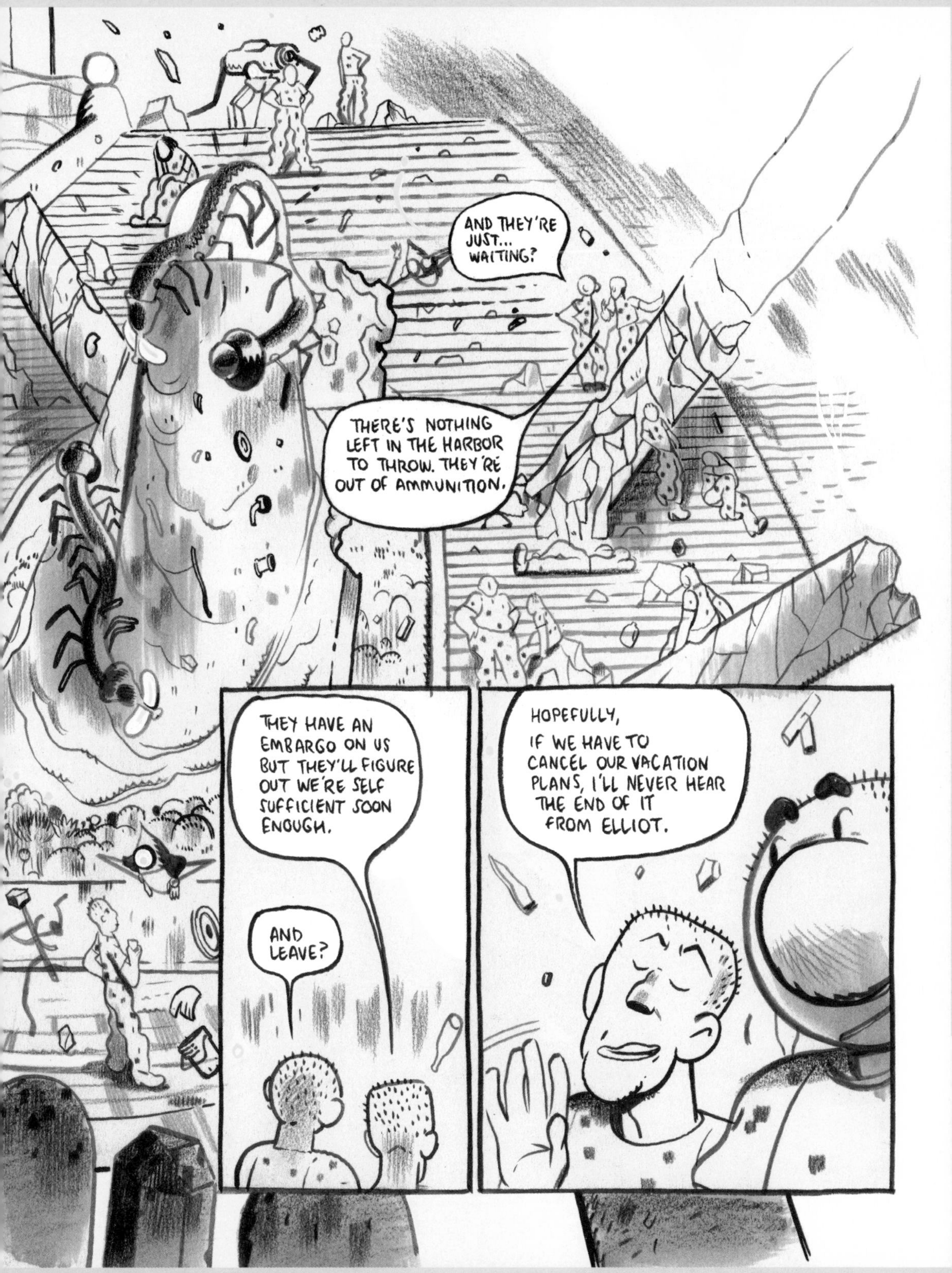
AND THEY'RE JUST... WAITING?
THERE'S NOTHING LEFT IN THE HARBOR TO THROW. THEY'RE OUT OF AMMUNITION.
THEY HAVE AN EMBARGO ON US BUT THEY'LL FIGURE OUT WE'RE SELF SUFFICIENT SOON ENOUGH.
AND LEAVE?
HOPEFULLY,
IF WE HAVE TO CANCEL OUR VACATION PLANS, I'LL NEVER HEAR THE END OF IT FROM ELLIOT.

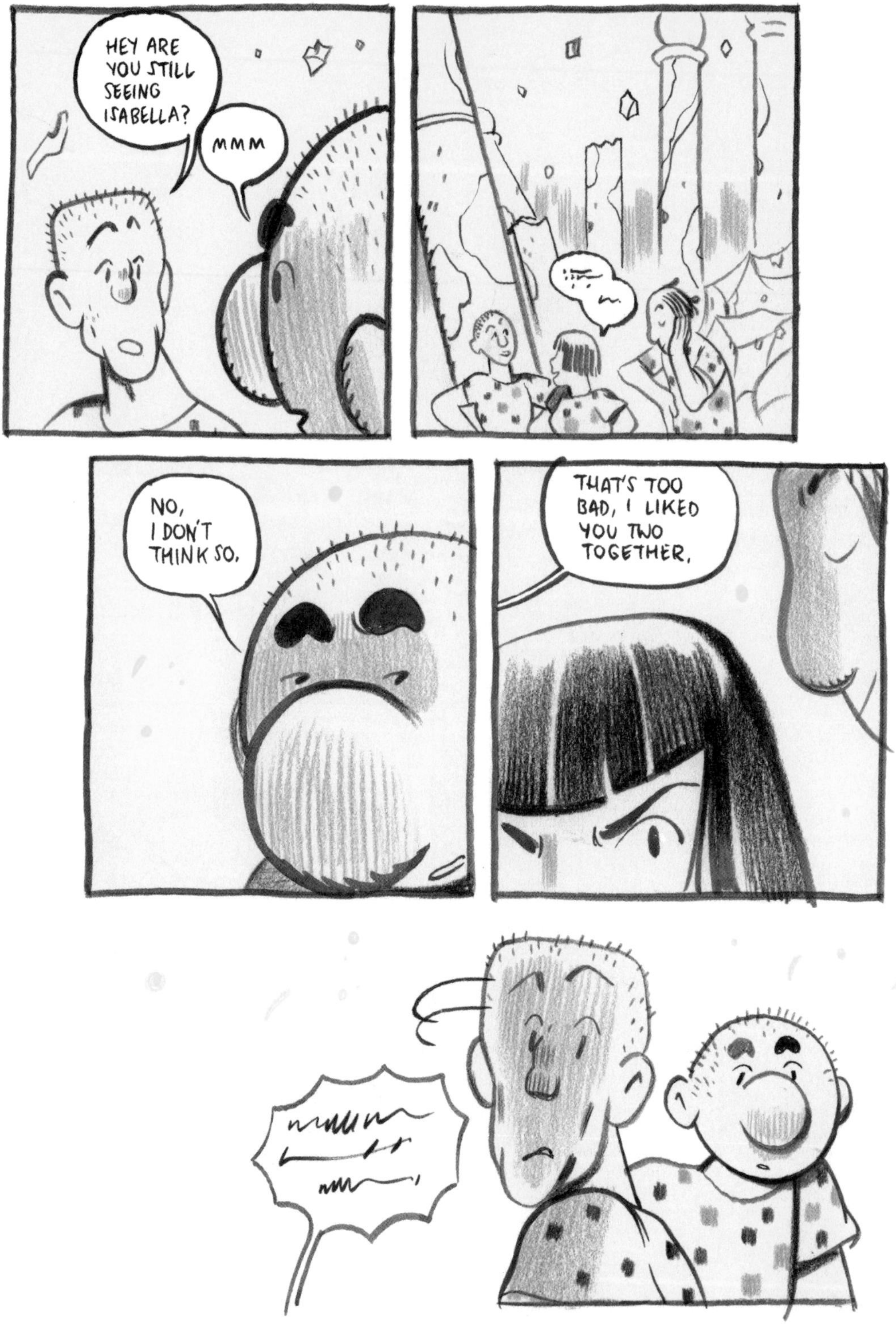
HEY ARE YOU STILL SEEING ISABELLA?
MMM
NO, I DON'T THINK SO.
THAT'S TOO BAD, I LIKED YOU TWO TOGETHER.

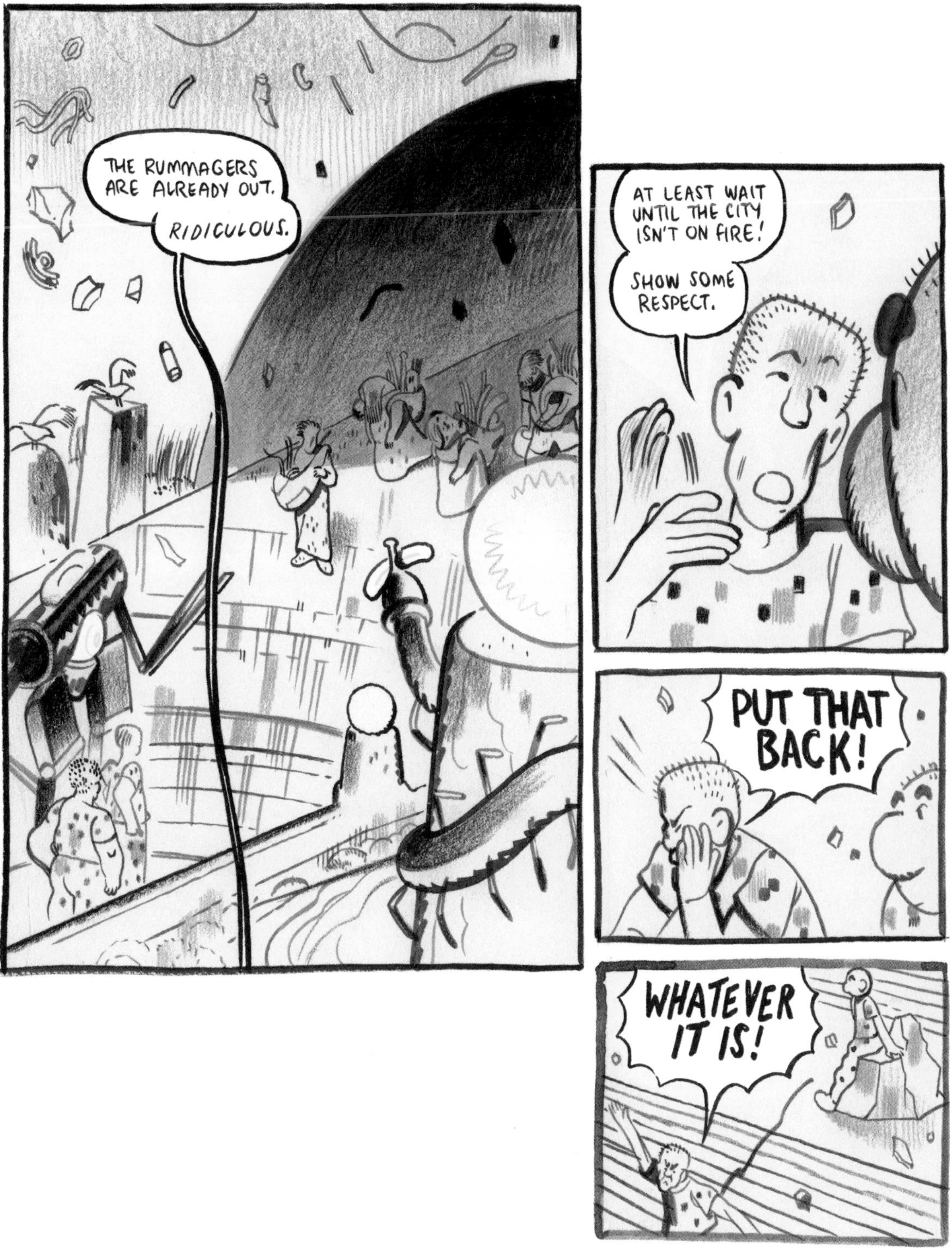
THE RUMMAGERS ARE ALREADY OUT.
RIDICULOUS.
AT LEAST WAIT UNTIL THE CITY ISN'T ON FIRE!
SHOW SOME RESPECT.
PUT THAT BACK!
WHATEVER IT IS!

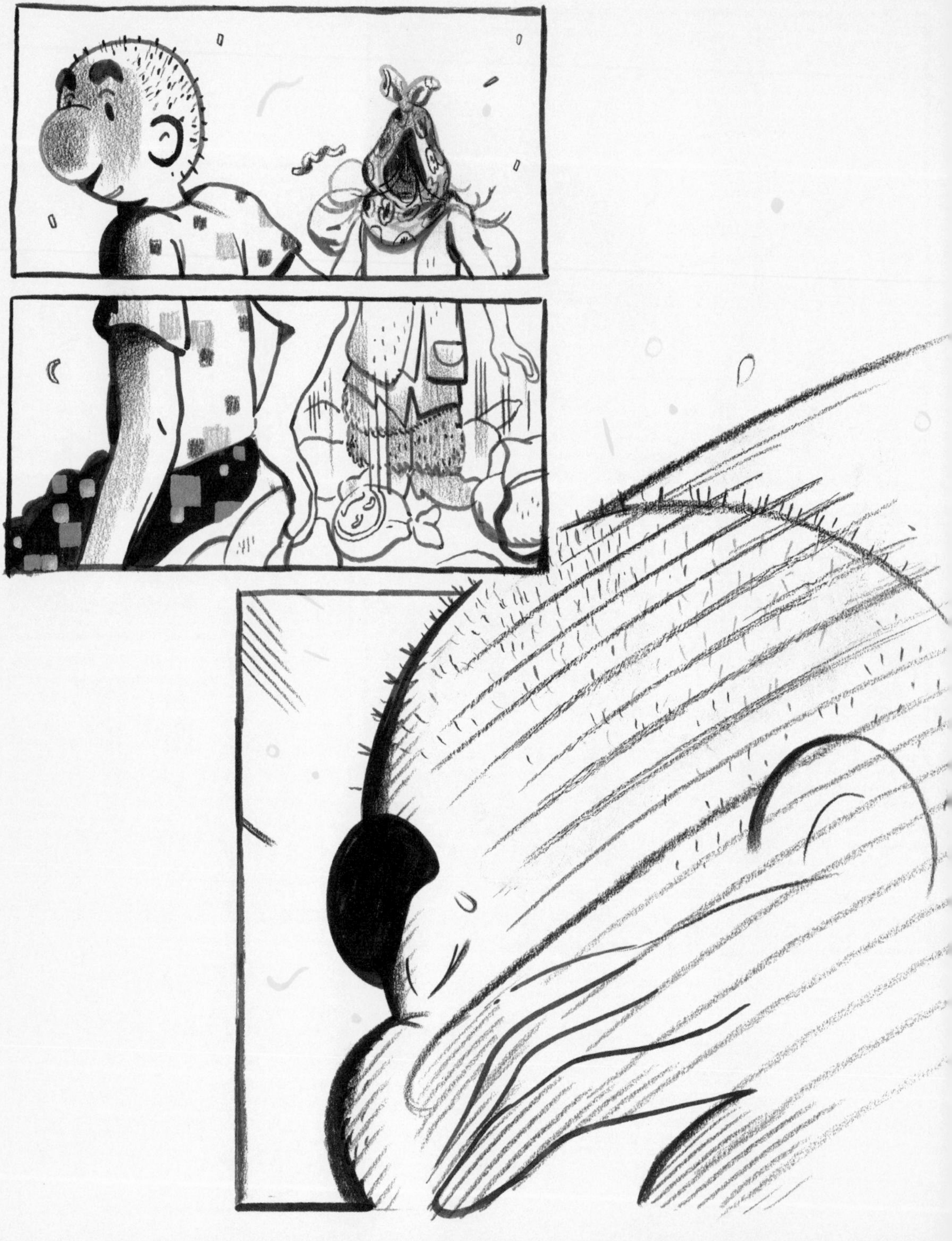

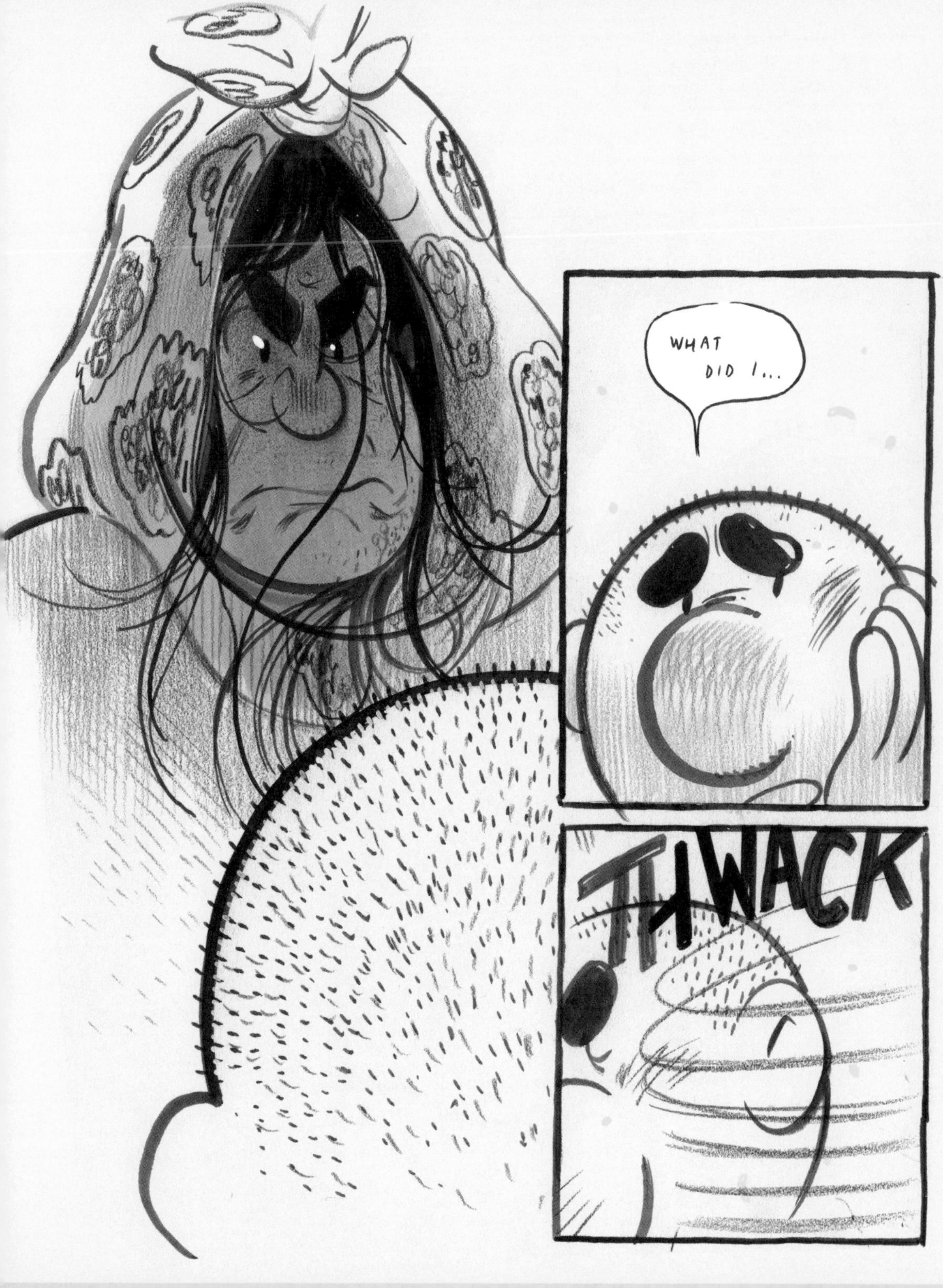
WHAT DID I...
THWACK

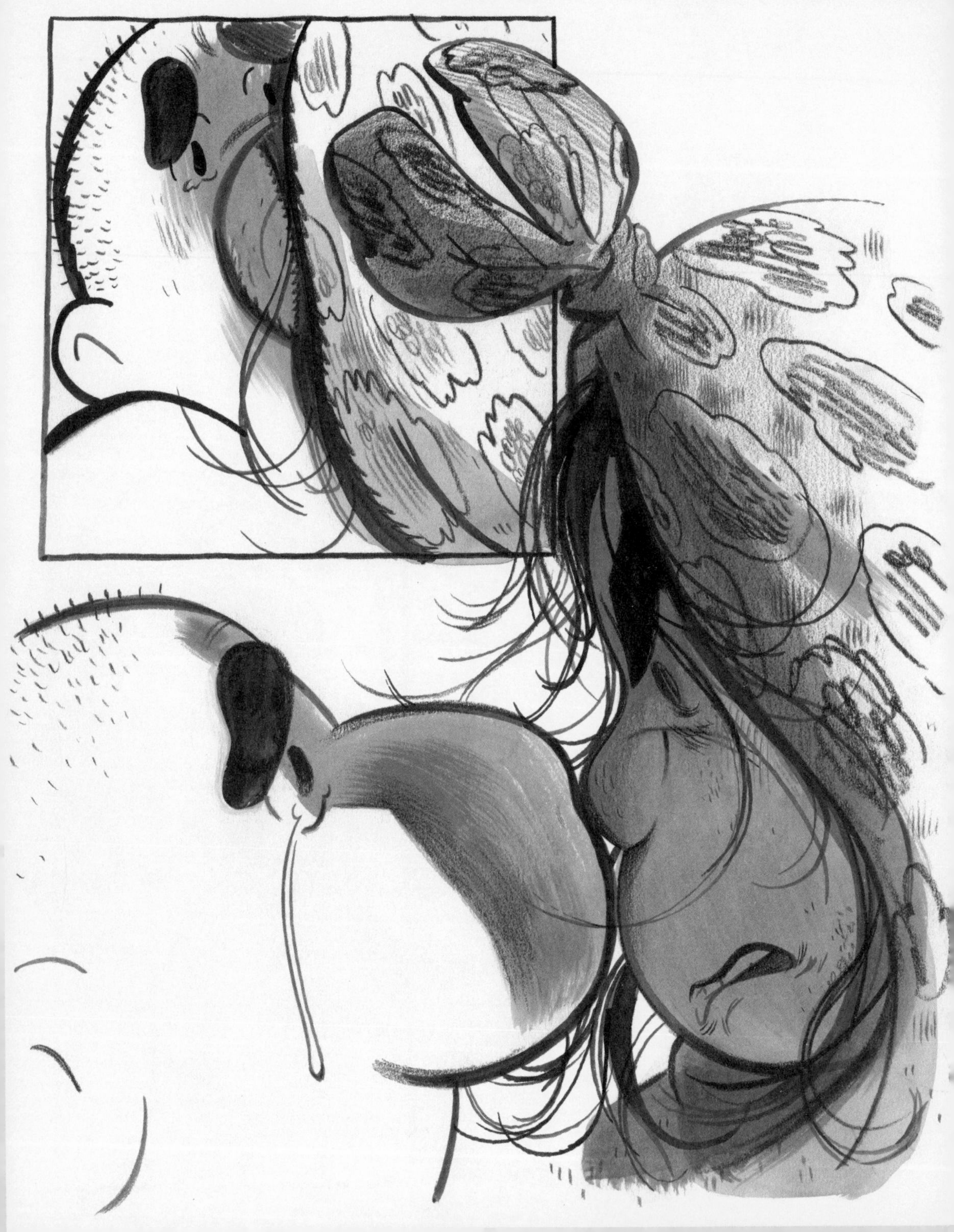

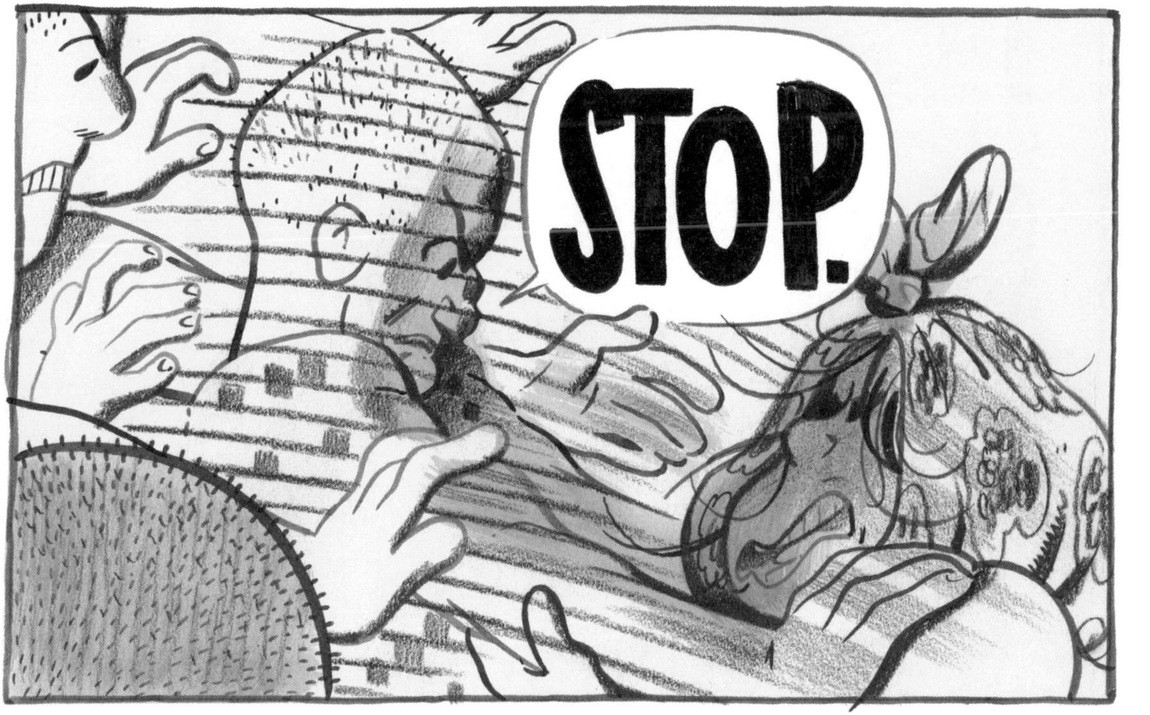
STOP.

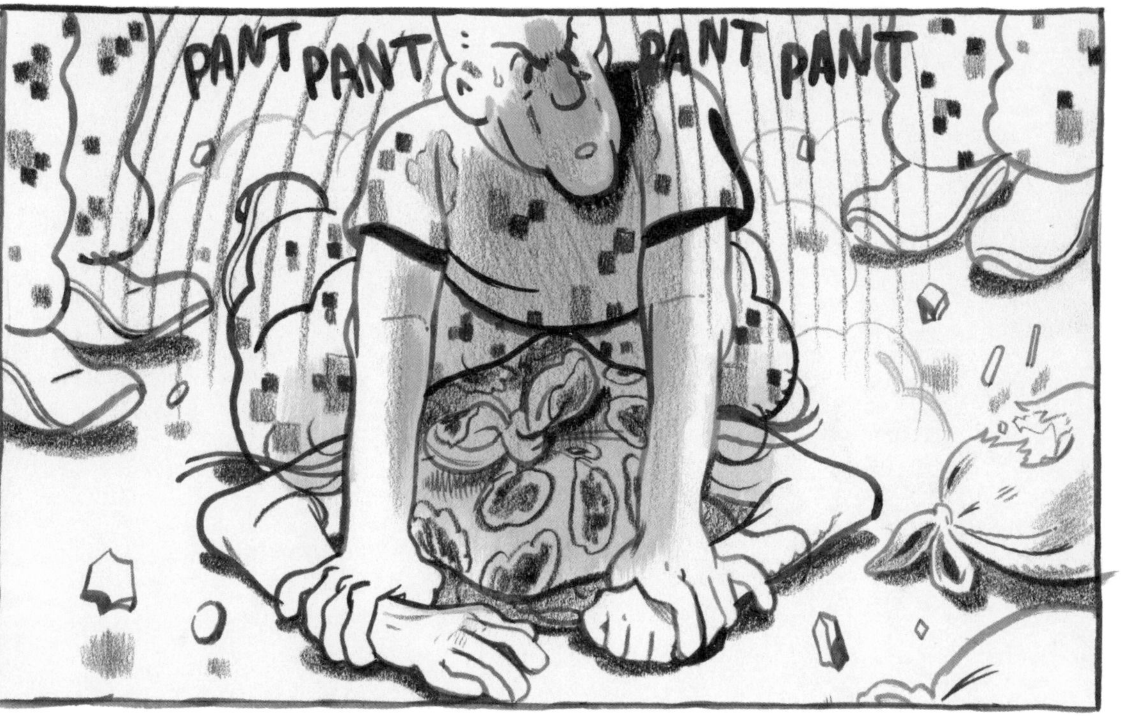
PANT PANT
PANT PANT

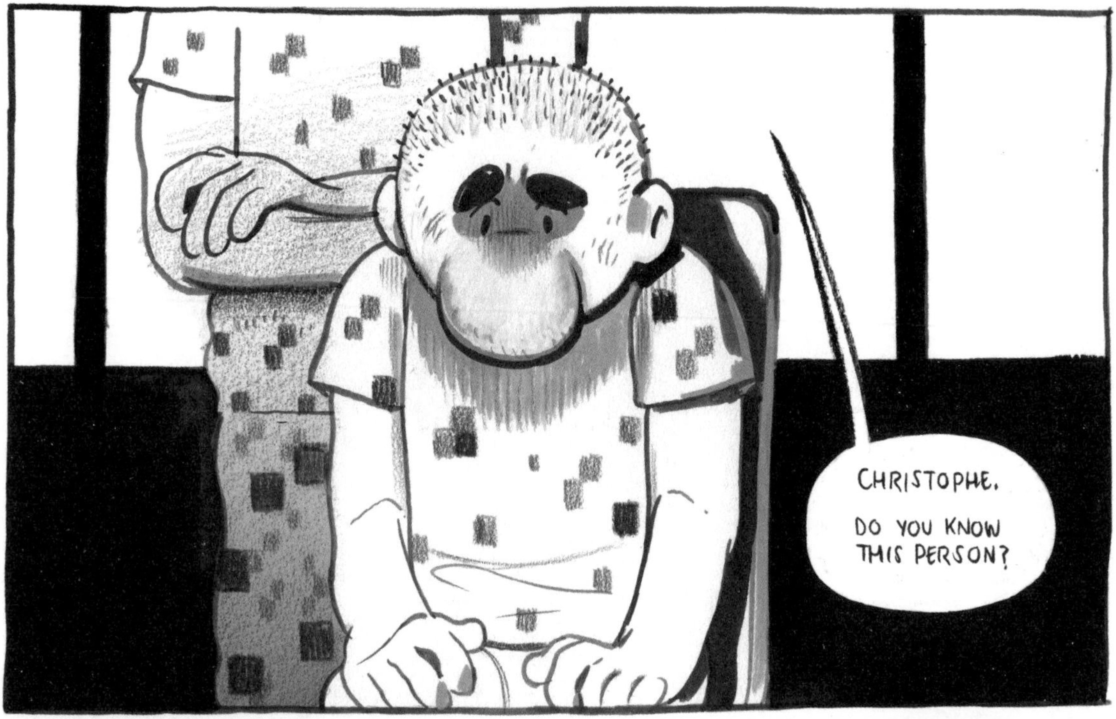
CHRISTOPHE.
DO YOU KNOW THIS PERSON?

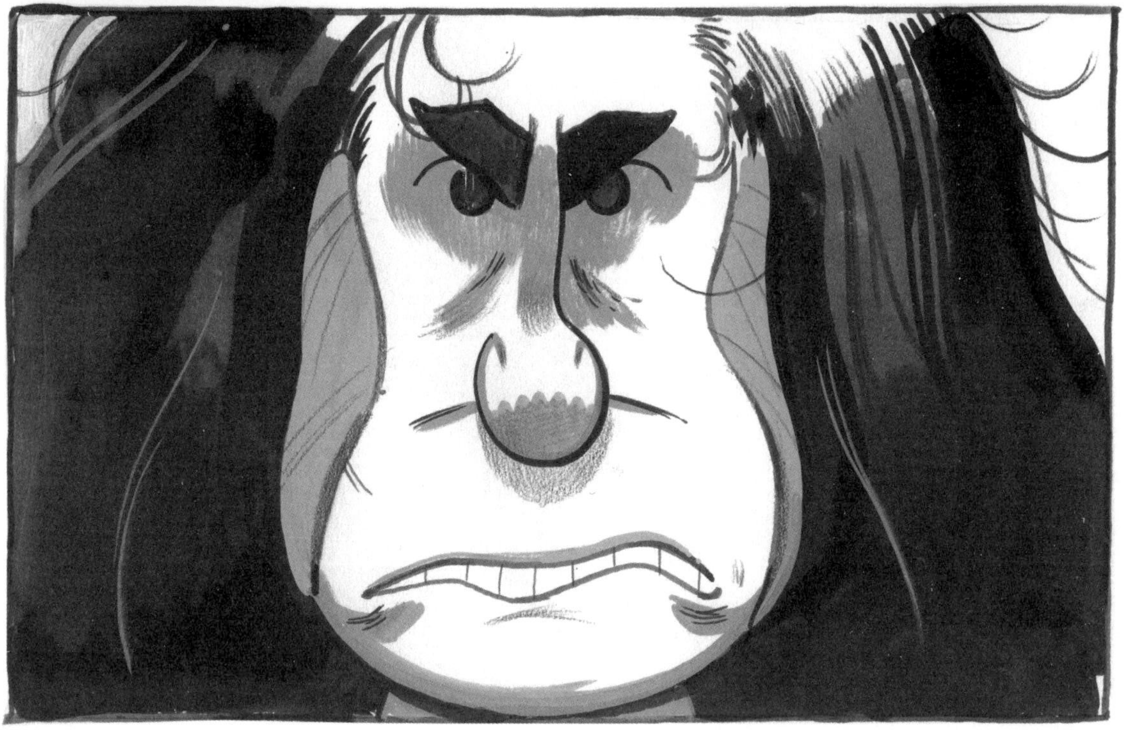

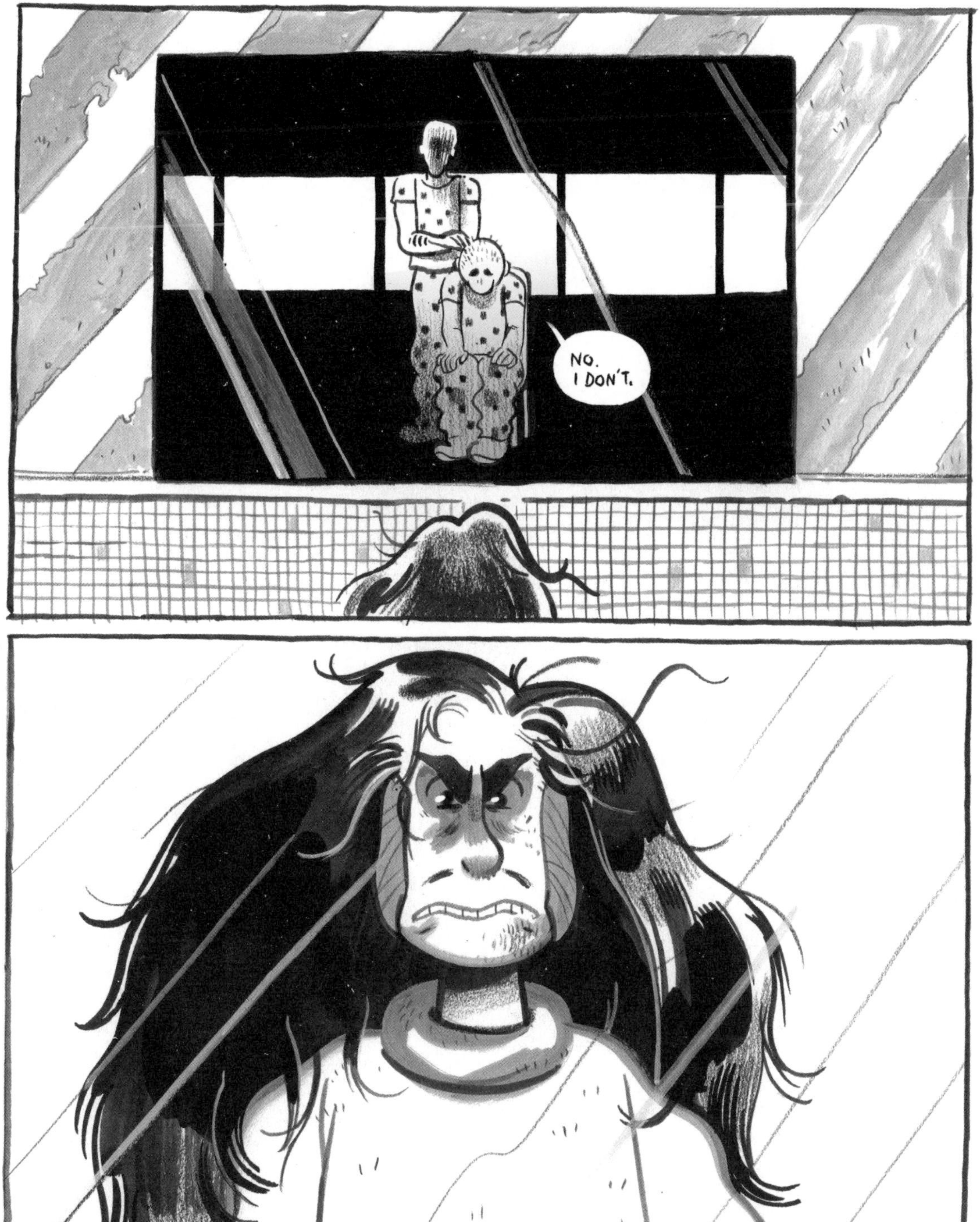
NO.
I DON'T.

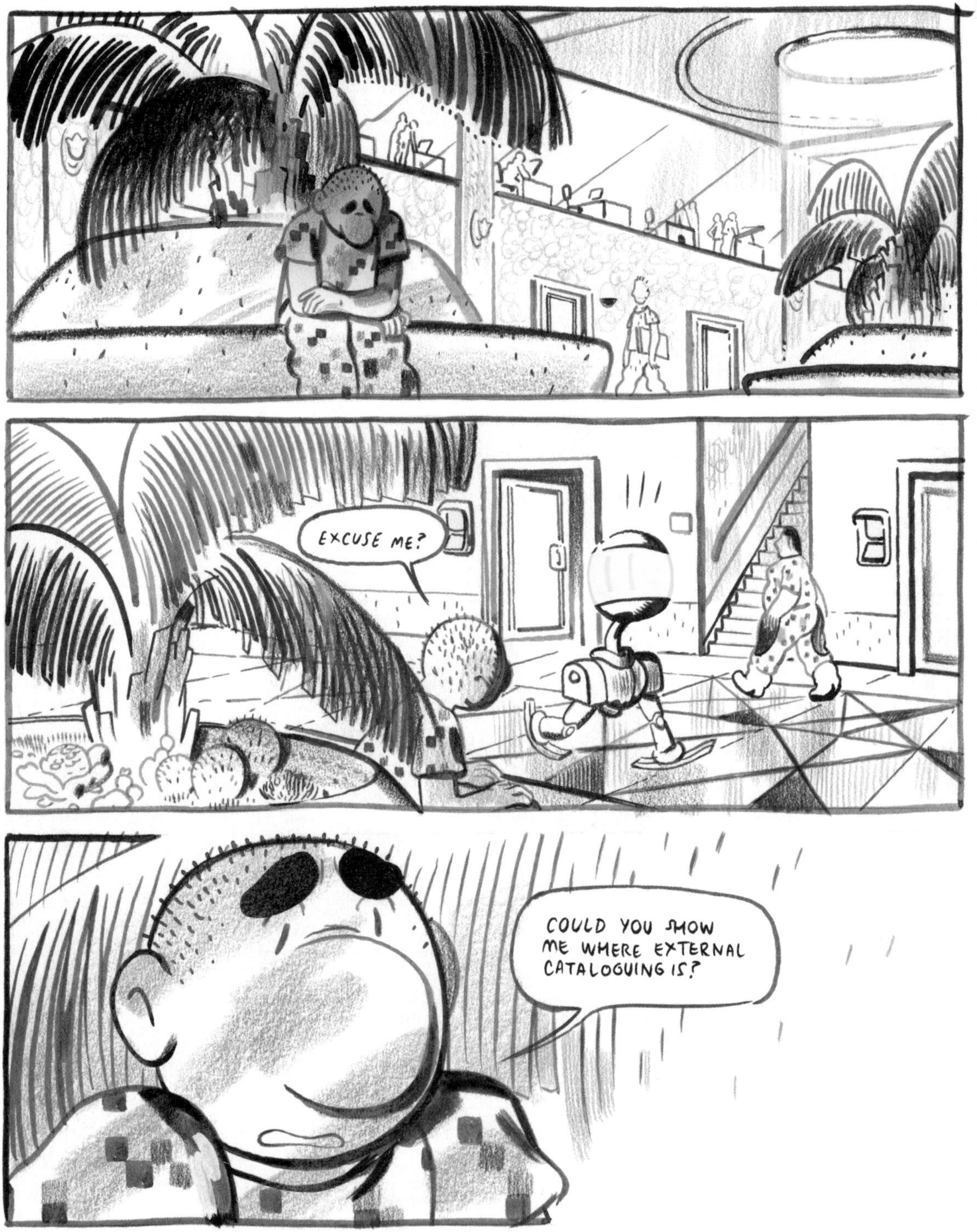
EXCUSE ME?
COULD YOU SHOW ME WHERE EXTERNAL CATALOGUING IS?

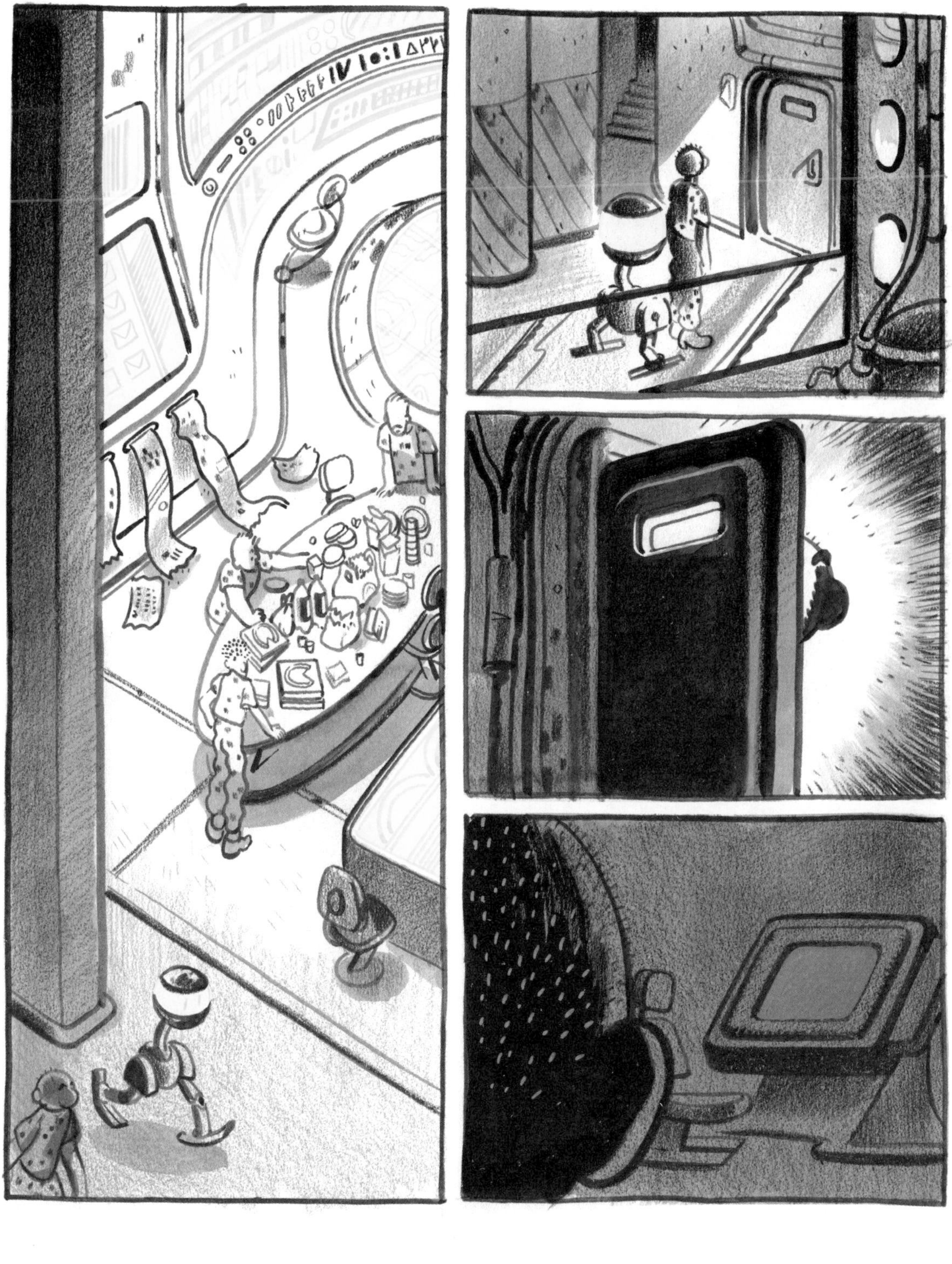

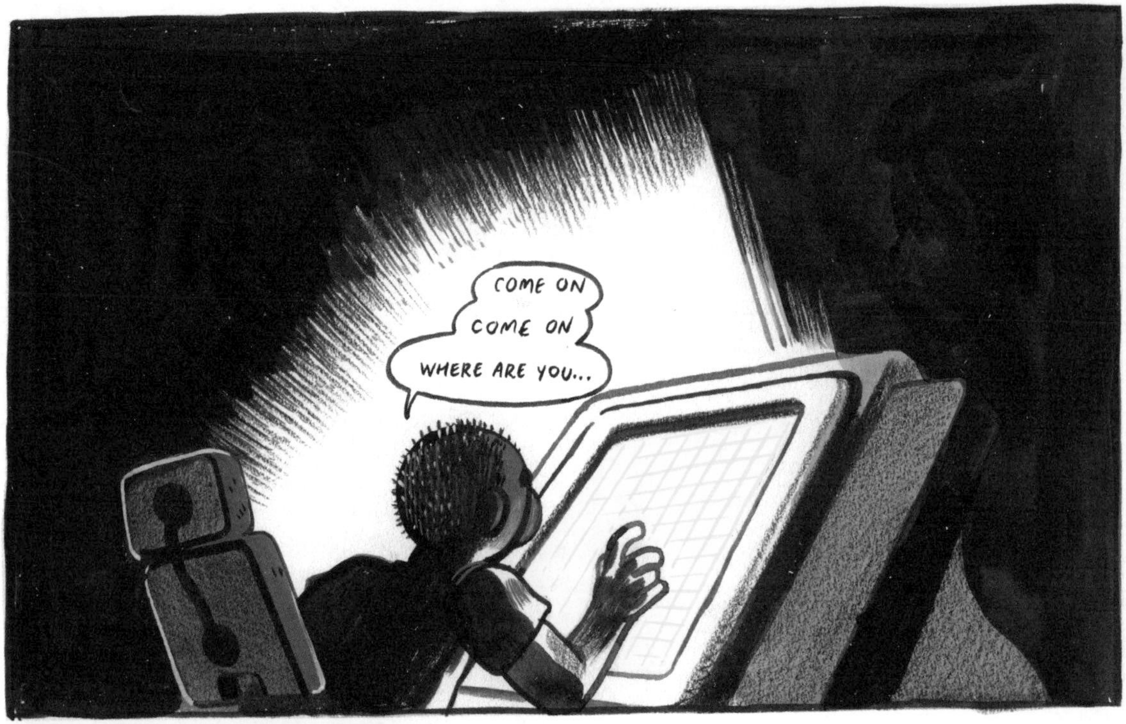
COME ON
COME ON
WHERE ARE YOU...

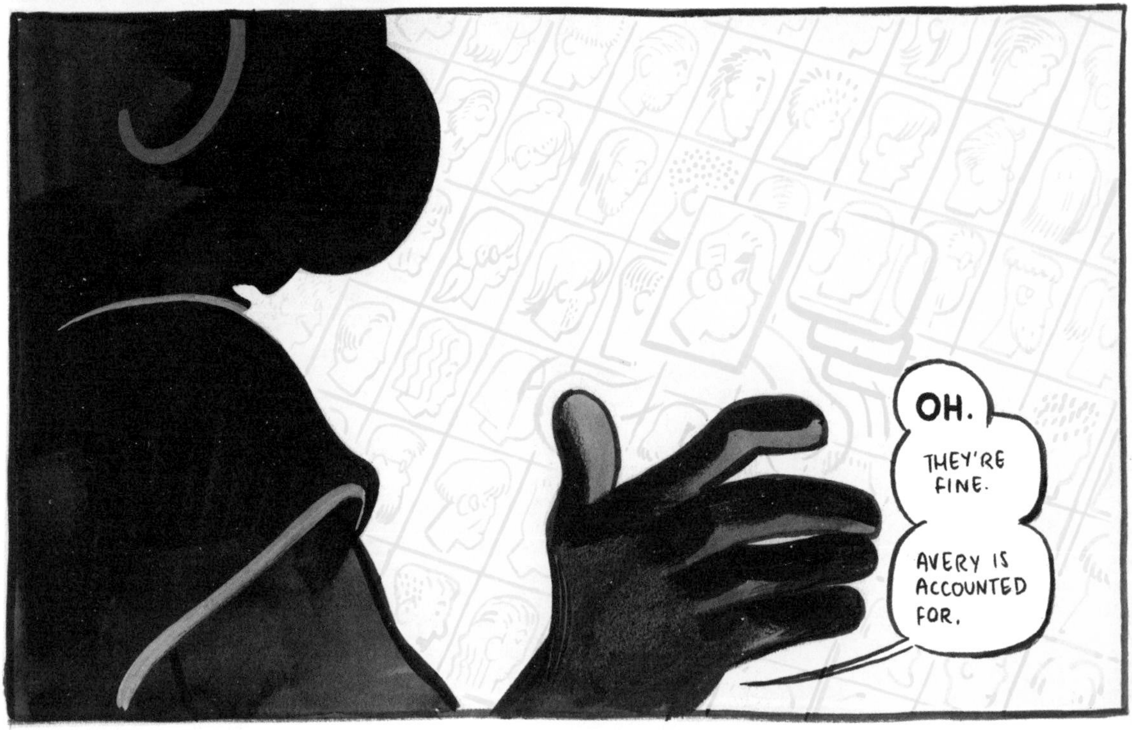
OH.
THEY'RE FINE.
AVERY IS ACCOUNTED FOR.

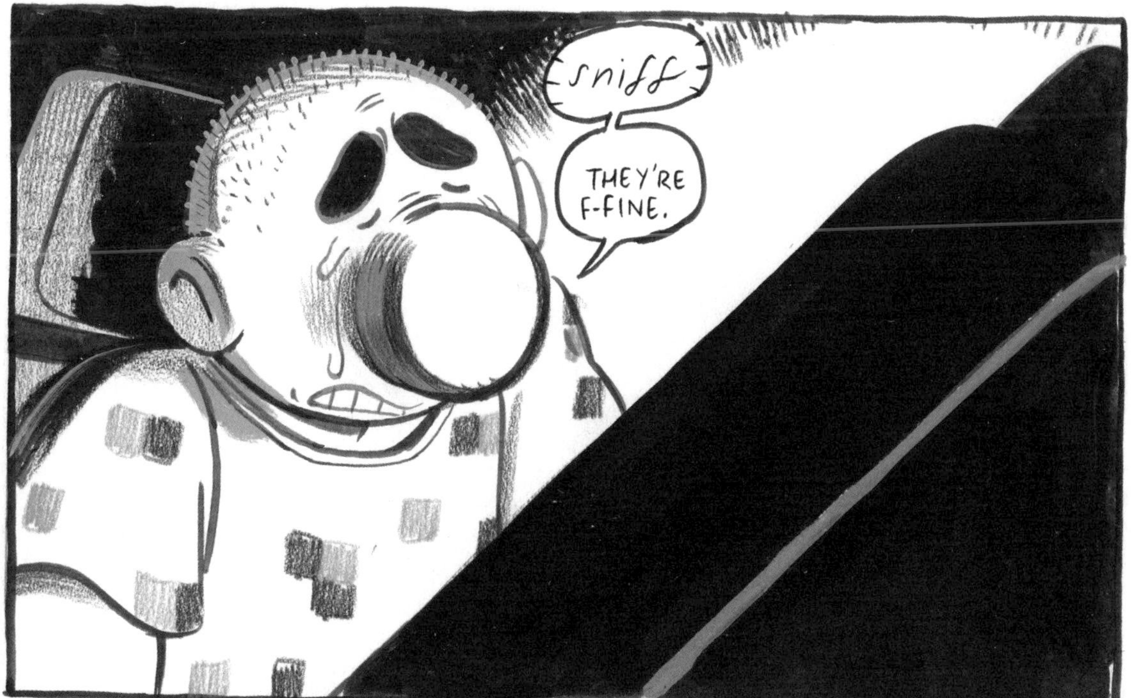
sniff
THEY'RE F-FINE.

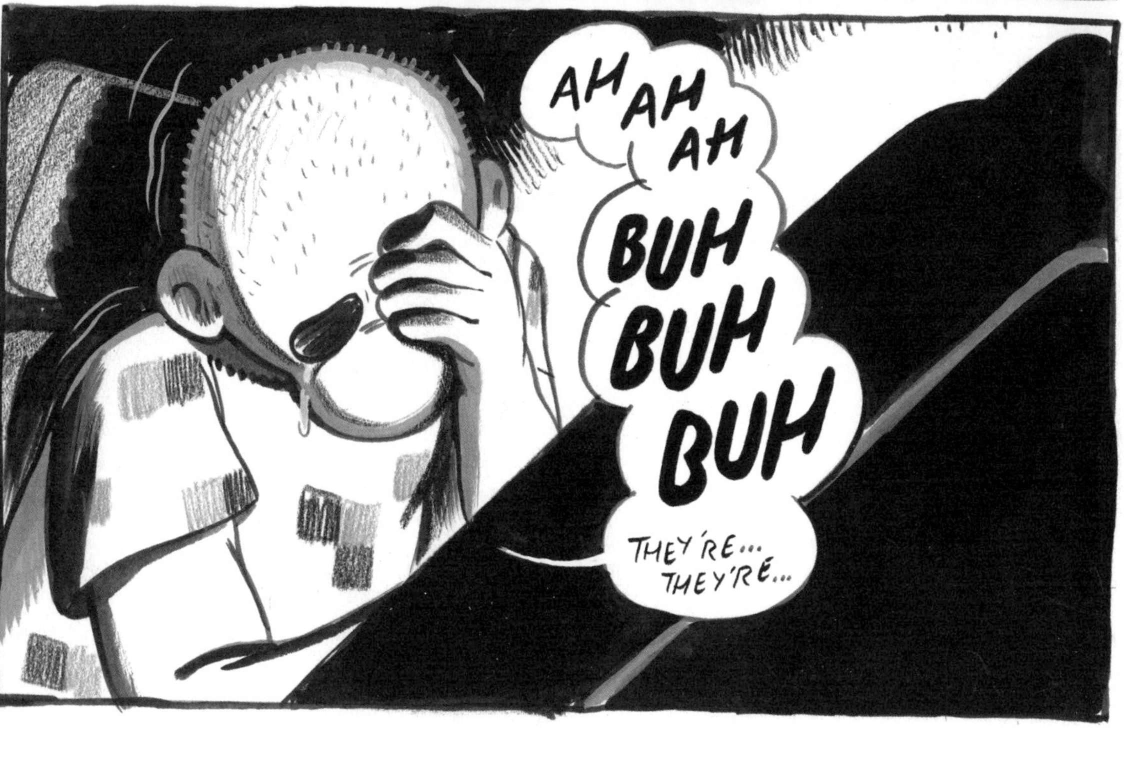
AH AH AH
BUH BUH BUH BUH
THEY'RE... THEY'RE...

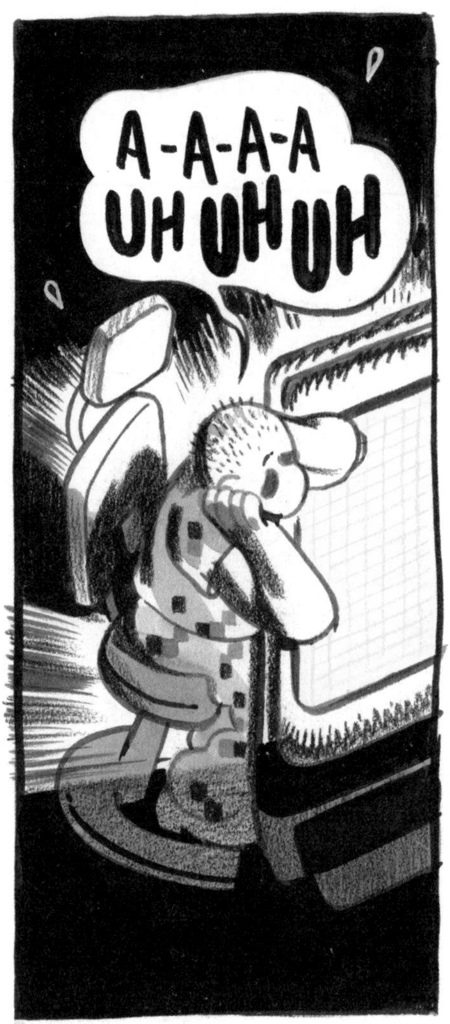
A-A-A-A UHUHUH

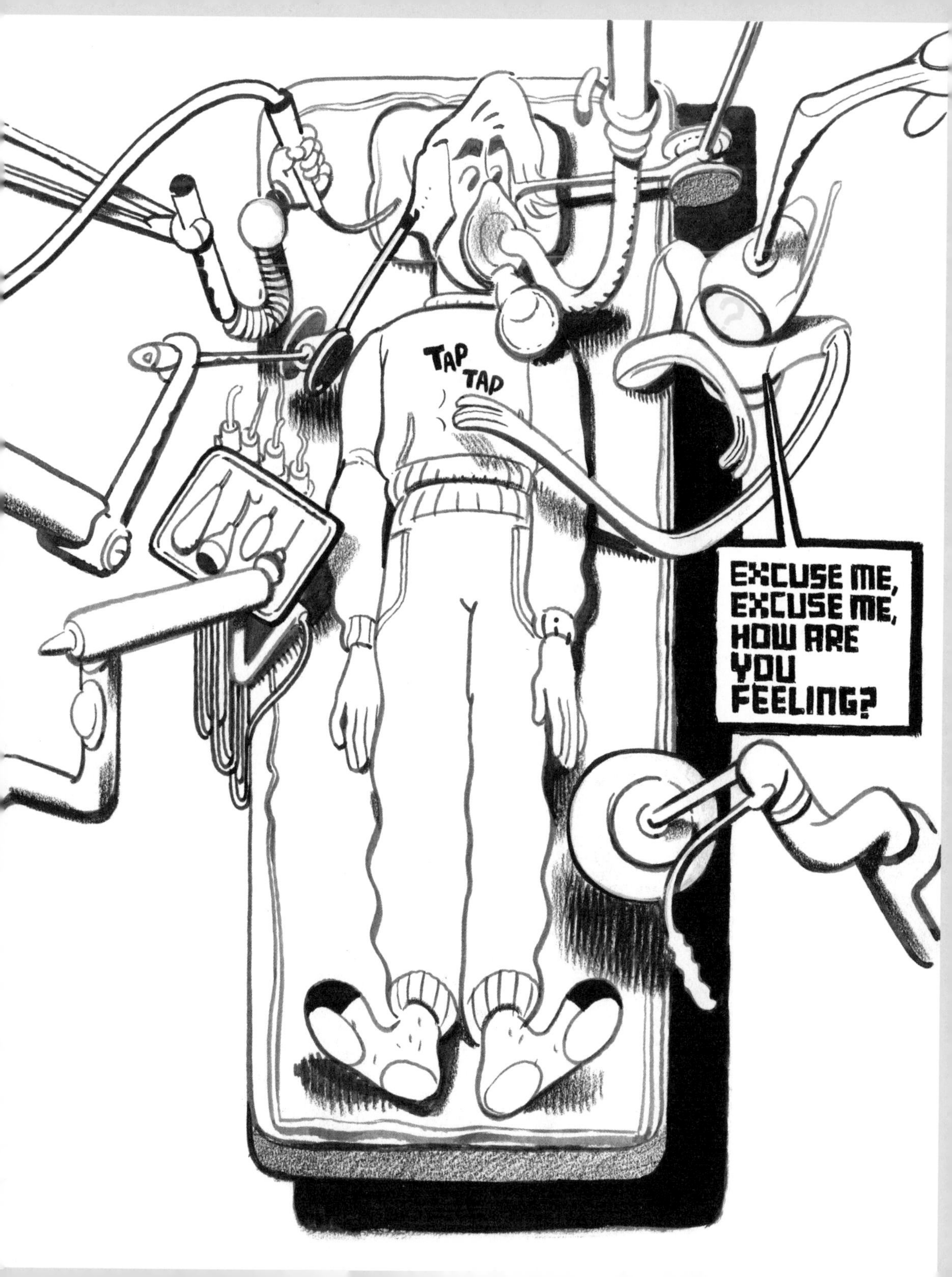
TAP TAP
EXCUSE ME, EXCUSE ME, HOW ARE YOU FEELING?

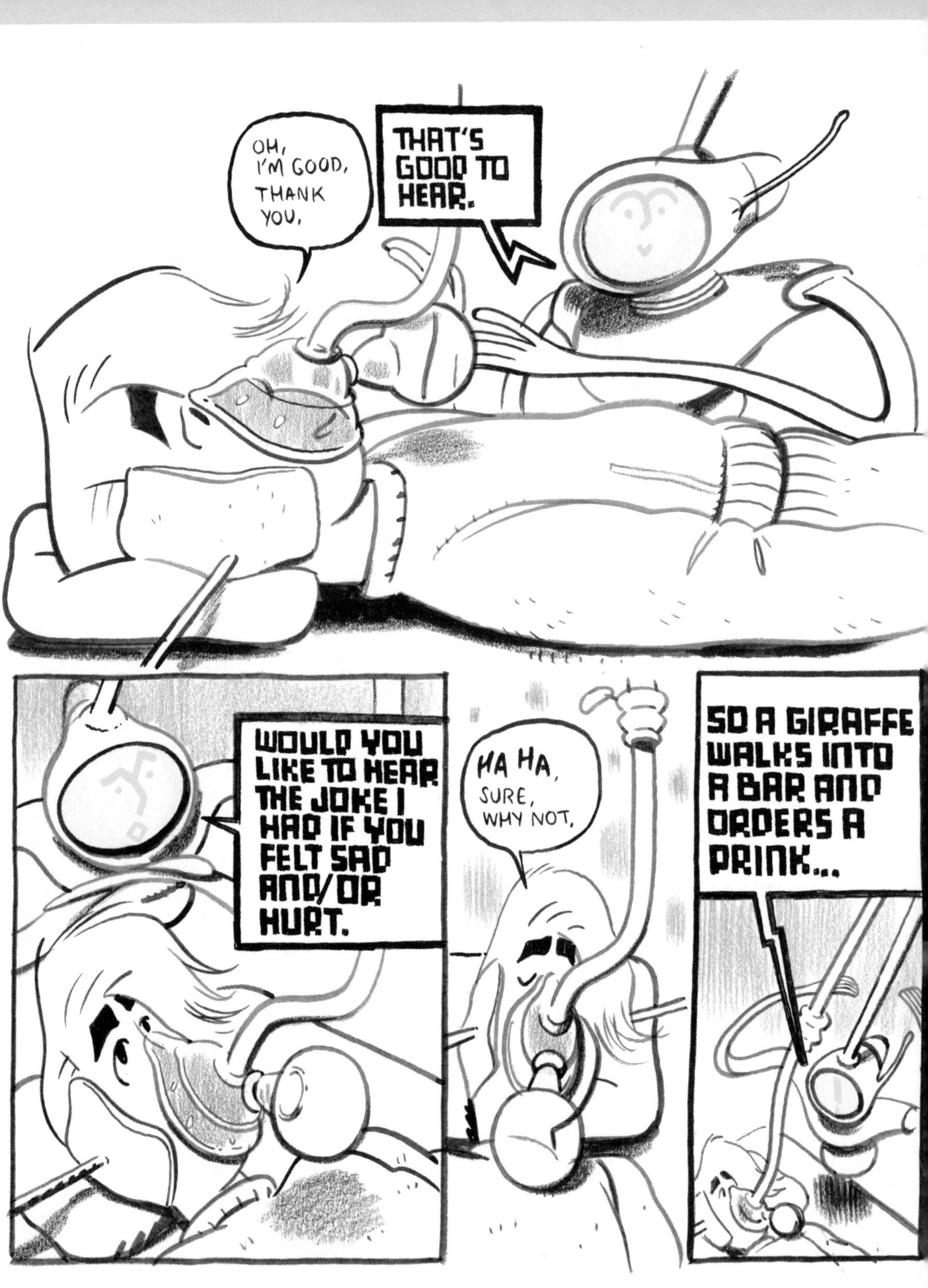
OH, I'M GOOD, THANK YOU.
THAT'S GOOD TO HEAR.
WOULD YOU LIKE TO HEAR THE JOKE I HAD IF YOU FELT SAD AND/OR HURT.
HA HA, SURE, WHY NOT.
SO A GIRAFFE WALKS INTO A BAR AND ORDERS A DRINK...

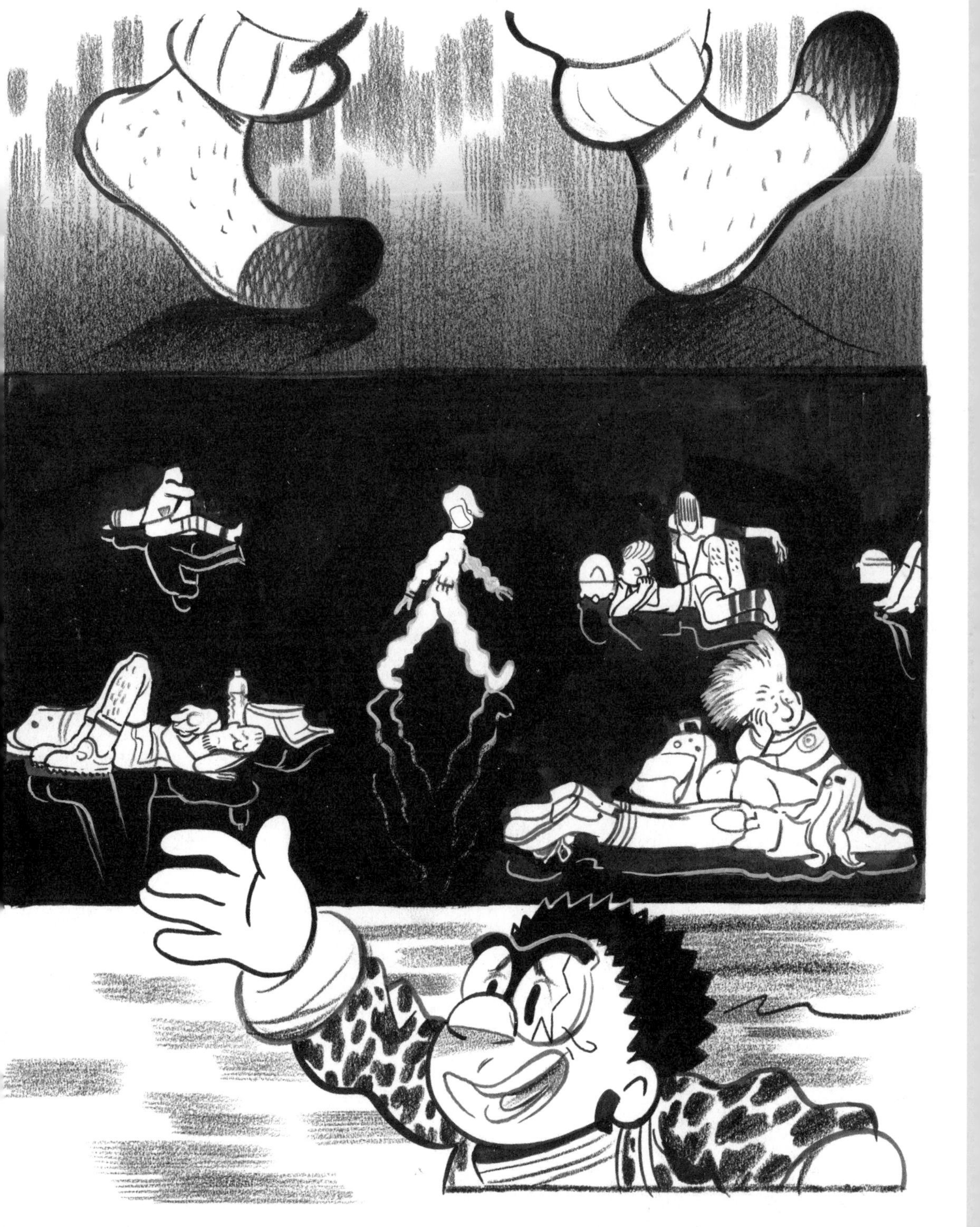

HEY.

OW.

WHAT DO YOU HAVE IN THERE?

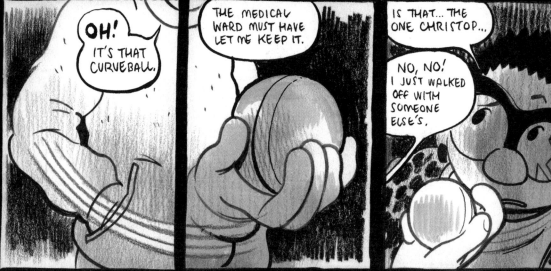

OH! IT'S THAT CURVEBALL.

THE MEDICAL WARD MUST HAVE LET ME KEEP IT.

IS THAT... THE ONE CHRISTOP...

NO, NO! I JUST WALKED OFF WITH SOMEONE ELSE'S.

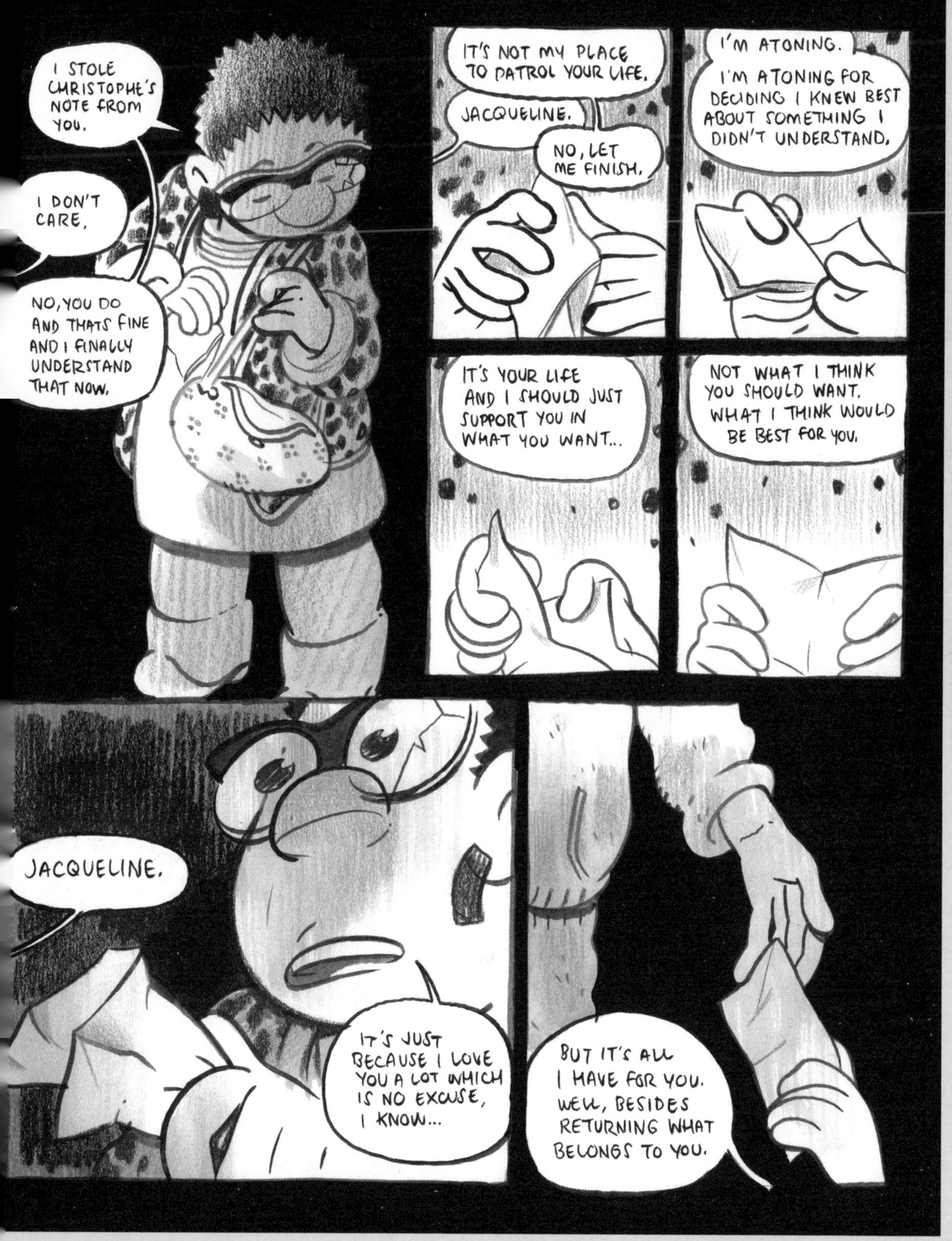

I STOLE CHRISTOPHE'S NOTE FROM YOU.
I DON'T CARE.
NO, YOU DO AND THATS FINE AND I FINALLY UNDERSTAND THAT NOW.
IT'S NOT MY PLACE TO PATROL YOUR LIFE.
JACQUELINE.
NO, LET ME FINISH.
I'M ATONING.
I'M ATONING FOR DECIDING I KNEW BEST ABOUT SOMETHING I DIDN'T UNDERSTAND.
IT'S YOUR LIFE AND I SHOULD JUST SUPPORT YOU IN WHAT YOU WANT...
NOT WHAT I THINK YOU SHOULD WANT. WHAT I THINK WOULD BE BEST FOR YOU.
JACQUELINE.
IT'S JUST BECAUSE I LOVE YOU A LOT WHICH IS NO EXCUSE, I KNOW...
BUT IT'S ALL I HAVE FOR YOU. WELL, BESIDES RETURNING WHAT BELONGS TO YOU.

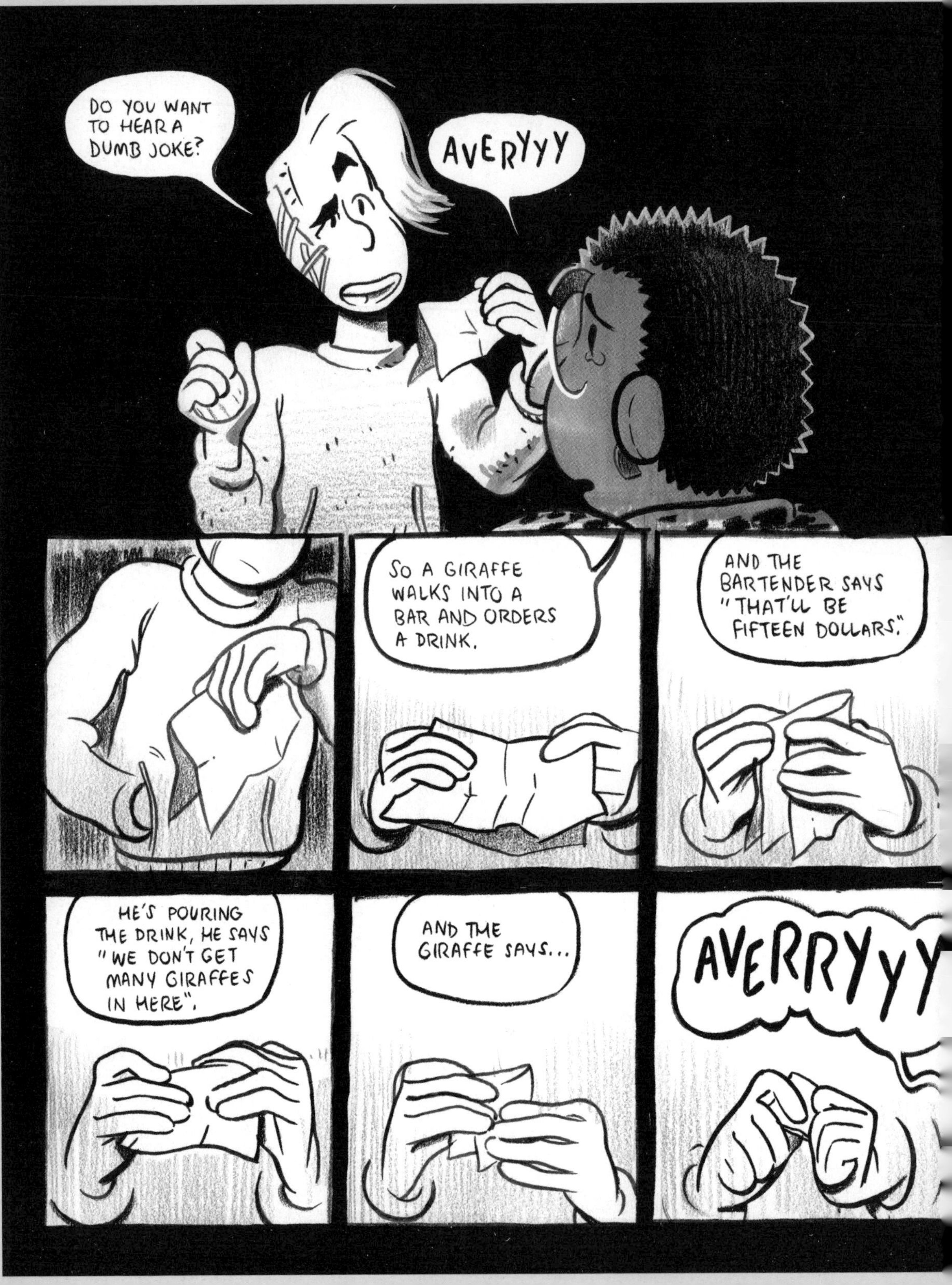
DO YOU WANT TO HEAR A DUMB JOKE?
AVERYYY
SO A GIRAFFE WALKS INTO A BAR AND ORDERS A DRINK.
AND THE BARTENDER SAYS "THAT'LL BE FIFTEEN DOLLARS."
HE'S POURING THE DRINK, HE SAYS "WE DON'T GET MANY GIRAFFES IN HERE".
AND THE GIRAFFE SAYS...
AVERRYYY

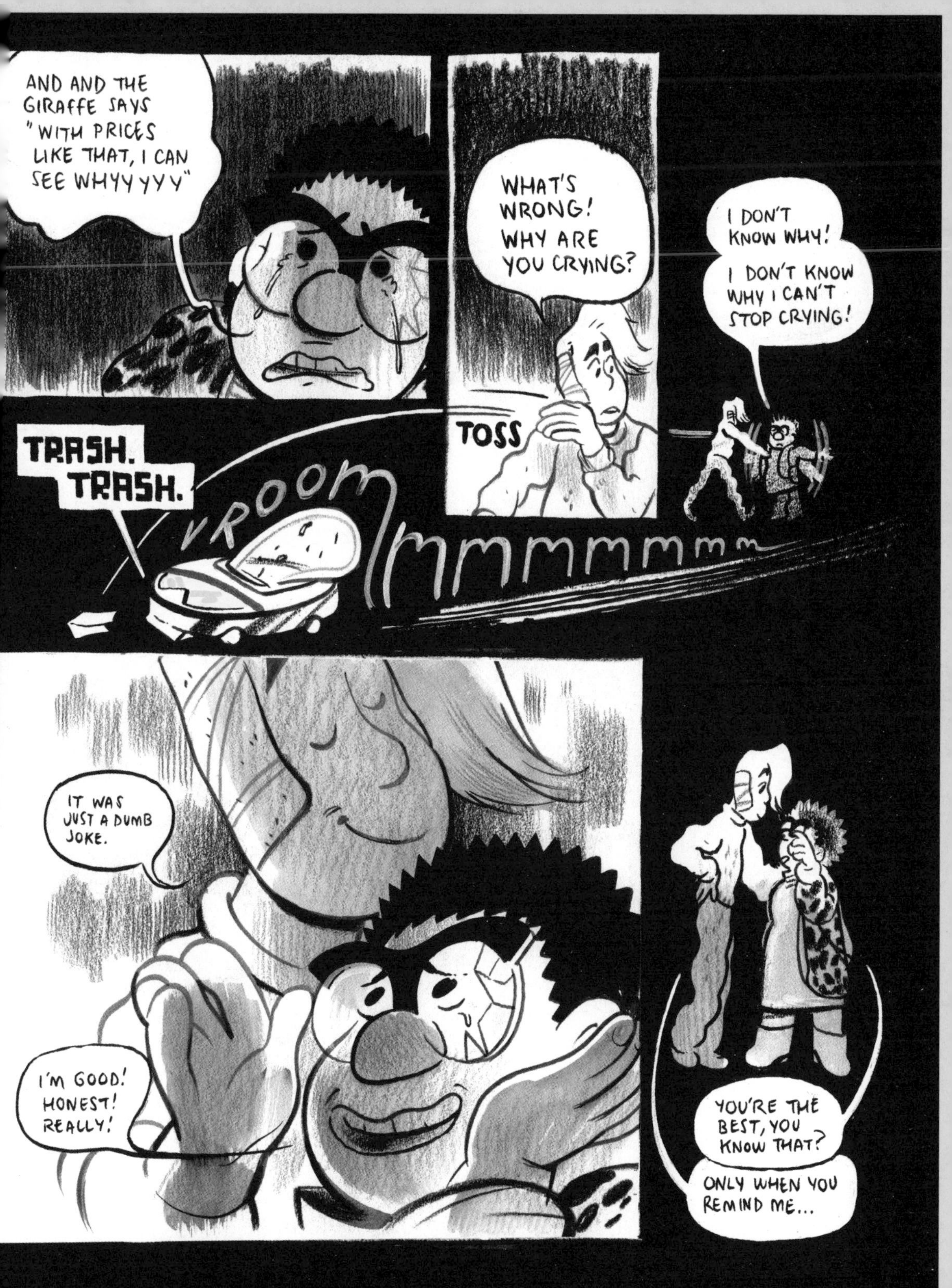
AND AND THE GIRAFFE SAYS "WITH PRICES LIKE THAT, I CAN SEE WHYYYYY"
WHAT'S WRONG! WHY ARE YOU CRYING?
I DON'T KNOW WHY!
I DON'T KNOW WHY I CAN'T STOP CRYING!
TOSS
TRASH. TRASH.
VROOMMMMMMMMM
IT WAS JUST A DUMB JOKE.
I'M GOOD! HONEST! REALLY!
YOU'RE THE BEST, YOU KNOW THAT?
ONLY WHEN YOU REMIND ME...

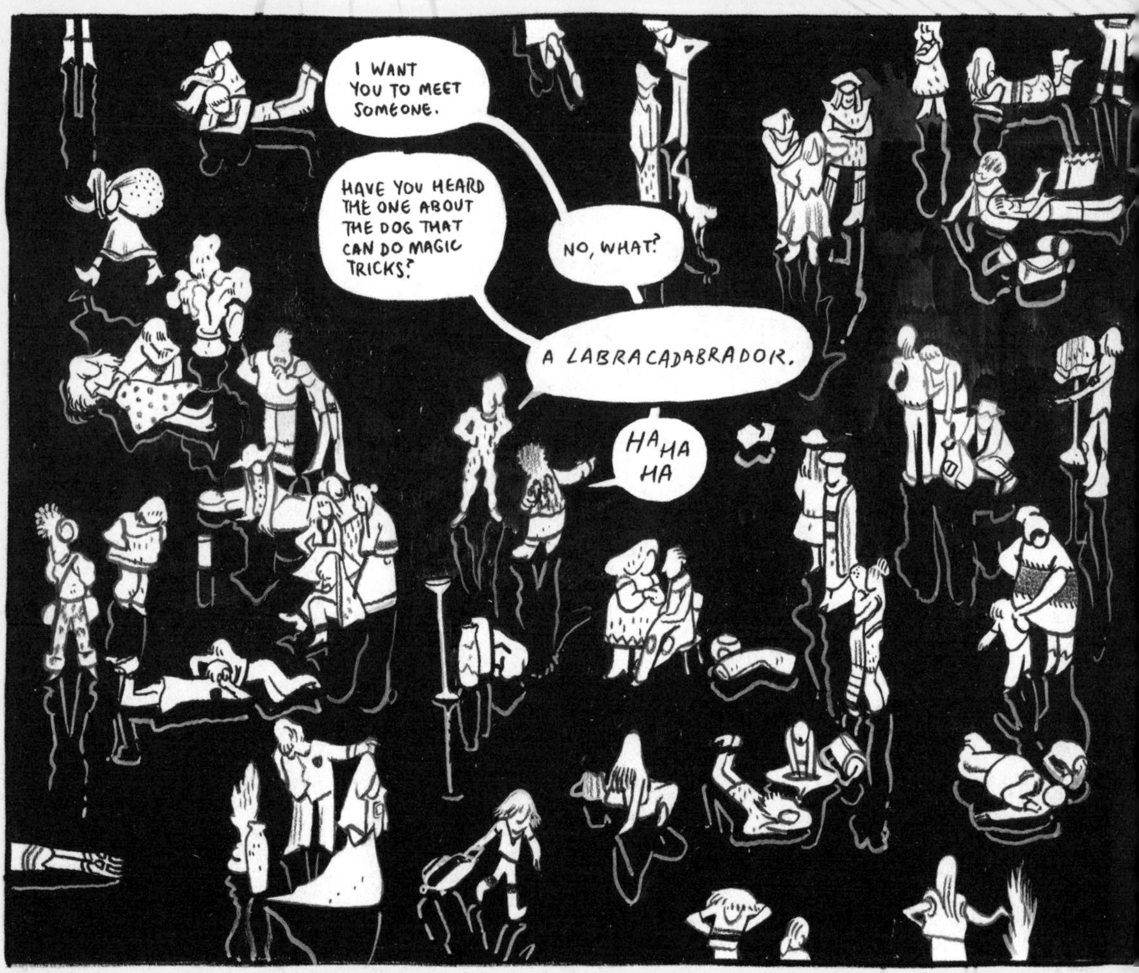
I WANT YOU TO MEET SOMEONE.
HAVE YOU HEARD THE ONE ABOUT THE DOG THAT CAN DO MAGIC TRICKS?
NO, WHAT?
A LABRACADABRADOR.
HA HA HA

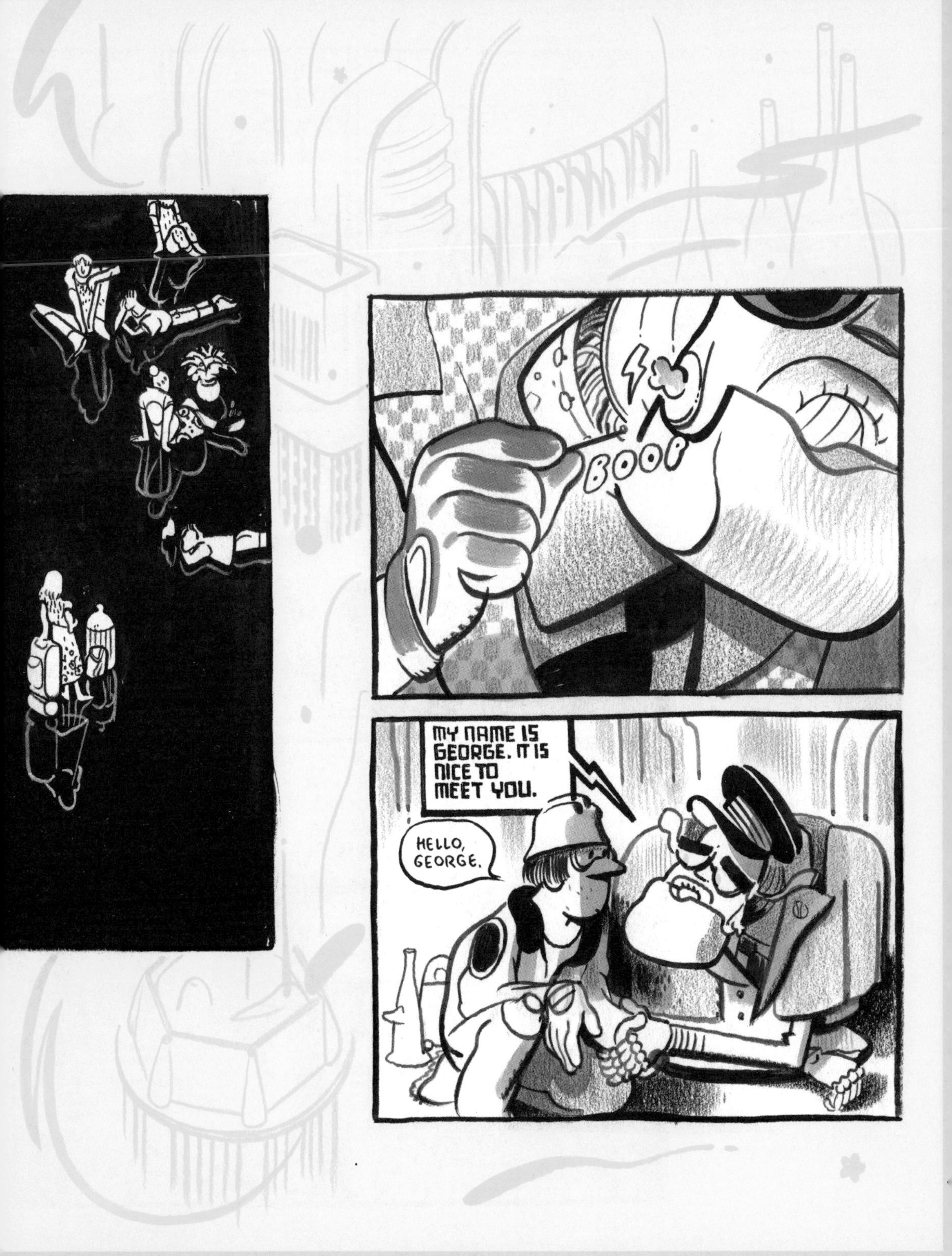
BOOP
MY NAME IS GEORGE. IT IS NICE TO MEET YOU.
HELLO, GEORGE.

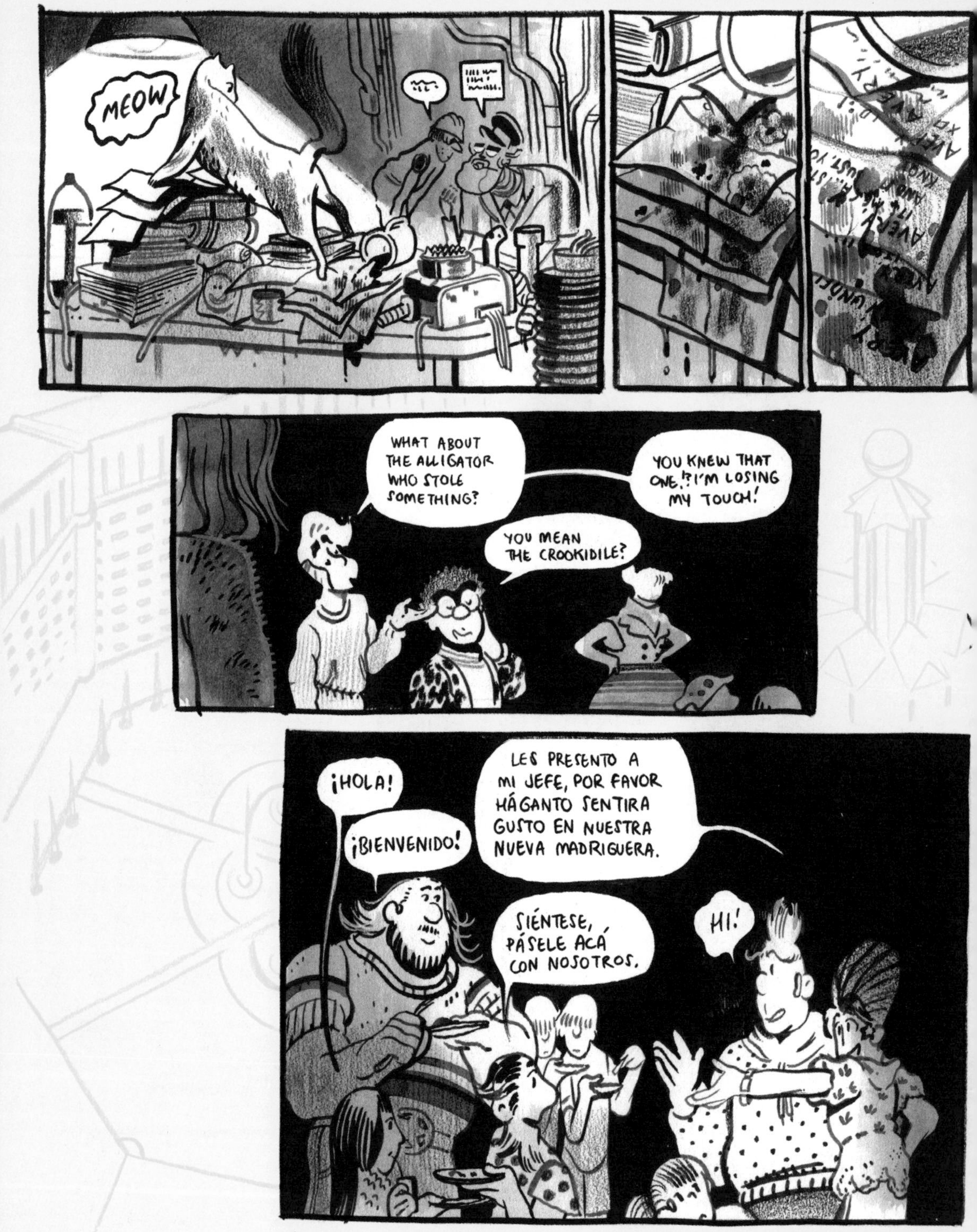
MEOW
WHAT ABOUT THE ALLIGATOR WHO STOLE SOMETHING?
YOU MEAN THE CROOKIDILE?
YOU KNEW THAT ONE!? I'M LOSING MY TOUCH!
¡HOLA!
¡BIENVENIDO!
LES PRESENTO A MI JEFE, POR FAVOR HÁGANTO SENTIRA GUSTO EN NUESTRA NUEVA MADRIGUERA.
SIÉNTESE, PÁSELE ACÁ CON NOSOTROS.
HI!

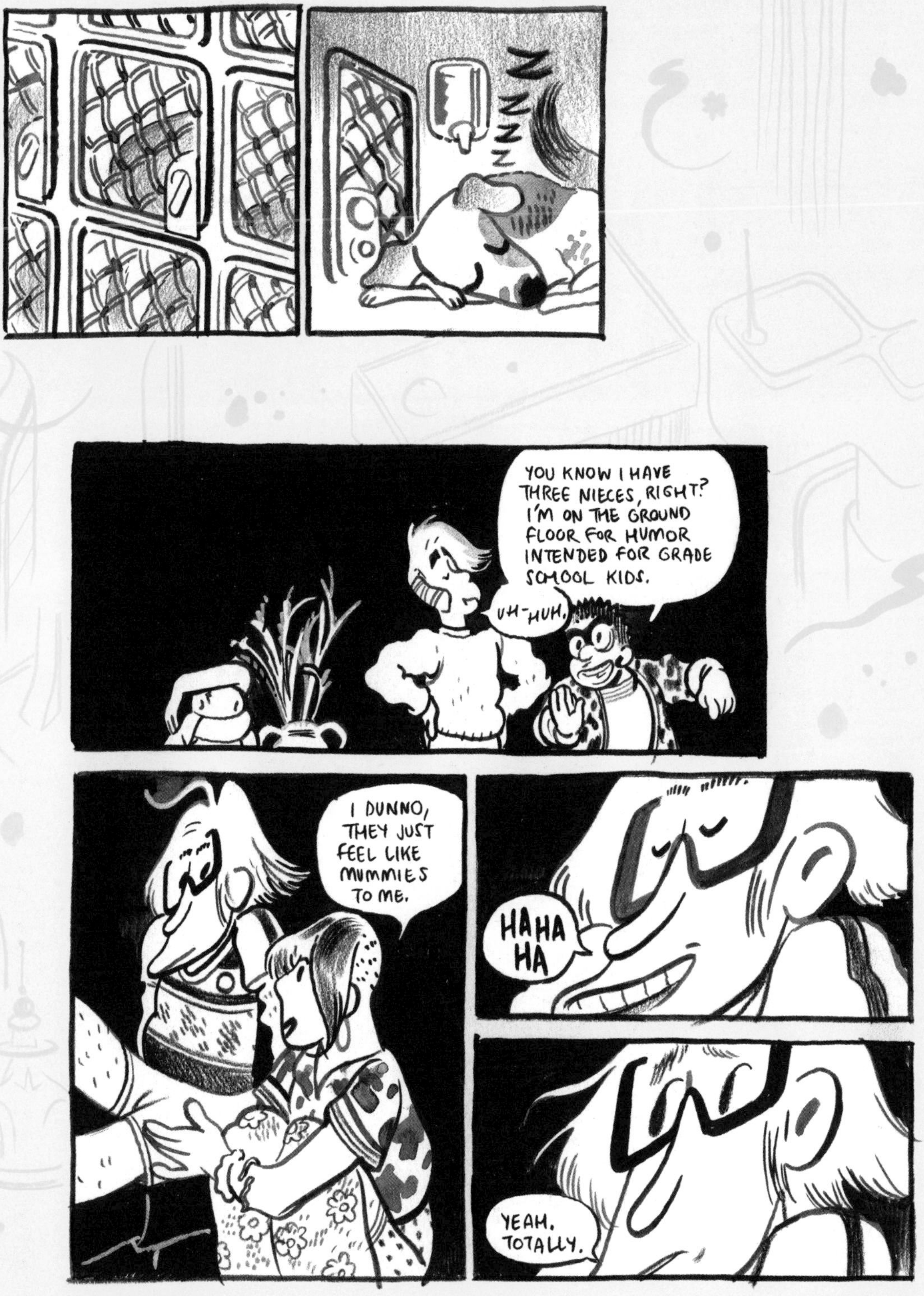
ZZZZZZ
YOU KNOW I HAVE THREE NIECES, RIGHT? I'M ON THE GROUND FLOOR FOR HUMOR INTENDED FOR GRADE SCHOOL KIDS.
UH-HUH.
I DUNNO, THEY JUST FEEL LIKE MUMMIES TO ME.
HAHA HA
YEAH. TOTALLY.

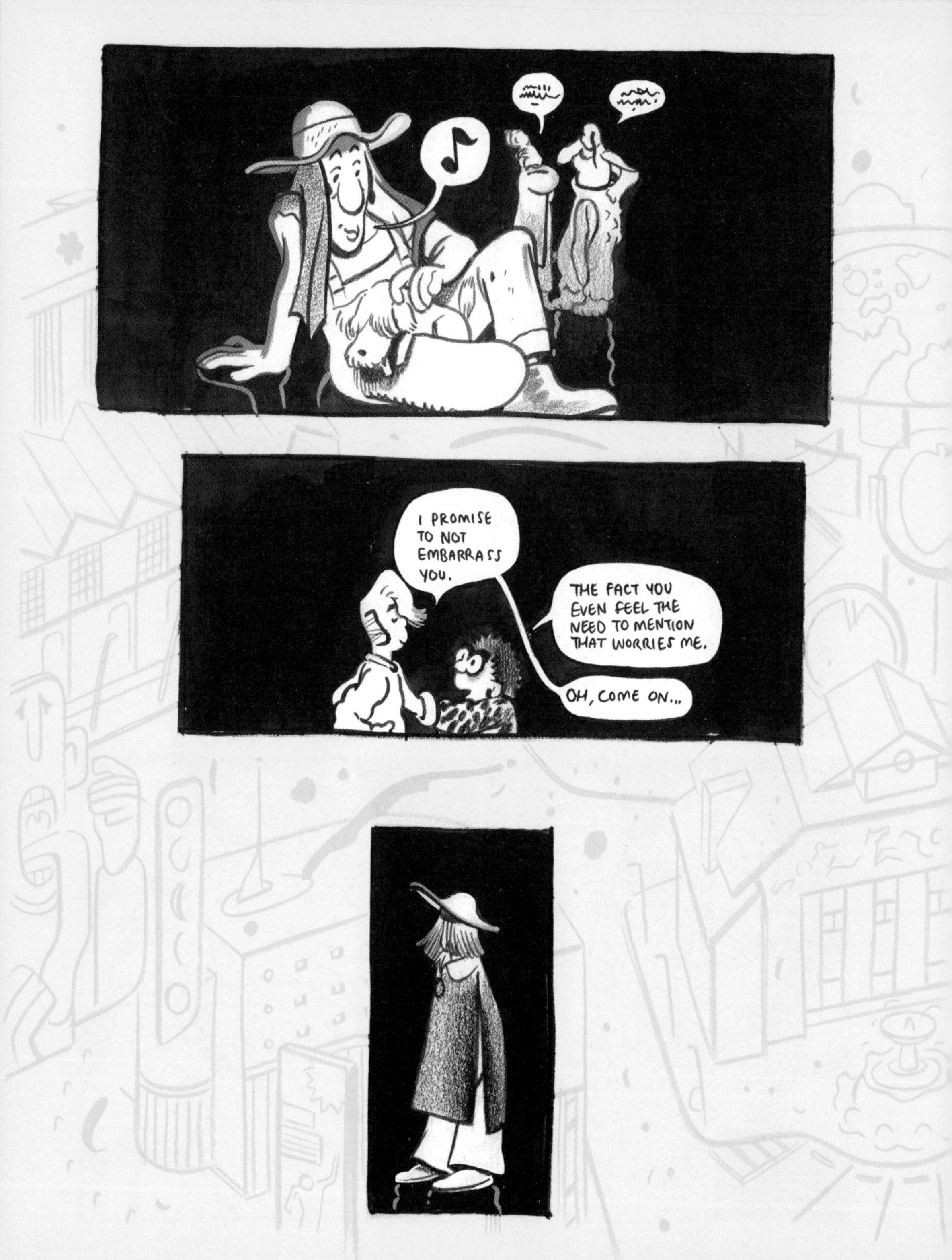
I PROMISE TO NOT EMBARRASS YOU.
THE FACT YOU EVEN FEEL THE NEED TO MENTION THAT WORRIES ME.
OH, COME ON...

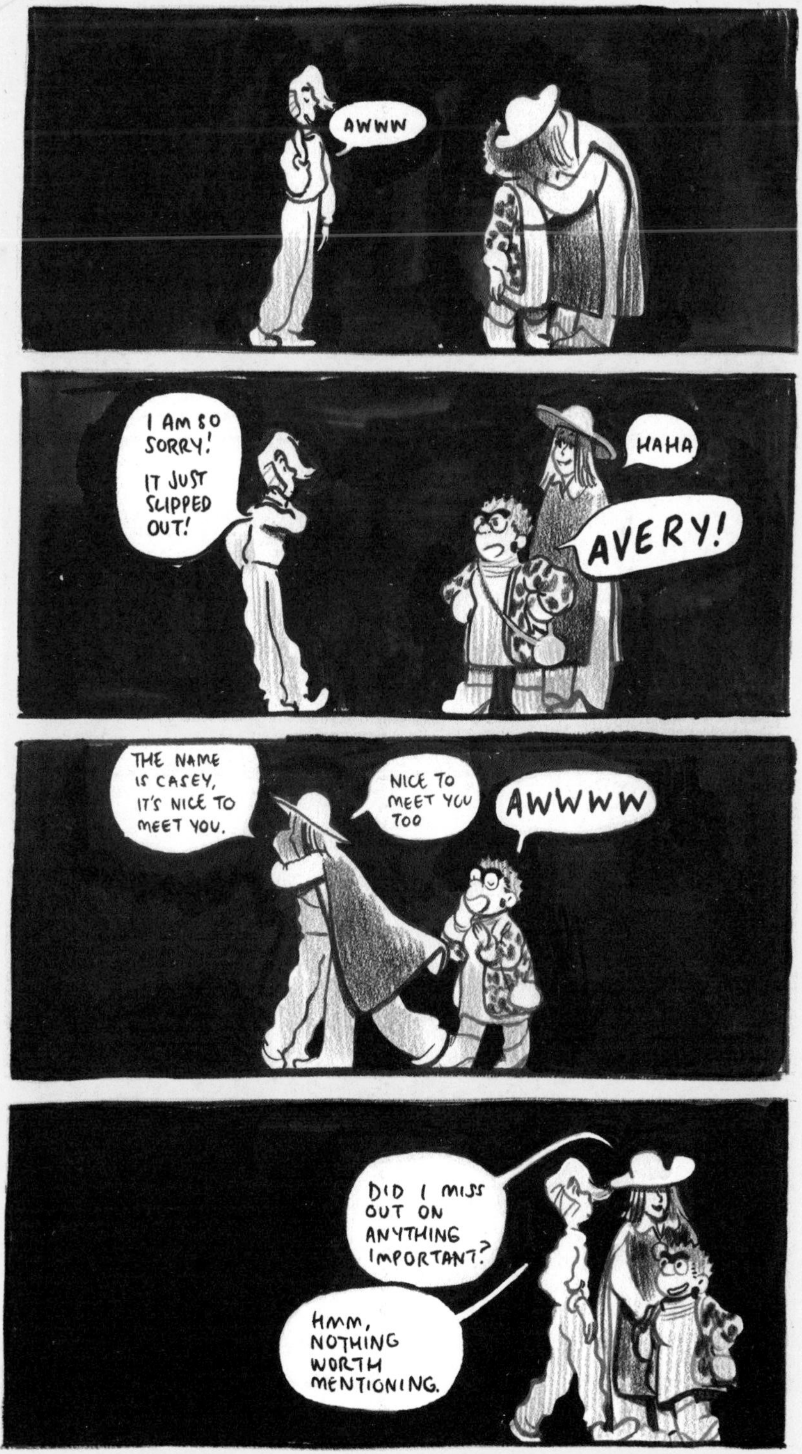
AWWW
I AM SO SORRY!
IT JUST SLIPPED OUT!
HAHA
AVERY!
THE NAME IS CASEY, IT'S NICE TO MEET YOU.
NICE TO MEET YOU TOO
AWWWW
DID I MISS OUT ON ANYTHING IMPORTANT?
HMM, NOTHING WORTH MENTIONING.

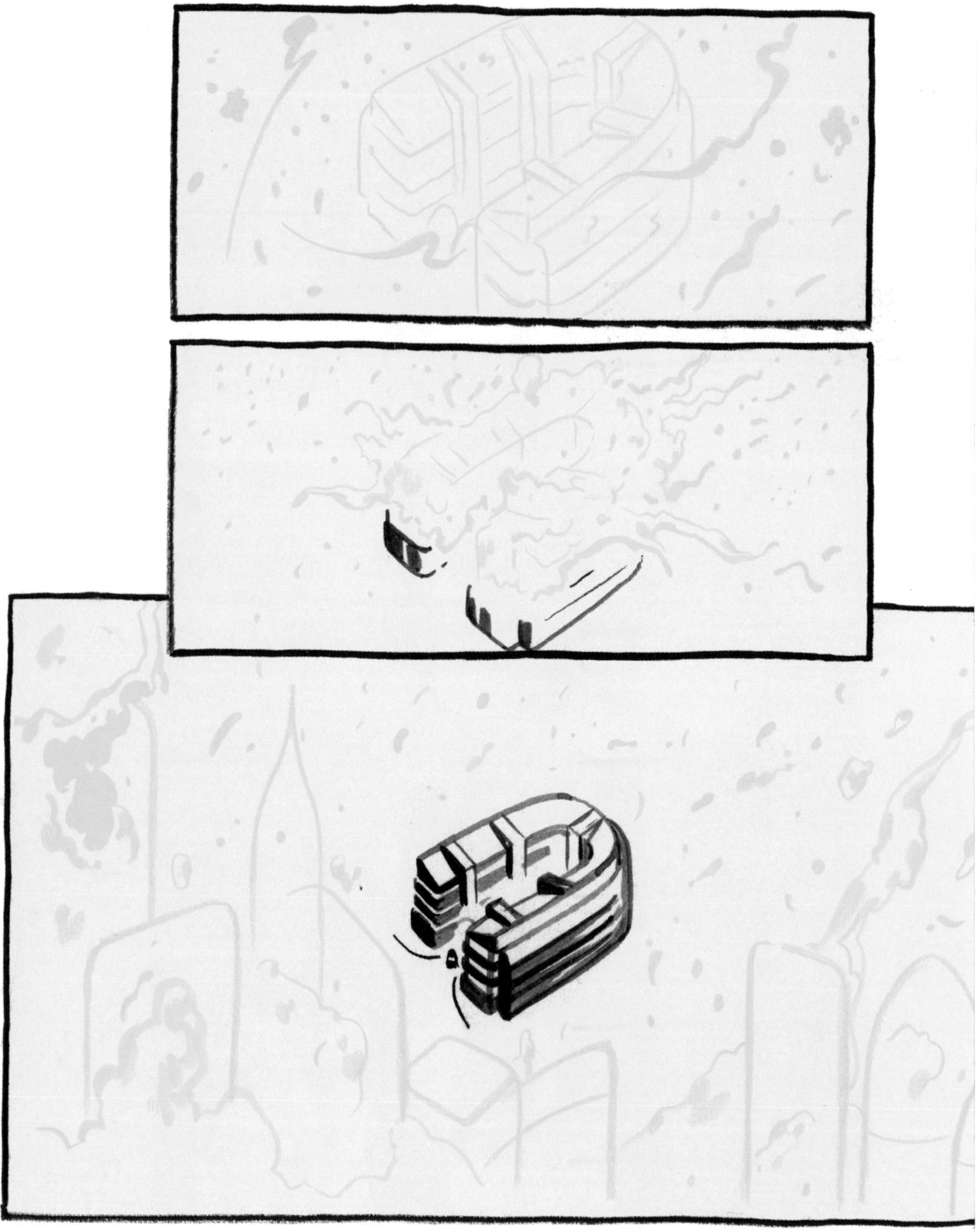